ADJUSTMENT
Applying Psychology
in a Complex World

Robert S. Feldman

University of Massachusetts

ADJUSTMENT

Applying Psychology in a Complex World

McGraw-Hill Book Company

New York | St. Louis | San Francisco | Auckland | Bogotá | Caracas
Colorado Springs | Hamburg | Lisbon | London | Madrid | Mexico | Milan
Montreal | New Delhi | Oklahoma City | Panama | Paris | San Juan
São Paulo | Singapore | Sydney | Tokyo | Toronto

ADJUSTMENT
Applying Psychology
in a Complex World

Copyright ©1989 by McGraw-Hill, Inc.

1 2 3 4 5 6 7 8 9 0   VNH VNH   8 9 3 2 1 0 9 8

ISBN 0-07-020406-3

This book was set in Caslon Book by Waldman Graphics Inc.
The editors were Alison Husting, James D. Anker, and David Dunham;
the designer was Nicholas Krenitsky;
the production supervisor was Diane Renda.
Drawings were done by Fine Line Studios.
Von Hoffman Press, Inc. was printer and binder.

Library of Congress Cataloging-in-Publication Data

Feldman, Robert Stephen (date).
    Adjustment : applying psychology in a complex world.
    1. Adjustment (Psychology)   2. Psychology, Applied.
I. Title.
BF335.F36   1989   150   88-9465
ISBN 0-07-020406-3

About the Author

Robert S. Feldman is Professor of Psychology at the University of Massachusetts at Amherst. A former Fulbright Senior Research Scholar and Lecturer, he is a Fellow of the American Psychology Association and author of more than seventy scientific articles, book chapters, and papers. He has also written or edited six books, including *Understanding Psychology* and *Social Psychology: Theories, Research, and Applications* (McGraw-Hill), and *The Social Psychology of Education* (Cambridge University Press). A committed teacher, Professor Feldman has taught for fifteen years. His spare time is most often devoted to serious cooking and inelegant, although painstakingly improving, piano playing. He lives with his wife, who is also a psychologist, and three children in Amherst, Massachusetts.

To

Wendy
Karl
Jon
Michael
Josh
Rachel
Dan
Sarah
Jessica
Matt
Andy

and their parents.

Contents in Brief

viii

CONTENTS IN BRIEF

CONTENTS

PART I

INTRODUCTION 2

Chapter 1
Living in a Complex World: Adjustment 5

CONTENTS

PART II

THE INDIVIDUAL   42

Chapter 2
Understanding and Thinking About the World   45

PART III

STAYING WELL: PHYSICAL AND MENTAL HEALTH   152

Chapter 5
Promoting Health and Coping with Illness   155

Chapter 8
Restoring Adjustment:
Treatment of Maladaptive Behavior   255

PART IV

Chapter 10
Friends and Lovers: Forming Relationships   321

Chapter 11
Together Forever?: Marriage and Divorce   355

Chapter 12
Sex and Life: Human Sexual Behavior   **387**

XX

CONTENTS

PART V

LIVING WITH OTHERS IN THE WORLD AROUND US   420

Chapter 13
Helping and Hurting: Prosocial Behavior and
Aggression   423

Chapter 14
Working for Life: The Psychology of Work   445

Chapter 15
The Places and Spaces of Our Lives: The Environment 485

Preface

War. Heroism. Crime. Politics.

The reader of any newspaper is well acquainted with the complexities of the world around us. Yet each of us, on a daily basis, leads a life equally intricate in its own way. Our relationships with others, our school and work performance, our motivation, our physical and mental health, and our understanding of our environment all interact to make life an exceedingly rich, complex, and challenging experience.

How to understand—and deal with—the varieties of challenges that are found in our lives is the underlying theme of *Adjustment: Applying Psychology in a Complex World.* The book is designed to be the basic textbook for a one-semester undergraduate course in psychological adjustment. Highlighting the applications that can be drawn from psychological research and theory, the book represents a broad overview of the ways in which psychology can provide guidance in meeting the challenges of daily living.

As the Table of Contents illustrates, the text consists of five parts and fifteen chapters. Beginning with a discussion of the individual in society, the way in which people understand and think about the world, developmental patterns, and motivation are considered. A discussion of health follows, examining both its physical and mental aspects. Next, the focus of the book turns to relationships with others, considering communication, liking, loving, and sexual relationships. Finally, adjustment in terms of the broader society is discussed, examining work, the environment, and formal strategies for better dealing with the world.

Although the text is based on current research and scientific experimental literature and theorizing, it does not dwell on the abstract. Instead, the focus is on concrete, everyday applications of psychology. In *Adjustment: Applying Psychology in a Complex World* readers can find a body of knowledge that has direct relevance to their lives and information that can be put to immediate use. To that end, it emphasizes up-to-the-minute information about current social issues of relevance—for example, AIDS, daycare, and changing family work patterns.

At the same time, the research and theoretical underpinnings of applied psychology are not ignored. Because research and theory provide a context for understanding the development of applications, it is critical that readers understand the fundamentals of how psychologists consider and evaluate information about the world. An important aim of this book, then, is to articulate the interplay between theory and applications so that readers get a sense of not just what psychologists have found of relevance to contemporary life, but how they have come to their conclusions.

Goals and Philosophy of *Adjustment: Applying Psychology in a Complex World*

There are several goals toward which *Adjustment: Applying Psychology in a Complex World* is oriented. First, it is designed to provide a broad overview of the applications of psychology, furnishing readers with a sense of what the field has to offer in terms of everyday living. An emphasis is placed on what is known, rather than the contradictions and uncertainties of the field. Moreover, no single theoretical approach or orientation is followed; instead, the text presents an objective, unbiased, and eclectic view of what the field has to offer.

A second major goal is to arouse readers' intellectual excitement over what the field of psychology has to offer by demonstrating how psychologists' research findings can be used in concrete ways to improve people's lives. To accomplish this goal, the book was written to capture the intellectual vitality of a growing and evolving field. It includes numerous vignettes and case studies, as well as exercises that students can try themselves. The book's structure, then, is intended to promote an interactive, involving experience for its readers.

Finally, the text is designed to facilitate student learning by encompassing the latest in instructional design features. The writing style is meant to be clear and interesting, and the text includes many pedagogical features, discussed below, that will enhance students' ability to fully understand and learn the core concepts.

Learning Aids and Features of *Adjustment: Applying Psychology in a Complex World*

Adjustment: Applying Psychology in a Complex World has several important features, including:

● *Chapter Outline.* Each chapter opens with an outline of the chapter. The outline serves as a chapter organizer, immediately making apparent the framework of the chapter for the reader.

● *Preview.* Every chapter begins with a short vignette about a person or event that has relevance to the major topic of the chapter. These vignettes clarify the relevance of the chapter content to everyday situations.

- *Coherent within-chapter organization.* Each chapter is subdivided into three major sections which stand relatively independent of the other parts of the chapter. Because research on instructional design has consistently shown that presenting material in small chunks enhances learning, recall, and understanding, this organizing structure is a major pedagogical device. Moreover, it allows maximum flexibility in tailoring the assigned readings to the order in which an instructor would most like to teach the topics.

- *To Review* and *Check Yourself.* Following each major section of a chapter, the key points covered are outlined in a To Review section. These are followed by a Check Yourself section, in which a series of questions on the content of the chapter are asked. These questions test the student's ability to both recall and apply the material. Answers to the questions are also included within the text.

- *Psychology for You.* Each of the three parts of every chapter concludes with a section that describes ways in which current findings from the field of psychology can answer questions and provide guidance on issues that are likely to be of major concern to readers. For example, the chapter on development includes techniques for raising children effectively; the chapter on understanding and thinking about the world discusses ways of forming more accurate impressions of other people; and the chapter on helping and hurting describes measures for dealing with anger. These Psychology for You sections, a unique feature of the book, demonstrate both the impact and promise that the field of psychology has on everyday living and adjustment.

- *Do It!* Each chapter has several Do It! boxes which provide a questionnaire or exercise for the reader to complete. For instance, the chapter on interpersonal relationships includes materials on measuring the reader's levels of jealousy.

- *Summary* A summary in a numbered list format is included at the end of each chapter. These summaries are concise reviews of each chapter's key concepts and, when used in conjunction with the opening chapter outlines, are effective study aids.

- *Key Terms and Concepts* The key terms and concepts, keyed to page numbers on which they are first introduced, are listed at the end of each chapter.

- *To Find Out More.* An annotated bibliography of suggested readings is included in every chapter. Publications that are both scientifically sound and of a self-help nature, as well as more technical books, make up these reading lists.

- *Glossary.* A glossary at the end of the book provides definitions of key terms.

Supplements

- *The Study Guide.* The *Study Guide to Accompany Adjustment: Applying Psychology in a Complex World,* written by Dr. Eric Duerr of the Georgia Institute of Technology, enables students to review thoroughly the major concepts in each chapter, personally involving them in the core concepts as well as testing them on their understanding of the text. Each chapter of the *Study Guide* opens with a complete list of learning objectives, benchmarks for progress in concept mastery. Students then can test their proficiency by completing twenty fill-in-the-blank questions, thirty-five multiple-choice questions, three Key Terms and Concepts sections, and six essay questions for each chapter. Finally, two Deepen Your Understanding exercises ask students to consider specific concepts they have learned in the text and apply them to hypothetical situations. The *Study Guide* helps link the course's theories, research, and applications to the students' own world, reinforces key topics and issues, and thoroughly prepares students for examinations.

- *The Instructor's Manual with Test Items.* The *Instructor's Manual with Test Items* is tailored to answer the needs of professors of varying levels of experience. Kenneth Thompson of Central Missouri State University has written a flexible resource guide for presenting chapter materials in a way that will complement professors' individual instructional needs and styles of teaching. Specific recommendations are provided for classroom activities, films, role-playing exercises, experiments, and other ways to creatively illuminate core concepts in each chapter. Whenever useful, step-by-step outlines of the activities accompany the suggestions. Beginning instructors are given advice on creating syllabi and exams. Also included are classroom discussion questions designed to spur student participation or to be used as essay questions in quizzes and exams. The test item portion of the manual provides a good sampling of multiple-choice, true-false, and matching questions. The *Instructor's Manual with Test Items* is a useful tool to enhance an instructor's personal teaching style, and I hope instructors will take advantage of its rich resources for use in their classes.

- *Computerized Testing.* A computerized testing system consisting of the questions found in the *Instructor's Manual with Test Items* is also available.

Acknowledgments

I am grateful to the following reviewers, who provided insightful, thoughtful comments on the manuscript at many stages:

Robert M. Adams, Eastern Kentucky University; John Altrocchi, University of Nevada School of Medicine; Cyrus Azimi, University of Central Florida; Eric Duerr, Georgia Institute of Technology; Thomas K. Eckle, Modesto Junior College; Richard Fuhrer, University of Wisconsin; William J. Gnagey, Illinois State University; Sidney Hochman, Nassau Community College; Louis J. King, California State Polytechnic University; Knud Larsen, Oregon State University; Carl Lutters, Clinton Community College; Louis A. Martone, Miami Dade Community College; Frederick Meeker, California State Polytechnic University; Donald M. Stanley, North Harris County College; Don Stephenson, College of Southern Idaho; Kenneth Thompson, Central Missouri State University; Patrick S. Williams, Wharton County Junior College, and David G. Weight, Brigham Young University.

There are several students who make the joys of professorhood particularly salient. Among them are (in totally egalitarian alphabetical order) Bob Custrini, Pierre Philippot, and Lee Rosen. Bob's unrelentingly clear view of the world, Pierre's combination of theoretical sophistication and good humor, and Lee's wit and honesty, along with much else, have stimulated me as much as any educational experience I have had, and I thank them for their input into my life on many levels.

My colleagues at the University of Massachusetts are to be thanked for making the University such a good place to work, and my friends for making Amherst such a good place in which to live. I must also acknowledge the still-vital role played by two primary professors from my past: Karl Scheibe of Wesleyan University and the late Vernon Allen, who was at the University of Wisconsin. I still marvel at their skill in teaching me the content, and values, of the discipline of psychology.

Were it not for the talents of several other people, you would not be reading this book. Jim Anker, my sponsoring editor, provided the spark that got this book going, and he remains a vital influence on it, as well as a friend. Alison Husting is a wonderful developmental editor, and her ideas, suggestions, and adept editorial direction could not be matched. And Rhona Robbin, although not working directly on this book, still provided a lingering presence in my psyche; I am unable to write a word without the feeling that she is looking over my shoulder, holding me to the highest standards. Finally, Carolyn Dash provided critical research and editorial assistance, and Kate Ward helped with the manuscript at every important juncture, and I thank them both.

My family is an ever-present and vital influence on my life, and there is little I do that does not reflect the experience of being a part of this large group. I am grateful to my brother, my sisters-in-law, brothers-in-law, and nieces and nephews; to my late mother-in-law, Mary E. Vorwerk; to Ethel Radler and Harry Brochstein; and especially to my parents, Leah Brochstein and the late Saul D. Feldman.

Finally, my wife, Katherine Vorwerk, and my children, Sarah, Joshua, and Jonathan, are, as ever, the bedrock of my life. I thank them, with love and fondness.

Robert S. Feldman

ADJUSTMENT
Applying Psychology in a Complex World

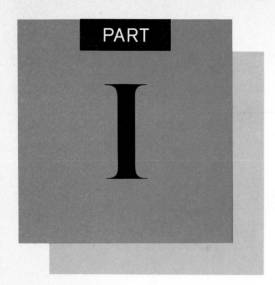

PART

I

INTRODUCTION

In this opening part of the book, we encounter a student who seemingly has everything going for him, yet he feels he doesn't know who he is or what is the meaning of his life. We meet another student who has just experienced the worst semester of his life; a woman whose dreams are shattered in a terrible accident; and a college graduate whose lack of career goals becomes a source of anxiety.

Each of these individuals faces challenges associated with adjustment, the efforts people make to meet the demands placed on them by the world in which they live. In the introductory chapter, we consider the ways in which people come to understand who they are, and the major approaches taken by psychologists in their quest to understand human behavior.

In Chapter 1, then, the focus is on the basic concepts that allow us to understand how people meet the demands and challenges placed upon them.

Living in a Complex World
Adjustment

CHAPTER

1

Chris O'Hara seemed to have it all: He was a good-looking guy, doing well in school, a great athlete, and he had a steady relationship with a woman for whom he felt great affection.

He was on the top of the world—or at least felt he should be. Yet there were things that were beginning to get him down. He was having trouble concentrating on his schoolwork, and things that had never bothered him before became major annoyances.

When he tried to identify the source of his disquiet, the best he could come up with were vague questions about the meaning of his very existence. Although not a terribly introspective person, he began to say to himself, "Is this all there is to life?"

When he received the letter from the dean of students, Harry Lennetti was aware of its contents without even opening it. After getting a D in his contemporary literature class, he knew that his grade point average was shot and that he would be put on academic probation, and the letter from the dean merely confirmed what he already knew. It had been, without a doubt, the worst semester of his life—and now he had to deal with the consequences.

Even though Rachel Langley hit the brakes as soon as she saw the other car sliding toward her on the icy road, she was not quick enough. In ten short seconds, her life was changed. Her automobile was a wreck, and so was her body: Her doctors told her that she would in all likelihood suffer pain in her legs, both of which were badly broken in the crash, for the rest of her life. Certainly, she would have to forget about her dream of making a career in ballet.

She knew that she had to make up her mind, but still had no inkling of which way to turn. When Susanne Katz began her last year of college, she had to make a decision about what she was going to do after graduation. Her friends were making their plans, and it seemed as if everyone else she knew was completely confident about their career choices. Her plans, on the other hand, were completely up in the air, and the anxiety she felt about her indecision was beginning to deeply disturb her. She was, in a word, scared.

Four people, four challenges. Like all of us, each of them finds life to be filled both with joys and with difficulties that must be confronted. To these four individuals, issues of **adjustment**—the efforts people make to meet the demands and challenges placed upon them by the world in which they live—are central to their lives.

Indeed, whether we are aware of it or not, adjustment plays a central role in everyone's existence. On some level, we all strive to achieve a happy, fulfilled life (although we may have different definitions of "happiness" and "fulfillment"), as we search for our place in the world and the meaning behind our daily activities.

In our efforts to meet the challenges of life, there are many maps that can be used to guide us. Some people choose to follow a philosophical path, others turn to theology, and still others to the physical sciences. Yet there is only one field that takes a systematic, scientific approach to the challenges of daily life: psychology.

Psychology is the scientific study of behavior and mental processes. As such, psychology attempts to find the causes that underlie behavior, and—like other sciences—to predict, control, and understand its phenomena. But the concerns that are of interest to psychology cut a wide swath, including not just what people do but also their thoughts, feelings, perceptions, reasoning processes, and motivations.

To understand these concerns, psychologists use scientific methods. Moving beyond intuition and hunches alone as sources of knowledge about the world, they use controlled, methodical research techniques to derive answers about problems that affect the individual.

In this chapter, we will introduce some of the major concepts of adjustment and discuss how psychology gives us insights into its processes. We begin by identifying the major kinds of challenges people encounter, considering the common obstacles that we face as we move through life. We also discuss the way in which each of us develops and maintains a uniqueness and the sense of ourselves as individuals.

The bulk of the chapter is devoted to a discussion of the central approaches devised by psychologists to explain human behavior—both our own behavior and that of others. We consider three very different conceptions of human beings that are used to guide the work that psychologists do to understand human adjustment.

You will also be introduced to the format of the book in this first chapter. *Adjustment: Applying Psychology in a Complex World* contains several features about which you should be aware. Each chapter is divided into three or four sections. Each section contains a Do It! box, which will give you the opportunity to experience some of the phenomena we have been discussing, and a Psychology for You selection, which explains exactly how the concepts you are learning about can be used to help in your own adjustments to life's challenges. A To Review segment, containing the key points presented in the section, and a To Check Yourself segment, which provides a series of questions that will allow you to test your understanding of the material, appear at the end of each section of the chapter.

Ultimately, the understanding you should gain from reading this book ought to help you attain a fundamental goal of this book: a greater ability to meet the demands and challenges placed upon you by the world in which you live.

1.1   **UNDERSTANDING THE ME I KNOW:**
The Challenges of Adjustment

Starting college . . . employment . . . the birth of a child . . . going to court . . . winning an election . . . sex . . . the death of a loved one . . . a new roommate . . . marriage . . . illness . . . having an accident . . . divorce . . . falling in love . . . drug use . . . promotion . . . pregnancy . . . moving away . . . attending a reunion . . . going on vacation . . .

The list could go on and on. No one's life lacks challenges, be they mundane (remembering where one left the car keys) or profound (falling in love or facing the death of a loved one). To begin our discussion of adjustment, we turn first to the question of how to identify and categorize the challenges of everyday life.

The Pressure Points of Life:
Identifying the challenges of everyday living

The specific challenges that we each face as individuals are unique, based on our genetic heritage and the particular experiences we have encountered throughout life. Yet there are several threads that run through the cloth of existence that are common to all individuals:

● *The challenge of defining and maintaining one's individuality in the world.* Despite the fact that most of us live within a rich social environment

Psychology includes the study of relationships. In considering a marriage, psychologists might ask why a husband and wife chose each other, what each of them expected from the relationship, and how the relationship evolved over the years.

Michael Weisbrot and Family

and are dependent on others, ultimately on some level we all must rely on ourselves and our own capabilities.

As we see in the first major section of this text, several challenges involve the individual. Each of us views the world from our own perspective and thinks about it in a unique way. Perceiving and thinking about the world in an accurate and effective way is a critical challenge, as these processes lie at the heart of the way in which we form our understanding of the world around us. We are also affected by developmental processes, the experiential and physical changes that occur.as we get older. Finally, the forces that motivate our behavior influence the particular challenges that we as individuals seek out, and they influence our capabilities in meeting such challenges.

● *The challenge of maintaining physical and mental health.* Given that at some very basic level we are biological creatures, we are faced with the necessity of maintaining healthy functioning. While this challenge appears on many levels, repeated exposure to the stresses inherent in everyday living can bring about both psychological and physical declines. As we shall see, illnesses such as heart disease and cancer, which once were thought to have only biological components, can be related to the ups and downs we commonly face. Finally, it is clear that mental health and psychological disturbances affect the ways we meet life's challenges.

● *The challenge of forming relationships with others.* The phrase "people are social animals" captures a primary aspect of human existence. We do not live as social isolates, but instead interact with others within a series of rich social networks. The nature of the relationships that we are able to form with others has an enormous impact on our psychological adjustment.

In this book we explore several aspects of the challenge of forming relationships with others. For example, we discuss the ways in which we communicate with others, on both a verbal and a nonverbal level. We also consider the rise (and fall) of relationships with others, including friendships, love affairs, and marriage. Finally, the challenges brought about by our sexual behavior and needs are discussed.

● *The challenge of living with others in a complex society.* On the broadest level, satisfactory adjustment is affected by events in the larger world around us. Given the complexities of our modern, technologically based world and our reliance on others, we are all members of a global society. Events in far reaches of the world can affect us in ways that cannot be avoided (for example, the Chernobyl accident in the Soviet Union, which sent clouds of radioactive dust around the world).

In the last section of this book we consider some of the broader issues that affect society as a whole. Means of reducing aggression and increasing altruistic behavior are examined. We also explore the role of work in everyday life, discussing the benefits that jobs and employment provide both to the individual and to society. Finally, the challenge of living effectively in a variety of environments is considered.

Although the number and kind of challenges that we face can appear overwhelming, most people cope quite well with them. Indeed, the challenges we find in everyday life offer an opportunity—an opportunity to grow and become more effective individuals, on both a personal and a societal level.

Who Am I, and Where Am I Going?:
Identity and adjustment

Central to the study of adjustment are issues dealing with **identity**—the sum total of the generalizations we make about ourselves, based on our thoughts, feelings, past behavior, and awareness of our own existence as human beings (Whitbourne, 1986). What makes up a person's identity? (Before examining this question, try completing the questions in the following Do It! box.)

DO IT!

WHO ARE YOU?

To get a better sense of who you are, write down fifteen things about yourself by completing each of the following statements:

_____ 1. I am _____

_____ 2. I am _____

_____ 3. I am _____

_____ 4. I am _____

_____ 5. I am _____

_____ 6. I am _____

_____ 7. I am _____

_____ 8. I am _____

_____ 9. I am _____

_____ 10. I am _____

_____ 11. I am _____

_____ 12. I am _____

_____ 13. I am _____

_____ 14. I am _____

_____ 15. I am _____

Now, place a 1 next to descriptions that relate to physical characteristics, such as appearance, size, or race. Place a 2 by those statements that refer to the different roles you play in life, such as student, gardener, son or daughter, and so forth. Next, put a 3 by statements that relate to specific sorts of traits or personal characteristics, such as being "cheerful" or a "lover of animals." Finally, put a 4 next to statements that are global and vague, such as "I am part of nature's firmament."

Now add up the number of responses that fall into each of the four categories. You also might want to ask a group of friends to carry out the exercise and compare your responses to theirs. Research has shown that students today are most apt to describe themselves in terms of category 3. In the 1950s, students were most likely to picture themselves in terms of category 2. Of course, there is nothing right or wrong about whatever category you find yourself using most frequently; each of us has a unique way of viewing ourselves.

Source: Kuhn & McPartland, 1954; Zurcher, 1977.

Part of identity lies in the **physical self,** our image of the physical aspects of our bodies. We all are intimately aware of our blemishes, protruding stomachs, long noses, muscular arms, or other idiosyncrasies. But even our more mundane features, which may be of no concern to us—our hair and eye color, for example—contribute to our overall physical selves.

The **social self** comprises the various roles that we play in life as part of our interaction with others. At the same time you are a student, you are also a son or daughter, a friend, a citizen, or perhaps an employee, lover, spouse, father, or mother. Each of these roles plays an important part in defining your overall identity and in some ways directs your behavior while in the role. For instance, as a student you may be outspoken and critical, while as an employee you may be more restrained in your criticisms of what your boss says. Despite the difference in the overt behavior, these roles contribute to your overall sense of who you are.

To a large measure, the social self is a reflection of the **looking-glass self**—the view of one's self that is provided by society and by other specific, significant individuals who populate one's world (Mead, 1934; Gergen, 1965). If we want to know how honest or trustworthy or happy we *really* are, we may seek out the opinions of others.

Of course, not everyone serves equally well as a source of information. Generally, we rely on the opinions of either people whom we hold in high esteem and whose opinions we particularly value, or—in a process called social comparison—individuals who are relatively similar to ourselves.

Social comparison is a phenomenon in which people depend on others to evaluate their own behavior, abilities, expertise, and opinions (Festinger, 1954; Goethals et al., 1986). But we do not choose just any other individuals to compare ourselves with; we tend to use people who are fairly similar to us on the dimensions that are most relevant to us in the specific area we are comparing.

The reason for relying more on similar, as compared to dissimilar, others, rests on the informational value of the two sources of information. For instance, suppose you want to know how you stack up as a tennis player. You probably already know you're not another Ivan Lendl, since he is so much better than almost everyone. On the other hand, it is probably less obvious how your playing compares to that of someone similar to you in terms of sex, body build, experience, and years of taking lessons. Using a similar person as a basis of comparison is likely to give you a clearer picture of your own abilities, as each of you are similar on other dimensions that are relevant to success at tennis.

We have seen how the self is made up of several components. But is there a component of the self that is uniquely personal to the individual and which does not rely either on physical aspects of our bodies, on judgments of ourselves made by others, or on comparisons with others?

The answer is yes. Each of us has a **personal self,** that private part of ourselves about which only we can know. It consists of the innermost experiences that we may or may not choose to share with others. Our personal selves are unique, comprising our view of the totality of our existence that allows us—with more or less ease—to meet the challenges that life places before us.

Accepting Yourself for Who You Are: Self-esteem

You would probably be the first to agree: You are not just a student, but a good, bad, or in-between one. Similarly, you probably don't think of yourself as simply having a face, but as having an attractive face or an unattractive one. In fact, you do not just have a self, but one that you evaluate as either positive or negative.

The fact that we make such judgments of ourselves indicates that there is an important evaluative component of self, known as self-esteem. **Self-esteem** is a person's general acceptance of himself or herself, or the degree to which people see themselves as individuals of worth. If you have high self-esteem, then, you generally feel respect for and accept yourself, while if you have low self-esteem, you generally lack respect for, reject, and negatively judge yourself.

Although all of us, on occasion, go through times of low self-esteem (following an undeniable failure, for example) some people routinely feel low in self-esteem. In extreme cases, the result can be physical illness, psychological disturbance, or a general inability to cope with challenges.

People with low self-esteem may also find themselves in a cycle of failure that is difficult to break. For example, a student with low self-esteem may begin studying for a test believing he is likely to do badly. This expectation may in turn lead him to reduce the amount of effort he puts forth—after all, if you are sure you are going to fail a test, why bother really trying to study? Moreover, because he is sure he is going to do poorly on the test, he also may feel elevated levels of anxiety, which may also hurt his test performance. Ultimately, of course, it is this pattern of beliefs that causes him to perform badly on the test, due to a combination of his lack of effort and his high level of anxiety. But rather than telling himself that his poor test performance is caused by low effort and elevated anxiety, he views it as an affirmation of his inferior ability—which, in turn, simply reinforces his low self-esteem.

One way of breaking such a self-defeating pattern is to increase an individual's sense of **self-efficacy,** the belief that one is personally responsible for and can regulate one's own behavior, thereby bringing about positive outcomes (Bandura, 1982). People with high self-efficacy tend to exert greater effort when faced with a challenge, which in turn increases the chances of success in dealing with it. For example, in one study children's feelings of self-efficacy were manipulated by providing them with goals that were represented as either attainable or unattainable. Those presented with attainable goals solved more problems and showed greater interest in the test than those given unattainable goals (Bandura & Schunk, 1981).

In sum, self-efficacy can help promote success in meeting the challenges of life. When people are convinced that they can indeed meet challenges, the resulting sense of self-efficacy will most likely place them in a cycle—a cycle of success.

Janice Fullman/The Picture Cube

The encouragement of an authority figure sometimes makes the difference between success and failure.

Although this book considers a variety of specific ways to help meet the kinds of challenges that life presents, there are certain broad principles that underlie every effort to adjust to the demands of the world around us. Psychologists Rudolf Moos and Jeanne Schaefer (1986) have outlined the major tasks that people must carry out in order to satisfactorily meet some of life's strongest challenges. These tasks include the following:

● *Establish the meaning and understand the personal significance of a situation.* In order to adjust to a particular situation, we must first come to grips with its meaning. Acceptance of life—as it is—is a prerequisite for taking subsequent steps to facilitate adjustment.

● *Confront reality and respond to the necessities of the situation.* Without a clear sense of what is happening to us, and without mapping out a series of steps that need to be taken to deal with a situation, we will be unable to cope with the challenges that confront us. For example, the death of a loved one may require both immediate responses (such as arranging the funeral) and longer-term responses (such as taking over the running of the household finances).

● *Sustain relationships with family members, friends, and others.* Although it is easy to withdraw into a shell when we encounter adversity, it is important to keep lines of communication open and to accept the help of others. Others can give objective advice, provide emotional support, and reassure us about our problems. In some cases, as we will discuss in future chapters, it may be useful to consult professional help-givers such as psychologists; in other cases one's own network of acquaintances is sufficient to provide help. No matter who one chooses to rely on, however, it is important to allow oneself a certain amount of dependence on others.

● *Maintain hope and optimism about the future.* Even in the face of extreme challenge, people who are able to maintain hope and optimism about the future are able to cope better with the difficulties they face than those whose outlook is negative. A sense of self-efficacy, competence, and mastery are particularly constructive in meeting life's challenges.

TO REVIEW

● Adjustment, the efforts people make to meet the demands and challenges placed upon them by the world, is a central task in most people's lives. The field that takes a scientific approach to understanding the challenges of life is psychology.

● Among the major challenges that people face are the challenge of maintaining their individuality, maintaining physical and mental health, forming relationships with others, and living with others in a complex society and world.

● Identity is the sum total of the generalizations we make about ourselves, based on our thoughts, feelings, past behavior, and awareness of our own existence. Identity is made up of the physical self, social self, looking-glass self, and personal self.

● Self-esteem refers to people's general acceptance of themselves, or the degree to which they see themselves as individuals of worth. One component of self-esteem is people's sense of self-efficacy, the belief that they are personally responsible for and can regulate their own behavior, and can thereby bring about a positive outcome.

CHECK YOURSELF

1. Match the situation described in the right column with the specific type of challenge it represents.

_____ Challenge of forming relationships with others

a. Chemicals from illegal dumping may be finding their way into our water supply.

_____ Challenge of maintaining physical and mental health

b. Les and Marion were finding it difficult to end their love affair and become just friends.

_____ Challenge of living with others in a complex society

c. Although her family and friends pressured her to take one job offer, Heather decided that it would be better for her to take another.

_____ Challenge of defining and maintaining one's individuality in the world

d. Gerry's doctor informed him that he would have to reduce the stress in his life and lower his blood pressure.

2. The opinion of ourselves that we form from the information we get from others similar to us, or from those whom we hold in high esteem, is called the:
    a. social self
    b. physical self
    c. personal self
    d. looking-glass self

3. The most useful comparisons a person can make of him- or herself are with those who are notably more competent or skilled. True or false?

4. Bandura believes that people can learn to become more successful in facing challenges and thereby enhance their sense of

_____.

5. One task that assists people in dealing with an adverse challenge is to rely on their inner strength and to disregard the views and advice of others. True or false?

_____

(See answers to these questions at the bottom of page 18)

1.2 THE FACES OF ADJUSTMENT:
Models of Personality and Human Behavior

To ancient peoples, difficulties in adjustment were brought about by the presence of evil spirits in the body. To purge those uninvited inhabitants, an operation known as "trephining" was performed. A hole was made in the skull with a sharpened stone instrument, thereby allowing the spirits to float out of the head.

Hippocrates, the famous Greek physician, had his own thoughts about the causes of adjustment difficulties. He felt that the body contained "humors," or fluids, that influenced people's behavior.

To the early American settlers, people who demonstrated difficulties in adjustment were thought to be possessed by the devil. Treatment typically involved whipping, immersion in hot water, starvation, or other tortures meant to make the afflicted's body inhospitable to the unwanted inhabitant.

It is easy to scoff at the views of the causes of behavior that lie behind each of these approaches to adjustment problems. Each example represents a view of the world that clearly has been disproven by scientific advances.

Yet, although most of us no longer consider behavior to be brought about by evil spirits, humors, or the devil, we still employ conceptual **models**—systems of interrelated ideas and concepts used to explain phenomena—to guide our understanding and investigations into psychological phenomena.

Such models provide a framework from which to view the various factors that affect behavior. Each model provides a different perspective, emphasizing different factors. Just as we may use several maps to find our way around a given geographical area—one to show the roads, another to locate the major buildings, and still another to follow the topography of the land—alternate models provide us with a means of understanding different components of behavior.

Psychologists have developed three major models—the psychodynamic model, the humanistic model, and the behavioral model—that are used to explain and understand human behavior and our own unique **personality**, the set of distinctive and stable characteristics that differentiates us from others and which provides consistency in our behavior across different situations. As we discuss each of the models, it is important to keep in mind that although no single perspective provides a complete account of all human conduct, each helps us to explain the extraordinary breadth of human behavior.

Finding the Inner Person:
The psychodynamic model

The party was without doubt one of the most boring Harry had ever attended—until, that is, Harry spotted the new arrival. A beautiful, friendly looking woman; she seemed perfect to Harry.

It was love at first sight, and Harry quickly began to make his way across the crowded room to see if he could get a conversation going. Thinking about his opening line, he decided he would say something like what he had seen in an old movie on TV the night before: "I don't believe we've been properly introduced yet." Not great, he thought, but it would do as an opening line.

As he approached the woman, Harry smiled at her and began to say what he had practiced in his mind. To his horror—and to the amusement of some bystanders who overheard him—what came out wasn't quite what he had intended: "I don't believe we've been properly seduced yet."

To those who overheard him, Harry's slip of the tongue suggested that something more than mere conversation was on his mind. And many psychologists—particularly those who subscribe to the psychodynamic model of human behavior—would be inclined to agree (Motley, 1987).

To such psychologists, appropriate explanations of human behavior ought to rest on processes and forces that emanate from within the individual. They focus, then, on a person's inner motivations, thoughts, feelings, and attitudes, rather than on the external environment. The psychodynamic model exemplifies this approach.

The psychodymanic model assumes that people have a rich inner life about which they are largely unaware, and which directs their outward behavior. Slips of the tongue, as well as dreams, are viewed as clues to the kinds of inner forces that bring about behavior. The **psychodynamic model,** then, is based on the belief that behavior is brought about by unconscious inner forces over which an individual has little control.

The person most directly associated with the development of the psychodynamic model was Sigmund Freud, a physician living in Vienna at the beginning of the century, who formulated psychoanalytic theory (Freud, 1922). **Psychoanalytic theory** states that unconscious forces act as determinants of personality. According to psychoanalytic theory, our behavior is produced in part by the thoughts, emotions, and desires harbored in the **unconscious,** the part of personality of which a person is not aware. Because many of life's experiences are unpleasant or painful, the unconscious provides a safe haven for recollections of them, where they will not disturb our

Sigmund Freud
formulated the
psychoanalytic theory.

Keystone/The Image Works

conscious existence. Moreover, the unconscious is said to contain **instinctual drives**—the infantlike wishes, desires, demands, and needs that are hidden from our conscious awareness because of the conflicts and pain they would cause us if they were part of everyday life.

According to Freud, personality has three separate, although interacting, parts: the id, the ego, and the superego. Although described as concrete objects, they are not actual physical structures, but rather parts of the abstract model illustrated in Figure 1-1.

The **id** is the raw, unorganized, inherited part of personality whose sole purpose is to reduce tension created by primary drives related to hunger, sex, aggression, and irrational impulses. The id operates according to a **pleasure principle,** in which the goal is the immediate reduction of tension and the maximization of satisfaction.

FIGURE 1-1
The three major structures of personality are the id, the ego, and the superego, according to Freud. However, as this figure shows, only a relatively small part of personality is conscious. It is important to realize that this figure represents a descriptive model of the interrelationships between the various parts of personality, and not an actual physical entity.

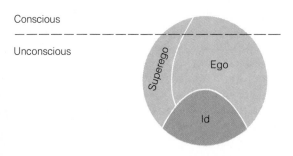

Conscious

Unconscious

Superego

Ego

Id

CHECK YOURSELF: ANSWERS
1. b, d, a, c **2.** d **3.** False **4.** Self-efficacy **5.** False

The id's desires cannot be consistently fulfilled, however, due to the presence of the second part of personality, the ego. The **ego** is the part of personality that provides a buffer between the id and the constraining realities of the objective, outside world. In contrast to the id's cravings for immediate gratification, the ego operates according to the **reality principle,** which holds that instinctual energy is restrained in order to maintain the safety of the individual and help integrate the person into society. Higher-order processes, such as thinking, decision-making, reasoning, and learning generally occur within the ego.

The third part of personality, the **superego,** is the seat of society's do's and do not's, as taught by parents, teachers, and other significant figures in a person's life. The superego becomes part of personality as children learn right from wrong and begin to incorporate the broad moral principles of the society in which they live.

While the superego and id appear to be opposites, in fact they both share an important feature: Each is insensitive to the demands of reality. If the id were to act without the constraints of the ego, a person's life would be primitive and directed solely toward seeking pleasure. On the other hand, a person whose superego is left unchecked would be a perfectionist, unable to make the compromises life requires. In sum, the ego must seek a balance between the irrational pressures of both the superego and the id.

Babies and sex: Freud's theory of psychosexual development.   One of Freud's most controversial assertions was that even the youngest of infants experiences sexual sensations, although the source of these sensations changes as the infant develops. He suggested that individuals move through a series of stages of **psychosexual development,** in which change occurs in the pleasure derived from particular areas of the body. As you can see in Table 1-1, the site of pleasure changes as the child matures. What is partic-

TABLE 1-1
The Stages of Personality Development According to Freud

STAGE	AGE	MAJOR CHARACTERISTICS
Oral	Birth to 12-18 months	Interest in oral gratification from sucking, eating, mouthing, biting
Anal	12-18 months to 3 years	Gratification from expelling and withholding feces; coming to terms with society's controls relating to toilet training
Phallic	3 to 5-6 years	Interest in the genitals; coming to terms with oedipal conflict, leading to identification with same-sex parent
Latency	5-6 years to adolescence	Sexual concerns largely unimportant
Genital	Adolescence to adulthood	Reemergence of sexual interests and establishment of mature sexual relationships

Alan Carey/The Image Works

According to Freud, infants go through an oral phase, during which the mouth is the center of pleasure and gratification.

ularly important about these stages is that experiences and difficulties during particular childhood stages are assumed to be related to specific sorts of idiosyncrasies in adult adjustment.

The **oral stage** is the first period of psychosexual development, lasting from birth to about 12 to 18 months of age. Infants of this age are apt to suck, mouth, and bite anything that can fit into their mouths, leading Freud to surmise that the mouth was the primary site of a kind of sexual pleasure. Moreover, he suggested that infants who are either overly indulged (perhaps by being fed at their every cry) *or* who are very frustrated in their quest for oral gratification might become fixated at this stage. **Fixation** refers to adult behavior which displays characteristics of an earlier stage of development. For instance, an adult who smokes, eats, or talks to excess, or one who is "bitingly" sarcastic, might be considered fixated at the oral period.

The next period is the **anal stage,** a phase in which a child's interests shift toward the anus. Beginning at around 12 to 18 months and ending at 3 years of age, children's major source of pleasure is the expulsion and retention of feces. Because this is the time in which society typically tries to assert its sway over the infant—in the form of toilet training—Freud felt that fixation at this stage is a distinct possibility, producing adults who are unusually rigid, orderly, punctual, clean, or sloppy.

Following the anal stage, the child moves into the **phallic stage,** which lasts from age 3 to around 5 or 6. At this point, interest shifts to the genitals and the pleasure derived from fondling them. The end of the stage also marks one of the most important milestones in development, according to Freud: the Oedipal conflict.

The **Oedipal conflict** represents children's awakening sexual interests in their opposite-sex parent. In the male, this interest becomes linked with the view that the father represents a rival—such a powerful one that the child feels threatened by the father. Due to the perceived threat, the Oedipal conflict is typically pushed to resolution through repression of desires for the mother and instead results in **identification** with the father, in which the son tries to be as similar to the father as possible.

The process is a bit different for females. Freud theorized (in a suggestion that brought about the accusation that he viewed women as inferior to men) that girls, who begin to encounter sexual interest in their fathers, experience **penis envy**—a desire to have the anatomical part that most distinguishes their fathers from them. They begin to blame their mothers for their lack of a penis but, finding such feelings unacceptable, instead begin to identify with their mothers.

Both males and females, then, are assumed to resolve the Oedipal conflict by identifying with their same-sex parent. At that point, Freud suggested that they enter the **latency period,** which lasts until puberty. During latency, little of sexual consequence occurs; it is not until adolescence, around age 12 or 13, that sexual interests reemerge. A person is then said to have entered the **genital stage,** which extends until death. The focus of the genital stage is on mature, adult sexuality—considered by Freud to be sexual intercourse.

Freud: The rights and wrongs   If at first glance Freud's theories seem to you to be unwarranted, you would be joining many critics who have come to a similar conclusion. Freud's psychoanalytic theory has been judged by many observers to be an untestable, unscientific set of propositions that do not allow us to predict behavior with much accuracy.

At the same time, many people find Freud's insights into individuals' development and behavior quite accurate and useful, and Freud's theory has had an enormous impact on the field of psychology specifically and on Western intellectual thought in general. The concepts of the unconscious, childhood sexuality, and fixation at early stages of development have all provided major contributions to understanding how people adjust to the world around them, and, as we will see in Chapter 8, there are a significant number of therapeutic techniques that are based on the Freudian approach. Psychoanalytic theory, then, has proved to be an influential and useful approach to helping people meet life's challenges.

What You Experience Is What You Are:
Behavioral models

In contrast to the psychodynamic emphasis on an individual's inner world, the **behavioral model** suggests that outward, observable behavior should be the focus of study when seeking to explain personality. To a behavioral psychologist, the most appropriate explanation for people's behavior rests in their environment. Internal aspects of the individual—such as thoughts, feelings, and motivations—are acknowledged but are not seen as major determinants of behavior. Behavioral theorists argue that the best explanation for people's behavior comes from examining the features of their environment.

The Bettmann Archive

John B. Watson originated
behaviorism in the 1920s.

According to B. F. Skinner, the most influential of the behavioral theorists, virtually all behavior—be it good or bad—is learned from environmental sources, and the key to understanding an individual's adjustment is
to focus on the rewards and punishments in the environment that have
shaped that person's behavior (Skinner, 1975). The behavioral approach
thus suggests that observable behavior should be the focal point of explanations of human behavior.

A sense of the behavioral approach's emphasis on the importance of
environmental factors comes from a famous comment made by John B.
Watson, the first major American psychologist who championed the behavioral model. He believed that by properly controlling a person's environment,
any desired sort of behavior could be obtained: "Give me a dozen healthy
infants, well-formed, and my own specified world to bring them up in and
I'll guarantee to take any one at random and train him to become any type
of specialist I might select—doctor, lawyer, artist, merchant-chief, and, yes,
even beggarman and thief, regardless of his talents, penchants, tendencies,
abilities, vocations and race of his ancestors" (Watson, 1924).

Stimulus and response: Classical conditioning   The behavioral approach
has identified several kinds of learning that underlie behavior. One of the
first was discovered by Ivan Pavlov, whose dogs became famous for their
digestive and especially their salivary activities (and, in fact, helped win
Pavlov the Nobel prize for his work on digestion). Pavlov is most remembered, though, for his work on learning, which identified a process known
as classical conditioning.

In **classical conditioning**, a person or animal learns a response to a stimulus that normally would not bring about that response. As used in classical conditioning, a **stimulus** is a source of physical energy that activates a sense organ, and a **response** is a reaction to a stimulus. For instance, Pavlov trained his dogs to salivate at the sound of a bell—a stimulus that would not typically bring about salivation. He did so by repeatedly pairing the previously neutral stimulus (the bell) with a stimulus that naturally brought about salivation (food, in this case). After a sufficient number of repetitions, the sound of the bell alone began to produce salivation.

To use Pavlov's terminology, the food represents an **unconditioned stimulus,** a stimulus that brings about a response without having been learned, while salivation is an **unconditioned response,** a response that is natural and needs no training (such as salivation at the smell of food). After repeatedly pairing the presentation of the food with the bell, however, the bell becomes a **conditioned stimulus** (a once-neutral stimulus that, due to its pairings with an unconditioned stimulus, brings about the same response as that of the unconditioned stimulus), and salivation in response to the bell is considered now to be a **conditioned response.**

Although Pavlov's experiments were performed with nonhumans, their potential for understanding people's behavior was quickly recognized. For example, how many of us fear such stimuli as thunderstorms, snakes, or spiders—stimuli which are, in reality, unlikely to harm us? It is unlikely that we were born with such apprehensions, but somehow we learned them as we grew up.

In a now-famous demonstration of the process through which such fears might be classically conditioned, Watson and Rayner (1920) exposed an 11-month-old infant Albert (who initially showed no fear of rats) to a loud noise at the same time that a rat was presented to him. The noise (an unconditioned stimulus) evoked fear (an unconditioned response); after just a few pairings, Albert began to show fear of the rat by itself. The rat, then, had become a conditioned stimulus that brought about the conditioned response, fear.

Classical conditioning underlies the development of many of our emotional reactions. Some of these reactions may be adaptive, as when we learn a healthy fear of hot stoves after being burned a few times. Other emotional reactions, such as irrational fears of other people, may be detrimental to proper adjustment and (as we shall discuss in Chapters 7 and 8) may require treatment aimed at "unlearning" the maladaptive behavior.

Reward and punishment: Operant conditioning   Not every behavior that people carry out is linked to some initially natural response such as salivation or fear of loud noises. Most of the complex behaviors that we perform, such as learning to read or playing a game of tennis, are unlikely to occur naturally. To account for such learned behavior, psychologists describe a second type of learning: operant conditioning.

When individuals learn by **operant conditioning,** they make responses because they have learned that positive or negative consequences are contingent (or dependent) on the response. Unlike classical conditioning (in which the original responses are the natural, biological outgrowth of the presence of some stimulus such as food, water, or pain), operant conditioning applies to voluntary responses, which an organism performs willfully in order to produce desirable consequences. The term **operant** emphasizes that the organism *operates* on its environment to produce some desired result. Thus, studying hard in order to get a good grade and practicing football diligently in order to earn the praise of friends for good performance are both examples of operant conditioning.

The consequences that shape and teach behavior are called **reinforcers,** which are stimuli that increase the probability that a preceding response will be repeated. A good grade reinforces the probability that we will study intensely in the future; congratulations from friends after making a touchdown during a football game will increase the likelihood that we will practice harder subsequently.

Although many reinforcers are **positive reinforcers**—stimuli *added* to the environment that bring about an increase in the response that preceded them—others are negative in nature. **Negative reinforcers** are stimuli whose *removal* is reinforcing, leading to an increase in the probability that a preceding response will occur in the future. For example, your car may have a buzzer that sounds if you do not fasten your seat belt. If the bothersome buzzer increases the frequency of your buckling up, it has operated as a negative reinforcer; the quieting of the buzzer is a negative reinforcer which leads to an increase in buckling-up behavior.

It is important to note that negative reinforcers are not the same as punishment. **Punishment** refers to unpleasant or painful stimuli or events that are *added* to the environment if a certain behavior occurs in order to *decrease* or reduce the behavior that preceded the stimuli or event. Thus, a parent who grounds a teenager for staying out past a curfew is *applying* a stimulus (grounding) in the hopes of *decreasing* undesired behavior. (Technically, there is also another type of punishment known as punishment by removal, in which a positive reinforcer is removed from the environment.)

Although the distinction between negative reinforcers and punishment can be tricky, there is one rule of thumb which helps to distinguish them: A negative reinforcer is meant to *increase* the incidence of a behavior preceding it, while punishment is meant to *decrease* the incidence of a behavior that precedes it.

Learning by imitating: Observational learning Both classical conditioning and operant conditioning assume that a-person has some previous experience with enacting a response before it can be associated with specific stimuli. In classical conditioning, that response must initially occur naturally, as part of an organism's biological makeup; in operant conditioning, the response must be emitted and then followed by a reinforcer for learning to occur. Yet there are many behaviors we learn prior to having any direct experience with relevant stimuli. Airplane pilots and brain surgeons do not learn to fly or operate through trial and error, modifying what they do through practice; instead, they first watch others, learning through the observation of others' technique.

To psychologist Albert Bandura (1977), a major part of human learning consists of **observational learning,** learning through observing the behavior of another person, or *model*. In what is now considered a classic experiment, Bandura and his colleagues demonstrated rather dramatically the ability of models to elicit learning. Young children saw a movie in which an adult wildly hit a five-foot-tall inflatable punching toy called a Bobo doll (Bandura, Ross, & Ross, 1963). Later, the children were given the opportunity to play with the Bobo doll themselves, and, sure enough, they displayed the same kind of behavior, in some cases mimicking the aggressive behavior almost identically.

In Bandura's view, observational learning takes place in four steps: (1) paying attention and perceiving the most critical features of another person's behavior; (2) remembering the behavior; (3) reproducing the action; and (4) being motivated to learn and carry out the behavior. Aside from learning through trial and error, then, with success being reinforced and failure punished, people can also learn through observational processes.

Of course, not all behavior that we witness is learned or carried out. Whether we later imitate a model depends, in part, on what eventually happens to the model as a result of the behavior. If we observe a friend who studies more frequently than we do and receives higher grades, we are more apt to model her behavior than if her studying leads to nothing more than a sharp decline in her social life and an increase in fatigue. Models who are

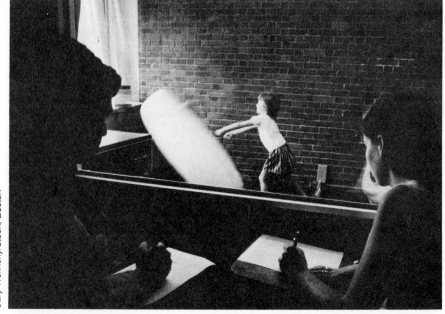

Cary Wolinsky/Stock, Boston

In Bandura's experiments, children who first watched an adult hitting the doll were more likely to play aggressively with the doll themselves than children who had not seen an aggressive adult.

seen receiving reinforcement for their actions are more likely to be mimicked than those who receive punishment.

To many psychologists, observational learning theory represents something of a hybrid theory. Rather than being purely behavioral—by ignoring the internal concerns of a person and focusing entirely on external, environmental factors—observational learning theory does consider mental activity to be a legitimate factor. In doing so, it has spawned some important treatment approaches (described in Chapter 8) for maladaptive behaviors which focus on modifying people's maladaptive thoughts and perceptions about the world.

Evaluating behavioral approaches   Despite observational learning theory's admission that at least some kinds of mental activity represent appropriate realms of investigation, critics of the behavioral approach sharply condemn the relative lack of interest in internal processes. To them, behaviorists miss the boat because of their reliance on events outside of the person and their propensity to ignore people's individuality and internal motivations.

On the other hand, proponents of the behavioral approach point to advances that have been made in understanding specific sorts of difficulties in adjustment (such as understanding the source of specific fears and phobias), as well as to several types of effective treatments that have grown out of behavioral approaches. Indeed, the amenability of everyday problems to behavioral treatment illustrates some of the merit of the approach.

The Goodness from Within:
The humanistic model

Moving slowly through the ward filled with children at the charity hospital, Mother Teresa reached out to wipe the forehead of one child, whose body was obviously wracked with pain. The child looked up at Mother Teresa, and—with obvious effort—attempted a smile. Mother Teresa smiled back, and offered a few words of comfort to the dying child. She then moved on to the next bed, filled with yet another homeless, poor, and sick child.

Mother Teresa, who won the Nobel prize for her efforts to help people who are unable to help themselves, displays the best that we can expect of ourselves as human beings. Yet, at the same time, the individuals to whom she offers aid and comfort reveal their own kind of dignity and uniqueness as individuals, sharing a basic humanity with Mother Teresa and all other people of the world.

The **humanistic model** emphasizes people's basic goodness and their natural tendency to rise to higher levels of functioning. In contrast to other approaches, which focus on the unseen, negative, unconscious forces controlling behavior (as in the psychodynamic model) or on situational rewards and punishments (as in the behavioral model), humanistic approaches spotlight the uniqueness of the individual. People are viewed as being consciously motivated to improve both themselves and the world in which they live. The humanistic view, then, is an optimistic, positive one; people are assumed to have it within themselves to strive for and attain a more fulfilling existence.

Although there are several versions of humanistic theory, probably the best articulated is that of psychologist Carl Rogers (1971). According to Rogers, individuals are constantly striving to reach a state in which their everyday needs are fulfilled and they have reached their highest potential and developed their capacities and talents to the fullest.

However, this drive toward self-fulfillment frequently conflicts with a need for **positive regard,** love, and respect that we seek from others. Because others provide this positive regard, we grow dependent on them, and we begin to see and judge ourselves through the eyes of others, relying on their values.

In Rogers' view, one outcome of placing so much emphasis on others is that there is often some degree of mismatch between a person's experiences and his or her self-concept. For example, if you consider yourself a generous, warm individual, and someone treats you as if you were greedy and cold, you will experience incongruence. If such discord is minor, there are few consequences. But larger discrepancies may affect adjustment adversely and may impede everyday functioning. One way to overcome such discrepancies between one's experience and self-concept is through the receipt of unconditional positive regard from others such as friends or a spouse. **Unconditional positive regard** consists of supportive behavior to-

Courtesy of Center for Studies of Person

Carl Rogers developed a humanistic approach to psychology, exemplified by client-centered therapy in which a therapist gives unconditional support to the client.

ward another person, regardless of what that person does. By receiving unconditional positive regard from others, individuals are taught that although their *behavior* may be legitimately evaluated as good or bad, they, as people, are still viewed positively. Such support provides a person with the opportunity to grow and develop a more realistic self-concept. (To get some insight into your own self-concept, see the following Do It! box.)

DO IT!

ASSESSING YOUR SELF-CONCEPT

How well do you know yourself? To get a sense of how you view yourself, place a checkmark next to each item that describes you, using the first column for your checks. Be truthful and honest with yourself. Next, go back over the list and place a check beside each item that describes your ideal self—the kind of person that you would like to be. (Use the second column for these ratings.) Work through the list quickly.

1. Absentminded _____ _____

2. Anxious _____ _____

3. Artistic _____ _____

4. Attractive _____ _____

5. Capable _____ _____

6. Charming _____ _____

7. Clear-thinking _____ _____

8. Clever _____ _____

9. Confused _____ _____

10. Courageous _____ _____

11. Dissatisfied _____ _____

12. Dreamy _____ _____

13. Emotional _____ _____

14. Energetic _____ _____

15. Enterprising _____ _____

16. Excitable _____ _____

17. Forceful _____ _____

18. Forgetful _____ _____

19. Gentle _____ _____

20. Good-looking _____ _____

21. Handsome _____ _____

22. Hardheaded _____ _____

23. Hasty _____ _____

24. Headstrong _____ _____

25. Hurried _____ _____

26. Imaginative _____ _____

27. Impatient _____ _____

28. Impulsive _____ _____

29. Industrious _____ _____

30. Ingenious _____ _____

31. Initiating _____ _____

32. Insightful _____ _____

33. Inventive _____ _____

34. Moody _____ _____

35. Irritable _____ _____

36. Nervous _____ _____

37. Original _____ _____

38. Persevering _____ _____

39. Pessimistic _____ _____

40. Polished _____ _____

41. Preoccupied _____ _____

42. Resourceful _____ _____

43. Restless _____ _____

44. Tactful _____ _____

45. Wise _____ _____

46. Witty _____ _____

SCORING Make three lists. In the first, list the terms that are characteristic of your real, not your ideal, self. In the second list, place those characteristics that you feel are your ideal, not your real, traits. Finally, make a third list of the characteristics that apply to both your ideal self and your real self.

The first list tells you things about yourself that are inconsistent with the way you would like to be. The second list gives you a sense of the way you would like to be but aren't. Finally, the last list shows you the traits on which you already match your ideal. How well do your ideal and real self-concepts match up?

Source: Byrne & Kelley, 1981.

Like other humanistic theories, Rogers' approach to human behavior is decidedly upbeat and optimistic. In contrast to both psychodynamic approaches, which view humans in a fairly negative light, and behavioral approaches, which take a neutral stance, humanistic theories see the individual from a positive vantage point. People are assumed to be inherently good and have worth and value, and they are thought to be striving toward self-improvement.

On the other hand, several criticisms have been leveled against humanistic approaches. For example, it is difficult, if not impossible, to verify some of the fundamental assumptions of humanistic approaches, such as the proposition that people are basically good and striving for fulfillment. Moreover, some of the major concepts of the humanistic approach are stated in fuzzy terms, lacking clear-cut definitions. Psychodynamic theorists argue that any account of human behavior that deemphasizes the unconscious—as do humanistic approaches—is bound to be incomplete. Still, the emphasis of humanistic approaches on allowing individuals to discover a sense of understanding and fulfillment in their lives makes it a theory that has a special relevance to people living in a world as complex as ours.

TO REVIEW

● Conceptual models, systems of interrelated ideas and concepts, provide a framework that can guide our understanding and investigations into the factors that affect behavior.

● The psychodynamic model is based on the belief that behavior is brought about by unconscious inner forces over which we have little control.

● Freud's psychoanalytic theory suggests that personality has three separate, although interacting, parts: the id, the ego, and the superego. His theory of psychosexual development suggests that people move through a series of stages in which the focus of pleasure shifts to different parts of the body. The stages are the oral, anal, phallic, latency, and genital periods.

● The behavioral model focuses on the person's overt behavior and the environment, deemphasizing the importance of internal events that are not directly observable.

- Among the major approaches that make up the behavioral model are classical conditioning, operant conditioning, and observational learning.

- The humanistic model emphasizes our uniqueness as individuals and our natural tendency to strive for higher levels of functioning.

- According to the major humanistic theory, proposed by Carl Rogers, people attempt to become self-fulfilled, although this may conflict with their need for positive regard.

CHECK YOURSELF

1. Psychodynamic, humanistic, and behavioral perspectives are examples of three guiding _____ in our search to understand human behavior and personality.

2. The instinctual drives arising from the *id* are tempered by the constraints of reality provided by the:
    a. ego
    b. pleasure principle
    c. superego
    d. conscience

3. Joseph is excessively compulsive about cleaning himself and his living environment. Freud would suggest that he is fixated at what stage?
    a. phallic
    b. anal
    c. oral
    d. psychosexual

4. According to Freud, adolescents eventually enter a stage of psychosexual development which extends until death. What stage is this?
    a. anal
    b. oral
    c. genital
    d. latency

5. Behavioral psychologists focus on the external determinants of behavior and deny the existence of internal aspects as having any effect on us. True or false?

6. The act of blinking when confronted with a flash of light in our face is an example of a(n):
    a. unconditioned stimulus
    b. conditioned response
    c. conditioned stimulus
    d. unconditioned response

7. Reading novels, because of the pleasure they provide, is an example of behavior resulting from _____ conditioning.

8. Running to get out of a cold rain is a response brought about through:
   a. punishment
   b. positive reinforcement
   c. classical conditioning
   d. negative reinforcement

9. Carl Rogers advocates the importance of being supportive of another individual, even if we do not approve of that individual's behavior, through the delivery of _____ _____ _____.

_____

(See answers to these questions at the bottom of page 34.)

1.3   WHICH IS RIGHT?:
Comparing Theories

The three major approaches to behavior—the psychodynamic, behavioral, and humanistic approaches—provide significantly different accounts of the forces that produce human behavior. Is one of the approaches the right one?

The answer is that such a question is an inappropriate one. Each theory looks at somewhat different aspects of behavior and holds different premises. In most instances, behavior can be reasonably considered from a number of perspectives simultaneously.

Take, for instance, the scenario regarding Chris O'Hara that opened the chapter. Chris, who seemed on the surface to be an individual whose life was free from problems, was having difficulties concentrating on his schoolwork and became easily distracted and annoyed. In addition, he was beginning to harbor questions about his purpose in life.

To understand Chris's problem, a psychodynamic theoretician would consider the unconscious forces that underlie his behavior. Chris's background and early development during childhood would be examined, and his current behavior would be seen in light of events that occurred earlier in his life.

In contrast, someone taking a behavioral approach would focus on the here and now. The rewards—and punishments—found in Chris's environment would be identified, and his observable behavior would be the focus of attention. Rather than his behavior being seen as a symptom of some underlying unconscious conflict, as emphasized in psychodynamic theory, a behavioral theoretician would consider Chris's behavior itself as a difficulty in need of modification.

A theorist employing a humanistic approach would focus on still another aspect of Chris's behavior. To a humanistic psychologist, there is something that is interfering with Chris's ability to achieve self-fulfillment, and it would be assumed that there is incongruence between Chris's actual and ideal self-concepts. In order to bring about a change in Chris's behavior, a humanistic psychologist's goal would be to release Chris's innate ability to deal with his problems, allowing him to develop more fully.

As you can see, each of the three theoretical perspectives takes a different approach and focuses on slightly different aspects of Chris's problem. Because of this, it is difficult to say that one theory is more "right" than another. The choice of which theory would be most appropriate depends, then, on the particular component of the problem that has greatest relevance to Chris. Moreover, each theory leads to different treatment strategies, as we will discuss in detail in Chapter 8. (For a sample of procedures that grow out of a particular theoretical approach, see the following Do It! box).

DO IT!

USING BEHAVIORAL APPROACHES TO MANAGE YOUR LIFE

The behavioral approach provides an example of how a theoretical perspective can be used to bring about change in your own life and behavior. After identifying a behavior that is in need of improvement, try following these steps (Royer & Feldman, 1984):

☐ *Specifying goals and target behaviors.* The first step is to identify your desired behavior change. Is it a loss of weight? An increase in amount of time spent studying? A decline in the number of fights you have with a roommate? The goals that lead to your specific targets must be specified in clear, observable terms. For example, if your desired change is a loss of weight, your goals might be "a loss of ten pounds in ten weeks" following a diet in which "calorie intake is reduced to 1,200 calories per day."

☐ *Designing a data recording system and recording preliminary data.* In order to determine whether you are successful in changing your behavior, you need to define your starting place. For instance, if your goal is to study more, you must be aware, with some degree of precision, how much time you now spend studying. This provides you with a baseline against which any subsequent change can be measured.

☐ *Selecting a behavior-change strategy.* This, of course, is the heart of a behavioral modification program. For example, in order to study more, you might work out a self-reinforcement system in which you "reward" yourself for increases in study time by purchasing a candy bar (obviously not the best choice if you are simultaneously trying to lose weight!). In addition, you might reward yourself by scheduling some "time off" every once in awhile, particularly after long periods of intensive study.

☐ *Implementing the strategy.* The next step is to institute the program of behavior change. It is important to maintain the program consistently in order for it to be effective. It is also crucial to continue keeping careful records of your progress toward the target behavior so that you will be aware of whether or not your program is working.

☐ *Evaluating and altering the ongoing program.* If you consistently advance in your program, getting closer and closer to your desired behavior, there is no need to modify the program. Once you have reached your goal, you can phase out the procedures. But if the program is not working, you should not hesitate to consider alternative approaches to modifying your own behavior.

Contrasting Theories:
Dimensions of comparison

Although the potential exists that someday there will be a common thread that can be used to explain all behavior, psychology has not yet reached that point. Until that happens, we are left with a series of disparate approaches. However, there are ways in which the theories can be compared and contrasted. Among the most important dimensions along which the theories differ are the following:

● *Unconscious versus conscious processes.* Humanistic theories place their emphasis on the conscious: Events are considered important only if a person actually is aware of them. In contrast, psychodynamic approaches emphasize the unconscious, suggesting that much of our everyday behavior is motivated by forces in the unconscious about which we are not aware. Behavioral theory takes a neutral stance, largely disregarding both the conscious and unconscious, emphasizing instead an individual's environment.

● *Nature (genetic factors) versus nurture (environmental factors).* Psychodynamic theory stresses genetic factors, which unfold during development in a natural progression; behavioral theory emphasizes environmental factors in determining behavior. Humanistic approaches take an intermediate view, stressing the interaction between both nature and nurture in producing behavior.

● *Freedom versus determinism.* Humanistic theories clearly emphasize the freedom that individuals have in making choices that affect their lives; other approaches stress **determinism,** the view that behavior is directed and produced by factors outside of people's willful control. Determinism is particularly evident in psychodynamic and behavioral approaches, which stress factors that are outside of people's voluntary control.

CHECK YOURSELF: ANSWERS
1. models **2.** a **3.** b **4.** c **5.** False **6.** d **7.** operant **8.** d **9.** unconditional positive regard

"The secrets of happiness revealed by psychologists."
"Cancer cured through psychology."
"Read others like a book."
"Stop smoking forever through hypnosis."
"Three easy steps to a better sex life."

You need only to turn to the psychology section of your local bookstore or peruse the newspaper and magazine rack next to the checkout counters at most supermarkets to see a multiplicity of titles such as these. Moreover, the number of self-help books now in print numbers well into the thousands, with no end in sight.

Can you, in fact, improve your adjustment (and become a better person to boot) by following the advice given by such books and articles? In general, the answer must be, "It depends." Not all such books and articles are written by reputable individuals, and just because something is in print does not

When choosing among the many self-help books published each year, it is important to ensure the advice is based on sound research.

Innervisions

mean it is accurate. You should proceed with great caution, then, before taking the advice of so-called experts in human behavior.

There are some general guidelines you can follow which will help you to distinguish between accurate and inaccurate statements about psychology.

● *The advice should be based on research findings, not the author's guesses about what works.* The author should refer to research that has been published in reputable journals, which you can look up yourself. Beware of advice that is not substantiated by research.

● *Changing one's behavior is not easy.* Don't be led astray by promises of quick change in your life. If changing your habits or solving your problems were as simple and easy as some authors would have you believe, you probably would have done it by yourself already. There is no free ride when it comes to changing well-entrenched patterns of behavior—it requires effort on your part.

● *There is no universal method that can solve everyone's problems.* The same approach will not work for all difficulties, and a particular technique may not work for all individuals.

Don't let these cautionary notes, however, mislead you into thinking that psychology has little to offer. On the contrary, psychologists have developed powerful techniques to improve the quality of your everyday life. In fact, by the time you have completed *Adjustment: Applying Psychology in a Complex World,* you will be familiar with a range of possibilities for improving your life. As you will see, psychology has much to offer.

TO REVIEW

● Each of the three major theoretical perspectives takes a different approach and focuses on particular aspects of behavior.

● Among the dimensions along which the theories can be compared are unconscious versus conscious processes, nature versus nurture, and freedom versus determinism.

● There are several rules of thumb that can be used to determine the accuracy of information about psychology.

CHECK YOURSELF

1. Whereas psychodynamic theory is more interested in unconscious processes, _____ theory is concerned more with conscious processes.

2.   When considering the role of nature versus nurture, what two theories take the most divergent positions?
   a.   humanistic versus behavioral
   b.   behavioral versus deterministic
   c.   psychodynamic versus behavioral
   d.   psychodynamic versus humanistic

3.   The view that behavior is directed and produced by factors outside of people's willful control is known as _____.

4.   Which of the following is *not* characteristic of sound psychological literature?
   a.   the admission by the author(s) that the advice may not be right for everyone
   b.   advice which does not rely heavily on research findings
   c.   a large bibliography of published studies
   d.   a statement indicating that positive behavior change may be slow in coming

(See answers to these questions at the bottom of page 38.)

TO SUMMARIZE

1.   When we speak of adjustment, we are referring to the efforts people make to meet the demands and challenges placed on them by the world. To understand adjustment, psychologists, who study behavior and mental processes, use scientific methods to predict, control, and understand phenomena.

2.   There are several major kinds of challenges that people face. Among the most important are the challenge of maintaining one's individuality in the world, maintaining physical and mental health, forming relationships with others, and living with others in a complex society and world.

3.   One of the central issues of adjustment relates to identity, the collection of generalizations we make about ourselves. Identity is made up of several components: the physical self, our image of the physical aspects of our body; the social self, the various roles we play in life; and the personal self, that private part of ourselves that is apparent only to us. The social self is a reflection of the looking-glass self, the view of one's self that is provided by society and by other specific, significant others. We use social comparison processes to obtain information relevant to the looking-glass self.

4.   Self-esteem refers to one's general acceptance of oneself, and it affects physical and psychological health and coping capabilities. It is also related to one's characteristic sense of self-efficacy, the belief that one is personally responsible for and can regulate one's own behavior, thereby bringing about a particular outcome.

5.   There are three major models—systems of interrelated ideas and concepts—used to explain behavior and our personality, the set of distinctive and stable characteristics that differentiate us from others and provide consistency in our behavior across different situations. These models are the psychodynamic model, the behavioral model, and the humanistic model.

6.   The psychodynamic model is based on the belief that behavior is brought about by unconscious inner forces over which an individual has little control. The psychodynamic model is represented by psychoanalytic theory, which was developed by Freud. Freud suggested that behavior is produced in part by the thoughts, emotions, and desires harbored in the unconscious, the part of personality of which the individual is not aware.

7.   Psychoanalytic theory proposes that there are three parts of personality: the id (containing instinctual drives), the ego (which provides a buffer between reality and the id), and the superego (containing society's do's and do not's). Moreover, it suggests that people move through a series of stages of psychosexual development, in which pleasure is derived from particular areas of the body. The stages include the oral stage, anal stage, phallic stage, Oedipal conflict, latency period, and genital stage.

8.   The behavioral approach focuses on environmental rewards and punishments and people's overt behavior, rather than their inner thoughts, feelings, and motivations. Proponents of behaviorism, the psychological model that suggests that observable behavior should be the focus of study, believe that behavior is affected primarily by factors outside the individual.

9.   Among the major kinds of learning identified by the behavioral approach is classical conditioning. In classical conditioning, a person or animal learns a response to a stimulus that normally does not bring about the response. For example, food to a dog represents an unconditioned stimulus, which brings about the unconditioned response of salivation. If a bell is paired repeatedly with the presentation of food, however, the bell will become a conditioned stimulus that brings about the conditioned response of salivation.

10. In operant conditioning, the focus is on learning in which people make a response because they have learned that positive or negative consequences are dependent on the response. The outcomes that shape and teach behavior are called reinforcers, stimuli that increase the probability that a preceding response will be repeated. Positive reinforcers are stimuli added to the environment that bring about an increase in the response that preceded them, while negative reinforcers are stimuli whose removal is reinforcing. In contrast, punishment refers to unpleasant or painful stimuli that are added to the environment in order to suppress behavior.

---

1. humanistic   2. c   3. determinism   4. b

11. In observational learning, behavior is learned through the observation of the behavior of another person, known as a model. Observational learning takes place in four steps: (1) paying attention and perceiving the most critical features of another person's behavior, (2) remembering the behavior, (3) reproducing the action, and (4) being motivated to learn and carry out the behavior.

12. Humanistic approaches emphasize people's basic goodness and their natural tendency to rise to higher levels of functioning. Among the best-known of the humanistic theories is that of Carl Rogers, who suggests people seek self-fulfillment.

13. Although it is natural to ask which approach is right, in actuality this is an inappropriate question. Each theory looks at somewhat different aspects of behavior and holds different premises. The theories differ on several major dimensions, including their emphasis on unconscious versus conscious processes, nature (genetic) versus nurture (environmental) factors, and freedom versus determinism.

KEY TERMS AND CONCEPTS

adjustment (p. 6)

psychology (p. 7)

identity (p. 10)

physical self (p. 11)

social self (p. 11)

looking-glass self (p. 11)

social comparison (p. 11)

personal self (p. 12)

self-esteem (p. 12)

self-efficacy (p. 13)

models (p. 16)

personality (p. 16)

psychodynamic model (p. 17)

psychoanalytic theory (p. 17)

unconscious (p. 17)

instinctual drives (p. 18)

id (p. 18)

pleasure principle (p. 18)

ego (p. 19)

reality principle (p. 19)

superego (p. 19)

psychosexual development (p. 19)

Oedipal conflict (p. 20)

identification (p. 21)

penis envy (p. 21)

latency period (p. 21)

genital stage (p. 21)

behavioral model (p. 21)

classical conditioning (p. 23)

stimulus (p. 23)

response (p. 23)

unconditioned stimulus (p. 23)

unconditioned response (p. 23)

conditioned stimulus (p. 23)

conditioned response (p. 23)

operant conditioning (p. 23)

operant (p. 24)

reinforcers (p. 24)

positive reinforcers (p. 24)

negative reinforcers (p. 24)

punishment (p. 24)

observational learning (p. 25)

humanistic model (p. 26)

positive regard (p. 27)

oral stage (p. 20)
fixation (p. 20)
anal stage (p. 20)
phallic stage (p. 20)

unconditional positive regard
(p. 27)
determinism (p. 34)

TO FIND OUT MORE

Grasha, A. F. (1983). *Practical applications of psychology.* Boston: Little, Brown.
Feldman, R. S. (1987). *Understanding Psychology.* New York: McGraw-Hill.
   Two overviews of the field of psychology, the first highlighting applications and
the second having a broader focus on research, theory, and applications.

Feist, J. (1985). *Theories of personality.* New York: Holt.
   A good overview of the major approaches to understanding personality and
human behavior.

Stanovich, K. E. (1986). *How to think straight about psychology.* Glenview, IL:
Scott, Foresman.
   An interesting guide relating how one goes about separating good psychology
from bad psychology, emphasizing the ways in which data can be collected and
quantified in an objective manner.

American Psychological Association (1988). *Careers in psychology,* Washington, DC:
American Psychological Association.
   This booklet describes the various types of psychologists in detail, with practical
advice regarding careers in psychology. It can be obtained—free—by writing to the
American Psychological Association, 1200 17th Street, N.W., Washington, DC 20036.

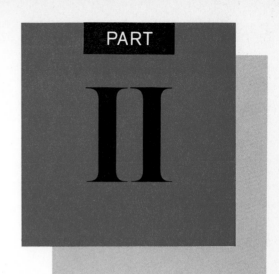

PART

II

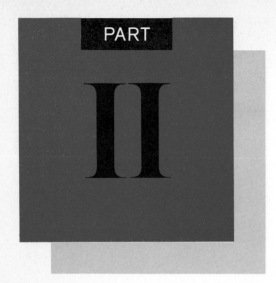

THE
INDIVIDUAL

In this part of the book, we encounter a racial incident with a deadly outcome. We meet two people, one of whom is viewed as old and the other as young—yet who are the same age. And we contemplate the bravery of a flier who manages to meet the challenge of a dangerous sea rescue.

This portion of the book considers the individual. We discuss the way in which individuals think about and come to an understanding of the world, and how that understanding colors their perception of others and their behavior. We examine how individuals grow and develop as they mature, and look at the critical changes that occur across the life span. Finally, we discuss the kinds of challenges people seek out, as we consider the factors that motivate our behavior and how our needs direct and energize behavior.

In Chapter 2, then, we focus on understanding and thinking about the world.

In Chapter 3, the discussion centers on development, beginning at birth and ending with death.

In Chapter 4, we concentrate on human motivation and the forces that underlie human behavior.

Understanding and Thinking About the World

CHAPTER

2

45

To a casual passerby, the Howard Beach area of Queens, New York, is a pleasant place, no different from hundreds of other urban areas in the country. Yet it was also the scene of one of the most jarring episodes of prejudice to occur in the United States in recent times.

In what the mayor called a "racial lynching" and "the most horrendous incident" of his nine years in office, four white teenagers chased and beat three black men whose only crime was walking through the neighborhood where the white teenagers lived.

The victims were pursued, taunted with racial insults, kicked, and beaten with fists, a baseball bat, and a tree limb. One of them escaped after being hit just once with a bat, while another was severely beaten until he pretended to be unconscious.

The least fortunate of the three, Michael Griffith, a 23-year-old construction worker, was viciously beaten and then was hit and killed by a car as he tried to escape from his attackers by running across a busy highway.

It would be easy to dismiss this episode as an isolated one, carried out by a few extreme, odd individuals. Unfortunately, though, this case is an example of a phenomenon—prejudice—which is far from rare in our world. How do people come to hold and act upon such extreme negative evaluations of others? This question, and ones related to it, comprise the central threads of this chapter.

In the chapter, we examine the way people think about and understand the world. We begin by considering the most basic processes that underlie our view and interpretation of the world around us. We examine the way in which people make sense out of the complex and varied sources of stimulation that they find in their environment. We then discuss how people form impressions about others and make inferences about the reasons behind others' behavior, as well as their own. Finally, we focus directly on prejudice in its many forms, considering both its impact on people's lives and techniques for reducing its occurrence and effects.

2.1   THINKING ABOUT THE WORLD:
Perception, Cognition, and Creative Problem Solving

Picture driving down a familiar road on a pleasant evening. It's dark, but the weather is clear and the traffic is light. Suddenly you hear a thud from underneath the car. You puzzle over the noise for a moment, decide it was either a piece of wood, a pothole, or some other obstacle, and drive on. Later that night, the police come to your home and tell you that one of two pedestrians walking along the road earlier has been struck by a car and killed. Badly shaken, the other person described your car and remembered your license plate number. You are arrested and charged with manslaughter. (Leibowitz & Owens, 1986, p. 55.)

As frightening as this scene may sound, it could happen to any of us. More than 50 percent of all traffic fatalities occur at night, even though far fewer miles are driven then than during daylight hours.

The explanation for this phenomenon rests on the way people perceive, think about, and come to understand the world. The fact that we are able to recognize old friends after many years apart, figure the square root of 25, and even turn the forms on this page into meaningful words and sentences merely scratches the surface of our wondrous abilities to sense and make sense of the world around us. At the same time, we are not infallible, and ultimately there are situations—such as that described above—that test the boundaries and limitations of our abilities and understanding of the world.

Understanding the World: Perception

If you believe that there are only five senses—vision, hearing, smell, taste, and touch—you are suffering from a common misconception. Psychologists specializing in the senses now suggest that each of these senses can be subdivided into others. For example, we can discriminate not only touch but related stimuli such as pain, pressure, temperature, and vibration. Similarly, the ear is not only sensitive to sounds but provides a sense of balance as well.

The discriminability of each of these senses is remarkable. For example, we are capable of seeing a candle flame 30 miles away on a dark, clear night; we are able to hear the ticking of a watch twenty feet away; we can smell one drop of perfume in a three-room apartment; and we can sense the touch of a bee's wing falling against our skin (Galanter, 1962).

However, it is not human beings' sensitivities that set them apart from other species in their ability to respond to and understand the world. (Dogs, for instance, have a far keener sense of smell, birds have better vision, and deer are better able to detect sound.) Instead, it is their ability to give meaning to stimuli that are sensed.

Perception is the sorting out, interpretation, analysis, and integration of stimuli from our sense organs. We use perception to process the raw sensory stimuli provided by our senses and to turn such stimuli into something meaningful and useful. Through perception, we are able to gather information from the environment and turn it into knowledge that defines and guides our view of the world.

One way of understanding the importance of our perceptual abilities is to consider what would happen if we did not have them. Suppose, for example, we responded to every stimulus that the world presented to us. Even sitting in a quiet library, glancing at a magazine, we would soon be over-whelmed with information, as the colors in the magazine's photos, the feel of the chair, the sound of the ventilation system, the smell of the books, and the taste of the gum we were chewing all made themselves known.

Fortunately, though, we engage in **selective attention,** a process in which we choose which stimulus to perceive and pay attention to. In fact, research in which two entirely different messages are presented simultaneously through earphones shows that people are capable of understanding only one of the messages at a time (Cherry, 1953). On the other hand, we are still capable of responding to alternate stimuli if the other stimuli are sufficiently intense, as anyone who has been engrossed in a book, yet hears the ringing of a phone, can attest to.

Moreover, there is a general sensitivity to information that is relevant to our goals, desires, and emotions. A person who is on a strict diet will often be unusually sensitive to stimuli relating to food. Similarly, individuals in a depressed state are more apt to be aware of and attentive to the unhappy stimuli in their lives—their poor relationships with friends or their bad grades—while at the same time they ignore stimuli related to more positive aspects of their lives, such as a good job or a happy marriage. This tendency to attend to the stimuli that are most relevant to us is another manifestation of selective attention.

Making sense of a changing world: simplifying the complex   As part of our efforts to understand the world, we often reduce the complex stimuli presented to us into more manageable, comprehensible stimuli. For example, rather than viewing Figure 2-1 as a series of unrelated blotches, we are able

FIGURE 2-1
Although the eye does the work of taking in the visual stimulus—in this case, black and white splotches—it is the brain that makes sense out of the splotches and sees a dog.

My phone number is area
code 604, 876-1569. Please call!

FIGURE 2-2
When you first look at this message, you probably read it as "My phone number is area code 604, 876-1569. Please call." But a closer look suggests that there are quite a few ambiguities. For instance, the word "is" and the number "15" are written identically, as are the "h" in "phone" and the "b" in the word "number." The fact that you likely had no difficulties in sorting out these ambiguities illustrates the impact of context on perception. (*Source:* Coren, Porac, & Ward, 1979).

to pick out the dog. Similarly, we see a complete message in Figure 2-2, even though individual portions are ambiguous.

Our quest to make sense of the world and our reliance on previous experience to evaluate stimuli sometimes result in oversimplification and consequent misperception. Take, for example, the high incidence of night-time driving accidents mentioned earlier. Most drivers assume that their vision is adequate for traveling after dark and consequently drive as if they were operating their vehicles in daylight. However, not only do the eyes and the rest of the visual sensory system operate much less efficiently in dimness, but various visual functions—such as the perception of color—are affected differently by the decline in light (Leibowitz & Owens, 1986). Our reliance on past experience, then, can result both in overconfidence and in potentially deadly errors.

Thinking Straight:
Cognition

Have you ever spent hours trying to solve a problem and suddenly—like the flashing of a lightbulb above someone's head in an old cartoon—had the solution come to you? Most of us have had a similar experience in which we attain **insight,** a sudden awareness of the relationship between various elements of a problem that had previously appeared to be independent of one another.

An understanding of the processes involved in the development of insight, as well as a broader concern over the way people think about the world, comes from the field of cognition. **Cognition** considers how people know and understand the world, process information, make judgments and decisions, and describe their knowledge and understanding to others (Bourne, Dominowski, Loftus, & Healy, 1986).

A chimp named Sultan actually provided the initial impetus for a good deal of inquiry into cognition. In the 1920s, Wolfgang Kohler, a German psychologist, studied problem-solving processes by placing Sultan in a cage with a bunch of bananas hanging high above his head. Kohler provided Sultan with the tools to reach them; some small boxes and sticks were strewn about the cage. Standing on a box, Sultan still could not reach the bananas. But if he stood on a box *and* reached with a stick, he could knock down the bananas, thereby attaining his goal.

49

Wolfgang Kohler used bunches of bananas, placed in plain sight but out of reach, to observe problem solving in chimpanzees. Here the chimp Sultan seems to display insight, without having been shown or taught that he can stack up boxes and climb on them to reach the bananas.

Sultan's behavior was enlightening. At first, he stomped around the cage in frustration. He stood on a box, he jumped, he threw the stick, but he still couldn't reach them. Eventually, while engaged in some entirely different activity, he suddenly grabbed the stick and stood on a box—and reached his bananas. According to Kohler, Sultan had attained insight into the situation.

Chimps, of course, are not the only ones with insight; people seem to come to solutions in an analogous fashion. For example, some people solve the problem illustrated in the Do It! box on the next page (Duncker, 1945) with a burst of insight.

On the other hand, most of us are unable to solve the problem initially, due to an impediment to problem solving known as **functional fixedness,** the tendency to think of an object only in terms of its typical use. In the candle problem, for example, functional fixedness occurs when the objects are inside the box, because the box's most typical use—as a container—interferes with a consideration of the box as a part of the problem's solution.

ILLUMINATE THIS QUANDARY

To try your hand at problem solving, consider the following problem:
You are presented with a set of tacks, candles, and matches in small boxes (see Figure 2-3). Your goal: Place three candles at eye level on the door so that wax will not drip on the floor as the candles burn. How can this be done?

Solution   The answer to the problem seems obvious when you see it illustrated in Figure 2-4. Actually, you might have solved it easily if the initial presentation of the problem in Figure 2-3 had shown the items lying on the table beside the boxes rather than lying inside the boxes. This problem, then, illustrates how functional fixedness can act as an impediment to problem solving.

Solving by the number: step-by-step solutions to problems   Consider the puzzle shown in Figure 2-5, which represents a simplified (although still difficult) version of a puzzle that a group of monks in Hanoi are said to be working on. The monks who came across this problem, known as the Tower of Hanoi puzzle, believe that the end of the world will be at hand when they solve it. (Because it is estimated that it will take approximately a trillion years for them to find the solution, you can rest easy.)

In our simpler version of the puzzle, there are three posts on which three doughnuts are to be placed in the order illustrated. The goal is to move

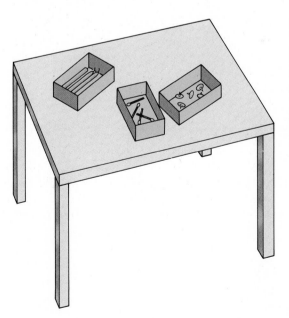

FIGURE 2-3
The problem here is to place three candles at eye level on a nearby door so that the wax will not drip on the floor as the candles burn—using only the materials in the figure (tacks, candles, and matches in small boxes).

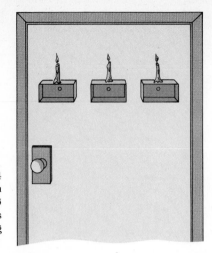

FIGURE 2-4
A solution to the problem
posed in Figure 2-3
involves tacking the boxes
to the door and placing
the candles on the boxes

FIGURE 2-5
The goal of the Tower of
Hanoi problem is to move
all three disks from the
first post to the last while
preserving the original
order of the disks, and
using the smallest number
of moves possible. Try it
yourself before you look at
the solution. (Solution:
Move C to 3, B to 2, C to
2, A to 3, C to 1, B to 3,
and C to 3.)

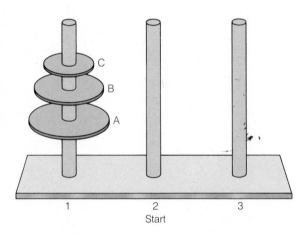

1   2   3
Start

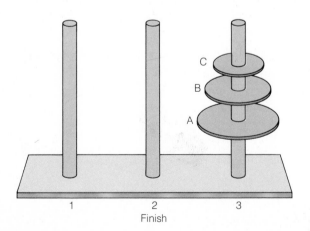

1   2   3
Finish

all three of the doughnuts to the third post in the same order, using the smallest number of moves. The rules are that only one doughnut can be moved at a time and no doughnut can ever cover a smaller one during a move.

While insight provides an explanation for the way in which some problems are solved, for this kind of problem insight would appear to be inferior to other problem-solving strategies—a conclusion borne out by researchers studying cognition. It turns out that rather than waiting for insight to occur, most people consider the problem systematically, using a logical, step-by-step approach.

People's tendency to look systematically for solutions can be viewed in terms of a series of stages typical of problem solving in general. The stages include three main activities: preparation, production, and judgment (Bourne, Dominowski, & Loftus, 1979):

● *Preparation.* During the preparation stage, people attempt to understand the problem. They try to ensure that they comprehend the initial information given to them and the solution that is sought. They also consider the problem in terms of those they have previously encountered. The outcome of this stage is the representation of the problem in their minds, divided into parts or looked at in a way that simplifies the information that is being considered.

● *Production.* In the next stage, people try to produce possible solutions. By recalling facts and procedures from memory and by employing trial-and-error procedures, they propose a solution to the problem.

● *Judgment.* In the final step of problem solving, the solutions that have been generated are evaluated. In problems such as the doughnut puzzle, in which there is a specific unique solution, judgment is straightforward. However, if the solution is ambiguous or there is more than one solution, the activities of this stage become more difficult. For example, people may have to develop rules or criteria to choose between alternative solutions.

Where the Obvious Solution Is Not Always the Best Solution: Creative problem solving

While the stages of problem solving help us understand how people approach and solve problems, they do little to explain why the solutions that some people come up with are better than those other people have to offer. Even the most simple of problems can elicit a wide range of responses from people.

Consider, for example, how you might respond to the question, "How many uses can you think of for a newspaper?" Compare your own responses to this one by a ten-year-old boy:

You can read it, write on it, lay it down and paint a picture on it. If you didn't have covers, you could put it in your door for decoration, put it in the garbage can, put it on a chair if the chair is messy. If you have a puppy, you put newspaper in its box or put it in your backyard for the dog to play with. When you build something and you don't want anyone to see it, put newspaper around it. Put newspaper on the floor if you have no mattress, use it to pick up something hot, use it to stop bleeding, or to catch the drips from drying clothes. You can use a newspaper for curtains, put it in your shoe to cover what is hurting your foot, make a kite out of it, shade a light that is too bright. You can wrap fish in it, wipe windows, or wrap money in it. . . . You put washed shoes on newspaper, wipe eyeglasses with it, put it under a dripping sink, put a plant on it, make a paper bowl out of it, use it for a hat if it is raining, tie it on your feet for slippers. You can put it on the sand if you had no towel, use it for bases in baseball, make paper airplanes with it, use it as a dustpan when you sweep, ball it up for the cat to play with, wrap your hands in it if it is cold. (Ward, Kogan, & Pankove, 1972.)

While it appears that this impressive list shows an extraordinary degree of creativity (from a child who, it should be added, is of normal intelligence), it is more difficult to understand the processes underlying **creativity,** which is usually defined as the combining of responses or ideas in novel ways.

One approach to understanding creativity relates to the presence of divergent thinking. **Divergent thinking** refers to the ability to respond with unusual, but still appropriate, responses to problems or questions. Divergent thinking is particularly apparent when compared to **convergent thinking,** the kind of thought that produces responses that are based primarily on knowledge and logic. For instance, convergent thinking is represented by a

Using an everyday object in an unexpected way is a mark of creativity.

Michael Weisbrot and Family

response, "You read it" to the query "What do you do with a newspaper?"; "You use it as a dustpan" is a more divergent response. Similarly, the problem of placing candles on a door in the Do It! box cannot be solved without using divergent thinking.

Because most tests of intelligence focus on convergent thinking skills— their problems are well defined and have only one acceptable answer— creative people who are divergent thinkers may find themselves at a disadvantage. This may explain why researchers consistently find that creativity is only slightly related to intelligence or school grades, particularly when intelligence is measured using typical intelligence tests (Barron & Harrington, 1981; Sternberg, 1986).

There are some factors that are, however, associated closely with creativity. For example, **cognitive complexity,** the use and preference of elaborate, intricate, and complex stimuli and thinking patterns, is typical of creative individuals. Similarly, creative people often have a wider range of interests and are more independent and more interested in philosophical or abstract problems than less creative individuals (Barron, 1969).

Why are some people less creative than others? One reason is that there are several deterrents to creativity (Simberg, 1971). As you can see in Table 2-1, these obstacles may be related to difficulties in perception or cognition, such as problems in precisely defining a problem or using all the stimuli that are available. Moreover, there are emotional blocks to creativity. For example, people may be afraid of appearing silly, or they may be so motivated to find a solution that they jump to the first solution they come to.

TABLE 2-1
Deterrents to Creativity

Blocks relating to perception and cognition
    Difficulty in isolating the problem
    Difficulty caused by narrowing the problem too much
    Inability to define terms
    Failure to use all the senses in observing
    Difficulty in seeing nonobvious relationships
    Difficulty in not investigating the obvious
    Failure to distinguish between cause and effect

Blocks relating to emotions
    Fear of making a mistake or making a fool of oneself
    Grabbing the first idea that comes along
    Rigidity of thought
    Overmotivation to succeed quickly
    Unusually strong desire for security
    Fear of supervisors and distrust of colleagues and subordinates
    Lack of drive in carrying a problem through to completion and testing
    Lack of drive in putting a solution to work

Source: Simberg, 1971.

You are faced with a thorny problem. Your roommate keeps inviting people to dinner, making elaborate meals, and serving expensive food. You and she have always shared food expenses evenly, but it is beginning to bother you that so much of the weekly food budget is going to feed *her* friends. How can you solve the problem?

Despite the deterrents to creative problem solving cited in Table 2-1, it *is* possible to become more adept at coming up with creative solutions to problems—whether they be everyday problems or more academic problems such as finding the solution to a problem on a test. In fact, several training programs have been developed that show success in raising the general level of creativity of participants (see, for example, Reese, Treffinger, Parnes, & Kaltsounis, 1976; Baron & Sternberg, 1987). Moreover, even training that concentrates on creativity in very specific areas—such as learning to find more creative uses for particular objects—has resulted in improvements in creativity that spill over into other areas.

Here are some specific suggestions from these training programs for solving problems of any sort more creatively:

● *Redefine the problem.* By looking at the problem in a different way, you can gain insight into its basic nature, opening up the potential for finding a creative solution that otherwise would not have occurred to you. For instance, rather than looking at your difficulties with your roommate as a social problem, think of the problem as an economic one. Find out how businesses share scarce resources, and turn what might be a delicate social interactional problem into an exercise in mathematics.

● *Think divergently.* Rather than looking for the most logical and direct solution (such as telling your roommate not to invite people for dinner), think divergently about the situation. Explore the reasons your roommate invites people over, and think how the problem could be resolved if the situation as a whole were to be changed in some significant way. Perhaps *you* could invite more people over, and balance the drain on the budget. It wouldn't save any money, but it might decrease your frustration and resentment over the situation.

● *Try brainstorming.* In **brainstorming,** people try to create as many ideas as possible, without regard to their sensibility or the feasibility of their implementation. Only after you have exhausted your ideas should you go back and evaluate them. The premise behind this technique is that creativity will be enhanced by the initial lack of critical evaluation, and you may produce ideas that you would not have thought of under more typical circumstances.

● *Take the perspective of another person.* Sometimes viewing the situation from the perspective of another individual—either someone who is involved in the situation or a disinterested bystander—can be helpful in bringing to mind new solutions. For instance, looking at the situation using your roommate's point of view might illuminate the fact that she does the cooking far more than you do and therefore feels free to invite people over for dinner.

● *Experiment with different solutions.* Explore in your own mind the likely outcome of as many solutions as you can think up. Consider each of their consequences if they were to be implemented, taking care to think of potential outcomes in as much detail as possible. As you work through the different scenarios, new solutions to the problem will likely become apparent.

Use of these strategies will not only maximize your creativity but will help you to view and approach the world around you more effectively.

TO REVIEW

● The processes of perception, which involve the sorting out, interpretation, analysis, and integration of stimuli, allow us to process the raw sensory stimuli from our sense organs and turn them into meaningful and useful information.

● Cognition considers the way we know and understand the world, process information, and make judgments and decisions.

● Problem solving typically encompasses three main activities: preparation, production, and judgment.

● Creativity is related to divergent thinking and preference for cognitive complexity.

CHECK YOURSELF

1. Henry was an accomplished rock climber. As he clung to the steep granite surface, he knew how important it was to block out all external stimuli and concentrate on the move before him. This would be considered an example of _____ _____.

2. Employing memory and trial-and-error tactics to seek out possible solutions to a problem occurs at what stage of problem solving?
   a. judgment
   b. insight
   c. production
   d. preparation

3. Generating novel but correct responses to problems is known as _____ thinking. By contrast, a more traditional approach to

problem solving that relies on past learning and acquired logic is known as
_____ thinking.

4.   The motivation to solve a problem quickly often leads to creative solutions. True or false?

_____

(See answers to these questions at the bottom of page 60.)

2.2   UNDERSTANDING OTHER PEOPLE:
Forming Impressions and Attributions

*What's Charlie like? Well, if I were to characterize him, I would probably
say that he's a rather warm person, industrious, critical, practical, and
determined.*

If you were to hear this from an acquaintance, you probably would view
Charlie as someone worth getting to know. But suppose you heard this
statement, identical in all respects except for one word:

*What's Charlie like? Well, if I were to characterize him, I would probably
say that he's a rather cold person, industrious, critical, practical, and
determined.*

Merely changing "warm" to "cold" probably makes a substantial change
in your overall view of Charlie. In fact, the way you interpret the other
adjectives might well differ depending on whether you hear "warm" or "cold"
first. For instance, research has found that the meaning of "industrious" is
quite different according to whether it describes a warm person or a cold
one (Kelley, 1950).

The fact that particular traits are especially influential in determining
our overall impression of others is one of the earliest findings in the field of
social cognition. **Social cognition** relates to the processes that underlie our
understanding of the social world—what others are like, what reasons lie
behind people's behavior, and how we organize and represent in memory
our experiences and the way the social world operates. Social cognition
allows us to categorize and interpret information relating to other people
(Fiske & Taylor, 1983, Gordon & Wyer, 1987).

Some of the earliest research on social cognition, which examined the
ways in which we make judgments of others, made clear that not only do
certain traits—called **central traits**— have an unusually strong influence on
the ultimate impression that is formed about others, but the order in which
information is given affects impression formation (Luchins, 1957). For example, we often weigh initial information about a person more heavily than
information we receive later. This **primacy effect** generally holds true even
when subsequent information contradicts earlier information entirely (see,
for example, Jones & Goethals, 1972). First impressions, then, *do* count.

It is not unusual to be presented with a series of descriptive adjectives about an individual—such as those in a newspaper or magazine biographical sketch—and, from this information, develop a general evaluation of the person in question. Knowing that certain characteristics, such as central traits, are unusually influential in determining our overall judgment is important in understanding how people form opinions about others.

These impressions do not represent the full story, though. In many instances, we do not receive a prepackaged listing of a given person's attributes but instead must rely on a potentially more ambiguous—yet far richer—source of information: observation of that person's behavior.

When we observe behavior, we make **attributions,** explanations for the reasons behind the observed behavior. Suppose, for instance, you observe that your classmate, Phil Anker, has failed a test, and you are interested in determining the reasons behind his poor performance—in other words, making an attribution for the failure.

If you are like most people, your first attribution will be made in terms of whether the cause is situational or dispositional (Heider, 1958). **Situational causes** are those brought about by something in the environment and not the person him- or herself. For example, you might attribute your classmate's poor performance to the difficulty of the test or to his being prevented from studying by his car's breaking down on the way to the library.

Susan Rosenberg/Photo Researchers

Most people make attributions regarding whether others' behavior is due to situational or dispositional causes. For example, is it through her own dispositional carelessness that this woman is wearing mismatched shoes, or is it due to situational circumstances beyond her control?

On the other hand, you might attribute your classmate's performance to a **dispositional cause**—a cause based on his personality characteristics or traits. For instance, if you think he failed the test because he was unintelligent or lazy and didn't study hard enough, you would be making a dispositional attribution.

How do we distinguish between situational and dispositional causes of behavior? To make this distinction, we typically put ourselves in the role of "naive psychologist" (Heider, 1958). As naive psychologists, we try to use some of the very same principles employed by a professional psychologist in determining the causes of behavior.

Most of us would have difficulty describing the principles that we do employ, since we usually are unaware that we are using them. However, people generally rely on three separate types of information to determine whether a behavior is caused by situational or dispositional factors: consensus, consistency, and distinctiveness. **Consensus information** comes from observing the degree to which several people behave similarly in a given situation. If we learned, for example, that almost everyone in Phil's class failed the test, this would suggest a situational cause: The test was too hard or poorly written.

Consistency information, the degree to which an individual behaves similarly in similar situations, provides us with another kind of data. If, for example, we learn that Phil seems to fail most tests in this class—consistency information—this provides a dispositional clue that it is he, and not the situation, that is the cause of the behavior.

Finally, we also use **distinctiveness information,** which considers the extent to which the same behavior occurs across different situations. If Phil not only fails tests but also has been fired from a job because of laziness, the similarity of such behaviors suggests that failure seems characteristic of Phil, independent of the situation.

Because in many, if not most, cases we have all three kinds of information—consensus, consistency, and distinctiveness information—available to us, the inferences we make are even more complex than when only one kind of information is present. We combine our findings from each of the different sorts of information and come to an overall judgment about the underlying cause of behavior. Despite the complexity of the attribution formation, however, it is clear that the process we tend to use to form attributions follows a lawful, rational pattern (Nisbett & Ross, 1980). Although we may well be "naive psychologists," the principles that we follow are surprisingly sophisticated.

CHECK YOURSELF: ANSWERS

1. selective attention **2.** c **3.** divergent, convergent **4.** False; overmotivation is considered a deterrent to creativity.

Errors of the Naive Psychologist:
Biases in understanding the world

Dear Ann Landers:

My boss, Waldo, is a selfish, self-centered, and demanding jerk. He asks the impossible of me. No matter how hard I work, he says I'm capable of more effort. I feel like I'm running on a never-ending treadmill. Last week, I finally blew my cool and threw a pile of papers at my boss when he gave me an assignment with a totally unreasonable deadline.

Don't tell me to quit; I don't know where I'd find another job. What should I do?

—Ursula

———————————————

Dear Ann Landers:

My office manager, Ursula, is without doubt the poorest worker I have ever had in my employ. She is lazy, incompetent, and sloppy. I have yet to find anything that she does well. And she's always complaining about working conditions. To top matters, last week she threw a pile of papers at me, after I'd given her an assignment with a perfectly reasonable deadline.

Don't tell me to fire her. If she weren't my wife's cousin, I would have done that a long time ago. What should I do?

—Waldo

To Ursula, it is clear that the source of her difficulties lies in situational factors beyond her control; her boss is a "jerk" who makes unreasonable demands. In contrast, Waldo's view of the situation places all the blame on Ursula's personal characteristics. To him, it is her incompetence that makes her behavior intolerable.

The different conclusions drawn about the same set of behaviors illustrates a pervasive tendency in attribution: We tend to attribute others' behavior to dispositional causes, but we tend to attribute our own behavior to situational causes. In fact, this tendency is so strong, it has been labeled the **fundamental attribution bias** (Watson, 1982).

The fundamental attribution bias illustrates that although we process information about others' characteristics and behavior according to a set of underlying guidelines, we are not infallible in our judgments (Funder, 1987). In fact, the fundamental attribution bias is but one of several biases that consistently color the accuracy of our judgments and attributions about others. In addition to the fundamental attribution bias, there are halo effects, the Pollyanna effect, assumptions of similarity, and self-serving biases. Understanding these biases can help you become a more perceptive and accurate judge of others and their behavior.

● *Fundamental attribution bias.* The fundamental attribution bias is one of the most powerful and pervasive of all biases. For example, analysis of letters written to advice columns such as Ann Landers and "Dear Abby" shows quite clearly that writers tend to attribute their own problems to situational causes, and they view the problems of others as resulting from dispositional causes (Schoeneman & Rubanowitz, 1985).

One reason for the bias relates to the nature of information available to people making an attribution. When we consider the behavior of another person, the most perceptually salient information is that person's behavior; he or she is the center of our attention. In turn, this leads to dispositional attributions. In contrast, changes in the environment are most obvious when we consider our own behavior, and we make attributions based on situational factors.

● *Halo effects.* Susan is intelligent, kind, and loving. Is she also hardworking? If you were to hazard a guess, your most likely response would be "yes." Your guess reflects the **halo effect,** a phenomenon in which an initial understanding that a person has positive traits is used to infer other uniformly positive characteristics. (The opposite would also hold true: Learning that Susan was unsociable and argumentative would probably lead you to assume that she was unhelpful as well.)

The reason for halo effects is that as naive psychologists we hold **implicit personality theories,** theories reflecting our notions of what traits are found together in individuals. These theories are based on a combination of experience and logic. Our perception of the world may be flawed, however, because application of our theory can be singularly inappropriate for a given individual, or it might simply be wrong. Most people have neither uniformly positive nor uniformly negative traits but instead reflect a combination of the two.

● *The "Pollyanna" effect.* In some respects, we have a blind optimism that is not too different from that of Pollyanna, who could see no evil in the world. Because we are typically motivated to view the world as a pleasant, enjoyable place, our perceptions of others are colored in a positive direction (Sears, 1982). This **Pollyanna effect** produces a tendency to rate others in a generally positive manner.

There are several examples of the Pollyanna effect. For instance, the public's evaluation of the President of the United States and other public figures is generally positive. Similarly, ratings of people in experiments normally fall in the positive range—even when the people have just met. Humorist Will Rogers may have been reflecting a widespread feeling, then, when he said, "I never met a man I didn't like."

● *Assumed similarity bias.* How similar to you—in terms of attitudes, opinions, and likes and dislikes—are your friends and acquaintances? (Before answering, you might want to try the exercise in the following Do It! box.)

THE ASSUMED SIMILARITY BIAS IN ACTION

Rate each of the following items, using this scale:

disagree 1 2 3 4 5 6 7 agree

Place your answers on the first of the three lines following each item.

1. I like sculpture more than paintings. _____ _____ _____

2. I like bananas more than spinach. _____ _____ _____

3. I prefer large parties to smaller, intimate ones. _____ _____ _____

4. I like basketball more than football. _____ _____ _____

5. I think the President is doing a good job. _____ _____ _____

6. I like rock and roll. _____ _____ _____

7. I like to sleep late in the morning. _____ _____ _____

8. I like classical music. _____ _____ _____

9. I would rather travel in the Orient than in Europe. _____ _____ _____

10. I think watching most movies is a waste of time. _____ _____ _____

Now that you have rated each of these statements, think of the name of a friend or acquaintance—someone with whom you are familiar but don't know all that well. Now go back over each item, but this time answer the way you think your acquaintance would answer each item. Use the second of the three lines to record your answer.

The next step is to get the acquaintance to complete the ten items; use the third line to record his or her responses (do not let your own answers be seen).

Finally, take the difference between the first and second responses for each item, and add up these differences (ignoring negative signs). This provides you with a figure showing the size of the difference between your own responses and your guess of your acquaintance's responses. Next, take the difference between the second and third responses for each item, and add up these ten differences (again ignoring negative signs). This provides the difference between your acquaintance's answers and your guess of his or her answers.

In most cases, the bigger difference will be the second one. The reason is that most people's guesses tend to be closer to their *own* preferences, rather than to the actual preferences of the person in question. In other words, we tend to assume that others are more like us than they really are—the assumed similarity bias in action.

Most people feel that their friends and acquaintances are fairly similar to themselves. But this feeling goes beyond just people we know; there is a general tendency—known as the **assumed similarity bias**—to think of people as being similar to oneself, even when meeting them for the first time (Ross, Greene, & House, 1977).

If other people are, in fact, different from oneself, the assumed similarity bias reduces the accuracy of the judgments being made. Moreover, it suggests an interesting possibility. It may be that one's judgment about another individual better defines the judge's characteristics than those of the person being rated. In some cases, then, the portrait we draw of another person—particularly one about whom we have little information—may in reality be a sketch of the way we view ourselves.

● *Self-serving biases.* If you do badly on a test, whom do you blame? If you are like many people, you will attribute your performance to poor teaching, poorly written test questions, the time of year, or most anything but the fact that—to put it bluntly—you are not smart enough to understand the material. On the other hand, if you had done well on the test, you would probably attribute your success not to its simplicity or the clearly written test questions but instead to your own talent and skill.

The reason for this difference in attributions concerns the self-serving bias. The **self-serving bias** is the tendency to view oneself and the judgments one makes in the most favorable light. The source of this bias is a desire to present oneself well and to preserve one's own sense of self-esteem.

There have been several demonstrations of the self-serving bias. For instance, teachers tend to attribute their students' success to their good teaching—while blaming their students for a lack of ability when they fail (representing an interesting reversal of students' perceptions of the situation; Beckman, 1970). Similarly, football coaches whose primary responsibility has been recruiting talented players blame losses on a lack of team effort; while coaches whose primary responsibility has been to motivate the team blame the same losses on a lack of team talent (Carver, DeGregorio, & Gillis, 1980). The self-serving bias, then, leads people to come up with attributions that are consistent with face-saving explanations.

In sum, people attempt to take credit for their successes—and blame others for their failures. Although susceptibility to the self-serving bias reduces the accuracy of people's judgments and the understanding they have of the world, they are able to preserve their self-esteem and maintain a positive view of themselves.

Anestis Diakopoulos/Stock, Boston

This coach, actively
involved in training his
players, may tend to
attribute a lost game to
poor recruiting rather
than inadequate training.

Psychology for You:
Judging others—and yourself—more accurately

*As you open your first freshman grade report, you already know it is going
to be a disaster. D in math, C's in French and English, B in humanities—
and, worst of all, F in geography. Your worst fears have come true. Your
classmates are smarter, you are in over your head, and it seems as if you
are just not cut out to be a college student. You seriously consider cutting
your losses and dropping out; it is clear you don't have the ability to do
well in college.*

The scene presented above is played out over and over in colleges across
the country. Most people enter college feeling concern over their ability to
measure up to the academic demands, and, if their initial performance is
poor, their assumptions that they lack sufficient ability to succeed are confirmed. This attribution may lead to anxiety, diminished effort, and ultimately, even poorer academic performance.

There are ways to break this cycle of failure, however. By making freshmen aware of how faulty judgments and attributional patterns can affect
their future performance, psychologists Timothy Wilson and Patricia Linville
(1982; 1985) developed a program to make students' judgments and attri-

butions more accurate—and, in the process, to improve their academic performance.

In the program, freshmen who had expressed a concern over their first-semester performance were shown statistics and videotaped interviews demonstrating that most students' grades improved over the course of their college careers. The information was intended to change the students' dispositional attributions—that they lacked sufficient ability—to situational attributions—that their initial college performance was due to temporary factors that could be overcome through increased effort.

The program worked. Students exposed to it improved about half a grade in their grade point average during the second semester of their freshman year—compared to a slight *decline* of .05 points for a group of students not involved in the program. In sum, increasing the accuracy of attributions by making students aware that situational factors have an important influence on academic performance proved to be an effective technique.

Here are several other strategies that can help us make more accurate judgments and attributions about the sometimes perplexing behavior of others:

- When sizing up another person, keep in mind the complexity of people's characteristics. People can, for instance, be both cruel and empathic, even though we don't expect such traits to occur together. The theories we use as naive psychologists, then, can sometimes be inaccurate.

- In making attributions about the cause of other people's behavior, it is important to realize that behavior is, at least in part, a reaction to the environment. Because of the fundamental attribution error, our tendency is to view others' behavior in terms of dispositional characteristics. We should try to view the situation from their perspective, acknowledging that they probably see themselves as responding to environmental factors. Our judgments of the reasons behind behavior can become more focused and ultimately more accurate, then, by considering how others view themselves and the situations in which they are operating.

- Be aware of the biases in person perception that we have discussed when making judgments of others and their behavior. Although we are imperfect observers and information processors, awareness, acknowledgment, and understanding of our limitations can help us to better understand the world around us.

TO REVIEW

- Social cognition relates to the processes that underlie our understanding of the social world.

- Acting as "naive psychologists," we form attributions to help us explain the reasons behind behavior that we observe.

- A primary dimension along which attributions are made involves whether a behavior occurs because of either situational or dispositional factors.

- The major sources of bias in social cognition and attribution include the fundamental attribution bias, halo effects, the Pollyanna effect, assumptions of similarity, and the self-serving bias.

CHECK YOURSELF

1. A poorly written report, resulting from the author's habitual tendency to put things off until the last minute, could be said to have what kind of cause?
   a. dispositional
   b. attributional
   c. situational
   d. primary

2. The fact that George was absent from work one Thursday was attributed to an outbreak of flu virus that had also affected other employees. This attribution was primarily based on what kind of information?
   a. distinctiveness
   b. consistency
   c. consensus
   d. dispositional

3. The fundamental attribution bias refers to our tendency to attribute our own behavior to dispositional rather than situational causes. True or false?

4. Jennifer's optimistic view of the world tends to bias the attributions she makes in a positive direction. This is an example of:
   a. the Pollyanna effect
   b. similarity bias
   c. fundamental attribution bias
   d. self-serving bias

(See answers to these questions at the bottom of page 68.)

2.3 WHEN JUDGMENTS GO WRONG:
Prejudice and Discrimination

Mr. X. *The trouble with Jews is that they only take care of their own group.*

Mr. Y. *But the record of the Community Chest campaign shows that they give more generously, in proportion to their numbers, than do non-Jews.*

Mr. X.   *That shows they are always trying to buy favors and intrude into Christian affairs. They think of nothing but money; that is why there are so many Jewish bankers.*

Mr. Y.   *But a recent study shows that the percentage of Jews in the banking business is negligible, far smaller than the percentage of non-Jews.*

Mr. X.   *That's just it; they don't go in for respectable business. They are only in the movie business or run night clubs. (Allport, 1954, pp. 13–14.)*

It is clear to anyone who reads this snippet of conversation that there is probably no evidence that Mr. Y could marshal that would result in changing Mr. X's views about Jewish people. His negative attitudes are so ingrained that no set of statistics or arguments would prove convincing to him.

The conversation exemplifies some of the difficulties that become apparent when we consider **prejudice,** evaluations or judgments of members of a particuar group based primarily on membership in that group and not on characteristics of those specific individuals. These evaluations can be negative as in the example above, or they can be positive, as when a member of a group holds more positive attitudes toward other members of the group solely on the basis of their membership. A member of the American Legion who evaluates other legionnaires positively *because* they are members of the group, then, is showing prejudice.

When people are prejudiced, they will most likely discriminate against members of a group. **Discrimination** occurs when members of a group are treated negatively or positively due to their membership in the group. Although prejudice and discrimination are closely linked, they do not always go hand in hand. For example, a person may be prejudiced against New Englanders, yet avoid displaying his or her prejudice in order to appear polite. Similarly, a person may obey laws against discrimination and therefore appear to be unprejudiced, while still harboring negative attitudes about certain groups.

Different People, Different Prejudice: Who are the targets of prejudice and discrimination?

Japanese are industrious.
Blacks are musical.
Italians are emotional.

We've all heard people making statements like these about members of particular groups. Perhaps you've even made similar comments yourself. Each of them, however, reflects a common **stereotype**—an overly simplified idea or expectation assigned to members of specific groups. Stereotypes are

CHECK YOURSELF: ANSWERS

1. a **2.** c **3.** False; we are apt to attribute our own behavior to situational rather than dispositional causes. **4.** a oversimplifications; because of our need to make sense of the complex social environment in which we live, we sometimes assume a uniformity to group members that is simply illusory. As a result, critical aspects of individuality are lost. (Before reading further, you might want to try the accompanying Do It! box.)

DO IT!

DO YOU KNOW YOUR STEREOTYPES?

Although most of us profess to be unprejudiced, many times we have little difficulty in identifying the most common stereotypes held by other people. To test your knowledge of stereotypes, consider the following descriptive terms:

ambitious
efficient
industrious
loyal to family ties
materialistic
meditative
methodical
nationalistic
pleasure-loving
scientific-minded
tradition-loving

Now write down four terms from the list above that you think are most applicable underneath each the three groups listed below:

Americans	Germans	Chinese
1.	1.	1.
2.	2.	2.
3.	3.	3.
4.	4.	4.

ANSWERS   According to a study of college students' stereotypes carried out by Karlins, Coffman, & Walters (1969), the adjectives most frequently applied to Americans were materialistic, ambitious, pleasure-loving, and industrious; Germans were most often designated as scientific-minded, efficient, nationalistic, and methodical; and Chinese people were most frequently described as loyal to family ties, tradition-loving, industrious, and meditative.

It is crucial to note, however, that these represent college students' *judgments* about what descriptors are appropriate for a given group; the study does not claim that these stereotypes are accurate.

There are actually several kinds of stereotypes. The most common involve racial and ethnic factors. For instance, if you asked a group of people to list characteristics of blacks, Chinese, Germans, Hispanics, and even groups who have little representation in the United States, such as Turks, you would probably find a surprisingly high degree of agreement among members of your survey group (Weber & Crocker, 1983).

Despite the degree of consensus, however, these stereotypes may be inaccurate. Beliefs can be widely held—people throughout the world once agreed that the earth was flat—and still be erroneous. And in fact, the accuracy of stereotypes is highly suspect, although in some cases they contain a kernel of truth when they are based on firsthand knowledge and information regarding the group being judged (Triandis & Vassilious, 1967).

Even when stereotypes contain some degree of truth, however, they reduce the accuracy of judgments made regarding individual members of a given group, since they may prevent us from perceiving critical characteristics and hinder our ability to make important distinctions between different individuals. Moreover, when we react toward others on the basis of stereotypes and not individual qualities, the effects can be quite harmful.

The Myths of the "isms": Sexism and ageism

While racial, religious, and ethnic-group membership have traditionally been viewed as the predominant source of stereotyping, two other categories are equally potent sources of stereotyping: sex and age. **Sexism** refers to negative attitudes and behavior based on an individual's sex, while **ageism** consists of negative attitudes and behavior based on a person's age. Although sexism is typically viewed in terms of prejudice and discrimination against women, and ageism usually concerns the elderly, the terms are broader, covering the effects of both phenomena on men and young people, respectively.

The prevalence—and subtlety—of sexism is illustrated by the difficulty that most people have in answering the following riddle:

A father and his son were driving along the interstate highway when the father lost control of the car, swerved off the road, and crashed into a telephone pole. The father died instantly, and his son was critically injured. An ambulance rushed the boy to a nearby hospital. A prominent surgeon was summoned to provide immediate treatment. When the surgeon arrived and entered the operating room to examine the boy, a loud gasp was heard. "I can't operate on this boy," the surgeon said. "He is my son." (Byrne & Kelley, 1981, p. 304.)

If you find this puzzling, it is because you have assumed that all surgeons are male. If you held no such assumption, the thought that the surgeon

Hazel Hankin

Sex discrimination is a
form of prejudice that
prevailed without much
question until recently.
Today, however, women
have more freedom than
their mothers had to
choose from a much wider
range of careers.

could be the boy's **mother**—which makes the incident immediately understandable—would have occurred to you more readily.

Sexism is found in many areas of our society. For instance, certain
professionals, such as physicians, truck drivers, and lawyers, traditionally
have been male; others, such as nurses and elementary school teachers,
usually have been female. Moreover, certain characteristics are traditionally
assigned to members of a given sex. Traits such as aggressiveness, bluntness,
and competitiveness have been viewed as masculine traits; traits of passivity,
tactfulness, and shyness have been seen as feminine ones (Basow, 1980;
Martin, 1987).

Although sexist stereotypes have undergone marked change over the
past twenty years, most people are still surprised when they encounter a
woman bus driver, a male secretary, or a female surgeon, and consider it
undesirable for a woman to act aggressively or for a man to respond passively. Stereotypes about appropriate behavior for men and women will continue to undergo modification, particularly as the roles of men and women
change with the demands of society. For instance, almost half of all women
with infant children are now working, suggesting that the traditional view
that a woman should be at home taking care of the children, while men
should pursue careers, may be a notion of the past.

Ageism is another form of stereotyping that may be affected by changes
in the social patterns of society. One of the most prevalent views of the
elderly suggests that they are passive, unsociable, and intellectually impaired

(Rodin & Langer, 1980). Yet such a view is far from accurate. As we will discuss when we consider adult development in Chapter 3, the elderly often continue the same activities that they enjoyed when young, and their degree of socializing is no different from that of earlier years. Intelligence in some areas continues to increase during the later years of life, although there are certain declines in the speed of problem solving. Moreover, the sex life of the elderly is often vigorous, a fact that is hardly congruent with ageism stereotypes.

In sum, stereotypes offer an oversimplified—and often erroneous—view of what characteristics and traits the members of certain groups share. As such, they reduce the accuracy of the impressions we form about others (Jussim, Coleman, & Lerch, 1987). Yet the most potent effect of such stereotypes is not the inaccuracy of judgments of other people, it is that they are used to maintain, justify, and perpetuate prejudice and discrimination.

Gauging the Consequences of Prejudice and Discrimination

There is no lack of data documenting the effects of prejudice and discrimination. For example, blacks and Hispanics, frequent targets of prejudice in the United States, have on the average lower incomes, less adequate housing, lower levels of education, and higher rates of unemployment than whites (U.S. Department of Commerce, 1980.) The consequences of prejudice are well illustrated by the plight of the blacks discussed in the passage at the beginning of this chapter.

Yet these obvious and fairly easily documented results of prejudice and discrimination mask even more subtle, and in some ways more significant and long lasting, outcomes. There are several psychological consequences of prejudice and discrimination that affect the psychological functioning of minority group members who are the targets of prejudice.

Self-esteem   Members of racial minorities may have lower **self-esteem**— feelings of personal self-worth—than do members of the predominant racial groups. When segregation—the forced separation of members of different groups—was legal in many areas of the United States (as recently as the early 1960s), blacks were forced to attend inferior schools, ride in the backs of buses, use separate drinking fountains, and suffer from a myriad of indignities that had no basis other than prejudice. It is not surprising that research showed that blacks, on the average, tended to have lower self-esteem than whites (Clark & Clark, 1947). As overt prejudice and discrimination have declined, however, the self-esteem of blacks has risen, and the differences between black and white self-esteem overall have decreased (Gray-Little & Appelbaum, 1979). Societal changes, then, seem to have brought about changes in the self-esteem of the targets of prejudice and discrimination (Simpson & Yinger, 1985).

Choosing your fate: locus of control   If you were discriminated against by being prevented from taking the job of your choice or moving into a particular neighborhood, might you eventually come to think that you had little control over your own destiny? People in this situation often do come to feel this way, and ultimately tend to view the world with an external locus of control. **Locus of control** is the degree to which we believe we are personally responsible for events in our lives. People with an external locus of control characteristically attribute events to other people or situations while those with an internal locus of control see themselves as the causes of events in their lives.

Probably because of the prejudice and discrimination they have experienced, blacks are more apt to hold an external locus of control than whites (Rotter, 1966). This difference has important consequences for the way many blacks view the world, and the way they strive for future success. Individuals who feel that the future is independent of how much effort they expend are unlikely to be motivated to put forward maximum effort; after all, why bother when the outcome is going to be dictated by forces beyond your control? In contrast, people with an internal locus of control are apt to feel that their effort will be rewarded by success and they'll be more motivated to give their best effort.

Another negative aspect of prejudice and discrimination is that it may result in **self-fulfilling prophecies**—expectations about the possibility of future events or behaviors that act to increase the likelihood that the event or behavior will occur. For instance, if a prejudiced person thinks that members of a particular group hold some negative trait, they may act in a way that actually produces manifestations of the trait on the part of that group (Skrypnek & Snyder, 1982). In one experiment that confirmed this principle, researchers found that a person who was told to expect that another individual was hostile ended up eliciting hostile behavior from the individual—while people who held no such expectation experienced no such behavior from the individual (Snyder & Swann, 1978).

It is clear, then, that the psychological characteristics that are associated with being a target of prejudice and discrimination are unfortunate. It is less obvious, though, that there are negative outcomes for the individuals guilty of prejudice and discrimination. For one thing, classifying people on the basis of membership in a particular group results in misperceptions, misattributions, and inaccuracies in understanding other people and the reasons for their behavior.

Perhaps the most subtle danger of prejudice and discrimination is a misperception of one's own groups—and even oneself. Because unduly *negative* perceptions of groups to which one does not belong tend to be accompanied by unduly *positive* perceptions of groups in which one holds membership, people who are prejudiced misperceive people with whom they have substantial contact—members of their own groups (Locksley, Ortiz, & Hepburn, 1980). In fact, it is possible that the overly positive evaluations of members of one's own group may lead to an inability to understand oneself accurately. In sum, prejudice and discriminative behavior act as blinders on people as they view others in the world around them.

THE INDIVIDUAL

Throughout this chapter we have discussed many sorts of impediments to thinking, perceiving, and understanding others, and nowhere are the dangers of these hindrances clearer than when we consider prejudice and discrimination. Psychologists have devised several approaches to help reduce and eliminate prejudice and discrimination. Among the most important are contact between people and methods whose goal is the unlearning of prejudice.

● *Contact between people.* If a white person holds blacks in low esteem, contact and interaction between them will reduce the prejudice, according to the contact hypothesis.

The **contact hypothesis** suggests that intergroup contact will reduce prejudice and discrimination—assuming that the contact is of an appropriate kind. Clearly, not all contact is going to be appropriate (a gang war between white and black gangs would hardly be expected to reduce prejudice, nor would having a black man serve a white man his dinner), and the trick is to determine what kind of contact will be most effective in reducing prejudice.

The answer appears to be that certain conditions must be met for contact between members of two different groups to be effective: (1) Members of both groups must have either the same status in the contact situation,

Studies indicate that many children have developed racial or ethnic prejudices well before they begin school. Integration in the classroom is intended to overcome these attitudes.

Erika Stone

or the status of minority group members must be the higher of the two; (2) authority figures in the situation must promote contact; (3) the contact should be pleasant or intimate; and (4) the groups must cooperate in an activity whose success depends on the contributions of them both (Amir, 1976; Norvell & Worchel, 1981).

Because these conditions are relatively stringent, contact does not invariably work. This fact is particularly obvious when considering the decidedly mixed results of school desegregation, in which black students have been brought into schools with student bodies that had previously been predominantly white (and vice versa) (Cooper, 1986). Yet in many cases contact does work. Although it may take time for the consequences of contact to become evident, the outcome is eventually positive (Amir & Sharan, 1984).

● *Unlearning prejudice.* Although prejudice is something that develops at an early age (children as young as 3 years old discriminate between whites and blacks), it is still possible to learn to be less prejudiced as an adult. Understanding the nature of stereotypes and the processes—and biases—that underlie person-perception is useful in broadening one's understanding of the reasons for one's own prejudice. Moreover, an awareness that stereotypes are overgeneralizations and that to understand people accurately it is necessary to consider each person as an individual helps to reduce prejudice. Finally, people who are given direct training in the meaning of subtle cues that occur during social interaction between members of different groups show a reduction in prejudice; they become, in essence, more accurate in their understanding of others' behavior (Landis, Day, McGrew, Thomas, & Miller, 1976).

In sum, it is critical to understand the subtle distinctions that exist between people. Although our thinking and perceptual limitations may reduce the accuracy of the judgments we make of others, it is ultimately possible to raise the level of proficiency with which we understand the world. In so doing, we can become less susceptible to the dangers of stereotyping, prejudice, and discrimination.

TO REVIEW

● Prejudice is the evaluation or judgment of members of a group that is based primarily on membership in that group and not on actual characteristics of individuals. Discrimination is the behavior associated with prejudice.

● Among the most common types of prejudice and stereotypes are racial and ethnic prejudice, sexism, and agism.

● Prejudice affects the self-esteem and the locus of control of its targets.

1.   An individual may be prejudiced without engaging in acts of discrimination. True or false?

2.   Whereas prejudice and discrimination have had a negative impact on the socioeconomic status of minority groups, the self-images of individual minority group members appear to have remained intact. True or false?

3.   A young Navajo Indian boy, faced with the unfavorable prospects of ever bettering his present status on the reservation, might be expected to develop an _____ locus of control.

4.   Once learned, prejudice is particularly resistant to change through education. True or false?

_____

(See answers to these questions at the bottom of page 78.)

TO SUMMARIZE

1. The way we perceive, think about, and understand the world is complex. Perception is the nervous system's interpretive function that sorts, analyzes, and integrates the stimuli from our sense organs. Through perception, we give meaning to these stimuli, helping to relate the external world to our personal internal worlds.

2. Because of the complexity of the environment, we cannot respond to all the stimuli around us, and therefore only a small proportion of stimuli are perceived at a given moment. Through selective attention, we choose which stimuli to pay attention to and interpret. We are especially sensitive to those external factors that are relevant to our goals, desires, and emotions. We also tend to reduce complex stimuli to more manageable, understandable stimuli. This process may lead to oversimplification and sometimes outright errors in perception.

3. We come to know and understand the world, process information, make judgments and decisions, and describe our knowledge and understanding through cognition. Insight, the sudden awareness of the relationship between various elements of a problem that had previously appeared to be independent of each other, is one of several important cognitive processes. Insight allows us to grasp ways in which objects can be used beyond their traditional functions in order to help us reach our goals.

4. Problem solving, another cognitive process, typically occurs in three main stages: preparation, production, and judgment. Although these three stages provide a general description of problem solving, they do not explain our creative thought processes. One factor that helps promote creativity is related to creativity in divergent thinking, which is the ability to contribute unusual, but still appropriate, responses to problems or questions. The use

of and preference for elaborate, intricate, and nonsimple stimuli and thinking patterns—known as cognitive complexity—is also associated with creativity. Among the strategies for increasing creativity are redefining the problem, thinking divergently, brainstorming, taking the perspective of another person, and experimenting with different solutions.

5. Social cognition describes the processes that we use to make sense of the social world—what others are like, what the reasons behind others' behavior are, and how we organize and remember our social experiences. Certain information, such as central traits, is weighted particularly heavily when we form impressions of others. Primacy effects, when we consider initial information about others as more influential than subsequent information, also affect impression formation and can cause us to view someone inaccurately.

6. We make attributions—explanations for the reasons behind others' behavior—when we observe behavior. Attributions are typically made in terms of situational causes (those causes relating to the environment or specific situation) or dispositional causes (causes based on a person's personality characteristics or traits). In determining whether to attribute a behavior to a situational or dispositional cause, we use three kinds of information: consensus, consistency, and distinctiveness information.

7. Attribution processes are prone to several kinds of errors and biases. The fundamental attribution bias is the tendency to attribute others' behavior to dispositional causes but to attribute our own behavior to situational causes. Halo effects occur when an initial understanding that a person has positive traits is used to infer other uniformly positive characteristics. The Pollyanna effect reflects a tendency to rate others in a generally positive manner; the assumed similarity bias occurs when we assume that others have characteristics similar to our own. Finally, the self-serving bias is the tendency to view ourselves and our judgments in the most positive light. Although these biases can be quite pronounced, they can be overcome, helping us form more accurate impressions of others.

8. Prejudice, another form of bias, occurs when evaluations or judgments of particular members of a group are based primarily on membership in that group, and not on the actual characteristics of specific individuals. When we prejudge others because of their group affiliation, we are said to discriminate against them.

9. Stereotypes, or overly simplified characteristics unrealistically assigned to every member of a group, can be used as a basis for prejudice and discrimination. In addition to stereotypes about racial and ethnic groups, there are common stereotypes regarding members of the two sexes (manifested as sexism) and different age groups (reflected as ageism).

10. Prejudice and discrimination have serious effects on their targets. For instance, members of racial minorities have lower self-esteem and an external locus of control. Moreover, self-fulfilling prophecies regarding the

negative behavior of the targets of prejudice may lead the targets to behave in a way that actually increases the likelihood that the expected behavior will occur.

11. Several strategies for reducing prejudice and discrimination have been devised by psychologists. Among the ones that have proven most successful are increasing contact between groups and educating people regarding the existence and dangers of stereotyping, prejudice, and discrimination.

KEY TERMS AND CONCEPTS

perception (p. 47)

selective attention (p. 48)

insight (p. 49)

cognition (p. 49)

functional fixedness (p. 50)

creativity (p. 54)

divergent thinking (p. 54)

convergent thinking (p. 54)

cognitive complexity (p. 55)

brainstorming (p. 56)

social cognition (p. 58)

central traits (p. 58)

primacy effect (p. 58)

attributions (p. 59)

situational causes (of behavior) (p. 59)

dispositional causes (of behavior) (p. 60)

consensus information (p. 60)

consistency information (p. 60)

distinctiveness information (p. 60)

fundamental attribution bias (p. 61)

halo effect (p. 62)

implicit personality theories (p. 62)

Pollyanna effect (p. 62)

assumed similarity bias (p. 64)

self-serving bias (p. 64)

prejudice (p. 68)

discrimination (p. 68)

stereotype (p. 68)

sexism (p. 70)

ageism (p. 70)

self-esteem (p. 72)

locus of control (p. 73)

self-fulfilling prophecies (p. 73)

contact hypothesis (p. 74)

TO FIND OUT MORE

Nickerson, R. S., Perkins, D. N., & Smith, E. (1985). *The teaching of thinking.* Hillsdale, NJ: Erlbaum.

Baron, J. B., & Sternberg, R. J. (Eds.) (1987). *Teaching thinking skills: Theory and practice.* New York: W. H. Freeman.

Want to think better? These books provide a variety of strategies to help you understand the world more effectively.

Fiske, S. T., & Taylor, S. E. (1983). *Social cognition.* New York: Random House.

A clear introduction to the burgeoning area of social cognition.

CHECK YOURSELF: ANSWERS

1. True **2.** False **3.** external **4.** False

Shaver, P. (1984). *An introduction to attribution processes*. Hillsdale, NJ: Erlbaum.
    An interesting, well-written guide to attribution which includes many examples.

Simpson, G. E., & Yinger, J. M. (1985). *Racial and cultural minorities: An analysis of prejudice and discrimination* (5th ed.). New York: Plenum Press.
    An outstanding, comprehensive compendium of the facts, figures, and theories of prejudice and discrimination.

Growing Up
Human
Development

No doubt about it, he was old. Past his prime. He would never be the same. As he walked away, the strength in his legs, which were already weak, seemed to sap away still further. He couldn't see all that well, and people laughingly called him Gramps—although not to his face. His time had come and gone.

No doubt about it, he was young. About to take the presidency of the richest and most powerful country in the world. People marveled at how someone his age could be so well prepared to lead the country. Although his star had already shone brightly, his vitality and youth and his handsome and vigorous demeanor led most people to bet that his time was yet to come.

What is perhaps most noteworthy about the descriptions of these two individuals—baseball star Ted Williams and President John F. Kennedy—is that they were written about two men who were the same age: 43 years old. At a point typically seen as being close to midlife, these two individuals were perceived by society in wildly divergent ways.

In this chapter, we examine adjustment across the life span. As the above example indicates, the effects of aging—both on ourselves and in the way that others perceive us—are not just results of the mere passage of time; rather, they reflect our individual circumstances, our genetic endowment, and the choices we have made in our lives.

Our focus will be on the physical, emotional, intellectual, and social changes that occur as part of **development,** the patterns of growth and change throughout life. We will see how the way we mature physically, our emotional development, and the way our thinking changes as we age reflect a complex interaction between biologically predetermined patterns of growth and the environment in which we find ourselves.

We begin by considering infancy and childhood. We discuss the interaction between heredity and environment and then look at how the patterns of cognitive growth change as we age. We also examine the crucial social relationships that develop during these early years and consider ways different parents raise their children.

The period of adolescence, the stage between childhood and adulthood, is our next focus of attention. We consider questions of identity and how it develops, and we examine moral development during this period.

Finally, we examine the bulk of the life span, adulthood and old age. We consider the transitions and passages through which people pass during adulthood and the way people adjust to the aging process. We conclude by looking at dying and death, considering the stages that people pass through as they reach this final milestone of life.

As you will see, concerns of adjustment are not relegated to any one part of the life span. Instead, they are part of an ongoing process that continues throughout people's lives.

3.1 • SETTING THE PATTERNS OF LIFE:
Infancy and Childhood

It is not very pretty, this entity that has just begun its journey through the world. Covered with fuzz and a white, greasy material, having a pushed-in nose and a flattened ear resting against its face in slightly the wrong place, it looks much like any other newborn. Yet this apparent similarity is deceiving: in the high-pitched cry, the grasping, flailing motions, there is more than a hint of uniqueness to this individual. Looking at this creature, one cannot fail to glimpse the special wonders of life ahead.

We all start life in the same way—as the union of an egg cell and a sperm cell. Yet from the moment of conception, each of us is unique, and the road on which we travel through life follows its own path.

Infancy and childhood represent a critical period of development. During this time, we develop patterns of behavior that have an impact on the effectiveness of our adjustment for the entire course of our lives.

Nature, Nurture, or Both?
Determinants of growth and change

To fully understand the nature of growth and change that occurs during infancy and childhood, it is necessary to consider the roots of development. Psychologists—and philosophers—have long argued whether the developmental changes that unfold during the course of our lives are due to nature or to nurture. Nature refers to **heredity,** causes that are transmitted biologically from one's parents; nurture relates to the **environment** and encompasses the influence of parents, siblings, family, friends, schooling, nutrition, and all the other experiences to which one is exposed. Do people begin life as the **tabula rasa** (or "blank slate") that the English philosopher John Locke suggested, or are they born with certain skills, propensities, talents, and predispositions regarding the way they view and understand the world?

The answer lies somewhere in the middle. People do not develop without being influenced by the specific environment in which they are raised, nor are they unaffected by the nature of their inherited characteristics. The predominant view, then, is an **interactionist** one: Both nature and nurture interact to determine the course of a specific individual's development (Eisenberg, 1987).

Some behaviors are more influenced by heredity, and some are more influenced by experience (see Table 3-1). But no developmental pattern is caused entirely by one or the other factor. Moreover, heredity presents a potential for particular traits or behaviors to occur and places limitations on the occurrence of others. For example, heredity provides you with the

TABLE 3-1
Characteristics with Strong Hereditary Components

Physical: Height and, to a lesser extent, weight; pulse and breathing rates; blood pressure; perspiration; patterns of tooth decay; voice tone and pitch; posture; age of first menstruation; and age of death.

Intellectual: Word fluency, memory, the timing of language development, maze-running abilities in rats, and scores on various tests of intelligence.

Personality: Shyness and outgoingness, emotionality, activity, depression, anxiety, and special aptitudes and interests, especially in the arts and athletics.

Source: Papalia & Olds, 1985.

potential for a certain level of artistic capability; whether you reach your potential depends on environmental considerations. Similarly, heredity provides you with physical limitations. No matter how hard you try, you will not be able to lift an object weighing 2000 pounds—the nature of the human body will simply not permit it.

Developing Our Thoughts:
Cognitive development

Just as our bodies are limited in the amount they can lift, our thinking is also affected by developmental factors. In fact, over the course of infancy and childhood there are considerable changes in the quality of our mental capabilities. These changes are no less dramatic than the developmental progression we view in infants who first learn to crawl and only after that learn to walk.

Jean Piaget, a Swiss developmental psychologist, believed that people universally move through a series of stages relating to **cognitive development,** the development of thinking, understanding, and knowing (Piaget,

During the beginning of Piaget's sensorimotor stage, a child is not yet ready to understand that objects continue to exist when they are not being seen, touched, or otherwise experienced through the senses.

Michael Weisbrot and Family

1970). According to him, these stages of cognitive development represent changes not only in the quantity of thought and information understandable to the child, but also in the quality of the knowledge and understanding children possess.

In Piaget's view, infants are in the **sensorimotor stage** from birth to around 2 years. Not only are their language skills at a low level, but even seemingly simple concepts, such as the fact that objects continue to exist when they are out of sight, are not understood. To an infant in the sensorimotor stage, what is "out of sight" is clearly "out of mind."

By the time children leave the sensorimotor stage, though, they have learned that objects have a permanence beyond their physical presence—they have developed the capability for internal representation of the objects. This prepares them for the next period, the **preoperational stage,** which lasts from about age 2 until age 7. During this stage they develop the use of language, which permits them to describe the world around them, and they engage in symbolic play, pretending to take on the roles of people they see around them—be it truck driver, mother, or physician.

Yet children's thinking during the preoperational stage still has rather unusual qualities. Children at this stage employ **egocentric thought,** in which the world is viewed entirely from their own perspective. They do not understand that others see things from a different vantage point. Because of their egocentric thinking, it is difficult to explain to children, for instance, that fighting is bad because it may result in someone else getting hurt; it is hard for children to understand the pain of others, since they can view things only from their own perspective.

Children in the preoperational stage are also unable to fathom the principle of conservation. **Conservation** is the knowledge that quantity is unrelated to the arrangement and physical appearance of objects. A child who does not understand conservation, then, may think that a ball of clay when it is formed into a snakelike shape has less clay than when it was in a ball. Even when the clay is returned to its original shape, children in the preoperational stage still insist that the different shapes contain different amounts of clay.

Usually by the age of 7, children have learned the conservation principle, and this marks the start of the **concrete operational stage.** Children begin to think more logically during this period and begin to overcome the egocentric thought that is characteristic of the previous stage. Their conceptions of time and space become more sophisticated, although they are still tied to the concrete, physical reality of the world; abstract thinking is still in the future.

The final period of cognitive development is the **formal operational stage,** which usually begins about 12 years of age. In this last period, which runs through adulthood, people are able to think on an abstract level. They can form hypotheses about the causes of phenomena, and they can test out these hypotheses in the form of "experiments," in which they systematically vary one factor after another to determine the effects of the manipulation. Reaching the formal operational stage, then, allows people to act as the "naive psychologists" that we discussed in Chapter 2. Still, a significant proportion of people never fully hone their formal operational skills and have difficulty solving problems that involve certain kinds of abstract thinking, even as adults (Keating & Clark, 1980). (See the following Do It! box for a test of your own skills).

TEST YOUR THINKING: THE PENDULUM PROBLEM

Although people generally move into the formal operational stage at around age 12, many older people have difficulty with certain types of problems that involve abstract thinking. To get a sense of your abilities, try the following problem:

You are given a string and several weights and asked to construct a simple pendulum. You are able to adjust the weight on the string, the length of the string, and the force with which you push the pendulum. The problem: What factor affects the rate of speed at which the pendulum swings—the weight, the length of the string, or the force used in pushing the pendulum? (After you have tried to solve the problem, read on.)

People in a concrete operational stage of thinking usually approach the problem haphazardly, and the answer they most typically give is that the weight is most important. On the other hand, people who use formal operational thinking approach the problem as an experiment, systematically varying one factor after another. Using this procedure, they conclude—correctly—that it is the length of the string that is the critical factor.

If you came up with the wrong answer, don't despair. Only about half of all college students get it right (Papalia, 1972). Moreover, if you try to do it in your head, without physically trying solutions out, the problem is almost impossible to solve correctly without an intimate knowledge of physics. Still, the fact that many people lack the ability to employ formal operational thought suggests that schools might well consider attempts to teach higher levels of thinking—a procedure that has been shown to be effective in several programs (see, for example, Nickerson, 1986).

Developing Our Relationships with Others
Social development

Most parents would be hard-pressed to say which was more important to them—their child's first word, a sign of increasing cognitive abilities; or his or her first smile, a recognition of the special social bond between parent and child. This difficulty reflects the fact that development proceeds simultaneously in many areas, each of which is related to crucial milestones as children grow into well-adjusted adults. One of the most crucial areas of growth and change relates to **social development,** the changes in relationships and interactions with others.

Attachment, the positive emotional bond that typically develops between parents and their children during infancy, represents a particularly important milestone of social development. Attachment helps infants survive by keeping them physically close to people who provide them with nourishment and protection. But it does more than that: It provides emotional security that permits them to interact with people in the outside world.

The development of attachment typically proceeds through four distinct stages (Bowlby, 1969; Ainsworth, Blehar, Waters, & Wall, 1978). Initially, infants are equally responsive to any adult. However, at the age of about 3 months they begin to discriminate and respond differently to their primary care givers, although they still do not protest if strangers appear.

The third stage, true attachment, begins at about 6 or 7 months of age. Infants now seek the physical presence of their primary care givers, and they react negatively when the care giver leaves. They also become wary of strangers, reacting with fear and withdrawal when left with someone they do not know.

The last stage of attachment is reached at 2 to 3 years of age, when children's increasing cognitive abilities allow them to interpret their care givers' behavior better. A child can understand, for instance, that when his or her mother leaves there is a strong likelihood that she will return. As a

Bettye Lane/Photo Researchers

After age 2 or 3, most children can separate from their parents with little anxiety.

consequence, the child's attachment becomes less rigid, and unhappiness at separation typically decreases.

One critical issue regarding attachment is the identity of the care giver. While early theorists focused solely on the attachment bond between mother and child, more recent work suggests that children become equally attached to their fathers (Lamb, 1982). In addition, it appears that the *quality* of interaction between care giver and child is considerably more important than the *quantity* of interaction in determining the strength of attachment, although clearly care givers must spend some minimum amount of time with a child (Belsky, 1985).

The importance of the quality of the interaction between child and care giver is suggested by the work of Harry Harlow (Harlow & Zimmerman, 1959). Harlow found that infant monkeys who were allowed to choose between a wire "monkey" that provided food, or a terrycloth "monkey" that was warm and soft—but did not provide food—invariably preferred the cloth monkey. It is clear that the cloth monkey gave greater comfort, and that simply providing food was insufficient to create attachment.

The issue of attachment is one of the greatest concerns that people cite when discussing the merits of day care, in which children are cared for by paid workers. Do children suffer emotional deprivation as a result of spending most of their waking hours with parent substitutes? Most research indicates that children who participate in day care are as attached to their parents as are children who have been raised at home. In addition, they typically prefer their parents over day-care workers (Belsky, 1985; Rutter, 1982; Ragozin, 1980). Day care, then, seems to produce no difficulties regarding attachment.

Expanding relationships   As children develop, the nature and importance of relationships with their care givers undergoes some critical changes. Rather than providing only physical care, parents begin to place a greater emphasis on socialization. **Socialization** is the process of learning and accepting society's values, attitudes, beliefs, and customs. In some societies, violent, aggressive play among children is not only permitted but encouraged; children are taught early on that aggression is an appropriate means of resolving problems. In other societies, however, parents teach their children that problems ought to be talked through and that punching a child who displeases them is inappropriate (Brake, 1985). Clearly, the nature of this socialization affects the behavior of these same children when they are adults.

Whatever the specific nature of socialization during childhood, it has important effects on children's development. In fact, some theorists—such as Erik Erikson (1963; 1986)—suggest that people's interactions and their understandings about one another present a series of critical crises or conflicts through which they must pass. The way these crises are resolved has a significant influence on people's ability to adjust to the demands that life places upon them.

According to Erikson, there are eight stages of **psychosocial development**—the growth and change of psychological orientation toward oneself and others. At every stage, a new level of social interaction with others is necessitated, and one is presented with a conflict or crisis that must be resolved. Each of the eight stages, then, is represented as a pairing of the most positive and the most negative aspects of the period. Although there is never a complete resolution of the conflicts presented in a given stage, one must resolve the current stage's crisis sufficiently to be able to deal with the new and increasingly complex demands of later stages.

Each stage is seen in terms of a matching of the most positive and negative aspects of the period's dominant crisis (see Table 3-2). First, the **trust versus mistrust** stage (birth to 1½ years) centers around the development of trust. Infants with warm, predictable, nurturant care givers develop a sense of trust that their needs will be met; infants whose needs are ignored or who are faced with inconsistent care and unpleasant interactions with others may fail to develop trust.

TABLE 3-2
Erikson's Stages of Psychosocial Development

STAGE NAME	APPROXIMATE AGE	MAJOR CHARACTERISTICS
1. Trust versus mistrust	Birth–1½ years	Feelings of trust from environmental support; or fear and concern
2. Autonomy versus shame	1½–3 years	Independence if exploration is encouraged; or self-doubt and shame
3. Initiative versus guilt	3–6 years	Identification of self as male or female; or guilt because of actions or thoughts
4. Industry versus inferiority	6–12 years	Development of sense of competence; or lack-of-mastery feelings
5. Identity versus role confusion	12–18 years	Awareness of uniqueness of self; or inability to identify appropriate role
6. Intimacy versus isolation	18–30 years	Development of loving, sexual relationships; or fear of relationship with others
7. Generativity versus stagnation	30–60 years	Sense of contribution to continuity of life; or trivialization of one's activities
8. Ego integrity versus despair	60–death	Sense of unity of life's accomplishments; or regret over lost opportunities

Charles Gatewood/The Image Works

Competence in academic and social skills is a mark of the industry versus inferiority stage, when children are developing a sense of themselves as individuals.

The **autonomy versus shame-and-doubt stage** marks the second phase (1½ to 3 years of age) of psychosocial development. During this period, children whose exploration and freedom are encouraged develop independence and autonomy and a sense of adequacy. In contrast, children who have been overly restricted and protected develop feelings of shame, self-doubt, and dependency.

The third period of psychosocial development is the **initiative versus guilt stage** (ages 3 to 6). During this period, children are capable of planning and initiating activities and play. If they are allowed some independence to do so, they will develop a sense of confidence about their own capabilities. On the other hand, adults who squelch children's attempts to direct and initiate activities will produce guilt and feelings of inadequacy.

If the crises of earlier stages have been successfully resolved, children reach the last of childhood's stages of psychosocial development, the **industry versus inferiority stage** (ages 6 to 12), ready to meet increasingly sophisticated challenges. Social play with others increases, and children begin to develop areas of special competence in school and sports. Successful resolution of the demands of this period results in the development of increasing adequacy in social interactions and basic skills. Moreover, children can begin to develop a sense of themselves as individuals. On the other hand, difficulties during this stage result in feelings of inadequacy and failure.

Psychosocial growth does not end at age 12; Erikson outlines four more stages of development, which we will discuss later in this chapter when considering adolescence and adulthood. It is clear, though, that the ground-work for successful resolution of later crises must be laid during childhood.

Psychology for You:
Dispelling the myth of the "right" way to raise children

A question that is universal to all new parents—and to those who even contemplate becoming parents—is whether they will be adequate to handle the task. Yet, despite the many books on the topic—take a look at the long list of titles on parenting at any bookstore—there is no secret formula. Because parents are only one of many influences in the complex environments in which children must be raised, and because of the important influence of inherited traits, parents cannot expect to mold their children into exactly the kind of human beings they wish for.

The notion that there is one "right" way to raise children is but one of several myths that are prevalent in our society regarding child-rearing practices (LeMasters, 1977). Among the others are:

● "Children will turn out well if they have 'good' parents." You probably know exceptions to this: Seemingly perfect parents produce children with many problems. Similarly, children from backgrounds filled with deficits often overcome them and go on to be extraordinarily productive members of society. As we discussed earlier in the chapter, development is a joint result of nature and nurture. Obviously, parents have no control over their children's biological inheritance, given that it is a function of chance genetic happenings at the moment of conception. Similarly, no parent can have complete control over a child's environment unless the child is raised without the benefit of social interaction outside the home. Whether the parents are "good," then, is not the sole criterion for successful child development.

● "There are no bad children—only bad parents." This is an unusually destructive myth. Clearly, the complex social relationships of children with their peers, and the behavior of siblings, schoolmates and teachers, and others with whom children come in contact, all have an effect upon children's behavior. Similarly, children inherit characteristics that have an important impact on the way they behave.

● "Child rearing is easier today because of modern medicine, modern appliances, and the insights of psychology." The same factors that led to the development of these advances work to make everyday living more complex. Despite these "advances," the concurrent increase in the complexity of the environment makes raising children increasingly difficult.

● "Love is enough to successfully raise children." Love by itself is *not* sufficient; parents must employ knowledge, discipline, and understanding in order to successfully raise children. On the other hand, the converse is also true: No amount of knowledge is sufficient to successfully raise children if such knowledge is not tempered with love and nurturance.

Knowing what's wrong is easier than knowing what's right: Raising well-adjusted children   While it is relatively easy to dispel myths about child rearing, it is considerably more difficult to present the other side of the question: What does one do to produce well-adjusted children? Although there are almost as many answers to this question as there are parents, there are several general points that can be made with confidence (Dwortzky, 1984; White, 1985).

● Do not exert excessive control over children. When parents try to control every aspect of their children's lives, they are probably more concerned with meeting needs of their own than their children's needs. To some degree, children need to make their own mistakes and learn to be independent. Without the chance to explore the world on their own, they will not be able to learn self-reliance and confidence.

● Avoid extreme permissiveness. When some limits are set on children, they are able to distinguish between desirable and undesirable behavior. Positive, socially acceptable behavior does not just spring forth from children; as we noted earlier, children must be socialized by those around them. Firmness, combined with open communication and explanations and rationales for decisions, seems to be an optimum approach to child rearing.

● A warm, accepting, and affectionate environment is a necessary condition for encouraging the development of well-adjusted children. Children must know that they are loved and that their parents accept them, warts and all.

● Be consistent and reasonable. If rules are constantly changing, children will never be able to understand them, let alone follow them. Moreover, discipline is accepted more readily when parents explain the rationale for rules and make it clear that parental decisions about the way children ought to behave are for the children's own benefit.

TO REVIEW

● Development is a joint function of heredity (causes transmitted biologically from one's parents) and the environment (causes relating to the influence of parents, siblings, family, friends, schooling, and other experiences).

● Piaget's theory of cognitive development suggests that children pass through four stages: sensorimotor, preoperational, concrete operational, and formal operational.

● Social development, changes in people's relationships and interactions, is marked by attachment, the positive emotional bond that typically develops between parents and their children. Another important aspect of social development is socialization, the process of coming to learn and accept society's values, attitudes, beliefs, and customs.

● Erikson proposes that there are eight stages of psychosocial development.

CHECK YOURSELF

1. The _____ view integrates heredity and environmental influence to explain human development.

2. Which statement about children in the preoperational stage is *not* true?
   a. Children have difficulty viewing the world from the perspective of others.
   b. Language develops.
   c. Children master the ability to understand how quantity relates to different physical shapes and arrangements of objects.
   d. Children take part in symbolic play.

3. At what stage does abstract thinking begin to develop?

4. Research suggests that in forming a strong attachment, the quality of care giver–child interactions may be more important than the quantity. True or false?

5. During which of Erikson's eight stages of development is the encouragement of a child's exploration and freedom considered important?

(See answers to these questions at the bottom of page 94.)

3.2   THE TRANSITION TO ADULTHOOD:
Adolescence

Of bodily desires it is the sexual to which they are most disposed to give way, and in regard to sexual desire they exercise no self-restraint. . . . They are passionate, irascible, and apt to be carried away by their impulses. . . . Youth is the age when people are most devoted to their friends or relations or companions. . . . If the youth commit a fault, it is always on the side of excess and exaggeration . . . for they carry everything too far, whether it be their love or hatred or anything else.

People were complaining about the behavior of adolescents even some 2000 years ago, as this quote from Aristotle attests, and we are still apt to encounter concerns about adolescents' rebelliousness, disrespect for society's values, and immorality (Brake, 1985). Yet **adolescence,** the period that marks the transition between childhood and adulthood, represents for most people a time of optimism and idealism in which their attitudes, values, and behaviors are shaped and molded in preparation for becoming full-fledged members of adult society. It is also, though, a time of such rapid social and physical change that a certain amount of turmoil is not uncommon.

Our focus here is on the crucial changes in social and moral development that occur during adolescence, particularly those involved with the development of identity. We will consider the important physical changes that occur during this same time when we discuss sexual behavior in Chapter 11.

Developing Our Relationships with Others: Social development

Who am I?

This fundamental question is one that you are likely to have asked yourself. As we discussed in Chapter 1, finding one's place in the world is one of life's major undertakings, and it becomes particularly salient during adolescence (Leahy, 1985).

Erikson's theory of psychosocial development—which we began discussing earlier in the chapter—proposes that questions of **identity,** the sense of one's unique value and position in the world, are of critical importance during adolescence. In the **identity versus role confusion stage** (which lasts from around age 13 until the beginning of adulthood in the early twenties), adolescents become less dependent on their families and concern themselves more with the world outside the home. As their interests widen, they try out more of society's roles. At the same time, though, they must learn to establish a coherent, integrated identity and view of themselves, one that recognizes both their strengths and their weaknesses. In Erikson's view, an integrated identity consists of four aspects: (1) learning to accept an adult view of one's own sexuality; (2) becoming an independent person, seen not as someone else's son or daughter but as a person in one's own right; (3) adopting a set of basic beliefs and values; and (4) choosing a set of social and career-oriented roles.

During the development of identity, Erikson suggests that people typically have an **identity crisis,** a state in which they are unsure, aimless, and confused about their identity. This crisis may ultimately have positive results, since it focuses people on the need to find a stable, workable, and realistic set of roles. For instance, a person set on a career in medicine who experiences an identity crisis when he finds he lacks the necessary aptitude in biology is better off avoiding such a career; the resolution of the crisis brought about by this revelation can prevent later failure and unhappiness.

CHECK YOURSELF: ANSWERS

1. interactionist   **2.** c   **3.** formal operational stage   **4.** True   **5.** autonomy versus shame and doubt

Susan Lapides/Design Conceptions

In developing their identity, people may try out a variety of roles.

On the other hand, unresolved identity crisis may be manifested in several ways. For instance, people may adopt a **negative identity**—a socially unacceptable role, such as that of a criminal or delinquent. A negative identity may be explicitly chosen (such as a punk rocker whose behavior is designed to "get even" with her parents) or may be relatively involuntary (as when a person using drugs becomes addicted to them and whose identity thereby comes to be centered around drug use).

Identity crises that are resolved too early by adopting a role without considering its implications may also bring about negative consequences. In a process known as **foreclosure,** an individual adopts an identity prematurely without making adequate preparation or a sufficient range of choices. A daughter who accepts her father's invitation to join the family business may be foreclosing other career choices without sufficiently considering her options. When foreclosure occurs, an identity crisis may be delayed until later in life. For instance, the daughter may come to regret her choice after participating in the family business for several years and have to face the trauma of searching for a new, more appropriate role.

Although the search for identity is most pronounced during adolescence and the identity versus role confusion stage, questions of identity arise at other times as well. When people go off to college, get their first jobs, marry, become parents, divorce, suffer the loss of a loved one, or encounter any of the other major turning points of life, they may once again come to question the meaning of their lives and their place in society. The degree to which they have successfully resolved issues of identity during adolescence affects their ability to cope with identity issues at later points in their lives.

Developing Our Sense of Justice: Moral development

Put yourself in the position of the man in the following story:

Your wife is near death from an unusual kind of cancer. There is one drug that the doctors think might save her—a form of radium that a scientist in a nearby city has recently developed. The drug is expensive to manufacture, and the scientist is charging 10 times what the drug costs him to make. He pays $1000 for the radium and charges $10,000 for a small dose of the drug. You have gone to everyone you know to borrow money, but you can get together only $2,500, which is one-fourth of what you need. You have told the scientist that your wife is dying and asked him to sell it cheaper or let you pay later. But the scientist has said, "No, I discovered the drug and I'm going to make money from it." In desperation, you consider breaking into the scientist's laboratory to steal the drug for your wife. Should you?

The answer you give to this question reveals a considerable amount about your level of morality, according to psychologist Lawrence Kohlberg (1984). In his view, people's responses to dilemmas such as this one differ according to the stage of moral development they have attained.

Kohlberg has identified three major levels of moral reasoning: preconventional, conventional, and postconventional. At the lowest level, **preconventional morality**, people follow unvarying rules based on rewards and punishments. For instance, at the preconventional stage you would evaluate the moral dilemma by saying that if you got caught while stealing you might go to jail, so it would probably not be worth doing.

Those people functioning at the **conventional morality** level approach moral problems in terms of their position as responsible members of society. For example, if you decided against stealing the drug because you thought you might feel guilty or dishonest for having done so, or if you decided to steal it because you felt you would never be able to face others because of your inaction, you would be reasoning at the conventional level of morality.

In contrast to people at lower levels of morality, individuals at the **postconventional morality** level invoke universal moral principles that are seen as broader than the particular society in which they live. If you, for example, had argued that stealing would lead you to condemn yourself because it had violated your own moral principles, or that if you didn't steal the drug you wouldn't be living up to your own standards regarding the sanctity of life, you would be reasoning at a postconventional level of morality.

There are pronounced age differences in the level of moral reasoning that people have attained. For example, prior to adolescence, children typically reason at the preconventional or conventional level; partially because of their inability to think abstractly, they are unable to view moral issues in terms of broad principles. During adolescence, however, people's increasing cognitive abilities may allow them to understand that there can be conflicts between socially accepted standards and their own personal principles, and they may choose to place their own ideals over those of society (Kurtines & Gewirtz, 1987).

Most people, though, never reach the postconventional stage of moral reasoning; Kohlberg estimates that only about 25 percent of all adults move beyond the conventional level. (To get a sense of your own moral reasoning, refer to the accompanying Do It! box.) Moreover, it seems as if the pattern of moral development identified by Kohlberg is more characteristic of males than of females (Gilligan, 1982). Women may be likely to understand morality more in terms of the specific relationships they have with the individuals involved in a moral dilemma and more in terms of the well-being of those individuals, than in terms of broad, universal, and abstract principles.

DO IT!

EXPLORING MORAL JUDGMENTS

To explore your moral judgments, read the following moral dilemmas and consider how you would resolve them (Colby, Kohlberg, Gibbs, & Lieberman, 1983, pp. 81–83):

> Judy was a 12-year-old girl. Her mother promised her that she could go to a special rock concert coming to their town if she saved up from baby-sitting and lunch money for a long time so she would have enough money to buy a ticket to the concert. She managed to save up the $15 the ticket cost plus another $3. But then her mother changed her mind and told Judy that she had to spend the money on new clothes for school. Judy was disappointed and decided to go to the concert anyway. She bought a ticket and told her mother that she had only been able to save $3. That Saturday she went to the performance and told her mother that she was spending the day with a friend. A week passed without her mother finding out. Judy then told her older sister, Louise, that she had gone to the performance and had lied to her mother about it. Louise wonders whether to tell their mother what Judy did.

To probe your moral reasoning, ask yourself the following questions:

☐   Should Louise, the older sister, tell their mother that Judy had lied about the money or should she keep quiet?

☐   In wondering whether to tell, Louise thinks of the fact that Judy is her sister. Should that make a difference in Louise's decision?

☐   Is the fact that Judy earned the money herself the most important thing in this situation?

☐   The mother promised Judy she could go to the concert if she earned the money. Is the fact that the mother made a promise the most important thing in the situation?·

☐   Why, in general, should a promise be kept?

☐   Is it important to keep a promise to someone you don't know well and probably won't see again?

Now consider this second scenario:

In Korea, a company of Marines was greatly outnumbered and was retreating before the enemy. The company had crossed a bridge over a river, but the enemy were mostly still on the other side. If someone went back to the bridge and blew it up, with the head start the rest of the men in the company would have they could probably then escape. But the man who stayed back to blow up the bridge would probably not be able to escape alive; there would be about a 4-to-1 chance he would be killed. The captain himself is the man who knows best how to lead the retreat. He asks for volunteers, but no one will volunteer. If he goes himself, the men will probably not get back safely.

To examine your moral reasoning, ask yourself these questions:

☐   Should the captain order someone else to go on this very dangerous mission or should he go himself?

☐   What is the best justification for saying it is right to send someone other than himself?

☐   Why or how do you say it is right to save more lives in this case, when it means ordering someone to his death?

☐   What is the best or most important reason for saying it is wrong to send someone else, when ordering someone else will save more lives?

☐   Does the captain have the right or the authority to give orders to a man as he thinks it best to? Why?

☐ Would a person have the right to refuse such an order?

☐ The captain has a family; the others do not. Should that enter into his decision?

☐ If he is going to pick someone to go, how should he choose?

Clearly, these questions have no right or wrong answers, but your responses to them should give you some insight into your own thinking about moral issues.

Adolescence is a period when both males and females may form a more sophisticated understanding of morality. It is also a time of change in the specific content of their moral values. At the start of adolescence, the values that are typically held most important include obedience, cheerfulness, and helpfulness. Later, however, these values become less important and are replaced with an increased sense of achievement, self-respect, broad-mindedness, and responsibility (Beech & Schoeppe, 1974).

What is particularly noteworthy about the values that evolve during adolescence is how similar they are to the values held by society as a whole. In fact, the notion that adolescents hold values that are strongly at variance with those of other stages in their lives as well as those of society as a whole is something of a myth. The fundamental values of adolescents most often mirror those of their parents. Any discrepancy is more likely to center on

Susan Lapides/Design Conceptions

Although adolescence is popularly characterized as a time of rebellion, the majority of teenagers share their parents' values and beliefs.

such mundane issues as noisiness and punctuality than on more basic issues, such as honesty and concern for others (Coleman et al., 1977).

Although the similarities between parents, other adults, and adolescents remain relatively high—at least in terms of basic values—there is a decline in reliance on adults for information and a shift toward using the peer group as a source of social judgment and comparison. The peer group becomes increasingly important, allowing adolescents to form close, adultlike relationships and helping to clarify their own personal identity.

Psychology for You:
Facing the quest for identity during adolescence

As we have seen, the development of a stable identity is a fundamental task that occurs during the years of adolescence—and recurs during later stages of development. Psychologists have identified several general points about the development of identity that are useful to keep in mind when exploring the question "Who am I?" Among them:

● Role models facilitate the development of identity. People who are searching for identity might do well to look around themselves and identify adults that they feel are successful. By talking to them, considering the things that they did to reach their current state in life, and thinking about ways in which their paths could be followed, people can help themselves in their own quest for identity. Remember that there are many forms of success, and the way success is defined is critical.

● People should not foreclose their options too early. Adolescence typically is and should be a time of exploration, in which individuals try out different activities and roles. It is a period in which to discover, through trial and error, what our potential is. Although this process may naturally entail some risk and anxiety, it is necessary to accept this risk—for without it, no growth would be possible.

● Keep in mind that we all wear many masks. Our identity has many facets, and it is not atypical to try out these different masks at different points and with different people. Although it is important to develop a good, firm sense of self, it is also necessary to understand that different people and situations will evoke different aspects of identity. You may not appear to be exactly the same person when you are around your parents as when you are with your friends. It is critical, though, not to be a chameleonlike creature that changes color depending on the nature of the environment; you should strive to develop a sense of what is unique and special about you, and be strong enough to allow your uniqueness to shine through in different situations.

● Remember that adolescence is but one period of our lives, and although it is a time of critical development and choices, it is not necessary to resolve all the questions or issues of life during this period. Development continues throughout the course of life, and we should not feel that it is necessary to make a lifetime's worth of decisions during adolescence. It is equally important to be aware that we should not unalterably rule out various paths and make decisions that would prevent us from choosing various options later on in life.

TO REVIEW

● Adolescence is the period between childhood and adulthood.

● Erikson suggests that the development of identity—the sense of one's unique value and position in the world—occurs during the identity versus role-confusion period.

● An identity crisis may occur during adolescence when people are unsure, aimless, and confused about their identity.

● According to Kohlberg's theory, the stages of moral development encompass preconventional, conventional, and postconventional morality. However, this sequence may be more descriptive of males than females, who appear to base their moral reasoning on specific relationships rather than on broad, universal principles of morality.

CHECK YOURSELF

1. Unresolved identity crises may lead people to adopt socially deviant roles through a process called "foreclosure." True or false?

2. You witness a young girl steal some fruit from a stand and take it to her younger brother. Both children appear hungry and impoverished. After thinking about it, you decide to turn the young girl over to the store owner, because you believe that stealing, under any circumstances, is not a socially acceptable act. At what stage of moral development are you, according to Kohlberg's scale?
    a. preconventional stage
    b. conventional stage
    c. postconventional stage
    d. immoral stage

3. If in the above example you felt that the children's needs outweighed the social wrongdoing, given the severity of their situation, your response would place you at what stage?
    a. preconventional stage
    b. conventional stage
    c. postconventional stage
    d. immoral stage

4. As one might expect, the values of adolescents differ dramatically from those of society as a whole. True or false?

(See answers to these questions at the bottom of page 102.)

GROWING OLD:
Adulthood, Old Age, and Death

We who are older have nothing to lose! We have everything to gain by living dangerously! We can be the risk-takers, daring to challenge and change systems, policies, lifestyles, ourselves.

Maggie Kuhn
Founder, Gray Panthers

For the majority of people who live into old age, the years from birth to adolescence mark a mere prelude to the remainder of life. Surprisingly, though, we know less about adulthood and old age than we do about the considerably shorter periods of infancy, childhood, and adolescence. One reason for the lack of emphasis on the majority of the life span is that the physical and intellectual changes occurring in adulthood are more subtle and gradual than those taking place earlier. Another reason is that developmental psychologists traditionally considered the psychosocial changes occurring after adolescence to be less pronounced, and the patterns of adjustment to be largely determined prior to adulthood.

In recent years, however, such views have largely been debunked, as psychologists have come to realize the critical nature of the changes that occur throughout life (Levinson, 1986; Rowe & Kahn, 1987). Because, with luck, most of us will reach a reasonably old age—the average life expectancy in the United States today is well into the seventies—the changes that occur during adulthood and old age hold a special significance.

The Passages of Adulthood:
Psychosocial development

To Erik Erikson, the start of adulthood marks yet another stage of development: the **intimacy versus isolation stage.** During this period, people focus on developing close relationships with one another. Those who are successful at resolving the crises of this stage, which lasts from the end of the teenage years until about age 30, are able to form relationships that are full on many different levels, including intellectual, emotional, and physical.

Early adulthood also marks a time in which people begin to solidify and hone the choices they have made earlier in their quest for identity. People become independent of their families and begin to view themselves as adults. They make career choices, settle into long-term relationships, consider and perhaps enter into marriage, and establish their own visions of what the future will hold.

CHECK YOURSELF: ANSWERS
1. False **2.** b **3.** c **4.** False

Yet people's lives continue to develop and grow, and their challenges become even broader. In the next major period, the **generativity versus stagnation stage,** people's major challenges are broader, says Erikson. Covering the entire period of middle adulthood, the crises of the stage concern generativity, which refers to a person's contribution to his or her family, community, work, and society as whole. If people are able to view their activities as contributing to the world and benefiting its future generations, their feelings during this stage will be positive. On the other hand, people who view their work or accomplishments as trivial and lacking in meaning will experience feelings of stagnation.

Psychologist Daniel Levinson (1986), who has studied adult development extensively, finds that middle adulthood frequently produces its own kind of identity crisis. Prior to midlife, people are guided by what Levinson calls "The Dream"—an all-encompassing notion about what goals are desired from life, be it writing the great American novel or becoming President of the United States. Around the age of 40 or 45, though, people begin to question their lives and their own particular "dream," as they enter a **midlife transition.** The thought that life is finite—always known but never felt so strongly before—begins to play an increasingly important role in everyday decisions, and people may come to the realization that "The Dream" is not going to be fulfilled—or at least not fulfilled in the way they had originally hoped.

Rather than looking forward in time, people in midlife begin to assess the past and their accomplishments, and they realize that there are limitations to how much they will accomplish (Gould, 1978). There are physical

Alan Carey/The Image Works

According to Levinson's studies, men in their late thirties or early forties may enter a period of midlife crisis, when they may become disillusioned with the career and lifestyle they chose in their twenties.

signs of aging—perhaps graying hair or "middle-age spread"—that no longer allow them to ignore the limitation of their bodies. Moreover, the events of life, such as the death of a peer, a child's trouble in school, or a divorce in the family, may make life seem frighteningly unstable.

If the midlife transition is perceived too negatively, people may enter a **midlife crisis** in which they question their contributions to the world and the very meaning of their existence. Even if they have been very successful—by all of society's benchmarks—they may feel that they have made errors in the choices that brought them to where they are. This crisis may lead to extreme changes in lifestyle, including career changes, marital changes, or upheavals in long-standing friendships (Tamir, 1986).

On the other hand, most people's midlife transition is relatively calm; it is the rare individual who leaves his or her spouse, takes on a lover, or quits his or her job and moves to Tahiti. Instead, this is a time of growth and continuing development. After the midlife transition people are less tyrannized by their inner conflicts and the demands of others, and they become more accepting of themselves. As their inner peace grows, they are able to be more compassionate and understanding of others (Levinson, 1986).

During middle adulthood, most people are seen by others, and come to view themselves, as senior members of their own particular worlds; for example, they may become master craftsmen or senior partners in a law firm. Not only do they see themselves as responsible for their own work and perhaps the work of those they supervise, but they view themselves in a broader light: They see their role as one of guiding the development of a new generation of adults who are soon to become the dominant generation.

Are women in this stage different from men? Although the work on midlife transitions has been well-substantiated, most of the research has concentrated on males. Research that has directly compared men and women or has focused on women has produced growing evidence that women make an important transition at around age 30 that may be even more important than the midlife transition of age 40 (Reinke, Holmes, & Harris, 1985).

According to this research, women in their thirties face family and job responsibilities that are often pressing. Single women in their thirties who want spouses may feel that time is running out. And for all women in this age bracket the end of the childbearing years comes into view. As their "biological clocks" tick on, moving toward the time when their age will not allow them to have children, childless women who desire to give birth may begin to feel the pressures of time. Although the notion is controversial, the age-30 transition may be more significant for women than the changes that typically occur at age 40.

Other research suggests that chronological age, by itself, may be an insufficient explanation for changes in women's adjustment as they get older. Instead, changes in family cycles and patterns—such as the start of children's schooling or the entry of a child into adolescence—seem more closely related to personal satisfaction and happiness than aging per se (Harris, Ellicott, & Holmes, 1986).

Psychosocial development in the elderly   Although many people assume that little change and development occurs during old age, it is actually a time of continued growth. According to Erik Erikson, it is not until late adulthood and old age that the last stage of psychosocial development, the **ego integrity versus despair stage,** is encountered. If the challenges of life are successfully met during this stage, the result is a sense of accomplishment and acceptance of one's inevitable and impending death. On the other hand, inadequate resolution during this stage leads to feelings of disgust with life and despair over what might have been but was not.

For some elderly people, the focus is on the "balance sheet of life," as they add up the pluses and minuses of the past. For these people, thoughts of the past are predominant, and they gradually withdraw from society (Frenkel-Brunswick, 1968). Yet others see themselves as functioning, active members of society and are fully involved in life's activities; their focus is more on the here and now.

These two phenomena among the elderly reflect differing theories that have been developed to explain successful patterns of aging: disengagement theory and activity theory. **Disengagement theory** reflects the view that the elderly make a gradual withdrawal from society on a physical, psychological, and social level (Cummings & Henry, 1961). On a physical level, their energy diminishes, reaction time declines, vision and hearing deteriorate, and smell and taste are not as sensitive. Psychologically, people in old age may look inward more than they did during their younger years, and they may reflect upon life more frequently. Finally, disengagement theorists suggest that the lower rate of interaction with others and the generally lower level of participation in the ongoing affairs of society are further reflections of a gradual withdrawal from society.

While disengagement seems at first to represent an unhappy, melancholy state of affairs, disengagement theorists suggest that this need not be

Joel Gordon

Late adulthood may reflect either disengagement, when an individual withdraws from social contacts, or continued activity, when people remain involved in stimulating pursuits.

the case and in fact may be the mark of positive adjustment. For example, disengagement allows for increased inward reflectiveness and a decline in the emotional investment in social relationships with peers, which, because of the inevitability of death, may be relatively transient.

Activity theory paints a different picture. It suggests that people who in old age maintain the interests, concerns, and activities of earlier years—as well as adding new activities—are likely to be more well-adjusted than those whose activities represent a sharp departure from the activities of earlier years (Blau, 1973; Streib, 1977).

Activity theory argues that the nature of old age in our society presents many possibilities for **role exits,** in which there is a termination of an on-going role. For example, people who retire give up their roles as wage earners. When a spouse dies, the role of husband or wife is no longer viable. According to activity theory, substitute roles and activities need to be found, and roles and activities from earlier years need to continue in order to maintain effective adjustment. Of course, aimlessly filling one's life with activities is no guarantee of happiness. Instead, the nature of the activities in which the elderly engage is crucial to the transition into later life (Gubrium, 1973).

Disengagement theory and activity theory suggest two very different descriptions of effective aging. Which presents a more appropriate view of adjustment in old age? We cannot say for sure. It is clear that some elderly people adjust quite adequately, despite numerous "role exits," without engaging in the activities of their past or developing substitutes for lost roles; they report being happy and view their lives in a positive light (Birren, 1985; Cummings & Henry, 1961).

On the other hand, many elderly who vigorously continue activities of the past and develop new ones are adjusting effectively to old age; they too report positive attitudes and self-concepts. Until more definitive evidence is found, then, it is premature to favor one form of adjustment in old age over another. The critical point is that psychosocial development continues during old age. Rather than being a period of waiting for impending death, old age is a time for important psychological growth and change.

The End of Life:
Death and dying

Our knowledge of the universality and certainty of death makes it no easier to accept. Death remains shrouded in mystery, uncertainty, and outright fear. Preparing for it and accepting the deaths of those close to us are among the major tasks of life. (To get a sense of your own attitudes toward death, try the questionnaire in the following Do It! box.)

HOW DO YOU FEEL ABOUT DEATH?

To assess your feelings about death, complete the following question-naire. For statements 1 through 11, use these scale labels:

1 = never; 2 = rarely; 3 = sometimes; and 4 = often

1. I think about my own death. _____

2. I think about the death of loved ones. _____

3. I think about dying young. _____

4. I think about the possibility of my being killed on a busy road. _____

5. I have fantasies of my own death. _____

6. I think about death just before I go to sleep. _____

7. I think of how I would act if I knew I were to die within a given period of time. _____

8. I think of how my relatives would act and feel upon my death. _____

9. When I am sick, I think about death. _____

10. When I am outside during a lightning storm, I think about the possibility of being struck by lightning. _____

11. When I am in a car, I think about the high incidence of traffic fatalities. _____

For statements 12 through 30, use these scale labels:

1 = I strongly agree; 2 = I somewhat agree;
3 = I somewhat disagree; and 4 = I strongly disagree

12. I think people should first become concerned about death when they are old. _____

13. I am much more concerned about death than those around me. _____

14. Death hardly concerns me. _____

15. My general outlook just doesn't allow for morbid thoughts. _____

16. The prospect of my own death arouses anxiety in me. _____

17. The prospect of my own death depresses me. _____

18. The prospect of the death of my loved ones arouses anxiety in me. _____

19. The knowledge that I will surely die does not in any way affect the conduct of my life. _____

20. I envisage my own death as a painful, nightmarish experience. _____

21. I am afraid of dying. _____

22. I am afraid of being dead. _____

23. Many people become disturbed at the sight of a new grave, but it does not bother me. _____

24. I am disturbed when I think about the shortness of life. _____

25. Thinking about death is a waste of time. _____

26. Death should not be regarded as a tragedy if it occurs after a productive life. _____

27. The inevitable death of humanity poses a serious challenge to the meaningfulness of human existence. _____

28. The death of the individual is ultimately beneficial because it facilitates change in society. _____

29. I have a desire to live on after death. _____

30. The question of whether or not there is a future life worries me considerably. _____

SCORING   If you rated any of these items: 13, 16, 17, 18, 20, 21, 22, 24, 27, 29, and 30, as 1, change your score to 4; those you rated as 2, change to 3; those you rated as 3, change to 2; and those you rated as 4, change to 1. Add up your scores.

Average scores on the scale typically range from about 68 to 80. If you scored about 80, death is something that seems to produce some degree of anxiety. On the other hand, scores lower than 68 suggest that you experience little fear of death.

Source: Dickstein, 1972.

Not every society finds death as difficult a topic as we do. In some cultures death is welcomed, viewed as a way of freeing oneself from one's earthly bonds. Yet in most Western societies the topic of death is avoided, and some people even refuse to acknowledge that death is a part of life.

If we are to understand and accept death, though, we must view it not as a fearsome stranger but as an expected companion in our lives. Elisabeth Kübler-Ross (1969), who has written extensively on death and dying, suggests that knowledge and awareness of death can bring us a better understanding of the meaning of life, allowing us to lead fuller and richer lives.

The physical side of death   One initial step in coming to terms with death is trying to understand it from a physical and biological perspective. Death due to aging has been addressed in two kinds of theories: genetic preprogramming theories and wear-and-tear theories (Bergener, Ermini, & Stahelin, 1985). **Genetic preprogramming theories** suggest that there is a built-in time clock that places limits on the reproduction of human cells. After a certain amount of time—determined by heredity—the cells will simply no longer divide, and the body declines until it cannot maintain itself. Another possibility is that there are certain "suicide" cells that are genetically preprogrammed to make the body self-destruct after a given period of time.

Wear-and-tear theories look toward the body's ultimate death from the standpoint of mechanics. In this view, the body just wears out in the same way that an old car eventually deteriorates. Wastes accumulate, and mistakes in cell reproduction are made. When enough things go wrong, the body simply wears out, and death occurs.

While we do not know which of these explanations is more accurate, it is important to note that both suggest that death is part of a natural biological process. In this sense, then, death is no more mysterious or unusual than is our ability to digest food.

The psychological significance of death   Of course, the psychological significance of death goes far beyond its biological underpinnings (Chirban, 1985). For example, Kübler-Ross (1969) found that there is a developmental sequence through which people pass when told that their own death is imminent. This sequence of stages includes denial, anger, bargaining, depression, and acceptance:

- *Denial.* A common reaction to news of someone's impending death is, "Oh, no!"—words of denial. Dying people are no different, except their denial is typically stronger and longer-lasting. Upon being informed that their chances for survival are slim, they may conclude that the diagnosis is wrong, the x-rays are incorrect, or the physicians involved are incompetent. In some cases, they simply refuse to listen to the unpleasant news.

- *Anger.* After people move beyond denial, they typically enter the second stage: anger. They may be angry at their families, at the medical staff, or at anyone who is healthy. They feel they have been treated unfairly, and ask the unanswerable question, "Why me?"

- *Bargaining.* Anger typically turns into bargaining, the third stage of the process. In this stage, a patient will search for ways to postpone death, even temporarily. For instance, a dying person may promise God to work with the needy—if he or she is spared.

● *Depression.* At some point it becomes clear to dying individuals that bargaining is of no use. In this fourth stage, depression typically sets in as patients are engulfed by a great sense of loss—loss of loved ones and loss of the future. In a sense, they are experiencing grief for themselves as individuals.

● *Acceptance.* In this final stage, people come to accept that the die is cast. They are no longer angry or depressed, but accept the coming end to their lives without emotion. Kübler-Ross suggests that patients in this stage have come to terms with their death and approach it with contemplative and quiet expectation. During this stage, the living become relatively unimportant to the dying person, and communication is often minimal. It is as if the dying individual has turned inward and has accepted his or her fate without concern. It is, in Kübler-Ross's words, the "final rest before the long journey" (Kübler-Ross, 1969, p. 100).

Of course, not all people experience dying in the same manner, and some may never reach the final stages, depending on their psychological makeup and the speed at which the dying process progresses. Some people may continue fighting until the end, refusing to accept the idea of their impending death, while others will die before they have had time to reach the stage of acceptance. In addition, the uncertainties of death mean that some people never receive the knowledge that their death is imminent—they may be continually waiting for new test results, or their physicians and families may not tell them that an illness is terminal—and they will have no chance to respond to the news.

When we add the lack of certainty about *how* we will die to the certainty that we *will* die, it seems clear that the contemplation of the meaning of death, far from being a taboo subject, may be a component of healthy adjustment. Understanding what dying people experience can help us understand our own coming death better—no matter how far off we expect it to be.

Psychology for You:
Dealing with loss and grief

Death is profoundly difficult not only for the dying person but for those who survive the loss of a loved one. All of us have experienced many forms of **loss,** a situation in which we no longer have something or someone of importance, during our lifetimes. Perhaps it was some treasured object that was damaged in an accident, the end of a relationship when a friend moved away, or a change in familiar environments when graduating from school. Each of these losses deprives us of something of value and typically results in sadness and sometimes fear for the future course of life.

Loss is part of life; because of the changes that occur during the course of people's lives, no one is able to lead a life that is free from loss. In fact, such a life would be one that shows no growth, since so many of life's important milestones (graduating from high school, leaving one's parents to live in one's own home, or leaving one job to take another) involve some component of loss. But death represents a different kind of loss, because its finality is so profound and because for most people it is so unwelcome. Coming to grips with losses due to death, then, is an important, and difficult, developmental task.

Dealing with death: The stages of grief   How does one deal with losses due to death? Most people pass through a series of stages of grief which are not all that dissimilar to the stages a dying person experiences (Greenblat, 1978; Malinak, Hoyt, & Patterson, 1979).

The first stage of grief is typically shock, denial, and disbelief, a stage that usually lasts a few days. During this period, people who have experienced the death of a loved one are often able to function quite well, at least in terms of surface activities; they may notify others of the death and arrange the complex details of a funeral. During this stage, denial may occur; the person may not admit the depths of unhappiness that such a loss would be expected to bring. In extreme cases, a person may refuse to admit that the death has occurred.

The next stage typically produces more outward and profound signs of distress: As denial of the death disappears, there is a deep sadness and depression, characterized by crying, sleeplessness, anxiety, and fear. People may feel immobilized, unable to see how their lives will ever be put back into order. This state usually peaks from five days to two weeks after the death, although it may last considerably longer.

Michael Grecco/Stock, Boston

The second stage of grief, marked by profound sadness and outward expressions of mourning, typically begins a few days after the death.

The last two stages bring an adjustment to the loss. In the third stage, people begin to resume their lives. They give up the notion that they will be able to recover what has been lost and instead begin to turn to others and loosen the bonds that connected them to the person who died.

Finally, the fourth stage brings about the development of a new identity, one that is independent of the dead individual. For instance, a woman who has lost her husband may begin to perceive herself as a "widow" or a "single person," as opposed to a "wife." Upon reaching this stage, people often feel that the death has given them new insight and that they have grown from the experience.

As is the case for the stages associated with dying, not all people experience the stages of losing a loved one in the same form or sequence. Some people may never reach the last stages and will experience a continuing sense of loss and grief. Moreover, if people hold ambivalent (positive *and* negative) feelings toward the dead person, or are a bit uncertain of their feelings toward the person who has died, guilt may lead to a prolonged grieving period. In most cases, though, the grieving process is complete within a year of the death, and people are able to carry on their lives with greater understanding about the world and themselves.

If you have suffered the loss of a loved one, how do you know that the grief you are experiencing is appropriate? The following symptoms signal that your reactions may be extreme:

● Grief continues for what you perceive as an unusually long period

● You are unable to carry out normal, everyday activities after a few weeks

● You develop physical problems

● Your personality changes

● You behave in ways that you do not understand or like

In these cases, professional help may be called for. In most cases, though, the loss of a loved one—however unwelcome and despite the pain it causes—brings the opportunity for psychological growth. Moreover, understanding how people typically react to death may help to prepare you for its inevitable entry into your life.

TO REVIEW

● As life expectancy increases, the psychological changes of adulthood and old age take on unusual importance.

● During adulthood, people pass through the intimacy versus isolation stage, in which they solidify and hone the choices they made earlier. Later, in the generativity versus stagnation stage, they consider their general contributions to society.

- The midlife transition may produce its own kind of identity crisis, known as a midlife crisis. The major turning point for men is generally age 40, and the age-30 transition may be more critical for women.

- Disengagement theory and activity theory present different conceptions of successful adjustment in old age.

- Dying people, and those who have experienced a major loss due to the death of a loved one, each pass through a series of stages.

CHECK YOURSELF

1. Independence from family, choice of career, and marriage typically mark Erikson's _____ versus _____ stage. Concern with contributions made to one's family, community, work, or society usually occurs in the _____ versus _____ stage.

2. Assessment of accomplishment and realization of life's limitations occur during the:
   a. "dream" period
   b. midlife crisis
   c. midlife transition
   d. intimacy versus isolation stage

3. For many women, a transition which may be more important than the midlife transition occurs at around age:
   a. 25
   b. 30
   c. 40
   d. 50

4. Carol has maintained her energy level and has sought novel ways of using her time well into her senior years. Her behavior is best explained by the _____ theory.

5. What class of theories suggests that "suicide" cells cause the body to self-destruct?

6. "If my family had taken better care of me and gotten me better medical care, I would probably not be dying now! They should be ashamed!" This comment might be expected at what stage of dying?
   a. anger
   b. bargaining
   c. depression
   d. denial

(See answers to these questions at the bottom of page 114.)

TO SUMMARIZE

1. Development, the patterns of growth and change throughout life, was discussed in this chapter. We saw how people's changes on physical, emotional, intellectual, and social levels affect adjustment patterns during the entire life span.

2. Heredity and the environment interact to determine the course of an individual's development. Most psychologists, then, take an interactionist point of view when considering the nature-nurture issue.

3. During infancy and childhood there are major changes in both the quantity and quality of cognitive development, the development of thinking, understanding, and knowing. According to Piaget, people pass through a series of stages, including the sensorimotor stage (birth to 2 years), the preoperational stage (2 to 7 years), the concrete operational stage (7 to 12 years), and the formal operational stage (12 years to adulthood).

4. Among the major milestones of cognitive development are the development of conservation abilities at the start of the concrete operational stage (in which children come to understand that quantity is unrelated to the arrangement and physical appearance of objects), and the ability to think abstractly during the formal operational stage.

5. Attachment, the positive emotional bond that typically develops between parents and their children, is an important part of social development during the early years of life. Attachment usually proceeds through four stages of development. One crucial factor that affects attachment is the quality, not just the quantity, of interaction between care giver and child.

6. As children develop, parents and other care givers begin to emphasize socialization, the process of coming to learn and accept society's values, attitudes, beliefs, and customs. Erikson suggests that as children gain more experience interacting with others, they pass through a series of stages relating to psychosocial development in which there is growth and change of psychological orientation to themselves and others. Each stage is viewed as representing a crisis, and the different stages are said to extend throughout the entire life span.

7. During childhood, the stages described by Erikson include trust versus mistrust (birth to 1½ years), autonomy versus shame and doubt (1½ to 3 years), initiative versus guilt (3 to 6 years), and industry versus inferiority (6 to 12 years).

8. There are several myths regarding child-rearing practices, including the notions that children will turn out well if they have "good" parents; that

CHECK YOURSELF: ANSWERS

1. intimacy, isolation; generativity, stagnation **2.** c **3.** b **4.** activity **5.** genetic preprogramming theories **6.** anger

there are no bad children—only bad parents; that child rearing is easier today than it used to be; and that love is enough to raise children successfully. On the other hand, there are several broad guidelines that suggest ways of raising well-adjusted children, including not exerting excessive control over them, avoiding extreme permissiveness; providing a warm, accepting, and affectionate environment; and being consistent and reasonable.

9. Adolescence, the period between childhood and adulthood, is particularly crucial. It is the period in which identity—the sense of one's unique value and position in the world—develops. Erikson suggests that issues of identity are crucial to the stage of psychosocial development that occurs during this period: the identity versus role confusion stage.

10. Some people experience an identity crisis in adolescence during which they are unsure, aimless, and confused about their identity. If the identity crisis is not appropriately resolved, they may adopt a negative identity or experience foreclosure, adopting an identity prematurely.

11. According to Kohlberg, there are three levels of moral development: preconventional, conventional, and postconventional. It is possible, however, that there are differences in the nature and sequence of moral judgments made by males and females, with Kohlberg's sequence representing a more accurate description for men than for women. There is also an important evolution in the values of adolescents, although in terms of basic values, adolescents are quite similar to their parents.

12. Psychosocial development continues during adulthood and even into old age. Erikson suggests that people pass through the intimacy versus isolation stage (early adulthood), the generativity versus stagnation stage (middle adulthood), and ego integrity versus despair stage (late adulthood).

13. Middle adulthood represents an important transition for most adults. Around age 40, many people enter a midlife transition in which they begin to assess their accomplishments and realize that there are limitations to what they will achieve during their lifetimes. In some cases, this precipitates a midlife crisis. There is also growing evidence that women may experience an even more powerful transition at age 30, and that age itself may be less important than the nature of family changes that women are experiencing.

14. Growth and change continue even after midlife. Two theories have been suggested to explain successful adjustment in later life for the elderly. Disengagement theory reflects the view that the elderly make a gradual withdrawal from society on physical, psychological, and social levels; activity theory suggests that adjustment is more successful for the elderly who maintain and even expand their interests, concerns, and activities of earlier years.

15. Aging and death are natural parts of the developmental process. Two theories have been proposed to explain why people age. Genetic preprogramming theories suggest that there is a built-in time clock that places

limits on the reproduction of human cells. Wear-and-tear theories view the body as a machine that eventually wears out.

16. People who are dying pass through a series of stages, including denial, anger, bargaining, depression, and acceptance. Grief at the loss of someone else also proceeds through several stages: shock, denial, and disbelief; deep sadness and depression; a resumption of one's life; and the development of a new identity that is independent of the dead individual.

KEY TERMS AND CONCEPTS

development (p. 82)

heredity (p. 83)

environment (p. 83)

tabula rasa (p. 83)

interactionist (p. 83)

cognitive development (p. 84)

sensorimotor stage (p. 85)

preoperational stage (p. 85)

egocentric thought (p. 85)

conservation (p. 85)

concrete operational stage (p. 85)

formal operational stage (p. 85)

social development (p. 87)

attachment (p. 87)

socialization (p. 88)

psychosocial development (p. 89)

trust versus mistrust stage (p. 89)

autonomy versus shame-and-doubt stage (p. 90)

initiative versus guilt stage (p. 90)

industry versus inferiority stage (p. 90)

adolescence (p. 93)

identity (p. 94)

identity versus role-confusion stage (p. 94)

identity crisis (p. 94)

negative identity (p. 95)

foreclosure (p. 95)

preconventional morality (p. 96)

conventional morality (p. 96)

postconventional morality (p. 96)

intimacy versus isolation stage (p. 102)

generativity versus stagnation stage (p. 103)

midlife transition (p. 103)

midlife crisis (p. 104)

ego integrity versus despair stage (p. 105)

disengagement theory (p. 105)

activity theory (p. 106)

role exits (p. 106)

genetic preprogramming theories (p. 109)

wear-and-tear theories (p. 109)

loss (p. 110)

TO FIND OUT MORE

Barocas, H., Reichman, W., & Schwebel, A. I. (1983). *Personal adjustment and growth: A life-span approach.* New York: St. Martin's Press.

Taking an in-depth developmental approach, this book considers adjustment and change throughout people's lives.

Bee, H. (1985). *The developing child* (4th ed.). New York: Harper & Row.

This is a fine introduction to the early years of life, providing a broad overview of the major milestones of development.

Rice, F. P. (1984). *The adolescent: Development, relationships, and culture* (4th ed.). Boston: Allyn & Bacon.

The sometimes difficult and stormy time of adolescence is captured in this text.

Schulman, M., & Meckler, E. (1986). *Bringing up a moral child.* Reading, MA: Addison-Wesley.

This volume discusses concrete procedures by which children can be brought up to behave—and think—morally.

Sheehy, G. (1976). *Passages.* New York: Dutton.

A rich, anecdotal account of the important transitions that people encounter during the adult years.

Kübler-Ross, E. (1969). *On death and dying.* New York: Macmillan.

This moving book dispels several myths about dying and brings the author's sensitive and thoughtful perspective to the topic of death.

The Forces Underlying Behavior
Motivation

CHAPTER 4

Despite the bad weather off the coast of Alaska, the rescue mission began routinely. Jake Jacques, a member of a rescue team that patrolled the ocean waters, was uneventfully lowered onto the deck of a fishing ship where an injured sailor, Sasha Gudkow, was lying.

Suddenly, though, after placing Sasha in the chopper's rescue litter basket, the mission became anything but routine. As the basket began to rise, a massive wave hit the ship, and as Jake wildly grabbed the cable, both he and the basket were flung over the sea. Because of the poor weather, the only escape was for Jake, now holding onto the cable with one hand, and the litter to be pulled up into the helicopter's belly. Yet Jake could barely hold on, for the steel braid of the cable cut into his skin like razor blades. His only hope was to flip himself onto the litter carrying Sasha, which was a few feet above him. But the task seemed almost impossible.

Jake tried repeatedly to flip his left leg up onto the edge of the basket. But he couldn't swing it high enough. If only this guy could help pull me onto the basket, Jake thought. *But Sasha was strapped down. Jake's body felt leaden. Now the wind was picking up. It puffed him around like a cotton ball.* Gotta hang on, *he told himself.* You can do it, Jake. *Just the way he always told Mary. Jake remembered his bride when she was in high school, practicing hurdles, her bright blond hair fluffing in the breeze. "You can do it, Mary," Jake had kept telling her. She had run in every state meet, and afterward she had told Jake his words had always echoed in her head: "You can do it!"*

Jake's shoulder was numb now. He knew he couldn't hold out much longer. He looked down. His stomach tightened. He was about 125 feet above the water. Your only chance is getting onto the basket. *He swung his leg in a wide circle and then arched his body with all his might. Once more, he dropped back heavily into space. He could almost hear the snap of his shoulder muscle. . . .*

Jake again looked down into the dark waters far below. They now seemed almost inviting. Soft. Deep. Soothing. Jake felt his grip loosening, his tension draining away. Somewhere far off, he heard Sasha's voice. How good it would feel, simply to relax and let go. *Then Sasha's voice came again, more insistent. Jake looked up. Sasha was staring straight at him, his eyes full of alarm.*

Jake tightened his grip on the cable. One more try, *he thought.* Gotta do it this time. Okay, bend the knee. Raise the foot. Now push upward with the body. Push, PUSH. *Jake closed his eyes against the pain. Up he came, and slowly his leg and then his body stretched across the litter, atop Sasha. Jake opened his eyes:* I did it! *(Reiss, 1985, p. 63–64.)*

120

For his role in the rescue mission, Jake Jacques received an Air Force Commendation medal. Yet his performance illustrates more than mere valor; it serves as an example of the strength of human determination and willpower.

In this chapter we discuss motivation and the factors that arouse, direct, and sustain behavior. We consider how people come to make choices in their lives, as well as how some of the basic biological processes—including eating and sleeping—operate to keep our bodies functioning almost automatically. We will also see how our own desires and concerns affect and interact with what once were thought of as solely biological functions.

We then discuss the ways people can fulfill psychological needs. We focus on several fundamental types of motivation, including the ways in which achievement, affiliation, security, consistency, curiosity, and creativity needs can be fulfilled. We also examine the significant individual characteristics that differentiate one person's needs from another's.

Finally, we consider cases in which needs get out of hand, as we discuss the irresistible needs that underlie addiction. The most common addictions are examined, including addictions to alcohol and cocaine.

Throughout our discussions, we will be concerned with human needs and the choices people make to fulfill them—as well as the consequences of those choices.

4.1   SKYDIVING VERSUS KNITTING:
Understanding Our Choices

As the stiff breeze blew over Mount Tom, Sally Fleming strapped her body into the hang glider poised over a sharp precipice. Never before had she experienced such a sense of vulnerability. Yet she felt as if she were compelled to start her journey in the tiny vehicle, powered only by the wind that blew over the mountains. As she willed herself to jump off the cliff and began to fly, her father's admonition—"Wouldn't you be just as happy knitting?"—ran through her head. She soon knew the answer: The thrill of moving silently through the air, gazing at the mountain below her, could not be matched. Her quest for excitement was leading her toward new challenges.

You may know someone like Sally Fleming—a person whose life is centered around challenges and who is never satisfied with the mundane. You may also know more sedentary people whose greatest thrill comes from eating a good home-cooked meal or sitting in an easy chair reading the newspaper.

To understand the kinds of challenges people seek and the factors that underlie the choices they make, we need to consider the concept of motivation. **Motivation** refers to the factors that arouse, sustain, and direct behavior toward attainment of certain goals, known as motives. Motivation may be directed toward goals as fundamental as acquiring food when we are hungry or more lofty goals centered around purely human endeavors, such as needs involving love and companionship.

To understand the motivation that underlies our behavior, we need first to consider several fundamental notions. Probably the most basic concept is that of **drive,** motivational tension or arousal that energizes behavior to fulfill some need. Some drives, known as **primary drives,** are related to the basic biological functioning of the body. These include hunger, thirst, sex, and sleep. People who seek out warmth to protect themselves from the cold are motivated by a primary drive.

On the other hand, not all drives have a biological basis; most of us have a desire to earn money and do well in school, activities that cannot be easily explained by examining the biology of human beings. Instead, it is clear that some of our motives are based on what are called **secondary drives**—learned drives in which no obvious biological need is being fulfilled. For instance, people who have a drive to be successful in business or to seek out risks are responding not to some biological need; they have learned, through past experience, the satisfaction that they achieve from seeking out these kinds of experiences (Sorrentino & Higgens, 1986).

Primary drives usually can be fulfilled in direct and obvious ways. If we are hungry, we seek out food; if we are thirsty, we look for water; and if we are tired, we look for a place to curl up and go to sleep. Such primary drives operate almost automatically, according to a principle called homeostasis. **Homeostasis** is the process by which an organism tries to maintain an optimal level of internal biological functioning. According to the principle of homeostasis, an imbalance in our internal biological state motivates us to compensate for the discrepancy from our optimal state. If, for instance, your level of food intake is too low to provide sufficient energy for your body to operate efficiently, a drive will lead you to seek out food. Hence, the hunger pangs you experience when you have not eaten for a while can be seen as your body's attempt to maintain homeostasis. Similarly, the feeling of fullness that follows a big meal makes you avoid food, thereby maintaining an equilibrium.

Coming in out of the rain is a behavior which represents largely a biological motivation: a need to stay warm and dry.

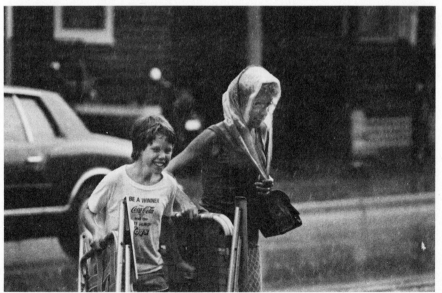

MacDonald/The Picture Cube

Although the concept of homeostasis is useful for explaining the operation of primary drives, it falls short when we consider secondary drives. It is difficult to identify the level of achievement or the sense of equilibrium we are seeking when we climb a mountain or drive a motorcycle at 80 miles an hour.

To compensate for the shortcomings of a model of homeostasis that relies on the maintenance of a biological equilibrium, some psychologists suggest that the secondary drives of human behavior might best be considered in the context of seeking an optimum level of stimulation and activity (Berlyne, 1967). According to this view, we all try to maintain a certain level of arousal. If our arousal is too high, we try to reduce it by disengaging ourselves from particular activities. For example, if our efforts to seek achievement result in too frenzied an existence, we may pull back and change jobs in an attempt to find a less harried way of life. On the other hand, if our lives produce too low a level of stimulation and activity, we may try to increase arousal by seeking situations that produce higher levels. (To get a sense of your own optimum level of arousal, see the following Do It! box).

DO IT!

DO YOU SEEK OUT SENSATION?

How much stimulation do you strive for in your life? Circle either A or B in each pair of statements.

1. A. I would like a job that requires a lot of traveling.
    B. I would prefer a job in one location.

2. A. I am invigorated by a brisk, cold day.
    B. I can't wait to get indoors on a cold day.

3. A. I get bored seeing the same old faces.
    B. I like the comfortable familiarity of everyday friends.

4. A. I would prefer living in an ideal society in which everyone is safe, secure, and happy.
    B. I would have preferred living in the unsettled days of our history.

5. A. I sometimes like to do things that are a little frightening.
    B. A sensible person avoids activities that are dangerous.

6. A. I would not like to be hypnotized.
    B. I would like to have the experience of being hypnotized.

7. A. The most important goal of life is to live it to the fullest and experience as much as possible.
    B. The most important goal of life is to find peace and happiness.

8. A. I would like to try parachute jumping.
   B. I would never want to try jumping out of a plane, with or without a parachute.

9. A. I enter cold water gradually, giving myself time to get used to it.
   B. I like to dive or jump right into the ocean or a cold pool.

10. A. When I go on a vacation, I prefer the comfort of a good room and bed.
    B. When I go on a vacation, I prefer the change of camping out.

11. A. I prefer people who are emotionally expressive even if they are a bit unstable.
    B. I prefer people who are calm and even-tempered.

12. A. A good painting should shock or jolt the senses.
    B. A good painting should give one a feeling of peace and security.

13. A. People who ride motorcycles must have some kind of unconscious need to hurt themselves.
    B. I would like to drive or ride a motorcycle.

SCORING   Give yourself one point for each of the following responses: 1A, 2A, 3A, 4B, 5A, 6B, 7A, 8A, 9B, 10B, 11A, 12A, 13B. To determine your total score, add up the number of points and then use the following scoring key:

    0–3 very low sensation seeking
    4–5 low
    6–9 average
    10–11 high
    12–13 very high

It is important to keep in mind, of course, that this short test provides only a rough estimate of your sensation-seeking tendencies. Its scoring is based on the results of college students who have taken the test. Moreover, as people get older, their sensation-seeking scores tend to decrease.

Source: Zuckerman, 1978.

There are wide discrepancies in the optimum levels of arousal people seek (Mineka & Henderson, 1985): Some of us will choose to be skydivers, while others will look for activities such as knitting or a game of checkers. Moreover, the level of arousal that we experience has implications for our success in performing different kinds of tasks. According to one of the oldest laws of psychology—the **Yerkes-Dodson law**—there is a specific level of motivational arousal that produces the highest performance on a task, with higher levels of arousal being most appropriate for easier tasks and lower levels being best for more complex ones (Yerkes & Morgulis, 1909).

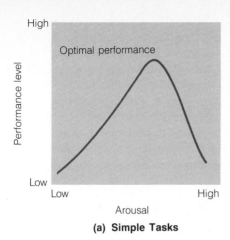

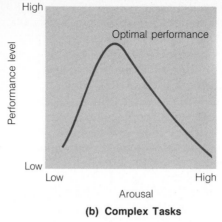

(a) Simple Tasks

(b) Complex Tasks

FIGURE 4-1
The Yerkes-Dodson law
states that optimal task
performance varies at
different levels of arousal.
When the task is simple,
as in (*a*), higher arousal is
optimal, while lower
arousal is optimal on
more complex tasks, as
shown in (*b*).

What is the explanation for the Yerkes-Dodson law? It seems that high levels of arousal help bring about maximum levels of performance of tasks in which the demands are not too great, while high arousal hinders performance of more complex tasks. Lower levels of arousal, then, are best for performing complicated tasks. Of course, if arousal is *too* high, performance of both simple and complex tasks suffers, as the arousal is distracting and anxiety-producing (see Figure 4-1).

Push and Pull:
Drives versus incentives

Are we driven by internal forces that propel us in certain directions in order to fulfill our inner needs? Or does our outward environment tug at us, pulling us toward certain stimuli and channeling our activities in particular directions?

These queries address two very different positions relating to human motivation, known as "push" and "pull" models (Hoyenga & Hoyenga, 1984). **Push models** suggest that our behavior is motivated primarily by our inner needs and desires; behavior is considered to be directed by inner forces that lead us to seek out stimuli and situations that will fulfill our inner needs. For example, the push model of motivation holds that our desire for food comes primarily from the internal "push" of hunger.

On the other hand, **pull models** examine the nature of external stimuli, called **incentives,** which attract or repel us. A delicious-looking piece of pie with a dollop of whipped cream may "pull" us—even if we have just finished a big meal and our internal hunger is relatively low. Similarly, finding a moldy piece of cheese in the back of the refrigerator may be enough to drive away any thoughts of eating. According to the "pull" view, then, the strength and nature of stimuli in the environment are the primary determinants of behavior.

Although the push and pull models of motivation represent two very different approaches, human behavior is sufficiently complex that it appears that push and pull processes are *both* at work. As we saw in Chapter 3, behavior is a joint function of heredity and environmental factors. Similarly, internal forces and external incentives interact with one another to produce behavior. We do some things because of inner forces pushing us in particular directions, while others are carried out primarily because of the nature of the incentives, demands, or requirements of the environment. But in neither case is "push" or "pull" the sole factor directing our behavior. Instead, internal drives interact with external stimuli in complex ways.

Arranging Our Motives:
Maslow's hierarchy of needs

Eleanor Roosevelt; an accomplished amateur painter; Abraham Lincoln; a nurturant mother.

Although a single classification for these four individuals is not readily apparent, to psychologist Abraham Maslow there is a commonality: They are all individuals who have reached and fulfilled the peak of motivational needs related to human behavior.

According to Maslow (1970), one can distinguish between two basic forms of motivation: deficiency motivation and growth motivation. In **deficiency motivation** people seek to maintain a physical or psychological equilibrium, while in **growth motivation** they attempt to move beyond what they

Self-actualization, when a person reaches his or her highest potential, can manifest itself in a wide variety of ways.

Elizabeth Crews/The Image Works

have accomplished in the past and seek greater fulfillment in their lives. Deficiency motivation provides for fulfillment of the basic biological requirements of human existence. Growth motivation propels people toward accomplishments of a uniquely human, more meaningful sort—accomplishments that provide an increase in people's overall capabilities as human beings.

In Maslow's view, people whose lives are dominated by deficiency motivation are unhappy and not well-adjusted psychologically. Rather than looking to accomplish meaningful and important growth in their lives, they tend to be complacent or bored with life. In contrast, individuals who have moved beyond deficiency motivation and instead center on growth motivation are apt to be more open, to be more accepting of others, and to have a better sense of themselves and their place in the world.

Maslow holds that different motivational needs form a specific order, or **hierarchy of needs,** in which fundamental, basic needs must be fulfilled before higher-order, more sophisticated—and, to Maslow, more significant—needs can be met. The needs are ordered according to the pyramid shown in Figure 4-2, in which the basic needs form the foundation for the higher needs at the top.

The most fundamental needs concern basic biological functioning such as hunger, thirst, and sleep. As long as these needs go unfulfilled, other needs will be less pressing. On the other hand, after biological needs are fulfilled, an individual is ready to meet the next level of needs, considered by Maslow to be safety needs, which encompass the safety of a secure and reasonably tranquil environment. Biological and safety needs are considered to be the "lower-order needs."

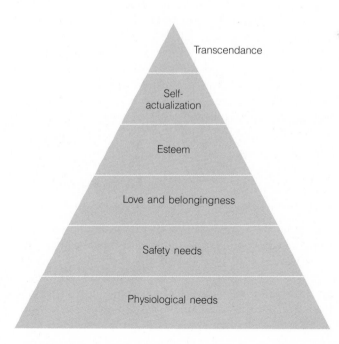

FIGURE 4-2
Maslow's hierarchy of needs illustrates how our motivation progresses from the broadest, most fundamental biological needs to higher-order ones. (*Source:* After Maslow, 1970).

Once the lower-order needs are fulfilled, a person is able to move toward higher levels, which consist of love and belongingness, esteem, self-actualization, and transcendence. Love and belongingness needs include being accepted by others, giving and receiving warmth and affection, and participating as a member of some group or society. Esteem needs encompass needs for a sense of adequacy, self-worth, competence, and a knowledge of one's value to others.

Not only are the highest-order needs—self-actualization and transcendence—most difficult to fulfill, they are also the most abstract concepts within the hierarchy. **Self-actualization** is a state in which other needs are fulfilled, and the individual focuses on personal growth and reaching his or her highest potential. Unencumbered by more everyday needs, people who reach the state of self-actualization are not searching for higher fulfillment; instead they feel a sense of satisfaction with what they are doing. They view themselves as fulfilled contributors to the world, and they concentrate on honing their skills, which have been developed to their fullest potential.

There is yet another stage in the hierarchy, identified in Maslow's later writings. In **transcendence,** people see themselves in a spiritual light, in harmony with nature, the world, and the universe. In a sense, their earthly, here-and-now needs are fulfilled, and they begin to consider their place in a grander scheme of things.

What is perhaps most important about Maslow's hierarchy is that it provides us with an explanation for the shifts in levels of needs that occur throughout our lives. During times of particular adversity, such as losing one's job or recovering from a physical disaster, or under conditions of especially high stress, people typically find themselves unable to focus on higher-order needs and instead are most concerned with maintaining more basic needs. When such lower-order needs are fulfilled, attention can be shifted to higher-order needs. Of course, movement up the hierarchy does not occur automatically; all of us must make the choice to focus our concerns on more lofty needs once the lower-order needs are fulfilled.

Maslow's model of the hierarchy of needs paints a picture of human motivation, using broad strokes. We'll now take a closer look at some of the specific kinds of motivation that guide human behavior, beginning with the primary drives of hunger and sleep. (Sex, a third primary drive, will be discussed in Chapter 11.)

Food for Thought:
Hunger

Most of us are reminded three times a day that we are creatures with biological needs, when we sit down to provide our bodies with food that can be converted into energy and the nutrients that help keep us alive. Yet anyone who has ever felt completely stuffed after a big meal, but who then consumes a tempting piece of layer cake for dessert, knows that biological needs are not the sole explanation for eating behavior.

There are, of course, several biological mechanisms that direct both the amount we eat and the specific choices we make. The **hypothalamus** of the brain seems to play a critical role, either by affecting the experience of hunger or by directing eating behavior (Stricker & Zigmond, 1976). For instance, one theory suggests that the hypothalamus may be related to the **weight set point,** a particular weight level the body strives to maintain (Nisbett, 1972). This acts like a thermostat, either calling for more food consumption when weight declines too much or slowing down consumption when weight overshoots the set point.

Other biological factors also affect food consumption. For instance, people on restricted diets or who lack certain nutrients tend to seek out foods that are high in the missing nutrients; there seems to be some internal mechanism that directs people toward foods that are lacking from their diets (LeMagnen, 1985).

Although biological needs play an important role in directing eating behavior, social factors are also important (Boakes, Popplewell, & Burton, 1987). The best example lies in our customary mealtimes: In the United States, most of us sit down to eat breakfast in the morning, lunch at midday, and dinner around six o'clock. There is no biological reason for this; it is a cultural custom—a fact that becomes particularly obvious when we consider cultures in which dinner is traditionally served at ten in the evening. Because we become accustomed to eating at a certain time, we often experience hunger based on what time it is, rather than on internal, biologically based cues. Similarly, our choice of foods is based on social factors. For example, in some cultures ants and grasshoppers are an unusual delicacy; in ours they generally are shunned (Polivy & Herman, 1985).

Hazel Hankin

A variety of factors, some genetic and some social, lead to obesity.

Social factors offer one explanation for **obesity,** in which a person weighs over 20 percent more than the average weight of people of his or her height. According to one theory, obese people have an oversensitivity to external, social cues (Schachter, 1971). Rather than attending to their inner, biologically determined hunger cues, obese people are assumed to be more influenced by the taste and attractiveness of food, by whether the clock says it is a customary mealtime, or by the ease with which food can be obtained. One experiment showed, for instance, that obese people ate considerably larger quantities of peanuts without shells than those with shells, since it takes more effort to open the shells. Nonobese individuals, in contrast, ate the same amount of peanuts with or without shells. For them, the effort involved was incidental to how much they ate.

In addition to being *over*sensitive to *external* cues, obese people may be *under*sensitive to *internal* hunger cues. For example, experiments have shown that there is only a weak association between how hungry obese people feel and the amount of time they have been deprived of food (Nisbett, 1968). Obese people, then, are relatively unaware of the information provided to them by their bodies.

In some extreme cases, eating behavior strays so much from the norm that it can be life-threatening (Bauer, Anderson, & Hyatt, 1986). **Anorexia nervosa** is an eating disorder in which people's lives begin to revolve around food. Anorexia nervosa ultimately may lead to starvation because anorectics develop an inaccurate perception of their bodies and refuse to eat, thinking (wrongly) that they look overweight.

Bulimia is a related disorder in which a person binges on large quantities of food. Often the binging is followed by "purging," in which the person induces vomiting. Because frequent vomiting can lead to a chemical imbalance or physical injury, death may occur—even though the bulimic's weight may appear normal. Both anorexia nervosa and bulimia, which afflict mainly females, are serious problems that demand professional intervention (Bauer, Anderson, & Hyatt, 1986).

The Stuff of Dreams: Sleep

Given that about a third of life is spent in bed, it seems obvious that sleeping fulfills some important human need. Surprisingly, though, just what this need is has yet to be identified: We still do not know specifically *why* it is that we sleep—although it is clear that we must.

Psychologists have, however, developed an extensive understanding of what goes on when we are asleep. Sleep is hardly a time of calm tranquility; instead, we pass through a series of diverse stages, characterized by different brain-wave patterns and body and eye movements.

There are four main stages of sleep, changing approximately every ninety minutes (see Figure 4-3). During these stages, the ease with which a person can be awakened varies. For example, in stage 1 sleep, which is characterized by relatively rapid, low-voltage waves, people are easily roused. In stage 2 sleep, characterized by a slower, more regular brain wave

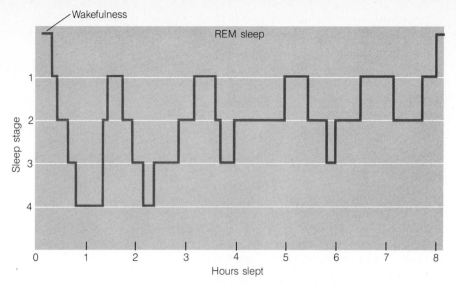

FIGURE 4-3
The stages of sleep change
in duration during the
course of an evening's
slumber. (*Source:*
E. Hartman, *The Biology
of Dreaming.* 1967.
Courtesy of Charles C
Thomas, Publisher,
Springfield, Illinois.)

pattern, it is more difficult to awaken a person. Stage 2 sleep accounts for about 50 percent of a college-age person's total sleep. Brain-wave patterns become even more regular and slower in stage 3 and stage 4 sleep, and people are least responsive to outside stimulation during these periods.

There is also a phase of sleep known as **rapid eye movement (REM) sleep,** which occupies about 20 percent of the average adult's total sleep. During REM sleep, the heart's rate increases and becomes irregular, blood pressure and respiration rate rise, males have erections, and voluntary muscles act as if they were paralyzed.

But the most surprising characteristic of REM sleep is the eye movements themselves: The eyes move back and forth behind closed eyelids, as if they were watching some action-packed scene. In fact, there *is* something the sleeper may be viewing: the action in a dream. People awakened during REM sleep report that they were dreaming, and evidence derived from research on people's sleeping habits suggests that the eyes move because they are following the dream's action (Dement, 1979; Borbely, 1986).

REM sleep seems to be essential to adequate functioning; people who have been deprived of it (by being awakened every time they enter the stage) make up their loss through a subsequent increase in REM sleep. Interestingly, though, we are still unable to say how much total sleep is necessary. Although most adults sleep between seven and eight hours a night, 20 percent sleep fewer than six hours a night, and 10 percent sleep more than nine hours a night.

Psychology for You:
Solving sleep setbacks

Anyone who has spent a night tossing and turning—a victim of **insomnia,** the inability to sleep—would vouch for the importance of a good night's sleep. Yet insomnia is one of the most common problems that people experience in their lives, with some one-third of adults reporting that they are suffering from it at any given time, and 15 to 20 percent saying that their insomnia problem is serious and chronic.

The causes of insomnia are varied, ranging from ingestion of too much caffeine (a potent ingredient in coffee and soft drinks), to being emotionally upset, to simply not being tired enough. In fact, insomnia may be brought about by such a wide variety of factors—psychological, biological, medical, emotional, and environmental—that its treatment can be difficult. However, there are several steps people can take to sleep better, suggests Peter Hauri, director of the Sleep Disorders Clinic at Dartmouth Medical School (Hopson, 1986):

● Keeping regular hours is a cardinal rule. Never oversleep because you haven't slept well during the night. If you suffer from insomnia, get up at the same time every day—it will help you sleep better that night. And try to go to bed at the same time every night.

● If you wake up during the night, relax in bed by reading or listening to music for a while. If you don't fall back to sleep soon, get up and engage in some quiet activity until you are tired; then return to bed.

● Avoid alcohol, cigarettes, tea, coffee, and soda for twelve hours before you go to bed. If you are particularly sensitive to them, eliminate them entirely from your diet.

● A bedtime snack of warm milk and crackers may actually help you sleep, but avoid large meals close to bedtime.

● Jot down your worries and concerns—and what you are going to do about them the next day—in the early evening.

● Exercise regularly, although not too close to bedtime. Not surprisingly, you'll sleep better if you are physically tired.

If these suggestions don't help your sleeping problem, you might consult a physician with experience in sleep disorders. In extreme cases, you might want to consider going to a sleep disorder clinic, several of which are found throughout the United States. It is important to be aware, though, that in many cases the mere passage of time brings about a cure: Insomnia is often a temporary condition.

TO REVIEW

● A drive is a motivational tension or arousal that energizes behavior to fulfill some need. Primary drives are related to basic biological factors, while secondary drives are learned drives in which no obvious biological need is being fulfilled.

● Although homeostasis—the process by which an organism tries to main-tain an optimal level of functioning—helps explain primary drives, it is less helpful in accounting for secondary drives.

● In "push" models, behavior is seen as motivated by our inner needs, while "pull" models view motivation in terms of external stimuli, or incen-tives.

● Maslow's model of motivation is based on a specific order, or hierarchy, of needs.

● Hunger and sleep are two of the most important primary drives.

CHECK YOURSELF

1. Beth's motivation to become an accomplished researcher in her field is based on a _____ drive.

2. Homeostasis is a useful concept to apply when attempting to explain secondary drives. True or false?

3. According to the Yerkes-Dodson law, a complicated task is best accom-plished when levels of arousal are:
    a. high
    b. variable
    c. low
    d. moderately high

4. "It's hard to explain. I just feel driven to complete my psychology paper early," June stated. Justin offered, "For me, I want to get it done early so that I can enjoy the weekend. Besides, I know the professor will appreciate it." June's motivation may be explained through a _____ model, whereas Justin's reasons may be better conceptualized through a _____ model.

5. Although Rick is in excellent physical condition, he is motivated to achieve a much higher level of fitness. Maslow would describe this type of motivation as _____ motivation, as opposed to _____ motivation.

6. People who have satisfied more basic needs and who feel fulfilled, seek-ing only to apply the finishing touches to their existing skills, are represented by what level of Maslow's hierarchy?
    a. esteem
    b. love and belongingness
    c. transcendence
    d. self-actualization

7. Janet is obsessed with dieting. Friends comment that she looks ema-

ciated, yet Janet perceives herself as still being overweight. She probably suffers from:

a. bulimia
b. low weight set point
c. anorexia nervosa
d. a hypothalamus disorder

8. One explanation for our body's increased activity during _____ _____ _____ sleep is that we are dreaming at the time.

_____

(See answers to these questions at the bottom of page 136.)

4.2   FULFILLING OUR PSYCHOLOGICAL NEEDS:
Secondary Drives

To Jim, competition was the key. Even when he was playing a game of checkers with his younger brother, he could not help but play to win. And when he lost, he felt so bad that you'd think he had failed in a major confrontation. But that was just his style; he competed against his room-mate, against his acquaintances, even against himself. For Jim, striving to achieve some hypothetical standard of excellence was a way of life.

_____

Phil never compared himself to others or against some standard. He didn't think much about grades or how much he was paid for his part-time job. He was content to try reasonably hard, and how well he did—or didn't do—just didn't concern him that much. As long as he had a lot of friends whom he could count on and do things with, and some close relationships in which he felt he could "let his hair down," he was happy.

You probably know people like Jim and Phil, who have widely divergent sets of goals and aspirations. To Jim, achievement is a major motivation factor; his strivings for success are clearly central to his everyday activities. Phil has a different agenda. His behavior is motivated more by needs of belonging and a desire to affiliate with others.

Needs for achievement and affiliation are just two of the major secondary drives (drives that are learned and have no biological significance) that dominate human life. Although the term "secondary" in one sense implies drives that are of lesser importance than primary drives, secondary drives are of major importance when we move beyond biological considerations and begin to examine needs that are more psychological in nature. It is these psychological needs that provide the impetus for the unique kinds of behavior that separate humans from other species.

The Drive to Excel:
Achievement motivation

What kinds of challenges do you seek out? If you typically search for tasks that are not too easy, yet not so difficult that your chances for success are low, then you are likely to have a strong need for achievement. **Need for achievement (nAch)** is a stable, learned characteristic in which satisfaction is obtained by striving for and attaining excellence (Heckhausen, Schmalt, & Schneider, 1985; McClelland, Atkinson, Clark, & Lowell, 1953). In contrast to Maslow's broader conception of motivation, nAch is theorized to be a specific, stable attribute held by an individual.

People who have a high need for achievement try to find situations in which they are able to compete against some standard of excellence and be successful at it. The specific nature of the task—be it getting good grades, making money, or doing well at checkers—is often less important than the challenge of seeking success. But how the task is perceived *is* critical to people with a high need for achievement; they consistently avoid tasks that they perceive as too easy or too difficult, and instead seek out tasks that seem to be of intermediate difficulty. The reason for this choice is clear: Easy tasks do not present a sufficient challenge, while difficult tasks are unlikely to produce a successful result.

In contrast to those with a high need for achievement, people with lower achievement motivation tend to be motivated primarily by a desire to avoid failure. They are likely to choose tasks that are either very easy or very hard and avoid tasks of intermediate difficulty (Atkinson & Feather, 1966). On easy tasks, they are reasonably sure to succeed (and thereby avoid failure); on difficult tasks almost everyone fails (making the consequences of failure relatively minimal).

While the notion that people have a stable need to achieve success or to avoid failure makes intuitive sense, there is also evidence that some people have a more surprising orientation: a **fear of success.** According to Horner (1972), certain individuals, and women, in particular, are concerned

Do some people have a fear of success? Despite her visible efforts to do well in her studies, this woman may fear the very success for which she strives.

about appearing *too* successful because of the negative consequences that may occur. For example, women tend to worry that success will make them seem less "feminine" and that, using a traditional view of the role of women, society will perceive success in a negative light. If this is the case, then, some women may actually strive to avoid high levels of achievement.

The existence of a fear-of-success motive is controversial, for experimental evidence supporting it is inconsistent (Hyland, Curtis, & Mason, 1985). However, it seems reasonable to assume that, at least as long as some members of society view the success of women in a negative light, some women may fear the very thing—achievement—that others are so motivated to attain.

Seeking the Company of Others: Affiliation needs

To some people, such as Phil in the example on page 134, success is measured less by how much they achieve than by the friendships they make, the closeness of the relationships they are in, and the degree of sharing and affection they experience with others.

People whose needs focus on the interpersonal sphere are said to have a high **need for affiliation,** a concern with establishing and maintaining relationships with others. Although most of us have some affiliation strivings—there are few hermits to be found in this world—people with a high need for affiliation are particularly involved in relationships with others. In college settings, such people are more apt to be concerned with their friends than with their studies, regarding the maintenance of friendships as being more important than high levels of achievement. In job settings they may be more concerned with getting along well with their coworkers than with getting the job done.

People who have a high need for affiliation may be particularly prone to **loneliness,** the inability to maintain the level of affiliation desired. Although there are several types of loneliness, the two major kinds stem from social isolation and emotional isolation. In **social isolation,** people feel cut off from the social support of family and friends, such as when they start a new job or leave home for the first time. **Emotional isolation,** in contrast, occurs when a person lacks a close, stable, and intimate relationship with another individual.

The two kinds of loneliness do not always go hand in hand. People may have a strong network of relationships with family and friends and still experience emotional isolation if they lack an intimate relationship with any one individual. Similarly, one can be in the midst of a crowd or be involved on a superficial level with many others and still experience a sense of

CHECK YOURSELF: ANSWERS
1. secondary **2.** False **3.** c **4.** push, pull **5.** growth, deficiency **6.** d **7.** c **8.** rapid eye movement (or REM)

loneliness, if there is a lack of emotional involvement and a sense of connectedness with other people.

On the other hand, being alone need not be unpleasant. Even people with a high need for affiliation can be in situations in which they are alone for relatively long periods without feeling lonely. What seems to be critical in determining loneliness is one's interpretation of being alone (Peplau, Miceli, & Morasch, 1982). If isolation is viewed as a consequence of relatively temporary, controllable factors ("Everyone is studying hard this semester and has too much to do to go out of their way to be friendly"), loneliness seems to be less difficult to deal with than if isolation is perceived as being due to one's own personal inadequacies ("I'm alone because I'm not a very likable or interesting person").

Better Safe than Sorry:
Security and consistency needs

As we saw in Chapter 2, we all try to make sense of and understand the world around us. In part, this is a function of **security needs,** needs to be safe in a world that holds all too many surprises and dangers. By understanding events and people around us, we are in a position to better predict future happenings, and we feel a sense of control.

In fact, our desire for consistency is so strong that we actively strive for a more orderly world and avoid cognitive dissonance. **Cognitive dissonance** is a state of psychological tension in which two or more conflicting thoughts or attitudes are held simultaneously (Festinger, 1957).

Smokers who deny that smoking is harmful, or who insist "I don't smoke that much," may be rationalizing to avoid experiencing cognitive dissonance.

There are many situations in which cognitive dissonance is aroused. For example, smokers who know that smoking is unhealthy, yet continue to smoke, feel dissonance between the two thoughts "smoking is unhealthy," and "I smoke." In order to reduce the dissonance that is aroused by these contradictory thoughts, smokers might change one (or both) of the cognitions. For example, they might modify a cognition (deciding that they really don't smoke all that much), change the perceived importance of one cognition (the evidence linking smoking to disease is weak), add cognitions (the amount of exercise they get compensates for their smoking), or simply deny that there is a contradiction (smoking really isn't linked to disease).

It is clear that our needs for security and consistency do not always lead us to think or behave in completely rational ways. It is somewhat paradoxical and ironic, then, that the very desire we hold to make the world more safe and understandable may lead us to misperceive its actual nature. On the other hand, this phenomenon allows us to reduce anxiety and psychological tension, and therefore may play an important role in our everyday lives.

What's New?:
Curiosity and creativity needs

While most conceptions of motivation suggest that we are driven to reduce tension or maintain some sort of steady state, not all needs can be explained in these ways. **Curiosity needs** (the desire to explore the world and receive novel stimulation), and **creativity needs** (needs to produce new ideas, works, or stimuli) are both examples of needs that, when fulfilled, may actually increase psychological tension and uncertainty.

Curiosity motivation is most apparent in infants, who appear driven to learn about the world and are constantly exploring their environment. By the time we reach adulthood, however, there is less uniformity in strength of curiosity needs, with relatively large individual differences. Still, an inquisitiveness about the world and the way it works appears to be characteristic of human beings in general (Deci & Ryan, 1985).

Curiosity needs are related to another set of needs: needs for creativity. Our curiosity needs lead us to explore the world around us, which in turn gives us the experience to behave creatively, juxtaposing novel ideas in unusual ways. Although there are wide individual differences in the strength of creativity needs, it is characteristic of human beings to want to create new things, be they works of art, inventions, or—in another sense—new individuals by having children. Creativity allows us to feel a special sense of accomplishment and pride for making a unique contribution to the world.

Psychology for You:
Directing your own motivation by setting goals

The models of the different kinds of motivation we have been discussing share a common trait: All are considerably clearer on how specific needs affect behavior than on how those needs develop in the first place. Of course, primary drives such as hunger and sleep are obviously largely biologically determined. But what of such needs as achievement, affiliation, and consistency, which—because they are related to secondary drives—are assumed to be learned?

Most secondary drives seem to develop largely through socialization by parents, teachers, and other significant individuals in a person's environment, and often at a very early age. For instance, people with a high need for achievement seem to develop such achievement needs by age 3; their parents tend to push them to excel and to compete against some standard of excellence, even while they are still toddlers, leading to the development of strong needs to achieve. Similarly, parents who are especially responsive to their infant's crying, rushing in to comfort them at their first cry, may unwittingly teach the infant that others play a particularly important role in the satisfaction of their needs—ultimately leading them to develop relatively high affiliation needs.

Because people's needs tend to be learned at an early age, they are relatively difficult to change. On the other hand, what is learned may be unlearned; new sorts of motivation may come to take the place of others as people age and develop. For example, when people have children, there are often major shifts in what they value and the needs they are seeking to fulfill.

Similarly, the environment can make demands upon people that lead to a modification of their own motivational structure. Consider Harry Truman. He claimed he was uninterested in the presidency of the United States, but then was thrust into the office after the sudden death of Franklin Roosevelt. He grew into the role, becoming what many historians consider one of the great Presidents. In the next election his desire for the presidency had increased sufficiently, and he set out to be elected in an arduous campaign of his own.

Rather than waiting for environmental demands to change the nature of your motivation, it is possible to actively bring about motivational changes yourself. Although Freud and other psychodynamic theorists might claim that many of our most important motives remain hidden in the unconscious, and there are times when we will be unaware of all the forces that are directing our behavior, it is still possible to explore and change the nature of the needs that underlie our behavior. You might consider taking the following steps:

● Examine your existing motivational structure. Before you try to change your motivational patterns, make some systematic effort to understand what they are at this time. Try the accompanying Do It! box, which will give you some insight into what values are most important to you.

● Determine what you want to accomplish. Rather than acting as a passive bystander and taking one day at a time, adopt a more active stance: Set both short-term and long-term goals for yourself, based on your values and an assessment of your own personal strengths and weaknesses.

● Set priorities for your goals. You may not be able to accomplish them all, but decide what goals are most important to you, and work toward them.

● Don't invest heavily in long-term goals; it is important to seek satisfaction from your short-term, daily activities. Choose long-term goals that can be accomplished through day-to-day activities that give you pleasure. If a long-term goal can be accomplished only through sheer drudgery, you might want to reconsider whether it is worthwhile.

● Periodically reconsider what is and is not important to you; your goals should not be etched in stone. As you continue your own development, your interests and priorities will likely change. You should be flexible enough to follow your interests to wherever they may lead you—even if it means giving up a goal in which you have invested much time and energy.

DO IT!

ASSESSING YOUR BASIC VALUES

Are your values in order? To assess how you prioritize the values that you hold most dear, rank and order the following, from most important (1) to least important (18):

_____ A comfortable life
_____ An exciting life
_____ A sense of accomplishment
_____ A world at peace
_____ A world of beauty
_____ Equality
_____ Family security
_____ Freedom
_____ Happiness
_____ Inner harmony
_____ Mature love
_____ National security
_____ Pleasure
_____ Salvation
_____ Self-respect
_____ Social recognition
_____ True friendship
_____ Wisdom

SCORING   After you have ranked and ordered these values—not a simple task—you might want to compare your responses to those of a national sample of Americans, who rated the values in this order: (1) family security; (2) a world at peace; (3) freedom; (4) self-respect; (5) happiness; (6) wisdom; (7) a sense of accomplishment; (8) a comfortable life; (9) true friendship; (10) salvation; (11) inner harmony; (12) equality; (13) national security; (14) mature love; (15) a world of beauty; (16) pleasure; (17) an exciting life; and (18) social recognition.

Source: Ball-Rokeach, Rokeach, & Grube, 1984.

TO REVIEW

● Need for achievement is a stable, learned characteristic in which satisfaction is obtained by striving for and attaining excellence. People with a high need for achievement seek out tasks of moderate difficulty; while people with low achievement motivation (with a high fear of failure) seek out very easy or very hard tasks.

● Need for affiliation reflects a concern with establishing and maintaining relationships with others. People with a high need for affiliation may be particularly sensitive to loneliness, the inability to maintain the level of affiliation one desires.

● Needs for security and consistency may lead to cognitive dissonance, a state of psychological tension brought about by the presence of incongruent thoughts or attitudes.

● Needs for curiosity and creativity also play an important role in human motivation.

● One way to bring about motivational change is through the use of goal-setting procedures.

CHECK YOURSELF

1. Martin knew that his chances of completing the triathlon were very slim. Nonetheless, he continued to train persistently for the event. Martin's behavior could be said to typify the actions of people with a high *need for achievement.* True or false?

2. Sarah is distraught. Her family and friends are close and supportive, but she yearns for a deeper, more intimate relationship. Although Sarah doesn't appear to suffer from _____ isolation, one could say she is experiencing _____ isolation.

3. Writing an innovative and effective classroom text would be an example of the author's fulfillment of a:
   a. curiosity need
   b. need for affiliation
   c. need for security
   d. creativity need

4. In changing one's own behavior, it is more important to keep thinking of achieving the long-term goal itself rather than working on the accomplishment of short-term goals that lead up to it. True or false?

_____

(See answers to these questions at the bottom of page 144.)

(See answers to these questions at the bottom of page 144.)

4.3   **IRRESISTIBLE NEEDS:**
                                    Addiction

My first contact with drugs was while I was a student at Madison High School. Back then it was pot and ludes. After I graduated and started making some money, I had friends in business and in nightclubs who had cocaine connections.

All the rich people, the politicians and the show-biz people, were using coke. I was just a working kid, so it was a big thing for me to try something that was a rich man's high.

About a year and a half ago, it got to be a habit for me. I had extra money and time to do it. If there was pressure at work, I'd run and get a gram of coke. I never cheated on my wife, but cocaine became my lover.

In the last six months, it's become unbearable. I've become paranoid. I can't go out of my house without looking behind me to see if I'm being followed. I break out in a cold sweat. I think people are watching me in my living room, that someone will jump through the window and take my cocaine.

I smoke an occasional joint, but nothing helps. I can hardly sleep. I go to work without sleeping, come home to get more cocaine to wake myself up. . . .

I've gone through most of my savings and borrowed from all the people I know. It's all gone up my nose and through my brain. (**The New York Times**, *1984, p. 50.*)

As this case suggests, human needs can sometimes be so compelling that they overwhelm people's efforts to lead a normal—and rational—existence. No matter how hard they try, their cravings for some substance, and the effects it produces, become irresistible, and people's lives become centered around it.

Although we are all experienced drug users—if you consider that coffee and soft drinks contain caffeine, a fairly potent stimulant, and most of us readily take vitamins, aspirin, and cold-relief medicine—relatively, few of us have chemical needs so strong that we cannot function without satisfying them. On the other hand, for some people, the need for a substance becomes so insistent that the result is **addiction,** a state in which an individual develops a physical or psychological dependence on a drug (Orford, 1985). Addiction may have a biological basis: The body becomes so accustomed to functioning with a drug present that in order to maintain homeostasis the drug *must* be present. In other cases, addiction may be primarily psychological, whereby people perceive that they are unable to respond to the normal stress of life without the presence of a drug (Carmi & Schneider, 1986).

Even everyday drugs have their addictive qualities. For example, the caffeine in coffee produces a physiological dependence, and it is common for coffee drinkers who sleep late and drink considerably less coffee on the weekend to find themselves with a headache caused by their body's reaction to a lack of caffeine. What follows is an evaluation of the addictive potential of three of the most commonly used, and potent, drugs: alcohol, cocaine, and marijuana.

The Legal Depressant: Alcohol

The cocktail party is drawing to a close. Some of the people are talking loudly, holding an animated, although not too coherent, conversation. In one chair, a man is sleeping heavily. Several other people are arguing, almost violently, about a trivial matter. And one woman is crying bitterly, complaining to no one in particular about her husband's infidelity.

In every case, the source of this behavior can be traced to the same drug: alcohol. If you don't think of alcohol as a drug or a potentially addictive substance, you are wrong on both counts: Alcohol is a **depressant,** a drug that slows the nervous system by causing nerve cells to fire more slowly. Moreover, in some individuals, alcohol has the potential for addiction (Heather, Robertson, & Davies, 1985).

Although alcohol initially increases people's sense of sociability and well-being, the release of tension and loss of inhibitions turns to depression as the amount of alcohol in the body increases. A person can begin to feel emotionally unstable, lose motor control, and hallucinate, and may eventually pass out.

Alcoholics—individuals who have a physical dependence on alcohol—have no control over their drinking (Knott, 1986). During the early stages of alcoholism, people begin to view drinking as a recreational activity and then begin to lose interest in activities that are not directly associated with drinking. They begin to drink secretly and need medical excuses from work. They may try to abstain from alcohol use but are unable to, jeopardizing jobs, families, and friendships. In later stages of alcoholism they drink indiscriminately. Prolonged drinking may lead to **delirium tremens (the D.T.'s)**—the extreme agitation, disorientation, or hallucinations that occur when alcohol is not available. There may be permanent liver and brain damage as well.

Determining where social drinking ends and alcoholism begins can be difficult.

Joel Gordon

Alcohol abuse represents a problem throughout American society; a recent poll found that some 32 percent of all families report alcohol-related problems (Harris, 1987). Moreover, the line between social drinking and problem drinking is a fine one, although there are guidelines to identify the nature of problem drinking behavior (see the accompanying Do It! box).

While it is not clear why some people develop an addiction to alcohol, several common factors are involved. Genetic factors may be important; a person with a family history of alcoholism is much more likely to become an alcoholic than is the person with no alcoholic relatives in earlier generations (Cloninger, 1987).

Other explanations for alcoholism focus on the reinforcing qualities of alcohol. Alcohol is able to decrease anxiety more effectively than almost any other substance, and thus its usage can be viewed as reinforcing. Over a period of time, people's use of alcohol may increase as they learn to associate it with anxiety reduction. But why some people are able to control their drinking—despite the reinforcing qualities of alcohol consumption—and others make its use habitual has not been fully explained (Heather, Robertson, & Davies, 1985). Some studies have suggested that sociocultural factors are to blame. For instance, there are ethnic and religious differences in drinking patterns. Moreover, peer pressure is associated with the use of alcohol, particularly during the initial stages of alcoholism. Still, the development of alcohol dependence has yet to be well understood.

CHECK YOURSELF: ANSWERS

1. False **2.** social, emotional **3.** d **4.** False

DISTINGUISHING SOCIAL DRINKING
FROM PROBLEM DRINKING

If you are concerned about your own drinking or that of someone you know, this scale provides insight into whether or not alcohol consumption is indicative of a problem.

1. Do you feel you are a normal drinker? (By normal we mean you drink less than or as much as most other people.) Yes _____ No _____

2. Does your wife, husband, a parent, or other near relative ever worry or complain about your drinking? Yes _____ No _____

3. Do you ever feel guilty about your drinking? Yes _____ No _____

4. Do friends or relatives think you are a normal drinker? Yes _____ No _____

5. Are you able to stop drinking when you want to? Yes _____ No _____

6. Have you ever attended a meeting of Alcoholics Anonymous? Yes _____ No _____

7. Has drinking ever created problems between you and your wife, husband, or other near relative? Yes _____ No _____

8. Have you ever gotten into trouble at work because of drinking? Yes _____ No _____

9. Have you ever neglected your obligations, your family, or your work for two or more days in a row because you were drinking? Yes _____ No _____

10. Have you ever gone to anyone for help about your drinking? Yes _____ No _____

11. Have you ever been in a hospital because of drinking? Yes _____ No _____

12. Have you ever been arrested for drunk driving, driving while intoxicated, or driving under the influence of alcoholic beverages? Yes _____ No _____

13. Have you ever been arrested, even for a few hours, because of other drunk behavior? Yes _____ No _____

Common Highs:
Cocaine and marijuana

People climbed down stairs into a blackened basement, sloshed through stagnant puddles, and knocked on a steel door. If they said the right words, they were in.

Awaiting them was a room bathed in candlelight where they could sit, listen to soft music, and buy and smoke cocaine until their pockets were empty. . . .

They might stay for a half hour. They might stay for days. But whenever their water pipes had burned their last pellets of crack, a highly addictive form of cocaine, the customers would experience a powerful yearning. And they would want to come back for more. (Kerr, 1986, p. 1.)

Although this scene sounds reminiscent of the kind of opium den portrayed in movies, it happens every day in hundreds of such "crack houses" now illegally operating in large cities throughout the country.

Although most cocaine use does not involve "crack houses," its use has grown to epidemic proportions during the last decade. **Cocaine,** which is inhaled (or "snorted") through the nose or smoked when it is in the form of "crack," produces a rapid high. In small quantities, cocaine produces euphoria, increased confidence, alertness, and a sense of well-being. Over the long term, though, users develop a powerful psychological craving for the drug, and their lives may begin to center on it—as suggested by the case described earlier at the start of this section. Moreover, they may begin to lose weight, become suspicious of others, and show little interest in anything not connected with cocaine. In extreme cases, cocaine can induce hallucinations.

Although cocaine was first thought to be relatively harmless, most experts now feel that the drug's psychological effects are addictive, and some researchers are coming to believe that the drug also produces a physical addiction (Baum, 1985; Eckholm, 1986). Moreover, the number of people using the drug is growing: There are some 5 million regular users of cocaine, and 30 percent of all college students will have tried cocaine by their fourth year of college (Martz, 1986). As these statistics—as well as incidents such as the overdose death of University of Maryland basketball star Len Bias—indicate, cocaine has become a major problem in the United States.

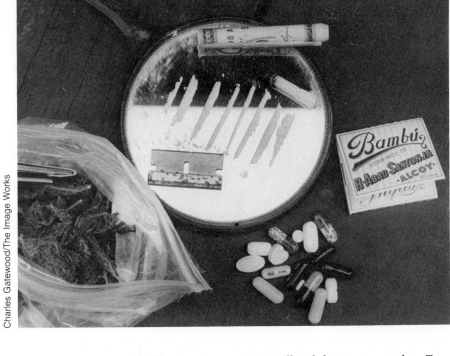

Charles Gatewood/The Image Works

Marijuana, cocaine, and pills such as amphetamines and barbiturates are sometimes used recreationally by people who insist, despite research findings to the contrary, that they are not harmful or addictive.

Marijuana is probably the most common illegal drug in use today. Typically smoked in cigarette form, marijuana has been tried at least once by one-third of all Americans over the age of 12, and among people in the 18- to 25-year-old range, close to two-thirds have tried it. More than 15 percent of the population over the age of 15 use it in a given week.

Marijuana generally produces a pleasant, relaxed feeling of well-being. The sense of time may be altered, and memory may be impaired. Sensory experiences become more vivid, and motor skills decline, making driving dangerous.

Is marijuana addictive? This question has aroused a good deal of controversy, although most research now suggests that usually marijuana is neither psychologically nor physically addictive (National Academy of Sciences, 1982). On the other hand, some research has indicated that there are decreases in the production of the male sex hormone testosterone associated with long-term, heavy usage (Miller, 1975), and there is clearly danger to the lungs from smoking large quantities of the drug, increasing the likelihood of cancer. Moreover, recent evidence suggests that marijuana affects the body's immune system, the natural defense against diseases (Friedman, 1986).

Psychology for You:
When your needs become addictions

While it is clear that in some cases our needs can be so overwhelming that they become physically or psychologically addictive, it is considerably less apparent why certain people are able to handle drugs without developing addictions. In some cases there may be genetic predispositions, while in others there seem to be environmental factors—such as prior learning, peer pressure, or sociocultural factors—that lead people to become addicted to drugs (Shiffman & WIlls, 1985).

Addictions are difficult to deal with. People with drug problems should seek professional help with the difficult, even dangerous, withdrawal period. There are several places to which people with drug problems can turn. Among them:

● Drug treatment centers and clinics

● Halfway houses, which provide residential treatment for those with drug problems

● Detoxification centers dealing specifically with alcoholism and related problems

● Alcoholics Anonymous, an organization that provides help and support to people who have problems with alcohol. Al-Anon and Alateen offer counseling and support to families and friends of alcoholics

● Mental health centers and counseling centers, which treat people with drug problems by dealing with underlying problems

When drug use turns to drug abuse, each of these sources offers help. The most important thing to keep in mind, though, is that if someone *seems* to have a problem, he or she probably does. Seeking professional help is the drug abuser's first step in controlling his or her needs.

TO REVIEW

● Addiction, which may be physical or psychological, is a state in which an individual develops a physical or psychological dependence on a drug.

● Alcohol is a depressant that reduces anxiety. Alcoholics develop a physical dependence on alcohol.

● Cocaine use is reaching epidemic proportions. It is clearly psychologically addictive.

● Marijuana is probably the most frequently used illegal drug. Although there is no evidence that it produces addiction, there are some concerns for long-term users.

CHECK YOURSELF

1. Although cocaine apparently does not produce physical dependence, it can still lead to *addiction* as we define it in this chapter. True or false?

2. Delirium tremens (the D.T.'s) may occur during the withdrawal from:
    a. marijuana
    b. alcohol
    c. caffeine
    d. cocaine

3. Brent's coworkers have noticed that he has become complacent about his work, looks thin and drawn, and has become suspicious of them. They suspect he is dependent on a drug. Which of the following drugs is Brent most likely using?
    a. marijuana
    b. cocaine
    c. LSD
    d. alcohol

4. Unlike cigarette smoking, consumption of marijuana poses no threat in terms of lung disease. True or false?

(See answers to these questions at the bottom of page 150.)

TO SUMMARIZE

1. Motivation refers to the factors that arouse, sustain, and direct behavior toward attainment of particular goals, known as motives. Drive is the motivational tension or arousal that energizes behavior to fulfill a need. If the drive is related to a basic biological function (such as hunger or sleep), we call it a primary drive; but if the drive is learned and there is no biological need that is being fulfilled, we call it a secondary drive.

2. Primary drives operate according to the principle of homeostasis, in which an organism tries to maintain an optimal level of internal biological functioning. But homeostasis does not explain secondary drives as effectively. According to one alternate view, we seek an optimum level of stimulation and activity relating to secondary drives. This view is consistent with the Yerkes-Dodson law, which states that there is a specific level of motivational arousal that produces optimum performance on a task.

3. Push models of motivation suggest that our behavior is motivated primarily by our inner needs and desires. Pull models, in contrast, suggest that external stimuli, called *incentives*, attract or repel us. Although the models appear contradictory, in fact, both factors are likely at work.

4. Maslow's theory of motivation allows us to distinguish between deficiency motivation (in which people seek to maintain physical or psychological equilibrium) and growth motivation (in which people move beyond what they have accomplished in the past and seek greater fulfillment). This hierarchy of needs suggests that fundamental basic needs must be fulfilled before higher-order needs can be met. The needs form a specific order: biological, safety, love and belongingness, esteem, self-actualization, and transcendence. Self-actualization is a state in which other needs are fulfilled

and the individual focuses on personal growth and reaching his or her highest potential, while at the transcendence level, people see themselves in a spiritual light.

5. Hunger has both biological and psychological aspects. The brain's hypothalamus affects eating behavior and may be related to the weight set point, a hypothetical weight level the body strives to maintain. Social factors also play a role in eating behavior, and they may affect obesity and the eating disorders of anorexia nervosa and bulimia.

6. Sleepers pass through four main stages of sleep, plus a kind of sleep called rapid eye movement, or REM, sleep. Dreams occur during REM periods. There are several strategies for dealing with insomnia, the inability to sleep.

7. The need for achievement is a stable, learned characteristic in which satisfaction is obtained by striving for and attaining excellence. People with a high need for achievement seek out tasks that are of moderate difficulty. Those who have a low need for achievement choose either very easy or very difficult tasks, and there may also be a fear-of-success motive.

8. The need for affiliation represents a concern with establishing and maintaining relationships with others. People with a high need for affiliation may be particularly susceptible to loneliness, the inability to maintain one's desired level of affiliation. Loneliness stems from social and emotional isolation.

9. Security needs arise from a desire to be safe in the world. These needs may lead to needs for consistency, which are reflected in our avoidance of cognitive dissonance, a state of psychological tension in which two or more thoughts or attitudes that are incongruent with one another are held simultaneously.

10. Two other important needs are curiosity and creativity. Curiosity needs are based on inquisitiveness and a desire to explore the world and receive novel stimulation, while creativity needs reflect the need to produce new ideas, works, or stimuli.

11. Motivational change can be brought about by systematic procedures. These include examining one's existing motivational structure, determining what one wants to accomplish, setting goal priorities, and periodically reconsidering goals.

12. Addiction is a state in which an individual develops a physical or psychological dependence on a drug. It can have both biological and psychological components. Among the most common addictions is the addiction to alcohol, a depressant. Addiction to cocaine can also occur; the craving for this drug is largely psychological. The question of whether marijuana is

CHECK YOURSELF: ANSWERS

1. True, it can produce psychological dependence **2.** b **3.** b **4.** False

truly addictive remains open. There are several sources of help for people with addictions.

KEY TERMS AND CONCEPTS

motivation (p. 121)

drive (p. 122)

primary drives (p. 122)

secondary drives (p. 122)

homeostasis (p. 122)

Yerkes-Dodson law (p. 124)

push models (of motivation) (p. 125)

pull models (of motivation) (p. 125)

incentives (p. 125)

deficiency motivation (p. 126)

growth motivation (p. 126)

hierarchy of needs (p. 127)

self-actualization (p. 128)

transcendence (p. 128)

hypothalamus (p. 129)

weight set point (p. 129)

obesity (p. 130)

anorexia nervosa (p. 130)

bulimia (p. 130)

rapid eye movement (REM) sleep (p. 131)

insomnia (p. 131)

need for achievement (nAch) (p. 135)

fear of success (p. 135)

need for affiliation (p. 136)

loneliness (p. 136)

social isolation (p. 136)

emotional isolation (p. 136)

security needs (p. 137)

cognitive dissonance (p. 137)

curiosity needs (p. 138)

creativity needs (p. 138)

addiction (p. 143)

depressant (p. 143)

alcoholics (p. 143)

delirium tremens (the D.T.'s) (p. 143)

cocaine (p. 146)

marijuana (p. 147)

TO FIND OUT MORE

Beck, R. (1983). *Motivation: Theories and principles.* (2nd ed.). Englewood Cliffs, NJ: Prentice-Hall.

A clear overview of the topic of human motivation, including many applications of the motivational theory and research.

Borbely, A. (1986). *Secrets of sleep.* New York: Basic Books.

Provides an accurate account of what is known about sleep, dreams, and sleep disorders.

Brownell, K. D., & Foreyt, J. P. (Eds.). (1986). *Handbook of Eating Disorders.* New York: Basic Books.

A comprehensive guide to eating disorders, including anorexia, bulimia, and obesity, by the foremost authorities in the field.

Mothner, I., & Weitz, A. (1984). *How to get off drugs.* New York: Rolling Stone Press.

Provides information on what to do if you are a habitual user of drugs—and how to avoid becoming addicted to drugs in the first place.

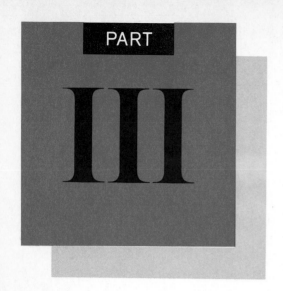

STAYING WELL

PHYSICAL AND MENTAL HEALTH

This part of the book takes us into diverse worlds. We meet a woman who fights the terror of cancer—and wins. We encounter a young policeman, at a loss over how to cope with the stress in his life. We consider a student so consumed with pervasive anxiety that she is forced to drop out of school. And we meet a therapist and client during their initial therapy session.

In Part III, we discuss physical and mental health. We look first at physical health, considering the challenges involved in leading a healthy life and coping with physical illness. We also focus on the stress of daily life—and the various ways of coping with it. The discussion then turns to various forms of maladaptive behavior, and the ways in which maladaptive behavior can be remedied.

In Chapter 5, then, the focus is on the maintenance of physical health and coping with illness.

In Chapter 6, we discuss stress and coping, emphasizing the ways in the which the stresses of daily life can be overcome.

In Chapter 7, failures of adjustment and the major forms of maladaptive behavior are considered.

Finally, in Chapter 8, we conclude this part of the book with techniques for treating instances of maladaptive behavior.

Promoting Health and Coping with Illness

155

Jean Marie was 20 years old and in Florida on vacation from her job at a Minneapolis day-care center, where she worked with preschool children. Suddenly she realized how extraordinarily tired she was—tired and weak and depressed. She went horseback riding one day and came back covered with bruises. She was black and blue from head to toe. "Surely," she thought, "this isn't normal." As soon as her vacation ended, Jean Marie visited the family doctor. He sent her directly to the hospital for tests, which revealed that she was suffering from acute myelocytic leukemia [cancer], a disease which until very recently was almost universally fatal in a matter of months.

The hematologist who examined Jean Marie's blood said . . . an experimental anticancer drug, daunomycin, would give her a 50-50 chance of remission (disappearance) of her cancer, but how long the remission would last no one knew.

The family gathered around and, with the doctor, broke the news to Jean Marie. "Oh, damn!" she blurted out and threw everything in reach onto the floor. Everyone cried, then Jean's younger brother said, "We're all with you. . . ." and Jean Marie decided she was going to fight for all she was worth. (Brody, 1977, p. 128.)

And so she did. Although it meant undergoing treatment that involved weeks of isolation, painful injections, some 125 blood transfusions, and seemingly endless tests, she gradually beat her cancer, eventually showing no signs of the disease. Her advice? "Really hang in there. You have to have a positive attitude. When I was in the hospital I didn't think about dying. I thought, 'this is something I have to get over.' I had a lot of people who hung in there with me, too." (Brody, 1977, p. 130.)

The soundness of Jean Marie's advice is becoming increasingly apparent, as evidence accumulates regarding the importance of people's attitudes, emotions, thinking, and behavioral patterns in determining the course of illness. What once were considered diseases that are purely biological in character—such as heart disease and cancer—are now being seen as having significant psychological components. Moreover, because many of the most significant health problems people face are related to behaviors that can be prevented—smoking is a prime example—maintaining health presents a significant challenge to adjustment.

The recent interest in the psychological aspects of health is a manifestation of one of the oldest problems in psychology: the mind-body question. Posed over the centuries by philosophers such as René Descartes, the **mind-body question** revolves around the relationship between the workings of the

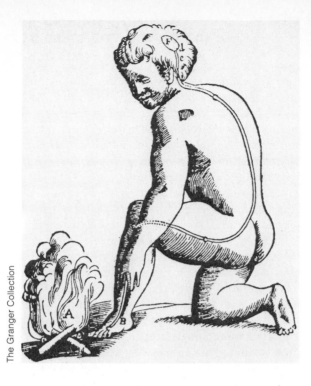

The Granger Collection

The mind-body connection is illustrated in this seventeenth-century diagram, in which Descartes shows the fire (*A*) conveying heat to the foot (*B*). The sensation travels up the spine to the brain (*F*), where the man becomes aware that his toes are getting burned.

mind—our individual consciousness, personality, and awareness of ourselves—and the physical activities of the body.

Because the concept of the mind is a subjective one and is difficult to measure in a concrete and objectifiable fashion, psychologists have shied away from its study. Recent work by psychologists specializing in health, however, has demonstrated unequivocally that the mind and body are closely related and interact with each other in important ways, and that it is insufficient to consider diseases from a purely biological standpoint.

This chapter begins with a discussion of the psychological components of two of the major health problems and leading causes of death in the United States—coronary heart disease and cancer. We consider the behavioral patterns that are associated with heart disease, how a person's reactions to a diagnosis of cancer may affect the course and outcome of the disease, and ways of coping with these serious medical problems.

We turn next to an examination of the nature of the relationship between physicians and their patients, noting that the way they communicate with one another affects the health of the patient. We then discuss ways of behaving as an effective patient.

Finally, we examine the factors that determine the degree to which people take health-related preventive actions. We focus primarily on smoking: the variety of diseases with which it is linked, how people begin to smoke and then get hooked, and several strategies for ending the habit.

MAKING YOURSELF SICK—
AND HELPING YOURSELF GET BETTER:
The Challenge of Staying Healthy

Harry Jackson tried never to waste a moment, and he was especially proud of the desk he built onto the front of his exercise bike. When seated on the bike, which he positioned in front of the television, he was able to get his daily exercise, sign letters, read, and view television—all at the same time. He noted that his wife could always tell when there had been an exciting football play: he pumped the pedals so quickly that she could hear the bike in the next room.

You may know people like Harry Jackson—individuals who hate to waste a second. Yet what you may not know is that such people are prime candidates for a heart attack. For, according to a growing body of work in the field of **health psychology,** the branch of psychology that explores the relationship between physical and psychological factors, such behavior may be related to a behavioral pattern that is associated with a heightened risk of coronary heart disease, the number one killer of people in the United States today.

Heart disease is not the only medical problem that we now know has important psychological components; in fact, people's behavior and even their attitudes are associated with several of what were once considered purely biological problems. We will consider the two most important health problems affecting people in this country, coronary heart disease and cancer, for it now seems clear that psychological reactions to the challenges of daily life are related to both their causes and their cures.

When It Is Better to Get a B than an A:
Behavior patterns and coronary heart disease

The process starts off silently in childhood. There is no symptom, no pain, no warning. A small globule of fat attaches itself to a wall in an artery leading to the heart. Slowly, as the years pass by, other fat cells join the first, building up a lingering deposit that eventually clogs the passageway through which oxygen-rich blood must pass. Then, one day, a blood clot breaks off in the blood stream. As it reaches the small passageway in the artery that is already obstructed with fat, the blood flow is cut off so much that a part of the heart dies from a lack of oxygen. The result: a heart attack.

This graphic description of the events leading to a heart attack is accurate, but a bit misleading: It paints a picture that is purely biological in nature, when in fact it is now known that social and psychological processes are important components in coronary heart disease.

Why should this be the case? Consider this fact: Adults living just sixty years ago had a slim chance of dying of a heart attack. Indeed, the mortality rate from cardiovascular disease in white American males is some five times higher than it was in the 1920s, when life moved at a considerably slower pace, and today coronary problems account for one-third of all deaths in Western society. Yet, even today there are cultural pockets in which heart attacks are rare: Asians living in the Orient have a much lower rate, as do the Amish sect in Pennsylvania. Clearly, cultural factors seem to be related to people's susceptibility to coronary heart disease.

The explanation for the increase in heart attacks in some, but not all, populations seems to rest at least in part on the rate of increase in industrialization and the pace of life. In fact, there appears to be a specific constellation of behaviors, referred to as the Type A behavior pattern, that is associated with a higher risk of heart attack. (To get a sense of where you stand in terms of these behaviors, you might want to try the questionnaire in the Do It! box before reading on.)

DO IT!

ARE YOU AN A OR A B?

To learn whether you are closer to a Type A or a Type B personality, answer each of the following questions:

1. I often try to think of more efficient ways of getting things done. Agree _____ Disagree _____

2. I think of myself as driven and ambitious. Agree _____ Disagree _____

3. I am almost always in a hurry. Agree _____ Disagree _____

4. I hate waiting in line. Agree _____ Disagree _____

5. I get annoyed when a car in front of me drives too slowly. Agree _____ Disagree _____

6. I play games to win—even when I'm playing with children. Agree _____ Disagree _____

7. I sometimes find myself thinking about or doing two or more things at the same time. Agree _____ Disagree _____

8. I tend to eat more quickly than other people. Agree _____ Disagree _____

9. I hate to be interrupted when I am working. Agree _____ Disagree _____

10. I often get angry at other people. Agree _____ Disagree _____

11. I am more interested in quantity than quality. Agree _____ Disagree _____

12. I feel guilty when I am relaxing. Agree _____ Disagree _____

13. I wish there were more than 24 hours in the day so that I could accomplish more. Agree _____ Disagree _____

14. I like to do better than other people. Agree _____ Disagree _____

SCORING This questionnaire is simple to score, since every statement is typical of a Type A behavior pattern. If you have agreed with most of the items, you might want to consider making some changes in your lifestyle to conform to the more easygoing Type B personality, which would be characterized by disagreement with all of the statements above. (The questionnaire is based on descriptions of the Type A behavior pattern in Matthews, 1982.)

The **Type A behavior pattern** is characterized by intense ambition, competitive drive, constant preoccupation with deadlines, and a sense of time urgency (Friedman & Rosenman, 1974). Type A people tend to speak rapidly and vigorously; they are tense; and they are prone to outbursts of hostility. Moreover, they are often driven, ambitious, and intensely competitive. They feel they never have enough time, and they may try to do or think about two or more things at a time. Type A's tend to measure their accomplishments in terms of quantity: number of courses taken, number of papers written, amount of money made.

But what are Type B people like? In most respects, the person exhibiting the **Type B behavior pattern** is everything the Type A person is not: relaxed, easygoing, uncompetitive, patient, and only rarely hostile. If we were to classify well-known individuals into A's and B's, we would probably find Ronald Reagan among the Type B's, while Lee Iacocca would be listed with the Type A's. Of course, people are generally not "pure" Type A's or Type B's; instead, they lie somewhere along a continuum marked by extremes at either end.

Type A and Type B individuals have work styles that are quite different.

George W. Gardner/The Image Works

The differences in the everyday lives of Type A and Type B people are many. In contrast to Type B's, Type A's arrive early for appointments; they perform more poorly on tasks that require slow, methodical responses, since they want to rush through the task; they tend to overestimate the passage of time; and they work at top speed, even at tasks for which there is no deadline (Gastorf, 1980; Burnam, Pennebaker, & Glass, 1975; Yarnold & Grimm, 1982). But they are, in general, more successful than Type B's: Type A's get higher grades in college, they earn more honors, and their socioeconomic status and occupational success tend to be greater (Ovcharchyn, Johnson, & Petzel, 1980; Waldron, et al., 1977).

The road from behavior to heart attack: Linking Type A behavior with coronary heart disease.   From the perspective of health, the most important feature of Type A behavior is evidence that it is associated with an increased risk of coronary heart disease. For instance, in a large, eight-year study examining more than 3,500 males, individuals who had been identified at the start of the study as having a Type A behavior pattern showed an incidence of heart disease twice as great as other subjects, had twice as many fatal heart attacks, and had five times as many recurring "coronary events" (Rosenman, Brand, Jenkins, Friedman, Straus, & Wurm, 1975). Moreover, the Type A behavior pattern was able to independently predict who was susceptible to heart disease at least as well as the other risk factors typically associated with heart problems, including age, sex, blood pressure, smoking patterns, and cholesterol levels in the body. In sum, there is evidence that the chances of having coronary heart disease are considerably greater if you are Type A than if you are Type B (Booth-Kewley & Friedman, 1987).

On the other hand, not all evidence consistently shows a link between Type A behavior and coronary heart disease, with some researchers claiming that the relationship is illusory (Tierney, 1985; Fischman, 1987). But the most recent and definitive summary of the literature finds that there is in fact a modest relationship between the two, although particular aspects of Type A behavior seem to be more closely associated with coronary heart disease than others (Booth-Kewley & Friedman, 1987). For example, the driven and competitive aspects of Type A people are major factors in coronary heart disease; speed seems less important. Overall, the most important concept to emerge from recent research is that people who experience frequent negative emotions—be it aggressive competitiveness, frustration, anger, depression, or some combination—are most prone to coronary heart disease. Because Type A people may be more likely than Type B's to experience such negative emotions, then, they are more apt to experience coronary heart disease.

What is the reason that Type A behavior might be linked to coronary heart disease? One important cause may be related to the finding that Type A individuals are more physiologically responsive to stress and challenge (Dembroski, MacDougall, Herd, & Shields, 1983). The response of Type A's is unusually vigorous; their blood pressure, heart rate, and rate of respiration increase to a greater extent than the responses of Type B's. Moreover, Type

A individuals tend to show higher levels of epinephrine and norepinephrine, hormones secreted by the body that are related to preparedness for emergency situatiuons, when they are under stress or are challenged. Such exaggerated physiological responsivity, in turn, seems to be tied to an increased incidence of cardiovascular disease.

From A to B: Transforming Type A's into Type B's.   If you feel that you readily fit into the Type A behavior pattern, you might be asking yourself whether you are destined to suffer from coronary heart disease.

The answer, for two reasons, is "probably not." First, the presence of the Type A behavior pattern increases only the *risk* of coronary heart disease and does not guarantee that a person will ultimately get it. In fact, there are a considerable number of Type A individuals who do *not* suffer from coronary heart disease—just as there are Type B's who do have heart attacks. But perhaps even more important, there is now evidence showing that Type A's can be trained to behave more like Type B's—and lower their risk of coronary heart disease.

The study that provides the evidence is known as the San Francisco Recurrent Coronary Prevention Project (Friedman et al., 1984). In it, a group of some 1000 volunteers—all of whom had already suffered a heart attack and whose risk of a subsequent attack was high—were randomly divided into two groups. In one group, the people were given conventional cardiovascular counseling, which included advice on diet, caffeine and alcohol intake, and exercise. In contrast, the experimental group was given the same kind of conventional counseling, but with an important addition: They were also intensively counseled on changing their Type A behavior to Type B behavior.

In the training, the participants were shown ways to restructure their thinking about situations that once would have made them experience stress. For example, if they were to find themselves in a long, slow-moving checkout line in a supermarket, they would be taught to use the time to contemplate their day's activities, rather than fuming about the time they were losing. (Part of the training, in fact, included teaching participants to choose the longest, slowest-moving lines.) In addition, they were trained to modify their physiological reactions to stress through such techniques as deep-muscle relaxation, which we will discuss in Chapter 6. They were also urged to make significant changes in lifestyle, including adopting new hobbies that were unrelated to their professions and cultivating old friendships.

The training appears to be successful. In measures of the participants' behavior patterns, Type A behavior, which was initially very high in almost all subjects, has been reduced substantially for those who have undergone training. But even more critical are the data on heart attack recurrence: The average annual recurrence rate for people receiving the traditional counseling was 6.6 percent—while for those who were taught to modify their Type A behavior, the recurrence rate was 3.0 percent, less than half as much.

In sum, the program has been a success. Type A's *can* be taught to act more like Type B's, and the resultant change in behavior is linked to a reduction in the incidence of coronary heart disease. Yet, there may be a trade-off involved: Because Type A behavior is linked to traditional measures of success (including grades and career success), people who modify their behavior to become more like Type B's may ultimately be less successful, at least in terms of society's measures of success. This may be a small price to pay, considering the alternatives.

Mind over Tumor?:
Psychological aspects of cancer

Probably no disease is more feared than cancer. Most people think of cancer in terms of lingering pain, and being diagnosed as having cancer is typically assumed to mean that death will follow shortly.

Although a diagnosis of cancer is not as grim as you might at first suspect—there are actually several kinds of cancer that have a high cure rate if found early enough—cancer remains the second leading cause of death in the United States, after coronary heart disease. Although the precise trigger for the disease is not well understood, the process by which cancer spreads is straightforward. Certain cells in the body become altered and multiply rapidly and in an uncontrolled fashion. As these cells grow, they form tumors, which, if left unchecked, suck nutrients from healthy cells and body tissue, ultimately destroying the body's ability to function properly.

While the process involved in the spread of cancer is basically physiological in nature, accumulating evidence suggests that the emotional response of cancer patients to their disease may have a critical effect on its course. For instance, one study examined the survival rates of women who had undergone the removal of a breast due to cancer. Both three months and ten years later, their survival rates differed significantly, depending on the attitude they held about their disease at the time of diagnosis (Pettingale, Morris, Greer, & Haybittle, 1985).

As you can see in Figure 5-1, women who stoically accepted their fate and did not complain ("Keep a stiff upper lip—don't complain"), and those who felt that the disease was hopeless and that nothing could be done to save them ("There's nothing to be done, I'm as good as dead"), had the lowest rate of survival: Most of these women were dead within ten years.

On the other hand, the survival rates were high for women who had a "fighting spirit" and who thought they would overcome the disease and planned to take steps to prevent its recurrence ("I'm going to conquer this thing"), as well as women who erroneously denied that they had cancer ("Despite the operation, I don't believe I really ever had cancer").

In sum, attitudes about their cancer at the time the disease was diagnosed were related to the women's long-term outcomes. Although the reasons behind this finding are not clear, one hypothesis is that the emotional state of a patient may affect the **immune system,** the body's natural defenses that fight disease. It is possible that certain kinds of emotional states may promote the production of natural "killer" cells that fight the cancer cells, thereby reducing the growth of tumors.

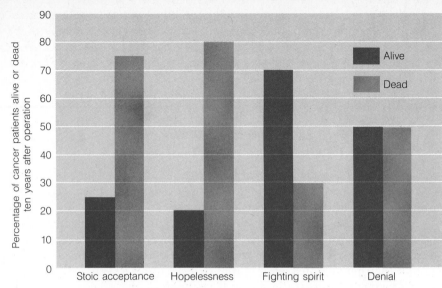

FIGURE 5-1
The relationship between people's psychological response to cancer three months after surgery and their survival rate ten years later. (Pettingale, Morris, Greer, & Haybittle, 1985).

Other research has examined the relationship between social support and the development of cancer. For instance, one fifteen-year-long study found that people who developed cancer reported that there was little closeness in their family (Thomas, Duszynski, & Shaffer, 1979). Moreover, researchers have tried to find whether a particular personality type is linked to cancer. Some findings suggest that cancer patients are less emotionally reactive, suppress anger, and lack outlets for emotional release. However, the data are still too tentative and inconsistent to suggest firm conclusions.

The research examining the link between cancer and psychological factors is controversial (Angell, 1985), although in recent years it has been accumulating. It is not unrealistic to suspect that in the future, attitudes and emotions will be viewed as important tools in the treatment of cancer.

Psychology for You:
Adjusting to a diagnosis of cancer

Can you beat cancer? The answer is yes, for a diagnosis of cancer is no longer a death sentence; if caught early enough, most cancers can be completely cured. Yet cancer remains a dreaded disease, and adjusting to it presents a unique challenge.

To meet the challenge of cancer, there are several strategies that are reasonable, including the following:

● Don't give up; fight to beat the disease. Your attitude makes a difference. Remember that cancer is curable, and that many people live with cancer for years.

● Understand your treatment. People who are involved in their treatment and who understand what options they have are likely to feel a greater sense of control over their disease. In turn, this sense of control can lead to more positive feelings. It is important, then, to participate in what is happening to you.

● Talk to others. Don't try to keep everything inside; be open and honest about your feelings. Most people will want to help you. Let them.

● Remember that no one can predict the future. Even if the outlook is not positive, take one day at a time. Enjoy the here and now, and keep in mind that medical science is inexact and the course of your own disease can never be precisely predicted.

TO REVIEW

● Both coronary heart disease and cancer—two major health problems—are related to psychological factors.

● The Type A behavior pattern, which is associated with a heightened risk of coronary heart disease, is characterized by intense ambition, competitive drive, constant preoccupation with deadlines, and a sense of time urgency. However, it does appear that the pattern may be modified, reducing the risk of coronary heart disease.

● The emotional response of cancer patients to their disease has an effect on the course of the disease. One explanation for this finding rests on the immune system, which may be affected by a person's emotional state.

CHECK YOURSELF

1. Classify the following behavioral descriptions as typical of either Type A or Type B behavior patterns:
   a. is even-tempered
   b. has a sense of urgency regarding time
   c. performs several activities at once
   d. is rarely aggressive
   e. is patient and methodical
   f. is extremely competitive

2. Evidence indicates that there is a clear causative link between Type A behavior and heart disease. True or false?

3. Which of the following were *not* included in the training Type A subjects received in the San Francisco Coronary Prevention Project?
   a. restructured thinking about stressful situations
   b. vigorous exercise

c. adopting new hobbies

d. deep-muscle relaxation

4. It is hypothesized that positive emotions may inhibit the growth of cancer by affecting the body's _____ _____.

5. Understanding treatment options usually results in cancer patients having a greater sense of control over their disease. True or false?

_____

(See answers to these questions at the bottom of page 168.)

(See answers to these questions at the bottom of page 168.)

5.2 PATIENT, HEAL THYSELF:
Physicians and Patients as Collaborators

Dr. Brenner: (To himself: Who's this guy? Oh, right, Jack Harrison. Haven't seen him in a while. Looks like an average 20-year-old to me; perhaps a bit skinny, but healthy enough.) *"And how have we been feeling, Jack?"*

Jack: (To himself: Why does he always talk to me as if I were two people?) *"Uh, pretty good, Dr. Brenner."*

Dr. Brenner: (To himself: I wonder what's really bothering him?) *"Well, that's just fine. But what brings you here today?"*

Jack: (To himself: Why doesn't he just examine me; maybe he'll find that lump on my arm and he can figure out what it is—although I'm sure it's nothing.) *"Actually, I've been feeling pretty good; I just want a checkup."*

Dr. Brenner: (To himself: I think there's something bothering him, but it seems like he's going to make me guess what it is.) *"Anything out of the ordinary you want me to take a special look at, Jack?"*

Jack: (To himself: Now's my chance to mention it . . . ; but, nah, it probably isn't important. I'll let it go, and if he notices it, fine. If he doesn't, it just means it wasn't all that important and I can forget about it. He's pretty busy anyway; why should I bother him with my worries?) *"Not really. I just want to make sure everything's in good shape."*

Dr. Brenner: (To himself: This guy is clearly not going to say a word. I hope I stumble upon what's eating him.) *"O.K., Jack, why don't you take off your shirt and sit on the examining table and we'll get started."*

Have you ever had a similar experience with a physician—not communicating some problem that has been bothering you? If so, you are not alone. Because of the view we have of physicians, their status, and their diagnostic abilities, many of us are surprisingly inhibited when it comes to exposing our real concerns.

In fact, many people view physicians as the auto mechanics of the body, thinking their precise inner workings can be fathomed solely by a skillful physical examination in the same way that an auto mechanic can find out what is wrong with an engine just by tinkering with it (Leigh & Reiser, 1980). Moreover, the relatively high social prestige and power of a physician may be intimidating to patients, making them feel that their problems are unimportant or that they are making themselves look bad in some way by admitting to some illness (Taylor, 1982).

Such perceptions are contrary to the reality of modern medicine, however. The notion that physicians can make accurate diagnoses without help from the patient is an inaccurate one: The human body is so complex that without information about the nature of a person's medical problem, physicians are severely limited in their ability to make accurate diagnoses (Mentzer & Snyder, 1982).

Healthy Communication:
Speaking about health

The difficulty that many patients have communicating their medical problems to physicians is indicative of a wide range of communication problems that underlie interactions between patients and health-care providers. In fact, communication problems are so profound at times that they threaten the well-being of patients.

Consider, for instance, the way physicians' instructions are communicated. How would you react if you were told to "reduce the hypertensive risk factor by lowering sodium intake"? Most people would prefer to be told that they could reduce risk of high blood pressure by reducing the amount of salt they put on their food. Yet even these simple instructions can be too complex for some individuals who may not understand what high blood pressure is and who lack even a basic knowledge about the workings of the human body (Ley & Spelman, 1967).

In addition, patients are often too embarrassed over their supposed ignorance to ask for clarification of physicians' instructions and suggestions. Surveys have found that about one-quarter of people who are taking a drug do not know why it has been prescribed for them. More incredible is the fact that some patients, queried as they are about to be rolled into the operating room, are not able to articulate why they are having surgery (Svarstad, 1976).

The importance of accurate communication of medical information is underscored by the finding that, in the absence of more precise information, people construct their own theories about their medical problems. In another example of our attempts to make sense of the world (discussed in Chapter 2), we tend to take the knowledge about medicine that we do have and weave it into a theory about what is wrong with us and how we can correct it (Leventhal, Nerenz, & Leventhal, 1985).

Someone who has been told to take pills daily for his high blood pressure, for example, may take them only when he has a headache, assuming (erroneously) that the headache is a symptom of the high blood pressure. This may be further reinforced if he measures his blood pressure when he has a headache and finds it high. (Of course if he were to take it at other

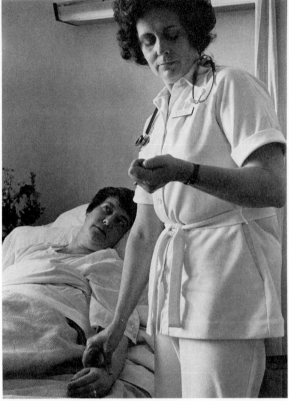

Frank Siteman/The Picture Cube

A patient who refrains from asking questions about her condition and treatment may do so because she feels health care workers are too busy to be bothered.

times, he would also find it high, exposing the inaccuracy of his theory.) Our misperceptions about medicine and the body, then, may lead us to behave in ways that are counterproductive to our own health.

The Interpersonal Dynamics of the Physician-Patient Relationship: Increasing patient control

The accuracy with which medical information is communicated is not the only factor that affects patients' understanding and ability to follow physicians' suggestions. The *way* in which information is imparted also plays a role. Medical personnel who are seen as being aloof, uninterested, or insensitive to the needs of their patients tend to elicit lower patient compliance to their suggestions than medical personnel who are warm and likable, and who seem to be interested in the plight of the patient (Davis, 1968).

CHECK YOURSELF: ANSWERS
1. Type A: b, c, f; Type B: a, d, e   **2.** False; causation has not been established   **3.** b
4. immune system   **5.** True

The reason for the greater success of physicians with better interpersonal skills rests, in large part, on the increase that occurs in patients' feelings of control over the physician-patient interaction. **Control** refers to a sense of mastery and power over events and one's environment. It appears that patients who experience feelings of control related to their health care may respond more successfully to medical treatment than those who have a lower sense of control over their treatment (Krantz, Baum, & Wideman, 1980). (For an assessment of some of your own attitudes toward health care, see the following Do It! box.)

DO IT!

HOW INVOLVED ARE YOU IN YOUR OWN HEALTH CARE?

To get a sense of your own attitudes regarding health care, complete the following questionnaire:

1. I usually don't ask doctors or nurses many questions about what they're doing during a medical exam. Agree _____ Disagree _____

2. Except for serious illness, it's generally better to take care of your own health than to seek professional help. Agree _____ Disagree _____

3. I'd rather have doctors and nurses make decisions about what's best than for them to give me a whole lot of choices. Agree _____ Disagree _____

4. Instead of waiting for them to tell me, I usually ask the doctor or nurse about my health immediately after an exam. Agree _____ Disagree _____

5. It is better to rely on the judgments of doctors (who are experts) than to rely on "common sense" in taking care of your own body. Agree _____ Disagree _____

6. Clinics and hospitals are good places to go for help, since it's best for medical experts to take responsibility for health care. Agree _____ Disagree _____

7. Learning how to cure some of your illnesses without contacting a physician is a good idea. Agree _____ Disagree _____

8. I usually ask the doctor or nurse lots of questions about the procedures during a medical exam. Agree _____ Disagree _____

9. It's almost always better to seek professional help than to try to treat yourself. Agree _____ Disagree _____

10.   It is better to trust the doctor or nurse in charge of a medical procedure than to question what they are doing. Agree _____ Disagree _____

11.   Learning how to cure some of your illnesses without contacting a physician may do more harm than good. Agree _____ Disagree _____

12.   Recovery is usually quicker under the care of a doctor or nurse than when patients take care of themselves. Agree _____ Disagree _____

13.   If it costs the same, I'd rather have a doctor or nurse give me treatments than do the same treatments myself. Agree _____ Disagree _____

14.   It is better to rely less on physicians and more on your own common sense when it comes to caring for your body. Agree _____ Disagree _____

15.   I usually wait for the doctor or nurse to tell me about the results of a medical exam rather than asking them immediately. Agree _____ Disagree _____

16.   I'd rather be given many choices about what's best for my health than have the doctor make the decision for me. Agree _____ Disagree _____

SCORING   Agreement with questions 2, 4, 7, 8, 14, and 16 indicates responses that show you wish to have a high degree of involvement in your own health care. On the other hand, if you agree with statements, 1, 3, 5, 6, 9, 10, 11, 12, 13, and 15, your tendency is to leave control over health-related decisions to others. Because higher degrees of control are associated with a more positive response to medical treatment, your patterns of responses should be of interest to you.

Source: Krantz, Baum, & Wideman, 1980.

Consider, for instance, what it is like to enter a hospital. First you must sign a myriad of forms that not only inquire about personal financial information, but require you to say you accept all aspects of treatment that may follow. After you are brought to your room, which probably contains one or more strangers, you are told to remove your own clothes and put on an anonymous hospital gown. Next comes a string of strangers, all of whom you must allow to poke and prod you and ask the most intimate of questions. There are few situations over which a person has less control, and it is not surprising that such circumstances might have a negative impact upon a patient's medical outcomes.

Like any bureaucracy, a large hospital can be intimidating. The added stress of knowing one is in ill health may make it difficult to cope with the many forms to fill out and procedures to follow.

Nowhere has the importance of control been illustrated more dramatically than in a study by Rodin and Langer (1980) of residents of a nursing home. Two groups of residents were given information that varied in terms of the degree of control that they had over their daily lives. For the high-control group, residents' choice, control, and responsibility were stressed; residents in the low-control group were given information that stressed the staff's control over their lives. High-control people were given a message from the chief administrator of the hospital that said, "I was surprised to learn . . . that many of you don't realize the influence you have over your lives here. . . . You should be deciding how you want your rooms to be arranged—whether you want them to be as they are or whether you want the staff to help you rearrange the furniture." The low-control residents were told, "I was surprised to learn . . . that many of you don't realize all you're allowed to do here. . . . We want your rooms to be as nice as they can be, and we've tried to make them that way for you."

The results of the study were dramatic. After just three weeks, residents encouraged to experience greater control reported that they felt more active and alert, were happier, and engaged in more activities than the low-control group—differences that were still apparent in an eighteen-month follow-up. But even more surprising was a comparison of the death rates of the two groups a year and a half later. Thirty percent of those in the low-control group were dead, while only 15 percent of the high-control group had died.

The outcome of this study has important implications for other medical settings (Rodin, 1986). For instance, patients in hospitals are made to experience even less control than patients in a nursing home, and the way in which they respond to such treatment affects the success of their hospitalization. According to health psychologist Shelly Taylor, most patients adopt what has been called the "good patient" role (Taylor, 1982). **Good patients** are patients who behave compliantly, cooperate with the hospital staff, are unquestioning and uncomplaining, and generally downplay their desires for more active involvement in their medical treatment. All told, good patients are rather passive.

Hospital staff tend to love good patients—especially when compared with their counterparts, the "bad patients." **Bad patients** are angry and hostile; they make frequent demands of the hospital staff; and their complaints about their treatment and their illness are many. Bad patients are constantly seeking information about their medical treatments. In some cases, their anger at being ill may be so intense that they sabotage their own treatment. At the very least, medical staff tend to avoid bad patients and at worst may return the bad patients' "bad" behavior, either by ignoring them or by behaving rudely.

It should be clear that neither extreme—good patient nor bad patient—is particularly desirable. Although good patients may be liked better by hospital staff for making the job of health care easier, such patients rarely take an active role in determining their course of treatment. Moreover, they may end up being misinformed about their condition and treatment, since they are hesitant to "bother" people with their questions.

Ultimately, the chronic good patients may enter a state of **learned helplessness** (Seligman, 1975), in which they feel that their attempts to control a situation will be unsuccessful, and they give up trying—even though if they did persist they might likely have been successful. Patients who have

TABLE 5-1

Good Patients and Bad:
The Consequences of Role Adoption for Hospital Patients

	"GOOD PATIENTS"	"BAD PATIENTS"
Behavior	Compliance; passivity; learned helplessness; inability to take in information; failure to provide information	Uncooperativeness; mutinous behavior; possible self-sabotage
Thoughts	Feelings of helplessness or powerlessness; possible denial or fatalism	Commitment to a right to know; suspicion regarding condition, treatment, and staff behavior
Emotions	Anxiety or depression	Anger
Staff response	Responsive to emergencies but routine failure to solicit information from patient	Condescension; ignoring complaints; "medicate to placate"; psychiatric referral; possible premature discharge

Source: Adapted from Taylor, 1979, p. 179.

come to believe that their efforts to control a medical situation are likely to fail, then, may enter a state of learned helplessness and come to feel that they are unable to control even the most minor aspects of their treatment.

The bad patient role is not a particularly healthy one, either. Medical personnel may grow so exasperated with the constant complaints of the bad patient that they may overlook significant problems that could signal a change in the patient's condition. Even more dangerous, they may decide, based on inadequate or unsubstantiated evidence, that the bad patient's agitation requires medication or that the bad patient is psychologically unbalanced and ought to receive counseling or therapy. (The consequences of acting as a good patient and a bad patient are summarized in Table 5-1.)

Psychology for You:
Being neither a good patient nor a bad patient—
but a healthy one

It should be clear that the best patient is neither a "good patient" nor a "bad patient." The good patient suffers silently in ignorance, while the bad patient alienates medical personnel. Both jeopardize their chances of receiving the best medical care. There are, however, some rational choices that patients can make to maximize their chances for good health. Among them:

● Choose a physician with whom you can develop a comfortable, relaxed relationship. Although basic credentials and training are important, so is

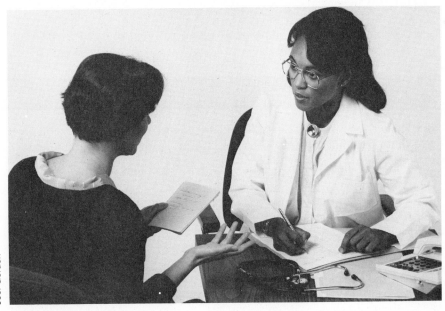

Joel Gordon

A visit to a physician can be made more productive by bringing along a list of symptoms and questions. Writing down the physician's answers and recommendations helps one remember to act on them later.

your ability to express yourself fully and effectively. If you feel inhibited, you will be unable to present your concerns well.

● Seek out information about your condition. If you don't understand something about your medical condition or your treatment, ask about it. If you have difficulty remembering your concerns in the presence of medical personnel, write down your questions. And if you have trouble recalling the answers to your questions, write them down as they are given to you. You can reflect on the responses later—and, if you have further questions, ask them again.

● Remember that medical treatment is a partnership between you and the health-care staff. You should not relinquish control to health-care providers, nor should you make all the decisions yourself. Just as a person who acts as his or her own lawyer has a fool for a client, a person who takes *complete* responsibility for his or her medical treatment often has a fool for a patient.

TO REVIEW

● There are several ways in which communication between physicians and patients can be difficult, including the accuracy with which instructions are understood and the way information is communicated.

● Perceived control, a sense of mastery and power over events and one's environment, is related to the success of medical treatment.

● The "good" and "bad" patient roles both have their drawbacks. The good patient role may lead to learned helplessness; the bad patient role may alienate the medical staff.

CHECK YOURSELF

1.   Medical personnel who show sincere concern for patients are likely to give those patients a greater sense of _____ over their interactions.

2.   Which of the following was *not* cited as a problem in patient-physician communication?
   a.   The physician may not use important technical terms in an attempt to avoid scaring the patient.
   b.   The patient may be too embarrassed or timid to ask for clarifications from the physician.
   c.   In the absence of accurate information, the patient may construct and act on his or her own theory.
   d.   The physician may not deliver his or her instructions clearly.

3.   When she was hospitalized, Nicolette asked many questions about her treatment, although she did so in a friendly, nonaggressive manner. As such, she was probably seen as a "good patient." True or false?

4.   "Good patients" may come to enter a state of _____ _____ wherein they feel incompetent to affect their medical care.

5.   "Bad patients" are likely to keep medical personnel especially attentive to changes in their physical condition. True or false?

_____

(See answers to these questions at the bottom of page 176.)

5.3   THE CHALLENGE OF STAYING HEALTHY:
Preventing Illness

Danger
Poison
XXX
Serious health hazard
Use may cause cancer and serious lung disease
Risky
Unsafe

Would you use a product with these labels attached? *Surely not,* you are probably thinking; *why would anyone use something that so clearly might be harmful?* But if you were told that the product was cigarettes, your answer might well be different—especially if you are among the millions of people to whom smoking is a habit.

However, despite the fact there are few people who would argue that smoking is anything but a dangerous and in many ways an unpleasant activity, the difficulty that smokers have in breaking the habit in some ways represents as much of a problem as do the addictions we discussed in Chapter 4. Similarly, although we all know the importance of exercising, eating well, brushing and flossing our teeth, and following a myriad of other rules, many of us have great difficulty in adopting those behaviors. Behaving in a way that will promote health, then, represents one of the most important—and difficult—challenges we face.

Preventing Illness:
Understanding health beliefs

If a physician tells you that you need to follow a difficult medical regimen in order to cure an existing medical problem, and—at the same time—that you ought to lose fifteen pounds because it will, in the long run, probably prolong your life, which advice are you more likely to take?

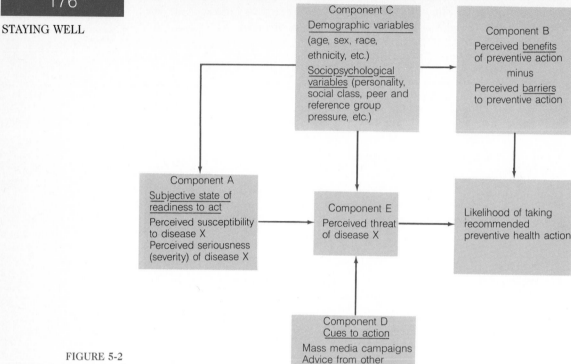

FIGURE 5-2
The interrelationships of
the major components of
the health belief model.
(*Source:* Becker &
Maiman, 1975; copyright
© 1975.)

If you are like most people, you are more apt to follow the advice that will cure your existing problem, rather than taking steps to prevent the possibility of ill health in the future. Over and over, research has shown quite clearly that medical instructions addressing a specific medical problem are more likely to be followed than those medical suggestions that are seen as being at our own discretion (Taylor, 1982). The reason has to do with a complex set of factors involving our beliefs about health.

According to the **health belief model** illustrated in Figure 5-2, there are several primary elements that guide our decision to undertake preventive health-related measures (Rosenstock, 1966; Becker & Maiman, 1975). The initial determinant is a person's perceptions of how susceptible he or she is to a disease and how severe that disease is (component A in the model). These perceptions directly affect the perceived threat of a disease (component E), which is also modified by factors such as demographic and so-

CHECK YOURSELF: Answers
1. control **2.** a **3.** False **4.** learned helplessness **5.** False

ciopsychological variables (component C) and the cues to action (component D).

The health belief model suggests that the ultimate likelihood of taking preventive health steps is a direct outcome of two components: first, the perceived threat of the disease (component E); and second, the perceived benefits, minus the perceived barriers to preventive action, of the action (component B).

The model has been used successfully to predict under what conditions people will follow health-related suggestions. For example, a comprehensive program was designed to carry out genetic screening for Tay-Sachs disease, a rare but fatal disease affecting one in thirty children in certain cultural groups (Becker, Kaback, Rosenstock, & Ruth, 1975). As predicted, participation in the screening was closely related to the degree to which the program was successful in raising the perception of susceptibility to the disease of the target population.

Although the health belief model has been successful in identifying the critical factors in producing compliance to health-related suggestions, it still does not allow precise predictions regarding when a person will follow health-related advice. In fact, the intricacy of the model mirrors the complexity of the problem in producing rational health-related behavior. For example consider a habit that represents one of the major avoidable health hazards of our time—yet one that is remarkably difficult to give up: smoking.

Keeping Life from Going up in Smoke:
Breaking the smoking habit

When June Rozinsky first began smoking in high school, she did it as a signal of her sophistication and liberation. Her "coolest" friends already smoked, and she thought she could fit in better with them if she, too, puffed away at a Marlboro. But what began as a conscious decision soon took on a life of its own; when she decided in college that she wanted to quit, she found she was unable to stop. Despite the nagging cough she developed, and the frequent chest colds to which she became susceptible, she still felt a perceptible physical pleasure when she lit up a cigarette—this left her with the feeling that she would never be able to give up the habit.

In 1982, the year that the surgeon general of the United States required that all packages of cigarettes carry the warning, "The Surgeon General Has Determined That Cigarette Smoking Is Dangerous to Your Health," some 130,000 people died from a cancer that was attributable to smoking. Countless others suffered from other smoking-related diseases, including heart disease, stroke, emphysema, bronchitis, and many other kinds of respiratory illnesses. The death rate among smokers is higher than among nonsmokers; it is no accident that life insurance companies charge lower rates to those who do not smoke than to those who do.

Smokers not only hurt their own health, but they bear social costs as well. Many communities have passed stringent laws regulating smoking in

Innervisions

In addition to the health risks it poses, smoking causes social conflicts.

public places, and smokers incur the wrath of others if they smoke in the "wrong" place at the "wrong" time. The yellowed teeth and bad breath that come from smoking are hardly an asset in social situations. And increasing evidence that "secondhand smoking"—breathing smoke that comes from smokers—can itself produce disease hardly endears smokers to those who don't smoke.

Yet, smoking remains a habit shared by millions of people. The most recent figures show that between 30 and 35 percent of all people smoke, and although cigarette consumption is declining among males, there is some evidence that smoking among females may have actually increased in recent years. Due to the sizable number of people who smoke, smoking is the greatest preventable cause of death in the United States.

A smoking habit doesn't start by accident. In fact, people go through several stages before becoming victims of a full-fledged smoking habit (Leventhal & Clearly, 1980; Hirschman, Leventhal, & Glynn, 1984). These stages include:

● *Preparation stage.* If cigarette manufacturers had their way, movies would always include beautiful heroines and handsome heroes puffing their way from beginning to end. As old-movie buffs know, cigarettes used to be a staple ingredient of the sex appeal of movie stars, and cigarettes and smoking became indelibly linked with glamor and sophistication. Even today, there are associations between cigarette smoking and maturity; teenagers may feel that smoking is a way of displaying their independence. Smoking may be viewed as being "cool," as an act of rebellion, or as a method of keeping oneself calm and collected under stressful situations. Developing attitudes such as these, then, marks the first milestone on the road to smoking.

● *Initiation stage.* Smoking is often a "rite of passage" for adolescents, seen as something that everyone should do as a part of growing up. Most people, at some point in their lives, try cigarettes. If they limit their experimentation to one or two cigarettes, they are unlikely to become hooked. But if they try even as few as ten, they stand an 80 percent chance of becoming regular smokers (Salber, Freeman, & Abelin, 1968).

● *Habit-formation stage.* This represents the crucial stage, when smoking moves from experimentation to habit. At this point, people begin to label themselves as smokers, and smoking is incorporated into their self-concept. In addition, an actual physical addiction develops as people become dependent on the effects of nicotine, the active ingredient in tobacco. Nicotine leads to the production of epinephrine, which increases general physiological arousal, producing a mild "high." Smokers become dependent on the presence of nicotine in their bloodstream, and they develop withdrawal symptoms when it is not available. A smoker deprived of nicotine may feel anxious, lethargic, tired, or nervous.

● *Maintenance stage.* In this final stage—which can last a lifetime—smoking becomes a well-entrenched habit with both biological and psychological aspects. Smokers learn to regulate their smoking, then, in an attempt to regulate both nicotine level (a biological factor) and emotional state (a psychological factor).

Psychology for You:
Smoke gets out of your eyes—quitting smoking

Given the many reasons that lie behind people's smoking behavior, it is no wonder that giving it up is difficult. In fact, it is so hard to stop smoking that only about 15 percent of those who try to quit are successful (Pomerleau & Pomerleau, 1977).

On the other hand, many people do decide to quit (see the Do It! box), and many manage to remain smoke-free for significant periods of time (Flaxman, 1978; Schachter, 1982). Among the myriad of strategies that will help you quit smoking are the following:

● Enlist the social support of your family and friends. Tell them you are quitting, and accept their encouragement and praise.

● Reward yourself. For every few days you go without cigarettes, give yourself some reward in the form of something that you would not otherwise do or receive: a movie, a ball game, a meal out, a new sweater, or some other reinforcer that will give you something to look forward to.

● Remember that the first few days are always the hardest. Because you have built up a biological dependence on the nicotine in cigarettes, it will take some time for your body to end its reliance on the drug's presence. After that, though, your dependence on tobacco will be reduced.

TO SMOKE . . . OR NOT TO SMOKE?

If you have ever thought of smoking, or are a smoker now, this questionnaire will allow you to organize your thoughts about smoking and may strengthen your resolve to avoid smoking entirely.

Give one of these numerical responses for each statement:

1: Strongly disagree   2: Mildly disagree
3: Mildly agree   4: Strongly agree

A. Cigarette smoking can make people seriously ill. _____

B. Smoking causes shortness of breath. _____

C. Cigarette smoking can have a harmful effect on health. _____

D. Cigarette smoking sets a bad example for others. _____

E. If someone stops smoking, it may influence others to stop. _____

F. Smoking influences others to take up or continue smoking. _____

G. I find cigarette smoking to be a messy kind of habit. _____

H. Cigarettes cause damage to clothing and other personal property. _____

I. Nonsmokers have a better sense of taste and smell than smokers. _____

J. Controlling cigarette smoking is a challenge. _____

K. Quitting smoking is a sign of willpower. _____

L. I do not like the idea of feeling dependent on smoking. _____

SCORING   Write the totals for the following groups of questions:

Add your responses to statements A, B, and C; they give your score for category 1 (health) _____
Add your responses to statements D, E, and F; they give your score for category 2 (looks) _____
Add your responses to statements G, H, and I; they give your score for category 3 (mess) _____
Add your responses to statements J, K, and L; they give your score for category 4 (control) _____

A score of 9 or more in one of the categories, which actually represent the four most common reasons people stop smoking, means you think that's a good reason to avoid smoking.

Source: Adapted from Malanka, February 1986.

● Remain smoke-free one day at a time. Don't think in terms of not smoking tomorrow, or next week, or next year; think that you just have to get through the rest of *today* without a cigarette.

● Avoid other smokers. Finding smoke in your eyes is sure to trigger old associations with smoking, so you'll want to avoid people who are still smoking. If this means avoiding old friends, console yourself with the fact that it is only temporary—until you have been cigarette-free for a reasonable length of time.

● When the urge to smoke is still strong, use imagery to visualize darkened, rotting lungs filled with smoke. Then think about the healthy, pinker lungs that you are going to develop as a result of not smoking.

● Start a regular exercise program. By making you feel better physically, exercise will help combat the nicotine withdrawal symptoms.

TO REVIEW

● The health belief model suggests the major components that underlie behavior related to the prevention of potential disease.

● Smoking is one of the major avoidable health hazards.

● The stages of smoking include preparation, initiation, habit formation, and maintenance of the habit.

● Although smoking is a difficult habit to break, there are several strategies that can help.

CHECK YOURSELF

1. Follow the progression of Jim's smoking habit by matching his experience in the right column with the corresponding stage in the left column.

A. _____ preparation

a. Jim is attracted to the image of the rock musician playing on stage with a cigarette dangling from his lower lip.

B. _____ initiation

b. Jim has, over time, developed a consistent pattern of smoking whereby he can maintain a mild nicotine "high."

C. _____ habit formation

c. Smoking for the first time with friends is a novel and exciting experience.

D. _____ mainte-
nance

d. Jim now views smoking as a crucial part of his self-image. It feels good to be smoking, but it doesn't feel great when he doesn't smoke.

2. Only about 15 percent of people who try to quit smoking actually succeed. True or false?

3. Which of the following strategies would probably *not* be effective for quitting smoking?
   a. Visualizing darkened smoke-filled lungs and then the healthy lungs you will develop.
   b. Rewarding yourself for not smoking.
   c. Avoiding smokers.
   d. Thinking about not smoking throughout the upcoming week.

4. Exercise helps to combat the symptoms of nicotine withdrawal. True or false?

5. Telling others that you are quitting smoking should help to gain their support. True or false?

(See answers to these questions at the bottom of page 184.)

TO SUMMARIZE

1. This chapter, which considers how attitudes, emotions, thinking, and behavioral patterns are related to health and illness, begins with a discussion of coronary heart disease. A specific constellation of behaviors, called the Type A behavior pattern, is associated with a heightened risk of coronary heart disease and heart attacks. The Type A behavior pattern is characterized by intense ambition, competitive drive, constant preoccupation with occupational deadlines, and a sense of time urgency. In contrast, people in the Type B behavior pattern are relaxed, easygoing, uncompetitive, patient, and only rarely hostile.

2. Although a causal link between Type A behaviors and coronary heart disease has not been fully documented, the association may be brought about by increased physiological responsivity of Type A's to stress and challenge. Type A's are not necessarily destined to have heart attacks, especially in light of the fact that Type A's may be changed to behave more like Type B's—and, in the process, lower their risk of coronary heart disease.

3. Cancer, too, has psychological components. It now appears that the emotional response of cancer patients to their disease may have a significant effect on its course. Although this work is still at the early stages and is controversial, the emotional state of patients may affect their immune system, the body's natural defenses that affect disease.

4. Because of our perception of physicians, their high status, and their diagnostic abilities, we are sometimes inhibited when it comes to commu-

nicating with them. Communication is also related to how well patients comply with their physicians' instructions about health care: Both the nature and the manner in which information is communicated affects the way patients understand and comply with physicians' suggestions.

5. Patients vary in their feelings of control, their sense of mastery and power over events and their environment. The degree to which patients feel a sense of control may affect the degree to which they respond to medical treatment: the more control patients have, the more likely they will respond to medical treatment.

6. "Good patients" are compliant, cooperative, unquestioning, and uncomplaining, and they do not communicate a desire to be involved in their medical treatment. In contrast, "bad patients" are angry, hostile, demanding, and complaining.

7. Good patients may enter a state of learned helplessness, in which they have learned that their attempts to control a situation will be unsuccessful and they give up trying, even when the situation is such that if they tried to bring about change they would likely be successful. Being a bad patient has its drawbacks, too: The patient may be ignored or considered in need of medication or counseling. For a patient, the best strategy is to be neither "good" nor "bad," but rather choose some middle ground.

8. The health belief model has been developed to explain behavior related to the prevention of potential disease. Among the most important factors are the way people perceive their susceptibility to a disease, its seriousness, and the benefits and costs of preventive action.

9. Cigarette smoking is one of the major preventable health hazards of our time. Smoking typically develops through a series of stages: preparation, initiation, habit formation, and maintenance of the smoking habit. There are several effective strategies for breaking the habit, yet it is a difficult task because the addiction to smoking is caused by both physiological and psychological factors.

KEY TERMS AND CONCEPTS

mind-body question (p. 156)

mind (p. 157)

health psychology (p. 158)

Type A behavior pattern (p. 160)

Type B behavior pattern (p. 160)

immune system (p. 163)

control (p. 169)

good patients (p. 172)

bad patients (p. 172)

learned helplessness (p. 172)

health belief model (p. 176)

preparation stage (in smoking) (p. 178)

initiation stage (in smoking) (p. 179)

habit formation stage (in smoking) (p. 179)

maintenance stage (in smoking) (p. 179)

TO FIND OUT MORE

Taylor, S. (1986). *Health psychology.* New York: Knopf.

A well-written, straightforward guide to the field of health psychology, written by one of the experts in the area.

DiMatteo, M. R., & Friedman, H. S. (1982). *Social psychology and medicine.* Cambridge, MA: Oelgeschlager, Gunn, & Hain.

Presents a good deal of information on the relationship between social factors and medical care, with an emphasis on the roles of patient and health-care provider.

Brown, B. (1984). *Between health and illness.* Boston: Houghton Mifflin.

A clear, engaging introduction to the state in which, the author claims, most people find themselves: a state of neither wellness or sickness.

Johnson, G. T., & Goldfinger, S. E. (1981). (Eds.). *The Harvard medical school health letter book.* Cambridge, MA: Harvard University Press.

One of the better health guides, providing a wealth of practical information on day-to-day health concerns.

CHECK YOURSELF: ANSWERS

1. A. a, B. c, C. b, D. d **2.** True **3.** d **4.** True **5.** True

Stress and Coping

After dropping off her daughter at the day-care center, Nora looked at her "must do" list for the day. With a sinking feeling in the pit of her stomach, Nora saw that her biology lab report was due at 4:00 PM, and in order to complete it she still had to run over to the lab to collect her last observations of those elusive fruit flies. She had to finish typing her history paper, and she also had a short homework assignment to complete. Somehow, she also had to fit in two 50-minute classes in the morning. To top it off, it was her mother's birthday, and she had to buy and send a card—or bear the consequences for the next two months.

While she sat in front of her list, contemplating how in the world she would ever complete everything, the phone rang. It was the director of the day-care center. Her daughter was complaining of a stomachache and had a slight fever, and Nora would have to pick her up immediately.

Nora found herself breathing rapidly. "How am I ever going to manage all I have to do?" she said to herself. She literally ran to the car to pick up her daughter, her mind a jumble. As she drove off, she found her hands clutching the wheel so hard that her knuckles turned white. "I've about reached my limit," she thought grimly as she drove off, almost in a panic.

Nora may be right in her assumption that she had almost reached her limit. People who experience too much of the kind of stress she is under are unable to continue their routine existence without reaching some sort of crisis. At the same time, though, people have enormous recuperative powers, and many of us are able to learn to cope with—and even thrive on—the kind of challenges that Nora is experiencing.

In this chapter we examine stress and coping. We begin by discussing the various kinds and sources of stress. We consider how stress may be sudden and surprising (as in a natural disaster) or how it may linger at low levels over long periods of time, and some types of stress are more costly than others.

We then examine both the physiological and the psychological reactions that result from stress. We discuss how our bodies respond to stress and the ways long-term stress can exact its toll. We also consider the behavioral and emotional outcomes of stress and how to choose whether to fight to overcome stress or to avoid situations that are stressful to us.

Finally, we turn to ways of coping with stress. We examine the positive actions that people can take to confront and alleviate stress in their lives, and we find that stress may be countered on many levels. At the same time, we consider why, paradoxically, stress-producing events may lead to personal growth.

Imagine this scene in a hospital emergency room: a young doctor in white confronts her patient—a young man with slitted eyes and slurred speech. He has taken a handful of sleeping pills—a suicide gesture, a very common episode. His girlfriend is standing by and looking perplexed. . . . Imagine that the time is 3:30 in the morning and the intern has been working since 7:30 the previous morning. Remember that she knows she will be on duty until 5:00 or 6:00 that night, and that her routine has been repeating itself every other night for more than a month. . . . Now ponder the emotional response that the intern might be experiencing. . . . Empathy? On TV, yes. From your easy chair, yes. In real life? Anger! The intern is numbed with fatigue. For her, rationality may be impossible. Her judgment is in flux. The patient becomes a problem to be solved—an assignment to be checked off. (Cook, 1973.)

Imagine this scene at a wedding boutique. The bride-to-be, not quite 21 years old, is putting on her gown for what she expects will be her final fitting before her wedding next Saturday. She comes out of the dressing room to hear a chorus of oohs and ahhs from her mother and the salesperson. But her mind is elsewhere—on the seating arrangement for the reception, on the honeymoon plans for Hawaii, and on the new apartment she and her future husband are furnishing. Her reveries are brought back to reality, though, when the salesperson asks, "Have you gained a few pounds, dear? I think we'll need to take out the waist a bit; the dress looks a little tight." Suddenly, all the tensions of the last few weeks are brought into focus, and the bride wants only to lash out at the salesperson. She feels anger, fatigue, and frustration as she blurts out, "Why can't you people leave me alone?"

Although the scenes are very different, the emotional reaction in each case is brought about by the same phenomenon: stress. **Stress** is the process of appraising events as threatening, challenging, or harmful, and responding to such events on a physiological, emotional, cognitive, or behavioral level. The triggering events themselves may be negative in nature, such as a physician confronted with a series of life-threatening crises, or they may be positive, such as a bride faced with a series of important, although desirable changes in her life. What defines events as stressful is the response that is made to them.

No one's life is totally free of stress—and, if it were, we would likely wish for *something* to happen that would relieve the consistency of a stress-free existence. Indeed, the only way in which life could hold no stress is if the environment would place no demands whatsoever upon us and if we had no needs of our own to fulfill. Given the unlikelihood and the undesirability of a life totally devoid of challenges, stress remains a central part of our lives.

The death of a loved one . . . being fired from a job . . . ending a relationship. It doesn't take a psychologist to know that events like these can produce stress. Yet when we try to identify other kinds of **stressors** (the circumstances and events that produce stress) the problem becomes a bit more complex.

Consider, for example, rock climbing. An individual who chooses to learn this sport may get nothing but joy from the opportunity to climb the sheer face of a deep ravine. Yet, for a person who has slipped into the same ravine and must climb up the rock wall to escape, the same climb can produce stress. Whether the situation is classified as stressful, then, depends on the way it is perceived and interpreted by a given individual (Fleming, Bann, & Singer, 1984).

What factors affect whether a particular event or circumstances produce stress? Generally, stress occurs when **cognitive appraisal**—the process by which people define and interpret events, occurrences, and other stimuli in their environment—reveals some kind of threat or challenge. The stimuli producing stress vary not only from one individual to another, but even within the same person from day to day (Paterson & Neufeld, 1987). For instance, you might find that getting a low grade on a test does not evoke stress if you attribute your failure to the difficulty of the test—especially if most of your classmates also do poorly. On the other hand, you likely will experience stress if you consider your poor performance a reflection of your intellectual shortcomings.

Despite the personal nature of the factors that produce stress in a given individual, stressors fall into several broad categories. These include cataclysmic events, personal stressors, and background stressors or minimum hassles (Lazarus & Cohen, 1977; Lazarus & Folkman, 1984).

Catastrophe: Cataclysmic events   When a devastating tornado ripped through Greene County, North Carolina, in 1984, there was widespread personal injury, loss of life, and extensive property destruction. To the survivors, the tornado was nothing less than a catastrophe, and it was no surprise that their stress levels soared (Long & Richard, 1986).

Cataclysmic events are stressors that occur suddenly and, most important, that affect many people simultaneously. Natural disasters, such as hurricanes and floods, fit into this category. So do catastrophes like nuclear accidents and plane crashes.

Although it might seem that cataclysmic events would produce the longest-lasting effects of any type of stressor, they actually may produce lower levels of long-term stress than do events and circumstances that are initially less intense. One reason is that they affect many people at the same time, so the difficulties a person encounters may be shared with others who can provide social support. Another factor is that cataclysmic events typically

Despite the magnitude of the devastation after a hurricane, the psychological response of victims of one-time, many-victim catastrophes is often relatively good.

have a clear end point; and once they are over, people can begin to rebuild their lives with the knowledge that the worst is behind them.

On the other hand, some victims of major catastrophes can experience **posttraumatic stress syndrome,** in which the original events and the feelings associated with them are reexperienced in vivid flashbacks or dreams. For example, many veterans of the Vietnam war suffer from posttraumatic stress syndrome, which leads to sleep difficulties, problems in relating to others, and (in some cases) alcohol and drug abuse. The fact that the suicide rate for Vietnam veterans is 86 percent higher than for the general population indicates the difficulties faced by veterans of this war (Blank, 1982). Similarly, victims of rape sometimes suffer from the symptoms of posttraumatic stress syndrome, facing major difficulties in adjustment following the event.

The stressors of life's changes: Personal stressors   The death of a friend, starting college, moving. Although normal parts of life, each of these changes can bring stress. **Personal stressors** represent major events in one's life that can produce an immediate stress reaction. Although the stress typically tapers off after sufficient time has passed, there can be lingering, long-term effects.

Which of life's many events can be considered stressful? In an attempt to answer this question, researchers developed the Social Readjustment Rating Scale (SRRS), a questionnaire for rating the number of life events—

both negative and positive—that a person has experienced during the past year (Holmes & Rahe, 1967). Because a large set of judges determined the typical importance of each event—starting with marriage, which was rated at an arbitrary 50 on the scale—during the development of the scale, it is possible to derive a total score for "life-change" events.

Several students have found that high scores on the SRRS are linked to subsequent illness or injury, and that—in general—stressful events are a factor in ensuing physical illness (Maddi, Bartone, & Puccetti, 1987). For instance, high levels of life events have been found to be associated with heart attacks, tuberculosis, diabetes, leukemia, and even accidents. Of course, we cannot necessarily assume that having many changes in one's life actually produces illness; there is merely an association between life changes and illness. It is possible, for instance, that people who experience significant life changes are also those who are more apt to be ill in the first place, or that being ill—one of the life events measured by the scale—causes one to experience more life changes (Schroeder & Costa, 1984). Similarly, because the experience of stress is based on the appraisal of the individual, we cannot assume that everyone reacts to a particular life change in the same way. Hence, the death of a disliked, quarrelsome spouse may be welcomed and ultimately produce less stress than if the spouse had continued to live.

Despite the deficiencies of the SRRS, it does provide a list of the most patent kinds of life events. Given that such events require both major and minor adjustments, their potential for causing stress is real. (To find out what the major life events in your own life are, see the following Do It! box, which presents a version of the SRRS modified for college students.)

DO IT!

WILL YOUR STRESS LEAD TO ILLNESS?

To find out whether the stress in your own life puts you at higher risk for illness, multiply the "stressor" value of each event you have experienced by its number of occurrences over the past year (up to a maximum of four).

50	Entered college
77	Married
38	Had trouble with your boss
43	Held a job while attending school
87	Experienced the death of a spouse
34	Had a major change of sleeping habits
77	Experienced the death of a close family member
30	Had a major change in eating habits

41	Changed choice of major field of study
45	Revised personal habits
68	Experienced the death of a close friend
22	Were found guilty of minor violations of the law
40	Had an outstanding personal achievement
68	Experienced pregnancy or fathered a newborn
56	Experienced a major change in the health or behavior of a family member
58	Had sexual difficulties
42	Had trouble with in-laws
26	Had a major change in number of family get-togethers
53	Had a major change in financial status
50	Gained a new family member
42	Changed residence or living conditions
50	Had a major conflict or change in values
36	Had a major change in religious activities
58	Experienced a marital reconciliation with your mate
62	Were fired from work
76	Were divorced
50	Changed to a different line of work
50	Had a major change in number of arguments with your spouse
47	Had a major change in responsibilities at work
41	Had your spouse begin or cease work outside the home
42	Had a major change in working hours or conditions
74	Experienced a marital separation
37	Had a major change in type and/or amount of recreation
52	Had a major change in use of drugs
52	Took on a mortgage or loan of less than $10,000
65	Had a major personal injury or illness
46	Experienced a major change in use of alcohol
43	Had a major change in social activities
38	Had a major change in amount of participation in school activities
49	Had a major change in amount of independence and responsibility
33	Took a trip or vacation
54	Became engaged to be married
50	Changed to a new school

41   Changed dating habits
44   Had trouble with school administration
60   Ended a marital engagement or a steady relationship
57   Had a major change in self-concept or self-awareness

SCORING   Now add up your points. If your score exceeds 1435, you are in a high-stress category, and you should consider the possibility that you are at risk for experiencing stress-related illness. Consider taking some of the steps that we discuss later in the chapter for dealing with stress.

Source: Marx, Garrity, & Bowers, 1975.

Hassles and uplifts: Background stressors   Just as you finally reach the bank teller, she puts out a "closed—use other window" sign, and you are forced to go to the back of another line. . . . A noisy motorcycle goes by your house, waking you out of a sound sleep. . . . An acquaintance asks—for what seems like the twentieth time—for help with a lab report.

Minor, everyday hassles such as this one can build up and cause a major stress reaction.

Steve Takatsuno/The Picture Cube

While none of these events is a major one, cumulatively they can take their toll. For most people, in fact, it may be life's minor, day-to-day hassles that are the source of most stress. **Background stressors,** or more informally, **daily hassles,** are minor irritations we face as we proceed through life. They may be inconsistent, one-time inconveniences or frustrations, or they may be longer-term in nature, such as dissatisfaction with a relationship, school, or job; a lack of privacy; or a fear of crime. By itself, no single hassle is sufficient to produce much stress, but when hassles add up, they may be enough to tip the balance toward a strong, stress-related reaction.

For example, there is a clear linkage between the number of daily hassles one experiences and the appearance of psychological symptoms such as depression and anxiety (Kanner, Coyne, Schaefer, & Lazarus, 1981). As you can see in Table 6-1, most people's hassles are relatively inconsequen-

TABLE 6-1

The Ten Most Frequently Reported Hassles and Uplifts*

ITEMS	PERCENT OF TIMES CHECKED
HASSLES	
1. Concerns about weight	52.4
2. Health of a family member	48.1
3. Rising price of common goods	43.7
4. Home maintenance	42.8
5. Too many things to do	38.6
6. Misplacing or losing things	38.1
7. Yardwork or outside home maintenance	38.1
8. Property investment or taxes	37.6
9. Crime	37.1
10. Physical appearance	35.9
UPLIFTS	
1. Relating well with your spouse or lover	76.3
2. Relating well with friends	74.4
3. Completing a task	73.3
4. Feeling healthy	72.7
5. Getting enough sleep	69.7
6. Eating out	68.4
7. Meeting your responsibilities	68.1
8. Visiting, phoning, or writing someone	67.7
9. Spending time with family	66.7
10. Home (inside) pleasing to you	65.5

*These are the items that a group of subjects identified as the hassles and uplifts they experienced most frequently over a nine-month period. The "percent of times checked" figures represent the mean percentage of people checking the item each month, averaged over the nine monthly administrations.
Source: Kanner, Coyne, Schaefer, & Lazarus, 1981, p. 14, table 3. Used with permission.

tial—the most common being concern about one's weight. The fact that such hassles are associated with psychological health suggests that the minor annoyances of life do add up.

On the flip side of hassles are **uplifts,** those minor *positive* events that make one feel good—even if it is only temporarily. As indicated in Table 6-1, uplifts range from relating well to a companion to finding one's environs pleasing. What is more intriguing about these uplifts is that they are associated with people's psychological health in just the opposite way that hassles are: The greater the number of uplifts experienced, the fewer the negative psychological symptoms experienced.

Of course the relationship between hassles, uplifts, and psychological symptoms is correlational. It suffers, therefore, from the same interpretive difficulties as the correlation found between major life events and physical illness discovered by the SRRS: We still cannot say that hassles produce stress, or that uplifts prevent it. Moreover, we have no objective assessment—other than people's self-reports—regarding the events that have caused them to feel that they have experienced a hassle or an uplift (Green, 1986). Still, the evidence is striking: Those daily hassles we all face are closely related to stress.

Identifying the causes of stress provides us with the first step in understanding how to cope with it. But to more fully understand how stress takes its toll, we must turn now from the causes of stress to its consequences.

When Stress Leads to GAS:
Physiological reactions to stress

When someone says, "I have been so furious with my boss lately, my blood boils every time I see him," few of us would expect to see whiffs of steam coming out of the speaker's ears when the boss enters the room. It is more likely that the employee would maintain a polite demeanor in front of the boss, disguising the anger hidden beneath the words.

The stress brought on by the boss may, in fact, be causing the symbolic counterpart of blood boiling in the form of heightened blood pressure. According to Hans Selye, a pioneering figure in research on the physiological characteristics of stress, stress can produce a variety of extreme biological outcomes.

Selye developed the **general adaptation syndrome (GAS),** a model of the stages through which one's body passes as it attempts to ward off the effects of environmental stressors (Selye, 1976). According to the model, depicted in Figure 6-1, we move through three major phases: alarm and mobilization, resistance, and exhaustion.

The **alarm and mobilization stage** represents the body's first line of defense against a stressor. When an organism is threatened by some stressor, it first prepares itself for battle. Regardless of whether the stressor is physical (such as a disease, an injury, or a loss of sleep) or psychological (such as the termination of a close relationship, anger over a boss's behavior, or a concern over one's safety), the body's reaction is similar: Heartbeat and blood pressure increase, muscles tense, sweating increases, production of the hormone adrenalin increases, and the organism attempts to meet the challenge of the stressor. In physiological terms, there is activation of the **sympathetic nervous system,** the part of the nervous system that is responsible for physiological responses to emergency situations.

If the stressor continues, the next phase of the GAS is reached. In the **resistance stage,** people prepare to fight the stressor, and they are generally able to cope with the stress-producing situation. But their physiological— and psychological—preoccupation with the specific original stressor makes them more vulnerable to other stressors. For example, if you are primarily concerned with meeting the demands of a difficult semester and concentrate your efforts on studying, you may be particularly irritable and unusually susceptible to illness. In fact, during the resistance stage, you are particularly prone to diseases of adaptation, or **psychosomatic disorders**—physical disorders in which emotions and thoughts play an important role. Psychosomatic disorders, which may include ulcers, high blood pressure, asthma, and skin problems, or more subtle problems such as insomnia or sexual problems (which are discussed more in Chapter 7), originate from people's attempts to adapt to stressors.

If attempts to meet the demands of a stress-provoking situation are inadequate, or if they continue for too long, the final stage of the GAS is reached: exhaustion. In the **exhaustion stage,** a person's ability to cope with stress declines to a point where the stressor is overwhelming. Almost no one is able to maintain a normal existence under continued high levels of stress. If the stressor continues unabated, the resultant stress leads ultimately to total exhaustion—and to the eventuality of death.

On the other hand, exhaustion may act to alter people's lives sufficiently to cause a decrease in the stressor and ultimately reduce the initial source of stress. For instance, a failing student who reacts to the stress of poor academic performance by studying so much that she ends up in the hospital

FIGURE 6-1
The three major stages in people's response to stress, according to the general adaptation syndrome (*Source:* Selye, 1976).

Stressor

Alarm and mobilization
Meeting and resisting stressor.

Resistance
Coping with stress and resistance to stressor.

Exhaustion
Negative consequences of stress (such as illness) occur when coping is exhausted.

may be given a medical withdrawal from all her courses, thereby terminating—at least temporarily—the initial stress-provoking stimulus. Her exhaustion, then, ultimately may produce something of a positive outcome.

Psychology for You:
Reappraising stress

It is clear that what constitutes a stressor is a very individualistic matter and may even vary from one moment to the next in the same individual. The fact that stress rests so much on the perceptions of the beholder suggests several tactics for turning what might be viewed as a stressful situation into one that is seen as something more positive. Although it is not always possible to avoid experiencing stress, you might find the following strategies helpful:

● Change your perceptions. Give new meaning to a situation. If you experience academic failure, tell yourself that you have an opportunity to begin anew, and that the challenge of academic excellence is one that you are willing to accept and act upon. Analogously, take the termination of a long relationship as a chance to meet new people and make new friends and an opportunity to learn how to have more satisfactory relationships in the future.

● Alter your behavior. If your job produces stress that leaves you feeling drained and uncomfortable, change it. Accept a transfer, or actively hunt

A heavy load of responsibilities and tight deadlines may cause some employees to feel job stress, while others may experience the same pressures as positive and stimulating.

Joel Gordon

for a new job. Alternatively, you can focus on ways of controlling a situation to improve it. Change the way you do things, change the way you interact with others, or change your reactions to others. The critical factor is to experience a sense of control over the situation so it becomes less threatening.

● Search for information. In many cases, knowledge *is* power, for just learning more about a situation can reduce the stress it produces. For instance, people suffering from chronic or life-threatening diseases respond more readily to treatment when they fully understand the problems they are likely to encounter (MacDonald & Kulper, 1983). In a way, knowing what to expect gives one the sense of having predictive control over future events, thereby causing the future to seem less threatening, (Thompson, 1983).

TO REVIEW

● Stress is the process of appraising events as threatening, challenging, or harmful, and responding to such events on a physiological, emotional, cognitive, or behavioral level. These events are known as stressors.

● Whether a situation is classified as stressful depends on the way it is perceived and interpreted.

● The three broad categories of stressors include cataclysmic events, personal stressors, and background stressors (or daily hassles).

● Selye's general adaptation syndrome suggests that the physiological response to stress follows three phases: alarm and mobilization, resistance, and exhaustion.

CHECK YOURSELF

1. Stress is defined as a response to negative events that are challenging or threatening. True or false?

2. Cindy was able to attribute her poor performance on the oral report to a lack of preparation time and insufficient sleep, thus reducing her level of stress. The process she employed is known as _____ _____.

3. Match each situation given in the right-hand column with the type of stressor it describes.

_____ personal stressor

a. Joyce has felt the tension build over the semester as a result of the crowded and noisy conditions in her dorm.

_____ cataclysmic event

b. Heather collapsed into her chair and muttered to herself, "I thought buying a house would make me feel content. Right now I'm a wreck."

_____ background stressor

c. Dennis and his family found themselves joining with other community members in an attempt to reduce the trauma they all experienced after the flood.

4. Physiological changes occurring at the onset of a stressor mark which of Selye's stages of the general adaptation syndrome?
    a. exhaustion
    b. resistance
    c. preoccupation
    d. alarm and mobilization

5. Continued exposure to high levels of stress, if unresolved, will ultimately lead to _____.

6. Educating oneself about the stressor one is experiencing is a way to help reduce stress. True or false?

_____

(See answers to these questions at the bottom of page 202.)

6.2   PSYCHOLOGICAL REACTIONS TO STRESS

"Have you done your paper for Professor Harrison's class yet, Jake?" asked Cary as he and Jake walked to the movies.

Jake swore under his breath and said, "I completely forgot about it. What in the world am I going to do?"

"How could you forget it? It's on the class syllabus, and Harrison made such a big deal about the assignment on the first day of class. I didn't think anyone could just **forget** *it."*

"I don't know how it happened, but it just slipped my mind. It's strange, too: I've looked at the syllabus probably a hundred times. And, come to think of it, I even remember jotting the assignment down in my notebook on the first day of class, thinking how awful it was going to be to write such a long paper and being scared to death by the thought of it. How could I have forgotten it?"

Rather than representing mere forgetfulness, Jake's behavior may signify something considerably more complex: his psychological reaction to the stress of the assignment. It turns out that the stressors of life do not just produce the kind of physiological reactions described by the general adaptation syndrome; there are also psychological reactions to stress. Such psychological outcomes range from active means of defending ourselves against stress (such as reacting to a stressor with aggression) to less obvious reactions (such as "forgetting" a stress-evoking assignment). We will consider the psychological reactions to stress in terms of the behavioral, emotional, and defensive responses it brings about.

Fight, Flight, or Not Quite: Behavioral reactions to stress

Depending on the way in which we appraise a stressor, there are several sorts of reactions that may occur on a behavioral level. For example, there may be a **fight response:** a direct attack on the source of stress. In its most fundamental sense, a fight response can involve actual aggression toward the source of stress. For instance, shooting a spouse's lover—a reaction to a not inconsiderable source of stress—is not as rare as one might imagine (and in some countries is even legal). More commonly, though, when aggression occurs, it takes a less extreme form. You might not physically attack a professor who gives a difficult assignment, for example, but you might argue bitterly with him.

"Fight" responses may also be more indirect. You may, for example, complain to a department head or a dean about a professor's unfair assignments, or you might try to organize your peers to protest the professor's behavior. Rather than confronting the source of stress directly, then, people may resist subtly. Assembly line workers sometimes sabotage the product they are working on, for instance, in anger over the stress their jobs produce.

Teri Leigh Stratford/Photo Researchers

A person may blow up under stress and behave violently, arguing, yelling, or even physically striking another person.

Although such a response does little to reduce the stress, it does provide an outlet for their discontent.

An alternative to a "fight" response is a flight response (Roth & Cohen, 1986). A **flight response** involves withdrawing from a source of stress. We can try to escape from a stressor or avoid it altogether. For instance, a student might drop a course that is a source of stress, or a worker may leave a job and choose one that produces less stress.

Although a flight response seems to imply that one is running away from one's problems, it may prove, in fact, to be a rational response to stress. If a situation cannot be changed, and there are viable substitutes to choose from, a flight response makes sense. Even temporary withdrawal may sometimes prove to be a reasonable response to stress, for it can provide the opportunity to find more acceptable alternatives.

In some cases, though, escape from stress may take maladaptive forms. Individuals may react to stress by becoming involved in substance abuse, or they may withdraw emotionally from others. In cases such as these, the kind of "flight" chosen has negative consequences.

A third behavioral response to stress involves a middle ground: compromise. Not quite fight or flight, the **compromise response** involves reacting to stress by attacking and changing some aspects of a source of stress while accepting others. For example, you might approach your boss with your complaints about your job, hoping to negotiate a compromise that would change certain aspects of it. While all your concerns about the job might not be satisfied, the situation may change sufficiently so that the level of stress is reduced.

When Stress Leads to Anxiety and Anxiety Leads to Stress: Emotional responses to stress

When Cindy returned home from the university, she could feel it gnawing at her. She didn't know why; her classes had gone O.K. that day, and she hadn't had any problems on the long commute home. But there it was. It could be felt in the pit of her stomach, vague, menacing, intangible—yet all so real. If only she could figure out why it was there, she thought to herself, she would feel so much better.

While this description may at first conjure up the image of some sort of parasite eating away at this unfortunate woman's body, in reality it represents the experience of a phenomenon that we have all felt at one time or another: anxiety. **Anxiety** is an emotional response characterized by feelings of fear, apprehension, and physiological tension.

CHECK YOURSELF: ANSWERS
1. False; the stressor need not be negative.   **2.** cognitive appraisal   **3.** b, c, a   **4.** d
5. exhaustion   **6.** True

Anxiety is a common response to stress. A stressor may lead us to be worried, frightened, or unable to think clearly. We typically experience obvious internal physiological reactions as well: a knot in the stomach, an increased heart rate, or muscle tightness. There may be outward physical signs of anxiety, obvious to observers, in which a person under stress sweats, trembles, or breathes heavily (Cohen, 1980).

Typically, there is a clear source of stress that produces anxiety. In some cases, however, anxiety is more generalized, occurring when there is no clear-cut, obvious stressor present. In such cases, the presence of anxiety can itself produce stress, as the individual tries, sometimes unsuccessfully, to determine why the anxiety is present. Anxiety, then, can occur as a *result* of stress, and it can also act as a *cause* of future stress. (Moreover, as we discuss in Chapter 7, the long-term, chronic experience of anxiety is also associated with several kinds of maladaptive, abnormal behavior.)

There are wide individual differences between people in the amount of anxiety they experience and how they experience and display it. Some people are more anxious than others, regardless of the nature of stress in their lives, while others experience relatively little anxiety, even in situations that would typically produce anxiety in others. (For a sense of the nature of anxiety in your own life, see the accompanying Do It! box.) People also have characteristic ways of experiencing and displaying anxiety due to stress; one person might, for instance, stutter when experiencing unusually high anxiety, while another's hands might shake.

DO IT!

HOW ANXIOUS ARE YOU?

To assess the degree of anxiety you typically experience, complete the following questionnaire by writing T (for true) or F (for false) following each of the statements:

1. I do not tire quickly. _____

2. I am troubled by attacks of nausea. _____

3. I believe I am no more nervous than most others. _____

4. I have very few headaches. _____

5. I work under a great deal of tension. _____

6. I cannot keep my mind on one thing. _____

7. I worry over money and business. _____

8. I frequently notice my hands shake when I try to do something. _____

9.   I blush no more often than others. _____

10.   I have diarrhea once a month or more. _____

11.   I worry quite a bit about possible misfortunes. _____

12.   I practically never blush. _____

13.   I am often afraid that I am going to blush. _____

14.   I have nightmares every few nights. _____

15.   My hands and feet are usually warm enough. _____

16.   I sweat very easily, even on cool days. _____

17.   Sometimes when I'm embarrassed I break out in a sweat, which annoys me greatly. _____

18.   I hardly ever notice my heart pounding and I am seldom short of breath. _____

19.   I feel hungry almost all the time. _____

20.   I am seldom troubled by constipation. _____

21.   I have a great deal of stomach trouble. _____

22.   I have had periods in which I lost sleep over worry. _____

23.   My sleep is fitful and disturbed. _____

24.   I dream frequently about things that are best kept to myself. _____

25.   I am easily embarrassed. _____

26.   I am more sensitive than most other people. _____

27.   I frequently find myself worrying about things. _____

28.   I wish I could be as happy as others seem to be. _____

29.   I am usually calm and not easily upset. _____

30.   I cry easily. _____

31.   I feel anxiety about something or someone almost all the time. _____

32.   I am happy most of the time. _____

33.   It makes me nervous to have to wait. _____

34.   I have periods of such great restlessness that I cannot sit long in a chair. _____

35.   Sometimes I become so excited that I find it hard to get to sleep. _____

36. I have sometimes felt that difficulties were piling up so high that I could not overcome them. _____

37. I must admit that I have at times been worried beyond reason over something that really did not matter. _____

38. I have very few fears compared to my friends. _____

39. I have been afraid of things or people that I know could not hurt me. _____

40. I certainly feel useless at times. _____

41. I find it hard to keep my mind on a task or job. _____

42. I am usually self-conscious. _____

43. I am inclined to take things hard. _____

44. I am a high-strung person. _____

45. Life is a strain for me much of the time. _____

46. At times I think I am no good at all. _____

47. I am certainly lacking in self-confidence. _____

48. I sometimes feel that I am about to go to pieces. _____

49. I shrink from facing a crisis or difficulty. _____

50. I am entirely self-confident. _____

SCORING   Give yourself one point for each statement that corresponds to the following key: 1.F; 2.T; 3.F; 4.F; 5.T; 6.T; 7.T; 8.T; 9.F; 10.T; 11.T; 12.F; 13.T; 14.T; 15.F; 16.T; 17.T; 18.F; 19.T; 20.F; 21.T; 22.T; 23.T; 24.T; 25.T; 26.T; 27.T; 28.T; 29.F; 30.T; 31.T; 32.T; 33.T; 34.T; 35.T; 36.T; 37.T; 38.F; 39.T; 40.T; 41.T; 42.T; 43.T; 44.T; 45.T; 46.T; 47.T; 48.T; 49.T; 50.F. The average score for college students is around 14 or 15. A score that is much higher than the average suggests that you experience an unusually high degree of anxiety.

Source: Taylor, 1953.

What You Don't Know May Help You:
Defensive reactions to stress

In the earlier example of the student who forgot an important assignment, we suggested that such behavior might actually be a reaction to stress rather than a chance, purposeless error. In fact, there is a whole class of reactions to stress—called defense mechanisms—that provide a psychological means of protecting ourselves from stress and for preserving our sense of self-worth.

Defense mechanisms are unconscious strategies people use to cope by concealing stress and anxiety from themselves and others. Although the notion of defense mechanisms was first developed as part of psychoanalytic theory, the idea that we employ psychological strategies, sometimes without

TABLE 6-2

Summary of the Major Defense Mechanisms

Repression	Pushing stressful, anxiety-producing thoughts or impulses out of conscious awareness
Suppression	Voluntarily attempting to push unpleasant thoughts out of one's consciousness
Displacement	Discharging negative feelings or thoughts regarding a more threatening, powerful person onto a weaker one
Projection	Attributing one's unacceptable ideas or thoughts to others
Rationalization	Distorting reality through justification of events
Regression	Retreating to an earlier stage of development
Denial	Refusing to accept or perceive reality
Fantasy	Gratifying one's desires by imagining satisfying events and achievements

our own awareness, to protect ourselves from stress has found its way into a variety of theories.

At one time or another, most of us use such mechanisms to protect ourselves from problems, difficulties, failures, and other sources of stress that we all face. Among the most important defense mechanisms are the ones that follow (as summarized in Table 6-2).

Repression The most frequently used defense mechanism is probably repression. In **repression,** stressful, anxiety-producing thoughts or feelings are pushed out of conscious awareness. In essence, one forgets that which is unpleasant. For example, as adults, some victims of childhood abuse are unable to recall events related to that abuse until they enter into therapy for some other, seemingly unrelated, problem.

In some cases, repression is helpful in dealing with stress. For instance, repression allows us to put problems and crises behind us and to concentrate on the here and now. On the other hand, forgetting that a paper is due is clearly dysfunctional—although it does allow us to avoid stress for at least a while.

Suppression If you consciously tell yourself to forget something that is bothering you, you are using a defense mechanism known as suppression. **Suppression** is the voluntary attempt to push unpleasant thoughts out of one's consciousness.

The primary difference between repression and suppression is that repression occurs unconsciously; we are not aware of it. In contrast, suppression operates within one's awareness—we *know* that we are trying to forget something when we employ suppression. Unfortunately for those trying to forget a cutting remark that someone has made to them, though, suppression is a considerably less effective protective device than is repression. Suppression is at best a stopgap measure; it is difficult to keep from thinking about something that one is trying not to think about.

Displacement   Your boss has just chewed you out for a minor mistake you have made in preparing a report. You feel upset and angry with the boss, but you know you must not reveal your feelings. Later, however, when your secretary makes an innocent remark about retyping the report, you really let her have it, screaming at her about her ineptitude. She looks at you in amazement, unable to fathom your behavior.

To a student of defense mechanisms, such behavior makes perfect sense. You are engaging in **displacement,** which occurs when negative feelings or thoughts regarding a more threatening, powerful person are discharged onto a weaker one.

Although displacement allows an individual to deal reasonably with a stressful situation at first, for the people onto whom the unacceptable feelings are displaced the story is quite different. For them, the person displays behavior that is incongruent with current circumstances, and therefore displacement may result in misunderstandings as well as strained or damaged relationships.

Projection   **Projection** is a defense mechanism in which people attribute their own unacceptable ideas or thoughts to other people. For example, a man who has sexual desires that he considers immoral may deal with such urges by unconsciously projecting them onto others, whom he then castigates for their "impurity." His own self-esteem is thus preserved—although at the expense of others.

Projection may be at the root of the phenomenon (discussed in Chapter 2) known as the "assumed similarity bias" (Ross, Greene, & House, 1977). You may recall that the assumed similarity bias represents the pervasive tendency to judge others as being similar to ourselves, particularly when we know little about them. For instance, happy people tend to think others are happy; creative people think others are creative. Moreover, we tend to think not only that others share our own traits, but also that their behavior in a given situation is due to the same causes that would guide our own behavior in the same situation. Because these assumptions can be wrong, projection may lead to misperceptions of others and their behavior.

Rationalization   Another defense mechanism that colors our perception of the world is rationalization. **Rationalization** is the distortion of reality in an attempt to justify thoughts, feelings, or events that make us uncomfortable. If you have ever done badly on a test, but then convinced yourself that it didn't matter because the test was unfair, the professor was inept, or the subject matter was unimportant anyway, you might well have been using rationalization.

Through rationalization, we are able to justify behavior that would otherwise make us feel guilty or unhappy. Rationalization is particularly difficult to detect, since—at least on the surface—our explanations make logical sense. However, the logic is often only surface deep, and careful scrutiny of the arguments made by a person employing rationalization will show them to be self-serving.

Fantasy   After graduating at the top of your medical school class, you receive a call from the President of the United States, who asks you to join his Cabinet as secretary of state. You refuse, saying that your research, for which you are about to receive a Nobel prize, is more important to you.

Each of us has our own secret **fantasies,** in which we are able to gratify our desires by imagining satisfying events and achievements. By using the fictional, dreamlike reveries of fantasy, we can gain a sense of control over the direction of our lives. Such fantasies can act as a defense mechanism, creating worlds without risk or pain and protecting us—at least temporarily—from our problems.

In moderation, fantasy can be a harmless and even a constructive process, for it allows us to try out future scenarios and eventualities. If, on the other hand, fantasy becomes a substitute for action, it can act as a destructive force in people's lives.

Regression   If you have ever stomped out of a room in anger, slamming the door behind you, your behavior might be considered an example of regression. In **regression,** people retreat to an earlier stage of development. For example, stress may cause a person who has given up smoking to take up the habit once again.

Denial   The first reaction of someone who has just received bad news is often to groan, "Oh, no." Similarly, many people claim that the possibility of nuclear war is remote and that there is little that they can do about it (Fiske, 1987). Both responses are probably an illustration of the defense mechanism of **denial,** in which there is a refusal to accept or perceive reality. By using denial, we are able to protect ourselves—at least temporarily—from painful or unpleasant circumstances in reality.

Psychology for You:
When flight beats fight

As a child, being called a "quitter" can have a particular sting to it. Even as adults, people are often told to "tough it out," to stick with stressful situations because that is the appropriate, adultlike behavior.

In reality, however, leaving a stress-producing situation is often a realistic, appropriate, and mature strategy (Roth & Cohen, 1986). There are some circumstances in which stress can best be dealt with by choosing "flight" over "fight." Among the indications that withdrawing from a stress-producing situation is more reasonable than attempting to remain in it are the following:

Joel Gordon

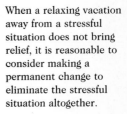

When a relaxing vacation away from a stressful situation does not bring relief, it is reasonable to consider making a permanent change to eliminate the stressful situation altogether.

● You have made an effort to reduce stress in the situation, but have been unsuccessful.

● You have sought out other options and found that alternatives to remaining in the situation are superior to, or at least as good as, staying in it.

● You have tried temporary respites from the stress-producing situation—such as a vacation or leave of absence—and still find that the stress is unmanageable.

● You have attempted to change other aspects of your life, making *them* less stressful, and still find that the level of stress is so high that you are unable to function adequately.

   In circumstances such as these, when even compromise looks doubtful, it is reasonable to seriously consider leaving the stress-provoking situation. In these cases, it is clear that "flight" beats "fight."
   If, on the other hand, you choose to remain in the situation, or if leaving is not an option, there are several useful, proven techniques for handling stress. In the remainder of the chapter, we discuss these ways of coping with stress.

TO REVIEW

● In addition to physiological reactions to stress, there are important psychological outcomes in terms of behavioral, emotional, and defensive responses.

● On a behavioral level, stress may bring about a fight or flight response. Another behavioral response is compromise.

● Stress may also produce an emotional response, particularly in the form of anxiety, an emotional response characterized by feelings of fear, apprehension, and emotional tension.

● Defense mechanisms, unconscious strategies that people use to conceal the source of stress from themselves and others, may also be a consequence of stress.

CHECK YOURSELF

1. Laura's supervisor has just reprimanded her. She feels that the action was unfounded. Three possible reactions are described in the right column. Match each item with the correct behavioral descriptor.

_____ Fight response

a. Laura calmly but assertively suggests that she and her boss discuss the issue rationally.

_____ Compromise response

b. Laura "snaps" at her boss, expressing her anger with harsh words.

_____ Flight response

c. Laura walks silently out of the office and considers finding a new job.

2. Anxiety can occur both as a consequence of stress and as a cause of future stress. True or false?

3. "I have too much going on to think about this right now. I'm going to forget about it until tomorrow." This statement is an example of which type of defense mechanism?
   a. rationalization
   b. repression
   c. suppression
   d. displacement

4. "The coach must really be having a bad day today. My performance couldn't have been bad enough to warrant her yelling at me." Which defense mechanism has the athlete employed?
   a. projection
   b. repression
   c. suppression
   d. rationalization

5. It is almost always a good idea to cope with a stress-producing situation until it is resolved rather than withdrawing from it. True or false?

(See answers to these questions at the bottom of page 212.)

The headaches I handle with aspirin, Gelusil for the stomachaches, and a drink for the nerves. It seemed to be working until last Sunday when I noticed my speech slurring and my hand getting numb, then my arm and the right side of my face. I had a stroke. Imagine me with a stroke. I'm not even forty years old, and I got a stroke. Maybe it's the stress of the job, who knows, but what's new? It's part of my job. Fortunately, the stroke went away with a little rest and medication in the hospital. Doctor said I should take it easy. 'I'll try, Doc, but can't promise. I mean, to be a cop is to be a stress officer. It's what the job is all about. If I can't cope out there, I might as well be a night watchman in a cemetery.' I guess I've just got to get tougher so the job doesn't get to me the way it does. But **how** *to do that is another matter. (Maslach, 1982, p. xii.)*

This police officer's concern about how to deal with the high levels of stress in his life reflects a problem that confronts all of us: finding an appropriate way to cope with the demands of the world in which we live. Yet, just as stress may appear in several guises, there are many ways in which **coping,** efforts to control, reduce, or learn to tolerate the threats that lead to stress, may take place (Holohan & Moos, 1987). We turn now to the most effective and proven strategies for dealing with stress.

Relax and Breathe Easy: Controlling your physiological reactions to stress

Recall the typical physiological reactions produced by stress: Our heartbeat and blood pressure increase, our muscles tense, we begin to sweat, and in general our bodies prepare themselves for either a fight or a flight response. It seems reasonable that if these reactions could be reversed, and perhaps even anticipated and thwarted from occurring in the first place, stress might be reduced. One mechanism for coping with stress, then, is to attempt to take control of the body's physiological reactions. Several techniques have been developed to do just that.

Meditation   Ohmm. Bahm. Rahn. Although at first they may seem to emanate from a marching band tuning up, sounds like these are often an intrinsic part of a procedure known as meditation. **Meditation** is a learned technique for refocusing attention that brings about an altered state of consciousness.

In most forms of meditation, people repeat a **mantra**—a sound, word, or syllable such as the ones above—or focus their attention on a particular picture, a part of the body, a plant, or some other stimulus such as a flame. The meditator's key to the procedure is to concentrate so thoroughly on the stimulus that he or she becomes unaware of outside stimulation, focusing entirely on the inner experience.

If meditation is carred out effectively, it brings about a decline in heart rate and blood pressure. Oxygen usage decreases, and even brain-wave patterns are altered (Wallace & Benson, 1972). Following about twenty minutes of meditation, people typically feel refreshed, relaxed, and less stressed.

Psychologists do not fully understand the processes underlying meditation, and there is some controversy regarding the explicit physiological processes affected by meditation (Holmes, 1985). Still, enthusiasts of a popular variant of meditation, called transcendental meditation (TM), claim that it also leads to better scholastic performance and decreased aggression, as well as several other benefits. While such claims have yet to be verified, it is clear that meditation is an effective technique for inducing relaxation and reducing stress (Benson & Friedman, 1985).

Progressive relaxation   A technique that focuses on the relaxation of specific muscle groups, as well as relaxation of the body as a whole, **progressive relaxation** is a coping technique that is more specific than meditation. In the procedure, various muscle groups are alternately tensed and then relaxed, allowing people to experience and learn what relaxation "feels" like.

The technique is based on the rationale that once our muscles are relaxed, we will interpret the physiological experience as one of tranquility. In turn, this leads to a reduction in the perception of stress (Jacobson, 1938). But more takes place than just a reduction in the *sense* of stress: Research has found that the use of progressive relaxation procedures leads to such benefits as a reduction in high blood pressure and other ailments such as headaches—even during periods when relaxation procedures are not being actively employed (Agras, Southam, & Taylor, 1983). (If you want to try a form of progressive relaxation yourself, see the Do It! box.)

DO IT!

RELAX!: A TECHNIQUE FOR LEARNING TO RELAX

To learn about the benefits of relaxation techniques for yourself, try this relaxation drill, which is a combination of several different methods:

1. Sit quietly in a comfortable position.

2. Close your eyes.

3. Deeply relax all your muscles, beginning at your feet and progressing up to your face. Keep them relaxed.

CHECK YOURSELF: ANSWERS
1. b, a, c **2.** True **3.** c **4.** d **5.** False

4. Breathe through your nose. Become aware of your breathing. As you breathe out, say the word "one" silently to yourself. For example, breath in ... out, "one"; in ... out, "one"; etc. Breathe easily and naturally.

5. Continue for ten to twenty minutes. You may open your eyes to check the time, but do not use an alarm. When you finish, sit quietly for several minutes, at first with your eyes closed and later with your eyes open. Do not stand up for a few minutes.

6. Do not worry about whether you are unsuccessful in achieving a deep level of relaxation. Maintain a passive attitude and permit relaxation to occur at its own pace. When distracting thoughts occur, try to ignore them by not dwelling upon them and return to repeating "ONE." With practice, the response should come with little effort. Practice the technique once or twice daily, but not within two hours after any meal.

Source: Benson, 1975.

Biofeedback We typically think of heart rate, blood pressure, and respiration as involuntary functions, out of reach of our willful control. Yet scientists have recently discovered that each of these responses can be directly controlled through a process called biofeedback.

Biofeedback is a procedure in which a person learns to control internal physiological processes through the use of electronic monitoring devices that provide continuous feedback on a given physiological response. For instance, a person concerned about headaches produced by muscle tension in her neck might have sensors connected to her neck muscles. By willfully trying to alter the tension, then receiving immediate and precise feedback from the electrical apparatus, she will learn to control the constriction and relaxation of the muscles. After several biofeedback sessions, she will probably be able to reduce the muscle constriction, even without being hooked up to the machine.

The significance of biofeedback for reducing the experience of stress is clear, since it allows people direct control of their physiological reactions to stress. Moreover, it can act as a preventive measure: By teaching people to reduce physiological tension in situations in which they normally would be expected to experience stress, they may be able to avoid the stress altogether.

Does biofeedback work? The procedure has been shown to be effective in a wide variety of settings and useful in controlling several different kinds of biological responses, such as headaches and pain (Miller, 1985). Although it is not successful in every case (Roberts, 1985), the potential of biofeedback in controlling stress is high.

Joel Gordon

Exercise can be very effective in reducing stress.

Exercise In meditation, progressive relaxation, and biofeedback, the emphasis is on coping with stress by controlling and *reducing* physiological reactions. Surprisingly, though, a technique that is quite effective in dealing with stress is one that initially *increases* physiological arousal: exercise.

Exercise tends to reduce stress in several ways. For one thing, heartbeat, respiration rate, and blood pressure—physiological responses sensitive to stress—tend to be lower in people who regularly exercise (although all these responses temporarily increase during exercise periods). Moreover, exercise gives people a sense of control over their bodies, plus a feeling of accomplishment. It even provides a temporary respite from the environment that is causing the stress in the first place, and it causes people to sleep better at night.

The most intriguing explanation of the benefits of exercise is a line of research that suggests that vigorous exercise releases **endorphins,** natural painkilling chemicals in the brain that may result in feelings of happiness and even euphoria (Watkins & Mayer, 1982). Endorphins may be responsible for the "runner's high," the positive feelings sometimes reported by long-distance runners following a long run (Hathaway, 1984). In sum, exercising may produce a naturalistic coping response in the body.

Diet Sometimes a change in diet is helpful in coping with stress. For instance, people who drink large quantities of caffeine are susceptible to feeling jittery and anxious; simply decreasing the amount they consume may be sufficient to reduce the experience of stress. Similarly, being overweight may itself be a stressor, and losing excess weight may be an effective measure for reducing stress.

Turning to Others:
Seeking social support

Our relationships with others may provide an important means of coping with stress. Researchers have found that **social support,** the knowledge that we are part of a mutual network of caring, interested others, enables us to experience lower levels of stress and to be better able to cope with the stress we do undergo (Schaefer, Coyne, & Lazarus, 1981).

There are several ways in which others can provide the social support that helps in dealing with stress (Taylor, 1986). For instance, others can provide emotional support by demonstrating that the person in need of their support is an important and valued member of a social network. Similarly, other people can provide information and advice about appropriate ways of dealing with stress—and they can be available as a sounding board.

Finally, people who are part of our social support network can provide us with tangible goods and services. For instance, they can supply a person whose house has burned down with temporary living quarters, or they can help a student who is experiencing stress due to academic performance to study for a test.

Relying on the social support of others, then, seems to be a reasonable strategy for dealing with stress. Not only does social support diminish the experience of stress, but it increases our ability to cope with it.

Thinking Stress Away:
Stress inoculation as a coping mechanism

I received a "D" on the first test of the semester. I'll never do well in the class now. I'll never catch up. I'm behind for good. I'm certain the professor thinks I'm stupid.

Have you ever heard someone present a situation in these black-and-white, unequivocal terms? To an observer it seems that such statements are illogical and irrational. It *is* possible to improve in a course after doing poorly initially; one *can* catch up after a poor start; and the professor has *not* necessarily formed an opinion about the student's intelligence.

Yet many of us use the same sort of self-defeating logic to deal with stress in our lives. According to psychologist Albert Ellis (1962), many of us hold irrational beliefs about our own behavior and the way others treat us. We assume that we should have love and approval all the time from all the people who are significant to us; we feel we must be completely competent, adequate, and successful all the time; and we think that it is terrible when things don't go the way we want them to.

Given such a set of beliefs, it is hardly surprising that the experience of stress is so common in people's lives. Yet the identification of these and other irrational beliefs suggests a means for coping with stress through an approach known as stress-inoculation training (Meichenbaum, 1977). **Stress-inoculation training** is a three-stage method for coping with and modifying people's thoughts about the stress and tension in their lives.

The first step in the procedure is to develop a greater awareness of one's behavior and thoughts. A daily log helps here; through it, a person can identify the specific circumstances that produce stress, learning the kinds of stimuli that bring about and maintain stress. Moreover, this process in and of itself can lead to a greater sense of control, as the person comes to understand the specific cause of his or her negative feelings.

In the second stage, a person mentally rehearses and begins to initiate behavior that is incompatible with any earlier irrational thoughts. Using the kinds of self-statements in Table 6-3, a person can learn the habit of coping with stress in a rational and constructive manner.

In the last stage of stress-inoculation training, a person is taught to apply the skills that have been learned. The skills are employed in increasingly stressful situations until the person is comfortable with the procedures. At this point, people can employ reinforcing self-statements.

It is important to realize that stress inoculation will not be effective one hundred percent of the time; there are times we simply cannot escape stress.

TABLE 6-3
Coping Self-Statements

The following statements are learned and used to cope with stress by replacing more irrational thinking in stress-inoculation training:

Preparation:
  What do I have to do?
  I can develop a plan to deal with it.
  Maybe what I think of as anxiety is eagerness to confront the stressor.
  Don't worry; worry won't help anything.
Confrontation:
  Take things one step at a time; I can handle the situation.
  This anxiety is what I thought would happen and have been told I would feel.
    It's a reminder to use my coping exercises.
  Relax; I'm in control. Take a slow, deep breath.
Coping:
  When fear comes, just pause a minute.
  Keep the focus on the present; what is it I have to do?
  I can't eliminate fear totally; just keep it manageable.
Self-reinforcement:
  It worked; I did it.
  Wait until I tell someone about this.
  It wasn't as bad as I expected.
  It's getting better each time I use the procedures.

Source: Adapted from Meichenbaum, 1977.

However, the procedure teaches the critical coping skill of preparation: To be forewarned about stress is to be forearmed.

Psychology for You:
Understanding the benefits of stress

We began this chapter by noting that a life totally devoid of stress would be routine and boring. Without challenges, we would lack many of the most important kinds of satisfaction we are able to attain in life, such as a job well done in the face of adversity. In an important sense, then, stress can produce personal understanding and growth.

There are several ways in which we can use stress, and our attempts to cope with it, to attain greater understanding of ourselves and the world. Consider the following ways in which stress can be of benefit:

● In stressful environments, people are motivated to understand better what is happening to them. This search for knowledge leads to greater awareness—not only of the world, but of themselves.

Research indicates that the stress of living in a busy crowded city may have a positive effect on many people.

Joel Gordon

● Stress can produce a reevaluation of our goals, making them more realistic. It can also save us from making the same mistake twice.

● The anxiety that accompanies stress can help us to be more vigilant about our surroundings. If the stress is not too high, we may learn things better and may operate at higher levels of efficiency than if no stress is present.

● Successful coping with stress can increase our own personal feelings of competence. Coping with stress allows us to assess ourselves in a realistic and honest way and come to an understanding of where our true strengths lie.

In sum, although coping with stress provides one of life's ongoing challenges, it can also provide a means of growing into hardier and better individuals, capable of reaching our own potential.

TO REVIEW

● Meditation is a learned technique for refocusing attention that brings about an altered state of consciousness.

● In progressive relaxation, people learn to alternately tense and relax various muscle groups, allowing them to learn to relax at will.

● Biofeedback is a procedure in which a person learns to control internal physiological processes with monitoring devices that provide feedback.

● Although exercise initially increases physiological arousal, it helps in coping with stress over the long term. A change in diet may also be effective in coping with stress.

● Social support, the knowledge from others that we are part of a mutual network of caring, interested others, enables people to experience lower levels of stress and to cope better with the stress they do undergo. Stress-inoculation training teaches people to more rationally think about and cope with stress in their lives.

CHECK YOURSELF

1. Meditation, progressive relaxation, biofeedback, and exercise are all techniques for reducing physiological arousal. True or false?

2. Endorphins are released during:
    a. exercise
    b. progressive relaxation
    c. biofeedback
    d. meditation

3.   During the second stage of stress-inoculation training, an individual learns to:
   a.   identify the conditions that bring about negative feelings
   b.   use self-statements that are incompatible with negative thoughts
   c.   extend his or her skills to increasingly stressful situations
   d.   self-reinforce

4.   Stress inoculation is a foolproof method of overcoming stress when it occurs. True or false?

_____

(See answers to these questions at the bottom of page 220.)

TO SUMMARIZE

1.   Stress is the process of appraising events as threatening, challenging, or harmful, and responding to such events on a physiological, emotional, cognitive, or behavioral level. Such events may be either negative (as in a life-threatening crisis) or positive (as the stress related to a happy event such as the birth of a child or a new job). Although stress is typically perceived as unpleasant, a life totally free of stress would hold no challenges.

2.   What constitutes a stressor—a threatening event—varies from one person to another, although there are general categories into which they may be placed. A cataclysmic event is a strong stressor that occurs suddenly and affects many people simultaneously. A personal stressor is a major event in a person's life that can produce an immediate stress reaction. Finally, background stressors (or daily hassles) are the minor irritations that people face in their day-to-day activities.

3.   Personal stressors have been found to relate to subsequent physical illness, and there is a link between daily hassles and the appearance of psychological symptoms. On the other hand, uplifts, those minor positive events that make people feel good, are associated with a lack of psychological symptoms.

4.   The general adaptation syndrome, or GAS, is a model developed by Hans Selye to explain the physiological characteristics of stress. According to the model, people react to stress in three stages. In the alarm and mobilization stage, the body prepares to battle a stressor. In the resistance stage, the person copes with the stressor. Finally, in the exhaustion phase, the person's ability to cope with stress declines to a point where the stressor is overwhelming.

5.   Behavioral reactions to stress may reflect either a fight or a flight response. If a person chooses a "fight" response, it may consist of a direct attack against the source of stress or an indirect one. If a flight response is chosen, the person tries to avoid the stressor. A third strategy may occur: In compromise, people react to stress by attacking and changing some aspects of a stressor while accepting others.

6. Anxiety, an emotional response characterized by feelings of fear, apprehension, and physiological tension, is a major consequence of stress. At the same time, anxiety can also act as a source of stress. Other psychological reactions to stress include the use of defense mechanisms, which are unconscious strategies people use to reduce stress and anxiety by concealing the source from themselves and others. The most important defense mechanisms include repression, suppression, displacement, projection, rationalization, fantasy, regression, and denial.

7. Coping consists of efforts to control, reduce, or learn to tolerate the threats that lead to stress. There are several coping techniques that encompass attempts to control one's physiological responses to stress including meditation, progressive relaxation, biofeedback, and exercise. Meditation is a learned technique for refocusing attention that brings about an altered state of consciousness. In progressive relaxation, various muscle groups are alternately tensed and then relaxed, allowing people to experience and learn to relax. Biofeedback is a procedure in which a person learns to control internal physiological processes. It entails the use of electronic monitoring devices that provide continuous feedback regarding the physiological response in question. Physical exercise and a change in diet are also effective techniques for reducing stress.

8. Social support is the knowledge that we are part of a mutual network of caring, interested others. Social support enables people to experience lower levels of stress and to be better able to cope with the stress they undergo.

9. Stress-inoculation training is another approach to coping with stress. It consists of a three-part procedure: developing a greater awareness of one's behavior and thoughts, mental rehearsal and initiation of behavior that is incompatible with any earlier irrational thoughts, and application of the skills that have been learned.

KEY TERMS AND CONCEPTS

stress (p. 189)

stressors (p. 190)

cognitive appraisal (p. 190)

cataclysmic events (p. 190)

posttraumatic stress syndrome (p. 191)

personal stressors (p. 191)

background stressors (p. 195)

daily hassles (p. 195)

flight response (to stress) (p. 202)

compromise response (to stress) (p. 202)

anxiety (p. 202)

defense mechanisms (p. 205)

repression (p. 206)

suppression (p. 206)

displacement (p. 207)

projection (p. 207)

CHECK YOURSELF: ANSWERS

1. False; exercise *increases* arousal. **2.** a **3.** b **4.** False

uplifts (p. 196)

general adaptation syndrome (GAS) (p. 196)

alarm and mobilization stage (of general adaptation syndrome) (p. 196)

sympathetic nervous system (p. 197)

resistance stage (of general adaptation syndrome) (p. 197)

psychosomatic disorders (p. 197)

exhaustion stage (of general adaptation syndrome) (p. 197)

fight response (to stress) (p. 201)

rationalization (p. 207)

fantasies (p. 208)

regression (p. 208)

denial (p. 208)

coping (p. 211)

meditation (p. 211)

mantra (p. 211)

progressive relaxation (p. 212)

biofeedback (p. 213)

endorphins (p. 214)

social support (p. 215)

stress-inoculation training (p. 216)

TO FIND OUT MORE

Nieves, L. R. (1984). *Coping in college: Successful strategies.* Princeton, NJ: Educational Testing Service.

If the stressors of college are getting you down, this book provides sound advice for ways of coping with academic challenges.

Brown, B. (1984). *Between health and illness.* Boston: Houghton Mifflin.

Written by one of the developers of biofeedback, this volume provides a lively view of the relationship between stress and health.

Cooper, C. L. (1985). (Ed.). *Psychosocial stress and cancer.* NY: Wiley.

A look at the links between stress and cancer, this volume demonstrates how stress may trigger the cancer process.

Selye, H. (1974). *Stress without distress.* Philadelphia: Lippincott.

Written by one of the pioneers in the area of stress, this book is a practical and useful guide for dealing with the stressors of daily life.

Kutash, I. L., & Schlesinger, L. B. (1980). (Eds.). *Handbook on stress and anxiety.* San Francisco: Jossey-Bass.

This group of papers on stress provides a good formal introduction to the area.

When Adjustment Fails

CHAPTER

7

Maladaptive Behavior

223

When the attacks first began, she was sixteen. Seated calmly at her desk, doing her homework, Madalyn Vestigio was suddenly overcome with the fear that something terrible was about to happen. As she experienced a feeling of impending doom, she was immobilized with fear. She could do nothing but sit quietly, with her heart pounding and sweat pouring from her body.

This time, the fear passed. But the attacks became more frequent. She was forced to drop out of school. Giving up her dream of becoming a lawyer and having a family, she lived a life of fear. Saddest, perhaps, was that she could never figure out what she was afraid of—only that she was so anxious that she feared for her life. "The Lord himself could tell me to get on with my life, and I wouldn't listen," she said. "I am so consumed with fear that it has taken over my life."

Although Howard Speer was doing reasonably well in his classes during his sophomore year of college, something was beginning to bother him. Always prone to short spells of depression, he was starting to experience them more and more. In fact, life was beginning to look awfully grim to him. As he confided to a friend, "I can't seem to get it together anymore. My love life stinks, most of my 'friends' are jerks, my parents are still giving me advice, and I don't have a clue about what I want to do after I finish school. Most of the time I just feel awful—tired, worn out, hopeless. I'll tell you the truth: I've been thinking that ending this rat race looks like a pretty good option to me."

When Marietta Hayes found the small lump on her arm, it confirmed her worst fears. "I knew I was going to get cancer. With all the medicine I've got to take for everything else that's wrong with me, I knew it was just a matter of time before I had a reaction. Now this." As she called her physician to make an appointment, she thought about how often she had done this in the past. "Most of the time I've recovered pretty well. This time, though," she mused, "I can see that my luck has run out."

Three people, three problems. All of us have our share, but some people's difficulties reach such proportions that they have difficulty meeting the everyday demands and challenges of the world. In this chapter we examine the kinds of psychological difficulties that beset some of us as we strive to function in society.

We begin with a discussion of the differences between maladaptive and adaptive behavior, and the surprising difficulties that arise when trying to make such distinctions. We consider several definitions of maladaptive behavior, and ultimately settle on an approach that can help us understand the two types of behavior. We also examine several different views of the origins of maladaptive behavior that help us understand the way such behaviors are manifested and treated.

We then begin an examination of the major forms of psychological maladjustment. Using a standard classification system, we examine anxiety and depression and discuss a major epidemic that exists today: suicide among young people.

Our focus turns next to disorders that cause an individual to experience physical symptoms without a medical cause. We discuss schizophrenia, a disorder in which there is a loss of reality. Finally, we consider personality disorders, in which there may be little sense of personal distress—it is other people, and society as a whole, that suffer most from the individual's maladjustment.

7.1   DISTINGUISHING MALADAPTIVE FROM ADAPTIVE BEHAVIOR

At the moment, as you probably noticed, I'm going through a spell of being depressed. I really couldn't tell you why it is, but I believe it's just because I'm a coward. . . .

This evening, while Elli was still here, there was a long, loud, penetrating ring at the door. I turned white at once, got a tummyache and heart palpitations. . . .

Is this woman mentally ill, or just having a bad day? It can often be difficult to distinguish between a normal, emotional response to problems and maladaptive behavior.

Joel Gordon

As you read this passage, you might think to yourself that, given the topic of this section of the chapter, the scene portrays maladaptive behavior. It seems reasonably obvious that someone suffering from a "spell" of depression of unknown origin, using the label "coward" because he or she feels depressed, and reacting to the ringing of a doorbell with such an extreme physiological response is suffering from some difficulties in adjustment.

Your opinion might well change, however, when you learn that this passage is drawn from *The Diary of Anne Frank* (1952), the true account of a young Jewish girl's day-to-day activities while she hid (ultimately unsuccessfully) from Nazi troops to avoid being banished to a concentration camp. Under the circumstances, who would not be depressed? Moreover, her strong reaction to the ringing of a doorbell can readily be explained as a reflection of the fact that its sound could signal the arrival of soldiers eager to search her hiding place.

As you can see, determining whether a particular behavior is maladaptive is not necessarily simple. (To experience some of the difficulties yourself, see the accompanying Do It! box.) Psychologists who have studied the issue have devised several general approaches to the problem.

DO IT!

DISTINGUISHING THE MALADAPTED FROM THE WELL-ADAPTED

Which of the following passages leads you to believe that the writer is revealing maladaptive behavior?

When what hugs stopping earth than silent is more silent than more than much more is or total sun oceaning than any this tear jumping from each most least eye of a star and without was if minus and shall be immeasurable happenless unnow. . . .

———————

Can't hear with bawk of bats, all thim liffeying waters of. Ho, talk save us! My foos won't moos. I feel as old as yonder elm. A tale told of Shaun or Shem? All Livia's daugher-sons. Dark hawks hear us. Night! Night! My ho head halls. . . .

———————

But then they danced down the street like dingledodies, and I shambled after as I've been doing all my life after people who interest me, because the only people for me are the mad ones, the ones who are mad to live, mad to talk, mad to be saved, desirous of everything at the same time, the ones who never yawn or say a commonplace thing, but burn, burn, burn like fabulous yellow roman candles exploding like spiders across the stars and in the middle you see the blue center-light pop and everybody goes "Awww!"

If you are an astute judge (or an English scholar), you will recognize that each of these passages was written by an acclaimed author and have been evaluated as literary masterpieces—and are not examples of maladjusted behavior. The first passage is from the poet e. e. Cummings (#16, 1981, p. 502), the second from James Joyce's *Finnegan's Wake* (1939), and the last from Jack Kerouac's *On the Road* (1957). It is probably clear to you that the distinctions between maladaptive and adaptive behavior are not always readily drawn.

Rare Is Wrong:
Maladaptive behavior as a deviation from the average

The most direct approach to identifying maladaptive behaviors is to examine their statistical incidence. According to this view, called the **deviation-from-the-average approach,** we simply determine whether and to what degree behavior deviates from the average. Behaviors that are infrequent or rare in our society, then, are considered maladaptive.

The drawback to such an approach is that some behaviors that are unusual hardly represent instances of maladaptation. If a person is unusually helpful, atypically brilliant, or extremely brave, it hardly seems reasonable to label his or her behavior maladaptive. On the other hand, if most people are rude and self-centered, it does not seem useful to consider their behavior

Mother Theresa's behavior and lifestyle are not typical of women in Western society, yet very few people would classify her as mentally ill.

Jerry Howard/Stock, Boston

adaptive merely because many people behave similarly. A definition of maladaptive behavior that rests on the behavior's statistical rarity does not, then, seem sufficient.

Perfecting the Imperfect:
Maladaptive behavior as a deviation from the ideal

Because the statistical average does not necessarily provide an appropriate standard against which to measure whether a behavior is maladaptive, it seems reasonable to turn to some other point of comparison. One possibility is to identify an appropriate standard or ideal against which to compare behavior. In the **deviation-from-the-ideal approach** to maladaptive behavior, the focus is on the degree to which a behavior differs from some ideal form of behavior. For instance, we might assume that intense, violent swings of mood are maladaptive due to their deviation from a more ideal situation in which mood swings are relatively insignificant.

Although it is an improvement over deviation-from-the-average approach, the deviation-from-the-ideal approach also has its drawbacks. The major one concerns identification of an appropriate standard or ideal. In a diverse world, there are many potential standards. To identify the ideal, some might look to religion, others to a particular philosophy, and still others (perhaps!) to psychology. There are few absolute standards about which most people would tend to agree. Moreover, because standards tend to change over time, the deviation-from-the-ideal approach to understanding maladaptive behavior is inadequate.

If It Feels Bad, It's Wrong:
Maladaptive behavior as a sense of subjective discomfort

Because both the deviation-from-the-average and deviation-from-the-ideal approaches to maladaptive behavior have their drawbacks, psychologists have turned to approaches that rely more on people's subjective feelings. One of the most useful revolves around the psychological consequences of people's behavior. According to the **subjective-discomfort approach,** a behavior is maladaptive if it produces feelings of distress, anxiety, or guilt or if it causes harm to other individuals. In this view, a behavior is maladaptive only to the extent that it causes psychological discomfort. For example, if a person experiences extreme guilt, anxiety, and unhappiness in school, this is an indication of maladaptive behavior, according to the subjective-discomfort criterion; but if his feelings are neutral or positive, his response is not maladaptive.

Even this approach, however, has its advantages. For instance, in some forms of severe maladaptive behavior, people feel elated and euphoric, regardless of the circumstances. Although to others their behavior seems inappropriate, such individuals feel no subjective discomfort. Moreover, such an approach to maladaptive behavior does not take into consideration the ability to function effectively as a member of society. Such concerns lead to a final approach to maladaptive behavior.

Michael Weisbrot and Family

The functional approach considers individuals to be mentally ill if they cannot meet their own basic needs, are not functioning in society, or pose a danger to themselves or others. Many homeless persons meet the first two criteria, but few meet the third.

The Continuum of Adaptive–Maladaptive Behavior:
A functional approach

An approach to maladaptive behavior that seems to best resolve the difficulties of earlier approaches considers the function that behavior plays in a given individual's life. According to the **functional approach,** a behavior is considered maladaptive if any of three criteria are met: (1) The behavior does not allow a person to function effectively with others as a member of society; (2) the behavior does not permit the person to meet his or her own needs; or (3) the behavior has a negative effect on the well-being of others.

Even with these criteria there is ample room for imprecision. In fact, behavior typically cannot be placed in absolute "adaptive" or "maladaptive" categories. Instead, it is more realistic to consider behavior as falling along a **continuum,** or scale, of behaviors, with adaptive behavior marking one end of the continuum and maladaptive the other. Looked at in this light, a given behavior can be considered in terms of how adaptive or maladaptive it is in a *relative* sense.

The ABCs of DSM:
Classifying maladaptive behavior

The difficulties in defining maladaptive behavior extend beyond merely distinguishing it from behaviors that are adaptive; devising a categorization system to classify different types of maladaptive behavior has proven to be a daunting task as well.

The classification system used by most mental health workers today is presented in the **Diagnostic and Statistical Manual of Mental Disorders, third edition—revised** *(DSM-III-R).* Published by the American Psychiatric Association in 1987, the manual represents a recent revision of the third major set of guidelines for classifying the entire spectrum of maladaptive behaviors. It includes definitions and descriptions of more than 230 individual categories.

While *DSM-III-R* provides a framework for discussing the continuum of maladaptive behavior, it is important to keep in mind that it has its drawbacks. For instance, labeling people as suffering from a specific sort of problem may pigeonhole them for life, even if the problem itself disappears; their diagnosis will remain in written records, and even their self-concept and the way in which they perceive themselves is likely to be affected by the label. Moreover, because *DSM-III-R* was devised not by psychologists but by psychiatrists (physicians who specialize in psychological problems) with minimal input from other mental health professions, some critics have noted that it tends to rely too heavily on physiological determinants of psychological disorders. It is important, then, to understand that—as with any classification system—*DSM-III-R* can be misused.

From Witchcraft to Science:
Models of maladaptive behavior

If you are certain that a person's maladaptive behavior is caused by her being possessed by a demon, would you feel justified in "treating" her through beatings and whippings designed to drive the demon away? Such treatment was standard for anyone who deviated too much from the rigid standards of eighteenth-century behavior in Puritan America. While you probably wouldn't condone such punishment, you'd understand that it does illustrate our tendency to treat maladaptive behavior in a way that we think reflects the cause of that behavior.

Happily, belief in demonic possession no longer dominates the way we view maladaptive behavior. There is, however, no universal agreement over the most reasonable approach to behavior, and we have several alternate views, or models, of maladaptive behavior. They include the medical model, the psychoanalytic model, the behavioral model, the humanistic model, and the sociocultural model. These models are important not only because they provide differing ways of understanding the genesis and nature of maladaptive behavior, but also because they ultimately suggest alternate treatment methods for the behavior.

The medical model   Advocates of the **medical model** believe that the root of maladaptive behavior lies in some physical dysfunction, such as a hormonal imbalance, biochemical deficiency, or injury to some part of the body. In fact, much of the terminology we use when we speak of mental *illness* or mental *hospitals* reflects the medical model.

Although the medical model is accurate in assuming that some maladaptive behavior is produced by physiological malfunctions (severe depression, for example, has been linked to a chemical imbalance in the brain), critics point out that there are many forms of maladaptive behavior in which no medical cause has been found. Moreover, the model suggests that for any maladaptive behavior there is a "cure" that can be found, and that such a cure is relatively independent of the actions of the person displaying the behavior (Szasz, 1982). Instead, responsibility for "curing" the behavior is left to the psychologist, psychiatrist, or physician. Hence, critics contend that the medical model places insufficient responsibility in the hands of the person with the problem.

The psychoanalytic model   Moving beyond the medical model, adherents of the **psychoanalytic model**—first introduced by Freud—hold that maladaptive behavior stems from childhood conflicts over opposing desires, particularly those regarding such basic impulses as sex and aggression. According to this view, we all pass through a series of stages during childhood in which sexual and aggressive impulses take different forms. If we do not successfully deal with these impulses, they remain unresolved in our unconscious and eventually reveal themselves through maladaptive behavior during adulthood.

Like the medical model, the psychoanalytic model has been criticized for its view that people have relatively little responsibility for their problems and difficulties. On the other hand, the notion that people have a complex inner life about which they are not aware is an important one, and the psychoanalytic model has produced important modes of treatment for maladaptive behavior.

The behavioral model   The **behavioral model** suggests that we should focus on a behavior itself, not on its underlying cause, when trying to understand maladaptive behavior. In this view, we need not look "inside" people to see what is causing their maladaptive behavior; we should look to their environment to see what is producing and supporting the behavior. Moreover, our attempts to resolve adaptive difficulties should focus on modifying the behavior itself rather than being concerned with any underlying physiological problems or conflicts suggested by other approaches. To proponents of the behavioral model, then, the focus is on observable behavior and devising ways of modifying specific maladaptive behaviors.

To rid a person of an unwanted behavior, the basic approach would consist of altering the maladaptive behavior or teaching the person new ways to behave to replace the old ones. While this strategy is effective in many cases, critics contend that the behavioral model ignores the underlying problems that caused the maladaptive behavior in the first place. Moreover, the de-emphasis of thinking and cognitive processes also has been a source of concern to critics, who suggest that people's thoughts and feelings are an important determinant of their behavior. Partially in response to such criticisms, some adherents of the behavioral model have begun to consider ways to modify the ways people think about the world or specific situations as they relate to their maladaptive behavior.

The humanistic model   Proponents of the **humanistic model** concentrate on what is uniquely human, particularly on the way people perceive and view themselves. Individuals are considered to be in control of their own behavior—including behavior that is maladaptive. According to this model, people set the limits of what is acceptable for themselves, and as long as it doesn't hurt anyone else or cause personal distress, they should be free to choose the behaviors in which they wish to engage.

The humanistic model, then, considers maladaptive behavior to be a natural response to the challenges of everyday life. Although critics contend that such an approach is vague and unscientific, the humanistic model has spawned a number of successful treatment approaches.

The sociocultural model   Rather than viewing a person as the source of his or her maladaptive behavior, the **sociocultural model** considers society to be the source of adjustment problems. Concentrating on factors such as racial prejudice, poverty, and economic discrimination, the sociocultural model views maladaptive behavior as a reflection of a person's way of functioning in society.

Although it provides relatively few suggestions for treatment, the sociocultural model is important in emphasizing society's contribution to adjustment problems. Moreover, it has the potential for suggesting ways of making society more supportive of its members.

Which model is best?: The eclectic approach   You might be wondering at this point which of these five models provides the most appropriate approach to maladaptive behavior. Unfortunately, the world is far from tidy, and no single approach is sufficient to treat all forms of maladaptive behavior. Most mental health workers are *eclectic:* They employ more than one model. For instance, we might consider a person's maladaptive behavior in terms of an underlying conflict between sexual and aggressive urges (a psychoanalytic approach), while simultaneously treating the symptoms with drugs (a medical approach) and teaching new behavior to the individual (a behavioral approach). The models, then, do not necessarily contradict one another, and all may be employed fruitfully.

Psychology for You:
Avoiding medical student's disease

As you begin to read through the various problems that people have, you may be surprised to find that you have experienced many of the symptoms yourself. Indeed, in some cases you may decide that your behavior is so similar to that described, you are certain that you suffer from the same maladjustment.

Michael Weisbrot and Family

Many successful therapists
use a blend of the various
models of psychotherapy.

Relax. In most cases, you are suffering only from "medical student's disease"—a malady that strikes people who are in the process of studying symptoms of any kind of illness, disease, or psychological disorder. In **medical student's disease,** students begin to feel that their own thoughts and behaviors bear an uncanny resemblance to the symptoms described in their textbooks and by their professors, and that they actually suffer from the dysfunction being studied.

In most cases, however, the resemblance is more apparent than real. Because the distinctions between adaptive and maladaptive behavior are so hazy, falling along a broad continuum, it is easy to interpret fleeting behavior as symptomatic of some underlying problem. We all experience wide swings of emotion. At times we are anxious, depressed, and fearful, and we fantasize about the most bizarre things. Only when such symptoms are persistent, deep, and consistent do they represent a real problem.

In sum, if you never questioned your adjustment before learning about the range of maladaptive behavior presented here, it is unlikely you ought to be seriously concerned now.

TO REVIEW

● Among the approaches to maladaptive behavior are the deviation-from-the-average, deviation-from-the-ideal, and sense-of-subjective discomfort approaches.

● The most reasonable approach is to consider behavior maladaptive if it meets any of three criteria: (1) the behavior does not allow a person to function effectively with others as a member of society; (2) the behavior does not permit the person to meet his or her own needs; or (3) the behavior has a negative effect on the well-being of others.

● Maladaptive-adaptive behavior lies along a continuum and is categorized using the DSM-III-R classification system.

● The major models used to explain maladaptive behavior include the medical, psychoanalytic, behavioral, humanistic, and sociocultural models.

CHECK YOURSELF

1. "Although he seems to function fairly well in social situations, it is clear that Steve's behavior is harmful to himself and adversely affects his family members. If you ask me, I'd call that maladaptive." Which approach to conceptualizing maladaptive behavior is being used above?
   a. the deviation-from-the-average approach
   b. the deviation-from-the-mean approach
   c. the subjective-discomfort approach
   d. the functional approach

2. It is most useful to think of behavior as falling along a _____ from adaptive to maladaptive.

3. A widely agreed upon advantage of DSM-III-R is that it emphasizes physiological determinants of maladaptive behavior. True or false?

4. Match each statement in the right column with the model it best fits.

_____ behavioral   a. Maladaptive behavior finds its roots in unresolved childhood conflicts.

_____ medical   b. One should look to the individual's environment to identify the factors that bring about and maintain maladaptive behavior.

_____ humanistic   c. Factors such as prejudice and economic discrimination are in large part responsible for maladaptive behavior.

_____ sociocultural   d. People choose to engage in some maladaptive behaviors in response to the challenges encountered in their lives.

_____ psycho-analytic   e. Chemical imbalances in the brain are responsible for much maladaptive behavior.

5. Most mental health workers employ components of all five models in their assessment of maladaptive behavior. That is, they are _____ in their approach.

_____

(See answers to these questions at the bottom of page 236.)

7.2   ANXIETY AND DEPRESSION

● *A truck driver was so consumed with the fear that he would stop in the middle of the Chesapeake Bay Bridge and jump over the side that he made his wife handcuff him to the steering wheel when it was necessary to drive across the bridge. Eventually, he could cross the bridge only in the trunk of his car while his wife drove.*

● *A woman was overcome with anxiety each time she walked down the aisles of a supermarket. "The food around me seemed piled so high, as if the aisles were closing in, and my head would start to swirl, and I'd just have to leave my cart right where it was and get out of there."*

● *A well-known public figure experiences anxiety when viewing bathwater running down the drain. If no one else is at home to pull the plug for him after a bath, he manages to pull it out, makes a mad dash for the door, while his heart pounds and he sweats profusely. (Adler, 1984.)*

At one time or another, we all experience **anxiety,** an emotional response characterized by feelings of fear, apprehension, and physiological tension. The anxiety we feel regarding an impending test, a public talk, or having to drive over an icy road—all stressful experiences—is a typical and quite reasonable reaction given the circumstances. However, in cases like the ones described above, anxiety occurs with little rational cause.

Indeed, we all experience adjustment problems—such as anxiety and depression—from time to time. For most of us, their relatively fleeting nature and superficiality represent normal parts of life. Yet for some people, the feelings linger, and their depth is such that they begin to interfere with the ability to meet the adjustive demands of daily life. When this occurs, the behavior of these individuals can be placed squarely at the "maladaptive" end of the continuum, and psychological intervention—which we discuss in Chapter 8—is called for.

Fear without Reason:
Anxiety disorders

When anxiety occurs without external justification and impedes people's daily functioning, it represents an **anxiety disorder.** There are several types of anxiety disorders, each of which we consider below.

Hazel Hankin

Does it make you feel uncomfortable to look at this picture? People with acrophobia have a severe fear of heights.

Generalized anxiety disorder   As you might assume from the name, people with **generalized anxiety disorders** experience long-term, consistent anxiety without knowing why. Those who suffer from the disorder know that something is bothering them, but they can never quite identify it. As their anxiety continues, and they are uanble to deduce what the source is, they may become overwhelmed by the anxiety, severely disrupting their daily lives. This was the case of Madalyn Vestigio, the woman we discussed at the start of the chapter.

Phobias   If you squeal at the sight of a mouse or cower when standing on the roof of a high building, you may know what it is like to have a phobic disorder. **Phobias** are intense, irrational fears of specific objects or stimuli. Rather than being characterized by vague anxiety—as in the case of generalized anxiety disorders—phobias are very specific to certain stimuli. Common phobias include a fear of closed spaces (claustrophobia), spiders (arachnophobia), snakes (ophidiophobia), or heights (acrophobia). In some cases, they may be rather odd: There are people who suffer from a fear of

CHECK YOURSELF: ANSWERS
1. d   **2.** continuum   **3.** False   **4.** b, e, d, c, a   **5.** eclectic

numbers (numerophobia), speaking aloud (phonophobia), and hair (trico-phobia).

In many cases, phobias may have only a minor effect on people's lives, if they can avoid the problem stimuli. In other cases, phobias may have a strong impact on everyday functioning. For example, students with a test-taking phobia will certainly be at a disadvantage in their academic endeavors.

Obsessive-compulsive disorder   Janet Moore, a sophomore, took the most meticulous notes you have ever seen. Not only would she write down every word the professor said—she took a shorthand course in order to be able to do it—but she also transcribed and typed her notes after every class. If she missed a word, she hounded her classmates in an attempt to include *everything* that was said in class. If she could not recreate every single word, she got anxious and afraid and was unable to sleep. Ironically, she was a mediocre student; the anxiety she experienced regarding note taking did not allow her much time to actually study the material she so meticulously collected.

Janet was suffering from an **obsessive-compulsive disorder,** in which she had **obsessions,** thoughts or ideas that kept recurring in her mind, and **compulsions,** urges to repeatedly carry out some act that seemed strange and unreasonable—even to her. Janet's obsession was her concern over documenting every word the professor spoke; her compulsion was producing the precise transcript of the lecture.

Many of us have mild obsessions from time to time (have you ever been plagued with the suspicion that you forgot to turn off your stereo when you left for the weekend?), but usually the thoughts persist for only a relatively short period of time. It is the long-term, irrational nature of obsessions and compulsions that makes them maladaptive.

Not Being in the Mood . . . for Anything: Depression and suicide

Everything I see, say, or do seems extraordinarily flat and pointless; there is no color, there is no point to anything. Things drag on and on, interminably. I am exhausted, dead inside. I want to sleep, to escape somehow, but there is always the thought that if I really could sleep, I must always and again awake to the dullness and apathy of it all. I doubt, completely, my ability to do anything well; it seems as though my mind has slowed down and burned out to the point of being virtually useless. The wretched, convoluted thing works only well enough to torment me with a dreary litany of my inadequacies and shortcomings in character, and to haunt me with the total, the desperate hopelessness of it all. What is the point in going on like this; it is crazy. I am crazy, I say to myself. Others say "It's only temporary, it will pass, you will get over it," but of course they haven't any idea how I feel, although they are certain they do. If I can't feel, move, think, or care, then what on earth is the point? (Goldstein, Baker, & Jamison, 1980, p. 182.)

As this articulate person makes clear, depression is one of the most debilitating of all psychological disorders. It is also one of the most common; from time to time we all suffer from feelings of sadness, worthlessness, self-blame, and lack of energy that are characteristic of **depression.** In most instances, however, depression is temporary, and people return fairly quickly to a more positive emotional state. Yet for some people the depth of their feelings is so profound and long-lasting that it affects their everyday adaptation to the challenges of life, and they are unable to function effectively.

The percentage of people likely to experience major depression during their lifetime is extraordinarily high—estimated at between 8 and 12 percent for men and between 20 and 25 percent for women (Boyd & Weissman, 1981). Moreover, depression is the most frequent problem diagnosed in outpatient clinics, affecting about a third of the patients (Woodruff, Clayton, & Guze, 1975; Winokur, 1983).

Although depression may take many forms, college students affected by it tend to exhibit several fairly consistent patterns (Blatt, D'Affilitti & Quinlan, 1976). They report that they are unusually dependent on others for help and support, they tend to exaggerate their own faults, and they may suffer from sleep and appetite disturbances. They also experience a sense that they are not in control of their own lives; events occur over which they feel they have no influence.

Because depression is such a common occurrence, it is sometimes difficult to distinguish "normal" depression from more serious forms. The distinction is primarily a matter of degree. In major depression, people may feel worthless, useless, and lonely, and they feel unrelenting despair that may linger for months. They may cry uncontrollably, and—in the most severe cases—they may be unable to eat or sleep.

Because of its frequency, depression has received much scrutiny, and several explanations have been suggested. Some investigators, particularly those relying on a psychoanalytic model, view depression as a result of anger directed at oneself; others see biological and genetic factors as playing an important role, particularly because major depression seems to run in certain families (McNeal & Cimbolic, 1986).

One current view of depression centers around the theme of **learned helplessness.** As we discussed in Chapter 6, people who come to feel that they are unable to escape from or cope with stress eventually give up even trying to change their environment. According to Martin Seligman (1975), depression may be a manifestation of such learned helplessness.

An Epidemic among Us:
Suicide

Dear Mom, Dad, Ron, and Friends,

I'm sorry I had to do this. I've had problems, and know that I'm running away. But I had to get away from them, and there was no other way out. I tried my hardest, but I couldn't face what was happening to me. I hurt so bad, and I knew that I would never be happy again after Julie and I broke up. It was my fault, and I couldn't live with it.

Love,
Billie

This note is representative of what has become a disconcertingly common phenomenon: suicide. Every year, some 200,000 people in the United States attempt suicide, and more than 10 percent succeed. More than 1000 of those committing suicide are college students, and the proportion of college students killing themselves is twice as great as the proportion of people in the same age range who do not attend college.

Even more surprising is the fact that within certain younger age groups suicide is on the rise, although it has declined slightly for some ages (see Figure 7-1). For example, teenage suicide has tripled in the last two decades, and suicide now ranks as the second leading cause of death for 15- to 24-year-olds in the United States. Because the actual number of suicides is probably even greater than these statistics indicate (physicians may report suicides as accidental deaths in order to spare a grieving family publicity, or people may disguise their suicides as auto accidents), the number of self-inflicted deaths has reached epidemic proportions among younger individuals.

What is the cause of this increase in suicides? Part of the answer relates to the fundamental causes of suicide: depression and stress, coupled with a view of the future as hopeless (Beck, 1985). People who are depressed often have a negative self-image, and they may come to view suicide as the only answer to their problems. Suicide is frequently precipitated by worries about academic performance, poor physical health, and—primarily—difficulties with relationships, although these problems may be outgrowths of a more fundamental depression. Moreover, although it would seem that scholastic failure might be associated with suicide, people who commit suicide tend to be relatively good students.

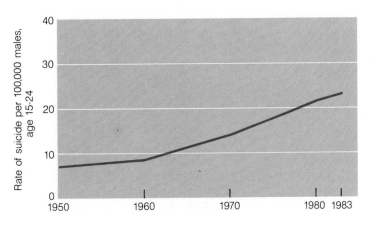

FIGURE 7-1
The rate of suicide in 15- to 24-year-olds has increased over the last two decades, as illustrated by these figures, which indicate the number of suicides per 100,000 white males. (*Source:* National Center for Health, 1985.)

While it is clear that depression is closely associated with subsequent self-destructive behavior, this fact does not explain the recent increase in suicide in younger age groups. Some observers have suggested that pressures on younger individuals have increased. There has been a rise in the use of drugs and alcohol, higher expectations for success, and exposure to temptations from peers. Moreover, suicide may sometimes represent "copycat" behavior: Several communities have experienced a rash of suicides following an initial self-destructive act by a high school student. It is likely, of course, that the individual who is influenced by a suicidal model is initially predisposed to suicide; being exposed to a model merely makes suicide a more viable option (Schneidman, 1985).

Although not simple, suicide can be prevented. As the Do It! box suggests, there are several signals indicating that a person is at risk for suicidal behavior. If you are ever told by someone that they are contemplating suicide, take them seriously, and urge them to seek professional help.

DO IT!

THE MYTHS AND REALITIES OF SUICIDE

Listed below are several statements about suicide. Which of these are true?

1. People who talk about killing themselves rarely do it.

2. Talking about suicide openly encourages people to kill themselves.

3. If a person tries suicide once, he or she is at higher risk in the future.

4. Women are more likely than men to commit suicide.

5. Individuals who have a concrete plan to commit suicide are more likely to try to kill themselves than those who have no detailed plans.

6. If a person is determined to commit suicide, there is nothing you can do to stop that person.

ANSWERS   1. False: Almost everyone who commits suicide provides some clue prior to the act itself. Take people seriously when they discuss suicide; 2. False: Discussing suicide is helpful and can potentially bring feelings to light that would otherwise be kept hidden;   3. True: People who have a history of attempted suicide have a greater potential for suicide;   4. False: Men are more likely to carry out suicide than women, and women are more likely to attempt suicide;   5. True: The greater the precision of their plan, the more likely they are to try it;   6. False: Most people who plan suicide *want,* on some level, to live; and intervention can—quite literally—save their lives.

Susan Lapides/Design Conceptions

The transition to college is distressing for many freshmen, particularly those who had a successful senior year in high school.

Psychology for You:
The special problems of college students

When you first began college, were you depressed, severely homesick, anxious, and withdrawn from others?

If so, you may have been suffering from **freshman adjustment reaction,** a psychological maladjustment unique to college students. Although it can happen to anyone, it is frequently most severe in students who had been particularly successful, either socially or academically, in their senior year of high school. When they enter college, suddenly lacking status and authority, many freshmen feel disoriented and distressed.

Although freshman adjustment reaction can be particularly painful for those in the midst of it, the passage of time is often sufficient for the syndrome to pass. But freshman adjustment reaction is just one of several problems of adjustment that college students encounter (Duke & Nowicki, 1979). Among the other most frequent concerns for male students are grades, social life, vocational decisions, the future, sexual relationships, peer pressure, adjusting to a new environment, leaving family for the first time, competition, and depression. For women, the list is a little different: What to do with their lives, the development of sexual and emotional relationships, strain from too much work, grades, general adjustment, gaining independence, forming an identity, pressure from parents, peer pressure, and morality top their concerns.

As you can see, many of these problems revolve around the specific demands of the college environment. Although, typically, none of them is severe, they can present a challenge to the well-being of students who experience them. Just knowing that others have the same anxieties may be sufficient to reduce their psychological bite and permit a person to deal with them more readily.

TO REVIEW

● Anxiety disorders are maladaptive responses in which anxiety occurs without external justification. Examples are: generalized anxiety disorders, phobias, and obsessive-compulsive disorders.

● Depression is characterized by feelings of sadness, worthlessness, and lack of energy. Depression is often linked to suicide, which is reaching epidemic proportions among young people.

● Freshman adjustment reaction is one of several problems of adjustment related to the college experience.

CHECK YOURSELF

1. Mandy's heart starts to pound whenever she raises her hand in class. Such a physiological response is generally considered maladaptive. True or false?

2. Identify the disorder described in the right column.

_____ phobia	a. Justin's chronic and debilitating anxiety appears to occur without specific causes.
_____ obsessive-compulsive disorder	b. Robin washes her hands at least four times an hour throughout the day and constantly worries about the germs they might be carrying.
_____ generalized anxiety disorder	c. Whenever Debbie enters the grocery store, she is overcome with fear and runs out. Strangely enough, entering other stores does not elicit the same response.

3. _____ is the most frequent psychological problem diagnosed in outpatient clinics.

4. The symptoms that characterize "normal" depression are quite different from those of major depression. True or false?

5. Which of these statements about suicide is *not* true?
    a. Suicide is now the second leading cause of death for 15- to 24-year-olds.
    b. Many suicides go unreported.
    c. College students and noncollege individuals of the same age group commit suicide at equal rates.
    d. More than 10 percent of those who attempt suicide succeed.

(See answers to these questions at the bottom of page 244.)

7.3 SOMATOFORM AND PSYCHOSOMATIC DISORDERS, SCHIZOPHRENIA, AND PERSONALITY DISORDERS

Mrs. L. was a deeply depressed woman of thirty-two—"in constant pain." Her pain was a muscular tension around the lower part of her back. She described it as a "burning, tearing, fiery-tongue-like, torturing" sensation. Neurologists, internists, surgeons were of no avail. . . .

"My whole life is concentrated on my back, and believe me, my pains are real. When I get my attacks, I scream like a wounded or tortured animal, and mind you, this goes on for hours at a time."

She was deeply offended when someone voiced the suspicion that she was "acting up" to torture her husband. "I don't believe that. I started having my attacks before my marriage. Too bad that marriage didn't cure the pain." (Bergler, 1974.)

When a string of medical specialists could find nothing physically wrong with this woman, suspicion turned to a psychological disorder—and this, as it happened, was the culprit. In the remainder of this chapter, we examine several additional psychological difficulties, beginning with problems of the sort besetting this woman.

Where the Physical Meets the Psychological: Somatoform and psychosomatic disorders

Most of us know someone who, when being asked how he or she feels, would regale us with something like the following:

I've been getting these headaches recently, and I've got a rash on my leg. Actually, I'm feeling better since I began to take the new kind of vitamins I found in the health-food store. But it's all relative; I still have less energy than most people. I think I have some low-level blood problem that is keeping me feeling run-down all the time. I have an appointment with a specialist to give me a really thorough physical. I'm really eager to get to the bottom of all these health problems; they scare me to death.

Such people, whose concerns about medical matters extend far beyond the norm, may be experiencing **hypochondriasis,** a fear of disease and a preoccupation with health. It is not that their physical symptoms are fabricated; people with hypochondriasis actually experience the many aches, pains, and other symptoms they describe (Costa & McCrae, 1985). The distinguishing characteristic is that they interpret such symptoms—erroneously—as signs of some underlying disease. These people, in fact, are relatively healthy.

Hypochondriasis is an example of a broader class of psychological difficulties called **somatoform disorders**—psychological problems that take on a physical form of some sort, despite the fact that there is no underlying biological cause. For example, a person may awaken one morning to find that he or she is unable to move a limb or is unable to hear. When physical examinations are unable to discover any cause—and if the person may be seen to move the "paralyzed" limb while sleeping—such problems are considered psychological problems and labeled somatoform disorders.

It is important to distinguish somatoform disorders, in which a physiological cause for medical problems is absent, from diseases of adaptation, or **psychosomatic disorders,** physical disorders in which emotions and thoughts play an important role. As first noted in Chapter 6, diseases of adaptation, which may include such disorders as ulcers, high blood pressure, asthma, skin problems, insomnia, or sexual problems, originate from our attempts to adapt to psychological stressors.

One of the characteristics of psychosomatic disorders is that they tend to be centered in a specific organ system, such as the digestive system (ulcers), circulatory system (high blood pressure), or respiratory system (asthma). Although the reason people develop problems in one system and not others is not clear, it does appear that there may be some predisposing biological and psychological factors that produce sensitivity in a particular system (Davison & Neale, 1982). For example, a person who has atypically sensitive or weak lungs may be particularly vulnerable to diseases related to that organ system, and develop asthma.

In sum, medical difficulties may present maladaptive problems in two forms. In somatoform disorders, there is no real underlying disease, yet the individual experiences symptoms of some form of medical problem. In contrast, people with psychosomatic disorders actually have a physical ailment, but the problem is brought about largely by psychological factors.

Losing Touch with Reality:
Schizophrenia

At first it was as if parts of my brain "awoke" which had been dormant, and I became interested in a wide assortment of people, events, places, and ideas which normally would make no impression on me. Not knowing that I was ill, I made no attempt to understand what was happening, but

CHECK YOURSELF: ANSWERS

1. False **2.** c, b, a **3.** Depression **4.** False **5.** c

felt that there was some overwhelming significance in all this, produced either by God or Satan, and I felt that I was duty-bound to ponder on each of these new interests, and the more I pondered, the worse it became. The walk of a stranger on the street could be a "sign" to me which I must interpret. Every face in the windows of a passing streetcar would be engraved on my mind, all of them concentrating on me and trying to pass me some sort of message. (MacDonald, 1960, p. 218.)

To Norma MacDonald, whose breakdown is chronicled above, reality was something different from that of other people. She was suffering from **schizophrenia,** a class of disorders whose symptoms include severe distortion of reality; disturbances in thinking, perception, and emotion; withdrawal from social interaction; and displays of bizarre behavior.

While there is no single pattern to schizophrenia, there are several characteristics—including its relative severity—that reliably distinguish it from other forms of maladaptive behavior. There are declines from earlier levels of functioning, in which a person is unable to carry out activities that were once possible. Thought and language become disturbed; reasoning becomes illogical, and conventional linguistic rules may be ignored. Coupled with this, people with schizophrenia often have perceptual disorders, manifested in abnormalities in vision, hearing, or the other senses. In fact, they may have **hallucinations,** the experience of perceiving things that do not actually exist.

People displaying the symptoms of schizophrenia also may have **delusions:** firmly held, unshakable beliefs with no basis in reality, consisting of the notion that they are being controlled by others or that they are being persecuted. Emotional responses in schizophrenia are also disturbed. People with the disorder may show either a bland lack of emotion or they may overreact emotionally, showing wide swings of emotion or emotion that is inappropriate to a given situation.

Finally, schizophrenia is marked by social withdrawal and isolation. People with schizophrenia lose interest in other people and events around them. In extreme cases they do not even acknowledge the presence of others. In many senses, then, people with a schizophrenic disorder appear to be living in their own private worlds.

Schizophrenia remains a baffling disorder; hence, several different approaches are being used to explain it (Watt, 1985). Part of the problem seems related to heredity; schizophrenia runs in some families. However, genetics does not supply the full story, since in many cases there is no family history of the problem.

Other explanations of schizophrenia focus on the biochemical aspects of the disorder. For instance, there is evidence that a biochemical imbalance in the brains of people with schizophrenia may produce chemicals that lead to hallucinations or disorganized thinking (Carson, 1983; Asnis & Ryan, 1983). In a sense, then, a self-generated drug overdose may lead to the symptoms of schizophrenia. Other theories suggest that schizophrenia is the result of excessive activity in areas of the brain that use the chemical

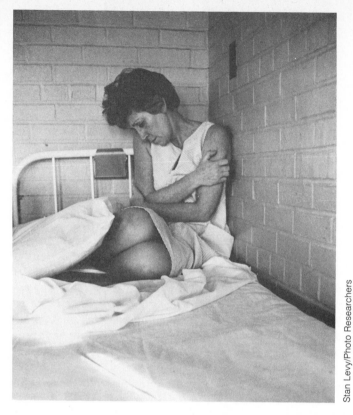

Stan Levy/Photo Researchers

In some cases of schizophrenia, the afflicted person may not acknowledge the presence of others.

dopamine to transmit impulses across nerve cells; still others hypothesize that there may be structural abnormalities in the brains of individuals with schizophrenia (Scheibel & Kovelman, 1986).

Finally, some explanations of schizophrenia rely on psychological factors. Psychoanalytic approaches suggest that schizophrenia is a manifestation of regression to an earlier stage of life. Another theory, the **double-bind hypothesis,** proposes that people with schizophrenia have in the past received simultaneous, yet contradictory, messages from significant figures in their lives. For instance, a parent who is verbally loving and supportive, yet who acts in an anxious and unsupportive manner on an emotional and nonverbal level, may produce such a high level of conflict in a child that schizophrenia is the eventual outcome.

The most accurate explanation of schizophrenia is one that considers several kinds of factors simultaneously. Known as the **predisposition model,** it suggests that people may inherit a predisposition or inborn sensitivity to schizophrenia, making them particularly vulnerable to stressful factors in the environment. Although the nature of the specific stressors may vary, ranging from a poor social environment to maladaptive communication patterns within the family, the outcome is the same if the stressors are sufficiently potent: schizophrenia. In this view, then, schizophrenia is not caused by any one factor but a combination of several.

Maladaptive Behavior without Distress: Personality disorders

I can remember the first time in my life when I began to suspect I was a little different from most people. When I was in high school my best friend got leukemia and died and I went to his funeral. Everybody else was crying and feeling sorry for themselves and as they were praying to get him into heaven I suddenly realized that I wasn't feeling anything at all. He was a nice guy but what the hell. That night I thought about it some more and found that I wouldn't miss my mother and father if they died and that I wasn't too nuts about my brothers and sisters, for that matter. I figured there wasn't anybody I really cared for but, then, I didn't need any of them anyway so I rolled over and went to sleep. (McNeil, 1967, p. 87.)

To the speaker of these words, a wealthy, successful actor, events that would typically bring about strong emotions—such as the death of a friend—are as insignificant as swatting a fly. He represents an example of someone suffering from a **personality disorder,** an enduring, inflexible, maladaptive pattern of behavior, thought, and perception. Unlike the other disorders we have been discussing, personality disorders often produce little personal distress. In fact, people with personality disorders often lead seemingly normal, successful lives. However, when their lives are examined more closely, they can be seen as having inflexible, maladaptive personality traits that prevent them from functioning effectively as members of society (Millon, 1981).

The **antisocial (or sociopathic) personality disorder** is one of the most significant types of personality disorders. People with this disorder, while often charming and fun to be with, can also make life miserable for those around them. They typically display no regard for the moral or ethical rules of society or the rights of others, manipulating people and situations for their own benefit. They display little guilt when they have injured someone else; they understand that they may have caused another person harm, but they feel no remorse.

The antisocial personality disorder may also be revealed through clashes with authority figures. Antisocial people are unable to withstand frustration, and they are impulsive; these traits frequently lead to stealing, lying, and cheating. At the same time, they may be quite adroit at getting what they want; they often have unusually good social skills, and their charm and apparent earnestness allow them to convince others to comply with their wishes.

The peculiar characteristics of the antisocial personality disorder are difficult to explain, and a variety of causes, ranging from the biological to the sociological, have been suggested. There is evidence that certain people suffering from the disorder grew up in environments in which there was little affection, a lack of consistent discipline, or outright rejection, but this background is far from universal. Because the antisocial personality disorder seems most prevalent in lower socioeconomic classes, it is also possible that there is a link between economic deprivation and the disorder. Despite the lack of a definitive explanation for why people develop antisocial personality disorders, it is clear that those marked by the disorder produce an inordinate amount of difficulty for others, as well as for society in general.

In addition to the antisocial personality disorder, there are several other types of abnormalities that fall under the personality disorder classification. For example, the **compulsive personality disorder** is displayed by people who have a preoccupation with rules, orderliness, efficiency, and detail. They are indecisive and have a restricted ability to express warm and tender emotion. In contrast, the **narcissistic personality disorder** is marked by a sense of self-importance, and there is a preoccupation with fantasies of unlimited success.

DO IT!

DIAGNOSING FROM AFAR

Now that you have been exposed to some of the basic categories of maladaptive behavior, you might want to try your hand at identifying the famous individual who is represented in each of these cases:

☐ After falling into a deep depression, he eventually overcame his adjustment difficulties to lead his country as president. Diagnosis: Major depression.

☐ He heard voices that urged him to kill presidential candidate Robert F. Kennedy. Diagnosis: schizophrenia.

☐ One of the richest men in the United States, he was obsessed with the possibility of being "contaminated" with germs, and made everyone with whom he came in contact wear surgical masks and gowns. Diagnosis: Obsessive-compulsive disorder.

ANSWERS   The first case is Abraham Lincoln, who suffered from bouts of depression throughout his life; the second is Sirhan Sirhan, Kennedy's assassin; and the third is aircraft manufacturer and multimillionaire Howard Hughes.

Psychology for You:
When you need help—and when you don't

Most people's adjustment problems don't manifest themselves in a clear break from reality, hearing strange voices, or feeling so anxious that immobility is the result. Instead, most adjustment problems are of a less dramatic type, and determining the way to best deal with them is not always clear. One of the greatest challenges people may face is determining when their problems have reached the point at which professional intervention is appropriate.

How do you decide whether or not you have a problem that is serious enough to warrant professional help? The following signals suggest that seeking help may be warranted:

- You feel psychological distress that lingers and interferes with your sense of well-being, competence, and ability to function on a day-to-day basis.

- You experience stress intense enough to make you feel that you are unable to cope effectively with a situation.

- You are depressed and feel hopeless for no appropriate reason, and these feelings occur on a long-term basis.

- You have a fear or phobia that prevents you from engaging in everyday activities.

- You have a minor problem that you are afraid will blossom into a large-scale problem.

- You feel that others are talking about you or plotting against you.

- You see, hear, smell, or feel things that others do not.

- You are unable to build friendships and loving relationships or interact well with others.

- You have physical symptoms for which physicians have been unable to find an underlying cause.

If you fit into one of these categories, you should consider seeking professional help. It is important to remember, though, that "maladaptive behavior" represents a vague concept, and absolute identification of a problem is not always easy. Moreover, it is important to recall the earlier discussions of medical student's disease; you should be wary about diagnosing your own behavior. Still, no one knows you better than you do, and if you suspect that you have a problem, it is important to seek professional advice. We discuss the kinds of help available for different disorders in the next chapter.

TO REVIEW

- Somatoform disorders are psychological difficulties that take on a physical form, although there is no underlying biological cause for the problem. One type of somatoform disorder is hypochondriasis, an exaggerated fear of disease and a preoccupation with one's health.

- Schizophrenia is a class of disorders in which there is severe distortion of reality; disturbances in thinking, perception, and emotion; withdrawal from social interaction; and displays of bizarre behavior.

- Personality disorders are enduring, inflexible, maladaptive patterns of behavior, thought, and perception. Among the different kinds of personality disorders are the antisocial or sociopathic disorder, the compulsive personality disorder, and the narcissistic personality disorder.

CHECK YOURSELF

1. Brenda's ulcer most likely resulted from the emotional stress brought on by her job situation. As such, her problem can be classified as a somatoform disorder. True or false?

2. "The President of the United States controls my behavior. I can take no responsibility for the things I do." This statement described a _____ which might be experienced by a person with a schizophrenic disorder.

3. The _____ model suggests that innate factors may predispose some individuals to the development of schizophrenia when they experience powerful stressors in their lives.

4. Although people with personality disorders may appear to be leading normal, successful lives, a look beneath the surface reveals that they live with a great deal of pain and emotional distress. True or false?

5. Which description of people exhibiting an antisocial or sociopathic personality disorder is *not* true?
   a. They display no regard for the moral and ethical rules of society.
   b. They are impulsive and unable to withstand frustration.
   c. They are often charming and fun to be around.
   d. They display deep remorse when they have hurt someone else.

(See answers to these questions at the bottom of page 252.)

TO SUMMARIZE

1. Determining whether a particular behavior is maladaptive is neither straightforward nor simple. One approach revolves around the behavior's statistical frequency. In this deviation-from-the-average approach, behaviors that are infrequent or rare are considered to be maladaptive. The drawback is that even positively valued behavior (such as unusually high intelligence) would be considered maladaptive. A definition of maladaptive behavior as behavior that deviates from an ideal is also inadequate, since there are no universal standards for society. Viewing behavior as maladaptive if it causes a sense of distress, anxiety, or guilt or if it causes harm to others is a better approach, although in some cases people with severe forms of maladaptive behavior feel no sense of discomfort or are not in touch with reality.

2. According to a functional approach to maladaptive behavior, a behavior is considered maladaptive if (1) it does not allow a person to function effectively with others as a member of society; (2) it does not permit the

person to meet his or her own needs; or (3) it has a negative effect on the well-being of others.

3. *DSM-III-R* (the *Diagnostic and Statistical Manual of the Mental Disorders,* third edition—revised) is the major classification system of maladaptive behaviors. There are also several models of maladaptive behavior that reflect an understanding of the causes of the behavior. The medical model suggests that maladaptive behavior is caused by some physical dysfunction, while the psychoanalytic model holds that it stems from childhood conflicts. The behavioral model suggests that we should consider only the behavior itself and not its underlying cause. The humanistic model sees people in control of their own lives and behavior, even behavior that others would consider maladaptive. Finally, the sociocultural model views maladaptive behavior as being brought about by societal forces.

4. When studying maladaptive behavior, it is important to avoid "medical student's disease." In this syndrome, students find that their own symptoms are similar to the symptoms they are studying and think that they have the same problems themselves.

5. Although we all experience anxiety, an emotional response characterized by fear, apprehension, and physiological tension, it can, in some cases, begin to interfere with everyday functioning. When anxiety occurs without external justification and impedes people's daily functioning, it represents an anxiety disorder. In a generalized anxiety disorder, people experience long-term, consistent anxiety without knowing why. Phobias are intense, irrational fears of specific objects or stimuli. Obsessions are thoughts or ideas that keep recurring in one's mind. Compulsions are urges to repeatedly carry out some act that seems strange and unreasonable.

6. Depression is characterized by feelings of sadness, worthlessness, and fatigue. The incidence of major depression among the general population is high: between 8 and 12 percent for men and between 20 and 25 percent for women. Depression may have several causes, including biological and genetic factors, or it may be caused by learned helplessness. Suicide, which is closely related to depression, has increased among 15- to 24-year-olds in the last two decades, reaching epidemic proportions.

7. College students may have special sorts of problems. They include freshman adjustment reaction, grades, social and sex life, overwork, and vocational decisions.

8. Somatoform disorders are psychological difficulties that take on a physical form of some sort, despite the fact that there is no underlying biological cause for the problem. One example is hypochondriasis, in which a person has a fear of disease and a preoccupation with health. In contrast, psychosomatic disorders are physical disorders in which emotions and thoughts play an important role in creating the medical problem.

9. Schizophrenia is a class of disorders in which there is severe distortion of reality; disturbances in thinking, perception, and emotion; withdrawal from social interaction, and displays of bizarre behavior. People with schizo-

phrenia may have hallucinations (the experience of perceiving things that do not actually exist) and delusions (firmly held, unshakable beliefs with no basis in reality). The best explanation for schizophrenia is the predisposition model, which suggests that people may inherit a predisposition or inborn sensitivity to schizophrenia, making them particularly vulnerable to stressful factors in the environment.

10. Personality disorders are enduring, inflexible, maladaptive patterns of behavior, thought, and perception. There is often little personal distress. One of the most significant forms of personality disorders is characterized by antisocial or sociopathic behavior, in which people have no regard for the moral or ethical rules of society or the rights of others. The compulsive personality disorder and the narcissistic personality disorder also fall into the personality disorder category.

KEY TERMS AND CONCEPTS

deviation-from-the-average approach (to maladaptive behavior) (p. 227)

deviation from the ideal approach (to maladaptive behavior) (p. 228)

subjective-discomfort approach (to maladaptive behavior) (p. 228)

functional approach (to maladaptive behavior) (p. 229)

continuum (p. 229)

Diagnostic and Statistical Manual of Mental Disorders, third edition—revised (*DSM-III-R*) (p. 230)

medical model (p. 230)

psychoanalytic model (p. 231)

behavioral model (p. 231)

humanistic model (p. 232)

sociocultural model (p. 232)

medical student's disease (p. 232)

anxiety (p. 233)

anxiety disorder (p. 235)

generalized anxiety disorders (p. 236)

phobias (p. 236)

obsessive-compulsive disorder (p. 237)

obsessions (p. 237)

compulsions (p. 237)

depression (p. 238)

learned helplessness (p. 238)

freshman adjustment reaction (p. 241)

hypochondriasis (p. 244)

somatoform disorders (p. 244)

psychosomatic disorders (p. 244)

schizophrenia (p. 245)

hallucinations (p. 245)

delusions (p. 245)

double-bind hypothesis (p. 246)

predisposition model (of schizophrenia) (p. 246)

personality disorder (p. 247)

antisocial (or sociopathic) personality disorder (p. 247)

compulsive personality disorder (p. 248)

narcissistic personality disorder (p. 248)

CHECK YOURSELF: ANSWERS
1. False, the disorder is real. **2.** delusion **3.** predisposition **4.** False **5.** d

Meyer, R. G., & Osborne, Y. V. H. (1982). *Case studies in abnormal behavior.* Boston: Allyn & Bacon.

A fascinating array of cases about individuals with different forms of maladjustment. Each case is explained by the authors of this interesting book.

Vonnegut, M. (1976). *The Eden express.* New York: Bantam.

A first-person case history of what it is like to suffer—and recover—from schizophrenia. Written by the son of author Kurt Vonnegut, it provides a frightening insight into the problem.

Agras, W. S. (1985). *Panic: Facing fears, phobias, and anxiety.* New York: W. H. Freeman.

For anyone who suffers from chronic anxiety, this book has much to offer, providing helpful advice on what can be done.

American Psychiatric Association (1987). Diagnostic and Statistical Manual of Mental Disorders. DSM-III-R (3rd ed., rev.). Washington DC: American Psychiatric Association.

This chapter has only scratched the surface of psychological disturbances. Although technical, this volume provides a sense of the range and comprehensiveness of the major system of disorders.

Restoring Adjustment

Treatment of Maladaptive Behavior

CHAPTER

8

255

Student *I've never been in this kind of situation before.*

Therapist *That's O.K. Many people find it difficult to talk to someone they have just met. Try to relax a bit, and tell me what brought you here.*

Student *(Pause.) Well, I'm not altogether sure. I feel nervous a lot.*

Therapist *What is the feeling like?*

Student *I don't know. It's a kind of feeling in the pit of my stomach. Almost like a knot. But sometimes it's a kind of uneasiness. I think there's something that's bothering me, but I can't put my finger on it.*

Therapist *Are there any particular situations that tend to make you feel nervous?*

Student *It's hard to come up with specifics.*

Therapist *I can understand how it might be hard to think of specific examples on the spur of the moment. But let's try this: Think back over the last few days, and tell me about any instances that made you feel especially anxious.*

Student *There was a time when I had to speak to my geology professor about a paper topic, and I felt really nervous about it.*

Therapist *Can you tell me more about that situation?*

Student *Well, my paper was late, and I thought the professor was going to be really angry with me.*

Therapist *Was she?*

Student *No, that's the funny thing. She didn't seem to care all that much.*

Therapist *Why do you think she didn't care?*

Student *I don't know. . . . Actually, it's the kind of thing that happens to me a lot, even when I was a little kid. I'd get real frightened about doing something bad. I'd expect my parents to come down hard on me, and then nothing would happen. They just didn't seem to notice. They just wouldn't care all that much.*

Therapist *They wouldn't care about what you had done or wouldn't care about you?*

Student *Care about . . . me.*

Have you ever wondered what kinds of things go on when someone seeks treatment for maladaptive behavior? The conversation above illustrates a typical initial therapy session. Perhaps as you read the interchange you envisioned it taking place in a darkened room, with the student lying on a

Innervisions

The popular image of therapy—where the client lies on a couch in a darkened room—is quite often inaccurate.

couch and a bearded therapist nodding sagely but mysteriously. While such a scenario is possible, it is only one of many that are representative of treatment. Treatment for psychological disturbances also occurs in brightly lit rooms, with both therapist and patient upright in easy chairs having an open discussion. Indeed, in some forms of treatment the patient's initial encounter with a treatment provider would consist of a thorough physical examination, and the course of treatment could be limited to medication.

There are more than 250 different kinds of treatments used by therapists today, ranging from one-session, informal discussions to treatments that last for years and involve powerful drugs. No matter what the treatment, though, all share a common goal: to eliminate maladaptive behavior and permit people to live fuller, more meaningful lives that meet the challenges of the everyday world.

In this chapter, we discuss the major forms of treatment that psychologists have devised for people with maladaptive behaviors. We begin by considering **psychotherapy,** psychological treatment in which patients (also called "clients") attempt to remedy psychological difficulties through discussions and interactions. We look at the different providers of treatment, discussing their training and qualifications.

We then discuss several of the most important forms of psychotherapy treatments, beginning with Freud's psychoanalytic approach and continuing with humanistic and behavioral approaches to maladaptive behavior.

Next we examine **biologically based therapy,** which takes a biological approach to treatment. We consider the use of drugs for dealing with maladaptive behavior, as well as more extreme measures such as electroconvulsive therapy and surgical techniques. Finally, we discuss the question of how well therapy actually works, and we consider how to find an appropriate therapist.

Solve your problems while gaining new insight into your behavior. I will help you discover the inner meaning of your dreams and desires. Soft, comfortable couch; long-term contracts available. Dr. George Rodinsky, (212) 587-4610.

Avoid costly, drawn-out therapy; do it the remarkably fast, modern way. With behavior therapy, we get to the heart of your difficulties immediately. In no time at all, we'll rid you of any problem you might display.

With this computer program you'll feel better in a snap. No more anxiety, no more rage; order this program, and you'll be a new person. Eric von Bulow, 45 Quaker Lane, Redmond Terrace, Montana.

Primal therapy: Compassionate, deep-feeling therapy available. Detroit (313) 783-2699, Houston (713) 256-8758.

DISCOVER YOU! Are you a 10 in looks, creativity, maturity (57 characteristics total)? Unique, confidential inventory. $1 for information. The Personality Market, 362 Middle Lane, Klaptree, R.I.

The classified section of many publications is filled with ads for psychological services only a little less sensational than the ones displayed above. (In fact, the last two are actual quotes.) The prevalance of this kind of advertising illustrates the bewildering array of different forms of treatment and types of therapists.

Yet one form of treatment is not the same as other forms; some problems respond more readily than others to certain kinds of treatment, and some therapists can better help particular individuals and problems. We begin our look at the major forms of treatment by discussing the distinctions between the various helping professionals.

Ph.D., Psy.D., M.D.:
Sorting out the ABCs of treatment providers

A look through the yellow pages of the telephone directory for any large city will demonstrate the varieties of help available, ranging from psychologists and psychiatrists to palm readers and mind readers. Obviously, some are more legitimate than others. Among the ones that are best suited to help:

● **Counseling psychologists** have Ph.D. or Ed.D. degrees in psychology or education. They are trained to deal with everyday adjustment problems and are often found in university counseling centers.

● **Clinical psychologists** typically hold Ph.D.'s or Psy.D.'s, although some have only Master's degrees. They specialize in the assessment and treatment of psychological disturbances.

- **Psychiatrists** have medical degrees. They are physicians who have received specialized training in maladjusted behavior. Because they have medical training they are able to prescribe drugs.

- **Psychoanalysts** have degrees in either medicine or psychology, and specialize in the psychoanalytic model developed first by Freud.

- **Psychiatric social workers** hold M.S.W.'s Master's degrees in social work. They treat people with adjustment problems in home or work settings, including individuals with marital or child-rearing problems.

How does one choose which of these professionals is most appropriate? In most cases, the nature of the difficulty a person is experiencing provides the best guide. If, for instance, a person is out of touch with reality, a psychiatrist would probably be the best choice, since most severe forms of mental disturbance employ drug treatments—which only a psychiatrist is qualified to prescribe.

On the other hand, if a person is suffering from a less extreme disorder, such as difficulty in adjusting to college or anxiety that impedes test-taking performance, a psychologist may be the most appropriate choice, since psychologists have been specifically trained to deal with problems encountered in everyday living.

Probably the most sensible way to begin looking for an appropriate help provider is to consult a local community mental health facility, college counseling service, or community health organization. After an initial consultation they often will help in the selection of an appropriate therapist.

It is important to keep in mind that a person's title alone is no guarantee of appropriate training. For example, someone using the title "therapist" can be completely unqualified, since in many states *anyone* is legally able to use the label. One way to determine the qualifications of a help provider is to ask whether he or she is state- or board-certified. Moreover, in cases in which there is no state certification system, affiliation with a university or teaching hospital is another useful criterion.

The View from the Couch:
Psychodynamic therapy and psychoanalysis

Patient (a fifty-year-old male business executive) *I really don't feel like talking today.*

Analyst *(Remains silent for several minutes, then) Perhaps you'd like to talk about why you don't feel like talking.*

Patient *There you go again, making demands on me, insisting I do what I just don't feel up to doing. (Pause.) Do I always have to talk here, when I don't feel like it? (Voice becomes angry and petulant.) Can't you just get off my back? You don't really give a damn how I feel, do you?*

Analyst *I wonder why you feel I don't care.*

Patient   *Because you're always pressuring me to do what I feel I can't do. (Davison & Neale, 1978, p. 472.)*

Perhaps this excerpt from a therapy session fits your idea of what therapy is all about: a patient discussing his concerns while a silent therapist asks probing questions and ponders what the patient says but reveals little of his or her own thinking.

In fact, this is not an altogether inaccurate interpretation of **psycho-dynamic therapy,** a form of therapy that is based on the premise that the source of maladaptive behavior is unresolved past conflicts and anxiety over the possibility that unacceptable, unconscious impulses will enter the conscious part of a person's mind. To keep this from happening, people use **defense mechanisms**—psychological strategies that protect them from their unconscious impulses (as discussed earlier in Chapter 6). In some cases, however, the defense mechanisms are not entirely effective and may lead to psychological distress and symptomatology.

The goal of therapy is to confront the unconscious conflicts and impulses that are at the root of anxiety by bringing them out of the unconscious part of the mind and into the conscious part. To do this, psychodynamic therapists use a variety of techniques, all of which consist of efforts to lead patients to consider and discuss their past experiences. Starting with their earliest memories, the goal is to dislodge long-hidden crises, traumas, and conflicts that are producing current distress and anxiety (Masling, 1986). In this way, patients will be able to "work through" their difficulties, thereby allowing the pain they cause to be dissipated.

Freudian therapy: Psychoanalysis   The psychodynamic therapy pioneered by Freud, known as **psychoanalysis,** is typically long and expensive. Patients often meet with their analyst for several hours each week (in some cases as many as five or six days weekly) for a number of years. During the sessions

In psychoanalysis, clients are asked to record their dreams for later discussion with their analyst.

they typically use **free association,** in which patients are told to describe whatever comes into their minds, whether or not it makes sense. In fact, patients are urged not to impose logic upon their thoughts, because it is assumed that important clues to the unconscious are provided by the patient's uncensored free associations.

Another important technique is **dream interpretation,** in which patients carefully describe their dreams. Psychoanalytic therapists look to the **manifest content of dreams** (their surface description) to provide clues to the **latent content of dreams** (the true message of the dream). To do this, they make interpretations of the meanings of dreams, often viewing the manifest content as a series of symbols about the underlying meaning of a dream. For instance, a dream in which the dreamer reports running back and forth through a subway station may be interpreted by an analyst as a frustration about sexual intercourse. (For an example of dream interpretation, see the Do It! box.)

DO IT!

INTERPRETING A DREAM

According to psychoanalytic theory, the content of dreams contains important clues to a person's subconscious. To get a feeling for how a psychoanalytically oriented therapist might interpret a dream, read the following dream and try to guess what its meaning might be:

I am in a gym, performing various exercises, with some other men. They are arranged in a line, in which they perform the exercises. I try to join the line at the head, but am rejected; I then try for the second place, and am rejected again; I try one place after the other till coming to the end of the line, and am rejected from every one of them.

This is what the patient's therapist had to say about the dream:

The analyst points out that the dream seems to involve men only. The dreamer then realizes that the men in the dream were actually boys from his all-male Catholic primary school, a place dominated by 'oughts' and 'shoulds.' With this come unpleasant memories of the gym class, which the dreamer hated passionately. The only reason he attended was because he was forced to; had it been left up to him he would not have shown up at any of the classes. As an afterthought, he adds that his mother also thought that 'it was good for you.' The imagery of the dream is direct and clear—the dreamer is being rejected from the line; he does not belong there. (Kaufmann, 1979, p. 111.)

Free association and dream analysis do not always proceed smoothly, due primarily to the phenomenon of resistance. **Resistance** is an inability or an unwillingness to discuss or reveal particular memories, thoughts, or motivations. Psychoanalysts assume that the same forces that work to keep past conflicts in the unconscious continue to operate, forcing the therapist to be constantly vigilant against resistance and to interpret its meaning. The person in our earlier example who said, "I really don't feel like talking today" is displaying resistance. **Transference,** in which patients come to see the analyst as symbolic of significant others (such as a parent or lover) from their past, can also occur during therapy. Transference can be seen in the example that starts this section: When the patient complains about the undue demands being placed on him by the therapist, he may be expressing resentment over his *parents'* treatment of him rather than that of the therapist.

Contemporary psychoanalytic treatment   Because the process of interpretation and revelation of unconscious conflicts is difficult, traditional psychoanalytic treatment is time-consuming and expensive. In fact, because there is no conclusive proof that years of therapy work much better than shorter versions, contemporary psychodynamic therapy tends to be shorter, usually lasting no longer than three months or twenty sessions (Garfield & Bergin, 1986). Moreover, rather than dwelling on a patient's childhood history and past conflicts, contemporary psychodynamic therapists concentrate on a patient's current relationships and level of functioning (Strupp, 1981; Reppen, 1981).

Although contemporary psychodynamic therapy has become considerably more affordable—both in time and money—it still has its critics. For instance, it is best suited to a particular kind of patient, sometimes called a YAVIS—young, attractive, verbal, intelligent, and successful (Schofield, 1964). Inarticulate and less intelligent patients find the requirement of rehashing their past to be difficult, even with the best of therapists. Moreover, the success of psychodynamic therapy is highest with a relatively limited range of adjustment problems, being most effective with patients with anxiety disorders. Patients with more severe problems are less likely candidates for psychodynamic therapy.

Client, Help Thyself:
Humanistic approaches to therapy

"Do it yourself." This might be the credo of **humanistic therapy,** which has as its basic premise the notion that people have control of their own behavior, that they can make choices—good and bad—about what happens to them, and that it is basically up to them to solve the difficulties that occur during the course of daily life. Instead of therapists being the relatively active and directive figures they are in psychodynamic approaches, humanistic therapists see themselves as guides or facilitators, leading people to the point where they can come to realizations about themselves and make changes in their lives.

Several different treatment approaches fall into the humanistic camp. In **client-centered therapy,** the goal is to enable people to better reach their potential for self-actualization (the state of self-fulfillment discussed in Chapter 4). According to Carl Rogers, the major proponent of client-centered therapy, therapists should provide **unconditional positive regard,** expressions of acceptance regardless of what the client says or does (Rogers, 1951; 1980). He reasons that the use of unconditional positive regard creates an atmosphere in which clients are able to come to rational and appropriate decisions about themselves and their own lives. A major goal of therapy, according to Rogers, is to allow people to accept their current self-concept. He suggests that rather than striving for some unobtainable and unrealistic ideal, they ought to focus on the positive aspects of themselves as they currently are.

Client-centered therapy makes use of a method called **nondirective counseling,** in which therapists clarify or reflect back in some way what the client has said, rather than interpreting or answering the client's questions. Consider, for instance, the following dialogue, typical of nondirective counseling:

Client   *I've been having trouble with my roommate. We haven't been getting along too well. I've been in a lot of arguments over little things with her lately and found it difficult to get over them. She's just started annoying me.*

Therapist   *You really are angry with her.*

Client   *Well, it's not that it's undeserved. She's gotten awfully thoughtless and inconsiderate. Last night she kept playing her record player, even though she knew I had to study. I just had to study for a biology test; she knew how much trouble I would be in if I didn't do well.*

Therapist   *It seems that you're not just upset about your roommate but about your studies as well.*

As you can see from this exchange, this therapist's role is primarily one of reflecting back and clarifying what the client has said. In client-centered therapy, therapists try to understand the world from the perspective of the client, honestly describing how they would feel in a similar situation.

Putting together the parts: Gestalt therapy   Remember the time your little brother broke your favorite toy? Do you recall how angry you were and how consumed with rage you felt? According to a group of therapists working from the gestalt perspective, that anger and rage may still be with you in some form, and the best way to rid yourself of it might be to hit a pillow, punch a punching bag, or scream in frustration.

In **gestalt therapy,** it is assumed that people carry with them conflicts from the past that affect their present-day relationships. According to Fritz Perls, who originated the therapy mode, the best way of dealing with the anger would be to reenact specific conflicts, taking the roles of various participants (Perls, 1967; 1970). For example, a client might first play the part of his brother, then himself, and then his mother, who may have been involved in the initial altercation. By seeing the situation through the eyes of other participants, people in therapy are assumed to understand their current problems better, and ultimately to experience life in a more complete way.

Client-centered therapy and gestalt therapy, the most representative of the humanistic therapies, share similar features. They emphasize that which is uniquely human and the degree to which individuals are in control of their problems. Rather than viewing people who are in therapy as "patients"—which implies a passive role—they view them as "clients," suggesting more of a partnership.

On the other hand, they share some of the criticisms that have been made regarding humanistic approaches. Conceptions of humanistic therapy are relatively imprecise, lacking some of the scientific and theoretical sophistication of other approaches. Moreover, humanistic approaches are best suited for highly verbal clients who have difficulties with anxiety, social skills, self-esteem, or the expression of feelings. As is the case with psychoanalytic approaches, more severe disorders are treated more effectively by other forms of treatment.

Group Therapy

In contrast to the other forms of treatment we have been discussing, some forms of therapy involve more than just one individual and therapist. For example, in **group therapy,** several unrelated people meet with a therapist to discuss some aspect of their psychological functioning.

In group therapy, people typically discuss their problems with the group, which is often centered around a particular difficulty, such as alcoholism or a lack of social skills. The other members of the group provide emotional support to members, as well as providing advice on ways in which they have coped effectively with similar problems.

Groups vary a great deal not only in the particular model that is employed (there are psychoanalytic groups, humanistic groups, and so forth), but also in the degree of directiveness the therapist takes. In some groups, the therapist is quite directive, while in others he or she allows the members of the group to set their own agenda and determine how the group will proceed.

Because several people are treated simultaneously in group therapy, it is a much more economical means of treatment. On the other hand, critics argue that the individual attention inherent in one-to-one therapy is lacking in group settings, and that especially shy and withdrawn individuals may not receive the necessary attention in a group.

Meri Houtchens-Kitchens/The Picture Cube

Group therapy may rely on the therapist to lead and guide the group, or it may be more loosely structured, as this parent support group.

Psychology for You:
Who makes a good therapist?

If you are considering entering therapy, one thing you probably want to know is just what sort of individual your therapist ought to be. Regardless of the specific form of treatment you enter, there are several guidelines that you can follow to determine whether a specific person will make a good therapist for you:

● Check the therapist's credentials. Therapists should have the appropriate degrees, certification, and licensing for the type of therapy you are entering. Just as the first thing you would ask a car mechanic is whether he or she is qualified and experienced with repairs on the make of car you have, you should ask a potential therapist to describe his or her background and experience with the kind of problem you are encountering.

● A therapist should be clear on the goals of treatment, the expected length of treatment, and criteria for assessing whether the goals of treatment are being attained. Although you should be wary of anyone who promises a "cure" by a certain date, it is reasonable to discuss estimates of how long the therapeutic process will continue and reassess progress after a reasonable trial period of treatment.

● You should feel a sense of trust for the therapist. If you feel uneasy after a few sessions because you are being treated in a way that bothers you, or if the therapist seems inept, dishonest, or unethical, follow your feelings. Try to discuss them honestly with the therapist, and if you remain dissatisfied, seek help elsewhere.

● The major providers of therapy are counseling psychologists, clinical psychologists, psychiatrists, psychoanalysts, and psychiatric social workers.

● Psychodynamic therapy is based on the premise that the basic source of maladaptive behavior is unresolved past conflicts and anxiety over the possibility that unacceptable unconscious impulses will enter the conscious part of the mind. Psychoanalysis is the type of psychodynamic therapy developed by Freud.

● The basic premise of humanistic therapy is the notion that people have control of their own behavior, that they can make choices about their lives, and that it is up to them to resolve their own problems. Among the two most frequently employed forms of humanistic therapy are client-centered and gestalt therapy.

● In group therapy, several unrelated people meet with a therapist to discuss some aspect of their psychological functioning.

CHECK YOURSELF

1.   Select the most appropriate treatment provider based on the problems presented in the right column.

_____ psychiatric social worker

a.   Jessica recently experienced an episode during which her sense of reality was severely distorted.

_____ clinical psychologist

b.   Martin cannot seem to handle the stress of adapting to his first semester in college.

_____ psychiatrist

c.   Christopher and Melanie both work full time and are concerned that the situation may be having an adverse impact on their young daughter.

_____ counseling psychologist

d.   Cathy fears that her psychological disturbances may be serious and would like someone to assess her problem and provide treatment.

2.   Sandy's therapist has asked her to blurt out whatever comes into her mind without attempting to make sense of the content. This psychoanalytic technique is known as:
   a.   dream interpretation
   b.   free association
   c.   transference
   d.   resistance

3.   The meaning underlying a client's detailed description of his or her dream is known as the _____ _____ of the dream.

4.   Modern psychoanalysis continues to rely heavily on the patient's distant history. True or false?

5.   Establishing an atmosphere of total acceptance is a basic tenet of:
   a.   client-centered therapy
   b.   psychodynamic therapy
   c.   gestalt therapy
   d.   psychoanalysis

_____

(See answers to these questions at the bottom of page 268.)

8.2   REPLACING BAD BEHAVIOR WITH GOOD BEHAVIOR:
Behavior Therapy Treatment Approaches

● You watch a plane fly overhead.

● You make a flight reservation.

● You drive to the airport.

● You buy a ticket for your flight.

● You step into a plane.

● You watch the plane's door closing.

● You listen to the engines start.

● You look out the window as the plane taxies down the runway.

● You feel the plane taking off.

● You are in the air.

If you had a flying phobia, this list might represent a set of your greatest fears, ending with the most unpleasant thought you can imagine. To a therapist using a behavioral approach, however, such a list might be the beginning of the end of your fear of flying. In fact, as we shall see in this part of the chapter, this is just one of a variety of procedures used by behavior-oriented therapists to deal with problems of adjustment.

Modifying Maladaptive Behavior:
Behavior therapy

Behavior therapy follows the premise that it is unnecessary to delve into people's past or dig into their psyches. Instead, it assumes that maladaptive behavior is learned, and that the goal of treatment is for the patient to either learn new behavior to replace the faulty skills that have been acquired or unlearn previously learned maladaptive behavior.

There are actually several distinct forms of therapy that are behavioral in nature. In **aversive conditioning,** basic principles of learning, first developed by Pavlov, are employed to teach people to have an unpleasant reaction to a stimulus that was initially enjoyed, but has become abused. For example, a woman with a drinking problem might be given an alcoholic drink at the same time she is given a drug that produces nausea and vomiting. After repeated pairings of the alcohol with the drug, the alcohol begins to be associated with vomiting and loses its appeal. Even the sight, smell, or thought of liquor may become sufficient to induce an aversive reaction.

Although aversive conditioning works effectively for several kinds of problems—including liquor and drug abuse and some kinds of sexual deviations—the positive effects are relatively short-lived in many cases. Moreover, there are important ethical problems regarding the use of aversion techniques that use potent stimuli such as electric shock (Sulzer-Azaroff & Mayer, 1986).

The counterpart of aversive conditioning is **systematic desensitization,** in which a stimulus that evokes pleasant feelings is repeatedly paired with a stimulus that evokes anxiety, in the hope that the positive feelings will eventually become associated with the anxiety-producing stimulus, thereby alleviating the anxiety (Wolpe, 1969; Rachman & Hodgson, 1980). For example, a person with a fear of flying might first be asked to construct a **hierarchy of fears**—a list, in order of increasing severity, of stimuli associated with his or her fears—such as the one that starts this section. After the hierarchy has been developed, the person is taught the kind of full-body relaxation techniques discussed in Chapter 6.

The next step in the process is for the therapist to teach the patient to put himself or herself into a relaxed state and then to ponder the fears in the first step of the hierarchy. Once the person can do that, he or she gradually moves up the hierarchy and is able to think about—and eventually experience—his or her most potent fears without feeling anxious.

Systematic desensitization has been shown to be an effective treatment for many sorts of problems, particularly phobias, anxiety disorders, and even some kinds of sexual problems such as impotence and fear of sexual contact (Karoly & Kanfer, 1982). It is possible, then, to learn to be comfortable with the things you once feared most.

Using reinforcement to shape adaptive behavior   The principle behind your grandmother promising you an ice cream cone if you behaved has been well established by behavior therapists. In one form of therapy sometimes used with severely disturbed patients in institutions, for example, people are rewarded with tokens such as poker chips or play money for displaying adaptive behavior. In this system, known as **token economy,** they can later exchange their tokens for some desired object or activity, such as a candy bar, new clothes, or more comfortable bedding.

CHECK YOURSELF: ANSWERS

1. c, d, a, b   **2.** b   **3.** latent content   **4.** False   **5.** a

Alan Carey/The Image Works

Mental hospitals
sometimes use a token-
economy system which
gives patients tangible
rewards for improving
their behavior.

Individuals with less serious problems may use another form of behavior therapy called contingency contracting. Suppose you were trying to lose weight. In **contingency contracting,** you would draw up a written agreement with your therapist, giving him or her a relatively large sum of money. If you reach your desired weight, the contract might allow you to reward yourself with the money the therapist has been holding—perhaps by splurging on a new jacket or by going to an expensive concert. If you fail, the contract might specify that the therapist give the money to an organization that you do not support, such as a group supporting a reduction in financial aid to students.

A more indirect form of therapy that employs reinforcement relies on **observational learning,** or **modeling** the behavior of others. Behavior therapists have used modeling to systematically teach people new skills and techniques for handling their fears and anxieties (Ciminero, Calhoun, & Adams, 1986). For example, children with fears of dogs have been shown movies of a child playing with a dog. The dog-fearing child watches the "fearless peer" walk up to the dog to touch, pet, and play with it (Bandura, Grusec, & Menlove, 1967). By observing the fearless peer's pleasure while playing with the dog, observers can shed their own fears.

Other procedures based on observational learning involve learning social skills, such as maintaining eye contact. A therapist may model appropriate behavior to teach it to a person who has never learned the skill (Sarason, 1976).

When Thinking Right Leads to Feeling Right: Rational-emotive therapy

● I must do everything right.

● I must be loved or approved by virtually every significant other person for everything I do.

● I should be thoroughly competent, adequate, and successful in all possible respects if I am to consider myself worthwhile.

● It is horrible when things don't turn out the way I want them to.

● This test can make or break my future.

Do you ever make such statements? Before you answer "no," consider this: According to one approach to therapy, developed by psychologist Albert Ellis, many of us do engage in this type of thinking, called **catastrophizing**. Ellis's premise is that many people suffer from psychological maladjustment because they harbor these kinds of irrational, unrealistic ideas about themselves and the world (Ellis & Grieger, 1986; Ellis, 1962; 1975).

The approach that Ellis takes to treatment is called **rational-emotive therapy**. Such therapy attempts to restructure a person's belief system into one that is more rational, realistic, and logical. To do this, the therapist offers strong, sometimes even blunt, arguments against the faulty beliefs, as illustrated in this example of a therapist's encounter with a woman whose love affair had ended:

"But you don't seem to understand," Myra wailed. "He has left me. I not only loved him, but had my whole future planned in and around him. Nothing has meaning any more. Everything I try to do, everywhere I go, everything I even try to think about is just plain empty without him." And she dived, for the twelfth time that session, for her wad of Kleenex tissues.

The therapist responds:

"Yes, I don't seem to understand. But I do understand; and it is you, in all probability, who don't. You don't—or, rather, I should really say you won't understand that it is over, and there's not a damned thing you can do about it right now to start it up again. And what you especially don't or won't understand is that the only sane thing to do, at the moment, is to start thinking about what else and who else can be interesting and enjoyable to you. No use repeating over and over that 'life is empty without Robert'—thereby making it as empty as you're saying it is. . . . I am sure,

*in fact I have every confidence, that you can go on telling yourself for the
next twenty-five years or so what a stinking, horrible, catastrophic shame
it is that Robert has left you and rendered your poor, poor life infinitely
barren. You can do it, all right, if you just keep telling yourself such non-
sense. On the other hand, if you decide that instead of sitting around in
feebleminded grief you'd like to develop an interesting and enjoyable life—
this you can do by saying different kinds of sentences to yourself and
learning to believe and act on them." (Ellis & Harper, 1961, pp. 116–117.)*

As you can see, this almost brutal interchange is quite different from
other forms of therapy we have discussed. (Consider, for example, how at
odds it is with how a client-centered therapist might respond to the woman's
concerns!) The excerpt does convey, though, many of the major characteristics of rational-emotive therapy, which include helping clients understand
that their anxiety is the result of what they are telling themselves about a
distressing situation and not as a result of the situation itself, training clients
to identify the irrational statements they make, and teaching alternative
statements that are more rational and helpful in dealing with the situation
(Bernard & Joyce, 1984). (To get an idea of how rational-emotive therapy
operates, see the Do It! box.)

DO IT!

REPLACING YOUR CATASTROPHIZING
WITH MORE RATIONAL THOUGHTS

At one time or another, most of us have found ourselves taking a test
during which we thought, "I don't know any of this material." To a
rational-emotive therapist, such a thought represents catastrophizing—it is ridiculous to say that we know *nothing* of the material. A more
reasonable—and certainly more adaptive—thought would be, "I'm
sure I know some of the material. I've got to slow down and recall the
material that I've studied. If I take it a little easy, things will come back
to me."

Below are some other kinds of catastrophic thoughts that people
frequently encounter when they are taking a test. Try to think of a
rational response to each. When you've gone through the list, refer to
the key at the bottom for some sample responses.

1. The test is so hard I'm sure to flunk.

2. I'm running out of time; everyone else is ahead of me.

3. If I don't get this important question right, I might as well not even
bother with the rest of the test.

4. The other people in the class are smarter than I am.

5. My mind is blank; I can't think of a thing.

6. I didn't study enough.

7. My life is going to be ruined if I fail this test.

APPROPRIATE RESPONSES

1. The test is so hard I'm sure to flunk. (There may be parts that are difficult, but some questions are going to be easier than others.)

2. I'm running out of time; everyone else is ahead of me. (While others may be leaving, not everyone is ahead of me. And even those who have left may not have been able to answer every question.)

3. If I don't get this important question right, I might as well not even bother with the rest of the test. (Every point counts, and I will pull up my score by answering as much of the test as I can.)

4. The other people in the class are smarter than I am. (There is a range of intelligence in every class; it is irrational to think that I am at the bottom of the distribution.)

5. My mind is blank; I can't think of a thing. (Slow down and relax. I have studied the material and knew it earlier today, so it is bound to come back to me.)

6. I didn't study enough. (I did spend some time studying, so what I have done will pay off.)

7. My life is going to be ruined if I fail this test. (I may feel unhappy, but my life is not going to be ruined if I fail.)

Rational-emotive therapy was the first of several outgrowths of behavioral approaches to therapy known as **cognitive-behavior therapy.** Unlike the original, "pure" forms of behavior therapy, which focus on people's outward behavior as the source of maladaptive behavior and pay little attention to their inner thoughts and feelings, cognitive-behavior therapy considers people's thoughts about themselves and the world as a legitimate focus of attention. In fact, the major purpose of such therapy is seen as an attempt to change people's thoughts; it is assumed that positive changes in behavior ultimately will follow.

Does It Work?:
Evaluating behavior therapy approaches to treatment

Both traditional forms of behavior therapy and cognitive-behavior therapy are quite effective in solving certain types of problems. Although it is dependent on the kind of problems being considered, the success rate for traditional behavior therapy ranges from 50 to 90 percent (Kazdin & Wilson, 1978; Garfield & Bergin, 1986). Behavior therapy is particularly effective for phobias and compulsions, for controlling impulses, and for training social skills. In addition, it works fairly rapidly.

On the other hand, behavior therapy has been criticized because of its inattention to the underlying problems that produce adjustment problems in the first place. Critics contend that by concentrating on overt behavior, this therapy ignores what may be the source of the disturbance. Moreover, in some cases, once one maladaptive behavior is eliminated, new ones sometimes crop up—a process called **symptom substitution.** Still, behavior therapy has a good history of success and is the therapy of choice for several kinds of adjustment problems.

Psychology for You:
Using behavior therapy to manage yourself

This discussion of maladaptive behavior and treatment has reiterated that you should be cautious about placing a diagnostic categorization on your own problems of adjustment. It follows, of course, that you should be even more hesitant about *treating* your difficulties on your own. Yet an approach to modifying your own behavior based on techniques developed by behavior therapists—called **behavioral self-management**—does allow you to act as your own therapist.

In behavioral self-management, people identify their problems and devise their own ways of using behavioral techniques. The technique is useful for a wide range of problems, including increasing exercise, becoming less sloppy, being better informed about current events, reducing smoking, studying more, working harder, and so forth. Although there are many different strategies for reaching such goals, the basic ones consist of altering the cues that promote an undesirable behavior (for example, by changing one's environment), directly modifying a response that should be changed, and/or providing reinforcement or punishment for desired or undesired behavior.

The difficulties associated with losing weight provide an excellent illustration of a problem that is responsive to self-management techniques. In the typical procedure, people are first asked to identify the cues and circumstances associated with eating. For a student named Jim, such cues included seeing food of any sort, being in the kitchen for any reason, watching TV or reading, talking with friends, boredom, or nervousness (Walker, Hedberg, Clement, & Wright, 1981).

To remedy his overeating, the general strategy employed was to find some way to reduce the number of cues that were associated with eating. To do this, a number of "rules" were set up about when, where, and how Jim could eat: He would not allow himself to eat unless he was seated at a table that had eating as its specific purpose (the kitchen table, dining commons table, or a restaurant). Moreover, he did not do anything except eat or speak to other people who were eating with him. This, of course, prevented snacking while watching TV, talking with friends, or doing most anything else. Finally, he stopped going into the kitchen for any reason but to prepare or eat a meal, and he kept all food in the kitchen inside cupboards to limit his exposure to foods that he was not preparing.

He also took several steps to try to weaken the association between the mere sight of food and eating. For instance, he took just one serving at each meal, and he never finished a portion. In addition, he would not sample anyone else's food. He also wrote down the time he ate, and would not eat again until at least three and a half hours had elapsed.

Using such self-management procedures, Jim was able to control his cravings for food and ultimately lose weight. Of course, there are other strategies available to him that might have been included in such a program. For instance, he could have developed a system for self-reinforcement, in which he would reward himself for a specified amount of weight loss by treating himself to a movie. The important point, though, is that behavioral self-management techniques provide a means by which you can, in one sense, be your own therapist.

Of course, as with any method, behavioral self-management does not work for every problem: If, for example, the difficulty involves a loss of touch with reality, this technique is hardly appropriate. But for many sorts of everyday problems that plague us, behavioral self-management has proven to be a viable and successful technique.

TO REVIEW

● Behavior therapy assumes that maladaptive behavior is learned, and that the goal of treatment is for the patient to learn new behavior to replace the faulty skills that were previously acquired, or to unlearn previously learned maladaptive behavior.

● Among the procedures used by behavior therapists are aversive conditioning, systematic desensitization, token economies, contingency contracting, and observational learning or modeling.

● Rational-emotive therapy, a form of cognitive-behavioral therapy, has the goal of restructuring a person's belief system into one that avoids "catastrophizing" and is rational, realistic, and logical.

● Behavioral self-management is a procedure for allowing people to modify their own behavior.

CHECK YOURSELF

1. Janet overcame her fear of dogs by learning to relax while imagining confronting an angry dog. This behavioral technique is called:
   a. observational learning
   b. a token economy
   c. aversive conditioning
   d. systematic desensitization

2. Which of the following strategies *does not* directly employ positive reinforcement?
   a. systematic desensitization
   b. token economy
   c. observational learning or modeling
   d. contingency contracting

3. Rational-emotive therapy helps clients explore the meaning underlying their negative self-statements. True or false?

4. Because rational-emotive therapy addresses an individual's thoughts and feelings, it is known as _____ - _____ therapy.

5. Behavior therapy can be used in some instances without the guidance of a professional therapist. True or false?

_____

(See answers to these questions at the bottom of page 276.)

8.3 MEDICINE TO HELP THE MIND:
Biologically Based Treatments

Every morning without fail, Coreen Irvine takes two pills. One is a simple vitamin, the kind many of us take routinely. The other is more extraordinary. Made of a powerful natural compound, the second pill contains a substance that allows Irvine to prevent what she fears most: a return to the nightmarish existence she had when in the throes of major depression two years before. Her therapist has explained that as long as she takes the drug she should be able to lead a normal existence. Without it, however, her symptoms of severe mental disorder are likely to return. Irvine knows that she must take the pill for the rest of her life, but it is a small price to pay: to her, the small pills represent nothing less than salvation.

The pills that Coreen Irvine takes daily represent a relatively recent innovation in the treatment of maladaptive behavior. In fact, the use of medicine to control maladaptive behavior is an example of just one of several treatment approaches that focus on biological, as opposed to psychological, means of treatment. Growing out of the medical model, research based on the medical model has identified several areas in which drugs and other biologically based therapies can be successfully employed to treat maladaptive behavior.

A Pill a Day Keeps the Psychologist Away:
Drug Therapy

There are several classes of drugs that provide the basis of therapy (called **drug therapy**) for maladaptive behavior. For example, **antidepressant drugs** are a class of medications used to elevate the mood of patients in severe

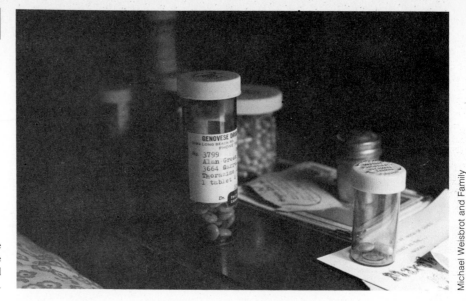

Drug therapy can be effective in controlling the symptoms of mental illness.

Michael Weisbrot and Family

cases of depression (McNeal & Cimbolic, 1986; Siris & Rifkin, 1983). Antidepressants are able to produce a long-term recovery from depression in 50 to 70 percent of patients. In some cases the depression does not return even after the drugs are stopped. In other cases, though, drugs must be continually taken in order to avoid a recurrence of the depression.

Antipsychotic drugs are responsible for the remarkable change that occurred in mental institutions during the 1950s. Before that time, such institutions were fearsome places, filled with moaning, rocking, clawing, and screaming patients, typically diagnosed as suffering from schizophrenia and being out of touch with reality. After the introduction of antipsychotic drugs, however, the scene became, almost overnight, more placid. Today, drug therapy is the treatment of choice for severe types of maladaptive behavior, such as schizophrenia, and some 90 percent of all hospitalized patients receive some form of medication (MacDonald & Tobias, 1976; Carson, 1983).

While antipsychotic drugs produce dramatic improvements in patient behavior, they do have several serious drawbacks. They may produce serious side effects, such as dizziness, dryness of the mouth and throat, and even the development of irreversible tremors and a loss of muscle control (Kane & Siris, 1983). Moreover, they do not produce a "cure" for maladjustment in the same way that taking penicillin cures an infection; once the drugs are no longer being taken, the original symptoms generally return.

CHECK YOURSELF: ANSWERS
1. d **2.** a **3.** False **4.** cognitive-behavior **5.** True

Perhaps the worst side effects, however, are psychological. As Mark Vonnegut (whose schizophrenia was considered in Chapter 7) describes, antipsychotic drugs have a numbing effect on one's perception of life:

What the drug is supposed to do is keep away hallucinations. What I think it does is just fog up your mind so badly you don't notice the hallucinations or much else. . . . On [drugs] everything's a bore. Not a bore, exactly. Boredom implies impatience. You can read comic books . . . you can tolerate talking to jerks forever. . . . The weather is dull, the flowers are dull, nothing's very impressive. (Vonnegut, 1975, pp. 196–197.)

The minor tranquilizers: Antianxiety drugs   What are the most frequently prescribed medications in the United States? If you guessed medication for stress and anxiety such as Valium, Miltown, or Librium, you're correct; drugs of this sort consistently make the "top ten" of physicians' prescription lists. In fact, some 10 to 15 percent of the population take Valium with some regularity.

Antianxiety drugs (or **minor tranquilizers,** as they are sometimes known) are designed to reduce the level of anxiety experienced by people, primarily by lowering excitability and partially by producing drowsiness. They are used not only to treat temporary and minor problems of adjustment (family physicians most often prescribe them to deal with tension and minor symptoms of anxiety, such as headaches and stomachaches), but as part of treatment programs for people with more serious disturbances, such as panic disorders.

In comparison to the more potent antidepressant and antipsychotic drugs, the effects of antianxiety drugs are less powerful, yet they still can produce relatively serious side effects. For example, they may produce fatigue and grogginess. Even worse, there is the possibility of dependence on the drug, causing people to take it whenever they feel upset. Finally, antianxiety drugs taken in combination with liquor can produce a fatal reaction.

Plugging into Treatment: Electroconvulsive therapy (ECT)

One of the most controversial treatments for psychological disorders is **electroconvulsive therapy (ECT),** whereby an electric current of 70 to 150 volts is passed through the head of a patient for about 1.5 seconds. The anesthetized, unconscious patient, who often undergoes ten such treatments in the course of a month, usually experiences a seizure during the administration of the current.

ECT often brings about the termination of severe symptoms of depression and sometimes schizophrenia, when drugs have proven ineffective. Although there can be side effects, most often a temporary loss of short-term memory, disorientation, and confusion, the benefits of the treatment seem to outweigh the obvious distastefulness of an approach that conjures up

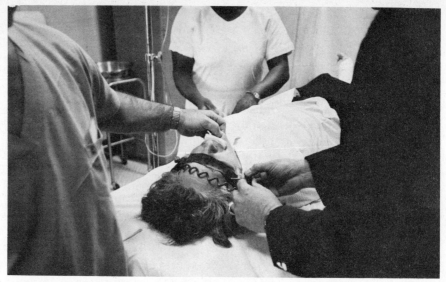

Paul Fusco/Magnum

Electroconvulsive therapy
is sometimes effective in
treating disorders, notably
severe depression, which
psychotherapy and drugs
have failed to alleviate.

images of capital punishment. ECT—as it is now carried out—is considered by most experts to be a humane procedure. Indeed, complications arise in only about 1 in 1700 treatments, and the risks do not seem any higher than when anesthetics are used alone (Holden, 1985). Still, there is controversy about the approach—some critics think it may cause permanent neurological damage—and it is usually used only as a treatment of last resort (Fisher, 1985; Sackheim, 1985).

Cut It Out:
Psychosurgery

If the root cause of mental disturbance is some dysfunction of the brain, why not sever the offending portion of the brain, hopefully ridding the patients of their symptoms? This is the reasoning behind the most controversial treatment for maladaptive behavior: psychosurgery. In **psychosurgery,** brain surgery is carried out to alleviate symptoms of mental disorder. The most typical procedure is the **prefrontal lobotomy,** which consists of surgically destroying or removing certain portions of a patient's frontal lobes, which are associated with emotions. In the 1930s and 1940s, people using this procedure assumed that patients would be less subject to emotional impulses, and thereby be in greater control of their own behavior.

In some cases, such assumptions were correct: patients with severe difficulties often improved. However, the cure was sometimes worse than the affliction, for patients often had marked personality changes and became dull, bland, and boring. Because of this kind of outcome, and due to the obvious ethical questions raised by the procedure, psychosurgery is almost never used today, except in instances in which drugs are ineffective in controlling aggressive or self-injurious behavior or there is intolerable, uncontrollable pain in terminal cases (Valenstein, 1986).

The Billion-Dollar Question:
Which treatment works best?

More than 2 million people in the United States are, at this moment, under formal treatment for some form of maladaptive behavior. Millions more are probably in need of treatment (see the Do It! box). With a problem this big, the question of "which treatment works best" takes on a new urgency. Moreover, it has an important economic aspect to it, given that the money spent on treatment easily runs into the billions of dollars annually.

DO IT!

THE MENTAL STATE OF THE UNION:
WHO NEEDS TREATMENT?

While the varieties of treatment are many, the question of which and how many people require treatment remains unanswered. To find an answer, the National Institute of Mental Health is carrying out a census to determine the kinds of disorders people are suffering from. Researchers have interviewed some 20,000 Americans and used the information they gathered to predict the kinds of disorders characteristic of the general population.

Before you see the numbers the study arrived at, take a minute to make some estimates of your own by filling in the blanks below.

1. Approximately _____ percent of all Americans currently suffer from some psychological disorder.
Of those people, there are about

2. _____ million who have an anxiety disorder

3. _____ million who have an obsessive-compulsive disorder

4. _____ million who have a panic disorder

5. _____ million who have schizophrenia

6. _____ million who have an antisocial personality

7. _____ million with an affective disorder, such as depression

ANSWERS   (1) 20 percent; (2) 13.1; (3) 2.4; (4) 1.2; (5) 1.5; (6) 1.4; and (7) 9.4.

The number of people projected to suffer from some form of major psychological maladjustment is probably larger than you might have anticipated. These are, indeed, troubled times.

In the current phase of the census, the researchers are seeking to determine which conditions seem to benefit most from what kinds of treatment. Ultimately, they will try to anticipate the kinds of events that trigger problems of adjustment.

Source of figures: National Institute of Mental Health, 1984.

Unfortunately, there is no simple way to determine who needs treatment and what treatment is best. It is necessary to ask a more fundamental question: Does *any* therapy really work?

At one time, most people simply assumed that therapy was effective. However, in the early 1950s psychologist Hans Eysenck published a literature review and claimed that people who received psychodynamic and related therapies were no better off at the end of treatment than people who were on a waiting list to receive therapy but who had not yet been able to start it (Eysenck, 1952). According to him, about two-thirds of people who had no treatment simply lost their symptoms of maladjustment—a process called **spontaneous remission,** in which a person recovers without treatment.

The study was controversial from the start. Criticisms centered around the inadequacy of the data Eysenck reviewed, which was lacking in many ways. For example, the data often were based on self-reports of therapists and patients, none of whom would be expected to be unbiased observers. Moreover, since the definition of maladaptive behavior is so unclear, the study had no easy way of distinguishing patients who had improved from those who had not.

Despite these problems, Eysenck's review served as an impetus for a long—and continuing—series of studies designed to demonstrate that therapy works, and most experts feel that therapy, in general, *is* effective (Garfield & Bergin, 1986; Casey & Berman, 1985; Smith, Glass, & Miller, 1980). Moreover, the rate of spontaneous remission is only around 40 percent, meaning that almost two-thirds of people with maladaptive behavior would not improve without intervention of some sort.

The harder issue is determining which form of therapy works most effectively. Because different treatments are appropriate for specific sorts of problems, it is inherently difficult to compare different forms of therapy and their rates of "cure." Compare, for instance, behavior therapy with psychoanalytic therapy: Is behavioral treatment that "cures" a fear of heights equivalent to psychoanalytic treatment that resolves a person's anxiety about a parent's death? Clearly, tallying cure rates is not without difficulties.

Despite these problems, researchers have attempted to compare rates of cure for people who enter a particular type of therapy, and the results are clear. If people make a reasonable initial choice—meaning that the kind of therapy they obtain is appropriate for the problem they have—then the rates of success for different therapeutic approaches are reasonably equivalent. Statistically, it appears that people who receive treatment appropriate to their problem have a 70 to 85 percent greater rate of improvement than people who do not receive treatment (Berman, Miller, & Massman, 1985; Orwin & Cordray, 1984; Smith, Glass, & Miller, 1980).

The crucial point here, of course, is choosing the appropriate therapy. We have discussed the forms of treatment that are most appropriate for a given type of problem, yet many people experiencing maladaptive disorders may find it difficult to identify what is and is not appropriate. The choice of what form of therapy to seek out, then, is critical.

One way of dealing with the problem is to choose a therapist who is identified as eclectic. **Eclectic approaches to therapy** employ a variety of techniques drawn from several different treatment approaches. By picking and choosing among various techniques, the eclectic therapist is able to choose a mix of treatment procedures that is most appropriate for the specific requirements of the difficulties for which a person is seeking help (Nelson, 1983).

Psychology for You:
Choosing the right form of psychotherapy

You've decided that a psychological problem you're experiencing is sufficiently bothersome to warrant some professional attention. Now what?

In addition to the necessity of determining the credentials of the therapist, which we discussed earlier in the chapter, there are several guidelines you can follow in choosing a way to enter therapy. Among the most important:

● Explore your difficulties initially with someone who will be able to give you general advice on the best course of treatment; *then* seek out a therapist who is able to provide such treatment. Health clinics, family physicians, and college health, counseling, and mental health services are good starting places for someone with a psychological problem.

● Choose a therapist in whom you feel a sense of trust. Research has shown that therapists who are seen as warm, caring, and sensitive produce better results than those lacking such qualities (Truax & Mitchell, 1971).

● If a therapeutic approach is clearly not working, don't feel too embarrassed or ashamed to discuss it with your therapist. Changing therapy providers makes sense if you are uncomfortable with your progress—or, worse yet, if you feel that your problems are mounting instead of being relieved.

● Remember that therapy requires a good deal of work on your part. It is not possible to sit back passively and let the therapist work *on* you; as with any change you want to bring about in yourself, it is *you* who must do most of the work. At times it may be painful; at times progress may appear to be slow; and at times you may want to just give up. Don't! The potential of therapy is great, for it may bring about a deeper understanding of yourself and a higher capability for dealing with the complex world around you.

The campus health center can be a good place to start when seeking help for a psychological problem. Although not all schools provide counseling or therapy, most can give reliable referrals.

Nancy Lutz/The Picture Cube

TO REVIEW

● Among the major drug therapies are antidepressant drugs, used to improve the moods of patients in severe depression, and antipsychotic drugs, used to control the severe manifestations of psychological disturbance.

● Antianxiety drugs or minor tranquilizers are designed to reduce anxiety levels, primarily by lowering excitability and partially by producing drowsiness.

● Electroconvulsive therapy and psychosurgery are less common biological therapies.

● The results of research on the effectiveness of therapy demonstrate that therapy is effective, as long as the treatment is appropriate for a given type of problem.

CHECK YOURSELF

1. Which of the following is *not* a potential side effect of antianxiety drugs?
    a. They may produce fatigue and grogginess.
    b. They can be fatal when combined with alcohol.
    c. They may lead to a loss of intelligence.
    d. They may produce a biological dependence.

2. Electroconvulsive therapy refers to the administration of shock to punish maladaptive behavior. True or false?

3. _____ _____ is a rarely used form of psychosurgery in which the portion of a person's brain associated with emotionality is destroyed or removed.

4. Hans Eysenck asserted in the early 1950s that two-thirds of untreated individuals simply lost their symptoms of maladjustment in a process known as _____ _____ .

5. An eclectic therapist is a specialist who treats only certain kinds of problems. True or false?
_____

(See answers to these questions at the bottom of page 284.)

TO SUMMARIZE

1. In this chapter we considered the varieties of treatments for maladaptive behavior. Treatment approaches tend to fall into two categories: psychotherapy, based on psychological approaches and accomplished through the interaction of therapist and patient (or client); and biologically based approaches, in which drugs and related therapies are employed. There is also a wide array of treatment providers, including counseling psychologists, clinical psychologists, psychiatrists, psychoanalysts, and psychiatric social workers.

2. Psychodynamic therapy is based on the premise that the sources of maladaptive behavior are unresolved past conflicts and anxiety over the possibility that unacceptable unconscious impulses will enter the conscious. To avoid this, people use defense mechanisms (psychological strategies to protect themselves from their unconscious impulses). The goal of therapy is to confront such buried impulses and bring them into the conscious. In psychoanalysis, the psychodynamic therapy developed by Freud, free association—a process in which patients describe whatever comes into their minds—and dream interpretation are employed. Contemporary psychodynamic treatment tends to be shorter and concentrates on patients' current relationships and levels of functioning rather than dwelling on the past. Psychodynamic therapy is best suited to relatively verbal and intelligent patients with anxiety disorders.

3. Humanistic therapy assumes that people are able to make choices in their lives, and it is basically up to them to solve their psychological difficulties. In one form of humanistic therapy, client-centered therapy, therapists provide unconditional positive regard to their clients, independent of what the clients do or say, thereby creating a supportive atmosphere that promotes rational decision making. Client-centered therapy also uses nondirective counseling, in which therapists clarify or reflect back what the client has said. In gestalt therapy, people are thought to carry with them conflicts from their past that affect their present-day relationships. To deal with these conflicts, clients are encouraged to reenact earlier conflicts, taking the roles of various participants. Although humanistic approaches emphasize that which is uniquely human and the degree of control people have over their own lives, they have been criticized for their relatively imprecise formulations and for being limited to clients with anxieties, social problems, low self-esteem, and emotional difficulties.

4. In group therapy, several unrelated people meet with a therapist in a group to discuss some aspect of their psychological functioning. Although this form of therapy is economical, some people may suffer from a lack of individual attention.

5. Behavior therapy assumes that maladaptive behavior is learned. The goal of treatment is for the patient to learn new behavior or to unlearn maladaptive behavior, rather than to examine underlying motivational conflicts or concerns. In aversive conditioning, people are taught to associate an unpleasant reaction to a stimulus that was initially enjoyed, such as pairing nausea with alcohol. In systematic desensitization, a stimulus that evokes pleasant feelings (such as relaxation) is repeatedly paired with a stimulus that evokes anxiety in order to associate the positive feelings with the anxiety-producing stimulus.

6. In another form of behavior therapy, reinforcement techniques are employed. Severely disturbed patients in institutions may be rewarded with tokens, which they can later exchange for a desired object or activity. A related use of reinforcement is contingency contracting, in which a therapist and client agree in writing to some behavior change. Reaching the goal produces a reward, while failing produces punishment. Finally, in observational learning, a client is exposed to a model who is reinforced for appropriate behavior.

7. Rational emotive therapy restructures a person's belief system into one that is more rational, realistic, and logical. The technique is designed to prevent catastrophizing, thinking that is irrational. Rational-emotive therapy is a form of cognitive-behavior therapy that considers people's thoughts about themselves and the world as a legitimate focus of attention.

8. Behavior therapies have good success rates, particularly for problems such as phobias, compulsions, impulses, and social problems. On the other hand, they have been criticized for ignoring the underlying problems that produce poor adjustment in the first place. Moreover, they may allow symptom substitution, in which the elimination of one form of maladaptive behavior is replaced by maladaptive behavior in another form. Still, behavior therapy is effective under many circumstances, including providing an approach to managing one's own problems (behavioral self-management).

9. Drug therapy uses drugs for the treatment of maladaptive behavior. Antidepressant drugs, for example, are a class of medications used to im-

CHECK YOURSELF: ANSWERS

1. c **2.** False **3.** Prefrontal lobotomy **4.** spontaneous remission **5.** False

prove the moods of patients in severe cases of depression. Antipsychotic drugs are used in cases of severely abnormal behavior. Such drugs have their drawbacks, however, including serious side effects, such as the development of irreversible tremors and loss of muscle control.

10. Antianxiety drugs (or minor tranquilizers) are among the most frequently prescribed medicines in the United States. They are meant to reduce people's levels of anxiety, primarily by lowering their excitability and partially by producing drowsiness. They are used to treat temporary and minor problems of adjustment and also for more serious disturbances. They, too, have their side effects, including the danger of dependence.

11. Other biologically based treatments include electroconvulsive therapy (ECT), in which an electric current is passed through a patient's head; and psychosurgery, brain surgery carried out to alleviate symptoms of mental disorder. Electroconvulsive therapy is still in use today—although it is a controversial treatment—but psychosurgery is almost never used.

12. Although difficult to ascertain, it does appear clear that therapy in general is more effective than no treatment. The rate of spontaneous remission—in which a person recovers without treatment—is only around 40 percent. It also appears that if people make good initial choices about a form of treatment appropriate to their specific behavior, the rates of success for different therapeutic approaches are reasonably equivalent. Statistically, it appears that people who receive treatment appropriate to their problem have 70 to 85 percent greater success than people who do not receive treatment.

KEY TERMS AND CONCEPTS

psychotherapy (p. 257)

biologically based therapy (p. 257)

counseling psychologists (p. 258)

clinical psychologists (p. 258)

psychiatrists (p. 259)

psychoanalysts (p. 259)

psychiatric social workers (p. 259)

psychodynamic therapy (p. 260)

defense mechanisms (p. 260)

psychoanalysis (p. 260)

free association (p. 261)

dream interpretation (p. 261)

manifest content of dreams (p. 261)

aversive conditioning (p. 268)

systematic desensitization (p. 268)

hierarchy of fears (p. 268)

token economy (p. 268)

contingency contracting (p. 269)

observational learning (p. 269)

modeling (p. 269)

catastrophizing (p. 270)

rational-emotive therapy (p. 270)

cognitive-behavior therapy (p. 272)

symptom substitution (p. 273)

behavioral self-management (p. 273)

drug therapy (p. 275)

latent content of dreams (p. 261)
resistance (p. 262)
transference (p. 262)
humanistic therapy (p. 262)
client-centered therapy (p. 263)
unconditional positive regard
(p. 263)
nondirective counseling (p. 263)
gestalt therapy (p. 264)
group therapy (p. 264)
behavior therapy (p. 267)

antidepressant drugs (p. 275)
antipsychotic drugs (p. 276)
antianxiety drugs (p. 277)
minor tranquilizers (p. 277)
electroconvulsive therapy (ECT)
(p. 277)
psychosurgery (p. 278)
prefrontal lobotomy (p. 278)
spontaneous remission (p. 280)
eclectic approaches to therapy
(p. 281)

TO FIND OUT MORE

Kroly, P., & Kanfer F. H. (1982). *Self-management and behavior change.* New York: Pergamon.

A self-help guide with scientific integrity, this guide to changing your own behavior can help you to modify a variety of the habits you like least.

Kanfer, F. H., & Goldstein, A. P. (Eds.). (1983). *Helping people change.* New York: Pergamon.

You will find a wealth of clearheaded advice in this volume, which discusses the various treatment techniques that are currently in use.

Masters, J. C., Burish, T. G., Hollon, S. D., & Rimm, D. C. (1987). *Behavior therapy.* (3rd ed.). San Diego: Harcourt Brace Jovanovich.

Written by experts in the field, this accessible book explores treatment based on behavioral approaches.

Belkin, G. S. (1984). *Introduction to counseling.* Dubuque, IA: Wm. C. Brown.

Gives an overview to the counseling process, illustrating the approaches used to help people with their difficulties.

Wedding, D., & Corsini, R. (1979). Great cases in psychotherapy. Itasca, IL: F. E. Peacock.

This volume illustrates some of the best-known cases of pioneering psychotherapists, including those of Freud and Rogers.

PART

IV

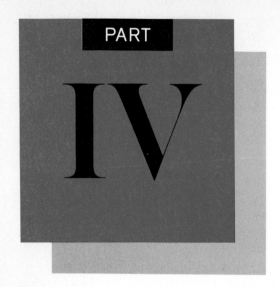

PART

IV

RELATIONSHIPS

In this part of the book, we encounter people in a variety of relationships and settings. We meet a professor whose interaction with his students relies on communication on both a verbal and nonverbal level. We encounter a man and woman who seem destined to spend their life together—until their relationship disintegrates. And we learn about how an adolescent is introduced to sex.

In Part IV, we consider the nature of the relationships which people form. We first discuss the means by which we communicate with others, using both verbal and nonverbal behavior. We then review specific kinds of relationships, considering the friendships we form with other people and the different aspects of love. Next we discuss a particular kind of relationship that is formalized by society—marriage—and focus on the factors that underlie success (and failure) in married couples. Finally, we consider sexual behavior, a fundamental aspect of some of our most important relationships.

In Chapter 9, then, the focus is on communication as it occurs on both a verbal and nonverbal level.

In Chapter 10, we discuss interpersonal liking and loving, emphasizing the factors that underlie the development of relationships.

In Chapter 11, marriage and divorce are considered.

Finally, in Chapter 12, we examine the impact of sexual behavior on people's relationships.

Communi-
cation

As Professor Feinman's eyes scanned the class, Harriet sank more deeply into her chair. The professor had a habit of calling on people in class when they didn't raise their hands, and Harriet certainly couldn't handle that today. Last night had been a late one for her: the "quick" movie and snack she agreed to have with Rick had run later than she'd anticipated, and she never got a chance to read the chapter in the textbook.

"Who can explain the dominant reaction to the wave of immigration in the nineteenth century?" she heard Professor Feinman say in a voice she found increasingly grating as the semester wore on. As he glanced toward her, she felt her muscles tense up. She did her best to look sufficiently interested and intelligent so he would look for someone who clearly didn't know the answer, someone he could have the pleasure of publicly humiliating. But at the same time, she tried not to look so very interested and intelligent that he would think she wanted him to call on her. It was a fine line to tread, but she thought she could do it pretty well—after all, she had been practicing since she first started school, and she knew how important it was to give the right impression.

Her thoughts were interrupted as she heard the professor say, "How about you, Harriet?" Quickly sitting up straight, her mind raced as she tried to come up with something. Trying to sound as if she knew what she was talking about, she mumbled something about the wave of immigration and the prejudices of the nineteenth century. But it wasn't good enough; Professor Feinman, sensing her basic ignorance, chose to ask a series of questions, a sardonic smile growing on his face. Finally, Harriet had to admit she hadn't done the reading. Her face flushed with embarrassment, and she silently cursed her bad luck.

While the moral of the above situation is obvious—it pays to complete one's assignments—it also provides us with an important lesson in communication. For as you consider what went on in Professor Feinman's class, you will notice communication that goes beyond just the words that are being spoken. Facial expressions, eye gaze, posture, tone of voice, and a host of other nonverbal behaviors provide information that is used by the participants to make sense of what is occurring. With and without words, we communicate impressive quantities of information.

This chapter examines the role that verbal and nonverbal communication plays in our lives. We begin by examining the spoken word, focusing first on the relationship between language and thought, considering how the way we communicate verbally may actually determine how we think about the world, and discussing how linguistic rules are used to facilitate social interaction. Finally, our examination of the spoken word concludes with a discussion of cultural variations in language.

Next, we turn to nonverbal behavior, considering facial expressions and how they are related to—and perhaps even produce—emotional reactions. We also look at eye gaze and body movements and their relationships to various emotional states, as we examine how well our nonverbal behavior actually reveals what we are experiencing.

In the final part of the chapter, we discuss how verbal and nonverbal behavior are combined as we communicate with others. We talk about some important cultural differences in communication and how we behave non-verbally when we hide our true feelings. Finally, we delve into ways that people might communicate more effectively with one another.

9.1   COMMUNICATING TO OTHERS WITH THE SPOKEN—AND WRITTEN—WORD

Although it had already left a blanket three feet deep, the snow showed no sign of abating. Paula, looking out the door of the cabin she was sharing with Ernie, was almost beside herself with glee. "Do you know what kind of snow this is?" she said as she peered out the door. "This is powder, and when it stops, we're going to have some terrific skiing. I haven't seen powder like this since I was in Montpelier three years ago. Usually you get frozen granular around here, but this is really different."

Ernie, unimpressed and ever skeptical, looked at the falling snow. "I admit it looks pretty," he said, "but what's all this about 'powder' and 'frozen granular'? To me, snow is snow; it all looks and feels the same."

"You'd feel differently if you were an experienced skier," replied Paula. "When you really get into skiing, you begin to talk about snow, and even think about it, in a different way."

If you have never skied, chances are you would agree with Ernie—snow is snow. While you might be able to tell the difference between snow that is easy to pack into snowballs and snow that is so powdery that it can't be packed, probably your understanding of snow is quite limited. On the other hand, the nature of snow is critically important to devoted skiers, and their awareness of such differentiations may well raise their level of skiing expertise.

The subtle variation in the way in which snow can be described illustrates an issue that is crucial to an understanding of language and the way it affects our everyday lives: the relationship between language and thinking. According to one theory, language and thought are linked together, with the language that we speak determining the way we think. In contrast, other theorists dispute this view, suggesting just the opposite—that language is a consequence of the way we think.

The view that language shapes, and may actually determine, the way people of a particular culture perceive, think about, and understand the world is known as the **linguistic relativity hypothesis** (Sapir, 1949; Whorf,

1956; Bloom, 1981). As an example of the kind of evidence used to support this hypothesis, consider the languages used by the Eskimos in the Arctic Circle and the Hanunoo tribe in Asia. It turns out that the Eskimo language has twenty or thirty different words for snow, and the language of the Hanunoo tribe differentiates between ninety-two kinds of rice. According to the linguistic relativity hypothesis, users of the Eskimo and Hanunoo languages think about snow and rice in a more sophisticated fashion than we English speakers, relegated as we are to so few words for each substance.

On the other hand, there is a clear alternative to the linguistic relativity hypothesis. Rather than language being the cause of the way we think about the world, language may be a result of our thinking. In this view, *thought* produces language. The only reason that Eskimos have so many words for snow and the Hanunoo so many words for rice is that snow and rice are considerably more relevant to them than they are to us. Following this logic, if we were to join their society, we could eventually learn to draw the distinctions between the different varieties of snow and rice, even if we did not learn their language.

Which sequence is correct—language shapes thought or thought shapes language? Although definitive work has not been done, it seems that there is no firm support for the linguistic relativity hypothesis. While language does have an influence on how we store information and how easily we remember it (Brown & Lenneberg, 1954; Brown, 1976), the statement that language determines the very way in which we think seems too strong (Au, 1983). Most researchers suggest, then, that the nature of our thinking shapes the language we use.

The Rules of Language
How language influences our interactions

While language may not determine our thinking about the world, there are many linguistic rules that have an important influence on the way we interact with others. For example, even simple conversations among English-speaking groups of people follow a ritualized set of rules that determine the order of conversation. Although we are not necessarily aware of the rules and probably could not, if asked, identify them, such rules are required to meet several underlying necessities of proper social intercourse: Each person must have a turn to speak, only one person may speak at a time, long silences in the conversation should be minimized, the order in which the speakers talk is not fixed ahead of time, and there needs to be a method to determine who speaks when (Clark & Clark, 1977).

The rules followed to meet these exacting requirements are relatively simple when just two people are conversing; the conversation simply alternates from one speaker to the other. But when more than two people are conversing, the interaction becomes more complex. However, it turns out that three simple rules underlie the coordination of such conversations:

Mark Antman/The Image Works

Most people would be unable to recite the socially agreed upon "rules" for conversation, yet we all follow them every day.

- Rule 1: The next turn goes to the person who is being addressed by the current speaker.

- Rule 2: The next turn goes to the person who speaks next.

- Rule 3: The next turn goes to the current speaker, if he or she resumes prior to anyone else beginning to speak.

These three rules form a hierarchy, with the first rule taking precedence over rules 2 and 3. If rule 1 is inappropriate, then rule 2 comes into play; and if rules 1 and 2 are inoperative, then rule 3 comes into effect. For instance, suppose Able, Baker, and Charlie are having a conversation. If Able asks Baker a question, then Baker should respond, and Charlie should not, according to rule 1. But if Able simply makes a statement, then either Baker or Charlie may speak next, according to rule 2. But if neither Baker or Charlie says anything, then Able is free to speak once more, according to rule 3. Of course, rule 2—which has precedence over rule 3—gives Baker or Charlie priority to speak next, even if Able wants to speak again.

Adjacency pairs   The rules of linguistic interaction go beyond merely indicating turn-taking behavior; they even shape the particular responses that we make in conversation. **Adjacency pairs** refers to sequential conversational turns, in which the second turn contains a reaction to the first turn.

There are several kinds of adjacency pairs, including the following:

- Question-answer sequence (A: "How's the weather?" B: "Rainy.")

- Greeting-greeting sequence (A: "Hi." B: "Howdy.")

- Offer-acceptance sequence (A: "Would you like a ride home?" B: "Sure.")

- Assertion-acknowledgment sequence (A: "Tom is putting on weight again." B: "He sure is.")

- Compliment–acceptance/rejection sequence (A: "Your tennis game is getting much better." B: "I wish you were right.")

- Request–grant/deny sequence (A: "Could you lend me your English lit notes?" B: "I guess so.")

While it may seem at first that these adjacency pairs represent a mere exchange of information, they do much more. Each pair carries with it the implicit notion that B is cooperating in the conversation by responding to A's first statement. In turn, this cooperation includes the implicit notion that the conversation can proceed.

The power of language: Saying who you are by how much you say "I would like you to meet Professor Robert Humbolt, Dr. Sandra Xavier, and Chief Justice Jonathan Cooper." If you were introduced to each of these people at a party, the nature of your conversation with them would probably be quite different than if they were introduced as "Bobby," "Sandy," and "Jonny."

The explanation for this difference lies in the power semantic and the solidarity semantic (Brown & Gilman, 1960). The **power semantic** is the power or status level that a speaker holds, while the **solidarity semantic** refers to the degree of shared social experience between two people. The power semantic suggests that people with high social status and power ought to be addressed with greater formality, while the solidarity semantic suggests that people with whom we share many social experiences can be addressed with less formality, even if they are of higher social status. Someone who lives next door to a distinguished judge might find it entirely appropriate to call him by his first name, given the shared social experiences of neighborhood life.

The power semantic and solidarity semantic affect the formality with which we address people, as well as the nature of the conversations we have with them. We are apt to be more comfortable disclosing personal information to people who are similar to us in social status, while conversations with higher-status individuals are likely to include less information regarding the personal details of our lives.

The *quantity* of speech is also related to the status of participants in a conversation. People of higher status tend to speak more than others, and, in group settings, more communications are addressed to them (Berger, Cohen, & Zelditch, 1973). In addition, the nature of communications received by high-status people is more positive than those directed at lower-status individuals (Forsyth, 1983).

Why do high-status people speak more than those of lower status? One reason is that people may assume that those of higher status have greater knowledge and understanding about the world, and so their opinion is sought out. It is also plausible that higher-status people attempt to maintain their higher status by speaking more frequently—or that they obtained their higher status in the first place, at least in part, because of their superior verbal skills. Although we don't know the specific reason for the higher verbosity of those of high status, it is clear that both quantitative and qualitative aspects of language reflect significant aspects of people's relationships with one another.

Nonstandard English: Cultural variations in language

Consider this dialogue between a 15-year-old named Larry and a questioner who is interested in Larry's feelings about God and life after death:

Q. *What happens to you after you die? Do you know?*

Larry *Yeah, I know.*

Q. *What?*

Larry *After they put you in the ground, your body turns into ah—bones. . . .*

Q. *What happens to your spirit?*

Larry *Your spirits—soon as you die, your spirit leaves you.*

Q. *And where does this spirit go?*

Larry *Well, it all depends. . . .*

Q. *On what?*

Larry *You know, like some people say if you're good . . . your spirit goin' to heaven . . . 'n' if you bad, your spirit goin' to hell. Well, [no]. Your spirit goin' to hell anyway, good or bad.*

Q. *Why?*

Larry *Why? I'll tell you why. 'Cause, you see, doesn' nobody really know that it's really a God. An' when they be sayin' if you good, you goin' t'heaven, tha's [wrong] 'cause it aint' no heaven for you to go to. (Labov, 1973, pp. 36–37.)*

On first reading, this passage seems to represent illogical reasoning and an unsophisticated grasp of the English language. Yet, if we look beyond the surface, we find a logical set of arguments. As linguist William Labov notes, an analysis of the passage reveals the following notions:

1. Everyone has a different idea of what God is like.

2. Therefore nobody really knows that God exists.

3. If there is a heaven, it was made by God.

4. If God doesn't exist, he couldn't have made heaven.

5. Therefore, heaven doesn't exist.

6. You can't go somewhere that doesn't exist.

7. Therefore, you can't go to heaven. Therefore, you are going to hell (Labov, 1973, pp. 36–37).

What makes the passage so difficult to understand initially is that Larry's use of English varies so much from standard usage. A 15-year-old black person from an impoverished background, Larry uses a form of **nonstandard English,** a variant of English which is spoken fairly consistently in some poor urban areas.

Despite its difference from standard English, nonstandard English follows regular patterns, including an absence of linking verbs ("she goin'" instead of "she is going"), improper verb agreement ("he come home" instead of "he comes home"), and omission of prepositions ("he teach Washington School" instead of "he teaches at Washington School"). In fact, the regularities are so great that some experts have argued that the use of nonstandard English ought to be allowed—and perhaps even encouraged—in school settings. They argue that nonstandard English meets the test of communicative competence by permitting speakers to communicate in an effective manner.

Speaking standard English at school may seem unnatural for a child whose family and neighbors normally use a nonstandard form of the language.

Susan Lapides/Design Conceptions

Other experts disagree, suggesting that the use of nonstandard English in broader society labels a speaker in socially undesirable ways. To these people, the use of nonstandard English should not be permitted in educational contexts, and children should be educated solely with traditional English.

Ultimately, the question boils down to a social issue and not a linguistic one. Given that speakers of nonstandard English are quite capable of communicating effectively within their own cultural group, neither standard nor nonstandard English can be said to be preferable to the other without making value judgments.

Psychology for You:
Avoiding sexism in language

In speaking at the leaste, let us kepe a natural order, and set the man before the woman for maners Sake. (Wilson, 1552, p. 189.)

If we were to take the advice of this sixteenth-century writer, our writing would continue to reflect the notion that men take precedence over women—not just in terms of language, but in everything else. As we discussed in Chapter 2, **sexism,** the view that women are inferior to men, is a pervasive prejudice with long-term historical roots.

The recognition that language might contribute to sexism grew out of the linguistic relativity hypothesis. Both linguists and nonexperts suggested that the use, for example, of "he" and "man" to refer to both men and women (as in "when the psychologist meets with a client, he is often . . ." or "man has but one heart, but two legs") helped to subtly promote and transmit from one generation to another the notion that men in some sense take precedence over women (Henley, 1977). Moreover, there was growing realization that primary school textbooks and stories often presented women in inferior roles (see the following Do It! box).

DO IT!

SEXISM IS NO FAIRY TALE

Even some of the most traditional stories place women and men in roles that convey messages that are, at best, questionable. Consider the story lines of the following well-known children's stories and try to identify some of the sexist elements in them:

1. "Snow White and the Seven Dwarfs"

2. "Cinderella"

3. "Lady and the Tramp"

4. "Rumpelstiltskin"

In "Snow White and the Seven Dwarfs," Snow White takes on the responsibility for taking care of the dwarfs; the dwarfs have a job, while Snow White cooks and cleans for them in their home in the woods. In "Cinderella," the motivation behind the prince's search for Cinderella is solely her beauty; they seemingly never hold any sort of meaningful conversation. The Walt Disney story of "Lady and the Tramp" shows Lady as petite and demure, while Tramp is wild and daring. Finally, in "Rumpelstiltskin," the heroine readily marries the prince, who has just previously forced her—upon threat of death—to spin gold for three nights.

The fact that some children's stories portray males and females in traditional or undesirable roles does not necessarily suggest that they should be rewritten. Instead, it illustrates that even well-known stories can subtly communicate messages with unintended sexism.

In order to prevent the transmission of sexism through the use of language, several suggestions for the use of language have been offered by psychologists and linguists (Longyear, 1983). Some of the major rules—which you might have noticed are incorporated into this text—are as follows:

● *Avoid the use of the generic male pronoun when referring to both sexes.* For instance, it is wrong to say, "When an adolescent starts to define himself as a person, he does so . . ." if you mean adolescent males and females. Instead, you might use the plural, saying, "When adolescents start to define themselves as persons, they do so . . ." or rewrite without personal pronouns, as in, "The adolescent who starts a process of self-definition as a person. . . ."

● *Avoid the use of occupational titles that have sexist connotations.* For instance, replace chairman with chair, coed with student, delivery boy with deliverer, fireman with fire fighter, policeman with police officer, and repairman with repairer.

● *Avoid language that is supportive of stereotyping.* Do not use "male nurse" or "lady doctor" or "woman anthropologist" unless you are also going to say "female nurse," "gentleman doctor," or "male anthropologist."

● *Avoid subtle sexist assumptions.* A writer who says, "Wave after wave of immigrants arrived from Europe, bringing with them their wives and children" is assuming that immigrants must be men. But what were the wives and children, if not also immigrants?

TO REVIEW

● In contrast to the view that thought produces language, the linguistic relativity hypothesis suggests that people's use of language affects the way they perceive, think about, and understand the world around them.

● Language incorporates many rules that help regulate our social interactions with others. For instance, there are rules regarding turn-taking in conversation, as well as the kind of responses we make during conversations.

● Nonstandard English follows regular patterns and is used consistently in some urban areas of lower socioeconomic status.

● Psychologists and linguists have offered several suggestions for the use of language to avoid sexist speech.

CHECK YOURSELF

1. The theory that language results from the common thoughts held by members of a society is called the linguistic relativity hypothesis. True or false?

2. In a group situation, Jenny is asked a question by Michael and responds. After a pause she continues to speak. According to the hierarchical rules underlying group conversations, which of the following possibilities best predicts what should happen next?
   a. The next turn goes back to Michael.
   b. Other members of the group wait for Jenny to resume before speaking themselves.
   c. Jenny forfeits her opportunity to continue speaking until after someone else has spoken.
   d. The next turn goes to Jenny or anyone else who speaks before she has had a chance to resume.

3. Match the example on the right with the correct adjacency pair listed on the left.

_____ question-answer	1. a. "Would you like to have dinner tonight?" b. "Sure, I'd love to."
_____ greeting-greeting	2. a. "Can I borrow your car this afternoon?" b. "Sorry, but I need it."
_____ offer-acceptance	3. a. "Have you completed the assignment?" b. "Yes, I just finished."
_____ assertion-acknowledgment	4. a. "You've lost weight. You look great." b. "Thanks, but I have more to lose."
_____ compliment–acceptance/rejection	5. a. "This heat is oppressive." b. "It sure is. I feel so lethargic."
_____ request–grant/deny	6. a. "Good morning." b. "Hello there."

4. "I remember first starting my degree program. I addressed all the faculty as 'Doctor' or 'Professor.' Now that I have collaborated with them for three years, I'm more comfortable using first names." In this example, the

_____ semantic shifted, with shared social experiences, to the _____ semantic.

5.   Nonstandard English violates regular English in that its language structure is highly irregular and, in fact, almost random. True or false?

_____

(See answers to the questions at the bottom of page 304.)

9.2   NONVERBAL BEHAVIOR:
Communicating Our Emotions

The woman was in tears, appearing to have just witnessed an event no less somber than the death of a close relative. To the casual observer, she could not have looked more grief stricken. In contrast, her husband, standing at her side, had happiness written all over his face. He wore a broad smile, and he threw his head back as a roar of laughter and glee shook his body. He looked as if they had just won the lottery.

In fact, they had. As you can see for yourself, the couple in Figure 9-1 have just learned that they have won a multimillion-dollar lottery. Yet their nonverbal behavior could not be more different.

As this photo illustrates, we use **nonverbal communication**—communication that is distinct from words—to make important inferences about others and the emotions that they are experiencing. In fact, the nonverbal information we receive from others is transmitted simultaneously across many different **channels,** pathways along which messages flow. To understand fully how individuals communicate with one another, it is necessary

FIGURE 9-1
This man and woman, although displaying very different facial expressions, are responding to the same situation—winning a million-dollar lottery. (New York Times/ Neal Bonezi)

to consider such separate channels as facial expression, eye gaze, body movements, and even tone of voice.

Does the Face Act as the "Mirror of the Mind"?: Facial expressions

Was St. Jerome, writing in the first century AD, correct in his assessment that the face is the "mirror of the mind"?

In many respects, he appears to have been accurate, for facial expressions often do provide a clear indication of the emotion being experienced by a person. (To test your own abilities at identifying the emotions behind a facial expression, see the Do It! box.)

DO IT!

NAME THAT FACIAL EXPRESSION

The following six photos represent the primary emotions that have been consistently identified as being distinguishable by untrained observers. Write in the name of an emotion represented by the face under each of the photos:

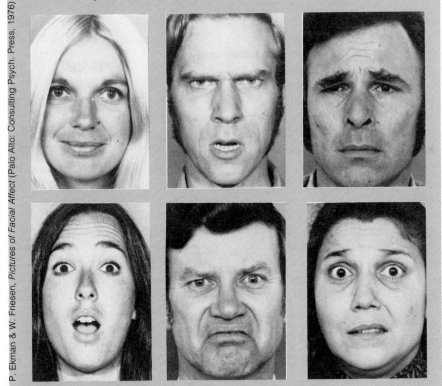

P. Ekman & W. Friesen, *Pictures of Facial Affect* (Palo Alto: Consulting Psych. Press, 1976)

ANSWERS   The six photos, in order of appearance, represent the emotions of happiness, anger, sadness, surprise, disgust, and fear.

The six emotions depicted in the Do It! box have been consistently distinguished in hundreds of experiments (Ekman, Friesen, & Ellsworth, 1982). These primary emotions are surprise, sadness, happiness, anger, disgust, and fear.

The six emotions represented in the photos are particularly noteworthy, as they are found not only in Western cultures but throughout the world. Regardless of where people have been raised or what learning experiences they have encountered, then, there seems to be universal expression of at least these basic emotions (Zivin, 1985).

To account for the similarities in the expression of the basic emotions, psychologist Paul Ekman suggests that facial expressions operate according to a facial affect program (Ekman, 1972). The **facial affect program** is analogous to a computer program that is turned on when a particular emotion is experienced. Assumed to be present at birth, the program activates a set of nerve impulses that control muscles to make the face display an expression characteristic of the emotion being experienced. For example, happiness is universally displayed by movement of the zygomatic major, a muscle that raises the corners of the mouth—forming what those of us who haven't taken a course in muscle physiology would call a smile.

Smile your troubles away: The facial feedback hypothesis   The lyricist who wrote the words "smile your troubles away" might well have been one of the first to suggest what has become known as the **facial feedback hypothesis.** According to the hypothesis, facial expressions not only *reflect* emotional experience, they are also important in actually *determining* how people experience and label emotion (Izard, 1977).

The fundamental notion behind the facial feedback hypothesis is that "wearing" a particular facial expression may cause us to experience the emotion that is congruent with the expression. Presumably, the expression provides muscular feedback to the brain, which produces the experience of the appropriate emotion. For example, the muscles that are activated when we intentionally frown may send a message to the brain indicating that we are unhappy—even if there is nothing in the environment to make us feel unhappy.

Some proponents of the facial feedback hypothesis take an even more extreme view, suggesting that appropriate facial expressions are necessary for an emotion to be experienced. In this view, if there is no facial expression there can be no emotion experienced (Rinn, 1984).

While evidence supporting the facial feedback hypothesis is not substantial, the results of one intriguing experiment—which you might want to try yourself—do lend it credence (Ekman, Levenson, & Friesen, 1983). In the experiment, a professional actor was asked to follow explicit directions regarding the movement of muscles (see Figure 9-2). Try it yourself, following these directions as they were given in the experiment:

CHECK YOURSELF: ANSWERS
1. False   **2.** d   **3.** 3, 6, 1, 5, 4, 2   **4.** power, solidarity   **5.** False

FIGURE 9-2
The instructions given this
actor were to (a) raise the
eyebrows and pull them
together; (b) raise the
upper eyelids; and
(c) stretch the lips
horizontally, back toward
the ears. If you follow
these directions yourself,
it may well result in your
experiencing fear.

- Raise your brows and pull them together.

- Now raise your upper eyelids.

- Now also stretch your lips horizontally back toward your ears.

If you carefully followed the directions—as the trained actor was able to do—you will have produced an expression that would look, to an observer, as if you were afraid. The important point, though, is what happens next: Does your fearful expression make you actually experience the emotion of fear?

If your experience is like that of the actor who participated in the experiment, you will show a rise in heart rate and a decline in body temperature, biological reactions that are characteristic of fear. In fact, the actors in the study showed physiological reactions congruent with the experience of each of the emotions for which they produced appropriate facial expressions.

In sum, the advice provided by the songwriter to "smile your troubles away" may not be much off the mark. If the facial feedback hypothesis ultimately proves valid, you might feel better just by smiling.

Windows of the Soul:
Eye gaze

Poets have always sung the praises of the eyes as a communication channel. Love, anger, power, and a wide variety of other emotions are thought to be revealed through people's eyes. As one ancient poet wrote, "The eyes without speaking reveal the secrets of the heart."

In many respects, research findings support such observations, for examination of the eyes reveals several consistent findings. One of the most stable findings regards eye gaze: the amount of eye contact between two people is a good indicator of the degree of interpersonal attraction between the two, with greater eye contact indicating greater attraction. This relationship holds not just for lovers, but for friends as well (Rubin, 1973; Exline & Winters, 1965; Kleinke, 1986).

The power of eye gaze is such that it not only reflects liking, but it can also *produce* attraction. In most cases, the more someone looks at us during social interaction, the more we like them—a fact not lost on salespeople, who learn early in their careers to look their customers straight in the eye.

On the other hand, not all cases of increased eye gaze are interpreted positively. In some situations, high levels of eye gaze are interpreted negatively. For example, a stranger who stares at you on the subway is not likely to engender much attraction; a quite opposite reaction, that of fear and anxiety, is a more probable result. The reason is that the eye contact is being interpreted as a hostile stare, a signal of aggression that exists throughout the animal kingdom (Greene & Reiss, 1984).

How does one distinguish between hostile and friendly gaze? In most cases, an analysis of the situation in which you find yourself will provide an answer. If high levels of gaze occur in a safe, secure context, the meaning of gaze is likely to be positive; but if they occur in a threatening situation, high levels of eye gaze are likely to be a deliberate display of hostility.

The Body Moves:
Communicating through kinesics

Although the face and eyes represent the major channels of nonverbal communication, the movements of the body also provide an important communicative medium. **Kinesics** is the study of how body language—movements of the hands, feet, and trunk—is related to communication.

Body movements, in some ways, lack the communicative abilities of both the face and eyes. The muscular structure of the body is less complex and does not allow the kind of fine movements of which the face is capable. Moreover, people are less used to employing movements of the body as a means of communicating, and therefore most people are relatively unaware of the messages that may emanate from it.

Still, body movements can and do provide important information about a person's psychological state. For instance, **adaptors** are specific behaviors that, at some point in a person's earlier development, were used for a specific purpose but are no longer a typical part of the person's everyday behavior. People under stress may sometimes rub their eyes, for example, similar to what they did as children when they hid their eyes to avoid viewing an unpleasant scene or situation. People may also cover their ears, as if trying to avoid hearing an unwanted message.

Illustrators are movements used to modify and augment spoken messages (Hager, 1982). If you were asked how to get to the campus library, you would probably employ an illustrator, pointing a finger in the appropriate direction as you explained verbally which way to go. Illustrators can also be used for emphasis, indicating, for example, the anger of someone who points her finger at you and declares how furious she is.

Finally, one of the most familiar body movements is the **emblem,** a body movement that replaces spoken language. Emblems are usually specific to

Maggie Steber/Stock, Boston

Body movements and postures provide clues to a person's emotional state. Former Ambassador to the United Nations Jeane Kirkpatrick appears to be feeling upset and discouraged in this photo.

a given culture, and they are understood by its members in the same way that most people understand the verbal language that is spoken.

Figure 9-3 illustrates several examples of common emblems and their meanings within our own culture. What is particularly interesting about emblems, however, is that the same emblem may have a very different meaning in another culture. For instance, the A-OK sign shown in the figure signifies the female sexual anatomy in many foreign countries and, if made by a man to a woman, represents a sexual proposition. Still another meaning is intended when one man makes the gesture to another; it is an insult to the second man's masculinity. It is easy to imagine the embarrassment gestures like this one can cause if used in the wrong environment.

FIGURE 9-3
Common emblems.

The thumbs up

The fingers cross

The fingertips kiss

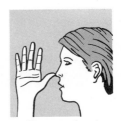
The nose thumb

The A-OK

Psychology for You:
Can you read a person "like a book"?

The authors of best-sellers such as *You Can Read a Person Like a Book* and *Body Talk* would have you believe people's nonverbal behaviors are an open tome in which their emotions and feelings are plainly written for all the world to see—if only others knew how to read them.

At best, such thinking represents an oversimplification; more likely, it is just plain wrong. Although nonverbal behavior does provide information about a person's emotional experience, it does not do so invariably. In fact, we monitor and control our nonverbal behavior in order to present ourselves effectively in social situations. Therefore, our nonverbal behavior may be more representative of what it is we are *trying* to convey to an observer than what it is we are actually experiencing. Moreover, because the same nonverbal behavior does not always represent the same thing, it is not reasonable to assume that there is a one-to-one relationship between a particular nonverbal behavior and a particular meaning.

There are, however, several principles that you can use to better understand the meaning of others' nonverbal behavior.

● Examine the social context in which nonverbal behavior occurs. Consideration of the situation and the environment will help you determine whether the behavior actually reflects the person's emotions and what message is being conveyed. For example, although a high level of eye contact is typically related to attraction, it may also be a sign of hostility; as we discussed earlier, only by considering the context in which it is occurring is it possible to understand the meaning of the behavior.

● Put yourself in the role of the communicator from whom you are receiving a message. What are his or her attitudes and background? What is he or she likely to be trying to convey? Can you perceive an underlying motivation behind the message that might affect how it is being conveyed? By considering such aspects of communication, you may be able to obtain a more accurate reading of the true nature of the message.

● Focus both on what people are saying *and* on what they are doing. Seeing a discrepancy between someone's verbal channel of communication and what they are doing nonverbally is an indication that you ought to monitor both channels more closely. In cases of inconsistencies between verbal and nonverbal communication, the nonverbal communication channel is often more accurate, since it is less easily manipulated than the content of what is being said (Ekman, Friesen & Ellsworth, 1982).

TO REVIEW

● Nonverbal communication, communication that is distinct from words, represents several channels of communication.

- Facial expressions reveal at least six basic emotions: surprise, sadness, happiness, anger, disgust, and fear. The facial feedback hypothesis suggests that facial expressions not only reflect emotional experience but also help determine how people experience and label emotion.

- Eye contact and body movement are also related to people's emotional experience. However, nonverbal behavior in general does not always provide an accurate assessment of a person's emotional experience.

CHECK YOURSELF

1. The facial feedback hypothesis suggests that distinct facial expressions result from experiencing certain emotions. True or false?

2. Depending on the circumstances, gazing into another's eyes can produce attraction or anxiety. True or false?

3. _____ is the study of how we communicate through body language.

4. When asked for her opinion of the restaurant, Monica held out her hand with an extended thumb pointing downward. She had communicated through a body movement known as a(n):
   a. adaptor
   b. emblem
   c. kinesic
   d. illustration

5. "Reading" people's body language to understand their underlying emotions can be done consistently with a high degree of accuracy. True or false?

(See answers to the questions at the bottom of page 310.)

9.3   GETTING IT TOGETHER:
Combining Verbal and Nonverbal Communication

You're at a crowded, noisy party. You've just been introduced to someone of the opposite sex, and the conversation begins in fits and starts as you go through the usual ritual about names, origins, year in school, and so forth. But something about the interaction strikes you as a little different. As the conversation continues, you notice the eyes of the speaker piercing into you, gazing with interest at your every word. The person moves closer, and the tone of voice that you both use takes on increasing intimacy. At one point in the conversation, you find yourself lightly touching this person's shoulder as you make a humorous point. Your new acquaintance smiles broadly, and you do the same. You begin to realize that the two of you are somehow in synch, and you hope you'll begin seeing a lot more of each other.

If you analyze the encounter described above, you'll see that it is based on several channels of communication—eye gaze, facial expressions, tone of voice, touching, and, of course, the conversation itself. Indeed, there are probably other communication channels, such as the posture of the participants, the way in which the trunk and limbs are moved, and even the way the two people are dressed that communicates information of one sort or another.

No one channel by itself produces the total effect brought about by the combination of all the individual channels. We turn now to the ways in which the composite of verbal and nonverbal messages communicates information—both voluntarily and unwittingly.

Communicating Our Feelings

When someone says, "I feel so embarrassed; my face must be red," or "I was scared to death when that big dog ran up to me; I was shaking all over," you probably know just how they felt. There is a close link between the way we speak about our feelings and the way such feelings are expressed and experienced nonverbally.

One explanation for the relationship between the physical experience of feelings, nonverbal behavior, and the language we use to communicate such feelings is the rather dramatic physiological reaction produced by strong emotions. Consider, for example, what happens if you are walking down a dark alley and find yourself confronted by a menacing stranger carrying a gun. As you experience a surge of fear, your body is probably reacting by activating the **autonomic nervous system,** which controls involuntary, biological functions such as heart rate and digestion. Among the specific changes that occur are the following:

- Rate and depth of breathing increase.

- Heart rate increases, pumping more blood through the circulatory system and causing the face to flush.

- The pupils of the eyes open wider, allowing more light to enter and thereby increasing visual sensitivity.

- The mouth becomes dry as the salivary glands and the rest of the digestive system stop functioning.

- The sweat glands increase their activity to allow a reduction in the increased body temperature.

- Hair all over the body stands on end as the muscles under the skin contract.

CHECK YOURSELF: ANSWERS

1. False   **2.** True   **3.** Kinesics   **4.** b   **5.** False

Due to the obvious nature of many of these internal biological changes, fear becomes apparent. Some theories of emotion suggest that the physiological reactions to a stimulus actually produce a particular emotion: You experience fear, for example, *because* your heart is beating rapidly and you are breathing deeply. Other theories suggest that the physiological reaction is a *consequence* of experiencing an emotion; in this view, your heart beats quickly and you breathe rapidly because you are afraid.

Although there is no definitive evidence to recommend one theory over the other (Scherer & Ekman, 1984), it is clear that emotional responses produce cues that are communicated to others. Yet not everyone is equally sensitive to the emotional cues produced by others; there are some important differences between various people in how well they understand the meanings of such cues.

On a general level, women appear to be more successful at identifying the meaning of emotional cues (Hall, 1985). Interestingly, there are also individual differences in the specific channels to which people pay attention. Some people, for instance, seem to focus primarily on facial channels, while others gain more information by listening to a person's tone of voice (Zuckerman, Lipets, Koivumaki, & Rosenthal, 1975).

DO IT!

THE EYES HAVE IT

To understand the subtleties involved in decoding the nonverbal behavior of others, look at the two photos in Figure 9-4 and decide which is the more attractive of the two:

FIGURE 9-4

Michael Weisbrot and Family

If you are like most people, you chose the second photo. The reason? The pupils of the woman's eyes have been slightly retouched in order to make them appear larger. This small change is enough to make most people prefer the second picture. In fact, male subjects tend to rate the woman with small pupils as cold, selfish, and hard, while the woman with larger pupils is viewed as soft, loving, and warm—even though subjects can't say why (Hess, 1975).

The Seeds of Miscommunication: Cultural differences in communication

As the white teacher asks her young black student a question, the student gazes at the floor. The teacher rephrases the question, and still the student averts his eyes, although this time he mutters "um-hum." Convinced that the student is not even paying attention to the question, the teacher sharply reprimands him.

If the teacher in the above scene had more awareness of the differences between white and black communication patterns, her response might have been quite different. For it turns out that there are several significant cultural differences between the behavior of whites and that of blacks relating to communication—differences that may lead to rather profound difficulties in cross-race communication.

For instance, although whites and blacks spend approximately the same amount of time gazing at a speaker's face when they are listening, the timing and sequence of gazing differs considerably (LaFrance & Mayo, 1976). Moreover, black parents sometimes teach their children that looking an adult in the eye is a sign of disrespect, while white parents typically tell their children just the opposite. The black child who looked away from his white teacher, then, may simply have been trying to convey a sense of respect.

Blacks' and whites' communicative patterns differ along other dimensions, as well. For example, there is a variation in **back-channel behaviors,** the short sounds that listeners make during a conversation to indicate that they are listening to what the speaker is saying. The typical back-channel pattern for white listeners is a nod of the head, accompanied by verbal responses such as "um-hum." Black listeners, on the other hand, use *either* head nodding *or* a verbal response to indicate that they are attending to what the speaker is saying (Erikson, 1979). What this suggests is that a black student who averts his eyes but who accompanies that nonverbal behavior with a back-channel verbal "um-hum" may be just as attentive as a white student who gazes directly at the teacher. A white teacher who knew more about the communicative behavior of blacks, then, might have avoided this cross-cultural miscommunication.

As you might imagine, the differences in communication styles are still greater when considering cultures that are even more disparate than white and black cultures. For example, consider the way in which friendship is communicated in certain cultures: "Men throw excrement at each other and comment loudly on the genitals of their respective parents when they meet; this behavior . . . is a proof of love to friends. In Tanzania, if a man meets a woman who is his special friend, he has the right to insult her and playfully pummel her like a punching bag" (Brain, 1977, p. 83).

In sum, there is ample opportunity for miscommunication to occur when people from different cultures communicate with one another. It is necessary, then, to carefully consider the meaning of each of the various communication channels, in isolation and together, when seeking to understand the behavior of people of a different culture.

Hiding Our Feelings:
Display rules

Your rich Aunt Minnie, who has always doted on you, gives you a small, elegantly wrapped box for your twenty-first birthday. You rip open the package, hoping for something great: expensive jewelry, maybe a stock certificate, or perhaps even the keys to a new car. As you get through the layer of tissue paper, though, the actual contents of the box becomes apparent: a set of six monogrammed handkerchiefs. Your disappointment is acute.

Does Aunt Minnie, eagerly waiting for your reaction, see your true emotions? Most likely not. Instead, you will probably lift up your head and give Aunt Minnie a dazzling smile, telling her that nothing could please you more than a set of handkerchiefs.

The reason Aunt Minnie may be fooled is due to your use of **display rules,** learned rules about the appropriateness of showing the proper emotion. Such rules, which are particularly applicable to nonverbal behavior, are learned during childhood. We are taught which emotions are appropriate to reveal and which are not (Feldman, 1982).

There are actually several ways in which display rules operate to control expressions of emotion: masking, intensifying, deintensifying, or neutralizing an emotion (Ekman, Friesen, & Ellsworth, 1972). In the case of Aunt Minnie, **masking**—one emotion disguised behind the facial expression for another—is occurring. **Intensifying** occurs when we exaggerate an expression, such as a smile, to indicate a greater degree of feeling than is actually being experienced. In **deintensification,** the opposite occurs: We mute or minimize our feelings, as when an opponent in a game is losing and we try to contain our feelings of pleasure. Finally, we may try **neutralizing** our facial expressions, blandly attempting to show no emotion at all. This might occur, for example, in a poker game, in which we try to reveal nothing about the merits of the hand we have been dealt (hence the term "poker face").

Which display rule operates in a given situation is based on several different factors. Some rules are elicited by the specific situation, others are cultural in nature, and still others are particular to a given individual (Ekman, Friesen, & Ellsworth, 1982). For instance, some situations have very explicit rules, allowing the display of certain emotions but not others. To

Dan Chidester/The Image Works

While loud, vehement cheering over a sports event on television is acceptable in a bar, it might be frowned upon in another situation, such as in a department store where television sets are sold.

take one example, it is considered appropriate to weep openly at funerals and to cheer and smile at a baseball game. At the same time, we are constrained by the same situational display rules from openly cheering at the funeral of a person from whom we will inherit millions of dollars, or, conversely, from crying over the losing streak of our favorite baseball team, no matter how unhappy we are.

There are also display rules that operate across particular cultures relating to the general display of emotion. For instance, in many Asian cultures it is considered inappropriate to display emotions in too extreme a form, while in Latin and Mediterranean cultures more volatile displays of emotion are acceptable.

Finally, individuals sometimes learn their own special set of display rules. A father might teach his son that it is "unmanly" to cry; the son might be taught to substitute the display of anger and aggression whenever he is experiencing sadness. In extreme cases, people learn such inappropriate display rules that their nonverbal behavior becomes maladaptive, and their behavior is perceived by others as being "odd."

The Truth about Lies:
Unmasking the truth using nonverbal behavior

Although display rules provide us with general guides for our communicative behavior, they are not the only consideration when it comes to understanding what it is that we communicate to others. Our communicative behavior is not always under our total control; in some cases feelings that we are trying to hide "leak out," despite our efforts to keep them under wraps. In fact, there is evidence that people who are trying to be verbally deceptive can sometimes provide good evidence, through nonverbal behavior, that they are lying (Zuckerman, DePaulo, & Rosenthal, 1981).

What cues reveal a person is being deceptive? Compared to truthful communications, lying seems to produce less eye contact, fewer head nods, less smiling, fewer gestures, more frequent shifts in body movement, less directness in postural orientation, changes in speech speed and pitch, and more discrepancies among various nonverbal behaviors (Miller & Burgoon, 1982).

It is interesting to note that the list of cues that most reliably reveal deception does not include language and most facial expressions—which as a rule provide the greatest amount of information about people's feelings. In fact, language and facial expressions provide relatively little information about whether or not a person is being deceptive. The reason is that those two channels have the greatest **controllability**—the ability to communicate what one intends to express.

The controllability of language and facial expressions is high for several reasons. We have the greatest experience in using them; we have received the most feedback from others regarding them, and thus we have learned to control the impression they make on others more effectively than we have with other communication channels. Moreover, the amount of control we can exert through our facial expressions and language is high. The face has many muscles, so it can be controlled to a considerably higher degree than other parts of the body. Conversely, the lack of skill we have in communicating via other parts of the body makes those a more accurate source of information about when a person is being deceptive. Because their controllability is so low, they reveal deception more readily.

Of course, the fact that certain channels are more indicative of deception than others does not mean that observers can successfully decode the meaning of such behavior. Indeed, research in controlled laboratory settings shows that observers accurately discern truthfulness or deceit 40 to 60 percent of the time (Miller et al., 1981). Although deception may be revealed through certain communication channels, then, we are not always able to detect it.

Still, there is a general lesson to be learned from research on deception: Honesty is the best (communication) policy. Because deceptive communications are apt to be revealed through several nonverbal channels, you reduce the possibility of cross-channel inconsistency by keeping deceptive communications to a minimum.

Psychology for You:
Communicating effectively

What is the best advice that can be given to people who wish to communicate effectively? Several broad principles can be suggested (Hart, Friedrich, & Brooks, 1975; Knapp, 1984):

● Show commitment to listeners, and demonstrate that their relationship with you is important. Respond to the feedback that they are giving you, and show immediate benefits that they can derive from perceiving your message.

● Demonstrate that you are committed to your message. Cite personal experiences, take firm stands, and be knowledgeable.

● Make it clear that you hope the relationship between you and the people with whom you are communicating will be an ongoing one. Show that they have an impact on you, and discuss what your future intentions are.

● Ensure that you are providing a message that is understandable and can be utilized. The worth and merit of a communication should be made apparent to listeners.

● Try to keep cross-channel communications consistent. Keep in mind that you are constantly transmitting messages via multiple channels, and there should be consistency across channels in order for a recipient of a message to get its full impact.

● Use feedback from others to modify your own communicative behavior. As you are interacting with others, note the reactions—both verbal and nonverbal—that your communications are producing, and, if they are not producing the intended reaction, change them.

● Be responsive to others. Remember that communication is a two-way partnership between you and the person who is receiving your messages. If you are not responsive to others, what you are trying to convey will soon fall on deaf ears—and blind eyes.

TO REVIEW

● The physical experience of feelings, nonverbal behavior, and the language we use to communicate such feelings are closely related.

● There are significant cross-cultural differences in communicative behavior.

● Display rules are learned rules that inform people about the appropriateness of showing emotion. We are not always effective in hiding emotion, however, since certain communication channels may reveal when we are being deceptive.

CHECK YOURSELF

1. Which of the following is *not* a response produced by the autonomic nervous system in reaction to a fearful situation?
   a. pupil constriction
   b. heart rate increase

c. breathing becoming faster and quicker

d. pupils opening wider

2. It is unclear whether we experience emotion as a result of a physiological reaction, or whether emotion precedes and produces the physiological reaction. True or false?

3. During a conversation in which they are asked a question, black people are more likely than white people to:

a. maintain *minimum* eye contact

b. maintain *maximum* eye contact

c. respond verbally

d. offer no response at all

4. Roger was determined to express disapproval if Peter made a racial comment at the party. Therefore, when Peter did make a racial slur, Roger flashed him an exaggerated frown. What type of expression did Roger use?

a. deintensification

b. neutralization

c. masking

d. intensification

5. Language and facial expressions most clearly convey that deception is occurring. True or false?

(See answers to the questions at the bottom of page 318.)

TO SUMMARIZE

1. The linguistic relativity hypothesis suggests that language shapes, and may actually determine, the way people of a particular culture perceive and understand the world. However, there is a clear alternative—that language is a result of our thinking, rather than a cause. In this view, thought produces language. Although there is no definitive evidence, most researchers now reject the linguistic relativity hypothesis.

2. Although we are generally unaware of them, there are several linguistic rules that determine the course of social interactions. For example, one set of rules determines speaking order and turn-taking behavior in conversations. Language also provides cues regarding the status of speakers through the power semantic (the power or status level that a speaker holds) and the solidarity semantic (the degree of shared social experience between two people). Finally, another linguistic rule concerns quantity of speech, which is related to the status of participants in a conversation. Higher-status people tend to speak more than lower-status individuals.

3. Some residents of poor urban sections of the United States speak a form of nonstandard English. Nonstandard English follows regular patterns, including an absence of linking verbs, improper verb agreement, and omission

of prepositions. The use of nonstandard English represents a social issue, not a linguistic one.

4. Standard language patterns may reflect sexism, the view that women are inferior to men. Nonetheless, many people eliminate this kind of unintentional bias using specific, nonsexist words and phrases.

5. The six primary emotions displayed by facial expressions are surprise, sadness, happiness, anger, disgust, and fear. Because of the universality of these emotions across different cultures, Ekman has suggested that facial expressions operate according to a facial affect program, analogous to a computer program that is turned on when a particular emotion is experienced.

6. The facial feedback hypothesis suggests that facial expressions not only reflect emotional experience but are also important in determining how people experience and label emotion. Thus, "wearing" a facial expression provides muscular feedback to the brain, which produces the experience of the appropriate emotion.

7. Eye gaze is a sensitive indicator of the nature of the relationship between people. For instance, the amount of eye contact between two people indicates the degree of interpersonal attraction between them, with greater eye contact indicating greater attraction. However, very high levels of eye contact may indicate hostility and aggression.

8. Kinesics is the study of how body language—movements of the hands, feet, and trunk—is related to communication. Among the kinds of body movements are adaptors (specific behaviors that, at some point in a person's development, served a special function or purpose but are no longer part of the person's set of everyday behaviors), illustrators (movements used to modify and augment spoken messages), and emblems (body movements that replace spoken language).

9. Because strong emotions produce dramatic physiological reactions, there is a relatively close relationship between the experience of emotions, nonverbal behavior, and the verbal language used to communicate our feelings. There are several theories regarding how people experience emotions; some suggest that physiological reactions produce emotions, and others suggest that physiological reactions are a consequence of experiencing an emotion.

10. There are several kinds of individual difference relating to communication. For instance, women are generally more sensitive to nonverbal cues. There are also cultural differences in communication. For example, the timing and sequence of gazing differs between whites and blacks. Back-channel behaviors, the short sounds that listeners make to indicate that they are listening to a speaker, also differ between whites and blacks.

CHECK YOURSELF: ANSWERS

1. a **2.** True **3.** a **4.** d **5.** False

11. Display rules are learned rules that inform people about the appropriateness of showing emotion. The primary display rules are masking, intensifying, deintensifying, and neutralizing an emotion. Despite the operation of display rules, however, our true emotions sometimes "leak out." In fact, nonverbal behavior can sometimes provide good evidence that people are being verbally deceptive.

KEY TERMS AND CONCEPTS

linguistic relativity hypothesis (p. 293)

adjacency pairs (p. 295)

power semantic (p. 296)

solidarity semantic (p. 296)

nonstandard English (p. 298)

sexism (p. 299)

nonverbal communication (p. 302)

channels (p. 302)

facial affect program (p. 304)

facial feedback hypothesis (p. 304)

kinesics (p. 306)

adaptors (p. 306)

illustrators (p. 306)

emblem (p. 306)

autonomic nervous system (p. 310)

back-channel behaviors (p. 312)

display rules (p. 313)

masking (p. 313)

intensifying (p. 313)

deintensifying (p. 313)

neutralizing (p. 313)

controllability (of verbal and nonverbal behavior) (p. 315)

TO FIND OUT MORE

LaFrance, M., & Mayo, C. (1978). *Moving bodies: Nonverbal communication in social relationships*. Monterey, CA: Brooks/Cole.

A lively introduction to the area of nonverbal communication, covering the major channels of communication.

Knapp, M. L. (1984). *Interpersonal communication and human relationships*. Boston: Allyn & Bacon.

With great accuracy, Knapp describes how communication processes affect the course of relationships in this well-written book.

Ekman, P. (Ed.). (1982). *Emotion in the human face*. Cambridge, England: Cambridge University Press.

Written by a series of experts, the chapters in this volume provide a look at recent work on facial expression.

Buck, R. (1984). *Nonverbal behavior and the communication of affect*. New York: Guilford.

A comprehensive look at the ways in which emotions are transmitted via the face and other channels of nonverbal communication.

Clark, H. H. (1985). Language use and language users. In G. Lindzey & E. Aronson (Eds.), *Handbook of social psychology*, (Vol. 2, 3rd ed.). New York: Random House.

Although technical, this volume is readable and interesting, elaborating on the information on verbal behavior discussed in this chapter.

Friends and Lovers
Forming Relationships

In the beginning, it seemed like the perfect match. Nothing could separate them. Jack Boggs was intelligent, charming, and good-looking; Ellen Ewing was bright, friendly, and vivacious. They first met in junior high school, but it wasn't until sophomore year of high school that they began dating seriously.

After high school they attended the same state university. They often took classes together, had the same friends, and spent most of their spare time together. Jack and Ellen were devoted to each other, and it seemed as if they were destined to be inseparable for the rest of their lives.

But after the start of their junior year of college, it all began to crumble. Ellen became dissatisfied with Jack's ambition—or lack of it, as she saw it—while he grew increasingly impatient with what he saw as her obsessive interest in a medical degree. They argued more and more frequently and started acting tense and irritable in each other's presence.

They understood now that something was wrong, but they couldn't pinpoint exactly what it was. All they knew was that their relationship—which had seemed to hold the potential for a lifetime of contentment—was all but over. Finally, they decided, it was time to split up.

Many of us have observed the course of relationships like this one, and some of us have been in them ourselves. How can we identify the factors that lead so many people to get together, form relationships, and eventually go their separate ways?

In this chapter, we examine the processes that underlie people's relationships. We begin by considering the factors that lead one person to be attracted to another, examining the role of physical attractiveness and liking.

Then we move from liking to loving. After discussing the ways to differentiate the two, we consider the ways love develops, and we distinguish between several kinds of love. How people go about maintaining loving relationships is also discussed.

To conclude the chapter, we consider the development, maintenance, and termination of relationships, examining how people's levels of relatedness vary and the kinds of behaviors that characterize developing relationships. Finally, we discuss the termination of relationships, citing the factors that can cause once-healthy relationships to wither and die, and recognizing a relationship whose end has come.

1. Do you have an aspirin?

2. Hi.

3. How long do you cook a leg of lamb?

4. Excuse me, I'm from out of town, and I was wondering what people do around here at night.

5. What kind of dog is that? He's great-looking.

6. Wow! What a beautiful day.

7. Please pass the ketchup.

8. Didn't I meet you in Istanbul?

9. Who's your dentist?

10. Don't tell me a beautiful girl like you doesn't have a date tonight.

According to one account, these remarks are among the fifty "best opening lines" of all time (Weber, 1970). (The worst range from "Do you think it will rain?" and "You look lonely" to "You are a beautiful person" and "Let's go to bed"; DuBrin, 1974).

That some authors feel that it is worthwhile to provide readers with comments that make good beginnings for relationships—and that there is a ready audience for such material—illustrates the importance our society places on the ability to initiate relationships with others. In fact, many people find meeting people and forming relationships to be among the most challenging tasks they face during the course of their lives. In this part of the chapter, we examine the major determinants that affect whether and how we become attracted to other people and ultimately develop relationships with them.

Near Is Better than Far:
Proximity

If you live in a dormitory or apartment house, reflect for a moment on the friends you made when you first moved in. Chances are you tended to form relationships with those who lived closest to you.

Proximity is, in fact, one of the factors that is most closely associated with attraction (Festinger, Schachter, & Back, 1950; Nahemow & Lawton, 1976). Psychologists have found that we tend to develop friendships with those who are located closest to us, and that we are least likely to develop friendships with those who live farthest from us. The basis for this finding is that people are able to obtain the social rewards that others provide—

People who live near each
other often form
friendships.

Susan Lapides/Design Conceptions

such as companionship, social approval, and help—relatively easily from
others who are geographically close, while it takes greater effort and time
to receive the same rewards from those who reside farther away.

Familiarity Breeds . . . Liking:
Mere exposure

Whoever coined the phrase "familiarity breeds contempt" needs to recheck
the psychology literature, for quite the opposite appears to be true: familiarity leads to attraction. If all other factors are constant, we tend to like
those to whom we are repeatedly exposed more than those to whom our
exposure is minimal.

This is partially explained by the **mere-exposure phenomenon,** in which
repeated exposure to any stimulus is sufficient to increase the positivity of
the evaluation of the stimulus (Zajonc, 1968; Birnbaum & Mellers, 1979).
The phenomenon occurs in a number of different arenas—not only do we
tend to be attracted to people to whom we are exposed more, but we also
like music, pictures, and even individual words to which our exposure is
high. Even animals do not seem immune to the effects of mere exposure:
In one experiment, rats were exposed to selections from Mozart or Schoen-
berg for twelve hours a day over a seven-week period. When the rats' musical
preferences were tested later by allowing them to shift their position in a
cage in a way that would activate a switch to play music of either one of the
two composers, rats chose the music with which they were most familiar
(Cross, Halcomb, & Matter, 1967).

Naturally, there are limits to the mere exposure phenomenon. Beyond
a certain point, exposure is not going to increase our attraction to an in-

dividual or another stimulus. Moreover, in cases in which the initial interaction with a person is strongly negative, repeated exposure is unlikely to
cause us to like the person more, and it may actually produce stronger
disliking for that person in the long run.

Do Birds of a Feather Flock Together . . .
or Do Opposites Attract?:
Similarity and attraction

If we were to use maxims and proverbs as a guide to understanding and
predicting human behavior, we would have a distinct problem, especially
when considering the two phrases "birds of a feather flock together" and
"opposites attract." Clearly, the two contradict each other. Psychological
research has provided us with a wealth of evidence on the issue, and the
results of the research have demonstrated that "birds of a feather flock
together." We find that people are attracted to others who hold similar
attitudes, values, and even personality traits (Byrne, 1969; Hill & Stull,
1981).

There are several reasons why similarity results in greater attraction.
For one thing, the discovery that people hold similar attitudes can be directly
rewarding to us, suggesting as it does that the views we hold are correct and
validated by others. Moreover, knowing that another person shares our views
allows us to more readily understand and predict how that person will behave. It also suggests that we will get along well with the person by engaging
in activities that are satisfying to both people.

Finally, knowing that another person is similar to us produces the phenomenon of **reciprocity of liking,** a tendency to like those who we think
like us. Reciprocity operates on several levels. Not only are we attracted to
people who like us, but the converse also holds true: If we like someone,
we tend to assume that they like us in return (Mettee & Aronson, 1974;
Burleson, 1984). Liking, then, is assumed to be a two-way street.

Where dissimilarity reigns: The need-complementarity hypothesis   There
are exceptions to the general case that similarity and attraction are found
together. People don't always seek out others like themselves; as one person
has commented, "I've known a lot of couples where the rocks in *her* head
seemed to fit the holes in *his*" (Howard, 1978).

In fact, some people seem to be attracted to others who are unlike
them. One reason is that we may be attracted to those people who fulfill
the greatest number of needs for us. Thus, a dominant person may seek out
someone who is submissive, while at the same time the submissive individual may be seeking someone who is dominant. Although by forming a relationship they are able to fulfill each other's complementary needs, their
dissimilarity often makes others expect them to be incompatible. The hypothesis that people are attracted to others who fulfill their needs—dubbed
the **need-complementarity hypothesis**—was first proposed in the late 1950s
in a classic study which found that a sample of married couples appeared

to have complementary needs (Winch, 1958). However, there has been little evidence since that time that supports the hypothesis, with most studies finding that attraction is related more to similarity in needs than to complementarity (e.g., Meyer & Pepper, 1977). In general, then, similarity—be it in attitudes, values, or personality traits—remains one of the best predictors of whether two people will be attracted to each other.

Beauty and the Beast:
Physical attractiveness and liking

Most of us would deny that physical attractiveness plays an important role in determining whom we like. In reality, however, it seems to be a critical factor in our relationships with others, particularly those involving the opposite sex.

In general, we like people who are physically attractive more than those who are unattractive. This phenomenon operates with startling consistency throughout the life span, beginning with infancy and operating into adulthood (Corter et al., 1978). Even in nursery and elementary school there is an association between children's physical attractiveness and their popularity with their peers and teachers (Dion & Berscheid, 1974), and this correspondence between physical appearance and liking continues through adulthood. For example, unattractive defendants in criminal cases are treated more harshly by juries than attractive people; attractive individuals receive greater help from others than unattractive ones; and attractive people receive greater cooperation from others than unattractive individuals (Berscheid, 1985).

Why is physical attractiveness so important in determining liking? One reason is that there is a **physical attractiveness stereotype** which suggests that the people who are physically attractive have a number of other desirable qualities. For instance, people tend to believe that the physically attractive not only have more desirable personality traits but that they are more likely to hold better jobs, have more successful marriages, and experience happier and more fulfilling lives than people who are less attractive (Adams & Huston, 1975). Given these assumptions about the lives of the physically attractive, it is not surprising that people are attracted to them more than to people who are physically unattractive. The latter, according to the stereotype, are less likely to have such positive qualities.

One of the surprising aspects of the physical attractiveness stereotype is that there may be a kernel of truth to it. Because the physically attractive are reacted to positively by others, they may develop more desirable personalities and more positive self-images, feel more self-confident, and ultimately become more successful than those who are physically unattractive. Moreover, people may prefer to interact with those who are physically attractive because of the prestige and increased status and esteem they feel by association. The physically attractive, then, may actually be more successful, in general, than those who are less attractive—thereby providing some validation for the stereotype.

Because most of the evidence regarding the importance of physical attractiveness is based on initial encounters between people, it seems reasonable to suggest that the importance of physical attractiveness would diminish over time. Unfortunately, this does not seem to be the case, although the evidence is sparse. In one study, college men and women agreed to have five dates with a member of the opposite sex. Instead of declining in importance, as we might expect, the importance of physical attractiveness in determining how much the partner was liked actually grew over the course of the five dates (Mathes, 1975).

Yet, for those of us with only moderate comeliness, findings such as these should not be viewed as entirely disheartening. For one thing, many unquestionably successful people would hardly be considered physically attractive; while being physically attractive is generally an asset, then, it is clearly not a necessary prerequisite to being a success in life.

Moreover, it turns out that physical attractiveness does not *always* prove to be critical or advantageous. For one thing, when people are asked to rank the factors that they find are important in a friend, physical attractiveness does not even make the "top ten" qualities (see the accompanying Do It! box). Moreover, in some cases physical attractiveness acts as a hindrance. For instance, success that comes to people who are unusually attractive may be attributed to their looks, as opposed to their skill. One study found that attractive women who were successful in business were disliked more than successful, unattractive women—because people thought they had achieved success not on their merits but because of their beauty. In the corporate world, then, physical attractiveness may have its drawbacks.

DO IT!

THE QUALITY OF FRIENDSHIP

What qualities do people find important in a friend? In a questionnaire, some 40,000 respondents were asked to rank the qualities that were most important to them. The following are the top ten, listed alphabetically. How would you order them?

_____ frankness

_____ good conversationalist

_____ independence

_____ intelligence

_____ keeps confidences

_____ loyalty

_____ sense of humor

_____ supportiveness

_____ warmth and affection

_____ willingness to make time

Another experiment that found disadvantages of physical attractiveness looked at the relationship between women's physical attractiveness in college and their adjustment and happiness twenty years later. What the study found was surprising: Women who had been attractive in college tended to be *less* happy and *less* well-adjusted in their later lives than those who had been relatively unattractive in college (Berscheid, Walster, & Campbell, 1974). Although the reasons are not clear, it may be that aging—and the perceived loss of one's "looks"—are more devastating to someone who was very attractive than to someone who was less attractive earlier in life.

Still, it is clear that physical attractiveness is an important factor in determining how much others are liked. Even in a society that professes to see beauty as "only skin deep," physical attractiveness seems, in most cases, to be a definite social asset.

Psychology for You:
Making friends

To the millions of people who have read Dale Carnegie's book *How to Win Friends and Influence People,* making friends is serious business. Yet you need not have reached the point of purchasing self-help books in order to feel apprehensive about initiating friendships. In fact, making friends and developing friendships is one of the most common concerns that people have throughout life.

Although there is no magic formula for making friends, several broad principles can be suggested for developing and maintaining friendships, based in large part on the psychological findings we have discussed.

● *Reveal yourself.* Others need to know who you are and what you are like before they can be attracted to you in any meaningful way. In order to facilitate relationships, it is appropriate to disclose information about yourself (Jourard, 1971). Don't assume that others will somehow divine your attitudes about the world without your revealing them; instead, be open and honest about the things you like and dislike. Only by honestly communicating your ideas and feelings will others learn the commonalities that you share—which, despite differences in surface attitudes, may be substantial when it comes to basic values and approaches to the world. (Of course, there are limits to this tactic; an inordinate degree of self-disclosure which comes prematurely in a developing relationship may backfire.)

Mike Mazzaschi/Stock, Boston

Lasting friendships often
develop as a result of
shared activities.

- *Let others know that you like them.* Given the findings relating to reciprocity of liking, it is clear that we like others who like us. If you like
someone, tell him or her—if not by words, then by deeds. Although being
honest about one's feelings may be risky in terms of opening oneself up to
rejection, it is also the only reasonable basis on which to develop a true
friendship.

- *Be accepting of others.* One mark of friendship is acceptance of people
the way they are, not the way you would like them to be. Do not impose
conditions on accepting others; keep in mind that no one is perfect, and
that everyone has both good and bad qualities.

- *Engage in shared activities.* The relationship between proximity and
attraction suggests that one important basis of friendships is engaging in
activities together. Friendships need time to grow, and sharing in mutually
satisfying activities—even if it is simply sitting and talking—sets the stage
for the development of lasting friendships.

- *Show concern and caring.* Although elusive qualities, concern and caring are prerequisites for the formation and continuation of friendships. One
must demonstrate an interest in the fortunes of others and share the sadness
of their adversity.

- Proximity is related to liking: We are friendliest with those who are physically closest to us.

- The mere-exposure phenomenon suggests that repeated exposure to any stimulus is sufficient to increase the positivity of the evaluation of the stimulus.

- Similarity in attitudes, values, and personality traits is associated with attraction. Moreover, the phenomenon of reciprocity of liking shows that there is a tendency to like those who we think like us.

- The need-complementarity hypothesis suggests that we are attracted to those who fulfill our needs—although the evidence in support of the hypothesis is minimal.

- The relationship between physical attractiveness and liking is clear: People who are more physically attractive tend to be liked more than those who are less attractive.

CHECK YOURSELF

1. "It was similar to situations in which you come to love an album after hearing it several times. The more time I spent with her, the more attracted to her I became." Which of the factors affecting attraction to another does this quote best describe?
   a. similarity
   b. complementarity
   c. proximity
   d. mere-exposure phenomenon

2. The greater accessibility of social rewards when people live near each other is probably the biggest reason that proximity occasions closer relationships. True or false?

3. The concept that attraction to those who are similar to us tends to be mutually felt is best labeled as:
   a. the mere-exposure phenomenon
   b. complementarity
   c. reciprocity of liking
   d. physical attractiveness

4. I became attracted to Janet because she made up for my flaws. Conversely, she may have been attracted to me because I had strengths in areas in which she felt weak." This statement exemplifies the _____ _____ hypothesis.

5. Is the hypothesis you labeled above well supported with current research evidence?

6. The physical attractiveness stereotype suggests that we are apt to assume that physically attractive people have objectionable personality characteristics. True or false?

(See answers to these questions at the bottom of page 332.)

10.2   **HOW DO I LOVE THEE?:**
                   Let Me Explain the Ways

The man and woman on the movie screen are talking about mundane, everyday matters: what food they like best, or perhaps how much exercise is really needed to prolong one's life. Suddenly, there is a lull in the conversation as they catch each other's glance, and the spoken conversation halts. As they gaze into each other's eyes for a few telling moments, one of them says to the other, "I think I'm falling in love with you." They lapse into silence, and then gradually inch closer together. They reach out to each other, embrace, and kiss passionately. Depending on the rating of the movie, the action either continues as the couple slowly sinks into a horizontal position, or else the film discreetly fades into a blackout. In either case, the result, to any savvy movie-goer, is clear: love—deep, passionate love—has dawned, at least for this couple. (Davis, 1973.)

How nice it would be if the world were this simple for the rest of us. Unfortunately, the development of love rarely proceeds in so uncomplicated a fashion as is shown on the movie screen.

We turn now from the phenomena that contribute to liking to those that contribute to love. According to psychologists—as well as those with any experience with it—love does not represent liking that is simply of greater intensity; it differs qualitatively from mere simple attraction (Walster & Walster, 1978). Moreover, not every kind of love is the same; there is a difference in the way you love a spouse, girlfriend, or boyfriend and the way you love your mother.

Investigators in the area, therefore, usually distinguish between two main types of love: passionate love and companionate love. **Passionate (or romantic) love** represents a state of intense absorption in someone. It includes intense physiological arousal, psychological interest, and caring for the needs of another. In contrast, **companionate love** is the strong affection that we have for those with whom our lives are deeply involved. Although passionate love may evolve, over time, into companionate love—at least for those relationships that are relatively enduring—the two differ in important ways, and each should be considered separately.

Joel Gordon

What does true love look like? It is important not to let the media dictate one's perceptions on this subject.

The Rages of Romance:
Passionate love

When poets and lyricists sing the praises of love, they are usually referring to passionate love. In fact, our society has very definite notions about what constitutes passionate love. According to the common view, if we are truly in love, our hearts ought to beat faster at the sight of our love, we should experience intense desire for him or her, and, no matter how we are treated, we must—if we really are in love—forgive his or her foibles and keep pursuing him or her. (See the following Do It! box.)

DO IT!

DOES YOUR LOVER MAKE YOU JEALOUS?

While we have all heard poets and philosophers describe jealousy, one of the darker emotions, few of us have taken the time to clarify our feelings about the kinds of things that make us jealous. To see how your answers compare to those of others who have completed the questionnaire, use the scale below to indicate how frequently you have engaged in each type of behavior.

CHECK YOURSELF: ANSWERS
1. d **2.** True **3.** c **4.** need complementarity **5.** No **6.** False

5 = frequently; 4 = somewhat often; 3 = sometimes;
2 = rarely; 1 = never

1. Took advantage of unplanned opportunities to look through a spouse's or lover's belongings for unfamiliar names, phone numbers, etc. _____

2. Intentionally looked through a spouse's or lover's personal belongings for unfamiliar names, phone numbers, etc. _____

3. Called a spouse or lover unexpectedly just to see if he or she was there. _____

4. Listened in on a telephone conversation of a spouse or lover or secretly followed him or her. _____

5. Extensively questioned a spouse or lover about previous or present romantic relationships. _____

6. Made nasty comments about or did something negative toward someone who had possessions you wished to have. _____

7. Made nasty comments about or did something negative toward someone who had a more successful career than you. _____

8. Made nasty comments about or did something negative toward someone whom your friends liked better than you. _____

9. Made nasty comments about or did something negative toward someone who was more attractive than you. _____

ANSWERS   The following are the average ratings found in the survey for each of the previous items: (1) 2.1; (2) 1.8; (3) 2.0; (4) 1.4; (5) 2.2; (6) 1.7; (7) 1.7; (8) 1.7; (9) 1.9

Source: Salovey & Rodin, 1985.

At least in the early stages of romantic relationships, this view is not too far from what people report they actually experience. People who are in love don't just *think* about their partners; they physically *feel* intense passion for them as well. Passionate love also often has a swift onset, in comparison to simple liking, which develops more gradually. Love can be more volatile; liking generally shows stability in its course. Love's greater intensity may result in relationships following a roller-coaster pattern of ups and downs. Some kinds of love also include relatively intense physiological arousal, as well as strong psychological absorption and interest in another person—often to the exclusion of everyone else (Walster & Walster, 1978).

In trying to draw clear distinctions between passionate love and liking, several approaches have been taken. For example, psychologist Zick Rubin developed two scales designed to measure liking and loving (Rubin, 1973).

TABLE 10-1

Sample Items from the Love and Liking Scales

LOVE SCALE

I feel that I can confide in _____ about virtually everything.
I find it easy to ignore _____'s faults.
I would do almost anything for _____.

LIKING SCALE

I think that _____ is unusually well adjusted.
I would highly recommend _____ for a responsible job.
I have great confidence in _____'s good judgment.

Source: Rubin, 1973.

Each scale consists of a series of ten items. To use the scale, a person fills in the name of someone to whom he or she is attracted and then indicates agreement with each statement on a nine-point scale (see sample items in Table 10-1).

The scale is generally successful in distinguishing between people who just like each other and those who are in a loving relationship. For instance, people who score high on the love scale tend to gaze into their partner's eyes more than those who score lower, and their love scores tend to predict how enduring their relationship will be. Moreover, the scores people obtain on the love scores scale are closely related to whether they expect to marry their partner, while scores on the liking scale show less of an association with marriage plans.

Although Rubin's scales help to distinguish people who are in love from those who merely like each other, they do not explain why passionate love is so different from liking. According to one explanation—dubbed the **two-factor theory of love**—people experience passionate love when two things occur together: intense physiological arousal and situational cues that suggest that "love" is the appropriate label for the feelings that are being experienced (Berscheid & Walster, 1974). Thus, when physiological arousal—be it from sexual arousal, excitement, rejection, fear, or anger—is thought to be caused by the situational cues suggesting that one is "falling in love," the arousal may come to be labeled as "passionate love."

The two-factor theory of love is particularly illuminating in explaining why people pursue love relationships when, under any other circumstance, they would have lost all interest in another person. For instance, often people who are rejected or hurt by a lover not only maintain their love for that individual, but actually may experience increased love. The reason, according to the theory, is that the rejection or hurt produces physiological arousal; if the arousal is attributed to being in love, the attraction to the person will be maintained, and, if the arousal is strong enough, it may actually increase.

Although there is no definitive evidence for the two-factor theory of love, there is indirect support. In one intriguing and imaginative experiment, an attractive, college-age woman stood at the end of a swaying 450-foot suspension bridge that spanned a deep canyon. The woman was supposedly conducting a survey, and she asked men who made it across the bridge a series of questions. She then gave them her telephone number, telling them that if they were interested in the results of the experiment they could contact her in the upcoming week.

In comparison to members of a control group that had completed the questionnaire after strolling across a stable bridge spanning a shallow stream ten feet below, the men who had come across the dangerous bridge showed significant differences in their questionnaire results: sexual imagery was considerably higher. Moreover, those crossing the dangerous span were sig-

One experiment indicated that fear—brought on by crossing a narrow bridge—may produce the perception of attraction.

Courtesy of Donald G. Dutton

nificantly more likely to actually call the woman in the upcoming week, suggesting that their attraction to her was higher. Presumably, then, the men connected the physiological arousal produced by the dangerous conditions with the woman, resulting in feelings of attraction (Dutton & Aron, 1974).

Naturally, other factors besides physiological arousal are related to perceptions of passionate love. For example, as Shakespeare's Montagues and Capulets found, much to their sorrow, parental interference in sons' and daughters' love affairs can actually increase desire and perceptions of love, rather than—as parents hope—decrease feelings of attraction. In what has come to be known as the **Romeo and Juliet effect,** researchers have found that the greater the levels of parental interference in dating relationships, the higher the levels of romantic love experienced by a couple (Driscoll, Davis, & Lipitz, 1972). On the other hand, as parental interference declines, dating couples begin to feel less intensely about one another. Interestingly, this does not hold true for married couples: There is little or no correspondence between parental interference and passion in married couples.

Love Without the Fury: Companionate love

For better or worse, most of us do not spend our lives in the heightened state of emotional and physiological arousal indicative of romantic love. Our love is more dispassionate and less volatile—the kind of love that has been labeled "companionate love."

What distinguishes companionate love from other forms of attraction? In comparison to liking, companionate love seems to be best characterized by relatively high levels of self-disclosure and the giving of material objects—such as gifts—as well as nonmaterial things such as emotional and moral support to the other person. Moreover, there tend to be more verbal and physical expressions of affection. People report feeling happier in the presence of loved ones and are more willing to tolerate their unpleasant characteristics than they are of people for whom they do not feel companionate love (Swensen, 1972).

Some conceptions of companionate love emphasize the altruistic nature of the relationship, in which people act to promote the welfare of a loved one, sometimes even above their own (Kelley, 1983). The Greeks, for example, spoke about a form of love called **agape,** a kind of loving represented by extremes of generosity.

The most critical distinction between passionate and companionate love, however, is the greater clarity and rationality with which two people in a companionate relationship are able to view each other and their relationship. Gone is the starry-eyed perception of one's lover, and in its place is a clearer understanding of the lover's virtues—and flaws. The awareness and acceptance of the good with the bad, however, marks in part the maturity of strong companionate love.

Not everyone agrees that love should be restricted to just the categories of companionate and passionate. In fact, the most contemporary theory of love, developed by psychologist Robert Sternberg, suggests that there are actually eight distinguishable forms of love (Sternberg, 1986b; Sternberg, 1987).

According to the theory, love is made up of three major components: intimacy, passion, and decision/commitment. The **intimacy component** encompasses feelings of closeness and connectedness; the **passion component** is made up of motivational drives relating to sex, physical closeness, and romance; and the **decision/commitment component** consists of the initial decision that one loves another and that there is a commitment to maintain that love.

By considering the presence or absence of each of the three components in a loving relationship, it is possible to derive the eight combinations of love illustrated in Table 10-2. The first kind of love, in which all three components are absent, is really nonlove; these relationships include the people with whom we have casual interactions during the course of our lives. Friendships form the second type of love, in which only the emotional component of love is present.

A third kind of love is infatuation, in which there is passion without intimacy and decision/commitment. "Love at first sight" falls into this category. The fourth type of love, called empty love, has only the decision/commitment component and lacks intimacy and passion. Relationships that have continued for many years and have grown stagnant are representative of empty love.

TABLE 10-2
The Kinds of Love

	COMPONENT*		
	INTIMACY	PASSION	DECISION/ COMMITMENT
Nonlove	−	−	−
Liking	+	−	−
Infatuated love	−	+	−
Empty love	−	−	+
Romantic love	+	+	−
Companionate love	+	−	+
Fatuous love	−	+	+
Consummate love	+	+	+

*+ = component present; − = component absent.
Source: Sternberg, 1986, table 2.

Romantic love is more complex than the other forms of love, since it contains the components of both intimacy and passion, although it lacks decision/commitment. People who are romantically in love are drawn together physically and emotionally.

Companionate love, in Sternberg's theory, is the result of intimacy and decision/commitment without passion. In one sense, it is a kind of long-term, committed friendship of the sort that might be seen in a marriage, where the physical attraction has been lost. In contrast, fatuous love has components of passion and decision/commitment but lacks intimacy. Relationships based on fatuous love may not be lasting, since an emotional component bonding the two people together is not present.

The eighth kind of love is consummate love. In consummate love, all three components of love are present. Although it is tempting to think of this kind of love as the "best," many fulfilling loving relationships are maintained for long periods with one or even two of the components only minimally present. In fact, the individual components vary in their influence over time and follow distinct courses, as illustrated in Figure 10-1. In strong, loving relationships, the level of commitment peaks and then remains stable, while intimacy continues to grow over the course of a relationship. Passion, on the other hand, shows a marked decline over time, reaching a plateau fairly early on in a relationship.

Psychology for You:
Maintaining loving relationships

You're in love . . . and you want it to last. What do you do to make sure the relationship doesn't falter? Although there are no infallible rules for maintaining a loving relationship, there are several things that can be done to help maintain one's love for another (Middlebrook, 1974).

● *Make the distinction between sexual attraction and love.* Although passion is obviously based in part on sexual interests, it is not enough to maintain an enduring relationship.

● *Examine the relationship.* Although it is not necessary to analyze and reanalyze every aspect of a relationship, it is necessary to think about what

FIGURE 10-1
The three components of love vary in strength over the course of a relationship.

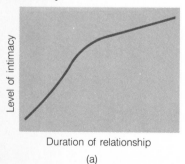

Duration of relationship

(a)

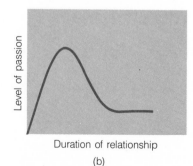

Duration of relationship

(b)

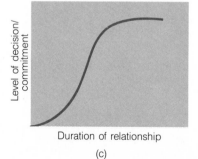

Duration of relationship

(c)

is and what is not important to you. Don't enter into a new relationship just to escape another part of your life that is less desirable, and don't let passion cloud your assessment of the benefits—and costs—of a relationship.

● *Keep lines of communication open.* In truly loving relationships, the partners are able to communicate what they are feeling. Don't delude yourself into thinking that your partner can read what is on your mind; you must articulate what you are thinking and feeling.

● *Don't think that you will be able to change or reform your partner.* If you don't like important aspects of your lover's personality now, it is unlikely that time will make your judgments less harsh. Of course, people do change their behavior over time, but you should not enter into a relationship thinking that you can bring about a profound change in your partner.

TO REVIEW

● Love differs from mere liking qualitatively, not just quantitatively.

● The two major categorizations of love are passionate love, in which there is an intense absorption in another, and companionate love, in which there is strong affection for those with whom our lives are deeply involved.

● The two-factor theory of love suggests that people feel passionate love when they experience (1) intense physiological arousal and (2) situational cues that suggest that "love" is the appropriate label for the arousal.

● Sternberg's theory of love proposes that there are three components that underlie love (intimacy, passion, and decision/commitment), resulting in eight forms of love.

CHECK YOURSELF

1. Passionate love, as explained by the two-factor theory, is experienced when what two things occur together?

2. Generosity, self-disclosure, and the lending of emotional and moral support are descriptive of _____ love.

3. According to the Romeo and Juliet effect, negative parental interference in their sons' and daughters' love relationships will frequently result in a (a) decay or (b) heightening of the amorous feeling.

4. Match the descriptions in the right column with each of Sternberg's eight forms of love listed in the left column.

1. _____ nonlove   a. passion and commitment without intimacy

2. _____ liking   b. passion only

3. _____ infatuated   c. commitment only
love

4. _____ empty   d. intimacy and passion without commitment
love

5. _____ romantic   e. intimacy and commitment without passion
love

6. _____ compan-   f. casual interactions
ionate love

7. _____ fatuous   g. all three components are present
love

8. _____ consum-   h. intimacy only
mate love

5. The theories discussed in this section support the view that the difference between liking and loving is mainly quantitative. True or false?

_____

(See answers to the questions at the bottom of page 342.)

10.3 DEVELOPING, MAINTAINING, AND ENDING RELATIONSHIPS

Attractive, petite woman needs/wants gentleman-companion. Needing-wanting serious meaningful forever-love, from-the-heart relationship. Both being sensitive, very supportive, loyal, honest, intelligent, dependable, neat, clean, healthy, respectful. Liking dancing, dining out, day trips, good conversation, togetherness, etc. Box S230H.

Male, 22, tall, attractive, perceptive, intelligent, athletic, artistic and professional, seeks the companionship and love of a singular woman who's slim, intelligent, comely, strong and sensitive. I enjoy good books, conversation, films, bicycling, music, cross-country skiing, fine arts, and more. Long-term relationships only. Box S222H.

Pretty, slim, witty, classy, intelligent, divorced, white female, 36, seeks attractive Ivy League type professional with humor, style, and integrity, for fun, growth, companionship, commitment. Box S234M.

As we see in these advertisements taken from the "Personals" section of a newspaper, forming relationships is an important—and sometimes elusive—goal for many individuals. Despite being attracted to numerous people, we ultimately develop meaningful relationships with relatively few of them. Moreover, no matter how a relationship begins, its course may take many routes and follow many different patterns. Our examination of liking and loving turns now to consideration of the rise—and fall—of relationships.

The Rise of Relationships:
Levels of relatedness

To understand the nature of relationships, we must begin by considering the different levels of relatedness that can exist between two people. Psychologist George Levinger (1974) suggests that there are three basic levels: unilateral awareness, bilateral surface contact, and mutuality. This conception, which is illustrated graphically in Figure 10-2, serves to illustrate the course that relationships typically follow.

The sequence begins with a zero contact point—those instances in which two people are completely unaware of each other. Obviously, most "relationships" would fall into this category, given that we are physically limited in the number of people with whom we may, in our lifetimes, come in contact.

Actual relationships cannot begin until people reach the stage of **awareness.** At this level we view others in terms of their outward characteristics. Those whom we perceive may not even be aware that they are being judged.

With **surface contact,** the next stage in the sequence, both people are aware of each other, and each forms attitudes and impressions of the other as well as attitudes and impressions regarding the relationship itself. The majority of our daily interactions with others fall into this category, as we encounter the same mail delivery person, janitor, or librarian, yet never form a deep or lasting closeness. In fact, the roles that such people play are typically more important to us than the specific individuals who occupy them.

It is not until a relationship reaches the stage of **mutuality** that it becomes truly personal. In mutual relationships, two people share knowledge about themselves with each other, feel some degree of responsibility for one

FIGURE 10-2
Levels of relatedness of two individuals. (*Source*: Levinger, 1974).

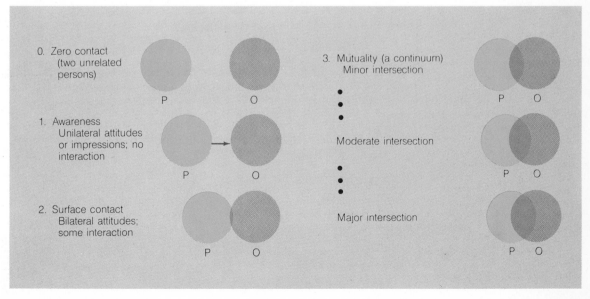

Interacting with someone frequently, for example in working on a class project together, is one step in the formation of a close relationship.

another, and develop their own patterns and rules of appropriate behavior that are unique to the relationship.

During the early stages of mutuality, referred to as "minor intersection" in the figure, people are hesitant about disclosing personal information about themselves. However, as the relationship progresses to the levels of moderate intersection and major intersection, self-disclosure increases, and the partners reveal intimate and meaningful attitudes and feelings. Moreover, they develop an awareness of the sources of the other person's happiness and satisfaction, and they begin to behave in ways that make the relationship increasingly rewarding.

Getting Closer:
Behavior in developing relationships

Although all relationships are unique, the behavior of people in developing relationships tends to change in fairly predictable ways (Berscheid, 1985; Burgess & Huston, 1979):

● They tend to interact more often, for longer periods of time, and in a widening array of settings.

● They seek each other's company.

CHECK YOURSELF: ANSWERS

1. intense physiological arousal, plus situational cues that suggest "love" is an appropriate label for the feelings being experienced **2.** companionate **3.** (b) **4.** 1. f; 2. h; 3. b; 4. c; 5. d; 6. e; 7. a; 8. g **5.** False

- They increasingly "open up" to each other, disclosing secrets and sharing physical intimacies. They are more willing to share both positive and negative feelings and are increasingly willing to provide praise and criticism. (To consider the ways self-disclosure increases with time, see the accompanying Do It! box.)

- They begin to understand the other person's point of view and way of looking at the world.

- Their goals and behavior begin to form greater synchrony, and they begin to share greater similarity.

- Their investment in the relationship—in terms of time, energy, and psychological interest—increases.

- They begin to feel that their psychological well-being is tied to the well-being of the relationship. The relationship comes to be seen as unique and irreplaceable.

- They begin to behave as a couple rather than as two separate individuals.

DO IT!

WHAT DO PEOPLE SHARE ABOUT THEMSELVES?

The nature of information that people are willing to share about themselves changes during the course of a relationship. To illustrate this concept, investigators in one experiment asked a group of people to imagine that they were watching a two-hour conversation between two individuals meeting for the first time (Berger, Gardner, Clatterbuck, & Schulman, 1976). These "observers" were then presented with a list of some 150 statements and were asked to sort them into fifteen-minute time slots during the two-hour conversation according to when the statement seemed most appropriate to be mentioned. The statements fell into regular patterns, depending on the duration of the supposed conversation.

The following are some representative statements from the study. Read through them and place them in the time slot that seems most appropriate:

Time slots:

A.	0–15 minutes	E.	60–75 minutes
B.	15–30 minutes	F.	75–90 minutes
C.	30–45 minutes	G.	90–100 minutes
D.	45–60 minutes	H.	100–120 minutes

I. Such a statement would not be made during a two-hour conversation between previously unacquainted persons.

1. I'm a volunteer at a local hospital. _____

2. I'm from New York. _____

3. My wife is a good cook. _____

4. I've been skiing only once. _____

5. I've never really had a vacation. _____

6. I wish I knew more about politics. _____

7. I am 35 years old. _____

8. It bothers me to hear young women cursing and swearing. _____

9. I don't like people who smile all the time. _____

10. People who don't finish what they start always annoy me. _____

11. I don't believe that there is an afterlife, but I'm really not sure. _____

12. I hate lying in bed at night listening to the clock tick. _____

13. I have a violent temper. _____

14. I find it difficult to respond rationally when I am criticized. _____

15. Sometimes I'm afraid I won't be able to control myself. _____

16. I wish my husband would feel free to cry as an emotional release. _____

17. I had my first sexual experience when I was 21. _____

18. I make $13,000 a year. _____

SCORING   Compare your responses to those of the subjects in the study, whose answers followed this pattern: 1. A; 2. A; 3. B; 4. B; 5. C; 6. C; 7. D; 8. D; 9. E; 10. E; 11. F; 12. F; 13. G; 14. G; 15. H; 16. H; 17. I; 18. I.

As you can see from the results, people expect a conversation to change significantly in two hours. Initially, they present superficial information. Only later do they disclose information about personal, sexual, and family problems—a sequence which mirrors what occurs in longer-term relationships.

Although the changes in relationships described above are fairly typical, the exact point in a relationship when these changes occur is difficult to predict. One important reason is that as relationships develop and mature, the people in them are also changing and growing as individuals. As the relationship itself evolves, then, the people who make it up may also be passing through personal changes of their own.

The Decline and Fall of Liking and Love:
Terminating a relationship

Although relationships often begin with the glow and promise of a lifelong commitment, many end without reaching the height of fulfillment that was originally expected and hoped for. Is there a way of determining which relationships will flourish and which will flounder?

To answer this question, we can investigate successful and unsuccessful relationships, comparing factors that might explain the different outcomes. In one study, Hill, Rubin, & Peplau (1979) examined some 200 couples who were dating at four Boston-area colleges. They found after two years had gone by that about 45 percent of the sample had broken up, while the rest were still involved and were either dating, engaged, or married.

Compared with those who were still together, couples who had broken up tended to be less intimate or attached to one another at the start of the two-year period, their degree of involvement in the relationship was unequal (either the man or the woman was more interested and invested in the relationship), and the two partners tended to be less similar to each other.

To determine the reasons for the couples breaking up when they did, both the men and the women were extensively interviewed at the end of the two-year period. As you can see in Table 10-3, the reasons that people gave for breaking up varied, and there were several significant differences between women's and men's reasons. Most agreed, however, that boredom with the relationship and differences in interests were major reasons for terminating the relationship.

TABLE 10-3
Reasons for the Termination of Dating Relationships

REASON	WOMEN'S REPORTS	MEN'S REPORTS
Becoming bored with the relationship	76.7%	76.7%
Differences in interests	72.8	61.1
Woman's desire to be independent	73.7	50.0
Man's desire to be independent	46.8	61.1
Differences in backgrounds	44.2	46.8
Conflicting sexual attitudes	48.1	42.9
Conflicting marriage ideas	43.4	28.9
Woman's interest in someone else	40.3	31.2
Living too far apart	28.2	41.0
Man's interest in someone else	18.2	28.6
Pressure from woman's parents	18.2	13.0
Differences in intelligence	19.5	10.4
Pressure from man's parents	10.4	9.1

Source: Adapted from Hill, Rubin, & Peplau, 1979.

The point at which the breakups actually occurred seemed to be systematic; couples tended to split up at the beginning of the fall semester or at the end of the fall or spring semester—natural breaking points for students. Moreover, although women were more likely than men to actually end the relationship, both men and women *perceived* that they were the ones who had initiated the breakup.

Endings: A model of relationship dissolution   Although learning the reasons people give to explain the end of a relationship is important, such information does not explain the processes that underlie breakups. One model that seeks to explain how relationships terminate suggests that there are four stages leading to the dissolution of a relationship (Duck, 1982). As you can see in Figure 10-3, the first phase occurs when the person passes a threshold and decides that he or she can no longer tolerate being in a relationship. During this stage, called the **intrapsychic phase,** there is a focus on the other person's behavior and an evaluation of the extent to which this behavior provides a basis for terminating the relationship.

In the second stage, called the **dyadic phase,** a person passes the threshold trigger in which he or she feels justified in withdrawing from the relationship. In the dyadic phase, the individual decides to confront the partner and determines whether to attempt to repair, redefine, or terminate the relationship. A repair of the relationship might attempt to keep it at its original status, while a redefinition might encompass a qualitative change in the level of the relationship ("We can still be friends" might replace "I'll love you forever").

If the decision to terminate the relationship is made, another threshold is reached. That is what Duck (1982) calls the "I mean it" threshold. The person then enters the **social phase,** in which there is public acknowledgment that the relationship is being dissolved and an accounting is made regarding the events that led to the termination of the relationship. At this stage, the fact that the breakup will have an impact on the broader social networks to which the people belong becomes apparent to both partners.

The last stage is the **grave-dressing phase,** in which the major activity is to physically and psychologically end the relationship. One of the major concerns of this period is to rethink the relationship, making what happened seem reasonable and fitting with one's self-concept.

Psychology for You:
Knowing when it's over

Strange as it may sound, it sometimes proves easier for people to remain in a bad relationship than to terminate one. People may grow to depend on the stability that a relationship provides. Their fears over facing the uncertainties of the future without their partners—even partners that no longer provide much in the way of positive outcomes—may be so great that they avoid facing the fact that the relationship is no longer viable.

BREAKDOWN: Dissatisfaction with relationship

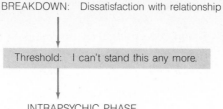

Threshold: I can't stand this any more.

INTRAPSYCHIC PHASE

Personal focus on partner's behavior
Assess adequacy of partner's role performance
Depict and evaluate negative aspects of being in the relationship
Consider costs of withdrawal
Assess positive aspects of alternative relationships
Face "express/repress dilemma"

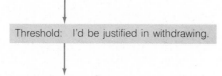

Threshold: I'd be justified in withdrawing.

DYADIC PHASE

Face "confrontation/avoidance dilemma"
Confront partner
Negotiate in "Our Relationship Talks"
Attempt repair and reconcilation?
Assess joint costs of withdrawal or reduced intimacy

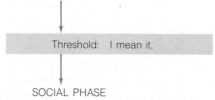

Threshold: I mean it.

SOCIAL PHASE

Negotiate postdissolution state with partner
Initiate gossip discussion in social network
Create publicly negotiable face-saving/blame-placing stories
  and accounts
Consider and face up to implied social network effects, if any
Call in intervention teams?

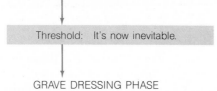

Threshold: It's now inevitable.

GRAVE DRESSING PHASE

"Getting over" activity
Retrospection; reformulative postmortem attribution
Public distribution of own version of break-up story

FIGURE 10-3
Phases of dissolving
personal relationships.
(Reprinted with
permission from Steve
Duck, "A Topography of
Relationship
Disengagement and
Dissolution." In *Personal
Relationships 4:
Dissolving Personal
Relationships*, edited by
S. W. Duck. New York:
Academic Press, 1982,
p. 16.)

In some cases, however, it is better to end a relationship that is no longer working than it is to continually suffer in a relationship in which the partners feel little, if any, attraction for each other. If you are in a relationship that is concerning you, you might take the following into consideration:

Couples may find counseling helpful in resolving conflicts that are damaging their relationship.

- *Keep in mind that no relationship is perfect.* Everyone has his or her faults, and every relationship has aspects to it that may produce negative feelings. It is important to weigh the benefits that you derive from the relationship against its costs—as well as considering the alternatives available to you.

- *Be analytical about a relationship that is troubling you.* Try to pinpoint the specific things that are bothersome about your partner—even if it means making lists, written or mental, of the positive and negative aspects of the situation. Once you understand the situation more precisely, you will be in a better position to make changes.

- *Seek out help for a sagging relationship.* In many cases, an outsider can be useful by providing a sounding board for your concerns, as well as by providing a fresh perspective on the situation. Professional counseling can play an important role in determining whether a relationship is worth saving.

- *Remember that change can foster growth.* Don't be afraid to leave a relationship because you are worried that the alternatives may not work out just the way you want them to. It is often better to face an uncertain future—with at least the potential for a more positive outcome—than to remain in the certainty of an unhappy relationship.

TO REVIEW

- There are three basic levels of relatedness: unilateral awareness, bilateral surface contact, and mutuality.

● People in developing relationships spend more time together and show greater self-disclosure, greater understanding of each other, and greater investment in the relationship.

● According to Duck's model of relationship termination, there are four stages that lead to the dissolution: the intrapsychic phase, the dyadic phase, the social phase, and the grave-dressing phase.

CHECK YOURSELF

1.   Robert and Katherine have progressed from their usual small talk and have now begun to share some aspects of their personal lives. According to psychologist George Levinger, their relationship has entered what level?
   a.   awareness
   b.   mutuality
   c.   surface contact
   d.   minor intersection

2.   Which of the following was *not* a finding in the Hill, Rubin, and Peplau (1979) study on breaking up?
   a.   Both men and women agreed that boredom with the relationship was a major reason for splitting up.
   b.   Men and women *both* perceived that they themselves were responsible for initiating the breakup.
   c.   Men were more likely to be the ones who actually ended the relationship.
   d.   Both men and women agreed that differences in interests was a critical reason for terminating a relationship.

3.   Match each statement in the right column with its corresponding phase in Duck's (1982) model:

_____ intrapsychic phase

a.   "I don't know if I can go on seeing Jim. I have some serious thinking to do about our relationship."

_____ dyadic phase

b.   "In retrospect, I can begin to understand why our relationship failed. It wasn't just Jim's fault or mine. We simply didn't work well as a couple."

_____ social phase

c.   "Yes, Lori, Jim and I are splitting up. Let me tell you more about it. . . ."

_____ grave-dressing phase

d.   "There's no question that we have to end our relationship. Now, I have to tell Jim."

(See answers to the questions at the bottom of page 350.)

TO SUMMARIZE

1. Proximity is one of the major determinants of attraction: We tend to be friendliest with those who are located closest to us. One explanation of the relationship between attraction and proximity rests on the mere-exposure phenomenon, in which repeated exposure to any stimulus is sufficient to increase the positivity of the evaluation of the stimulus. Mere exposure applies not only to people but to inanimate objects as well.

2. The relationship between similarity and attraction is also well established. People who hold similar attitudes, values, and personality traits like each other more than those who are dissimilar. Moreover, there is reciprocity of liking, a tendency to like those who we think like us. Although there is some evidence that supports the need-complementarity hypothesis—which suggests that we are attracted to others who fulfill our needs—most studies suggest that similarity is a more influential determinant of attraction.

3. Physical attractiveness is another factor that results in liking, beginning at a young age. The stereotype for physical attractiveness suggests that the physically appealing also hold other desirable traits (such as a more desirable personality) and generally experience happier, more fulfilling lives. Although there may be some truth to these generalizations, it turns out that physical attractiveness is burdensome in some situations.

4. Love differs from the more common liking in several respects. It often has a swift onset, is more volatile, and may include relatively intense physiological arousal. Two kinds of love are usually distinguished from each other: passionate (or romantic) love, which represents a state of intense absorption in another, and companionate love, the strong affection that we experience regarding those with whom our lives are deeply involved.

5. Passionate love has been explained by the two-factor theory. The theory states that people experience passionate love when there is intense physiological arousal and situational cues that suggest that "love" is the appropriate label for the feelings that are being experienced. The theory is supported by research showing that feelings of attraction are produced by dangerous situations. However, the two-factor theory is not the sole explanation for passionate love. For instance, there is the Romeo and Juliet effect, which demonstrates that parental interference in dating relationships may lead a couple to feel more intensely about each other.

6. Companionate love is characterized by relatively high levels of self-disclosure and such behavior as the giving of material objects and physical expressions of affection. Other conceptions of companionate love emphasize the altruistic nature of the relationship. People who experience companion-

CHECK YOURSELF: ANSWERS

1. b **2.** c **3.** a, d, c, b

ate love are usually able to view the other person and the relationship more realistically than people who experience passionate love.

7. According to Robert Sternberg's model, there are actually eight distinguishable forms of love. The model suggests that there are three major components of love: intimacy, passion, and decision/commitment. By considering whether each of these components is present or absent, eight different forms of love can be distinguished.

8. Although we are attracted to many people, we pursue relationships with only a few, and these relationships vary in intensity. According to one model of relationships, there are three basic levels of relatedness: awareness, surface contact, and mutuality.

9. As relationships develop, there are several characteristic behaviors that emerge. For example, people in developing relationships interact with each other more often, for longer periods of time, and in a widening array of settings; they seek out each other's company; they increasingly "open up" to each other; they tend to understand their partner's point of view more; their goals and behaviors begin to form greater synchrony; their psychological investment in the relationship grows; and they begin to relate to others as a couple rather than as individuals.

10. When relationships end, they do so for a variety of reasons. Among dating couples in college, the major causes that the couple themselves report are boredom with the relationship and differences in interests. There are also systematic points in the course of the year during which breakups tend to occur, as well as biases in the perception of who initiated the breakup.

11. There are four stages leading to the dissolution of a relationship. The first stage is the intrapsychic phase, in which there is a focus on the other's behavior. The second stage is the dyadic phase, in which a person decides whether to repair, redefine, or terminate the relationship. The social phase is the third stage. Here there is public acknowledgment that the relationship is being terminated. The last stage is the grave-dressing phase, in which the major activity is to physically and psychologically end the relationship.

KEY TERMS AND CONCEPTS

mere-exposure phenomenon (p. 324)

reciprocity of liking (p. 325)

need-complementarity hypothesis (p. 325)

physical attractiveness stereotype (p. 326)

passionate (or romantic) love (p. 331)

companionate love (p. 331)

decision/commitment component of love (p. 337)

awareness level (of relatedness) (p. 341)

surface contact level (of relatedness) (p. 341)

mutuality level (of relatedness) (p. 341)

intrapsychic phase (of relationship dissolution) (p. 346)

two-factor theory of love (p. 334)
Romeo and Juliet effect (p. 336)
agape (p. 336)
intimacy component of love
(p. 337)
passion component of love (p. 337)

dyadic phase (of relationship
dissolution) (p. 346)
social phase (of relationship
dissolution) (p. 346)
grave-dressing phase (of
relationship dissolution) (p. 346)

TO FIND OUT MORE

Hendrick, C., & Hendrick, S. (1983). *Liking, loving, and relating.* Monterey, CA: Brooks/Cole.

Rubin, Z. (1973). *Liking and loving: An invitation to social psychology.* New York: Holt.

Each of these books presents an attractive introduction to the field of liking and loving. The first volume particularly emphasizes the growth of relationships, while the second—although a bit dated—provides a clear, witty overview of the area.

Knapp, M. L. (1984). *Interpersonal communication and human relationships.* Boston: Allyn & Bacon.

A well-written and interesting book, this volume contains a comprehensive review of the ways in which communication patterns affect the course of people's relationships.

Walster, E., & Walster, G. W. (1978). *Love.* Reading, MA: Addison-Wesley.

An introduction to the specific area of love, including a special emphasis on how it can be studied scientifically.

Together Forever?
Marriage and Divorce

CHAPTER

11

On Monday Corporal Floyd Johnson, 23, and the then Mary Ellen Skinner, 19, total strangers, boarded a train at San Francisco and sat down across the aisle from each other. Johnson didn't cross the aisle until Wednesday, but his bride said, "I'd already made up my mind to say yes if he asked me to marry him." Thursday the couple got off the train in Omaha with plans to be married. Because they would need the consent of the bride's parents if they were married in Nebraska, they crossed the river to Council Bluffs, Iowa, where they were married Friday. (San Francisco Chronicle, cited by Burgess & Wallin, 1953, p. 151.)

If there ever were a courtship and marriage that could be characterized as "whirlwind," this one would be it. But few of us enter into marriage so easily; for most people, the decision to marry and the choice of a husband or wife take considerably more time.

In this chapter we focus on marriage. We examine how decisions are made about whether to marry and whom to marry, and what courses marriages tend to follow. Moreover, we consider how and why some marriages fail, and we discuss alternatives to traditional marriage.

We will begin by considering the choices people make regarding marriage. We first look at the factors that help people decide to marry and the ways they choose a specific individual as a partner. We also examine the stages through which marriages pass and the means by which people deal with marital discord.

Next we consider divorce. The chapter covers the factors that lead to a decision to terminate a marriage and the effects a divorce has on those involved. We also consider remarriage, discussing how second marriages differ from first ones.

The chapter concludes with a discussion of alternatives to marriage, including living together without marriage and several nontraditional forms of marriage. Finally, we discuss the consequences of being single.

11.1   LOOKING FOR MR. OR MS. RIGHT:
Choosing—and Keeping—a Spouse

Karen Evans O'Leary and Douglas F. Keenan were married at St. Brigid's Church in Amherst. The bride, daughter of Mr. and Mrs. Mark O'Leary of Hingham, graduated from Regis College. She is vice president of Office Mart Publishing House. The bridegroom, son of Mr. and Mrs. William Keenan, is a sales representative for the Mensum Corporation and is a graduate of Cunningham College. The couple will live in Boston after a trip in Hawaii.

What is interesting about this announcement, so typical of the thousands published daily in newspapers throughout the country, is that it reveals so little about who these two people actually are and the factors that drew them together. In this part of the chapter, we consider why people decide to marry and, more specifically, how they come to choose a particular individual as their spouse.

Choices:
To be or not to be . . . married

Why do two people decide to get married? If you asked most people raised in our Western culture, they would probably respond with the same answer: "love." In our society, love is the major reason people cite for deciding to get married, and you would find few people who would admit that they would even contemplate marrying someone with whom they were not in love (Simpson, Campbell, & Berscheid, 1986).

Moreover, most people think that even after they get married, love remains an essential ingredient of the marital relationship. Individuals typically feel that love is a requirement for maintaining a marriage, and love's termination is viewed as a sufficient reason for ending a marriage. In fact, most of the 75,000 women answering a survey about love and marriage reported that love was the key factor in the success of their marriages and in their initial decisions to marry (Tavris & Jayaratne, 1976).

Yet love is not the only reason people cite when asked why they married a particular individual. Most people also rate companionship and the need for a stable, intimate relationship as important. Husbands and wives seem

Sharing recreational interests is one component of a stable, satisfying marriage.

Alan Carey/The Image Works

to fulfill several kinds of roles in this regard (Nass, 1978). In the **therapeutic role,** the husband or wife helps the spouse with problems, perhaps dispensing advice or acting as a sounding board. In the **recreational role,** husband and wife share activities of a recreational nature—participating in sports, going to the movies, or engaging in other leisure-time undertakings.

Moreover, spouses fulfill a **sexual role.** For some individuals, marriage provides the only morally acceptable avenue for sexual activities. Although societal pressures are more lenient than they once were, and sex prior to marriage is generally viewed as less objectionable than it once was (as we discuss in Chapter 12), marriage still is viewed by many people as providing the most reliable, long-term avenue of sexual fulfillment.

Marriage also allows what is still the most socially acceptable means of having and raising children. Although the number of unwed parents has grown considerably over the past decade, most people still consider marriage a prerequisite for parenting.

Finally, some people view marriage as a means of providing economic security. For example, marriages in many cultures are still arranged on an economic basis. A bride who brings a large dowry to her marriage is seen as considerably more attractive than one whose dowry is small. Although the economic factor is certainly less important than it once was in Western society—few people admit they are marrying for financial security—it still plays a role in marital decisions. For example, parents may object to a son's or daughter's choice of mate if the potential spouse does not come from an "appropriate" economic background or if his or her financial prospects do not appear promising.

Choosing That Certain Someone:
Selecting a mate

We have seen that there are several factors that underlie people's desire to get married. But how do people move from a generalized motivation to marry to choosing a particular individual as their partner?

One answer to this question is provided by a model developed by Janda and Klenke-Hamel in 1980. The model suggests that just as we sift flour to rid it of the undesirable coarser particles, people choosing a mate typically screen potential partners through a **filtering process,** in which "candidates" are considered through successively finer-grained filters. According to the filtering model illustrated in Figure 11-1, the first filters are loosely woven, eliminating candidates who lack such basic characteristics as proximity and availability. For those candidates who survive this first filtering, the next filter reflects consideration of potential partners on the basis of similarity and complementarity of needs.

Then comes a filter that sifts for interpersonal attractiveness. The finest filter screens people on the basis of compatibility of expectations and notions of what role each is to play in a partnership. Presumedly, there are only a few people who make it all the way through the sifting process.

Although people may not be aware of the filtering process they employ

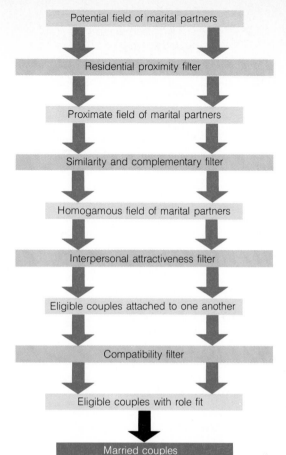

Potential field of marital partners

Residential proximity filter

Proximate field of marital partners

Similarity and complementary filter

Homogamous field of marital partners

Interpersonal attractiveness filter

Eligible couples attached to one another

Compatibility filter

Eligible couples with role fit

Married couples

FIGURE 11-1
The filtering model of partner selection. According to the model, potential candidates are considered through a series of successively finer-grained filters. (*Source*: Janda & Klenke-Hamel, 1980).

when choosing a mate—and presumedly the order in which filters are used may vary from one person to another—people are explicit about the characteristics they are looking for in a potential husband or wife. For instance, as you can see in Table 11-1, the list of the most important characteristics identified in one survey of unmarried undergraduates was topped by the traits "kindness and understanding," "exciting personality," and "intelligence." There are also some reliable sex differences: Physical attractiveness was significantly more important to men than to women, and good earning capacity and a college education were characteristics more important to women than to men (Buss & Barnes, 1986).

Beyond the Courtship:
Charting the course of marriage

Deciding to get married and identifying a mate are, of course, only precursors to marriage itself. Although many people consider married life to be a relatively stable, unvarying state, in reality matrimony is multifaceted, and

TABLE 11-1

**Preferences Concerning a
Potential Mate**

RANK	CHARACTERISTIC
1	Kind and understanding
2	Exciting personality
3	Intelligent
4	Physically attractive*
5	Healthy
6	Easygoing
7	Creative
8	Wants children
9	College graduate[†]
10	Good earning capacity[†]
11	Good heredity
12	Good housekeeper
13	Religious

*More important to males than to females.
†More important to females than to males.
Source: Buss & Barnes, 1986.

over the course of any marriage people move through several different stages. We now consider some of the major factors that influence how the typical marriage—in which the couple marries and raises children—unfolds over the years.

Early marriage: Choosing roles   Once the honeymoon comes to an end, the realities of married life come as a shock to many newly married couples. The excitement of their wedding and the trip that traditionally follows it begin to wear off, and couples face the critical task of adjusting to the challenges of marriage.

One of the first tasks that most couples face is deciding who does what. In the past, society provided clear guidelines regarding this distribution of activities. The husband was in charge of fixing the car, repairing appliances, building bookshelves, and—most important in the traditional view—earning a living. The wife, on the other hand, was to care for the house (cook, clean, and shop) and care for the children.

Obviously, times have changed; it is no longer assumed that society's traditional distribution of household activities is appropriate. Indeed, society itself has changed, and the view that particular household activities should not automatically be restricted to one or the other partner in the marriage is very much a part of contemporary society.

On the other hand, even among couples who consciously strive for an equitable distribution of household activities, the specific activities that the husband and wife carry out often fall into traditional patterns. Even the

Peter Simon/Stock, Boston

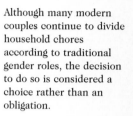

Although many modern couples continue to divide household chores according to traditional gender roles, the decision to do so is considered a choice rather than an obligation.

most successful career women may assume traditional roles at home (Burros, 1988).

Even with a satisfactory distribution of household chores, however, there is bound to be some degree of discord between husband and wife. There are several areas in which disagreements are likely to arise. For example, one survey found that the most frequent sources of conflict were money, sex, in-laws, recreation, friends, drug use, religion, and children (Knox, 1979). Sexual difficulties and occupational and child-rearing decisions can present especially difficult challenges. Resolving such conflicts represents an important challenge to the individual partners and the couple's collective adjustment.

Prior to marriage, conflicts are often resolved easily; partners readily acquiesce in order to avoid disrupting the romantic glow they feel envelops their relationship. After marriage, however, disagreements may take on a harsher reality, and husband and wife may be less apt to compromise and avoid issues for the sake of avoiding argument.

The communication style that a husband and wife adopt can have a substantial effect on their success in resolving their conflicts (Miller, Nunnally, & Wackman, 1975). For example, in some marriages, the dominant means of communication is **speculative communication,** in which problems are acknowledged, but the conflict is not dealt with in detail. (For example, "I apologize for getting angry; I just don't know what got into me" is a statement that admits there is a problem, but does little to resolve it.) In contrast, in **open communication,** couples speak honestly of their feelings, employing statements that reveal their own perceptions and providing reasons for their actions (as in "I apologize for getting angry; when you asked me to wash the dishes, I felt unappreciated, and what I thought you meant was that your time was more valuable than mine.")

The childbearing years of marriage   One of the major decisions facing couples is whether or not to have children. If a couple decides to raise a family, how many children should they have? How far apart? When? To a surprising extent, these decisions are affected by social conventions. For instance, in the 1940s two children was considered the ideal; in the 1950s, four children was thought optimal. In the 1960s, however, the trend reversed itself; the number declined. Currently, the average number of children in the family hovers at around two. Moreover, as more people postpone marriage and the proportion of women who delay their first birth until their middle and late thirties increases, the number of childless and one-child families will probably rise (Westoff, 1986). In fact, the percentage of couples with no children at all has doubled in the last few decades. In 1960 around 10 percent of married women between the ages of 25 and 34 were childless, while today the figure is closer to 25 percent.

What lies behind the rising rate of childlessness? There are several issues. As women have moved into well-paying, demanding careers in record numbers, many have found that motherhood requires too many sacrifices. For instance, as they see other couples juggling career and family, married couples may judge the competing demands as too difficult to successfully balance and decide against having children. Moreover, an economic analysis of the costs of child rearing may certainly weigh against having children; experts now estimate that parents must spend more than $135,000 to support a child through college (Kantrowitz, 1986).

In most cases, though, it is not the demands of childrearing, nor the economic drawbacks, that tip the scales against having children, but rather a conscious choice of priorities in a couple's lives. To some couples, the loss of freedom and the perceived potential costs to the closeness of their existing relationship make them decide against having children. As more and more people decide not to have children, childlessness may have little or no social stigma attached to it.

Despite the rise in the number of childless couples, most marriages still, at some point, produce offspring, and the advent of children into a marriage can produce several kinds of challenges. In addition to rather drastic shifts in activities that occur when the roles of "father" and "mother" are added to the other roles a couple occupies, there are ongoing questions that arise relating to child-rearing practices. Who should be the primary care giver? Should the child attend day care? How does one choose an appropriate school for one's child? What activities should the child be encouraged to engage in? How does one deal with school problems? What sorts of friendships should be encouraged? How can one deal with the problems that affect every child in our society, such as the ready availability of drugs? Each of these areas presents a challenge to parents, who must try to chart an optimal course for their children.

Marriage after the children have gone: The "empty-nest" stage of life   For couples with children, an important milestone occurs at the point when the

Ellis Herwig/Stock, Boston

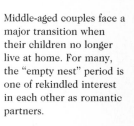

Middle-aged couples face a major transition when their children no longer live at home. For many, the "empty nest" period is one of rekindled interest in each other as romantic partners.

children leave home—to get jobs, to get married, to go off on their own, or to go to college. Whatever the reason, the departure of a family's children can produce a new set of challenges and adjustments. Typically, for some twenty years the primary roles husband and wife have played have been parental ones, but now their primary roles revert back to being husband and wife. This period of life is sometimes called the **empty-nest syndrome.**

As people live longer, the empty nest syndrome has tended to lengthen. For some people, the empty nest stage is welcomed, as couples rediscover their own freedom. For others, however, the period is less rosy. For home-makers whose lives are centered around their families, the departure of children may result in the feeling that their major role in life is over. More-over, because middle age brings with it some clear signs of aging (as we discussed in Chapter 3), people at this stage may begin to feel dissatisfied with their lives.

Still, there are unlikely to be any major changes in the quality of a marriage just because children have grown up. Marriages that were satis-factory when the children were home are likely to remain satisfactory, while marriages with problems are apt to continue to produce dissatisfaction (Duberman, 1974). (To gain some insight into the factors that characterize successful marriages, see the Do It! box.)

DO IT!

MARRIAGES MADE TO LAST

In an effort to determine the factors that make for happy marriages, Lauer and Lauer (1985) surveyed couples with enduring marriages and asked about the most important factor that accounted for their marriage's success. Below are the six most frequently cited reasons by both husbands and wives:

My spouse is my best friend.

I like my spouse as a person.

Marriage is a long-term commitment.

Marriage is sacred.

We agree on aims and goals.

My spouse has grown more interesting.

Now see if you can predict how husbands and wives differed in the frequency with which they chose these six factors by ordering them in the appropriate column below:

Husbands	Wives
1.	1.
2.	2.
3.	3.
4.	4.
5.	5.
6.	6.

ANSWER: In the survey there was *no* difference between husbands and wives in the frequency with which they cited the six items; each listed the six in the order printed above. Men and women, then, were similar in their views of the reasons behind the success of their marriages.

Source: Lauer & Lauer, 1985.

Psychology for You:
Preventing marital discord

We have seen that there are several areas that may produce conflict in marriage. There are, however, several techniques that can be used to reduce the destructiveness of discord, including the following (Knapp, 1984; Goleman, 1985):

● *Focus conflict on one topic at a time, and provide a rationale and an explanation for your behavior.* You might say, for example, "What you are doing makes me particularly upset right now, not because of anything you did, but because I got stuck in traffic on the way home from work."

● *Avoid direct criticism.* Instead of saying, "You are the most selfish person I know," say, "It seems as if your behavior in this instance does not take my interests into account." By using this maneuver, you discuss a person's behavior—which is relatively amenable to change—rather than criticizing his or her character and personality.

● *Communicate in terms of specific changes in behavior you would like to see in your partner.* Don't label undesired behavior in a manner that is bound to cause offense. A spouse who is told, "I feel exploited by having to pick up your dirty clothes from the floor" is likely to react more positively than one who is told, "You are a lazy slob, and I'm tired of having to pick up your clothes from the floor."

● *Try to "stop the action" and enter a cool-off period during a conflict.* The "stop the action" technique allows both partners to become less enveloped in the discord, lessening the chances that the conflict will escalate into a major battle.

● *Avoid "mind reading," pretending to know another person's thoughts or feelings.* Think how you would react if someone said to you, "You can't fool me; I can read you like a book"; "I know that you've had a bad day; don't try to hide it"; or "You're so depressed; you must be getting your period." You should be cautious in making judgments about the causes of another person's behavior, because the way in which you make attributions will have important consequences for the nature of your relationship (Fincham, Beach, & Baucom, 1987).

TO REVIEW

● People marry because they are in love and because marriage provides companionship. Marriage can also provide a stable, intimate relationship, an avenue for a socially sanctioned sexual relationship, children, and economic security.

● A mate is typically chosen via a filtering process, in which candidates are considered through successively finer-grained filters.

● During the earliest stage of marriage, husband and wife choose roles and attempt to deal with conflict.

● The second major stage of marriage occurs during the childbearing years, when couples make choices regarding their children and how to raise them.

● In the post-children period of marriage, sometimes called the empty-nest syndrome, parents once again assume the primary family identities of husband and wife instead of father and mother. Marriages that were successful tend to remain successful during this stage, while marriages that produced dissatisfaction continue to be unsatisfactory.

CHECK YOURSELF

1.   Kevin thought to himself, "She is very attractive, but I know her culture and religion are very different from mine, so maybe I won't introduce myself." Screening potential partners in this manner has been referred to as a _____ _____.

2.   Couples who strive for equitable relationships usually find themselves performing only those tasks not typically ascribed to their gender. True or false?

3.   Which one of the following reasons was *not* cited in the text as a reason for an increase in childlessness?
   a.   Economically, childrearing is becoming prohibitively expensive.
   b.   The demands of childrearing for dual-income couples are considered too burdensome to undertake.
   c.   More marriages are ending in divorce, upsetting couples during the childbearing years.
   d.   Couples now seem to prioritize their personal closeness and perceive childbearing as too great a sacrifice.

4.   Unsatisfactory marriages often improve dramatically with the departure of the children. True or false?

5.   Rather than criticizing each other's characters or personalities, couples should identify specific instances of each other's _____.

_____

(See answers to the questions at the bottom of page 368.)

11.2   'TIL DEATH DO US PART?:
Divorce and Remarriage

"Al, I don't love you any more. I want a divorce."
I couldn't believe my ears. A divorce! . . . My mind was spinning. Everything was a jumble, fragmentary images of what we were and what Jean was saying. This couldn't be. This couldn't be the same Jean, the Jean I had known and loved all those years. I couldn't find words to answer immediately. My mind and my voice were in two different places. Finally, I half cried and half choked, "You can't mean that. Why? What for? What about us? What about the kids?" (Martin, 1975, pp. 5–7.)

Scenes such as the one reported above are far from rare in contemporary American society. The statistics are hardly surprising: Some 1 million divorces occur each year, and more than 40 percent of all new marriages are likely to end in divorce.

Yet divorce is not inevitable; most marriages still remain intact, and many thrive and provide a lifetime of happiness and contentment to the participants. Moreover, since 1981 the number of marriages has increased by 3 percent, while the number of divorces has declined by 5 percent (Harris, 1987).

What are the factors that lead to divorce? As you can see in Table 11-2, investigators have found several factors that are associated with a higher or lower probability of divorce. These factors do not necessarily identify the specific cause of a divorce; they are merely elements that correlate with a higher probability of marital instability and divorce.

Some psychologists have approached the issue of divorce by examining the rewards a couple gets from marriage, the barriers against divorce, and the alternatives to marriage that are available to the couple (Levinger, 1979). For instance, marriage provides material rewards, such as family income. It may also provide status, affection, companionship, and sexual fulfillment.

TABLE 11-2
Likelihood of Marital Instability and Divorce

FACTORS ASSOCIATED WITH HIGHER PROBABILITY OF DIVORCE

Urban background
Marriage at very young age (15 to 19 years old)
Short acquaintanceship before marriage
Short engagement or no engagement
Parents with unhappy marriages
Kin's and friends' disapproval of the marriage
General dissimilarity in background
Membership in different religious faiths
Failure to attend religious services
Disagreement of husband and wife on role obligations

FACTORS ASSOCIATED WITH LOWER PROBABILITY OF DIVORCE

Rural background
Marriage at average or older ages
Acquaintanceship of two years or more prior to marriage
Engagement of six months or more
Parents with happy marriages
Kin's and friends' approval of the marriage
Similarity of background
Membership in same religious faith
Regular attendance at religious services
Agreement of husband and wife on role obligations

Source: Goode, 1976, pp. 537–538.

Jeffrey Dunn/The Picture Cube

Seeking a divorce entails many major decisions. While legal considerations are often in the forefront, the divorce also carries great emotional weight.

There are several barriers to divorce, including financial and legal expenses and complications, feelings regarding the welfare of the couple's children, and religious and societal constraints against divorce.

Finally, even when both the rewards of marriage and the barriers against leaving a marriage are perceived as low, individuals still consider the nature of alternatives available to them before deciding to terminate a marriage. If the alternatives are worse or no better than the current relationship, people may remain in a less-than-satisfying marriage.

Ironically, the frequency of divorce in our society may itself be a reason for relationships to flounder. As divorce becomes more commonplace, the perceived barriers against it appear to diminish. Certainly, the societal stigma against divorce has declined in the last few decades. (To see how your own views of marriage and divorce match up with those of other college students, see the Do It! box).

CHECK YOURSELF: ANSWERS
1. filtering process **2.** False **3.** c **4.** False **5.** behavior

MARRIAGE . . . AND DIVORCE

To get a sense of how well your own feelings about marriage and divorce match up with those of other college students, indicate your agreement with each of the following statements, using this five-point scale:

1 = strongly agree
2 = agree
3 = not certain
4 = disagree
5 = strongly disagree

1. I believe marriage is a lifelong commitment. _____

2. I believe divorce is acceptable except when children are involved. _____

3. I view my parents' marriage as happy. _____

4. I believe I have the skills to make a good marriage. _____

5. If I have a child, I feel only one parent should work so the other can take care of the child. _____

6. I believe children are not necessary in a marriage. _____

7. I believe household chores and tasks should be equally shared between marital partners. _____

8. If my spouse is offered a job in a different locality, I will move with him or her. _____

9. I do not believe extramarital sex is wrong for me. _____

10. I believe friendships outside of marriage with the opposite sex are important in a marriage. _____

11. I believe the major social functioning in a marriage should be with other couples. _____

12. I believe married couples should not argue in front of other people. _____

13. I want to marry someone who has the same social needs as I have. _____

14. I believe religious practices are important in a marriage. _____

15. I would not marry a person of a different religious background. _____

16. If I do not like my spouse's parents, I should not be obligated to visit them. _____

17. I feel parents should not intervene in any matters pertaining to my marriage. _____

18. I feel I need more education on what to expect from marriage. _____

19. I believe counseling is only for those couples in trouble. _____

SCORING   Compare your responses with those of more than 5000 college students. The numbers given are the most popular answers for each item: (1) 1; (2) 4; (3) 1; (4) 2; (5) 4; (6) 2; (7) 2; (8) 2; (9) 5; (10) 2; (11) 2; (12) 2; (13) 2; (14) 1; (15) 4; (16) 4; (17) 1; (18) 2; (19) 4. Note, of course, that these responses are only those of the majority. They are not right or wrong—they simply reflect people's opinions.

Source: Martin & Martin, 1984.

In addition, as more people are divorced, the number of alternative relationships grows because more people join the pool of potential partners. Partners, thus, are forced to continually reevaluate their present relationship, which itself becomes a cost of maintaining the relationship (Berscheid & Campbell, 1981).

Uncoupling:
The outcomes of divorce

No one comes through a divorce unscathed; it is a difficult experience for everyone involved, as it affects them on several different levels. Specifically, divorce has an impact in the following areas (Bohanan, 1970):

● *Emotional.* The relationship between the two individuals, once characterized by love and affection, deteriorates into a very different set of emotions. There also can be emotional withdrawal or mutual antagonism.

● *Legal.* Divorce takes place within the context of the legal system. Because of the complexity of the law in many states, the legal aspects of divorce can be time-consuming and expensive and can add to the emotional strain on both parties involved.

● *Parental.* When children are involved, a couple must make decisions regarding child custody and support. While in the past custody has been awarded, almost automatically, to the wife, contemporary law allows either parent to have primary responsibility for the children. In some cases, in fact, husband and wife receive joint custody of the children.

● *Community.* The divorce alters relationships with friends and acquaintances. Many divorced people find that their social relationships with other couples no longer function effectively, and they must develop new relationships.

● *Psychological.* People may face changes in their own psychological makeup, including changes in self-esteem or a sense of autonomy. They must separate themselves psychologically from the influence of a spouse and learn to function more independently.

Each of these areas is associated with its own challenges to the adjustment of the parties involved. As with any challenge, however, the outcome need not be negative. Beginning a new life after divorce can provide important psychological and adjustive growth.

Starting Over:
Remarriage

For most people, divorce does not mark the final curtain in the drama of marriage: 75 to 80 percent of those who get divorced get married once again, usually within two to five years. They typically marry a person who has also experienced divorce, in part because those are the people who are most likely to be available, and in part because they share similar experiences.

There are several reasons why remarriage following divorce is so prevalent. For one, newly single people raising children may feel that it is better for their children to have an intact family structure. Moreover, much of the

Michael Weisbrot and Family

For divorced men and women with children, the decision to marry and form a "blended" family has far-reaching consequences and signifies a major adjustment for everyone involved.

social life that divorced individuals have previously experienced probably centered around married couples, and as single people they may be excluded from the social patterns with which they are familiar. When these factors are added to the reasons people marry in the first place—love, companionship, economic security, and so forth—remarriage may appear to be a highly desirable option.

Unfortunately, remarriage does not always work out in the way people hope, and in fact the statistics regarding the success of second marriages are not comforting. The percentage of second marriages that end in divorce is even higher than for first marriages, and the average second marriage is shorter-lived than the first marriage.

There are several reasons second marriages have a higher rate of failure than first marriages. For one thing, divorced people may marry "on the rebound," seeking to overcome the pain they have experienced during divorce, and they may not fully consider the possible negative aspects of their relationship. Moreover, there are strains on second marriages that are not present in first marriages, often in terms of having to integrate children from two families.

On the other hand, many second marriages are successful. Second marriages that last several years can give people satisfaction that does not differ substantially from that in successful first marriages (Glenn & Weaver, 1977).

Many people report being significantly happier with their second marriage than with their first. This greater satisfaction can come from several sources. People who have gone through divorce may enter into a second marriage with a clearer sense of reality and expectations about what a marital relationship can and cannot provide. Participants in second marriages are likely older and, therefore, emotionally more mature. Finally, they are less apt to compare a present partner to some abstract, ideal spouse; and any comparison to a previous spouse would likely favor the current partner.

Remarriage, then, brings with it the possibility of learning from one's mistakes—or the potential for recreating one's failures. Whatever the outcome, it is clear that, for most people, marriage remains a preferred option.

Psychology for You:
Dealing with marital problems

You've suffered along for months, perhaps years. You are unhappy in your marriage, and you've begun to think that divorce may be a reasonable solution to your problems. Yet, at the same time, you want to do your best to avoid a divorce. What can you do?

● *Communicate with your spouse.* Don't let things seethe inside of you; let your spouse know that you are upset and the extent of your dissatisfaction with the marriage. None of us are mind readers, and a spouse simply may be unaware of what it is about the marriage that bothers you.

● *Don't stay married for the sake of the children, your parents, or anyone else's feelings.* You do no one else any good—and you potentially harm yourself and your children—by remaining in a relationship that is miserable for you. Consider the way you feel and the quality of your life in making decisions about your marital relationship.

● *Seek professional help.* A trained marriage counselor can provide help to couples that are motivated to save their marriages. As with any mental health professional, it is important that the therapist have the right credentials; for instance, members of the American Association for Marriage and Family Therapy must meet strict membership criteria.

● *Don't equate divorce with failure.* Even if you attempt to save your marriage, it may ultimately be impossible. If this is the case, it is important not to characterize yourself as a failure. The reasons for the marriage's end may be out of your control, or circumstances may have conspired to provide you with no other reasonable choice. Moreover, people make mistakes, and for many people, marrying the wrong person for the wrong reasons is one of their biggest. Whatever the reason, divorce can be one of life's most significant challenges, providing the potential for personal growth.

TO REVIEW

● Divorce is a frequent phenomenon in our society. There are about 1 million divorces each year, and more than 40 percent of all new marriages are likely to end in divorce.

● People decide to get divorced by considering the rewards they receive from marriage, the barriers against divorce, and the alternatives to marriage that are available to them.

● Divorce has an impact on emotional, legal, parental, community, and psychological levels.

● The rate of remarriage for divorced people is high: Some 75 to 80 percent of those who get divorced get married again. Although the divorce rate for remarriages is even higher than for first marriages, many remarriages are successful.

CHECK YOURSELF

1. Even in a relationship in which few rewards exist, couples may decide against divorce as an alternative for several reasons. List three.

2. An increase in the rate of divorce has made divorce a more socially acceptable alternative and, as such, may serve as a reason for relationships to falter. True or false?

3. Match the statements on the right with the appropriate area of impact of divorce on the left.

_____ emotional	a. "Susan and I both want custody of Tom."
_____ legal	b. "It's hard to believe we were so close, and now we can't look at each other."
_____ parental	c. "I have to regain my confidence, now that I'll be facing life alone for a while."
_____ community	d. "I don't know how I'll be able to pay the attorney's fees for this."
_____ psychological	e. "They're our best friends, and now neither of us are comfortable around them."

4. Approximately _____ to _____ percent of individuals who get divorced marry a second time.

_____

(See answers to the questions at the bottom of page 376.)

11.3 OPTIONS:
Alternatives to Marriage

Are there advantages for me to not being legally married? I was brought up with traditional values. You must get married, that type of thing, and have that piece of paper, but I feel the commitment is mental, and emotional. It's stuck in my head, not on a piece of paper. . . .

If he had said to me, "Let's get married," I don't know how I would feel. I haven't thought of it. I think I'd rather stay the way it is now. I think it gives me more of a sense of my own identity. Sometimes people say I don't want to because it leaves me free to split or whatever I want to do. But I don't think of it that way. If I want to leave, I'm going to want to leave, whether I've got that paper and a thousand other papers and a hundred wedding gifts and the whole bit. (Fleming & Washburne, 1977, p. 274.)

Not everyone chooses to follow the traditional path of marriage. For the woman quoted above, for instance, the state of matrimony provides no advantages over the situation in which she and her partner simply live together. We turn now to a consideration of this and other alternatives to traditional marriage.

Love Without the Legalities:
Cohabiting couples

The Bureau of the Census calls it POSSLQ—persons of opposite sex sharing living quarters. Some people label it "shacking up." Whatever term is used,

cohabitation—in which an unmarried male and female live together and have an intimate relationship—has been on the rise in our society.

The common stereotype of cohabiting couples is that they are young, irresponsible, and uncaring of the traditional norms of society. In every respect, such a stereotype tends to be overdrawn. There are people of every age who live together without marriage (including the elderly); there is no evidence that they are more or less responsible than any other category of individuals; and they are quite sensitive to the traditional norms of society. In many instances, in fact, it is a careful and thoughtful consideration of society's norms that has led them to choose an alternative to marriage.

The figures on how many people cohabit are not easy to determine, but it has been estimated that 20 to 35 percent of all college students have cohabited, and more than 2 million Americans are "living together." In about one-quarter of these cases, there are children involved. By and large, cohabiting couples who have not previously married are better educated than married couples, and they are found more often in urban areas (Glick & Spanier, 1980).

Why do people choose cohabitation over marriage? Some people feel that the risks of marriage are so great that they ought to first experiment by living together, thereby being able to reassure themselves that their partner is indeed the person with whom they want to share the rest of their lives. Others cohabit because they have experienced a painful divorce, and they are hesitant to resume the commitment that marriage implies, feeling that it is easier to end a nonmarried relationship than a marriage.

Still others decide that the legalities and social implications of marriage are undesirable, and they cohabit to avoid being cast into the roles of "hus-

John Coletti/Stock, Boston

Cohabitation without marriage is an alternative chosen by couples of many ages and socioeconomic levels.

band" and "wife." (On the other hand, the outcomes of recent "palimony" legal cases—in which one partner sues the other for support after a relationship had ended—suggest that there may be an implicit legal contract that exists between unmarried partners in long-term relationships, even if it is an unwritten one.)

Ironically, however, long-term cohabiting couples often find it just as hard to end a relationship as do long-term married couples. In fact, the kinds of lives that cohabiting couples lead are not all that different from those of married couples. The nature of adjustments that must be made to the partners, the requirement that people choose and negotiate specific roles in the relationship, and the decisions and adjustments that revolve around children are also necessary for cohabiting couples.

Whatever the reasons that people cohabit, it is clear that societal norms against cohabitation are much less restrictive than in previous eras. While in the past women who lived with men were viewed as "loose" and morally corrupt, today the social stigma of cohabitation has diminished considerably.

Despite society's increasing tolerance of cohabitation, there are still serious problems that may be associated with it. For example, the lack of legal sanction of the relationship—sometimes viewed as an advantage—can present difficulties when children are born. Moreover, if cohabiting is used as a means of avoiding the emotional responsibilities inherent in long-term relationships, the costs of such an arrangement may be considerable.

Expanding the Limits of Married Life:
Open marriage and group marriage

For some people, traditional married life, which carries the responsibilities of sexual and emotional fidelity to one's spouse, is too restrictive. To overcome such limitations, Nena and George O'Neill developed the concept of **open marriage** in the early 1970s to describe marriages in which sexual encounters with people outside the marriage are acceptable. (To test your feelings about some of the major propositions of open marriage, see the following Do It! box.)

CHECK YOURSELF: ANSWERS

1. Financial and legal expenses and complications; the perceived welfare of the couple's children; religious and/or societal constraints **2.** True **3.** b, d, a, e, c **4.** 75 to 80

WHAT ARE YOUR VIEWS ON OPEN MARRIAGE?

To assess your agreement with the major notions of open marriage, check the alternative in each pair of items that best describes how you feel (if you are not married, place yourself in the role of spouse):

1. _____ My spouse and I feel that our marriage is going to last forever, OR
_____ My spouse and I realize that our marital relationship is subject to changes which might result in our going separate ways.

2. _____ My spouse and I feel that it is important to spend some of our vacation time apart, OR
_____ My spouse and I don't believe in separate vacations.

3. _____ My spouse and I keep certain dreams and fantasies to ourselves to avoid hurting each other, OR
_____ My spouse and I share our dreams and fantasies even if they reveal "forbidden" desires.

4. _____ My spouse and I often exchange roles for convenience sake, OR
_____ My spouse and I have our ascribed roles in our marriage.

5. _____ My spouse and I feel that it is a risk to our marriage for either of us to develop a caring relationship with someone of the opposite sex outside of our family, OR
_____ My spouse and I feel comfortable with each other developing caring relationships with individuals of the opposite sex outside of our family.

6. _____ My spouse and I pursue our own unique lifestyles, OR
_____ My spouse and I have evolved a compromise lifestyle.

7. _____ When either spouse is away, we are concerned about what the other might do, OR
_____ Neither of us has any qualms about what the other might do when he/she is away.

SCORING   For each odd-numbered item, give yourself one point if you preferred the second of the two statements. For each even-numbered item, give yourself one point if you preferred the first of the two statements. The higher the total number of points, the more you agree with the basic assumptions of open marriage; the lower your score, the more comfortable you are with traditional forms of marriage.

Source: Items were drawn from a scale developed by Wachowiak & Bragg, 1980.

According to O'Neill and O'Neill (1972), the ideal open marriage differs from traditional marriage in several key respects:

- There is an emphasis on the here and now, rather than on the long-term goals typical of traditional marriages.

- There is greater respect for personal privacy than in traditional marriage, allowing people to lead personal lives that they do not necessarily feel they must share with a spouse.

- Open marriages have greater role flexibility.

- Couples engage in open companionship, avoiding the traditional notion of acting as a couple. This may involve developing deep emotional and even sexual relationships with people outside the marriage.

- Open marriages show greater equality in power and responsibility.

Although there are quite a few people who are, in some degree, sympathetic to the philosophy of open marriage, the number of individuals who actually adhere to all its principles is a small minority of married couples. The major difficulty comes in the sexual and emotional arenas; the vast majority of married people are unable to openly accept extramarital liaisons on the part of their spouses without experiencing jealousy and personal conflict.

Group marriage, in which three or more people consider themselves married, is another alternative to traditional marriage. In group marriage, the partners form intimate emotional and sexual bonds with one another, although the nature of the specific relationships with the group marriage varies from one to another.

As you might expect, the complexities involved in maintaining a group marriage are enough to make Mideast peace negotiations look simple. Consequently, group marriages are quite rare, and—where they do exist—they are fragile and prone to breakups. In one study, for instance, the average length of a group marriage was just a year and a half, with many lasting just a few weeks (Constantine & Constantine, 1970).

Going It Alone:
Staying single

When the findings were announced, they created an immediate stir. A study of marriage trends in the United States found some startling statistics: College-educated white women born in the 1950s who are still unmarried at age 30 stand only a 20 percent chance of ever tying the knot. At age 35, their chances slip to 5 percent, and by age 40 they almost stand a better chance of winning a lottery, as the odds of getting married are reported to be at just 2.6 percent (Bennett, Craig, & Bloom, 1986).

For those women who had postponed marriage under the assumption that they would marry when they felt the time was appropriate, the statistics came as an unpleasant shock. Many women felt suddenly pressured to "search" for a husband, while others resigned themselves to being single for the rest of their lives.

On the other hand, for those women who had chosen to be single, the news had little impact. Some 5 percent of the population in the United States never marry, and many of those who remain single make a deliberate decision to pursue life without a spouse.

Moreover, the statistics had little relevance to men. For one thing, the projections pertained only to women; oddly enough, the census data on which the findings of the study were based were insufficiently reliable to draw conclusions regarding males. Moreover, society places considerably fewer sanctions on unmarried men, who are permitted more flexibility in their marital state than women. Whereas it is acceptable for an older man to marry a younger woman, society frowns on marriages in which the woman is substantially older than the man. Even the labels traditionally used to describe unmarried women—"spinsters" and "old maids"—are pejorative, while unmarried men are called "bachelors," a word with more positive connotations.

Despite the difficulties unmarried women face, many women—and men—are choosing to remain single. Being single may be perceived as offering several advantages. There is typically greater freedom and flexibility of lifestyles for unmarried individuals than for those that are married. Moreover, some people may wish not to become highly dependent on any single individual, or may reject the idea that living with another person requires the legal sanction of society.

Greater sexual freedom is also offered by being single. For example, the ability to have multiple sexual liaisons, without the concern of fidelity to a spouse, is offered by a single lifestyle (although the AIDS epidemic has made relationships with multiple sexual partners unwise). Finally, for the estimated 10 percent of the population that is homosexual, legalized marriage is not a viable option.

On the other hand, there are losses brought about by being unmarried. Single people do not have a traditional family with whom to share their joys and their problems, nor do they have the long-term emotional attachments that marriage can ideally provide. There are economic costs, as well. Married couples who each work can have a higher standard of living by pooling their two salaries than can a single person living on one salary, given the proportion of income that must be applied to housing costs. Remaining single in this traditional society can ultimately present serious challenges to adjustment given that our social structure is organized in terms of couples. The problem is even more difficult for people who remain single but who would like to get married; they must get beyond feelings that they have failed in an important social sense, and instead accept their situation as a valid and positive lifestyle, perceiving the very real advantages that only single people experience.

Psychology for You:
Is POSSLQ a possibility?

Dear Abby:

I am a 20-year-old, third-year college student with a big problem. Four months ago I moved in with my boyfriend, and since that time my family has thrown more guilt my way than a person can deal with in a lifetime. My mom says I will roast in hell and she will never accept my boyfriend as a son-in-law. (We plan to marry next year.) The last time my mom called, she begged me to move out, saying my sinful action is killing my grandparents—that my grandfather has removed all my pictures from their house and refuses to speak my name. My mom says my grandparents cry all the time and may never let me in their house again. Also, their 50th wedding anniversary party has been called off because I chose to live with my boyfriend.

Don't you think I am old enough to make my own decisions for my life, or should I allow my family to "blackmail" me into a decision made by them? I want to do the right thing.

—Lost in Portland ("Dear Abby," November 18, 1986).

In a very real sense, this letter to advice columnist Abby Van Buren (who, by the way, told the letter writer that she was old enough to make her own decisions about whom she lived with) illustrates some of the difficulties faced by people who find themselves as POSSLQ—persons of opposite sex sharing living quarters. Choosing to live with another person is a weighty decision, one that requires much forethought. But it is also one that is made with increasing frequency among college-age individuals.

How do you know whether such a move is appropriate for you? Among the issues to consider are the following:

● Living together should not be done on a whim. You should have a strong, loving relationship with the person with whom you intend to live. You should not have to be talked into living together; it should be a decision shared by both partners.

● Work out ground rules before you move in together. How will finances be managed? How will household chores be shared? What friends will be invited to visit, and how often?

● Carefully examine your moral, religious, and ethical background. Even if you feel that cohabitation is morally appropriate, you may still experience feelings of guilt if you perceive you are defying important moral strictures that were taught to you as a child.

● Consider how your family feels about your behavior. If you are close to your family, and they disapprove, it is reasonable that you will experience conflict over cohabitation.

Innervisions

For college-age couples, the decision to cohabit may be strongly influenced by whether their parents approve of the arrangement.

TO REVIEW

● Cohabitation, in which an unmarried male and female live together and have an intimate relationship, is far from rare in our society.

● In an open marriage, sexual encounters with people outside the marriage are considered acceptable.

● Choosing to remain single is a viable alternative for people, although females face negative stereotypes regarding unmarried women.

CHECK YOURSELF

1. Which of the following is *not* considered an important reason for deciding to cohabit?
    a. Living together allows for experimentation before making a marriage commitment.
    b. Ending a relationship would be considerably easier to handle emotionally.
    c. The couple may view the legalities of marriage as undesirable.
    d. Socially, couples do not want to be typecast as "husband and wife."

2. What is the major difficulty most often encountered in open marriages?
   a. lack of long-term goals
   b. violation of individual privacy
   c. unstable balance of responsibility and power
   d. jealousy and conflict from extramarital emotional and sexual relationships

3. Group marriage is becoming more popular as an alternative to traditional marriage. True or false?

4. Despite advantages to remaining single, there are several potential disadvantages that may result. List three.

5. Simply making the decision to cohabit outside of marriage is a strong indicator that moral dilemmas will not arise. True or false?

(See answers to the questions at the bottom of page 384.)

TO SUMMARIZE

1. When asked to indicate the reasons that they marry, most people focus on love. However, there are many other reasons to marry, including companionship; the need for a stable, intimate relationship; a morally acceptable avenue for sexual activities and parenting; and economic security. Mates tend to be selected via a filtering process, in which candidates are screened through successively finer-grained filters.

2. Marriages pass through several stages. During the early years of marriage, a primary task is choosing roles. Traditionally, husbands earned a living while wives tended the house and children. Today, however, the roles are considerably more flexible. During the next stage of marriage—the childbearing years—couples decide whether they want children and, if so, how many to have. Finally, in the postchildren phase of marriage, couples face the "empty-nest" syndrome, in which the couple's children leave home and the husband and wife are once again alone.

3. Techniques for preventing marital discord include focusing conflict on one topic at a time; providing rationales for one's behavior; trying to stop the action and enter a cooling-off period during a conflict; avoiding direct criticism, talking about specific changes in behavior; and avoiding "mind reading," an attempt by one person to predict another person's thoughts.

4. Around 1 million divorces occur each year, and more than 40 percent of all new marriages are likely to end in divorce. Divorce occurs through a consideration of the rewards a couple gets from marriage, the barriers present against divorce, and alternatives to marriage that are available to the partners.

5. The decision to divorce has an impact in several important areas. For example, there are emotional and legal outcomes, effects relating to parenting, impacts on the level of community relationships with friends and acquaintances, and psychological difficulties that are related to divorce.

6. For people who divorce, remarriage is frequent; 75 to 80 percent of those who divorce remarry, usually within two to five years. Unfortunately, the rate of divorce in second marriages is even higher than that in first ones. Still, many second marriages prosper and endure.

7. There are several principles involved in dealing with marital problems. They include communication with one's spouse, not staying married for the sake of children, seeking professional help, and realizing that divorce is not the equivalent of failure.

8. There are several alternatives to traditional marriage. One is cohabitation, in which an unmarried male and female live together and have an intimate relationship. Estimates suggest that from 20 to 35 percent of all college students have cohabited at some time. Societal norms against cohabitation are much less restrictive than they once were.

9. Open marriage, another alternative to traditional marriage, holds that sexual encounters with people outside the marriage should be acceptable. Group marriage, in contrast, is an alternative in which three or more people consider themselves married. Both open marriages and group marriages are rare in our society.

10. Staying single provides an alternative to marriage. Unmarried people have greater freedom and flexibility: They are not dependent on another individual, and they may have greater sexual freedom. On the other hand, they do not have traditional families, nor do they have the long-term emotional attachment with one person that marriage can provide. Women, especially, may face negative stereotyping as "spinsters" and "old maids."

11. In deciding whether cohabitation is a viable alternative, people should consider the strength of their relationship; their moral, religious, and ethical background; and the attitudes of their families. Moreover, ground rules should be worked out before moving in together.

KEY TERMS AND CONCEPTS

therapeutic role (of marriage) (p. 358)

recreational role (of marriage) (p. 358)

sexual role (of marriage) (p. 358)

filtering process (p. 358)

speculative communication (in marriage) (p. 361)

open communication (in marriage) (p. 361)

empty-nest syndrome (p. 363)

cohabitation (p. 375)

open marriage (p. 376)

group marriage (p. 378)

TO FIND OUT MORE

Hendrick, C., & Hendrick, S. (1983). *Liking, loving, and relating.* Monterey, CA: Brooks/Cole.

This volume provides extensive coverage on ways in which marriages and other loving relationships develop, maintain themselves, and sometimes decline.

Bernard, J. (1972). *The future of marriage.* New York: World.

A classic book, written by a well-known sociologist, discusses the shape of marriage.

Wallerstein, J. S., & Kelly, J. B. (1980). *Surviving the breakup: How children and parents cope with divorce.* New York: Basic Books.

A helpful guide to the effects of divorce, including ways in which people actively cope with its problems.

CHECK YOURSELF: ANSWERS

1. b **2.** d **3.** False **4.** (a) Single people lack the benefits of sharing that a family may provide. (b) Long-term emotional bonds may be lacking. (c) Shared incomes allow for a higher standard of living. **5.** False

CHAPTER

12

Sex and Life
Human Sexual Behavior

Where did I find out about sex? It certainly wasn't from my parents. If I had depended on them, I still wouldn't know the first thing about sex. Oh, I remember some stilted conversations when I asked about where babies came from (I think my father's response was to leave the room, and my mother mumbled something about—believe it or not—the stork, and that I still wasn't old enough to understand it all that well). Later on, as I approached adolescence and tried once more to find out something about sex, my parents' responses were even more evasive and embarrassed, and I gave up ever finding out anything from them.

I turned, instead, to the library, where I furtively looked through books that had sexually explicit passages. The really "good" books, I found out, were under lock and key, behind the librarian's desk, and of course I could never get up the nerve to ask for one of those. But I got quite an education just from randomly taking books off the shelves, although I'm still not sure how accurate these sources were.

At the same time I was conducting my compulsive literature search, I was also playing scientist, using myself as my only subject. Even before I had run across any reference to it, I discovered masturbation. "Discover" is the right word; I thought I was the only one in the world to masturbate, and thought there was something incredibly unusual about my body that allowed it to feel so good. Each time I masturbated, I vowed that it would be my last time; I was sure I would get cancer or some equally dread disease because of my depravity. Unfortunately, my vows, while made with great earnestness, would never hold; I soon found myself unable to control my urges.

My initiation into sex with a partner was equally uninformed, and had overtones of excitement, guilt, and disaster. Oh, it felt good to finally be doing the thing that I read so much about; but I was so scared that the pleasure and passion that I thought sex was always supposed to bring—at least in the books I had found—was pretty well lost to the moment.

I still don't understand why my initial experiences with sex were so difficult. Why should sex, which is so much a part of everyone's lives, be so difficult a topic to discuss and think about in a rational way?

The question that ends this passage is one we might all well be asking. As this person notes, there is no more basic a behavior for human beings than sex. Unfortunately, though, many people's initiations into sex contain elements that are similar to the one described above, and coming to grips with human sexuality remains a critical challenge throughout most people's lives.

In this chapter, we consider how human sexuality is related to everyday living. We begin by discussing the physiological aspects of the human sex organs, examining some of the biology that underlies the sex act. We also look at the factors that explain what arouses us sexually and explore the patterns of human sexual responsivity.

We turn next to the various patterns and alternatives involved in sexual behavior. We examine such basic practices as masturbation, heterosexuality, homosexuality, and bisexuality, considering their manifestations in people's lives.

Finally, problems in sexual adjustment are discussed. We focus on the primary example of nonconsenting sex—rape—and AIDS, the major health problem relating to sexual activity. Also, we examine the most common sexual dysfunctions, problems that are surprisingly frequent in many people's lives. The chapter ends with a discussion of treatment strategies for sexual difficulties.

As we review the various forms of sexual behavior, it is important to keep in mind that it is impossible to consider sex without reference to one's underlying moral and ethical values. Each of us must decide for ourselves what sexual activities are appropriate—or inappropriate—for us; not friends, family, nor any psychology book can determine what is sexually right or wrong. It is only when we thoughtfully consider our sexuality in the broader context of our lives that we can make informed decisions about this most basic aspect of our humanity.

12.1 THE FACTS OF LIFE:
Basic Sexual Biology

And then, without saying a word, he began to undo the tiny buttons up her arms, revealing the creamy flesh underneath, and kissing her as he did so. And then, removing first the heavy ropes of pearls he had given

Although popular romances may excite sexual fantasies, they are unreliable as a source of information about sexuality.

Innervisions

her, he began to undo the myriad tiny satin buttons down the front of her dress, revealing the exquisite cleavage, covered by the perfectly sculpted satin slip, and finally the lacy corset . . . this was precisely as she had dreamed it . . . plunging into her with his full desire unleashed within, she moaned not with pain but with pleasure. . . . He brought her an exquisite agony she had never even dreamed of, and she brought him to heights so pure and so lovely that he almost cried in her arms, as he lay there, spent, with his head cradled on her bosom. (Steel, 1983, pp. 131–132.)

It is unfortunate that the primary source of many people's knowledge about human sexuality comes from sources no more accurate than that represented by this passage from Danielle Steel's novel, *Thurston House.* Yet, for almost everyone except characters in popular novels, sex is considerably more complex and involved than a series of overwhelming, all-encompassing orgasms, one following another in rapid, heart-stopping succession. In fact, to understand the realities of human sexuality, we first need to consider the basic physiology of the human sex organs.

Factors of Physiology:
The human genitals

An understanding of the **genitals,** the male and female sex organs, is the first step in comprehending human sexual behavior. Shown in Figure 12-1 are the female **ovaries,** sex organs which produce eggs and **estrogen,** the female sex hormone. The greatest production of estrogen occurs during **ovulation,** when an egg is released by the ovaries, typically every 28 days. At this time, a woman is at the height of her fertility. During ovulation, if a male's sperm is deposited into the **vagina** (the barrel-shaped female organ into which the penis is inserted during sexual intercourse) and reaches the egg, conception will occur.

The **penis,** or male external sex organ, is the vehicle through which sperm travel into the vagina, and it is a male's most sexually excitable organ. During sexual arousal, the penis becomes erect, which in turn allows it to enter a woman's vagina during sexual intercourse.

The **testes** produce sperm and **androgen,** the male sex hormone. Androgen produces secondary sex characteristics, such as pubic hair and a deepening of the voice, during puberty. It also controls a male's sex drive. Unlike estrogen, whose production rises and falls cyclically in females, androgen is produced fairly constantly in males. Men, then, are less apt to experience cyclical changes in sex drives than are women.

Despite differences between males and females in the production of sex hormones, and thus sex drive cycles, both men and women are interested in and receptive to sex on a fairly consistent basis. Unlike other animals, whose sexual arousal is dependent primarily on their production of sex hormones and the presence of a receptive partner, humans are exquisitely sensitive to a wide array of stimuli that provoke sexual arousal.

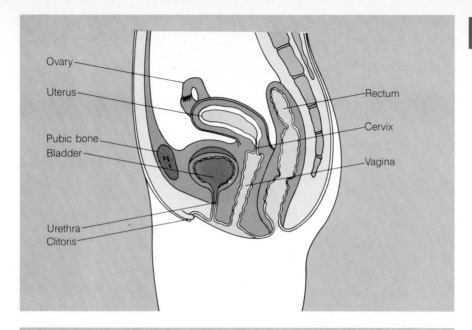

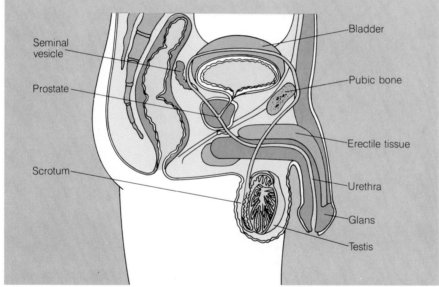

FIGURE 12-1
Cutaway side views of the
female and male
sex organs.

Turning On:
Sexual arousal, the genitals—and the brain

The brain is the site of sexual arousal.

Strange as it may sound, there is good reason to accept such a statement, for whether we consider a stimulus as sexual is very much a function of how we evaluate it cognitively. For some people, sexual arousal may be associated with the smell of a certain perfume, the sound of a particular song (remember "Bolero" in the movie *10*?), or the sight of lacy underwear. For others, it is the thought of a woman's breast, a man's buttocks, or a fantasy involving sex between two people.

Fantasies—thoughts and images in people's minds—play a particularly important role in producing sexual arousal. Around 60 percent of all people report experiencing fantasies during sexual intercourse, with relatively little difference between those of men and women, as you can see in Figure 12-2 (Sue, 1979). It is important to note that fantasies do not signal a desire to actually act out their content; they are merely images that enhance sexual arousal. Moreover, they do not indicate disloyalty to one's sexual partner, but should be viewed as a means of enhancing sexual arousal.

The variety of fantasies that people have is congruent with the notion that what is one person's sexual turn-on is another's turn-off. Much of what people find exciting and **erotic**—that is, sexually stimulating—is a matter of prior learning. In certain cultures, for instance, extreme obesity was once considered to represent the height of human sexuality, while contemporary America views slimness as a sexual virtue. Similarly, in some cultures today, elongated labia majora (the pads of fat on either side of a woman's vaginal opening) are thought of as sexually attractive, and women in those cultures

FIGURE 12-2
The kinds of fantasies that men and women have during sexual intercourse are relatively similar. (*Source*: Sue, 1979, table 3.)

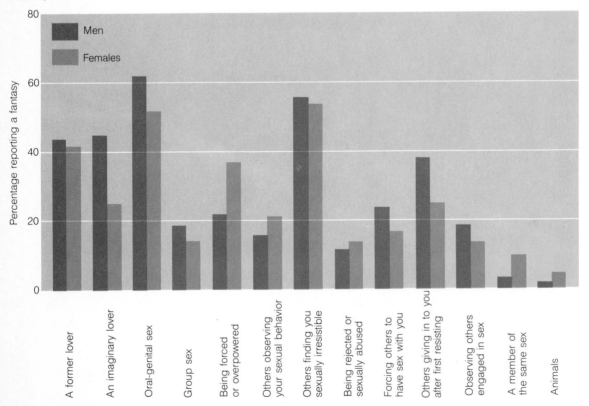

frequently tug on them to make them longer. It is not that human sexual physiology is different across cultures; rather, it is the social and cultural meaning that has been given to a particular physical characteristic that has been modified.

Analogously, there are no specific areas on the human body that, when touched, automatically produce sexual arousal. A physician who touches a woman's breast or examines a male's penis typically does not provoke sexual arousal; the situation is, by definition, a nonsexual one. However, the information sent to the brain from such **erogenous zones**—areas of the body that are particularly sensitive because of an unusually rich array of nerve receptors—is essentially the same as when a lover touches them. The difference in response resides in the brain's interpretation of the meaning of the touch. Only when we interpret touch as being associated with sexuality are we likely to respond with arousal. In at least this sense, then, it is accurate to argue that the brain is the site of sexual arousal.

The Rise and Fall of Sex:
Human sexual responsiveness

Independent of what does and does not turn people on, human sexual responsivity follows fairly regular patterns, although there are some important differences between men and women. Typically, there are four phases of sexual responsivity: excitement, plateau, orgasm, and resolution (Masters & Johnson, 1966).

In the **excitement phase,** the genitals become prepared for sexual activity following exposure to an arousing stimulus. In males the penis swells. In females, the **clitoris**—the female sexual organ particularly responsive to sensation—enlarges, and the vagina becomes lubricated. Females may also experience a "sex flush," in which they get a redness over their chest and throat.

The second stage is the **plateau phase,** in which the body prepares for orgasm. The highest level of sexual arousal occurs at this point, as the penis and clitoris swell. Heart rate, respiration, and blood pressure increase, and muscles tense up as the body prepares itself for the next stage—orgasm.

Orgasm is one of those things in life that is next to impossible to describe, although, as the saying goes, you know one when you have one (see the following Do It! box). Saying it is an intensely pleasurable experience does not quite do it justice. Physiologically, however, orgasm is easy to define: there are rhythmic muscular contractions that occur in the genitals every eight-tenths of a second. In the male, the contractions expel **semen,** the fluid containing sperm, from the penis, in a process known as **ejaculation.** For both men and women, there is a sharp rise in pulse and respiration rates.

WHOSE ORGASM IS THIS?

Do males and females experience orgasms differently? If you think so, try to identify whether each of these descriptions was made by a man or a woman:

1. Your heart pounds more than 100 miles per hour; your body tenses up; you feel an overwhelming sensation of pleasure and joy.

2. An orgasm feels like blood pulsating through my body, rushing essentially to the genital area, a surge of contraction-like waves paired with a rapidly beating heart and strong pulse; my heart feels like someone is squeezing it, painful, and I have trouble breathing deeply.

3. Feels like being plugged into an electric socket, but pleasureful rather than painful. Nearly indescribable!

4. It's as if every muscle in your body is being charged with intense electricity; your mind is incapable of thinking about anything, and you become totally incoherent. All the nerves in your body tremble, and you have trouble breathing, and get the urge to scream, or yell, or do something wild.

5. An orgasm to me is like the sensations of hot and cold coming together in one throbbing, thrusting, prolonged moment. It is the ultimate excitement of my passion.

6. Like exquisite torture. The sudden release of all the primal urges in the body. The gladness and yet the sadness that the fun is over.

7. An orgasm is that point when you don't care if anyone hears you screaming out your pleasures of ecstasy.

8. It's like all the cells in my brain popping at once and whirling around, while all the muscles in my body heave upward till I reach ultimate sensory bliss.

9. Tingling, throbbing, pleasureable feeling. Breathing is very fast and not rhythmic. Tend to hold my breath at peak. Possible shaking afterward and tightening contraction of muscles.

10. An orgasm is a heavenly experience. It can be compared to nothing.

ANSWERS If you thought that men and women perceive orgasms in very different ways, you might be surprised at how hard it is to tell the difference from the descriptions, as the following answers will probably indicate to you: 1. M, 2. F, 3. M, 4. F, 5. F, 6. M, 7. F, 8. M, 9. F, 10. M.

Following orgasm, people move into the **resolution stage.** During the resolution stage, the body returns to its normal state, reversing the changes brought about by arousal. The genitals return to their original size, and heart and respiration rates return to normal.

During the resolution stage, there is a marked difference between men and women, as illustrated in Figure 12-3. Men enter a **refractory period** during resolution; they are not able to be aroused, and thus are unable to have another orgasm and ejaculate until some time has passed. The time spent in the refractory period may be just a few minutes, or—in older men—may last as much as a few days.

Women, in contrast, have no refractory period; they are immediately capable of cycling back into the orgasm phase and experiencing repeated orgasms. Eventually, of course, women move through the resolution stage and return to their normal, unaroused state.

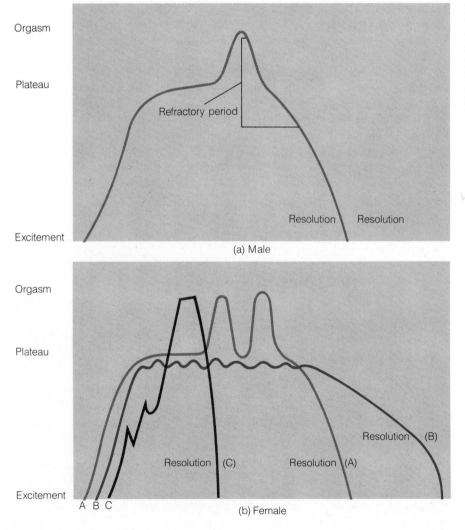

FIGURE 12-3
The pattern of men's and women's sexual response differs. In (*a*), a male pattern is shown; in (*b*), three female patterns are displayed. (*Source*: After Masters and Johnson, 1966).

Interestingly, recent evidence has challenged the conventional wisdom that males are unable to experience multiple orgasms without an intervening refractory period. In several studies, males have reported that they are able to experience multiple orgasms prior to ejaculation (Hartman & Fithian, 1984; Robbins & Jensen, 1978). In one survey, for example, some 12 percent of males said they had multiple orgasms, and work examining their physiological responses confirms their reports. It may be that orgasm and ejaculation are actually two independent biological processes, and that although in most males they occur simultaneously, some men have learned to separate them—a knack as yet undeveloped in most males.

Psychology for You:
Evaluating the "goals" of sex

As we discuss sexual performance, it would be easy to conclude that sex is a goal-oriented activity that is designed to produce an orgasm. In fact, the terminology that we use to discuss sex—sexual *performance,* sexual *foreplay* (as if it is just a prelude to the important main event), and even the idea of *climaxing* or *achieving* an orgasm—hint at society's views on the preeminent importance of orgasm.

However, such an orientation misses much of the pleasure that sex can offer. Many experts argue that one can enjoy the aspects of sex that come before and after orgasm as much as an orgasm itself, and that sexual practices should not be oriented toward "attaining" orgasm.

Rather than turning sexual activity into a situation in which you either achieve or fail at reaching an orgasm, then, it is important to evaluate what it is that you want to get out of sexual activity. If you are keeping score on

A sexual experience can be more pleasurable and rewarding if it is not just focused on achieving the goal of orgasm.

Barbara Alper/Stock, Boston

your "success" rate, you may be missing out on some of the most positive aspects of sex. Every sexual practice can give pleasure, whether or not it ultimately enhances the chances of having an orgasm, and sexual activities should be enjoyed for the pleasure they bring at a given moment.

TO REVIEW

● The male and female sex organs are known as the genitals.

● Because sexual arousal is determined by the interpretation given a stimulus, it is accurate to say that the brain is the site of sexual arousal.

● The four phases of sexual responsivity are excitement, plateau, orgasm, and resolution. Unlike women, men enter a refractory period, during which they are unable to have an orgasm.

CHECK YOURSELF

1. An increase in the production of estrogen in a woman marks a period of infertility. True or false?

2. _____ is the male sex hormone produced in the testes.

3. The brain can be considered the site of sexual arousal in the sense that:
   a. the brain signals the production of sex hormones
   b. the brain interprets the meaning of potentially sexual forms of stimulation
   c. imagined fantasies are necessary for sexual behavior
   d. messages from the brain block physical sensation in the erogenous zones

4. Match the description in the right column with the appropriate phase in the left.

_____ excitement phase   a. rhythmic muscular contractions in the genitals

_____ plateau phase   b. highest level of sexual arousal; heart rate, respiration, and blood pressure increase

_____ orgasm   c. male erection and lubrication of the female's vagina

_____ resolution phase   d. the body returns to its normal state

5. During ejaculation, the male expels _____, the fluid containing _____.

_____

(See answers to the questions at the bottom of page 398.)

A boy will not feel so vigorous and springy; he will be more easily tired. . . . He will probably look pale and pasty, and he is lucky if he escapes indigestion and getting his bowels confined, both of which will probably give him spots and pimples on his face. . . .

The results on the mind are the more severe. . . . A boy who practices this habit can never be the best that Nature intended him to be. His wits are not so sharp. His memory is not so good. His power of fixing his attention on whatever he is doing is lessened. . . . A boy like this is a poor thing to look at. . . . [He is] untrustworthy, unreliable, untruthful, and probably even dishonest. (Schofield & Vaughan-Jackson, 1913, pp. 30–42.)

The source of all these maladies? To the authors of this early twentieth-century sex manual, "What Every Boy Should Know," it all stemmed from one vile practice: **masturbation,** or self-stimulation producing sexual arousal.

Yet, if the writers of this passage were correct, the world would be a sorry place, since some 97 percent of all males have masturbated at some point in their lives. Women, who presumably would suffer equally dire consequences from masturbation, would also be in bad shape, given that around 78 percent of all females masturbate at one time or another during their lives (Miller & Lief, 1976).

Happily, contemporary views of masturbation have changed drastically; a practice that was once thought to produce everything from insanity to warts is now considered a natural form of sexual expression which is neither physically nor psychologically harmful. However, negative attitudes toward masturbation still linger, and people who consider it immoral may experience regret or guilt over the practice.

The changes in views regarding masturbation illustrate the deep-seated difficulties that society has in determining the appropriateness and "normality" of various sexual behaviors. Historically, it has always proven to be particularly difficult to draw concrete distinctions between sexual behavior that is indicative of positive adjustment and that which is maladaptive.

For example, one way of defining adaptive sexual behavior is to rely on a particular societal standard or norm. However, depending on the standard one uses—be it a particular philosophy, the Bible, one's parents—a given sexual behavior may be seen as completely normal, or it may be viewed as deviant. Given that societal standards undergo drastic shifts over the course of time, and that our multicultural society has few agreed-upon standards in the first place, such a definition of sexual adjustment seems inadequate.

Another approach to defining sexually adaptive behavior is to consider sexual behavior in light of the degree to which it deviates from the "average"

CHECK YOURSELF: ANSWERS

1. False; this marks the height of a woman's fertility.   **2.** Androgen   **3.** b   **4.** c, b, a, d
5. semen, sperm

in society. However, the fact that a particular sexual behavior is rare does not imply that it is maladaptive; if someone prefers sex in the back seat of an automobile to sex in the bedroom, there is no logical reason to assume that what might be unusual from a statistical point of view is necessarily maladaptive.

According to most psychologists, the most reasonable approach to understanding what is sexually adaptive behavior is one that considers the psychological consequences of sexual behavior. In this approach, sexual behavior is considered maladaptive if it produces a sense of distress, anxiety, or guilt—or, of course, if it is harmful to another individual. In this view, then, sexual behavior is viewed as maladaptive only to the extent that it produces a negative impact on an individual's sense of well-being or on the well-being of others.

It is important to realize that the rights and wrongs of sexual behavior, and the dos and don'ts associated with sex, are very much a reflection of each individual's own and society's values. Over the course of just a few years, there can be—and have been—dramatic shifts in what is considered appropriate. As we discuss the various forms that human sexual expression takes, then, keep in mind that there are few universal principles to guide people's sexual behavior.

Men and Women Together:
Heterosexuality

The most common form of sexual behavior involving two people is **heterosexuality,** or sexual behavior between a man and a woman. Although heterosexuality encompasses a variety of sexual acts—starting at the level of holding hands and kissing—most researchers have focused on sexual intercourse as the primary means of gauging heterosexual behavior.

Premarital sexual intercourse   Nice girls don't do it. "It," of course, is premarital sexual intercourse, and until very recently premarital sex for women represented one of society's major taboos. Until the night of her wedding, a woman was expected to remain a virgin. For men, on the other hand, society held no such expectations; not only was premarital sex permissible, men were almost expected to have premarital sexual experience.

To view that premarital sex is permissible for males but not for females, known as the **double standard,** was dominant as recently as twenty years ago. For instance, a survey in the mid-1960s found that around 80 percent of adult Americans believed that premarital sex is always wrong. However, by the 1970s a dramatic shift occurred, with only about one-third of respondents in one survey reporting that sex prior to marriage was wrong (Reiss, 1980). Moreover, the differences regarding the acceptability of sex for men and not women also shrank: The standards for women, while still stricter than for men, were not prohibitive. Have changes in the acceptability of premarital sex been matched by actual changes in sexual practice? The answer is affirmative. In one survey, for instance, about 80 percent of women under the age of 25 said they had experienced premarital intercourse, while just over 20 percent of those over 55 years of age reported having had premarital sexual intercourse (Horn & Bachrach, 1985).

Males have also shown an increase in the rate of premarital intercourse, although the increase has not been as dramatic as it has been for women—most likely because the male rates of premarital sexual intercourse were already high. For example, the earliest surveys we have show that 84 percent of all men in the 1940s had premarital intercourse; in the early 1980s, the figure had risen to closer to 95 percent. In addition, the age at which men had intercourse for the first time has steadily declined, and some 76 percent of college-age males have had intercourse by the time they finish college (Arena, 1984).

The decline of the double standard has not meant that *all* standards have been abolished and that **promiscuity**—indiscriminate, casual sex—is now the norm. Instead, new standards have arisen which appear to be based less on the status of the legal relationship between two individuals and more on the qualitative nature of their relationship. According to one standard, that of "permissiveness with affection," premarital intercourse is permissible for both males and females if the partners have a stable, loving, and committed relationship (Reiss, 1980). Whether a couple is legally married, then, appears to be less of an issue than in previous years.

Marital sex   Most people find it difficult—if not impossible—to envision their parents engaging in sexual intercourse. Still, it is hard to argue with the reality that few of us were delivered by a stork, and that even the most sedate married couples—yes, even one's own parents—are likely to have a sex life that includes sexual intercourse.

Just how active that sex life is depends, among other things, on the age of the couple. Although the average frequency of sexual intercourse across all married couples is around eight times per month (Westoff, 1974), younger couples tend to have intercourse more frequently than older ones (see Figure 12-4).

But mere numbers do not explain the quality of sexual activity engaged in by married couples, and here there is wide variation. For example, while for some couples sex becomes dull and commonplace, in others there is a gradual awakening of the sexuality of the partners, and sex becomes fuller and more meaningful as the years go on. For instance, one woman described the change in the sexual patterns within her marriage in this way.

After we'd been married a while, we felt there was a lot happening that we didn't understand, so I asked my husband if he and I should try to read up on it. So we went out and bought three books, and through them we found all different ways of caressing, and different positions, and it was very nice because we realized that these things weren't dirty. Like I could say to my husband, "Around the world in eighty days" and he'd laugh and we'd really go at it, relaxed and having fun. (Hunt, 1974, p. 183.)

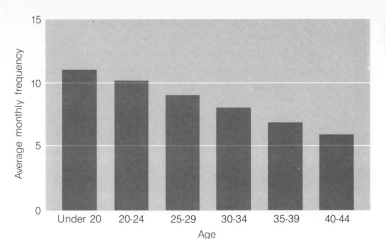

FIGURE 12-4
The average monthly
frequency of sexual
intercourse between
married couples,
according to the age of
the wife. (*Source*: Westoff,
1974, table 2).

As these comments suggest, (1) the stereotype that sex becomes boring
with age and with the same partner is not accurate and (2) sexual intercourse, while often viewed as the "goal" or "endpoint" of sexual activity,
need not be seen as the only, or necessarily the predominant, form of sexual
behavior in which couples engage. Touching, caressing, kissing, and manual
stimulation of the genitals are all pleasurable sexual behaviors, whether or
not they ultimately lead to sexual intercourse.

Whatever the nature of sexual activity between married couples, it is
now clear that sex remains an important factor well into old age. While the

The popular assumption
that senior citizens are
"too old" to engage in sex
has little basis in fact.

Hazel Hankin

stereotype of the elderly typically omits any thought of sexual activity—most people look at sexuality in an 80-year-old as somehow indecent—in reality there is no reason why even the most elderly person cannot have an active sex life. Recent research now suggests that as long as a person remains in good health there is no reason that sexual activities need to be curtailed, and surveys suggest that about 10 to 20 percent of healthy people over the age of 78 regularly engage in sexual intercourse (Pfeiffer, Verwoerdt, & Wang, 1968). (Interestingly, a major source of decline in sexual function appears to be a lack of regular sexual expression. Because of changes in the physiology of the sex organs, sexual inactivity can lead to a permanent loss of functioning. For the elderly, then, the best advice might be, "Use it or lose it!")

Independent of the frequency or nature of sexual behavior that occurs with married couples, a couple's perception of the quality of their sex lives—in whatever way they define "quality"—is related to their overall satisfaction with their marriage (Tavris & Sadd, 1977). It is not how often a couple has sexual intercourse, then, that seems to matter, but the meaning the couple places on their sexual activities.

Extramarital sex   There is no clearer indicator of marital dissatisfaction than the presence of **extramarital sex**—sexual activity between a married person and someone who is not his or her spouse. And clearly such activity is on the rise, particularly among women. For example, in the 1940s, about half of all married men and one-quarter of all married women admitted to having had sex at least once with a partner other than their husband or wife. More recent surveys have shown a slight increase for men and a significant rise for women. In fact, some researchers suggest that the rate for females has almost reached the rate for males (Thompson, 1983).

Despite the increase in the incidence of extramarital sex, most people still highly disapprove of such activity, both in general and particularly for their own marriages. For instance, around 75 percent of the women and 60 percent of the men agreed that mate-swapping is wrong, and between 80 and 98 percent of both men and women said that they would not want their own spouse to be involved in sexual activities with another person (Hunt, 1974).

Men with Men, Women with Women, Men with Women: Homosexuality and bisexuality

Consider each of these statements about **homosexuality,** sexual attraction to a member of one's own sex:

● True or false: Homosexuality is very rare.

● True or false: People are either completely homosexual or completely heterosexual.

● True or false: As a group, homosexuals are not as well adjusted as heterosexuals.

Joel Gordon

Homosexuality, among both men and women, is more prevalent than many people realize.

If you believe any of these statements are true, you are wrong: Each, although indicative of common stereotypes about homosexuality, is simply untrue.

In fact, the number of people who are involved with same-sex partners is considerable. About 20 to 25 percent of males and around 15 percent of females have had at least one homosexual experience during adulthood, and between 5 and 10 percent of both men and women are estimated to be exclusively homosexual during extended periods of their lives (Hunt, 1974; Kinsey, Pomeroy, & Martin, 1948).

Actually, the statistics on homosexuality are often confusing, primarily because the distinction between heterosexuality and homosexuality is not as clear-cut as we might at first expect. Heterosexuality and homosexuality actually mark the end points of a continuum, rather than being separate, black-and-white categories. As pioneering sex researcher Alfred Kinsey found when he carried out extensive surveys on sexual experience in the 1940s, a scale such as the one shown in Figure 12-5 is more precise and better reflects reality than merely categorizing people as *either* homosexual or heterosexual. Indeed, there are a considerable number of people who fall in the middle, and who might best be classified as **bisexuals,** people who experience sexual attraction to members of both sexes.

Despite the conceptual difficulties involved in categorizing people according to their sexual orientation, one thing is clear: There is no relationship between sexual preference and psychological adjustment (Reiss, 1980). No significant differences between the physical and mental health of homosexuals, bisexuals, and heterosexuals have been documented, and the disparities that have been found may be attributed to the harsh views that many in society still hold toward homosexuality.

Bisexual behavior						
0	1	2	3	4	5	6
Exclusively heterosexual behavior	Incidental homosexual behavior	More than incidental homosexual behavior	Equal amount of heterosexual and homosexual behavior	More than incidental heterosexual behavior	Incidental heterosexual behavior	Exclusively homosexual behavior

FIGURE 12-5
The Kinsey Scale was designed to define the degree to which a person's sexual orientation was heterosexual, homosexual, or bisexual. (*Source*: After Kinsey, Pomeroy, & Martin, 1948.)

Despite the lack of evidence relating to any harmful effects of homosexual behavior and the relative frequency of homosexual activity in our society, stereotypes regarding homosexuality remain quite negative. Male homosexuals are thought of as effeminate and females as mannish; male homosexuals are often seen as child molesters; and many people believe that homosexuals are suffering from a curable disease.

In fact, there is no basis for such stereotypes. In most cases, one cannot tell homosexuals from heterosexuals by their appearance, most child molestation is carried out by heterosexuals, and homosexuality is neither a disease nor something that needs to be "cured." Yet, such stereotypes linger, causing some experts to describe the attitudes of many people as representative of **homophobia,** a strong, irrational fear of homosexuals. Evidence of homophobia in job discrimination, jokes, and derogatory comments about homosexuals presents people whose sexual orientation is primarily homosexual with strong challenges regarding adjustment. Because of society's disapproval, homosexuals may have to cope with stress that heterosexuals do not experience.

Psychology for You:
Making choices

We have seen that there are wide variations in sexual behavior, and choosing what is appropriate for you is hardly an easy task. However, there are several points to consider prior to engaging in sex-related behavior.

● *Frequent does not equal appropriate.* No matter how frequent a behavior is in our society, it is not necessarily appropriate for *you* as an individual. Even if 99.9 percent of the population engaged in premarital sex, this does not mean that you should feel compelled to do so. Only after an examination of your own attitudes, values, and moral and religious beliefs can you be certain that a given choice is appropriate for you.

● *Communicate.* Except for masturbation, all sexual activities involve two people. As in any human interaction, then, the desires and needs of one's partner can be misunderstood and misperceived. It is crucial that every possible line of communication—both verbal and nonverbal—be kept open. No one should be expected to read a partner's mind; if you want something about your sexual relationship changed, let your partner know about it. (To enhance your own abilities at communicating your sexual needs, some experts suggest carrying out the exercise presented in the accompanying Do It! box.)

● *Don't be a spectator.* When you are engaging in sexual activity, don't feel that you must evaluate your—and your partner's—every move for evidence of success or failure as a lover. Instead, enjoy the moment. Sex is not a contest in which you must measure your performance.

● *Normal is what you make it.* As we discussed in our consideration of sexual normality, it makes sense to adopt a functional approach to sexual behavior: If a sexual behavior produces a sense of distress, anxiety, or guilt, or if it is harmful to some other individual, it should be considered maladaptive. In contrast, if a sexual behavior has no negative impact on one's own psychological functioning or on the well-being of others, there is no reason why any specific behavior should be looked upon—in and of itself— as something that is wrong. Sex is not something in which we *must* engage, nor is it something that we must *not* do—but rather something that can enrich us and provide an important source of fulfillment.

DO IT!

INTRODUCING—YOUR BODY

In order to communicate your sexual needs to someone else, it is first important to understand your own body. Try the following exercise, which is designed to increase your knowledge of your own body and its sexual responsivity:

☐ Undress and stand completely naked in front of a full-length mirror, taking a good look at yourself. Notice the curves, the contours, the blemishes, the things that you like, and the things that you dislike. Try saying them out loud to yourself.

☐ Run your fingers over your body, from your head to your toes, slowly. How does it feel? Which parts are particularly sensitive, and which are relatively insensitive? Are there any parts that you are avoiding touching? Why would this be?

☐ Explore your genitals. If you are male, look directly at them, and then explore them with your fingers, paying attention to the particular sensations you are experiencing. If you are a female, use a hand mirror to see how others view your genitals. Also explore them with your fingers. (If you become sexually aroused, that is O.K.; your genitals are designed to be responsive to touch.) Try to figure out what feels best, and which areas are the most sensitive.

☐ Now that you know what feels best, you'll be better able to communicate this new information to your partner.

Source: Hyde, 1986; Brenton, 1972; Heiman, LoPiccolo, & LoPiccolo, 1976; Zilbergeld, 1978.

TO REVIEW

● Masturbation, once thought of as an activity fraught with dangers of many kinds, is now considered a natural part of sexual expression. As such changing views illustrate, the nature of sexual adjustment is difficult to define in an absolute, invariant sense.

● The double standard—the view that sexual activity is permissible for males but not for females—has declined as the dominant view, and sexual practices have tended to match the change in attitudes. The double standard has largely been replaced with the standard of "permissiveness with affection."

● There is wide variation in both the amount and the nature of sexual activity across married couples.

● Sexual orientation is not simply categorized as heterosexual or homosexual. What is clear is that there is no relationship between sexual orientation and psychological adjustment.

CHECK YOURSELF

1.   The most useful way of discerning adaptive from maladaptive sexual behavior is to consider it in light of:
    a.   psychological consequences resulting from the behavior
    b.   one's individual sensation of pleasure
    c.   societal standards and norms
    d.   the extent to which it deviates from the societal average

2.   "As a man, I feel it's important to have sexual experiences prior to marriage. But, I would like the woman I marry to be a virgin." This type of statement, not uncommon twenty years ago, represents the _____ _____.

3. Through years of marriage to the same partner, the quality of sex almost invariably declines. True or false?

4. Recent surveys indicate that extramarital sex has:
   a. decreased slightly for men
   b. risen significantly for women
   c. remained approximately the same for men and women
   d. decreased slightly for women

5. _____ refers to an irrational fear of homosexuals.
   _____

(See answers to these questions at the bottom of page 408.)

12.3 CHARTING A SEXUAL COURSE:
Problems in Sexual Adjustment

When Mary Riley was raped, nobody heard about it. Nobody read it in the papers. There was no trial, no investigation.

Nobody knew but Ms. Riley—and the man who raped her.

Ms. Riley (not her real name) was a freshman at a large Southern university when it happened. She was with a date at his fraternity for a party. It was getting late when Ms. Riley's date said he felt sick. He went upstairs to his room. She followed, to see if she could help. In the room, when the door was closed, the man raped her.

"Even as I say this now it sounds crazy to me, after what he did to me," Ms. Riley recalled. "But I didn't scream. Not because I didn't think to scream. . . . I decided not to scream because I didn't want to embarrass him." (Meyer, 1984, p. 1.)

Sex—an activity that offers some of the most meaningful and intimate experiences in life—can, under the wrong circumstances, be characterized by violence and aggression in its most brutal and damaging form, as in the rape described above. And even when sexual problems are less acute than rape, they still may represent challenges to adjustment of the most profound kind. We turn now to several of the more difficult problems of adjustment related to sexual activity.

Sex Without Consent:
Rape

Rape is more a crime of violence than a crime of lust. Most experts feel that the underlying motivation of rapists is not sexual gratification, but power and control over the victim (Groth, 1979).

While you might think of rape as relatively rare, it is not. For instance, in 1982 there were 77,763 reported cases of rape, and the FBI suggests that only 20 percent of all rapes are actually reported. Other figures are even higher. On the basis of a series of in-depth interviews one survey projected

Miro Vintoniv/The Picture Cube

Date rape can be avoided if both people agree that dating conveys neither the right nor the obligation to engage in sex.

that there is a 26 percent chance that a woman would be raped at some point in her life (Russell & Howell, 1983).

Rather than rape being committed by strangers, it is most often carried out by an acquaintance of the victim. For example, in one extensive survey of college students, one out of eight college women reported having been raped, and of that group about half said the rapists were first dates, casual dates, or romantic acquaintances—a phenomenon known as **date rape** (Sweet, 1985).

These high figures are less startling when we consider society's attitudes regarding violence toward women, which may act to legitimize rape in the minds of some perpetrators. For example, when a group of high school students were asked under what conditions it would be acceptable for a man to hold a woman down and force sexual intercourse, only 44 percent of the females and 24 percent of the males answered that no circumstances warranted forced sex (Mahoney, 1983). The remainder thought that forced sex is appropriate under certain conditions, depicted in Figure 12-6. College-age students are not appreciably different in their responses; when a group of college males were asked whether they might ever commit rape, fully 35 percent reported that, under the right circumstances, they might (Malamuth, 1981).

Victims of rape typically experience **rape trauma syndrome**, psychological and physical damage that occurs following rape (Burgess & Holmstrom, 1979). The syndrome generally consists of two stages, an acute phase and

CHECK YOURSELF: ANSWERS

1. a **2.** double standard **3.** False **4.** b **5.** Homophobia

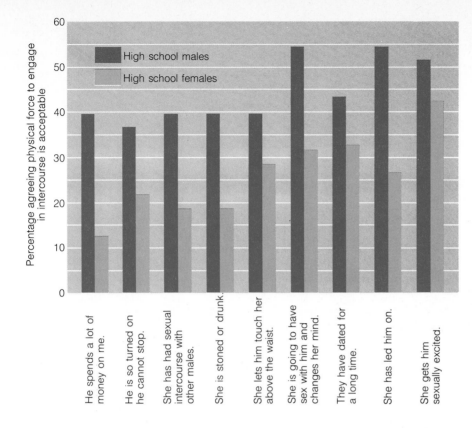

FIGURE 12-6
A sample of high school students indicated the conditions under which they felt it was permissible to force a woman to have sexual intercourse. Only a minority of both men and women felt that the use of force was never permissible. (*Source:* Mahoney, 1983).

a long-term reorganization phase. In the acute phase, a woman may first experience an expressive reaction, in which she cries and feels fearful, anxious, angry, and tense. These overt symptoms then subside, and women tend to subdue or mask their feelings, appearing—at least on the surface— calm and composed. Fear and self-blame tend to be dominating reactions during this period.

Following the acute phase, there is a long-term reorganization phase, in which the lasting effects of the rape appear. Some women change jobs or careers, move, or avoid environments that are similar to the ones in which they were raped. Some rape victims also suffer from sexual difficulties.

Ultimately, most rape victims recover and are able to put their lives together again. Still, rape is an extremely traumatic event for women, and, in almost every case, victims benefit from counseling, which can provide support and the opportunity to express pent-up feelings about the rape and rapist.

The Threat of Sexually Transmitted Disease: AIDS

It is 8 o'clock on the evening of November 21, 1991, and the president of the United States is on television. His mood is somber. "My fellow Americans," he says, "I want to talk to you tonight about one of the most dan-

gerous public-health problems this nation has ever known—the disease we call AIDS. As you know, the AIDS epidemic is now killing nearly 60,000 Americans a year, placing enormous burdens on our system of medical care, and creating tragic and bitter divisions in our society. Nearly a decade of intensive effort by medical science has failed to produce a preventive vaccine or a cure—and though we must not give up hope, we must now confront the growing threat of AIDS courageously and decisively.

Tomorrow I will ask Congress for new legislation to combat this national emergency. My program will include a substantial increase in funding for scientific and medical research. It will call for comprehensive reform of the structure and financing of the nation's health-care system. And it will confer wider legal authority on the National Commission on AIDS—specifically, the power to test the blood of any person believed to be afflicted with this dreadful disease. (Morganthau, 1986, p. 30.)

This grim scenario may become a reality if current projections hold true. By 1991, some 270,000 Americans are likely to have been diagnosed as having **AIDS (acquired immune deficiency syndrome)** and the virus will have spread to between 5 million and 10 million people. Perhaps half of these will eventually die of the disease—although no one really knows for sure.

Without doubt, no factor has had a greater influence on sexual behavior than the specter of AIDS. A sexually transmitted disease, AIDS was at first largely confined to homosexuals. However, it is rapidly spreading to other groups, causing widespread changes in sexual habits.

For some people, for instance, the days of casual sex are over, since it is difficult to determine reliable information about a partner's prior sexual encounters. Indeed, because the AIDS virus can remain dormant for years, one's partner may not even know if he or she has been infected with the disease (Masters, Johnson, & Kolodny, 1988). As a result, the use of condoms during sexual intercourse has increased, along with other measures that promote what has come to be called "safe sex" (see the accompanying Do It! box).

DO IT!

"SAFE SEX"—SEXUAL PRACTICES THAT HELP PREVENT THE TRANSMISSION OF AIDS

Despite the specter of AIDS and other sexually transmitted diseases, people need not become celibate. Experts on AIDS and other sexually transmitted diseases suggest the following practices to minimize the risks:

☐ *Know your sex partner—well.* Sexual activities with someone whose sexual history is unfamiliar are risky. Before entering into an intimate physical relationship with someone, be aware of that person's background.

☐ *Avoid the exchange of bodily fluids, particularly semen.* In particular, most experts recommend the avoidance of anal intercourse. The AIDS virus can spread through small tears in the rectum, making anal intercourse without using condoms particularly dangerous.

☐ *Use condoms.* Condoms are the most reliable means of preventing transmission of the AIDS virus.

☐ *Consider the benefits of monogamy.* People who are in long-term, monogamous relationships with partners who have been faithful are not at risk (with the exception of intravenous drug users or those who have received a transfusion of contaminated blood—something that is close to impossible today).

Mass educational efforts are being made to inform us that AIDS is a danger to people in all walks of life.

The adjustment problems associated with AIDS present problems as difficult to deal with as the physical aspects of the disease (Morin, Charles, & Malyon, 1984). People with diagnosed cases of AIDS, for example, must deal with the fact that there is no cure and that they are likely to die, probably within two years. Moreover, people who learn through a blood test that they carry the virus—but do not yet have the disease or its symptoms— stand a risk of unknown probability of eventually coming down with AIDS. Dealing with this kind of uncertainty is a difficult proposition, and support groups and individual counseling have been used to help people deal with the effects of the disease (McKusick, Coates, & Horstman, 1985).

Finally, the AIDS epidemic has produced repercussions even for those who are not at risk for the disease. For instance, some people have inordinate fears of catching the disease from everyday contact with those suffering from AIDS—although scientific evidence suggests that it is only through the exchange of bodily fluids that the disease is spread—while others' fears are so great that they have called for such extreme measures as quarantines for AIDS victims. People with such concerns must have their fears and anxieties addressed. Moreover, the families and lovers of those with AIDS, who must often face the impending deaths of victims, frequently can be aided by counseling.

Gonorrhea, syphilis, and genital herpes   Although AIDS presents the greatest risk, there are several other sexually transmitted diseases that warrant concern. **Gonorrhea** is almost as frequent as the common cold—there were 4 million reported cases in 1982. The disease is characterized by discharge from the penis or vagina, and may include a burning sensation during urination in men. **Syphilis** first appears as a round sore about the size of a dime on the genitals, and in later stages its symptoms may include a rash, fever, headache, or sore throat. If untreated, it eventually may produce severe circulatory and neurological problems and lead to death. Both gonorrhea and syphilis can usually be treated with penicillin.

Genital herpes is a virus related to cold sores that sometimes appear around the mouth. It first appears as small bumps, blisters, or sores around the genitals; the sores later break open, causing severe pain. These sores heal after a few weeks, but the disease eventually reappears after an unpredictable interval, and the cycle repeats itself. There is no cure for genital herpes, and during the active phases of the disease it can be transmitted to sex partners.

Secrets of the Bedroom:
Sexual dysfunctions

Although you might blithely admit to a stranger that your finger is infected or that you've sprained your ankle and have difficulty walking, it is likely that any sexual difficulties you have experienced might well be the source of deep embarrassment and concern, something that you might find hard to admit to even your most intimate friends.

However, there is no logical reason that problems regarding sexual behavior should, by definition, have greater importance than physiological or other problems that afflict us. It is only because our society stresses the importance of sexual functioning that it is of such concern.

Among the most common sexual problems for males, and the one that produces the most anxiety, is **erectile failure,** the inability to achieve or maintain an erection. Indeed, it is a rare male who has not experienced erectile failure at least once. This is not particularly surprising, given that erectile capabilities decrease in the presence of drugs, liquor, anxiety, or fears about the ability to "perform" sexually. Erectile failure becomes a problem only when it occurs frequently.

Premature ejaculation—in which a man is unable to delay ejaculation— is another common sexual problem. Because men's definitions of how long they desire to delay ejaculation vary, premature ejaculation is a difficult problem to pin down. In fact, the problem may sometimes be "cured" by simply having a man redefine how long he wants to sustain his erection before he ejaculates. **Inhibited ejaculation** is the opposite problem; here, the difficulty is that a male is able to have an erection but is unable to ejaculate.

Anorgasmia is a woman's inability to have an orgasm. There are two major subcategories of anorgasmia: primary and situational. In **primary orgasmic dysfunction,** a woman has never experienced an orgasm, while in **situational orgasmic dysfunction,** a female is able to have an orgasm only under certain conditions—such as during masturbation—but not during sexual intercourse. Because such a high percentage of women do not experience orgasm during intercourse (at least one-third), generally because of the lack of sufficient stimulation, some experts have suggested that situational orgasmic dysfunction is simply a normal part of female sexuality and not dysfunctional at all (Kaplan, 1974).

Psychology for You:
Treating sexual problems

Given the complexity of sexual behavior, it should not be surprising that treatment is equally complicated. Sexual problems may stem from biological or psychological causes (or both), and each must be considered in treatment. However, despite the wide variety of treatment approaches to sexual problems, there are basically three major classes of psychological treatment: behavior therapy, marital therapy, and individual psychotherapy (Sotile & Kilmann, 1977).

● *Behavior therapy.* The most prominent approach to sex therapy, exemplified by the treatment used by sex therapists William Masters and Virginia Johnson, assumes that sexual dysfunctions are learned, and that the goal of treatment is to unlearn dysfunctional behavior. Requiring that husband and wife participate in therapy together, they teach couples new techniques and procedures for sexual behavior, stressing that sex should not be oriented toward "performing" in a certain manner.

For example, couples are told to use a process of **sensate focus,** in which attention is directed away from intercourse and toward other behaviors that feel pleasurable to the partner, such as caressing the neck or massaging the back. By relieving couples of the notion that they must achieve certain sexual feats (reaching simultaneous climaxes, for instance), they often are able to relieve anxiety associated with sexual behavior—which in turn leads a couple to experience greater satisfaction with their sexuality.

● *Marital therapy.* Marital therapy views sexual problems as symptomatic of problems with a couple's marriage. In marital therapy, an attempt is made to improve the functioning of the marriage in a general sense, which in turn is assumed to lead to an improvement of the couple's sexual functioning.

● *Individual psychotherapy.* To some experts, sexual dysfunction is simply one kind of symptom produced by inner conflicts which may have nothing to do with sexuality. If this is indeed the case, the most appropriate means of treatment is to identify the conflicts through some of the types of individual therapy approaches we discussed in Chapter 8. By resolving the person's general psychological difficulties, then, sexual functioning may be improved.

Which approach to resolving sexual problems is most appropriate? Unfortunately, there is no agreement among sex researchers as to which type of treatment works best. Indeed, as with the kinds of therapy for psychological disturbances that we discussed in Chapter 8, it is likely that no one procedure is going to be universally effective. Different people have different sorts of problems, and for many individuals, some combination of the three might be most appropriate.

For a person with a sexual problem, the best advice would be to consult a physician, a psychologist, or a sex therapist. Unfortunately, in most states almost anyone can call oneself a sex therapist, and many people with little training beyond their own active sex lives have gone into the sex counseling business. It is particularly important, then, to ensure that someone using the title "sex therapist" is certified by the American Association of Sex Educators, Counselors, and Therapists, a national professional organization.

TO REVIEW

● Rape, in which one person forces another to submit to sexual activity, is more often a crime of violence than one of sex. Rape is also surprisingly frequent in our society.

● AIDS, acquired immune deficiency syndrome, is a deadly, sexually transmitted disease that is having profound consequences on sexual practices.

● Among the most common sexual dysfunctions are erectile failure, premature ejaculation, inhibited ejaculation, and anorgasmia.

● The major forms of treatment for sexual problems are behavior therapy, marital therapy, and individual psychotherapy.

CHECK YOURSELF

1.   Overt expressions of fear, anxiety, and anger, followed by inner feelings of fear and self-blame, describe the typical repercussions experienced by a woman who has been raped. These experiences are known as _____ _____ _____.

2.   Fortunately, heterosexuals need not take precautions against acquiring AIDS in their sexual activities. True or false?

3.   "It was embarrassing to have an orgasm so quickly." This man's statement indicates that he experienced the problem of:
   a.   inhibited ejaculation
   b.   erectile failure
   c.   anorgasmia
   d.   premature ejaculation

4.   "Unless the situation is just right, I just don't reach orgasm." This woman is describing _____ orgasmic dysfunction.

5.   Match the descriptions in the right column with the proper type of therapy listed on the left.

_____ behavior therapy   a.   problems in the couple's relationship underlie sexual problems and are treated

_____ marital therapy   b.   the couple works together to unlearn sexual dysfunction

_____ individual psychotherapy c.   sexual dysfunction is symptomatic of personal inner conflicts

(See answers to these questions at the bottom of page 416.)

TO SUMMARIZE

1. The male and female sex organs are known as the genitals. The female's ovaries produce estrogen, the female sex hormone, on a cyclical basis, with greatest production during ovulation, when an egg is released by the ovaries. If a male's sperm is deposited in the vagina and reaches the egg during ovulation, conception occurs. The male's testes produce both sperm and androgen, the male sex hormone.

2. Human sexual arousal represents a combination of basic physiology and learned responses to particular stimuli. Fantasies—thoughts and images in people's minds—play a particularly important role in producing sexual

arousal. Although the body is endowed with erogenous zones, areas that are particularly sensitive to touch, such zones do not automatically produce arousal when touched. It is only when people interpret the touch as sexual that arousal is likely to occur.

3. There are four phases to human sexual responsiveness. In the excitement phase, the genitals become prepared for sexual activity. In the plateau phase, the body prepares for orgasm, and the level of sexual arousal increases. The orgasm stage provides an intensely pleasureable experience and is characterized by rhythmic muscular contractions in the genitals. Finally, in the resolution stage, the body returns to its normal state, reversing the changes brought about by sexual arousal. Men, unlike women, enter a refractory period during which they are not able to be aroused and have another orgasm. In contrast, women are capable of having multiple orgasms.

4. The approaches used to define sexual "normality" include reliance on some societal standard or norm or consideration of sexual behavior in terms of how much it deviates from the average in society. A more reasonable approach is to consider the psychological consequences of sexual behavior. In this view, sexual behavior is considered maladaptive if it produces a sense of distress, anxiety, or guilt, or if it is harmful to some other person.

5. Masturbation, sexual self-stimulation, was once thought to be harmful. Today, however, it is viewed as being a natural form of sexual expression. It is also a common behavior, with some 97 percent of males and 78 percent of females reporting that they have masturbated at some point in their lives.

6. Heterosexuality, or sexual behavior between a man and woman, is the most common form of sexual behavior involving two people. Until recently, premarital sex for women was considered taboo. However, the double standard, the view that premarital sex is permissible for males but not for females, is on the decline, and the incidence of premarital sex for women has increased.

7. Married couples have active sex lives, although the frequency of sexual intercourse is related to the age of the couple. Couples vary not just in the quantity of intercourse, but in the quality of their sex lives. A couple's perception of the quality of their sex life is related to their overall satisfaction with their marriage.

8. Despite stereotypes to the contrary, homosexuals (people who are sexually attracted to members of their own sex) are as well adjusted as heterosexuals. There is also a relatively large number of people who have had homosexual experiences.

9. Rape, where one person forces another to submit to sexual activity, is more a crime of violence than one of sexual passion. Moreover, most rapes

CHECK YOURSELF: ANSWERS

1. rape trauma syndrome **2.** False **3.** d **4.** situational **5.** b, a, c are committed by acquaintances of the victim. The frequency of rape is not rare; some statistics suggest that a woman has a 26 percent chance of being raped sometime in her life. There is also a surprising acceptance on the part of society regarding violence toward women.

10. Acquired immune deficiency syndrome, or AIDS, has had a profound influence on sexual behavior. By 1991, it is predicted that the AIDS virus will have spread to between 5 million and 10 million people, about half of whom may eventually die. Although initially a problem among homosexuals, drug users, and certain other groups in the population, the disease is spreading throughout all segments of society. There are other sexually transmitted diseases as well; these include gonorrhea, syphilis, and genital herpes.

11. Erectile failure, the inability to achieve or maintain an erection, and premature ejaculation, in which a man is unable to delay ejaculation, are among the most frequent sexual dysfunctions in men. In women the inability to have an orgasm is called anorgasmia. In primary orgasmic dysfunction, a woman has never experienced an orgasm; in situational orgasmic dysfunction, a woman is able to have an orgasm only under certain conditions but not during sexual intercourse. Behavior therapy, marital therapy, or individual psychotherapy is used in the treatment of such sexual problems.

KEY TERMS AND CONCEPTS

genitals (p. 390)

ovaries (p. 390)

estrogen (p. 390)

ovulation (p. 390)

vagina (p. 390)

penis (p. 390)

testes (p. 390)

androgen (p. 390)

fantasies (p. 392)

erotic (p. 392)

erogenous zones (p. 393)

excitement phase (p. 393)

clitoris (p. 393)

plateau phase (p. 393)

orgasm (p. 393)

semen (p. 393)

ejaculation (p. 393)

resolution stage (p. 395)

refractory period (p. 395)

masturbation (p. 398)

heterosexuality (p. 399)

double standard (p. 399)

promiscuity (p. 400)

extramarital sex (p. 402)

homosexuality (p. 402)

bisexuals (p. 403)

homophobia (p. 404)

rape (p. 407)

date rape (p. 408)

rape trauma syndrome (p. 408)

AIDS (acquired immune deficiency syndrome) (p. 410)

gonorrhea (p. 412)

syphilis (p. 412)

genital herpes (p. 412)

erectile failure (p. 413)

premature ejaculation (p. 413)

inhibited ejaculation (p. 413)

anorgasmia (p. 413)

primary orgasmic dysfunction (p. 413)

situational orgasmic dysfunction (p. 413)

sensate focus (p. 414)

TO FIND OUT MORE

Masters, W. H., Johnson, V. E., & Kolodny, R. C. (1985). *Human sexuality*. Boston: Little, Brown.

Written by acknowledged experts in the field, this book provides a well-written, accurate overview of human sexual behavior.

Killman, P. R., & Mills, K. H. (1983). *All about sex therapy*. New York: Plenum.

A layperson's guide to sex therapy, useful for those contemplating treatment for sexual problems.

Pritchard, C. (1985). *Avoiding rape on and off campus*. Wenonah, NJ: State College Publishing Company.

A guide for people concerned about the prevention of rape, oriented toward college students.

Hite, S. (1981). *The Hite Report on Male Sexuality*. New York: Knopf.
Hite, S. (1976). *The Hite Report: A Nationwide Study of Female Sexuality*. New York: Macmillan.

Although neither of these studies represents a truly representative and scientific survey, both provide a wealth of quotations about people's sexual experiences.

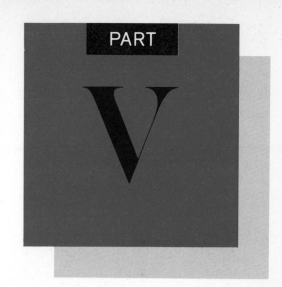

PART

V

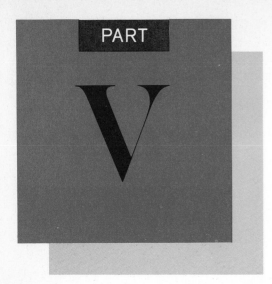

THE WORLD AROUND US

We encounter a variety of people in this part of the book. We see a man who goes out of his way to help someone in distress. We meet people who work at jobs ranging from dishwasher to editor. And we hear the complaints of the occupants of an overcrowded dormitory room.

In this final part of the book, we turn to the issues that involve our interactions with the wider world around us. We first look at how our behavior helps or hurts others, and ways of increasing helpful behavior and reducing behavior that is harmful. Next, we turn to the world of work, an activity which takes up a good part of most people's adult lives, and discuss the ways in which we can work together most effectively with others. Finally, we end this part—and the book itself—with a look at environmental psychology, as we examine our social and physical environments.

In Chapter 13, then, we consider the causes and consequences of behavior that helps and hurts others.

In Chapter 14, we examine the psychology of work, focusing on the role of work in our lives and the factors that lead us to determine our goals and choose a particular career path.

Finally, in Chapter 15, we discuss both the social and physical environments in which we live.

Helping and Hurting
Prosocial Behavior and Aggression

As Jack Higgins, an 18-year-old freshman at City College, jogged through Prospect Park in New York City, his mind was not on running but on his upcoming exams. He was deep in thought when he caught a flash of color in a ravine that ran just below the path he was following. He almost kept going, when he heard a muffled yell. Now interested and a bit worried, he turned off the path, heading toward the sound.

For Sondra Okum, a 15-year-old girl, Higgins's decision was the luckiest of her life. For at that moment she was being sexually assaulted by 29-year-old Mark Cauldwell, a previously convicted sex offender. She had been walking through the park when Cauldwell pulled her off the path and into the ravine, hitting her and telling her to be quiet or he would kill her.

Cauldwell had just ordered her to take off her clothes when Higgins arrived on the scene. Without hesitation, Higgins jumped Cauldwell, wrestled him to the ground, and held him in a hammerlock until Sondra Okum stopped another passerby and asked him to call the police.

To Sondra Okum, Jack Higgins was a hero. Higgins himself was more modest in his assessment. He said later, "I was just following the Golden Rule. If I was in trouble, I would hope that somebody would come to help me out."

In this incident, we see the best and the worst of human behavior. Aggressiveness and hatred characterize the perpetrator of the assault on Sondra Okum. Sexual assault is but one of a wide range of harmful acts, including petty unkindnesses that we may encounter every day and enormous crimes of war that inflict pain and suffering on millions of innocent people.

On the other hand, helpful and self-sacrificing behavior is not all that uncommon. While the news media report the more dramatic instances of helping—such as rescuers who help a disaster victim at great risk to themselves—there are untold instances of helping, or **prosocial behavior,** that occur constantly. These range from assisting a youngster who is trying to cross a busy street to donating money to a charity. It is these small acts that make prosocial behavior a crucial part of the social fabric of society.

In this chapter we examine both helpfulness and aggression, two very different sides of human nature. We'll first consider prosocial behavior and the factors that lead people to aid others. We discuss emergency situations and more general instances in which helping is called for. We see how moods and emotional states affect prosocial behavior, and consider ways of assisting most effectively.

The chapter then considers aggression. The issue of whether aggressive behavior is instinctive or learned is discussed, as are the ways aggressiveness

Melissa Shook/The Picture Cube

Prosocial behavior, such as stopping to help a stranded motorist, is an important part of our social fabric.

in the media affects viewer belligerence. We also examine pornography and violence toward women, and then investigate ways anger can be dealt with.

The chapter concludes with ways helping may be increased and aggressive behavior reduced. We review the results of moral admonitions and compare their effectiveness with that of the observation of models who act helpfully and nonaggressively. The chapter ends with techniques for enhancing moral behavior in general, including ways people's values may be clarified and their moral reasoning made more sophisticated.

As you will see in this chapter, although acting in a helpful and non-aggressive manner is not simple, aggression is not a necessary component in an individual's life. People can become more helpful and giving—to the betterment of society as a whole.

13.1   HELPING OTHERS:
Behaving Prosocially

A 29-year-old unemployed father of eight children leaped onto the tracks of a Greenwich Village subway station yesterday morning and saved the life of a 75-year-old blind man who had stumbled and fallen between the cars of a train that was about to pull out.

"I wasn't thinking about the danger, just that, hey, somebody needs help," said Reginald Andrews, who tore ligaments in his right knee as he pulled the confused, bleeding victim into a narrow crawlspace under the edge of the platform while others tried frantically to halt the train.

"I'd do it again—I'd do it for anybody who needs help," said Mr. Andrews. (**The New York Times,** *December 21, 1982.*)

As Cindy Serbun lay in bed in the throes of a bad case of the flu, her roommate, Carol O'Conner, told her not to worry about the term paper that had to be delivered to Professor Kagan by three o'clock that afternoon. "I'll be able to drop it off for you before then," she told Cindy.

"But Carol," replied Cindy, "it's way out of your way. And I know that you've got a lot to do yourself today."

"Don't worry about it. You're really too sick to go out. I'll be able to fit it in after lunch."

Consider, for a moment, the commonalities between the two situations described above. Although the first is by far more dramatic than the second, each contains elements of human selflessness and generosity.

Helping, or prosocial behavior, is acting in a way that benefits other people. The deed may be as minor as stopping for a hitchhiker, or as major as risking one's life to save that of another from disaster. It may be thoughtful and deliberate, as when a benefactor makes a major donation to a charity, or impulsive and impetuous, as when a person rushes into a burning building to save a child calling for help. The common element in these examples is the benefit that others, and society in general, receive from the assistance.

Emergency!:
Helping in times of need

Suppose you are talking with a small group of students, discussing personal problems associated with college life. Suddenly, you hear one of them say the following:

I-er-um-I think I-I need-er-if-if could-er-er-somebody er-er-er-er-er-er-er give me a little-er-give me a little help here because-er-I-er-I'm-er-er-h-h-having a-a-a real problem-er-right now and I-er-if somebody could help me out it would-it-would-er-er s-s-sure be-sure be good ... because-er-there-er-er-a cause I-er I-uh-I've got a-a one of the-er-sei—er-er-things coming on and-and-and I could really-er-use some help so if somebody would-er-give me a little h-help-uh-er-er-er-er-er c-could somebody-er-er-help-er-us-us-us [choking sounds].... I'm gonna die-er-er-I'm ... gonna die-er-help-er-er-seizure-er-[choking sounds, then silence]. (Latané & Darley, 1970, p. 379.)

Then, before you know it, he has lapsed into what seems to be an epileptic seizure. Would you rush to the aid of the victim, or would you remain seated and assume that someone else would provide help?

Although the question is not easy to answer, there is one factor of particular importance that would influence your response: the number of people nearby. Surprisingly enough, a large body of research shows that a major determinant of whether you would help depends not so much on the victim's plight but instead on the number of other potential helpers who are

Yan Lukes/Photo Researchers

Bystander apathy occurs
often on busy city streets,
where each person
assumes that others, who
are also failing to address
a problem, will help.

also present. The specific nature of the findings is probably not what you'd expect; they clearly indicate that the *greater* the number of people present the *less* likely you would be to help the victim.

The explanation for this finding rests on the concept of **diffusion of responsibility,** the tendency for people to feel that responsibility for helping is shared among those present. The more people nearby, then, the less personally responsible each individual feels—and therefore the less help will be provided (Latané & Nida, 1981).

Experiments investigating the diffusion-of-responsibility phenomenon have repeatedly shown that the greater the number of bystanders in an emergency situation, the less likely is the chance that any one of them will help. For example, in the study during which the above "seizure" took place, observers found that in groups of two people, 85 percent of the subjects helped; in groups of three, 62 percent helped; and when six people were present, just 31 percent responded (Latané & Darley, 1970). It is clear, then, that subjects were more apt to come to another's aid when there were fewer people present than when they thought there were several others with whom they were able to share responsibility.

The discovery of the diffusion-of-responsibility phenomenon led to the development of a more general model to explain how other factors lead to helping in emergency situations (Latané & Darley, 1970). According to the model, helping proceeds along four basic steps (see Figure 13-1):

1. *Noticing a person, event, or situation that may require help.* If we are not aware that something out of the ordinary has occurred, we clearly are not going to provide aid.

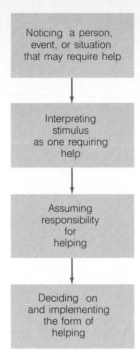

Noticing a person,
event, or situation
that may require help

Interpreting
stimulus
as one requiring
help

Assuming
responsibility
for
helping

Deciding on
and implementing
the form of
helping

FIGURE 13-1
The Latané and Darley
model outlines the basic
steps of helping. (*Source:*
Latané & Darley, 1970.)

2. *Interpreting the event as one that requires help.* Even if a situation is noticed, it must be unambiguous enough to be perceived as an emergency situation. The presence of others first becomes important here, for if others are seen as nonresponsive to the situation, it provides a clue that the situation is not an emergency.

3. *Assuming responsibility for taking action.* If others are present, diffusion of responsibility may occur. Moreover, if the others who are present are seen as particularly skilled—as, for example, a physician might be—then bystanders are less likely to help.

4. *Deciding on and implementing the form of assistance.* If a person assumes responsibility for helping, the last step is to decide *how* to help. The variety of possibilities is great here, ranging from the indirect—such as calling the police—to direct forms of assistance, such as actually providing first aid or bringing the victim to a hospital.

The specific nature of help that will be provided typically follows a **reward-cost analysis,** in which a person psychologically weighs the rewards that will come from helping against the costs that will be incurred from the help. According to this concept, only when the rewards outweigh the costs will a particular form of helping be implemented (Lynch & Cohen, 1978).

Not all help, however, follows a reward-cost analysis. Some prosocial behavior seems to be **altruistic,** helping that is beneficial to another while requiring sacrifice on the part of the helper. A person who saves her children while sacrificing her own life during a sea disaster and a soldier who pulls several members of his platoon to safety while exposing himself to enemy fire are both exhibiting altruism.

Although it would at first seem to be fairly straightforward, the notion of altruism presents some conceptual difficulties. For example, we cannot infer altruism simply by looking at someone's objective behavior. A rich person who donates thousands of dollars to her alma mater may be generous only because she expects to receive the praise of others or to see her name over the front door of a new building. Moreover, such an act requires little in the way of self-sacrifice. In contrast, a poor person who gives just a few dollars to a charity may be making a greater sacrifice, in relative terms, than the richer one.

Altruism, then, is dependent to a large extent on the intent of the helper. If there are no external rewards and the act is not coerced by others, acts of helping can be considered altruistic.

Do unto Others:
The norms of helping

Do unto others as you would have them do unto you.
Kindness is its own reward.
He who helps others helps himself.

The first platitudes that people learn often have to do with society's positive view of prosocial behavior. These sayings reflect **norms,** or generalized expectations that are held by society regarding appropriate behavior in a given social situation.

Much of our helping behavior is brought about by the norms we hold in regard to aiding others who are in need. Although most people have general norms regarding the importance of helping, there are also more specific norms that lead to prosocial behavior, including the norms of social responsibility, norms of equity, and norms of reciprocity. (To examine some of your own norms, you might try out the questions in the accompanying Do It! box.)

DO IT!

NAME YOUR NORMS

The following statements assess people's personal norms about various kinds of helping behavior. After responding to each of the questions, compare your answers with those of large samples of college students.

1. If a stranger needed a bone marrow transplant and you were a suitable donor, would you feel a moral obligation to donate bone marrow?

Obligation not either way		No obligation to donate			Strong obligation	
−1	0	1	2	3	4	5

2. If a close relative of yours needed a heart transplant and you were a suitable donor, would you feel a moral obligation to arrange to donate your heart to him or her upon your death?

Obligation not either way		No obligation to donate			Strong obligation	
−1	0	1	2	3	4	5

3. How much of a moral obligation would you feel if the State Employment Service requested you to employ a delinquent youth who had a police record?

Strong obligation to refuse		No obligation either way		Strong obligation to agree		
−3	−2	−1	0	1	2	3

4. How much personal obligation would you feel to talk to a stranger in a movie theater?

Some obligation not to	No obligation either way	Slight obligation	Somewhat more obligation	Strong obligation
−1	0	1	2	3

5. How much personal obligation do you feel to help other people in trouble?

Some obligation not to	No obligation either way	Slight obligation	Somewhat more obligation	Strong obligation
−1	0	1	2	3

6. If a school for the blind asked you to read school books to blind children a few times a week in the afternoon or evening, would you feel a moral obligation?

Obligation to refuse	No obligation either way	Weak obligation to agree	Obligation to agree	Strong obligation to agree
−1	0	1	2	3

7. If the president's office for volunteer services asked you to work a few hours per week as an aide in a neighborhood day care center, would you feel a moral obligation?

Obligation to refuse	No obligation either way	Weak obligation to agree	Obligation to agree	Strong obligation to agree
−1	0	1	2	3

8. If a solicitor for the school for the blind came to your door and requested a $1 contribution, would you feel a moral obligation?

Obligation to refuse −1	No obligation either way 0	Weak obligation to agree 1	Obligation to agree 2	Strong obligation to agree 3

SCORING The following are the percentage of responses falling into each category by a sample of college students who were asked the same questions:

1. −1: 12%; 0: 36%; 1: 12%; 2: 13%; 3: 8%; 4: 9%; 5: 10%

2. −1: 5%; 0: 11%; 1: 3%; 2: 7%; 3: 10%; 4: 16%; 5: 49%

3. −3: 11%; −2: 5%; −1: 5%; 0: 9%; 1: 13%; 2: 38%; 3: 19%

4. −1: 39%; 0: 52%; 1: 7%; 2: 2%; 3: 7%

5. −1: 7%; 0: 4%; 1: 18%; 2: 45%; 3: 33%

6. −1: 4%; 0: 12%; 1: 28%; 2: 41%; 3: 19%

7. −1: 6%; 0: 36%; 1: 24%; 2: 25%; 3: 9%

8. −1: 6%; 0: 2%; 1: 5%; 2: 29%; 3: 64%

Source: Schwartz, 1977.

The **norm of social responsibility** suggests that we expect people to respond to the needs of others who are dependent upon them. When the Red Cross solicits blood by asking you to "be a good neighbor," it is invoking the norm of social responsibility to increase the chances that you will help.

Two of the major factors that affect whether the norm of social responsibility will lead to helping are the degree to which a person feels that a potential recipient of aid is truly dependent and in need of help, and whether that neediness is due to factors that are beyond the victim's control. People who are seen to be in need because of some fault of their own—be it incompetence at managing their affairs or some moral transgression—are less apt to receive help than those whose problems are due to circumstances out of their control. For example, in one study of the patterns of contributions to the "*New York Times*'s 100 Neediest Cases," an annual fund-raising drive, researchers found that the greatest proportion of aid went to victims of such problems as child abuse and illness—events that could in no way be seen as brought about by the victim. On the other hand, people with problems which might be seen as having been brought on themselves, such as individuals who had committed moral transgressions, received proportionally lower contributions (Bryan & Davenport, 1968).

While the norm of social responsibility suggests that helping behavior should be motivated by a sense of caring for people in a general sense, without regard for the benefits that the helper himself or herself might

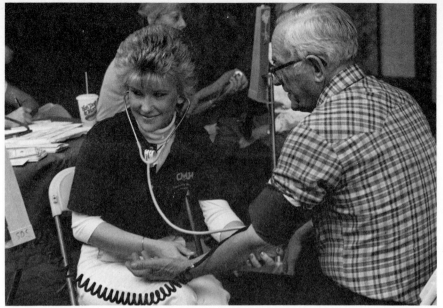

In order to raise funds, charity or volunteer programs, such as this blood-pressure screening clinic in a shopping mall, may promote the perception that recipients are worthy or deserving.

Arvind Garg/Photo Researchers

receive, the norms of equity and reciprocity take a different approach. Both norms suggest that helping behavior should be considered in light of our notions of justice and fairness, rather than the more abstract idealistic social good that comes from helping the needy.

The **norm of equity** says that people should be rewarded in proportion to their costs and that they should suffer in proportion to their transgressions. If people are thought to be suffering beyond what they deserve—in other words, suffering beyond what is equitable—then equity norms require that they be helped out of a sense of fairness and justice. On the other hand, if they are seen to deserve to suffer in some way, then their neediness is likely to be perceived as being just and fair, and they are less likely to be helped by others.

The **norm of reciprocity** suggests that one reason for helping others is to receive some future benefit oneself. The rationale that lies behind the norm is that in return for providing help to others we can expect that the helping will be reciprocated. And this is, in fact, the case. Research on prosocial behavior has found that not only do people reciprocate help to a specific individual who has helped them in the past, but they are more likely to give help to others if they themselves have received help (Staub, 1978).

I'm in the Mood for . . . Helping:
Emotional states, personality, and helping

You've just received an A on a test, and you are feeling terrific. As you leave the classroom building, test in hand, a fellow ahead of you drops his books to the ground, and papers scatter in the wind. Is your good mood likely to make you stop and help him, or are you more apt to rush ahead, eager to celebrate your good fortune with your friends?

The answer, in most cases, is that you would be more apt to stop and help—particularly in comparison to a student who has just found out that she failed the test. People in a good mood are more likely to help than people in an unpleasant mood (Rosenhan, Moore, & Underwood, 1976; Carlson & Miller, 1987). And the circumstances that evoke the good mood need not be extreme: In one study, for instance, people who found a dime in a phone booth coin return slot (planted, of course, by the experimenter) were more likely to later help a person in need than people who had not found any money (Isen & Levin, 1972).

Empathy, a state in which a person experiences the emotions of another individual, can also increase prosocial behavior. People who observe the distress of a person in need and put themselves in the place of the victim may begin to feel a sense of distress themselves. This is likely to increase their motivation to help (Eisenberg & Miller, 1987).

Some individuals are particularly prone to feeling empathy for others, and this personality trait is related to their general level of helpfulness. People who are characteristically high in empathy tend to help others more than people who, for the most part, lack the trait (Eisenberg-Berg & Mussen, 1978).

Are there other personality traits that are related to helping behavior, and, more specifically, are there people who are consistently good Samaritans? Most of the work on helping behavior and personality traits has yielded a negative conclusion: There is no single personality factor or set of attributes that differentiates helpers from nonhelpers. Most people are not characteristically helpful or unhelpful, in a general sense. Instead, factors specific to a given situation play the dominant role in determining whether a person chooses to provide aid to someone in need.

Psychology for You:
Helping others

As her chauffeur maneuvered the car through the heavy traffic, Elizabeth Barnsworth, a noted benefactor of the poor and downtrodden, wondered to herself why her gifts of turkeys to the homeless men's shelter had not been greeted with more enthusiasm. "Why," she sniffed to herself, "these men ought to act more grateful for my help. After all, I've gone way out of my way for them. The least they could do is show some appreciation."

If Ms. Barnsworth were a bit more sensitive, she'd realize that her help, in order to be appreciated, must be given in a more thoughtful manner. The fact that people are receiving economic or material benefits from someone's help does not necessarily mean that the psychological outcomes of the aid are positive. Indeed, recipients of aid may feel defensive or unhappy because of their neediness (Fisher, Nadler, & Whitcher-Alagna, 1982).

There are, however, several ways an individual may provide aid and promote a positive reaction. Among them:

● *Inquire about and listen to what a person's needs are.* Before assuming that someone needs a particular form of assistance, be sure the person really does have a need.

● *Allow the recipient of aid to reciprocate in some way.* The norm of reciprocity is a strong one—even on the part of recipients of aid—and providing a person the opportunity to "repay" help allows that norm to be fulfilled.

● *Provide help in a way that does not threaten the recipient's sense of control or autonomy as an individual.* For example, recipients of aid might be allowed to choose the form of aid that they will receive.

● *Provide aid that is appropriate.* Sometimes it is the smallest favor that can mean the most to someone else. In fact, just spending time with and listening to a person can provide help of the most important kind.

TO REVIEW

● Prosocial behavior refers to behavior that benefits other people.

● Because of diffusion of responsibility, the greater the number of people present during an emergency, the less likely help is to be provided.

● The four steps relating to help-giving behavior in an emergency include (1) noticing a person, event, or situation that may require help; (2) interpreting the event as one that requires help; (3) assuming responsibility for taking action; and (4) deciding on and implementing the form of assistance.

● Although there are some personality characteristics, such as empathy, that relate to helping behavior, generally there is little evidence of a "prosocial" personality type.

CHECK YOURSELF

1. For helping behavior to be termed "prosocial," it must be planned and deliberate. True or false?

2. The diffusion-of-responsibility phenomenon shows that the *greater/ lesser* (select one) the number of observers in an emergency situation, the less likely it is that anyone will offer help.

3. Dr. Gunstone sacrificed her entire afternoon to help her student work out the procedures of a novel experiment. As a result, they were able to complete the experiment and publish a paper under both their names. Would Dr. Gunstone's help be considered an act of altruism?

4.	Julie was quick to donate money to an organization that provides assistance to juvenile offenders. After all, this was the same group that helped her several years back when she had committed a legal offense. Julie's donation was an act arising from the norm of:

a.	social responsibility
b.	reciprocity
c.	justice
d.	equity

5.	One of the basic tenets put forth by Carl Rogers, founder of nondirective psychotherapy, is that the therapist needs to attempt to feel the client's problem himself or herself. This state, which has been shown to increase prosocial behavior, is known as _____.

6.	Providing help to the needy may be done more positively by allowing the recipient to somehow repay the favor. True or false?

_____

(See answers to these questions at the bottom of page 436.)

## 13.2	HURTING OTHERS:
Aggression and Anger

The passenger was one of four in the subway car, waiting for the arrival at the next station. Suddenly, without warning, a tall man walked up to the passenger, announced it was a robbery, and demanded the passenger's money. Not hearing over the din of the moving subway car, the passenger asked him to please repeat what he had said. It proved to be a deadly mistake: The man pulled out a gun, and shot the passenger in the head. The victim slumped forward, dead. The other passengers were too dazed to act, and, as he ran away, the gunman yelled to the others to forget what they had just seen.

Despite the gunman's admonition, it is unlikely that any of the witnesses would ever forget such an act. Unfortunately, this random case of violence, while still shocking to us, is not all that rare in a world filled with war, terrorism, and crime. We turn now from helping behavior—the more optimistic side of human nature—and consider its flip side, aggression and anger.

Interestingly, despite their prevalence, aggression and anger have proven difficult to define precisely. Aggression, in particular, presents some knotty conceptual problems. Clearly, a surgeon who performs an emergency tracheotomy without anesthesia on a person who is choking in a restaurant produces excruciating pain. Yet few of us would think of the surgeon's behavior as aggressive. On the other hand, if the surgeon were a Nazi doctor who carried out the operation in an experiment on concentration camp victims, the label "aggressive" might well be appropriate. (To consider some other examples of aggression, refer to the accompanying Do It! box.)

WHAT IS AGGRESSION?

Consider each of the following examples. Which acts are aggressive, according to your own sense of what constitutes aggression?

1. A soldier shoots an enemy at the front line.

2. The warden of a prison executes a convicted criminal.

3. A juvenile gang attacks members of another gang.

4. Two hungry men fight for a piece of bread.

5. A man viciously kicks a cat.

6. A man, while cleaning a window, knocks over a flowerpot, which, in falling, injures a pedestrian.

7. A girl kicks a wastebasket.

8. Mr. X, a notorious gossip, speaks disparagingly of many people of his acquaintance.

9. A man mentally rehearses a murder he is about to commit.

10. An angry son purposely fails to write to his mother, who is expecting a letter and will be hurt if none arrives.

11. An enraged boy tries with all his might to inflict injury on his antagonist, a bigger boy, but is not successful in doing so. His efforts simply amuse the bigger boy.

12. A man daydreams of harming his antagonist, but has no hope of doing so.

13. A senator does not protest the escalation of bombing to which she is morally opposed.

14. A farmer beheads a chicken and prepares it for supper.

15. A hunter kills an animal and mounts it as a trophy.

16. A Girl Scout tries to assist an elderly woman, but trips her by accident.

17. A bank robber is shot in the back while trying to escape.

18. A tennis player smashes his racket after missing a volley.

CHECK YOURSELF: ANSWERS
1. False   **2.** greater   **3.** no   **4.** b   **5.** empathy   **6.** True

19. A person commits suicide.

20. A cat kills a mouse, parades around with it, and then disca[rds]
it.

After deciding whether each of these acts is aggressive, u[se this]
more formal definition: Aggression is the "intentional injury [or harm]
to another person." Which of the examples change in ligh[t of this]
definition?

ANSWERS   When intent is taken into account, the following items would be
considered aggressive: 1, 2, 3, 4, 5, 10, 11, 14, 15, and 20.

Source: Based, in part, on Benjamin, 1985, p. 41.

The difference between the two examples, of course, is intent: In the first case, the surgeon is acting to save the victim's life; in the second case, the surgeon's intent is quite different. Most experts feel that the intent behind an activity is the key to determining whether an act should be considered aggressive, and they would define **aggression** as the intentional injury or harm to another person (Berkowitz, 1974).

Roots of Hostility:
The origins of aggression

Coming up with an appropriate definition of aggression still does not explain its pervasiveness within the human condition. One perspective suggests that aggression is **innate**—or inborn—in human beings. According to this reasoning—expounded first by Freud—aggression is so common that people must be genetically predisposed in some way to behave aggressively (Freud, 1920). In fact, an extreme form of this hypothesis is that human beings have a fighting instinct, in which aggressive energy is constantly being built up within a person until it is discharged. The process through which people discharge their aggressive feelings is known as **catharsis,** and may range from physical aggression to more mild forms, such as yelling or swearing. According to Freud and to Konrad Lorenz (1974), who studied animal aggression extensively, the longer such energy is built up, the greater will be the magnitude of the aggression that is eventually discharged.

The innate view of aggression has led to the controversial notion that society ought to provide "acceptable" means for the release of aggression through such activities as participation in, or viewing of, violent sports and games. In fact, some therapists suggest that people actively seek out ways of expressing their inner aggression and rage, such as by pummeling a pillow or going into a room by themselves and screaming as loud as they can. In the view of such theories, people's innate aggressive urges thereby can be expended in socially tolerable ways, and people will be less apt to engage in violence that is harmful to society.

While an appealing view—especially for people who seek an excuse to watch a lot of football on TV—there is little evidence to support the hypothesis that people who are involved in sporting activities behave any less aggressively than those whose most violent pastime consists of an afternoon spent at the library. In fact, there is some evidence to the contrary. Participants in and observers of sporting events are just as likely to show subsequent aggression as those who do not participate, and subjects in experiments who are rewarded for hitting an object are no less aggressive—and are at times more aggressive—than subjects who have not hit an object previously (Walters & Brown, 1963; Berkowitz, 1973; Tavris, 1983).

The lack of definitive evidence in support of innate explanations of aggression has led psychologists along other avenues. One of the major alternatives that has been proposed is the frustration-aggression hypothesis. According to this view, aggression tends to occur in the presence of **frustration,** a thwarting or blocking of some ongoing, goal-directed behavior. The hypothesis suggests that frustration leads to a readiness to act aggressively. Whether or not aggression actually occurs depends on the presence of **aggressive cues,** stimuli that have been associated in the past with actual aggression or violence and that consequently trigger aggression when a person is frustrated (Berkowitz, 1984). These aggressive cues may range from such obvious stimuli as weapons or pain to more subtle ones, such as hearing the name of a person who has been associated with aggression in a movie that has been viewed recently (Berkowitz & LePage, 1967; Berkowitz & Geen, 1966).

Rather than providing a harmless outlet for aggression, sports events may incite violence, as happened at this soccer match in Belgium. The scoreboard vainly exhorts fans to "be aware that the misconduct of a minority disturbs the pleasure of the majority of the spectators."

Reuters/Bettmann Newsphotos

An alternative to both the innate view of aggression and the frustration-aggression hypothesis considers aggressive behavior primarily in terms of learning. According to **observational learning theory,** we learn to be aggressive, employing processes no different from those that explain the way we learn everything else (including learning to be helpful to others). Rather than viewing aggression as an inevitable part of the human condition, then, social learning theory considers aggression as a learned response that has occurred due to the presence of various rewards and punishments in a person's environment (Bandura, 1986). People who are rewarded (from peer accolades, for example) for behaving aggressively or who are punished for nonaggression (a child whose parent scolds her for behaving too timidly when accosted by a bully, for example) are more likely to behave aggressively in the future.

Some of the most telling evidence for the validity of the observational learning approach to aggression has come from experiments that consider the way in which the observation of *others'* aggression leads to aggression in the observer, when the person who is being observed appears to be rewarded for the aggression. It seems that merely observing the positive consequences that accrue to people who behave aggressively is sufficient to foster aggression on the part of an observer. For example, in one classic experiment, children who watched an aggressive adult model hitting a large blow-up clown subsequently displayed significantly higher levels of aggression than subjects who first saw the adult sedately playing with Tinker Toys (Bandura, Ross, & Ross, 1963). It is clear from studies such as these that the observation of aggression can lead to its imitation, particularly when the consequences of the aggression to the original model are positive.

Mary Poppins versus Miami Vice:
Media aggression

In a society in which the average child between the ages of 5 and 15 is exposed to no fewer than 13,000 violent deaths on television, it is reasonable to ponder the effects of such a constant barrage of media aggression—especially in light of the evidence showing that, at least under some circumstances, observation of aggression can lead to its imitation (Freedman, 1984; Gerbner, Gross, Jackson-Beeck, Jeffries-Fox, & Signorielli, 1978).

Because there is clearly no ethical way of experimentally controlling the amount or nature of what a person views throughout his or her lifetime, it is hard to conduct experimental research to determine whether observing large quantities of media violence directly *causes* aggression in viewers. However, nonexperimental research clearly demonstrates that, at the very least, there is a relationship between the amount of violence viewed and viewer aggression (Friedrich-Cofer & Huston, 1986).

For example, one study examined children's television viewing over a one-year period (as assessed by parental diaries) and found that subsequent aggression was related to children's viewing of programs that were high in aggressive content (Singer & Singer, 1981). Moreover, another long-term

Alan Carey/The Image Works

Although the cause-and-effect relationship is arguable, there is a clear correlation between aggressive behavior in children and their viewing of violent television shows.

study found that there was a relationship for male subjects between viewing violence, in the case of this study at age 8, and their aggression ten years later (Eron, Huesmann, Lefkowitz, & Walder, 1972).

Of course, such findings are merely correlational; although they report associations between viewing media aggression and displaying aggressive behavior, we cannot assume that watching media that contain aggression actually produces aggression in the viewer. Consider, for instance, one plausible alternative hypothesis: People who are aggressive are predisposed to watch aggressive media presentations. For instance, it is quite likely that people who are already aggressive tend to choose to watch shows involving violence, while those who are unaggressive prefer less aggressive fare—a possibility borne out by some data (Freedman, 1986). It is also possible that some other factor, such as socioeconomic status, leads simultaneously both to higher levels of television viewing with high levels of aggressive content *and* viewer aggression.

Still, despite the difficulties in determining cause-and-effect relationships, most psychologists agree that, under many circumstances, exposure to violence causes subsequent aggression in viewers (Geen & Thomas,

1986). One can only wonder what is the cumulative toll, in terms of aggressive behavior, of the constant barrage of violence that television presents to viewers of all ages. (To get a fuller idea of the aggression that occurs even in shows supposedly geared toward children, just take a look at Saturday morning cartoons.)

Violence against Women:
Pornography and aggression

Not too long ago, the attorney general of the United States formally accepted the report of a commission convened to examine the effects of pornography—as he stood, ironically, under the unclothed statue of some ancient Greek god. Although many of the findings of the report were controversial, with some members disavowing its conclusions, one finding was incontrovertible: The amount of pornography containing depictions of violence against females had grown significantly in the last decade (Meese Commission, 1986).

Given the relationship that exists between exposure to media violence and subsequent aggression, does the appearance of pornography containing sexually explicit violence against women represent a dangerous situation? To many psychologists, the answer is affirmative, based on experimental evidence collected to examine the issue. For example, some research demonstrates that people exposed to pornographic materials that include aggressive content are more likely to admit a willingness to rape a woman than those who are exposed to pornographic material that is nonaggressive (Malamuth & Donnerstein, 1982). Similarly, angered male subjects who viewed an erotic movie that contained violence toward a woman showed significantly more subsequent aggression toward a female than if they had viewed an erotic movie that contained no violence (Donnerstein & Berkowitz, 1981).

In sum, the viewing of media pornography that contains depictions of violence against women can lead to increased aggression toward women (Check & Malamuth, 1986). It is important to note, though, that it is not pornography per se that is related to the increased aggression, but rather erotic materials of a specific sort: those that contain violence toward women.

Psychology for You:
Dealing with your anger

When angry, count ten before you speak; if very angry, an hundred.

—Thomas Jefferson

When angry, count four; when very angry, swear.

—Mark Twain

Although anger, and remedies for dealing with it, have been around for centuries, it still remains one of the most frequent encounters of everyday life. **Anger** consists of feelings of displeasure or rage. In contrast to aggression, anger is an emotional state, rather than a behavior directed toward another. Of course, if a person's anger is strong enough, it may well result in overt aggression.

Anger is a common outcome of any number of life's everyday frustrations and annoyances: heat, noise, crowding, exercise, drugs, and alcohol all can lead to anger. In other cases, it is the perceived provocation of others that results in anger. The person who cuts in front of us in a line, the boss who publicly derides our performance on a project, or the clumsy individual who bumps into us as we leave the supermarket, knocking all our groceries to the ground, all might be expected to produce anger.

While the causes of anger are not hard to fathom, there is little agreement among psychologists about the best techniques for dealing with the emotion. Just as the catharsis hypothesis suggests that aggression is best discharged through a process in which aggressive energy is "ventilated," some psychologists suggest that anger can be reduced through the expression of verbal or even physical aggression. However, careful study has shown that aggression produces catharsis only under certain conditions: the retaliation is directed at the appropriate person (for example, either the one who made you angry or someone deserving of the blame); the retaliation must be at an appropriate level, neither too strong nor too weak; and the retaliation must not provoke a retaliatory reaction from the target (Konecni, 1975). Given the difficulty in simultaneously fulfilling all these conditions, it seems unlikely that the expression of aggression is an appropriate means of dealing with one's anger.

On the other hand, there are situations in which the verbalization and expression of anger are appropriate (Tavris, 1982). Anger has communicative value; it can alert people around us that something is amiss. It also can produce feelings of control, reducing our sense that we are powerless and unable to change a situation. But the expression of anger must be *thoughtful* in order to bring about change. Rather than anger being manifested in a spontaneous outburst, it should be displayed in a manner that can potentially produce a desired change in a situation.

TO REVIEW

● Although difficult to define, aggression is generally considered the intentional injury or harm to another person.

● The innate view of aggression suggests that aggression is inborn in human beings, with aggressive energy constantly being built up until it is discharged through catharsis.

● The frustration-aggression hypothesis suggests that frustration leads to a readiness to act aggressively; whether the aggression actually occurs depends on the presence of aggressive cues.

- Observational learning theory presumes that people learn to be aggressive through rewards and punishments.

- While the evidence is not firm, most experts feel that viewing media violence produces subsequent aggression in viewers. Moreover, viewing pornography that contains violence against women can lead to increased aggression toward women.

CHECK YOURSELF

1. Jim believes that when he trains for boxing, he releases the aggressive tension within him. Freud would term this release of aggression _____.

2. The theory that predicts that aggressive tendencies are more apt to be acquired in settings where aggression is commonly witnessed is the:
    a. aggressive cue theory
    b. observational learning theory
    c. innate view
    d. frustration-aggression hypothesis

3. While there is a strong correlation between media violence and viewer aggression, it is still unclear whether media violence actually causes aggression in the viewer. True or false?

4. There is a clear link between exposure to all forms of pornographic material and subsequent violence against women. True or false?

5. Communicating anger in a way that is constructive is best accomplished when the individual expressing anger does so in what way?
    a. in a retaliatory fashion
    b. by telling a friend about it
    c. as a spontaneous outburst
    d. thoughtfully, to those involved in the anger-producing situation

(See answers to these questions at the bottom of page 444.)

13.3   GOOD VERSUS BAD:
Increasing Helpful Behavior, Reducing Harmful Behavior

Generally you enjoy baby-sitting, but the Harris kid is about to sour you on all children. Always a bit whiny, today he has outdone himself, making one demand after another.

    It is late in the afternoon, and both you and he are exhausted. Suddenly, in one of the rare moments you let him out of your sight, you find that he has knocked over a vase you had warned him a dozen times to stay away from. You know he did it on purpose, since he needed to climb up on a chair to reach it.

You feel you are about to snap. You begin to shout hysterically; you scream and rant and rave until he begins to cry and cower in the corner. Although you feel a certain grim satisfaction in reducing the kid to tears, you also feel wonder—and a certain disgust at yourself—at how easy it is for you to fall into behavior that you know is inappropriate. What happened to all your good intentions about helping people, rather than harming them?

Although few of us would profess to *want* to behave harmfully toward others, it is not rare to find ourselves acting aggressively and hurting people, through either our words or our deeds. As we have seen before, aggression is, unfortunately, a staple of daily life throughout the world. (See the following Do It! box.)

DO IT!

PREDICTING AGGRESSION TOWARD OTHERS

Consider the following scenario:

A subject in an experiment is told he is to act as the teacher of another person in a study having to do with learning. As the teacher, the subject is told he is to give increasingly strong electrical shocks to the student each time the student makes an error, using a shock generating machine. The shocks start out at a relatively mild 30 volts, and move in 15-volt increments up to 450 volts. The highest voltage levels are labeled "Danger—Severe Shock" and marked with three ominous looking red X's. The lesson to be taught consists of a long list of paired words—the kind of task that is likely to provoke a good deal of mistakes on the part of the learner. Even if the subject protests, the experimenter urges that he continue with the experiment, sayng that the shocks will cause no permanent damage, and that in any event he will take full responsibility.

The question for you: What percentage of subjects who took part in the experiment would ultimately give the highest level of shocks? (Write your response here: _____%.)

The actual answer is likely to startle you, as it did a group of expert psychiatrists who were polled prior to the experiment actually being run. The psychiatrists predicted that less than one in a thousand would

CHECK YOURSELF: ANSWERS

1. catharsis **2.** b **3.** True **4.** False **5.** d

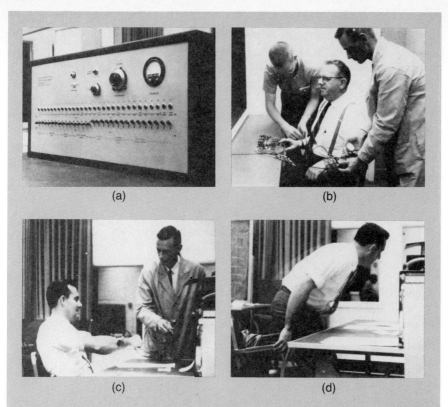

(a)   (b)

(c)   (d)

In these scenes from the film *Obedience* (copyright 1965 by Stanley Milgram), a shock generator (a) was used to deliver shocks to the "learner" (b), a confederate of the experimenter. To demonstrate the supposed severity of the shocks, the subject (c) received a "sample" shock. After delivering shocks to the learner in accord with the experimenter's instructions, this subject refused to continue and left the control room (d). (Copyright 1965 by Stanley Milgram. From the film *Obedience*, distributed by the New York University Film Division and the Pennsylvania State University, PCR.)

reach the highest level, and that most people would not go beyond the 150-volt level.

In actuality, the results showed that fully 65 percent of subjects placed in the experiment gave the highest-level shock of 450 volts (Milgram, 1974). Although these surprising results are tempered by the fact that in all cases the recipient was a confederate of the experimenter and actually did not receive any electric shocks, this is small consolation, because the subjects did not know this. They thought they were administering painful shocks to the "learner."

When asked afterward why they continued administering seemingly painful shocks, most subjects blamed their behavior on the experimenter, saying that they were merely following his orders. Yet this is hardly a comforting (or even legitimate) reply, given that this was the excuse used by hundreds of war criminals who said that they, too, were only following the orders of their superiors when they carried out atrocities of all sorts.

While we may debate the generalizability (as well as the ethicality) of this study, it is an important one. Never before had the fact that authority figures so easily can induce people to perform aggressive acts been made with such clarity—and with such frightening implications.

Yet the world is also filled with kindnesses. Mothers and fathers care for their children and willingly make sacrifices for them. People enter low-paying, low-prestige professions, devoting their life's work to uncelebrated causes because they want to help the world. Others give generously of their time, energy, and money to any number of causes, ranging from the political to the social.

Clearly, the goal of any reasonable person would be to attempt to reduce the incidence of aggressive behavior and to heighten helping. Psychologists have considered this goal long and hard and have identified several approaches to the issue; we turn now to the ways in which people's aggression may be diminished and their prosocial behavior increased.

Do as I Say, Not (Necessarily) as I Do . . . : Moral admonitions

When parents tell their children to do as they say (and not necessarily as they do), they are practicing a long-established procedure for producing prosocial behavior and reducing aggression. Unfortunately, it is not a particularly effective one, for words alone—if unaccompanied by deeds—do not have much of an effect as a model for other people's behavior.

For example, research has shown that those who *preach* generosity are far less effective in eliciting charitable behavior from observers than those who actually *behave* generously (Grusec & Skubiski, 1970). Even when preaching is effective, broad generalizations of the type that parents and other models are apt to impart ("it's good to help others in any way you can") have been shown to be less effective than more specific admonitions ("it's good to donate money to these specific poor people") (Grusec, Kuczynski, Rushton, & Simutis, 1978).

Leading people to contemplate the importance of helping has also been found to be relatively ineffective in increasing prosocial behavior. In one thought-provoking study, for instance, a group of theology students were asked to deliver a talk either on the good Samaritan parable (the biblical tale in which a Samaritan stops to help a fallen victim who has been robbed and beaten) or on a topic unrelated to helping (Darley & Batson, 1973). On the way to the talk, each student passed a confederate of the experimenter who lay slumped in an alley, coughing and groaning as the subject walked by.

It turned out that the degree of help provided by subjects was unrelated to whether or not they were giving a talk about helping. What *did* determine the degree of aid provided, however, was whether the subject was late for the talk: Subjects who were late provided significantly less help than those who were not late.

Results such as these clearly suggest that merely telling people to be helpful and leading them to think about the importance of helpfulness is a relatively ineffective strategy for producing increases in prosocial behavior. Moreover, there is no evidence that admonishing people to be less aggressive is any more effective in producing declines in aggression than is admonishing them to become more helpful. More direct means of evoking prosocial behavior and reducing aggression, then, are necessary.

Rewarding the Righteous and Punishing the Pernicious: Reinforcing helpfulness and punishing aggression

When a child behaves aggressively, the most frequent response of parents is to invoke some form of punishment: In some cases a verbal admonition to behave better, and in others some form of physical punishment, such as a spanking. Indeed, such an approach mirrors that of society, which is apt to punish severe aggression with prison terms and, if the act is sufficiently profound, with death.

Despite the prevalence of the use of punishment, it generally is not effective in curbing aggression. For one thing, physical punishments are likely to lead to anger and ultimately may produce more aggression on the part of the person being punished—if not toward the person administering the punishment, then toward some more vulnerable victim. Even worse, people administering punishment act as models themselves, and their behavior may be imitated in the future. Finally, and perhaps most important, the effects of punishment in general are relatively transitory; while it may temporarily bring a halt to aggression, the reduction typically does not last long (Sulzer-Azaroff & Mayer, 1986).

In contrast to the use of punishment, rewards provided for prosocial and nonaggressive behavior do tend to be effective in bringing about desired behavior. At a very basic level, of course, children learn very early in their lives that sharing and generosity will bring them rewards of a tangible nature, such as receiving an ice cream cone for unusually helpful behavior. Later, though, the rewards tend to be less concrete, consisting of verbal praise.

Corporal punishment was considered an appropriate response to crime and misbehavior until fairly recently.

Through this process, people ultimately learn that there are rewards associated with prosocial behavior, and they develop an internal morality that provides them with a sense of self-satisfaction when they have behaved in a helpful manner.

Do as I Do, Not (Necessarily) as I Say . . . :
Modeling desired behavior

Driving along a busy highway, you see a woman on the side of the road struggling to change a flat tire. Do you stop to help her?

According to the results of a classic experiment, your answer to the question would likely depend on whether you had earlier passed by a man who was helping another woman change a flat tire. If you were like other subjects in this experiment who had seen the helpful model, you would be twice as likely to stop and help than if you had not seen the model earlier (Bryan & Test, 1967).

The evidence is clear: Viewing another person who behaves helpfully leads to increased helpfulness on the part of observers, and models who exhibit nonaggressive behavior lead to declines in aggression. In contrast, if a model behaves selfishly or aggressively, observers tend to become more selfish and prone to aggression (Staub, 1971).

Prosocial and nonaggressive models are effective in eliciting prosocial behavior and reducing the incidence of aggression for several reasons. In cases in which models receive rewards for their behavior, observers may experience a sense of being rewarded themselves, and thus may be more apt to behave in a similar fashion, in the phenomenon of **vicarious reinforcement.** Moreover, modeling goes beyond simply mimicking the behavior of others. For instance, people can learn to construct abstract rules and principles through a process called **abstract modeling** (Bandura, 1977). Rather than modeling others' specific behaviors, people can draw generalized principles that underlie the behaviors they have observed. Thus, after observing specific instances of helping behavior, people may construct abstract principles regarding the importance of helping behavior in situations that go beyond the one in which they initially viewed the model.

Models who behave helpfully or nonaggressively also make helping and nonaggression more salient in a situation, helping to define the kinds of behavior that can be considered appropriate. Finally, models may help define the nature of a situation: Particularly when events are ambiguous, the specific nature of a situation may not be apparent. By acting in a particular way, a model can help clarify that help or nonaggressive behavior is the right action.

In sum, models who behave helpfully and in a nonaggressive manner can play an important role in increasing helpful behavior and reducing harmful behavior. Yet, apart from the examples of a relatively few truly selfless individuals, such as Gandhi or Mother Teresa, most of the news we hear and the historical examples to which we are exposed present models of a very different sort, making exposure to helpful and nonaggressive models a relatively (if unfortunately) rare happenstance. However, as we shall see next, psychologists have developed several procedures for directly enhancing prosocial behavior that have proven to be quite effective (Eron, 1986).

Psychology for You:
Learning moral behavior

When schools were first formally organized in the United States, one of their dominant goals was to communicate and teach moral values. Although this goal has largely been forgotten—except in religiously oriented education—there are several techniques that have been used to enhance moral behavior: values clarification and the enhancement of moral reasoning. These techniques are designed to overcome the limitations of moral admonitions.

● *Values clarification.* In **values clarification,** the goal is not so much to promote a particular brand of morality, but rather to encourage an examination and increased understanding of the values that a person holds. It is assumed that by clarifying a person's existing values, gaps and contradictions that exist will be made more explicit, leading people to adopt moral values that are more beneficial to them and society. To do this, people being trained in values clarification participate in a series of exercises that are designed to make them aware of their own values and the relationships among them.

● *Enhancing moral reasoning.* In **enhancing moral reasoning,** people are directly taught to reason about moral issues in a more sophisticated manner than their current approach. Based on Kohlberg's model of the development of moral reasoning (discussed in Chapter 3), this method includes the presentation of moral dilemmas, the creation of conflict, and attempts to make people more aware of others' perspectives in order to teach that moral issues involve many points of view that must be weighed simultaneously (Hersh, Paolitto, & Reimer, 1979).

Examination of the effectiveness of values clarification and moral reasoning enhancement has shown that they are both effective in doing what they set out to do: People become more aware of their values, and their level of moral reasoning increases. However, it is less clear that they promote actual changes in moral *behavior,* as opposed to changing the way they think about morality (Kaplan, 1983). Still, enhancing the clarity of people's values and making their moral judgments more sophisticated are clearly the first, and most necessary, steps in making them more likely to behave prosocially and nonaggressively.

TO REVIEW

● Moral admonitions, if unaccompanied by congruent behavior, are not particularly effective in promoting prosocial behavior and reducing aggression.

● Although rewards are generally effective in producing prosocial and non-aggressive behavior, the use of punishment has some important limitations.

● Models who behave helpfully and nonaggressively lead to increases in prosocial and nonaggressive behavior on the part of observers.

● Values clarification and enhanced moral reasoning sophistication lead to changes in the way people think about morality, although it is not clear if there are actual behavioral changes.

CHECK YOURSELF

1. Informing people of the value of prosocial behavior is usually sufficient to produce such behavior in those individuals. True or false?

2. Which of the following have been found to be consequences of the use of punishment?
   a. The punisher's act may be imitated in the future by the punished.
   b. The effects of punishment are usually short-lived.
   c. Punishment may produce aggressiveness by the punished.
   d. All the above are true.

3. The fact that Helen had watched someone help an elderly man to cross a busy road probably influenced her decision later to help a young child who was struggling to tie his shoe. This scene represents an example of _____ _____.

4. The process of engaging people in exercises designed to enhance awareness of their values is known as _____ _____.

5. Values clarification and enhancement of moral reasoning may be a worthwhile initial step, but they have not been demonstrated to change actual behavior. True or false?

_____

(See answers to the questions at the bottom of page 452.)

TO SUMMARIZE

1. Helping, or prosocial behavior, refers to behavior that benefits other people. One important area of helping relates to behavior in emergency situations, in which it turns out that the more people there are present, the less likely it is that any one individual will help a victim. The reason for this phenomenon is diffusion of responsibility, the tendency for people to feel that when many people are present, each person is less individually responsible.

2. Helping in emergency situations follows a four-step model: noticing a person, event, or situation that may require help; interpreting the event as

one that requires help; assuming responsibility for taking action; and deciding on and implementing the assistance required. The specific kind of help that will be provided typically follows a reward-cost analysis, in which the rewards that will come from helping are weighed against the costs. However, some helping behavior may be altruistic, in which the costs of helping are greater than the rewards.

3.   Norms, generalized expectations that are held by society regarding the appropriateness of certain behavior in a particular social situation, affect helping behavior. Among the most important are the norm of social responsibility (suggesting that we expect people will respond to the needs of others who are dependent upon them), the norm of equity (which states that people should be rewarded in proportion to their costs and that they should suffer in proportion to their transgressions), and the norm of reciprocity (which suggests that people help others in order to receive some future benefit for themselves).

4.   Helping is affected both by people's moods and by their characteristic level of empathy, the degree to which they experience the emotions of others. However, there appears to be no particular personality factor or trait that differentiates helpers from nonhelpers in general; situational factors are critical.

5.   Aggression can be defined as intentional injury or harm to another person, although labeling a particular behavior as aggressive may be ambiguous, due to the difficulty in determining the person's intent. Some psychologists feel that aggression is innate (inborn), and suggest that people feel that aggression must be discharged in a process called catharsis. However, others suggest that aggression occurs when a person is frustrated and in the presence of aggressive cues—stimuli that have been associated in the past with actual aggression.

6.   Observational learning theory suggests that we learn to be aggressive through the observation, and subsequent imitation, of others' behavior. This approach explains the effects of the observation of media violence, which most experts believe produces subsequent aggression in viewers—although the evidence is not conclusive. In addition, the observation of media pornography that depicts violence against women can lead to increased aggression toward women.

7.   Moral admonitions, in which people preach particular modes of behavior without practicing the behaviors themselves, are not particularly successful in producing increases in helping behavior and declines in aggression. However, direct rewards, as well as providing models of prosocial behavior, are more effective.

8.   Both values clarification techniques and procedures in which people's moral reasoning is made more sophisticated have been shown to be effective in changing people's views of morality. It is not clear, though, that they promote actual changes in moral behavior.

KEY TERMS AND CONCEPTS

prosocial behavior (p. 424)

diffusion of responsibility (p. 427)

reward-cost analysis (p. 428)

altruistic (p. 428)

norms (p. 429)

norm of social responsibility
(p. 431)

norm of equity (p. 432)

norm of reciprocity (p. 432)

empathy (p. 433)

aggression (p. 437)

innate (p. 437)

catharsis (p. 437)

frustration (p. 438)

aggressive cues (p. 438)

observational learning theory
(p. 439)

anger (p. 442)

vicarious reinforcement (p. 448)

abstract modeling (p. 448)

values clarification (p. 449)

enhancing moral reasoning (p. 449)

TO FIND OUT MORE

Latané, B., & Darley, J. M. (1970). *The unresponsive bystander: Why doesn't he help?* New York: Appleton-Century-Crofts.

A prize-winning classic, this book chronicles the reasons bystanders are unlikely to help in times of need.

Kurtines, W. M., & Gewirtz, J. L. (1984). *Morality, moral behavior, and moral development.* New York: Wiley Interscience.

This book presents a series of chapters by experts in the area of moral behavior, discussing the factors that influence positive moral actions.

Malamuth, N. M., & Donnerstein, E. (1984). *Pornography and sexual aggression.* New York: Academic.

The relationship between pornography and sexual aggression is explored in this book, which reviews the most definitive evidence.

Goldstein, A. P. (Ed.). (1983). *Prevention and control of aggression.* New York: Pergamon.

Taking a multidisciplinary approach, this book provides practical advice on avoiding and dealing with aggression in a variety of areas.

CHECK YOURSELF: ANSWERS

1. False **2.** d **3.** abstract modeling **4.** values clarification **5.** True

Working for Life

The Psychology of Work

The job wasn't really that great. I washed big pans that were used to cook the short ribs. They were about five feet long and two feet wide. They were covered with grease, and I would push this cart along the line and collect the dirty pans and then bring them over to the washer. I would stack them on these racks and then wheel the racks into this big washer. Then I would start the pulley and open the wash valve and wait for them to come out the other end. This might take a minute, maybe two. I don't really remember. When they came out, I would wheel them back to the other end of the line, unload them, and pick up some more dirty pans.

I used to joke at lunch. I'd say, "If anybody hears that layoffs are comin', do me a favor. Send in my name." Then a funny thing happened. I got laid off. I couldn't believe it. First, I thought it was one of the guys pulling a joke. But then I heard other people got notices, too, and I knew it wasn't a joke. I felt like a kid who wet his pants. I was afraid to go home and tell my wife. The rest of the day, nobody talked to me. They looked at me like I had cancer. . . . The end of the day, I didn't want to leave. I even thought about just working through the next shift. It was crazy, like I thought if I didn't leave the pan washer they couldn't lay me off. But the afternoon shift guy came, and I had to leave. (Landy, 1985, pp. 374–375.)

That even the most mundane jobs have immense meaning to the people who perform them is evident from this dishwasher's account of the shock of being laid off from his job. Work encompasses much more than merely a series of activities that must be carried out; rather, it has a profound impact on people's very identities and perceptions of themselves and their self-worth.

In this chapter we explore the effects of work on people's lives. We begin by discussing the function that work plays in people's lives and the different kinds of motivation that underlie the need to work.

Next, we consider how people make choices about their careers and how such choices can be made most effectively. We discuss the stages through which people progress as they think about their careers, and we look at the effect of sex on the nature of employment and career choices.

Finally, we examine the factors that lead to satisfaction on the job. We see how satisfaction is related to job performance, and we discuss strategies for increasing work satisfaction in job settings.

As we will see, working plays a central role in people's lives. As such, it presents one of life's major, ongoing challenges.

*Why do I work? Well, there are the obvious reasons: money for shelter, food, and the other necessities of life. I like to feel that I'm doing something for society, too, contributing in even a small way. But when it comes down to it, I **like** to work. I enjoy the things I do in the office, I like to talk to people on the job; I enjoy working with other folks, and, although I hate to admit it, I'm happy that I achieve things that other people don't. I'm awfully competitive, and I'm always trying to outdo my fellow employees. Oh, there are days when I'd rather not get out of bed in the morning; my job certainly isn't perfect. But when it comes down to it, I have more fun doing my job than a lot of other things I do in life.*

When people discuss the role that work plays in their lives, it soon becomes clear that the jobs they have play a much larger role in their lives than merely providing a means for earning a living. Instead, work contributes to their broader world in many ways.

When Work Is More than Earning a Living:
The functions of work in people's lives

If nothing else, jobs provide an income to workers—no small reward in a society in which life would be nearly impossible without money. Yet the accumulation of wealth, beyond some minimum that permits people to feel reasonably satisfied, is not the primary reason that many people engage in work.

Many people subscribe to the **Puritan work ethic,** the notion that work is important in and of itself. According to this view, the simple act of earning a living is of value and can provide satisfaction to workers. The Puritan work ethic is a norm that is widely held in American society and sometimes has been cited as a reason for the economic success of cultures that live by it.

But work also provides individuals with personal satisfactions that are related to their own particular needs (Repetti, 1987). For instance, one's job provides a source of personal identity. Consider, for example, the kinds of questions we ask people when we first meet them. After finding out their names and where they come from, the question that is most often asked next usually has to do with their occupational roles—information that is then used to make judgments about what they are like. In important respects, people define themselves according to the jobs they have—be they custodians, lawyers, or gardeners.

Work also affects people's social lives. Because we spend so much time in work situations, important relationships often develop, and the friendships that develop at work often spill over into non-work-related areas of

The careers people choose
are often a reflection of
their personal values
and attitudes.

Innervisions

our lives. And even when our primary social life does not revolve around work, there are often social obligations, such as inviting the boss to dinner or the annual office Christmas party, that must be fulfilled.

The kinds of work we do also relate to our personal values and interests. Individuals in a given profession frequently show similarities in their attitudes, and their values tend to mirror those of their coworkers. For example, one survey found that business people tended to place particular emphasis on economic and political values, while college professors and high school teachers were particularly concerned with social and religious values (Huntley & Davis, 1983).

Of course, such results merely indicate that there is a correlation or association between the values and interests of workers and the professions that they are in. We cannot tell whether initially holding these particular values led similar sorts of people to choose a certain profession, or if holding similar values is a consequence of working in the profession. Nonetheless, it is clear that our sense of what is and is not important tends to be shared by our coworkers in the particular job we are in. (For a look at the kind of job that would be particularly appealing to you, try the following Do It! box.)

DO IT!

WHAT'S IMPORTANT IN A JOB?

The following are ten job criteria that were listed most frequently in a nationwide survey related to the kinds of attributes that people look for in their jobs. Place a check by the ones that are most important to you, and then consider the results of the survey:

_____ Friendly, helpful coworkers
_____ Work that is interesting
_____ Opportunity to use your mind
_____ Work results that you can see
_____ Pay that is good
_____ Opportunities to develop skills/abilities
_____ Participation in decisions regarding job
_____ Getting help needed to do the job well
_____ Respect for organization you work for
_____ Recognition for a job well done

ANSWERS   The survey results found that the percentage of people who checked a particular criterion are: Friendly, helpful coworkers: 70%; Work that is interesting: 70%; Opportunity to use your mind: 65%; Work results that you can see: 62%; Pay that is good: 61%; Opportunities to develop skills/abilities: 61%; Participation in decisions regarding job: 58%; Getting help needed to do the job well: 55%; Respect for organization you work for: 55%; and Recognition for a job well done: 54%.

Source: Yankelovich, D., 1974.

The nature of our jobs also has an important effect on our **status**—the evaluation by others of the roles we play in society. As you can see in Table 14-1, there are significant differences in the status inherent in various professional roles, with physicians and college teachers at the top of the list and ushers and shoe shiners falling to the bottom.

In addition, there is a clear relationship between a job's status and people's attitudes toward their work: The higher the status of a person's job, the more likely that person is to say that he or she would choose it again (Yankelovich, 1974). Moreover, the status of the entire family can be influenced by the job that is held by the head of the household.

TABLE 14-1
Occupational Status for
Different Occupations

In a series of national surveys conducted
between 1972 and 1982, Americans were
ranked by a variety of occupations in terms
of prestige. The highest possible score was
90, the lowest 10. Some of the results are
presented below.

OCCUPATION	SCORE
Physician	82
College teacher	78
Lawyer	76
Dentist	74
Bank officer	72
Airline pilot	70
Clergy	69
Sociologist	66
Secondary schoolteacher	63
Registered nurse	62
Pharmacist	61
Elementary schoolteacher	60
Accountant	56
Painter	56
Librarian	55
Actor	55
Funeral director	52
Athlete	51
Reporter	51
Bank teller	50
Electrician	49
Police officer	48
Insurance agent	47
Secretary	46
Air traffic controller	43
Mail carrier	42
Farm owner	41
Restaurant manager	39
Automobile mechanic	37
Baker	34
Salesclerk	29
Gas station attendant	22
Waiter and waitress	20
Laundry operator	17
Garbage collector	17
Janitor	16
Usher	15
Shoe shiner	12

Source: NORC, 1982, pp. 299–314.

For Money or Love?:
Intrinsic and extrinsic motivation

Underlying many of the major reasons that people work are intrinsic and extrinsic motivation. **Intrinsic motivation** is motivation that causes people to participate in work for their own enjoyment, not for the reward it will bring them. In contrast, **extrinsic motivation** is motivation that causes people to work to obtain tangible rewards.

Some researchers have argued that, in contrast to extrinsic motivation, intrinsic motivation causes people to persist longer, work harder, and produce work of higher quality (Deci & Ryan, 1985; Lepper, Greene, & Nisbett, 1973). On the other hand, given our discussion of the range of factors that lie behind the reasons people work, neither intrinsic or extrinsic motivation alone seems sufficient to explain why people work, although there are certain conditions under which the arousal of particular kinds of motivation has been found to bring about better performance. For example, intrinsic motivation is enhanced by increasing workers' sense of self-determination on the job and by providing them the opportunity to make choices, such as what tasks to work on or in what order to carry out various activities. Moreover, intrinsic motivation can be facilitated by increasing workers' perceptions of competence and expertise through the use of positive feedback (Steers & Porter, 1983; Harackiewicz & Larson, 1986).

On the other hand, external rewards, which produce an increase in extrinsic motivation, can also enhance worker performance. For instance, external rewards are effective when they are important to a worker, when they depend on the nature of the worker's performance, when a worker's performance is measured accurately (so that workers can determine the level of their performance), when the worker understands the reward system, and when there is trust between workers and employers (Lawler, 1981). In contrast, when rewards are provided regardless of the quality of a worker's performance, extrinsic motivation is undermined.

Although people work for reasons that are related to both intrinsic and extrinsic motivation, the degree to which intrinsic versus extrinsic factors dominate in determining people's work performance is not clear (Locke & Henne, 1986). It is apparent that people work for reasons that go well beyond just bringing home a paycheck.

In the Company of Others:
Working together in groups

Lee felt fortunate when he got a job as editor with the major advertising firm of Hegel, Bach, and Rosen. Of course, it was just a first step in what he felt confident would be a successful career, but even as "assistant editorial associate," he felt sure he would soon leave his mark on the company.

The job itself was almost laughably simple: It consisted of looking up words in the dictionary to make sure they were used properly in advertisements that the creative staff had written. In fact, Lee soon found that he could work almost twice as fast as his coworkers, who had been on the job for quite some time. He felt his superior performance would soon be recognized by his supervisor, and he couldn't help but think that he would quickly be moving up in the company.

Instead, Lee began to notice something else happening. His coworkers, who had initially been friendly and welcoming, began to act cool and disapproving. Even worse for a person like Lee, so intent on climbing the corporate ladder, his supervisor seemed displeased in subtle ways by his obviously higher productivity. After just a few weeks it seemed that Lee had alienated just about everyone with whom he worked.

Rethinking his strategy for corporate success, Lee seized a solution. He gradually began to slow down, matching more closely the productivity of his fellow employees. His instincts were right: Gradually, his coworkers became friendlier, and his boss seemed relieved and considerably more complimentary about Lee's performance, telling him that he now seemed to have "learned the ropes" of the business. It seemed clear to Lee that he had made the right move in slowing down—and that despite his shaky start, he could once again begin fantasizing about making it to the top.

The lesson that Lee had learned was an important one. As psychologists have found, the influence that coworkers have on work performance is substantial and oftentimes more important in determining what goes on in the workplace than the formal goals that an employer might have in mind. For example, the results of a now-classic series of studies carried out in the 1920s demonstrate clearly the important influence that coworkers have on performance.

The feeling that management is taking notice and listening can boost productivity on the assembly line, sometimes more than a change in working conditions would.

In the studies, a team of investigators studied working conditions at a telephone-manufacturing facility—the Hawthorne plant of the Western Electric Company (Mayo, 1933; Roethlisberger & Dickson, 1939). They began by considering the effects of changes in illumination intensity on the productivity of workers assembling telephone components. Gradual increases in lighting were made, and each change brought about an increase in productivity. Surprisingly, however, productivity continued to increase even when the lighting was increased to a point where the room was flooded with bright light. And even more intriguing, productivity rose once again when the researchers began to *decrease* the lighting! It became apparent that it was the special attention that the workers were receiving from the researchers that led to their productivity increases, rather than the particular nature of the changes made by the researchers—a phenomenon that became known as the **Hawthorne effect.**

The Hawthorne effect spawned a series of studies that revealed quite clearly the extent to which workers are influenced by interpersonal factors and the degree to which informal norms regarding appropriate behavior can supplant the formal norms of employers. This fact was demonstrated quite graphically by what the researchers found in a switchboard wiring room, in which the formal management goal was the production of two and a half switchboards each day.

In contrast to the formal goal, the researchers found that the workers held to an informal norm of producing two switchboards a day. Workers who either exceeded or produced fewer than the informal goal of two per day received verbal abuse for their transgressions: Underproducers were called "chiselers," and overproducers were called "speed kings" or "rate busters." The overproducers were also physically punished by being punched in the arm by their coworkers in a not-too-subtle attempt at enforcing the informal goal.

What is particularly important about these informal norms is that they are at odds with the best financial interests of the workers. Because the pay of the employees was based on productivity, workers who decreased their production suffered financially in order to meet the informal norms of their work group.

The reason that workers were willing to make financial sacrifices for the sake of the informal group norms seems to be due to the high degree of cohesiveness of the group. Group **cohesiveness** is the degree to which group members are attracted to the group as a whole, and to other members individually (Forsyth, 1983). Groups that are high in cohesiveness tend to produce a number of consequences, including higher self-esteem for group members, a higher likelihood of membership maintenance, and greater adherence to the group's norms.

In the case of the switchboard wiring room—just as in our earlier example in the advertising agency—the group cohesiveness was probably high, leading to relatively stringent enforcement of the informal norms relating to the accustomed level of productivity. In cases of high group cohesiveness in the workplace, then, people may choose to honor their friendships more than their pocketbooks.

THE WORLD
AROUND US

Before you are able to make choices about specific career paths that you might follow, you must have a general notion of what it is you wish to get from your work. One approach to identifying your work priorities is based on the **balance sheet approach** to decision making. Useful in making any kind of decision, the balance sheet is a list of positive and negative outcomes that might occur as a result of a particular decision (Janis & Mann, 1977; Janis & Wheeler, 1978). By making explicit both the pros and cons of each potential choice, people later report feeling more satisfied with the decisions that they do make, as well as being more aware of the positive and negative aspects of decisions.

To produce a balance sheet, the following information should be listed:

● *List the tangible gains and losses for yourself.* First consider what *you* will gain (such as a particular income level or interest in your work) or lose (such as spare time, if the job requires long hours) from a particular profession.

● *List the tangible gains and losses for others from the potential decision.* Perhaps a high income will provide your family with many luxuries; or, in terms of losses, perhaps you will lose a close family life, if the profession requires a good deal of travel.

● *List the projected self-approval or self-disapproval from the potential choice.* You might feel pride over being a member of a particular profession, or, on the negative side, you may be embarrassed about being a member of a profession which has low prestige and status.

● *List the projected social approval or disapproval you will receive from others.* Consider how others will react to your choice of career. Project the kinds of positive responses from others the choice will bring about (you might receive respect and admiration for a given choice), and consider the negative outcomes of a potential decision (perhaps your social life will be largely restricted to members of the profession you choose).

By explicitly listing both the positive and negative potential outcomes of several potential decisions on a balance sheet, you will be in a much better position to make informed judgments about the kind of career path you might want to follow.

TO REVIEW

People work not only to earn money but for reasons related to the Puritan work ethic, personal identity, their social lives, values, and status.

Underlying these reasons are intrinsic and extrinsic motivation.

Both formal and informal goals may exert an influence in work settings, dependent, in part, on work-group cohesiveness.

CHECK YOURSELF

1. Which of the following was *not* cited in the text as a reason that people work?
   a. People define themselves according to their jobs.
   b. Friendships develop at work.
   c. Coworkers hold diverse interests, thereby adding more richness to one's social life.
   d. The act of earning a living is highly valued.

2. Rachel has been working 12-hour days to finish a project, just so that she can get the raise promised her. In all likelihood, she is driven primarily by _____ motivation to finish the project.

3. Studies on the Hawthorne effect have demonstrated that the lighting level in a factory is a major factor affecting productivity. True or false?

4. Group cohesiveness
   a. has no substantial effect on productivity, according to decades of research
   b. is unrelated to a work group's informal norms
   c. produces sticky spots on factory floors
   d. may produce either a rise or a decline in productivity, depending on the nature of the group's informal norms

(See answers to the questions at the bottom of page 466.)

14.2 IT'S MORE THAN A JOB:
Choosing a Career

How did I decide to become a lawyer? The answer to that question is actually quite embarrassing, as I look back now. At the start of my senior year of college, I suddenly realized that I better get on the stick and decide what it was that I wanted to do when I "grew up"—something that suddenly seemed to be looming just around the corner. At the time, the Iran hearings had just ended, and I was fascinated with the role that the legal profession was playing in the hearings. At the same time, I was a faithful follower of L.A. Law, and I had this romantic view of myself in one of those big corner offices. For these reasons—and just about no other ones, I'm ashamed to admit—I took the law boards and applied to law school.

Given the importance of a job in most people's lives, it is surprising that many people's choices regarding their life's work follow this kind of haphazard pattern. For instance, some people "fall into" jobs, depending on what is available or convenient. Moreover, people from economically disadvantaged and minority backgrounds may have fewer choices to consider than people from middle- and upper-class backgrounds. For most, however, the choice of a career is made relatively systematically, often following a series of phases that may extend over a person's entire working life.

From Fantasy to Reality:
The stages of choosing work

According to Eli Ginzberg (1972), the first phase of career choice is the fantasy period. During the **fantasy period,** which lasts until about age 11, career choices are based on personal desires without regard to a person's ability, competencies, training, or available job opportunities. A child who wants to be an astronaut—but who overlooks the fact that he or she suffers motion sickness in a car—is in the fantasy period.

The **tentative period,** which spans ages 11 to 18, marks the point in which realistic considerations begin to be taken into account. During this time, people become aware of whether and to what degree their particular abilities, values, and goals will allow them to pursue a particular career choice, and they begin to make tentative career choices. Although this phase begins with an emphasis on people's determination of what their interests

Fantasy can be an important step in the process of choosing a career.

Michael Douglas/The Image Works

CHECK YOURSELF: ANSWERS
1. c **2.** extrinsic **3.** False **4.** d

are, it ends with them matching the opportunities in the world around them with an increasingly accurate assessment of their own strengths and weaknesses.

Finally, people enter the **realistic period,** which generally coincides with high school graduation at around age 18. During this phase, specific career options are explored, either through actual work experience or through training that is oriented toward a particular career. Following a period of exploration, people begin to narrow their career alternatives to a few choices and ultimately specify their commitment to a particular career.

However, even after settling on a particular career choice or job, people make, revise, and sometimes completely change their earlier choices. Indeed, the choices characteristic of the realistic stage can continue throughout a person's lifetime. For most people, though, the process of choosing a career is complete by middle age.

Ginzberg's three-phase model has been supported by several surveys. For example, in one study a group of students were followed as they moved through the eighth, tenth, and twelfth grades, and then two years after graduation. The dominant trend was a change from a more idealistic orientation to a more realistic one as they reached twelfth grade (Gribbons & Lohnes, 1965).

Although Ginzberg's model of career choice identifies the periods through which people pass, it is less illuminating in terms of the factors that actually influence career and job choices. What specific influences affect people's occupational interests and aspirations?

One important influence is parents' motivations for their children's occupational success. Generally, the higher the parents' aspirations for their children, the higher the children's desires for success, independent of the intelligence or social and economic status of the family. Parental occupational status and attitudes toward work are also important factors. Families in which the parents have high occupational status and positive attitudes toward work are more likely to have children who seek out high-status careers and have positive work attitudes. Parents who have lower occupational status and less positive attitudes toward work tend to have children with lower career aspirations (Marini, 1978).

Peers also play an important role in determining career choices and aspirations. Although the research on females is less conclusive, it is clear that the career aspirations of adolescent males are related to the aspirations of their friends (Marini, 1978). Boys whose friends have high career goals tend to be influenced by those goals; those whose peer groups have relatively low aspirations tend to have low aspirations themselves.

Finally, career and job choices are affected by an individual's personal characteristics. Not surprisingly, higher intelligence is related to higher career aspirations. Moreover, people with higher intelligence tend to make occupational decisions that are more realistic in terms of their actual abilities, interests, and the job opportunities that are available. Similarly, personality characteristics, such as high levels of achievement motivation (discussed in Chapter 4), are associated with higher career aspirations.

Women's Work, Men's Work:
Sex and career choices

The last few decades have seen nothing less than a revolution in women's lives. In the last twenty years, the number of women in the labor force has more than doubled; women now make up more than 55 percent of the work force (Stark, 1987). Women in the labor force now outnumber women who are not working, and 60 percent of married mothers with children younger than 6 now work outside the home (Gerson, 1985). Indeed, the traditional "housewife" role is fast becoming as archaic as the Model T: Only one in a thousand females in their first year of college plans on a career as a house-wife, and fewer than 11 percent of all women today can be considered the stereotypical housewife—a married mother who is not working outside of the home. Moreover, elderly women now represent the largest proportion of housewives (Russell, 1985).

If women are no longer the housewives they once were, what are they doing? There are increasing numbers of women in what once were male-dominated occupations, such as medicine, engineering, carpentry, manage-ment and administration, and finance. (At the same time, the number of men in what were traditionally female-dominated professions, such as teach-ing and nursing, is increasing.)

Despite the movement of women into occupations that were tradition-ally male-oriented, most traditionally female jobs are still relatively low-paying and have relatively low status. As you can see in Figure 14-1, around 80 percent of all clerical workers are women, while only 25 percent of

FIGURE 14-1
Despite the movement of women into occupations that were traditionally male-oriented, women make up the majority of workers in many low-status and low-paying jobs. (*Source:* Women's Bureau, U.S. Department of Labor, October, 1980. "Women Are Under-represented as Managers and Skilled Craft Workers." Washington, D.C.: U.S. Government Printing Office.)

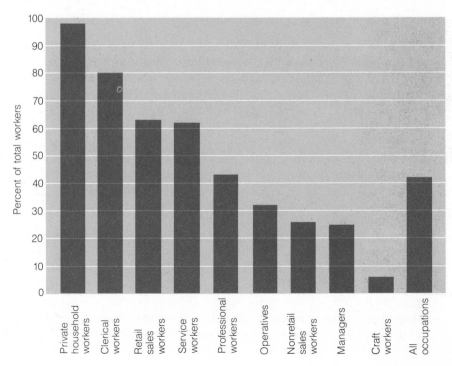

managers are female. Moreover, if you refer back to the occupations with the highest prestige in Table 14-1, you will see that the jobs with the highest prestige attached to them are the ones least apt to include many women.

Still, the barriers erected by society to the success of women can be overcome. As more women enter the work force, issues relating to women will likely become more prominent in the minds of employers, and inequities between men and women may be reduced. Moreover, there is now a body of federal legislation making discrimination in the workplace illegal. Both men and women, then, can reasonably make career choices on the basis of what is best for them as individuals, rather than what is "appropriate" for someone of their sex.

Psychology for You:
Making career choices

Given the importance of work in people's lives, making career choices represents one of the most important challenges each of us faces. Yet few people make career decisions systematically, and many rely on rumors, misinformation, or unreliable sources to make choices that may affect them for the rest of their lives.

There are, however, several ways in which career choices can be made effectively. Among the key points that psychologists have identified:

● *Don't be rushed into a decision.* If you feel uncertain about career choices, take your time in exploring the various options that are available to you. Remember that career choices are not made only once in a lifetime but at several junctures.

● *Systematically investigate the nature of various jobs and career opportunities.* Libraries contain a wealth of information on career options, and college counseling centers typically contain material that can help you make intelligent career choices.

● *Know yourself.* Carefully and realistically assess your strengths and weaknesses in terms of your aptitudes, abilities, and interests (see the accompanying Do It! box). If your performance in science classes is not strong and you have little interest in biology, it is probably not reasonable to hold onto any vague desires you might have to be a physician, no matter how much you think you'd like to treat patients or earn a large salary. You should focus instead on those possible jobs where your talents lie. College counseling centers are helpful in this respect, too: They can administer tests that allow you to determine what your major strengths are. You can also use the balance sheet approach, described earlier in the chapter, to make decisions about specific careers.

● *Learn from your mistakes; don't suffer with them.* If you have settled on a career choice and it is not panning out, realize that your decision can be changed. A considerable number of people make career changes, even

Arthur Tress/Photo Researchers

When a career that was once enjoyable no longer provides satisfaction, it may be wise to consider making a change.

in middle age and later. Don't allow yourself to be locked into a decision that was made at an earlier point in your life. The world changes, as do your interests and abilities.

DO IT!

WHAT DO YOU WANT FROM YOUR JOB?

The most common—and best—advice that people who wish to identify a career path are given is to determine what their skills, values, and interests are in order to find a job that makes use of them. To get started doing that, the following exercise may be helpful:

1. Write the question "Who am I?" at the top of ten sheets of paper.

2. Now go back and write one answer to the question on each sheet. The answers might take the form of being "a woman" or "a good dancer" or "a go-getter" or "a neat person." Be honest and accurate.

3. Now go back to each sheet and, looking at the answer, write what it is about that answer that is *interesting* and *exciting* to you.

4. Next, arrange the ten sheets of paper in order of priority. Place your most important aspect of your identity on the top and the least important on the bottom.

5. Examine each of the answers you wrote about what is interesting and exciting to you, and try to identify any common denominators. Write these common denominators on another sheet of paper. For example, they might be attributes such as "I like taking initiative" or "I enjoy working with other people."

6. The items on this last list suggest the components a job ought to have in order for it to be fulfilling and for you to feel effective and satisfied. Using this list, see if you can be explicit about what these components are.

This exercise provides one method for identifying what it is you are looking for in a career. The more you can do to recognize what you want from a job and what your own particular strengths are, the more successful you will be in making informed, suitable choices.

Source: Bolles, 1988.

TO REVIEW

● Career choices are typically extended over three phases: a fantasy period, a tentative period, and a realistic period.

● Among the influences on career choices are parents' motivations for their children's occupational success, parental occupational status and attitudes toward work, peer aspirations, and the individual's personal characteristics.

● Despite the movement of women into occupations that were traditionally male-oriented, most women's jobs are still relatively low-paying and have low status.

CHECK YOURSELF

1.   Match the statement in the right column with the stage it best typifies in the left column.

_____ fantasy

_____ tentative

_____ realistic

a. "I'm really good at math and science . . . and I like them. Maybe I *should* be a chemist."

b. "I really enjoyed that research assistant job. I guess I will enter the psychology program after all."

c. "Dennis wants to be a senator one week, and a fisherman the next!"

2. Parents who express high expectations for their children often find, paradoxically, that their children become underachievers instead. True or false?

3. Most women:
   a. have jobs of lower status than men
   b. are paid less than men in comparable jobs
   c. no longer fit the traditional role of "housewife"
   d. experience all the above

(See answers to the questions at the bottom of page 474.)

14.3 TURNING WORK INTO PLAY:
Job Satisfaction

My job was stacking the Ping-pong paddles into piles of fifty. Actually, I didn't have to count all the way up to fifty. To make it a little easier, they told me to stack 'em in circles of four with the first handle facing me. When there got to be thirteen handles on the second one from the front, then I'd know I had fifty. After a while of stacking, I didn't have to count anyway. I could tell fifty by just looking at the pile.

Maybe it wouldn't have been so bad if I could have seen all the piles I stacked at the end of the day. But they were taking them down as fast as I was piling them up. That was the worst part of the job.

No . . . that wasn't the worst part. The worst part was that you had to stand up all day doing it.

You couldn't talk either. You wouldn't want to anyway because it was too noisy, and the way we were all spaced apart, you'd have to lean over and shout. But if you ever tried to talk, Alma would come running over with a whole lot more paddles. Or she'd yell, "Why aren't you finished yet?" (Garson, 1975, pp. 1–2.)

How satisfied with your job would you feel if you were in this person's place? You don't need to be a psychologist to detect the unhappiness, frustration, and anger that a job of this sort would bring about, and job satisfaction would hardly be expected to be high.

Yet most jobs are not as unambiguously tedious and unpleasant as this one, and researchers have been left to sort out the factors that make for satisfaction with one's work. It is not a simple task, for it is not just the nature of work that affects the degree of a person's satisfaction but a complex interaction involving both the job and a person's individual needs, personality traits, demographic background, and skill level. (To get a sense of how your own level of job satisfaction can be measured, see the Do It! box.)

ASSESSING JOB SATISFACTION

One way of measuring job satisfaction is to assess the way employees act with respect to their jobs, rather than the more direct assessment technique relating to how they feel about their jobs. To get a sense of how this works, answer each of the following questions in terms of a job you now hold—which might well be the "job" of full-time student.

1.   When you wake up in the morning, do you feel reluctant to go to work? Yes _____ No _____

2.   Do you ever feel reluctant to go home from work at night because of the enjoyment you are getting from the job? Yes _____ No _____

3.   Do you often feel like going to lunch at work sooner than you do? Yes _____ No _____

4.   Do you feel like taking a coffee break more often than you should? Yes _____ No _____

5.   Do you ever wish you could work at your job on evenings or weekends? Yes _____ No _____

6.   Are you sometimes reluctant to leave your job to go on a vacation? Yes _____ No _____

7.   When you are on vacation, do you ever look forward to getting back to work? Yes _____ No _____

8.   Do you ever wake up at night with the urge to go to work right then and there? Yes _____ No _____

9.   Do you ever wish holidays or weekends would end so you could go back to work? Yes _____ No _____

10.   If you were starting over in your career, would you lean toward taking the same type of job you have now? Yes _____ No _____

11.   Would you be tempted to recommend your present job to a friend with the same interests and education as yours? Yes _____ No _____

SCORING   Add up the responses that agree with the following key: 1. N; 2. Y; 3. N; 4. N; 5. Y; 6. Y; 7. Y; 8. Y; 9. Y; 10. Y; 11. Y. The higher your score, the more satisfied you are with your work.

Source: Locke, 1976.

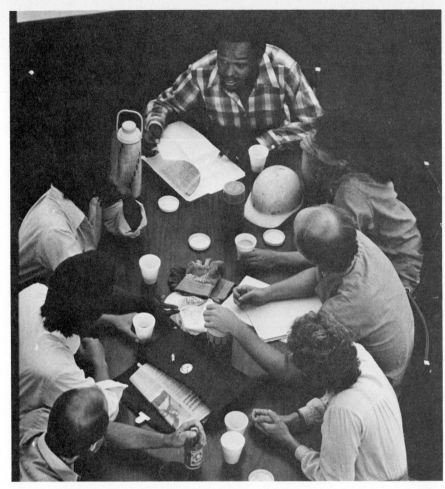

David Powers/ Stock, Boston

When workers are given
decision-making power,
employee morale and
productivity are likely to
improve significantly.

Not surprisingly, however, there are several key factors that are associated with job satisfaction (Mitchell, 1982). For instance, pay and promotional opportunities are of primary importance. However, it is not only pay in an absolute sense that affects satisfaction but also pay relative to the level of effort that is expended and pay as it compares to that of one's coworkers. For instance, it is quite possible for someone making $25,000 a year to be more satisfied (with both the pay and the job) than someone earning $100,000 a year, if the $25,000 is perceived as high in terms of the salaries that coworkers are earning, while the higher salary is viewed as being inequitable relative to what others in a similar position are getting.

Of course, job satisfaction is not determined by salary and promotional

CHECK YOURSELF: ANSWERS
1. c, a, b **2.** False **3.** d

opportunities alone (Szilagyi & Wallace, 1987). The ability of workers to set their own goals is typically related to satisfaction. Workers who are able to participate with their employers in the determination of both the nature and quantity of their production are apt to be more satisfied than those who have goals imposed upon them.

Job clarity, the degree of explicitness of the rules that determine what is expected of a worker, is also associated with job satisfaction. Jobs that have well-defined expectations about the kinds of things that the worker is to accomplish generally produce higher levels of job satisfaction than those in which job clarity is relatively low.

Similarly, jobs that are high in **role conflict**—contradictory demands placed on a worker by employers—are likely to produce dissatisfaction (VanSell, Brief, & Schuler, 1981). When there are role conflicts, a worker who meets one set of demands may be unable to fulfill another that may be of equal importance. For example, an executive in an advertising agency who must make sure that the employees in her unit are highly productive and efficient, and are simultaneously operating at their peak of creativity, may find herself in a no-win situation. If she allows her employees more time to be creative, efficiency is reduced; but if she pushes her employees too hard to maximize efficiency, their creativity may suffer.

In other cases there can be conflict between a person's occupational role and that outside of the job. The most prevalent example of this sort of role conflict is the dilemma faced by working parents and particularly by working mothers (Baruch & Barnett, 1986). Women who are simultaneously wage earners, mothers, and homemakers face extraordinary demands on their time and energy. Consider, for example, a single mother who is about to depart on a business trip when her child becomes ill. She is faced with the dilemma of leaving the sick child or canceling her trip; the latter choice may cause her to jeopardize her chances for career advancement. No matter which option she chooses she may face conflict and guilt (Skinner, 1986).

Finally, the degree of satisfaction experienced in a job is, of course, related to the specific content of the work itself. Work that is perceived as challenging, interesting, and able to be accomplished successfully produces higher levels of job satisfaction than work that is perceived as tedious, mo-notonous, and repetitive.

What is particularly noteworthy about this conclusion is that it is the workers' *perception* of their jobs rather than the actual content of the jobs that leads to different levels of job satisfaction. Particular kinds of jobs do not automatically lead to job dissatisfaction. Rather, whether workers are dissatisfied rests on their own backgrounds and competencies and the way they view the world. Thus, a job that might be perceived as boring and tedious by one person—thereby producing job dissatisfaction—might be viewed as sufficiently interesting to another individual and promote job sat-isfaction (Locke, 1976). (For other factors that are important in determining job satisfaction, see Table 14-2.) Probably the overriding factor in deter-mining people's satisfaction with their jobs, then, is the match between the nature of the job and their particular skills.

TABLE 14-2

Work Satisfaction: Effects of Various Events, Conditions, and Agents on Job Satisfaction

SOURCE	EFFECT
EVENTS OR CONDITIONS	
Work itself: challenge	Mentally challenging work that the individual can successfully accomplish is satisfying.
Work itself: physical demand	Tiring work is dissatisfying.
Work itself: personal interest	Personally interesting work is satisfying.
Reward structure	Just and informative rewards for performance are satisfying.
Working conditions: physical	Satisfaction depends on the match between working conditions and physical needs.
Working conditions: goal attainment	Working conditions that facilitate goal attainment are satisfying.
AGENTS	
Self	High self-esteem is conducive to job satisfaction.
Supervisors, coworkers, subordinates	Individuals will be satisfied with colleagues who see things the same way they do.
Company and management	Individuals will be satisfied with companies that have policies and procedures designed to help the individual attain rewards.
	Individuals will be dissatisfied with conflicting roles and/or ambiguous roles imposed by company and/or management.
Fringe benefits	Benefits do not have a strong influence on job satisfaction for most workers.

Source: Landy, 1985, p. 399.

I Can't Get No Satisfaction:
The impacts of job satisfaction on job performance

Is a satisfied worker a better worker? Common sense would suggest an affirmative response, and in some respects the notion appears to be correct. Workers who report being satisfied with their jobs are likely to have lower rates of absenteeism than those who are less satisfied (Steers & Rhodes, 1978). Moreover, job satisfaction leads to lower rates of job turnover (Mobley, Horner, & Hollingsworth, 1978).

On the other hand, job satisfaction is not always related to better performance. For instance, it does not seem that more satisfied workers necessarily do a better job than less satisfied workers on a day-to-day basis

Ellis Herwig/Stock, Boston

In addition to financial hardship, unemployment brings problems in emotional and physical well-being.

(Iaffaldano & Muchinsky, 1985). One reason may be that the productivity of workers is controlled more by factors such as the possibility of pay raises or promotions due to good performance than by job satisfaction. Even workers who are dissatisfied with their jobs may be willing to work hard if the job provides other, more tangible rewards, especially if other jobs are scarce and there are few opportunities for alternative employment.

It is also clear that having a job is preferable to not having one. In general, unemployed people have poorer psychological and physical health than people with jobs. Losing one's job results frequently in feelings of anxiety, depression, insomnia, irritability, lack of self-confidence, and an inability to concentrate (Warr, 1983; Walker & Mann, 1987).

Even aspects of unemployment that might seem positive—such as the increase in free time that it provides—typically produce negative consequences. For example, unemployed people show declines in attendance at voluntary organizations, their use of libraries declines, they read less, and their sense of time seems to be affected, as demonstrated by the fact that they are less punctual for meals and appointments (Jahoda, 1982; Fryer & Payne, 1986). Given the many functions that jobs play in people's lives, such negative responses to a lack of work are hardly surprising.

Psychology for You:
Increasing your work satisfaction

Given that job satisfaction is the result of an interaction of factors having to do with the individual's particular capabilities and interests and the nature of the job itself, how does a person go about ensuring job satisfaction?

While there is no foolproof formula that can guarantee job satisfaction, there are several steps that can be taken to maximize one's chances for work satisfaction.

● *Make wise career choices.* It is unlikely that you will ever be satisfied in a job for which you are not qualified. As we discussed earlier, there are several systematic ways to choose a job. Use them, and avoid finding yourself in a no-win position.

● *Restructure your job to fit your needs.* There are several ways in which jobs can be redesigned to make them more satisfying. For instance, **job enlargement,** in which the number and variety of tasks assigned to a job are increased, has been found to be effective in raising job satisfaction. Similarly, increasing the autonomy and responsibility of workers has positive effects on job satisfaction.

Autonomous work groups, in which small groups of employees work together to produce a product, are a particularly effective means of increasing satisfaction. Replacing traditional assembly line methods (in which there are a series of tasks performed sequentially by different workers with each worker carrying out the same task over and over) with autonomous work groups allows workers to complete a series of tasks as a group. Workers also take part in scheduling and decision making. Because each person in the group is capable of carrying out the entire job alone, the members of the group are able to switch jobs, as long as the group as a whole produces at a specified rate. Although initially developed as a procedure for use in factories, autonomous work groups can also be used in other settings.

Many employers sponsor stress-reduction seminars and promote group discussions of other nontraditional methods to increase their employees' ability to cope.

Michael Weisbrot and Family.

- *Change yourself to fit your job.* There may be no such thing as the "perfect" job, and expecting to find one can be self-defeating. If a person generally feels positive toward his or her job and it is impossible to change those specific aspects of the job that are bothersome, it is reasonable to attempt to change one's perceptions of the job's negative aspects.

For instance, in the same way that we discussed changing the perception of threat into that of a challenge when we discussed stress in Chapter 6, a person might attempt to change his or her perceptions of and reactions to the job. One way would be to meet informally with coworkers and supervisors for the purpose of sharing job concerns, which can be useful in learning new perspectives on work-related issues. Similarly, some work organizations arrange for workers to engage in sensitivity training, in which they teach workers to be more aware of their own feelings and values as well as those of others. The greater understanding brought about through this process often allows people to be more at ease with the negative aspects of their jobs.

TO REVIEW

- Work satisfaction is produced by an interaction between a person's individual needs, personality traits, demographic background, and skill level, and the nature of the job itself.

- Among the factors most directly affecting job satisfaction are pay and promotional opportunities, goal-setting capabilities, job clarity, and role conflict.

- Although job satisfaction is related to job absenteeism and rate of turnover, it is not closely related to productivity.

- To increase job satisfaction, one should make wise career choices, restructure a job to fit one's needs, or change oneself to fit the job.

CHECK YOURSELF

1. Workers are typically more satisfied with their jobs when they are allowed to participate with their employers in setting goals. True or false?

2. "If you could just be more specific about what it is you want me to do, I think I could do a fine job!" This worker is dissatisfied with the level of _____ _____ that has been expressed to her by her employer.

3. Conflict between an individual's occupational role and his or her role outside of work appears most prevalent in:

    a. single males
    b. working mothers

c. working fathers

d. single females

4. "I wish they would lay me off! I could find plenty of enjoyable things to do with all that free time." Based on research cited in the text, would this person's prediction be accurate?

_____

(See answers to the questions at the bottom of page 482.)

TO SUMMARIZE

1. Work plays several central roles in people's lives. For example, many people subscribe to the Puritan work ethic, the notion that work is important in and of itself. Work also provides personal satisfaction related to one's needs, including offering a source of personal identity. Finally, work is related to people's social lives and their personal values and interests.

2. Intrinsic and extrinsic motivation underlie many of the major reasons that people work. Intrinsic motivation is motivation that causes people to participate in work for their own enjoyment, not for the rewards it will get them. In contrast, extrinsic motivation is motivation that causes people to work to obtain a tangible reward. Most people work for reasons relating to both intrinsic and extrinsic motivation.

3. As the Hawthorne studies illustrated, work groups that are high in cohesiveness—the degree to which group members are attracted to the group as a whole and to the other members individually—are more likely to exert influence in the form of informal group norms.

4. The choice of career typically proceeds in three major stages. In the fantasy period, career choices are based on personal desires without regard to a person's ability, competence, training, or opportunities. In the tentative period, which spans ages 11 to 18, reality plays more of a role, as people become increasingly accurate in assessing their own strengths and weaknesses. Finally, people enter the realistic period, generally following high school graduation. In this period, people explore actual options and begin to narrow their alternatives to a few choices.

5. Among the factors that influence career choice are parental aspirations for their children's occupational success, parental occupational status and attitudes toward work, and peer aspirations. Finally, career and job choices are affected by such personal characteristics as intelligence and achievement motivation.

6. The role of "housewife" is becoming increasingly rare, with women in the labor force now outnumbering women who are not working. However, most women's jobs are relatively low-paying and have low status. When women enter high-prestige professions in large numbers, the prestige of the profession starts to drop, and salaries begin to decline.

7.   Job satisfaction is affected by an interaction involving both the nature of a person's job and a person's individual needs, personality traits, demographic background, and skill level. Among the most important factors are salary and promotional opportunities, as well as the alternatives available to the individual.

8.   Greater job satisfaction is also related to higher job clarity, the degree of explicitness of the rules that determine what is expected of a worker, and lower role conflict, in which there are contradictory demands placed on a worker. In addition, of course, the specific content of a job is associated with job satisfaction.

9.   Not surprisingly, job satisfaction leads to lower rates of absenteeism and job turnover. However, higher levels of satisfaction are not necessarily related to better performance. To increase job satisfaction, people should make reasonable career choices initially, restructure their jobs to fit their needs, or change themselves to better fit the job.

KEY TERMS AND CONCEPTS

Puritan work ethic (p. 457)

status (p. 459)

intrinsic motivation (p. 461)

extrinsic motivation (p. 463)

Hawthorne effect (p. 463)

cohesiveness (p. 463)

balance sheet approach [to decision making] (p. 464)

fantasy period (of career choice) (p. 466)

tentative period (of career choice) (p. 466)

realistic period (of career choice) (p. 467)

job clarity (p. 475)

role conflict (p. 475)

job enlargement (p. 478)

autonomous work group (p. 478)

TO FIND OUT MORE

Frost, P. J., Mitchell, V. F., & Nord, W. R. (1986). *Organizational reality: Reports from the firing line* (3rd ed.). Chicago: Scott, Foresman.

A series of vignettes describing people's work lives, with an emphasis on working in organizations.

Landy, F. J. (1985). *Psychology of work behavior*. Homewood, IL: Dorsey.

A detailed account of the relationship between work and psychological variables, this book provides a clearly written, current look at the impact of work on people's lives.

Forsyth, D. (1983). *An introduction to group dynamics*. Monterey, CA: Brooks/Cole.

A very well written, interesting guide to group behavior, including extensive coverage of groups in work settings.

Terkel, S. (1974). *Working.* New York: Avon

To find out what people have to say about work, journalist Studs Terkel extensively interviewed people—ranging from accountants to prostitutes—about their jobs. The meaning of work is made clear in the eloquent comments presented in this volume.

Bolles, R. (1988). *What color is your parachute?* Berkeley, CA: Ten Speed Press.

This volume provides useful information for people seeking answers to occupation-related questions in a clever, practical manner.

CHECK YOURSELF: ANSWERS

1. True   **2.** job clarity   **3.** b   **4.** No

The Places and Spaces of Our Lives
The Environment

CHAPTER 15

The dorm room was already full to capacity, you thought. Then, the university, in its typical wisdom, decided to add a third person to the room in which you had spent the first three weeks of the term.

Sure, you understood that there was a housing crisis; more people had shown up at the start of the fall semester than the university had anticipated. But why should their poor planning screw up your life? Didn't the administration understand that it was bad enough having two people live in an area not much bigger than a closet?

You felt an instant dislike for your new roommate, and you felt a premonition that you were not going to get along with him. In fact, as he began to shove his clothes into what, until a few moments ago, had been your closet, you felt a tangible sense of violation. "Let me help you with that," you felt compelled to say, when in reality all you wanted to do was throw his possessions out the window—with him behind them.

As is plain from this episode, the environment in which we live plays a crucial role in our perceptions of the world and our reactions to people around us. Our view of others, and even of ourselves, is in large part dependent on the acceptability of our surroundings.

It is only in the past few decades that psychologists have recognized the impact of the environment on our adjustment. Consequently, the specialized field of environmental psychology developed as a way to study the environment's influence on our behavior and emotions. **Environmental psychology** considers the relationship between the environment and people's behavior and sense of well-being.

In this chapter, we begin by discussing the psychological sense of ownership we have over our surroundings and the things we do to protect ourselves from the intrusions of others. The chapter investigates how we use "bubbles" of space—the different distances we maintain between our bodies and others, depending on the nature of the situation—to regulate social interaction with others. Moreover, the ways in which people react to the use of space by others is discussed.

Finally, we consider the factors that lead to the experience of crowding. We examine various explanations for how we react to high-density situations and the ways crowding affects us. We also look at ways in which the experience of crowding can be reduced.

Throughout the chapter, the underlying goal is to delineate the ways in which the physical environment affects behavior. Through this knowledge, improvements in the environments in which we live can be achieved.

15.1

STAKING OUT YOUR TURF:
Territoriality

487

THE PLACES
AND SPACES
OF OUR LIVES

As Mike walked into the library, his mind was on his upcoming physics test. How am I ever going to remember all those formulas, he asked himself anxiously.

Making his way between the stacks, he was relieved to find that his favorite table was unoccupied. Although the table had six seats around it, Mike spread out his books all across the table's top and placed his sweater and jacket on two of the chairs. Then he sat down in a third. As he did so, he felt just a twinge of guilt for taking so much room, but he knew that anyone seeing that much stuff spread over the table would keep away—which was, of course, his goal.

At the same time he felt a wave of relief that he would be able to study, unbothered by the presence of others, in his favorite spot. After all, he rationalized to himself, he had spent so much time studying at this table that he had earned the right to its use—it was, by this point in the semester, **his** *table.*

Anyone who has a favorite spot in which to study can understand Mike's feelings. We all develop special locations, such as park benches, offices, parking spots, or particular seats at our kitchen tables, that we consider ours—even if, in the legal sense, we have no ownership of them.

Psychologists have adopted the term **territoriality** from research on animal behavior to describe these possessive feelings. When we experience feelings of territoriality over an area, we typically try to personalize the region and defend it against the intrusions of others (Holahan, 1982).

There are actually three categories of territories, and the extent to which people will defend them depends on which category they're in (Altman, 1975; Taylor & Stough, 1978):

● **Primary territories** are under the complete, long-term control of their users, and they are perceived in that manner by both their owners and other people. The notion that a person's home is his or her castle stems from the fact that living spaces are primary territories: Intrusions by others are looked upon as the most serious of transgressions. To a lesser extent, people's dormitory rooms or offices represent primary territories. People's identities are often tied up in their primary territories.

● **Secondary territories** are areas that are used regularly by a person but are under less permanent control and are used by more than one person during the course of a day. A table in the library is a good example of a secondary territory, as is a desk in a college classroom. People using a secondary territory are assumed to have legitimate rights to an area while they are using it, but their rights end as soon as they leave. However, should they return, they can temporarily reclaim a secondary territory as their own.

A territorial message can be conveyed without words: Spreading one's belongings out clearly says, "Keep out of my space."

Cary Wolinsky/Stock, Boston

● Finally, **public territories** are areas of temporary personal control that can be occupied by anyone at any time. A public phone booth or a bench in a bus terminal waiting room are both examples of public territories. Anyone who wants to occupy them has the right to use them, and people relinquish their rights to the area as soon as they leave. For example, if you left your seat in an airport to buy a book for your flight, you would not expect to find the chair you vacated still waiting for you after you completed your purchase.

Personalizing Your Place:
Territorial markers

If you are a male dog, the way you indicate what territories are yours is simple, if somewhat undignified: You urinate on the edges of the territory. Humans tend to use more refined means of indicating their territories, although their intent in keeping out undesired others is no different.

People employ several kinds of **territorial markers,** objects and behavior used to personalize and defend their territories. One fundamental type of territorial marker can be seen through the use of fences, hedges, locks and

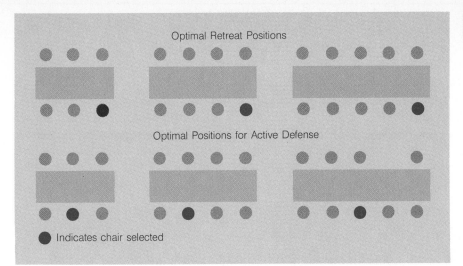

FIGURE 15-1
Those seats marked with
an X show the choices
made by most people
according to whether they
want to defend against or
accept intrusion in their
territorial possession of a
table. (*Source:* Sommer &
Becker, 1969.)

chains, and "no trespassing" signs. These sorts of markers make it clear that
the area being protected is a primary territory and that violations of the
space may be dealt with harshly.

Territorial markers of secondary and public territories tend to be more
subtle, since the areas are not truly "owned" by users in the same sense
that primary territories are owned. At a library table, for instance, people
might use the same tactic used by Mike when he spread objects around on
the table and chairs. However, certain items are more effective than others
in maintaining exclusive use of a territory; research shows that personal
items—such as clothing—are more effective than impersonal objects in preventing others from invading a space under crowded conditions (Sommer
& Becker, 1969).

Choice of a particular seating location also helps to indicate territoriality to even a casual observer, as the results of one experiment showed
(Sommer & Becker, 1969). As illustrated in Figure 15-1, subjects asked to
indicate which seat they would sit in to actively "defend" a library table
against intruders most often chose the middle seat. In contrast, a decision
to retreat was indicated by the choice of a corner position. (Seating position
is also related to particular activities, as you can find out for yourself in the
following Do It! box.)

DO IT!

CHARTING THE SPACES OF OUR LIVES

The importance of territoriality in people's lives is indicated by the high degree of agreement that is generally found when they are queried about the significance of particular seating positions. To see how closely you agree with others, look at the following four seating positions shown in Figure 15-2, and indicate which you would choose if you were conversing, cooperating, doing something independently, or competing.

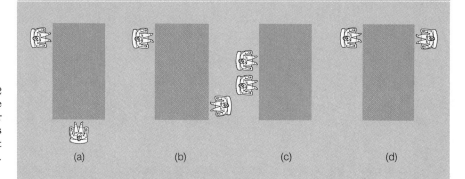

FIGURE 15-2
As you examine these seating positions, consider the most likely activities that would be carried out at each one.

(a)   (b)   (c)   (d)

One survey found that most people choose position (d) if they want to converse with one another. Cooperative behavior is considered most likely in position (c). If people are doing something independently, they tend to prefer arrangement (b), and if they are competing, they prefer position (d). Position (a) is rarely preferred for *any* activity. How closely do your answers compare to those of the people queried in the survey?

Source: Sommer, 1969.

Why We Guard Our Turf:
The purposes of territoriality

The zealousness with which people defend their territories is an indication of the significant role that territoriality plays in our everyday lives. For example, territoriality helps us organize and understand the world around us. On the most basic level, a sense of territoriality keeps others from wandering through our homes at any time of the day or night. Moreover, it allows us to predict what others will do in a given situation. If we did not experience territoriality at the kitchen table, for instance, the seating pattern at every meal would have to be negotiated.

Territoriality also provides a means of clarifying and maintaining social organization. Social roles and status can be indicated through the territory that a person occupies. For instance, office and desk size often are primary indications of the importance a person has in an organization, and promotions often bring with them an increase not just in salary but in the size of a person's office.

Perhaps the primary role played by territoriality relates to people's identity. If you consider the questions you ask when you meet someone for the first time, "Where do you live?" and "Where were you raised?" are probably among the most common. The reason is that such questions relate to the function that territoriality plays in permitting the development of a sense of group and personal identity (Edney, 1975).

People who share a territory often undergo similar experiences and develop a common base of knowledge: They use the same stores, their children attend the same schools, and they may share the same frustrations with their local government's inability to keep the streets clean or plowed in wintertime. Due to these shared experiences, people may develop a common group identity, which can be demonstrated through similarity in dress, the use of particular kinds of language, and celebration of particular holidays.

In extreme cases of territoriality, public territories may be taken over by residents of an area, with outsiders being discouraged from and even harassed for entering an area that is claimed by a particular group. For instance, when street gangs have well-defined areas of ownership, intruders from other gangs understand that violence may ensue if they cross a territorial boundary. In some cases, in fact, the territorialities are marked by graffiti on walls and buildings, indicating where one gang's territory begins and another's ends (Ley & Cybriwsky, 1974). Interestingly, such clear-cut territorial markers tend to prevent intergroup violence, compared to situations in which the boundaries between territories are ambiguous.

Dan Chidester/The Image Works

Members of a community may join together to defend their territory, as these neighbors did to protest the building of a large hotel.

Territoriality also helps to promote a sense of personal identity, in addition to helping develop shared identity. People typically label themselves in geographic terms: The phrases "I'm a New Yorker" or "I'm a Southerner" indicate the importance of territoriality in determining identity. Moreover, knowing where someone hails from may lead to stereotypic labeling processes. For example, we may assume that a person who chooses to live in rural Kansas has very different characteristics from someone who lives in downtown Los Angeles.

The importance of territoriality in defining one's personal identity also is indicated by the efforts people put into personalizing their own territories. For instance, children increasingly personalize their bedrooms into the teenage years, at which point they typically contain little of what their parents have provided (or would even like) in the way of decoration (Altman, 1975).

Residents of dormitory rooms, too, usually decorate their rooms as the first activity they undertake upon moving in at the start of the fall term. By putting up pictures and posters, rearranging the furniture, and otherwise acting to make the space more personalized, they are able to make the room more reflective of their own interests, attitudes, and values. Moreover, as the school year goes on the amount of personalization in dormitory rooms increases. Indeed, researchers have found that students who do not personalize their rooms, or who decorate them only with items relating to personal relationships outside of school (such as photos of their family) are more likely to drop out of college by the end of the year than those who personalize their rooms (Henson & Altman, 1976).

Such findings suggest that creating a sense of territoriality in one's living environment can have a positive impact on adjustment. Even if you share a dormitory room or bedroom with others, it seems reasonable to personalize at least some specific area of the space that you inhabit, for territoriality clearly plays several important functions in regulating people's everyday lives. By staking out our territories, we are able to maintain a sense of group and personal identity, as well as helping to manage our social interaction with others.

Psychology for You: Making territories work

Although few of us have the luxury of designing our living spaces from the ground up, environmental psychologists have suggested several principles to keep in mind if the opportunity ever arises—be it renting a new apartment, moving into a new dormitory, or purchasing a home (Fisher, Bell, & Baum, 1984; Holahan, 1982). Among the most important:

● *There should be specific areas that are designed to be primary, secondary, and public territories.* Rather than letting usage patterns determine the kind of territory a particular space is, building designers should determine in advance of construction how spaces are to operate. Some of the

FIGURE 15-3
The Pruitt-Igoe housing
project in St. Louis was so
poorly designed that,
twenty years after it was
built, it was virtually
uninhabitable and was
destroyed. (*Source:*
UPI photo.)

worst public housing design blunders of recent years have occurred when
secondary territories (such as halls and play areas) have functioned instead
as public territories, thereby inviting crime and vandalism when people had
no sense of "ownership" over a particular area. (See Figure 15-3 for the
consequences of one of the biggest mistakes.)

● *Territories should permit personalization.* Apartments and dorm rooms
in which there are stringent rules about what and how things can be attached to the walls might well be avoided, as it is clear that the ability
to personalize an area with one's own possessions is related to residents'
satisfaction.

● *Territories should be designed to permit residents to experience a sense
of control over their environment.* Any design features that allow people to
make changes in their territories are desirable and preferable to features
that cannot be changed. If you have a choice, then, between a dorm room
with furniture built in and bolted to the floor and one in which the furniture
can be moved around, the best option is most likely the latter.

TO REVIEW

● Territoriality, the sense of ownership that develops over a particular
geographic area, is related to three kinds of territories: primary territories,
secondary territories, and public territories.

● People use territorial markers to personalize and defend their territories.
They may be concrete—such as "no trespassing" signs—or more subtle, as
with the use of clothing.

● Territoriality functions to help us organize and understand the world, provides a means of clarifying and maintaining social organization, and provides a source of shared and personal identity.

CHECK YOURSELF

1. Match the statement in the right column with the type of territory, listed in the left column, that it describes.

_____ primary territory   a. Sally and her two office mates finally had to work out a schedule to use the desk their computer was on.

_____ secondary territory   b. Jenny thought all week about a visit to her secluded lakeside cabin on Friday night.

_____ public territory   c. Frank likes to sit near the front of the bus, but today all those seats were occupied.

2. Derek left half a cup of coffee and a notebook on the table as _____ _____ to ensure that his seat would still be unoccupied when he returned.

3. Which of the following is *not* identified as a purpose territoriality might serve?
   a. To provide insight into a person's identity
   b. To promote group identity and cohesiveness
   c. To decrease defacement of public property, such as writing graffiti, by establishing a sense of pride in one's shared territory
   d. To convey a sense of leadership, such as in the way an organization's president might arrange his or her office

4. College students typically decorate their dorm rooms with personal items early in the semester, but decrease the personalization of their rooms as the year passes. True or false?

5. It is probably better to choose a living environment in which there exist many options for rearranging furniture. True or false?

(See answers to the questions at the bottom of page 496.)

15.2   TOO CLOSE FOR COMFORT?:
Personal Space

As she settled into her seat on the bus, Cheryl planned to get a bit of reading done. Sitting by the window, she looked out for a moment and then began reading her book.

At the next bus stop, another woman got on and, although there were quite a few other empty seats, sat down beside Cheryl. The woman was heavy, and she leaned against Cheryl as she settled into the seat. What was worse was the woman began asking Cheryl a series of questions, trying to involve her in a conversation. Even this wouldn't have been so bad if the woman hadn't kept her face so close to Cheryl's that she could feel the woman's breath as she talked.

Cheryl was disgusted and responded quickly. She gathered up her belongings and got off the bus at the next stop. Better to spend the time waiting for another bus, she thought to herself, than to have to put up with that woman any longer.

Perhaps you have been in a similar situation—someone moves so close to you that your immediate reaction is to get away as fast as you can. The cause of your discomfort and Cheryl's is a violation of personal space. **Personal space** is the zone around a person's body into which other people may not enter. This area, which is analogous to an invisible bubble around our bodies, protects us from the intrusions of others in a way that is comparable to the protection provided by territoriality.

Although personal space was initially thought of as a circular bubble surrounding people, research has found that different areas of the body have different spatial requirements (Hayduk, 1978). For instance, the personal space zone for the top half of the body is greatest, and it dwindles in magnitude below the waist, tapering as it approaches the floor (see Figure 15-4). In addition, personal space is not rigid; it grows and compresses according to the nature of the situation, the individuals with whom one is interacting, and one's personality characteristics. (To get a sense of the shape of your own personal space, consult the following Do It! box.)

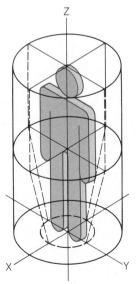

FIGURE 15-4
Our personal space zone forms this three-dimensional shape around our body. (*Source:* Hayduk, 1978.)

SHAPING YOUR PERSONAL SPACE

To find out the shape of your own personal space zone, imagine that you are at the center of Figure 15-5 and each of the eight numbers represents a door through which a person is about to enter. You are facing door number eight, and your back is to door number four.

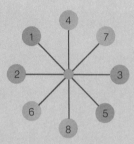

FIGURE 15-5
Diagramming the shape of
personal space.

Now place a mark on each of the eight lines at the point that indicates how close you would allow the imaginary person to come before you began to feel uncomfortable. Connect the eight points—and you'll know the general shape of your personal space (Duke & Nowicki, 1972).

After carrying out this exercise, you might want to experiment a bit with your actual personal space zone. Enter into conversation with different people—friends, professors, strangers, salesclerks—and note how close you are standing to them. Your personal space zone, indicated by the distance you maintain between you and the other person, will likely vary, depending on the intimacy of the relationship with the person with whom you are interacting.

There are, for example, general standards for spacing that depend upon the intimacy of the interaction (Hall, 1966). These spacing criteria include:

● The **public interaction zone** extends from 12 to 25 feet from the body and encompasses formal contacts between a person such as a politician, a lecturer, or an actor.

● The **social interaction zone,** used for impersonal and businesslike contacts, extends from 4 to 12 feet.

CHECK YOURSELF: ANSWERS
1. b, a, c **2.** territorial markers **3.** c **4.** False **5.** True

● The **personal interaction zone** is used for most of our contacts with close friends, as well as everyday interactions with acquaintances. The personal zone encompasses 18 inches to 4 feet.

● The **intimate interaction zone** is used when making love or comforting another person, playing physical contact sports, and displaying extreme emotions. The intimate zone extends to 18 inches out from the body.

In addition to personal space determining how closely we interact with others, we use the distance from us that people stand to draw inferences about how much people are attracted to us. For example, one experiment found that people who were asked to imagine that another person was standing 3 feet away thought that they would be liked significantly more than when the other person was imagined to be 7 feet away. Another experiment, in which subjects were asked to space themselves as if they liked or disliked another individual, revealed that subjects chose to stand considerably closer to people they liked (Mehrabian, 1968a, 1968b).

One of the most intriguing properties of personal space is that different cultures seem to have very different norms regarding what is the appropriate distance to maintain when conversing with another person. For example, Arabs tend to sit closer to one another than Americans do when talking (Watson & Graves, 1966). In fact, Arabs most times converse casually at a distance of just 1 foot—whereas Americans tend to hold nonintimate con-

Gale Zucker/Stock, Boston

Close friends and relatives generally converse at an "intimate" range and may often touch each other as they talk.

versations at distances of 4 to 12 feet. Arab tradition holds that it is important to breathe on the person with whom one is speaking, for it is assumed that inhaling a speaker's breath is a sign of politeness and that those who do not follow the practice are acting ashamed or embarrassed.

In addition to cross-cultural variations in personal space, there are differences in the use of the personal space zones according to the sex of the two people interacting with each other. Men, in general, have larger personal space zones than women, and when two men converse, they keep a significantly greater distance from each other than do two women interacting with each other (Hayduk, 1983).

The state of one's mental health also seems to be related to the size of one's personal space zones. When we experience anxiety, for instance, we typically maintain more personal space than when we are relaxed (Hayduk, 1983). In severe cases of mental disturbance, such as chronic schizophrenia, personal space zones may be unusually large or uncommonly small. In some cases, people suffering from schizophrenia may invade the personal space of others or may actually have an inaccurate sense of where their own bodies end and where the rest of the world begins (Arrowitz, 1968).

Facing Spacing:
The functions of personal space

Consider what it would be like if we had no personal space zones. People could come so close to us that we would smell their breath (and probably feel it as well), have a close-up view of every blemish on their faces, and hear every nuance of their voices.

Such a scenario illustrates one of the most important functions of personal space zones: protecting ourselves from stress brought about by the potential intrusiveness of others. When others come too close, they bring with them the potential of producing emotional and physical stress. For instance, we may experience high levels of noise, and, in extreme cases, we may open ourselves to the aggression of others when we allow them to interact with us at too close a range. In sum, personal space may provide us with protection from unwanted stressful stimuli.

But personal space plays another role in people's lives: It protects us from information overload. **Information overload** refers to situations in which we receive so much physical and visual stimulation that we are unable to process and comprehend critical data coming from the environment. By keeping others at a distance, then, we are able to maintain control over the stimulation to which we would otherwise have to pay attention (Evans, 1974).

Finally, personal space plays a communicative function in people's lives. Because the amount of space that people maintain between themselves is an indication of the nature of their relationships, personal space can communicate the feelings two people have for each other.

The importance of personal space is indicated by the reactions that people have to its violation, which typically leads to stress, discomfort, and—if the violation is extreme—fleeing from the situation. One illustration of this comes from an experiment in which college students sitting at a table in the library had their personal space violated by a confederate of the experimenter, who sat either directly across from them or right beside them (Sommer, 1969). When the confederate sat across from the student, reactions were fairly subdued. However, when the confederate sat down next to the students, reactions were much more pronounced: The students shifted posture, moved their chairs, or displayed anger in some manner. When these tactics proved ineffective in driving the confederate away, most of the students chose the most direct route to resolving the situation: They packed up and left. In fact, within half an hour of the confederate's arrival, three-fourths of the students had left.

On the other hand, not all violations of personal space may have detrimental consequences. For example, in one study potential helpers' personal space was invaded when they were being asked for aid. If the need of the person requesting the aid was perceived as high, such invasions actually led to a greater willingness to help than in cases in which personal space was not invaded. On the other hand, if the neediness of the person requesting the help was perceived as low, personal space invasions led to less help being offered than when personal space was not violated (Baron, 1978). It seems as if the invasion of personal space under conditions of high neediness led to interpretations of greater neediness than when there was no invasion of personal space. In some cases, then, violations of personal space may have a beneficial effect.

Psychology for You:
Designing around your personal space

Before architects produce designs, they typically hold discussions with representative users. For example, before an architect designs a new dormitory, standard operating procedure would be to hold a series of discussions with each set of users—students, university officials, and maintenance staff—to determine what their needs are. If you were asked to give advice to an architect eager to produce designs that reflect what environmental psychologists have discovered about personal space, you might suggest the following points:

● *Design features that force people to interact with others at an inappropriate distance are likely to be experienced negatively* (Duffy, Bailey, Beck, & Barker, 1986). For example, fixed seating arrangements, such as those typically found in airports and other waiting rooms, are likely to discourage interaction if they do not take into account people's personal space zones. Thus, many waiting rooms have chairs that are bolted to the floor, one next to another, either facing in the same direction or back-to-back.

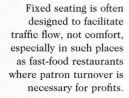

Fixed seating is often designed to facilitate traffic flow, not comfort, especially in such places as fast-food restaurants where patron turnover is necessary for profits.

Michael Weisbrot and Family

Such an arrangement makes it impossible to hold a conversation with anyone other than the person seated immediately to one's right or left, and even then one must contort one's body (Sommer, 1974). (Interestingly, designers of waiting rooms in airports and bus and train stations are often aware of the consequences of such design features and employ them in order to *prevent* socialization—thereby leading people to avoid sitting in their seats and instead spend their money on concessions!)

● *Seating positions can be arranged to influence the nature of social relationships between people.* For instance, research on patient behavior in therapeutic settings has found that patients become more open and relaxed when clinicians seat themselves close to the patients than when they are farther away (Jourard, 1970). Moreover, counselors who seat themselves across a table from their clients are likely to be viewed less positively than counselors who are seated corner-to-corner at a table.

Students' classroom behavior, too, can be affected by their seating position (Sommer, 1969). In seminar rooms, students who sit directly opposite the instructor tend to participate most often, while those seated at the side of the table are the next most frequent participants. People seated immediately to the left or right of the instructor are the ones most unlikely to participate.

In larger classrooms, students' grades are related to where they sit. Both in situations in which students are permitted to choose their seats and those in which the teacher assigns seats, students in the front and middle of large classrooms tend to have higher grades than those at the rear and sides (Stires, 1980). The explanation underlying these findings is related to the amount of eye contact possible with the instructor: The greater the degree of eye contact with the teacher, the more involved students seem to feel, and consequently they are more apt to participate and feel motivated to do well in the class.

● *In order to promote more intimate social interactions, architects should consider designing buildings that include open spaces.* The reason can be found in research suggesting that the more enclosed an area is, the more personal space is desired by those using it. As room size or ceiling height is decreased, then, people are more motivated to maintain a greater amount of personal space. Moreover, they try to preserve greater personal distance when they are located in corners of rooms than when they are at its center (Savinar, 1975; Tennis & Dabbs, 1975). What such findings suggest, then, is that architects wanting to decrease interaction distance among residents of a particular structure should include larger, more open spaces.

TO REVIEW

● Personal space, the zone around a person's body into which other people may not enter, is greatest for the top half of the body and dwindles in size below the waist, tapering toward the floor.

● In Western society, the standards for spacing include the public interaction zone (12 to 25 feet), the social interaction zone (4 to 12 feet), the personal interaction zone (18 inches to 4 feet), and the intimate interaction zone (up to 18 inches).

● There are cross-cultural differences in personal space, as well as differences related to sex and mental health status.

● Personal space protects us from stress, avoids information overload, and communicates feelings in a relationship.

CHECK YOURSELF

1.   Match the description in the right column with the appropriate personal zone in the left column.

_____ public interaction zone

_____ social interaction zone

_____ personal interaction zone

_____ intimate interaction zone

a.   Mark leaned over and kissed his wife on the cheek as she toiled away at her work.

b.   The crowd burst into applause as the singer walked onto the stage.

c.   Barbara walked over to the coffee machine every morning to say hello to Cheryl.

d.   Don and Janet sat across from each other at the conference table as they critiqued the upcoming budget.

2.   Women tend to have a smaller personal space zone than men. True or false?

3.   Phillip had to leave the party and step outside for a few minutes. The room was so crowded, smoky, and noisy that it had produced a situation referred to as _____.

4.   When an individual's personal space is invaded for an extended period, he or she, as a last resort, would be most apt to:
   a.   lash out physically at the intruder
   b.   raise his or her voice so that others would hear
   c.   escape the situation by leaving
   d.   strike up a conversation with the intruder

5.   Invasions of personal space by strangers always produce a negative effect. True or false?

6.   If you wanted your points to be heard by the group leader at a business meeting, it would probably be best to sit:
   a.   close to the leader's side
   b.   at the end of the table to the leader's right
   c.   at the end of the table to the leader's left
   d.   directly across the table

(See answers to the questions at the bottom of page 504.)

15.3   TWO'S COMPANY, BUT WHAT'S A CROWD?:
Crowding and the Social Environment

All summer the beach had been yours and yours alone: It was an isolated, solitary strip of sand on the west side of the island; no tourists had found it, and you had almost become convinced that its out-of-the-way location would never succumb to the annual intrusion of the hordes of out-of-towners.

One day, though, your worst fears were realized. As you woke up from a nap, you saw three people lying on **your** *beach. Although the beach was hundreds of feet long, you felt exposed and violated. In fact, you felt as if the beach were now populated beyond your tolerance, and you left to seek out another, less crowded beach.*

It was an exhilarating experience. Here, in the midst of Shea Stadium, you were one of thousands of people waiting for the appearance of Bruce Springsteen. Other people were screaming and chanting all around you, and everywhere you turned people were milling about the stadium. The noise was almost beyond belief, and when Springsteen walked onto the stage, the sound level got even higher. But you didn't care; the crowd invigorated you, and somehow you wished there were even more people around to share the moment.

The experiences of these two people illustrate the difficulties psychologists face when attempting to understand the effects of crowding, one of the most critical factors influencing our perceptions of the environment in which we live. Clearly, crowding is not just a matter of the number of people occupying a particular amount of space; as illustrated by the cases described above, a person may feel crowded on an open beach or experience no sense of crowding in a packed baseball stadium.

Most scientific definitions of crowding, then, consider the phenomenon in psychological terms (Fisher, Bell, & Baum, 1984). According to this psychological perspective, **density** refers to the purely physical and spatial aspects of a situation—the number of people per unit of space. In contrast, **crowding** is an unpleasant psychological and subjective state relating to how a person *reacts* to the physical density of the environment.

High density alone, then, does not inevitably result in the perceptions of crowding. Rather, additional factors of a psychological nature—situational conditions like the amount of time spent in the setting, the presence of other stressors, or the nature of the person's relationship with others—influence whether a particular level of density is experienced as crowding. (To recognize the conditions under which you feel the most crowded, consider the questions in the following Do It! box.)

DO IT!

OUR CROWDED SPACES AND PLACES

To gain some insight into your reactions to various environments, consider each of the following places, and rank them according to the amount of *crowding* (an unpleasant psychological and subjective experience) you felt. Put your rankings on the first line following the situation.

the room in which you last slept _____ _____

the classroom in which you took your most recent psychology class _____ _____

the last party you attended _____ _____

the last concert you attended _____ _____

the last time you studied in the library _____ _____

the last meal you ate _____ _____

the last line you stood in _____ _____

the last test you took _____ _____

the last movie you attended _____ _____

the last time you took public transportation _____ _____

Now go back and rank each of the situations according to their *density,* based on the physical and spatial aspects of the situation, with the lowest numbers for the lowest density. (Write your rankings on each second line.)

Now compare your two responses. What is the relationship between the experience of crowding and that of density? What was the reason that some situations that were relatively high in density produced a relatively low sense of crowding? Are there any commonalities among the situations that produced the most crowding—and the least?

Why can high density result in the experience of crowding? Several explanations have been suggested, including the following:

- *Stimulus overload.* According to the **stimulus-overload explanation,** high density produces excessive stimulation that overwhelms and ultimately overloads people. The presence of others is viewed by this model as not particularly different from any sort of extreme stimulus, be it noise, heat, or light. In order to reduce such excessive stimulation, people may try to escape it, either by leaving the area or by psychologically "tuning out" the presence of others.

- *Loss of control.* The **loss-of-control explanation** of crowding suggests that people in high-density settings experience a decreased sense of control over their environment. Because, as we have discussed in Chapters 5 and 6, losing control and freedom leads to negative reactions, the high density produces an unpleasant experience—leading to a sense of crowding (Burger, Oakman, & Ballard, 1983).

- *Focus of attention.* According to the **focus-of-attention explanation,** high-density situations may lead to shifts in the kinds of things people pay attention to, and the nature of the shift determines whether a sense of crowding will be experienced. If people's attention becomes focused on the presence of other people, they are likely to experience crowding. On the other hand, if attention is primarily focused on some other aspect of the situation—such as the loudness of a band or the kind of food being served at a party—crowding will not be experienced (Worchel & Brown, 1984; Webb, Worchel, Riechers, & Wayne, 1986).

- *Density-intensity.* The **density-intensity explanation** of crowding suggests that high density does not inevitably lead to negative consequences. For example, if you think back to the last large party you enjoyed, it is quite

CHECK YOURSELF: ANSWERS

1. b, d, c, a   **2.** True   **3.** information overload   **4.** c   **5.** False   **6.** d

Crowding can be an
exhilarating experience in
situations where the
people are present
by choice.

possible that the physical density of the setting was quite high. The fact that you could still have a good time—even in a setting that might normally seem crowded—suggests that the presence of many people does not necessarily have negative effects. In fact, the presence of a large number of people in a relatively small area might even have added to your enjoyment of the party.

According to the density-intensity explanation, however, the high numbers of people do have an effect: They increase the intensity of a person's reactions to the setting. If the situation is perceived as basically a pleasant one, such positive feelings will tend to be magnified by the high density. In contrast, if the situation is thought of as negative, these feelings will be intensified, and the individual will experience crowding (Freedman, 1979).

The density-intensity theory helps explain why we might find someone at a party irresistible but later, in the cold light of day, find that person not quite so attractive. The high density at the party leads to intensified attraction. (Of course, the opposite phenomenon also ought to hold true: Those to whom we react negatively at a party will probably seem less repellent subsequently, when the density of the situation is lower.)

A Matter of Life and Death:
The outcomes of crowding

While we still do not know which explanation of crowding provides the most accurate account of the phenomenon, we do know that—by definition—crowding results in an unpleasant state. But the consequences of crowding go well beyond merely negative emotional states, becoming, in some instances, a matter of life and death.

In one particularly striking example, the death rates for inmates in a state psychiatric prison were found to be closely associated with the population density. As the prison population grew, so did the per capita death rate; and as the population fell, the death rate followed suit, as illustrated in Figure 15-6 (Cox, Paulus, & McCain, 1984; Paulus & McCain, 1983).

Other research has shown that students living in high-density dormitories visited the student health center more frequently than those living in lower-density housing (Baron, Mandel, Adams, & Griffen, 1976). Similarly, another study of prison inmates found that prisoners living in crowded housing units had a higher number of complaints of illness (Cox, Paulus, McCain, & Schkade, 1979). Crowding, then, is related to an increased level of health problems—which may, in the extreme case, even result in death.

There are other difficulties associated with crowding. For instance, our attraction to others is negatively related to the density of the setting in which we are interacting. In one study, roommates living in crowded rooms liked each other less (and viewed each other as less cooperative) than roommates who were living in less crowded rooms (Baron, Mandel, Adams, & Griffen, 1976; Aiello, Vautier, & Bernstein, 1983). Similarly, crowding has been found to lead to declines in helping behavior. It heightens aggression and impairs performance of a variety of tasks (Holahan, 1986).

The negative consequences of crowding have also been found to be related not only to the number of people in a given area but also to the configuration of a given area. In a comprehensive study of dormitory use at a large state university in New York, reactions to various dormitory floor plans were assessed (Baum & Valins, 1977; 1979). The major comparison was between residents assigned to dormitories arranged in a typical pat-

FIGURE 15-6
The death rate in this prison population rose as its population increased, indicating a startling outcome of crowding. (*Source:* Cox, Paulus, & McCain, 1984.)

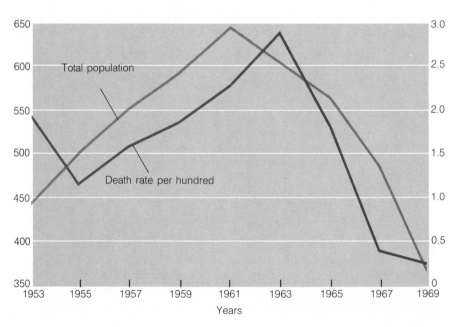

tern—a series of bedrooms located along a long corridor, with a central bathroom and shared lounge—versus residents assigned to dormitories in which three to four bedrooms were arranged in a suite, with a bath and living room shared only by the occupants of the few bedrooms (see Figure 15-7). The corridor and suite designs had virtually identical space per person and number of residents per floor.

The effects on the occupants of the two different floor plans were dramatic. Residents of the corridor-style dormitory reported feeling significantly greater crowding, felt they had less privacy, and reported the desire to avoid others considerably more frequently than residents of the suite-style dormitories. Moreover, while suite dwellers reported no differences in their perceptions of crowding according to which room they had in the suite, there were strong differences in reported crowding according to the location of corridor-style dorm dwellers. Students who lived near the bathroom or the lounge reported feeling considerably more crowded than those farther away (presumably because of the increased traffic near their rooms). Finally,

FIGURE 15-7
The configurations of these two types of dormitories, although similar in square footage, had dramatically dissimilar results on the occupants. (*Source:* Baum & Valins, 1977.)

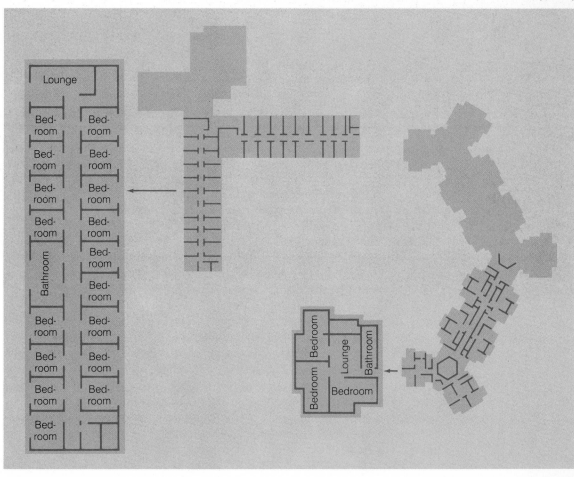

corridor residents felt that they were forced into interacting with others much more frequently, they were less sure of what their neighbors thought about them, and they were less apt to perceive similarities in attitudes among themselves and their neighbors.

One of the most intriguing findings to emerge from the study was that the effect of the configuration of the living quarters lingered even after the residents left the setting (Baum & Gatchel, 1981). When participating in laboratory experiments designed to assess their personal space zones, residents of the corridor-style dormitory tended to sit farther away from a confederate and looked at the confederate less. They also performed worse than suite residents on a task that required cooperation, and better when the task required a lower level of personal involvement.

In sum, the configuration of the dormitories had a significant effect on whether the residents experienced crowding and the way they responded to such crowding. A dorm, then, may have a significant impact on its inhabitants—well beyond its basic function as a place in which to sleep.

Turn That Radio Down:
Noise and heat

Obviously, spatial density and crowding are not the only aspects of the physical environment that have important influences on human behavior. Consider, for example, the students of a New York City public school, which was located directly adjacent to an elevated railroad track on which trains screeched by every five minutes. When a train was passing by, teachers could not be heard for a thirty-second period unless they screamed.

As you might expect, the effects of such periodic high levels of noise were profound. Students in classrooms closest to the railroad had significantly lower reading scores than students who were in classes on the opposite side of the building, where the noise levels were somewhat lower (Bronzaft & McCarthy, 1975).

Findings such as this clearly illustrate the harmful nature of high levels of noise. But it is not just loud noise that can have negative effects, as anyone who has ever suffered through a night of listening to a slowly dripping faucet can confirm. The predictability, duration, fluctuations, and sound level of the noise, as well as the listener's attitudes toward the noise source, the listener's activity, and the time of day the noise occurs all influence the way in which the listener will be affected by a noise source (Kryter, 1985).

Other physical aspects of the environment also affect people's behavior and attitudes. The temperature is a primary one. As the temperature rises, so do people's tempers: Aggression increases, and even the rate of violent crime rises (Anderson, 1987). On the other hand, if it gets *too* hot, aggression seems to decline: It seems as if people may prefer to do nothing rather than act aggressively toward others.

Psychology for You:
Controlling crowding

We have seen that there are a considerable number of problems related to crowding. There are, however, several ways in which crowding can be controlled. Among the most useful suggestions made by environmental psychologists are the following:

- *Increase people's sense of control.* Because of the plausibility that a lack of control leads to the experience of crowding, any efforts that can be made to increase the sense of control over the environment are reasonable. For example, environments could be designed to give residents a choice in how they use space and the activities in which they engage. Walls and partitions might be movable, and furniture could be designed to be easy to rearrange. Moreover, because people who are warned prior to being placed in a high-density situation react more favorably than those who are not forewarned—presumably because a warning enhances their sense of control—acknowledging that one's environment may have a high density may be helpful in alleviating a sense of crowding (Baum, Fisher, & Solomon, 1981).

- *Change the focus of attention.* The focus-of-attention explanation for crowding suggests that design features that shift attention away from the presence of other people and toward the environment would lead to per-

Paolo Koch/Rapho/Photo Researchers

Responsible urban planning can make high density less problematic. This Tokyo street is reserved for pedestrians on Sundays, a major shopping day; during the rest of the week the street is a busy thoroughfare for auto traffic.

ceptions of less crowding. Such features as bright posters or pictures, then, might cause people to pay less attention to others and more attention to the environment.

● *Employ architectural designs that decrease feelings of crowding.* There are several features that reduce the perception of crowding, including greater ceiling height and rectangular—as opposed to square—rooms (Fisher, Bell, & Baum, 1984).

Even if these suggestions fail in alleviating people's sense of crowding, it is important to remember that living in crowded conditions is not invariably bad. For example, studies of residential areas such as Hong Kong, one of the most densely populated areas of the world, show few negative effects that can be attributed directly to housing density (Mitchell, 1982). We may eventually adapt to high density—especially if our friends and neighbors share our plight.

TO REVIEW

● While density refers to the purely physical and spatial aspects of a situation (in terms of number of people per unit of space), crowding is a psychological and subjective state that relates to a person's reaction to the physical density of the environment.

● There are several explanations for the experience of crowding, including the stimulus-overload, loss-of-control, focus-of-attention, and density-intensity explanations.

● Crowding is related to higher mortality rates, health difficulties, decreased liking for those in the setting, declines in helping behavior, heightened aggression, and deterioration in task performance.

● Noise and temperature are aspects of the physical environment that affect behavior.

CHECK YOURSELF

1. _____ is a phenomenon that refers to an unpleasant psychological state related to the _____ of the environment.

2. Match the subjective experiences described in the right column with the appropriate theory on crowding.

_____ stimulus overload

a. "I just feel like I'm at the mercy of the crowd when I'm in that place."

_____ loss of control

b. "The number of people wouldn't be so bad if the room weren't so small."

_____ focus of attention

c. "This bus terminal is too noisy and crowded for me. I have to step outside for a minute."

_____ density-intensity

d. "I was so interested in the singer that I hardly even heard the noisy crowd."

3. "I rushed right out to buy their album after the concert, and now I hardly ever listen to it. How could I have thought it was so good?" Which of the explanations listed in question 2 best accounts for this person's experience?

4. Which of the following was *not* identified as a negative consequence of crowding?
   a. decreased attraction for others
   b. apathy in resolving conflict
   c. an increase in the level of health-related problems
   d. higher death rates in crowded institutional settings

5. Negative behaviors resulting from the configuration of a setting have been found to disappear immediately when the person changes to an improved setting. True or false?

_____

(See answers to the questions at the bottom of page 512.)

TO SUMMARIZE

1. Among the most important aspects of environmental psychology, which considers the relationship between the environment and people's behavior and sense of well-being, is territoriality. Territoriality describes the feelings of ownership that develop over a particular geographic area. As a response to territoriality, we usually try to personalize particular areas and defend them against the intrusions of others.

2. The extent to which people defend a territory depends on which of three kinds of territories it belongs in. Primary territories are under the complete, long-term control of their users, and they are perceived as such by both their owners and others. In contrast, secondary territories are used regularly by a person but are under less permanent control and are used by more than one individual during the course of the day. Finally, public territories are areas of temporary personal control that may be occupied by anyone at any time.

3. We use territorial markers to personalize and defend an area. The types of territorial markers range from fences, hedges, locks, and "no trespassing" signs to clothing and books. Territories are defended because of the important roles they play in people's lives, including allowing us to organize and understand the world, providing a means of clarifying and maintaining social organization, and providing a source of shared and personal identity.

4. Personal space is the zone around a person's body into which other people may not enter. Personal space protects us from the intrusions of others in the same way we are protected through territoriality. The major standards for personal spacing in our culture include the public interaction zone (from 12 to 25 feet), the social interaction zone (4 to 12 feet), the personal interaction zone (18 inches to 4 feet), and the intimate interaction zone (contact to 18 inches). There are, however, major cross-cultural and individual differences in the use of personal space.

5. Personal space plays several important roles in our lives. It protects us from the stress brought about by the potential intrusiveness of others and from information overload, and it communicates the feelings two people have for each other in a relationship.

6. It is important to distinguish between density (the physical and spatial aspects of a situation), and crowding (an unpleasant psychological state relating to how a person reacts to the physical density of the environment).

7. There are several explanations that have been suggested to account for the experience of crowding. The stimulus-overload explanation suggests that high density produces excessive stimulation that may overwhelm and overload people. The loss-of-control explanation suggests that people in high-density settings experience a decreased sense of control, while the focus-of-attention explanation suggests that crowding occurs when our attention is focused on the high density of a setting. Finally, the density-intensity explanation suggests that high density increases the intensity of a person's reactions to the setting. If the situation is seen as an unpleasant one, negative feelings will be intensified.

8. Crowding is associated with several unfavorable outcomes. Among them are higher mortality rates, health difficulties, decreased liking for those in the setting, declines in helping behavior, heightened aggression, and deterioration in performance on a variety of tasks.

9. The level, predictability, duration, and sound level of noise, as well as the listener's attitudes toward the noise source, the listener's activity, and the time of day the noise occurs all affect people's reactions. Higher temperatures are related to aggression, although when it gets *too* hot, aggression seems to decline.

KEY TERMS AND CONCEPTS

environmental psychology (p. 486)   secondary territories (p. 487)

territoriality (p. 487)   ·   public territories (p. 488)

primary territories (p. 487)   territorial markers (p. 488)

CHECK YOURSELF: ANSWERS

1. Crowding, density   **2.** c, a, d, b   **3.** density-intensity   **4.** b   **5.** False

personal space (p. 495)
public interaction zone (p. 496)
social interaction zone (p. 496)
personal interaction zone (p. 497)
intimate interaction zone (p. 497)
information overload (p. 498)
density (p. 503)
crowding (p. 503)

stimulus-overload explanation
(of crowding) (p. 504)
loss-of-control explanation
(of crowding) (p. 504)
focus-of-attention explanation
(of crowding) (p. 504)
density-intensity explanation
(of crowding) (p. 504)

TO FIND OUT MORE

Fisher, J. D., Bell, P. A., & Baum, A. (1984). *Environmental psychology* (2nd ed.). New York: Holt.

An interesting introduction to the field of environmental psychology, written by three well-known experts in the area.

Stokols, D., & Altman, I. (1986). *Handbook of environmental psychology*. New York: Wiley.

A collection of articles by the foremost researchers in the field, covering the most current and representative work in environmental psychology.

Fisher, C. S. (1984). *The urban experience* (2nd ed.). New York: Harcourt Brace Jovanovich.

If you ever wondered what it is like to live in a city, this book will most likely provide you with the answers to all your questions.

Glossary

(Numbers in parentheses indicate the chapters where the terms are discussed.)

abstract modeling Modeling in which abstract rules and principles are constructed (13).

activity theory Suggests that people who in old age maintain the interests, concerns, and activities of earlier years are more likely to be well-adjusted than those whose activities represent a sharp departure from the activities of earlier years (3).

adaptors Nonverbal behaviors used for a specific purpose but no longer a typical part of everyday behavior (9).

addiction A state in which an individual develops a physical or psychological dependence on a drug (4).

adjacency pairs Sequential conversational turns in which the second turn contains a reaction to the first turn (9).

adjustment The efforts people make to meet the demands and challenges placed upon them (1).

adolescence The period that marks the transition between childhood and adulthood (3).

agape A kind of loving represented by extremes of generosity (10).

ageism Negative attitudes and behavior based on a person's age (2).

aggression Intentional injury or harm to another person (13).

aggressive cues Stimuli that have been associated in the past with actual aggression or violence and that consequently trigger aggression when a person is frustrated (13).

AIDS Acquired immune deficiency syndrome, a disease transmitted primarily through sexual activity (12).

alarm and mobilization stage [of the general adaptive syndrome] The body's first line of defense against a stressor in which it prepares itself for battle (6).

altruism Helping that is beneficial to another while requiring sacrifice on the part of the helper (13).

androgen The male sex hormone; produces secondary sex characteristics (i.e., pubic hair, deepening of the voice) (12).

anger Emotion consisting of feelings of displeasure or rage (13).

anorexia nervosa An eating disorder in which people develop an inaccurate sense of the actual gauntness of their bodies and refuse to eat (4).

anorgasmia A woman's inability to have an orgasm (12).

antianxiety drug Drug designed to reduce the level of anxiety experienced by people by lowering excitability and partially by producing drowsiness (8).

antidepressant drug Elevates the mood of patients in severe cases of depression (8).

antipsychotic drug Meant to reduce psychotic behavior; responsible for change in mental institutions in the 1950s (8).

antisocial (sociopathic) disorder Individuals exhibiting this maladaptive behavior are charming and fun to be with, but can also make life miserable for those around them (7).

anxiety Emotional response characterized by feelings of fear, apprehension, and physiological tension (6, 7).

anxiety disorder A disorder in which

anxiety occurs without external justi-fication and impedes people's daily functioning (7).

assumed similarity bias The bias in which people are thought of as being similar to oneself (2).

attachment The positive emotional bond that typically develops between parents and their children during infancy (3).

attributions Explanations for the reasons behind the observed behavior (2).

autonomic nervous system Controls involuntary, biological functions such as heart rate and digestion (9).

autonomous work groups Small groups of employees who work together to produce a product (14).

autonomy versus shame and doubt The period during which, according to Erikson, toddlers (ages 18 months to 3 years) develop independence and autonomy if exploration and freedom are encouraged, or shame and self-doubt if they are restricted and overprotected (3).

aversive conditioning Employs the basic principles of learning, to teach people to have an unpleasant reaction to stimulus initially enjoyed (8).

awareness Viewing others in terms of their outward characteristics (10).

bad patients Angry and hostile patients who make frequent demands of the hospital staff and who have many complaints about their treatment and illness (5).

back-channel behaviors Short sounds that listeners make during a conversation to indicate that they are listening to what the speaker is saying (9).

background stressors Daily hassles and minor irritations that we face as we proceed through life (6).

balance sheet approach (to decision making) Technique for identifying what a person wants from work by systematically considering options (14).

behavior therapy Treatment that focuses on changing behavior, and which suggests that it is unnecessary to delve into people's past or dig into their psyches (8).

behavioral model A model that focuses on behavior itself, not its underlying cause, in trying to understand maladaptive behavior (7).

behavioral self-management A procedure in which people learn to identify and resolve their problems using techniques based on learning theory (8).

biofeedback Procedure in which a person learns to control internal physiological processes through the use of electronic monitoring devices that provide continuous feedback (6).

biologically based therapy Biological approach to treatment of maladaptive behavior (8).

bisexuals People who experience sexual attraction to members of both sexes (12).

brainstorming Creating as many ideas as possible without regard to their sensibility or the feasibility of their implementation (2).

bulimia An eating disorder in which a person binges on large quantities of food, followed by purging (vomiting) (4).

cataclysmic events Stressors that occur suddenly and affect many people simultaneously (6).

catastrophizing Making a relatively minor issue a life-or-death one (8).

catharsis Process by which people discharge their aggressive feelings (13).

channels [of communication] Pathways along which messages flow (9).

chemotherapy Therapy based on the use of drugs (8).

client-centered therapy Therapy designed to enable people to better react to their potential for self-actualization (8).

clinical psychologist A psychologist who specializes in assessment and treatment of psychological difficulties (8).

clitoris Female sex organ particularly responsive to sensation (12).

cognition Considers how people know and understand the world, process information, make judgments and decisions, and describe their knowledge and understanding to others (2).

cognitive appraisal The process by which people define and interpret events, occurrences, and other stimuli in their environment; reveals some sort of threat of challenge (6).

cognitive-behavior therapy Considers people's thoughts about themselves and the world as a legitimate focus of attention (8).

cognitive complexity The use and preference of elaborate, intricate, and complex stimuli and thinking patterns (2).

cognitive development The development of thinking, understanding, and knowing (3).

cognitive dissonance A state of psychological tension in which two or more conflicting thoughts or attitudes are held simultaneously (4).

cohabitation Situation in which an unmarried male and female live together and have an intimate relationship (11).

cohesiveness Degree to which group members are attracted to the group as a whole and to other members individually (14).

companionate love Strong affection that we have for those with whom our lives are deeply involved (10).

compromise Involves reacting to stress by attacking and changing some aspects of a source of stress while accepting others (6).

compulsions Urges to repeatedly carry out some act that seems strange and unreasonable (7).

compulsive personality disorder A disorder in which people are preoccupied with rules, orderliness, efficiency, and detail (7).

consensus information Information obtained by observing the degree to which several people behave similarly in a given situation (2).

conservation The knowledge that quantity is unrelated to the arrangement and physical appearance of objects (3).

consistency information The degree to which an individual behaves similarly in similar situations (2).

contact hypothesis Suggests that intergroup contact will reduce prejudice and discrimination (2).

contingency contracting Acting upon a written contract between a therapist and a patient (or parent and child, etc.) that sets behavioral goals, with rewards for achievement (8).

continuum A continuous measurement scale (7).

control Sense of mastery and power over events and one's environment (5).

controllability (of communication channel) Ability to communicate what one intends to express (9).

conventional morality Morality in which people approach their problems in terms of their standing as responsible members of society (3).

convergent thinking The kind of thought that produces responses that are based primarily on knowledge and logic (2).

coping Efforts to control, reduce, and learn to tolerate the threats that lead to stress (6).

counseling psychologist A psychologist who specializes in treatment of day-to-day adjustment problems (8).

creativity The combining of responses or ideas in novel ways (2).

creativity needs Needs to produce new ideas, works, or stimuli (4).

crowding Unpleasant psychological and subjective state relating to how a person reacts to the physical density of the environment (15).

curiosity needs The desire to explore the world and receive novel stimulation (4).

date rape Rapes occurring on first dates or casual dates, or with romantic acquaintances (12).

decision/commitment component (of love) Consists of the initial decision that one loves another and that there is a commitment to maintain that love (10).

defense mechanisms Unconscious strategies people use to cope by concealing stress and anxiety from themselves and others (6, 8).

deficiency motivation Motivation based on the maintenance of a physical or psychological equilibrium (4).

deintensification Muting or minimizing of our feelings (9).

delusions Firmly held, unshakable beliefs with no basis in reality (7).

denial Refusal to accept or perceive reality (6).

density Purely physical and spatial aspects of a situation; the number of people per unit of space (15).

density-intensity An explanation based on the fact that "crowded" situations that seem negative become more negative, while those that seem positive become more positive (15).

depressant A drug that slows the nervous system by causing nerve cells to fire more slowly (4).

depression A disorder characterized by strong, consistent feelings of sadness, worthlessness, self-blame, and lack of energy (7).

development The patterns of growth and change throughout life (3).

deviation-from-the-average approach (to maladaptive behavior) Considers whether and to what degree behavior deviates from the average (7).

deviation-from-the-ideal approach (to maladaptive behavior) Considers the degree to which a behavior differs from some ideal form of behavior (7).

diffusion of responsibility The tendency for people to feel that responsibility for helping is shared among those who are present (13).

discrimination When members of a group are treated negatively or positively due to their membership in the group (2).

disengagement theory Reflects the view that the elderly make a gradual withdrawal from society on a physical, psychological, and social level (3).

displacement A defense mechanism in which negative feelings or thoughts regarding a more threatening, powerful person are discharged onto a weaker one (6).

display rules Learned rules about the appropriateness of showing an emotion (9).

dispositional causes (of behavior) A cause based on personality characteristics or traits (2).

distinctiveness information Considers the extent to which the same behavior occurs across different situations (2).

divergent thinking The ability to respond with unusual, but still appropriate, responses to problems or questions (2).

double-bind hypothesis An explanation in which people with schizophrenia have in the past received simultaneous, yet contradictory, messages from significant figures in their lives (7).

double standard   The view that premarital sex is permissible for males but not for females (12).

the "dream"   An all-encompassing notion about what goals are desired from life (3).

dream interpretation   Process in therapy in which patients describe their dreams, which are interpreted by a therapist for signs of underlying conflicts (8).

drive   Motivational tension or arousal that energizes behavior to fulfill some need (4).

DSM-III-R   Diagnostic and statistical manual of mental disorders, third edition revised; classification system used by most mental health workers today (7).

eclectic approach (to treatment)   Employs a variety of techniques drawn from several treatments (7, 8).

ego   the part of personality that provides a buffer between the id and the constraining realities of the objective, outside world (1).

ego integrity versus despair   Last stage of psychosocial development (3).

ejaculation   The process in which semen is released from the penis (12).

electroconvulsive therapy (ECT)   Treatment involving the administration of an electric current to a patient's head to treat depression (8).

emblem   Body movement replacing spoken language (9).

emotional isolation   Where a person lacks a close, stable, and intimate relationship with another individual (4).

empathy   A state in which a person experiences the emotions of another individual; may increase prosocial behavior (13).

empty-nest syndrome   When the husband and wife revert to their earlier roles as husband and wife rather than mother and father (11).

endorphins   Natural, pain-killing chemicals in the brain that may result in feelings of happiness and even euphoria (6).

environmental psychology   The branch of psychology that studies the relationship between the environment and people's behavior and sense of well-being (15).

erectile failure   The inability to achieve or maintain an erection (12).

erogenous zones   Areas of the body that are particularly sensitive because of an unusually rich array of nerve receptors (12).

erotic   Stimuli that are sexually stimulating (12).

estrogen   The female sex hormone (12).

excitement phase (of sexual arousal)   The genitals become prepared for sexual activity following exposure to arousing stimuli (12).

exhaustion stage (of the general adaptation syndrome)   Person's ability to cope with stress declines to a point where stressor is overwhelming (6).

extramarital sex   Sexual activity between a married person and someone who is not his or her spouse (12).

extrinsic motivation   Motivation that causes people to work to obtain tangible rewards (14).

facial affect program   Analogous to a computer program, activated when a particular emotion is experienced (9).

facial feedback hypothesis   Suggests that facial expressions not only reflect emotional experience, but that they are also important in actually determining how people experience and label emotion (9).

fantasy   A defense mechanism which we use to gratify our desires by imagining satisfying events and achievements (6).

fantasy period (of career choice)   Phase in which career choice is based on personal desires without regard to one's ability, competencies, training, or available opportunities (14).

fight response   A direct attack on a source of stress (6).

filtering process   Concept that marriage candidates are considered through successively finer-grained filters.

flight response   Involves withdrawing from a source of stress (6).

focus-of-attention model (of crowding)   An explanation based on the fact that an attempt to determine what aspect of a stimulating situation is causing one's arousal can lead to a feeling of being crowded or of being comfortable (15).

foreclosure   A process in which an individual adopts an identity prematurely without making adequate preparation or a sufficient range of choices (3).

formal operational stage   According to Piaget, the final period of cognitive development, beginning at about age 12 (3).

free association   A Freudian therapeutic technique in which patients say everything that comes to mind to give the therapist a clue to the workings of the patient's unconscious (8).

freshman adjustment reaction   Psychological maladjustment unique to college students (7).

frustration   A thwarting or blocking of some ongoing, goal-directed behavior (13).

functional approach (to maladaptive behavior)   A behavior is considered maladaptive when any of three criteria are met: (1) the behavior doesn't allow a person to function effectively with others as a society member, (2) the behavior does not permit the person to meet his or her own needs, or (3) the behavior has a negative effect on the well-being of others (7).

functional fixedness   The tendency to think of an object only in terms of its typical use (2).

fundamental attribution bias   The tendency to attribute others' behavior to dispositional causes, and to attribute one's own behavior to situational causes (2).

general adaptation syndrome (GAS)   Model of stages through which one's body passes as it attempts to ward off the effects of environmental stressors (6).

generalized anxiety disorders   Characterized by the experience of long-term, consistent anxiety without knowing why (7).

generativity versus stagnation stage   According to Erikson, the stage in which people's major challenges are broader (3).

genetic preprogramming theories   Suggest that there is a built-in clock that places limits on the reproduction of human cells (3).

genitals   The male and female sex organs (12).

genital herpes   Virus related to cold sores that sometimes appear around the mouth (12).

gestalt therapy   An approach that attempts to integrate thoughts, feelings, and behavior into a whole (8).

gonorrhea   Sexually transmitted disease, almost as frequent as the common cold (12).

good patients   Patients who behave compliantly, cooperate with the hospital staff, are unquestioning and uncomplaining, and generally downplay their desires for more active involvement in their medical treatment (5).

grave-dressing phase (of relationship dissolution) Major activity is to physically and psychologically end the relationship (10).

group marriage A situation in which three or more people consider themselves married (11).

group therapy A procedure in which several unrelated people meet with a therapist to discuss some aspect of their psychological functioning (8).

growth motivation Where people attempt to move beyond what they have accomplished in the past and seek greater fulfillment in their lives (4).

habit formation stage (of smoking) Stage in which smoking moves from experimentation to habit (5).

hallucinations The experience of perceiving things that don't actually exist (7).

halo effect A phenomenon in which an initial understanding that a person has positive traits is used to infer other uniformly positive characteristics (2).

Hawthorne effect A phenomenon in which the special attention workers received from researchers, rather than the particular nature of the changes made by the researchers, led to productivity increases (14).

health belief model A model of the primary elements that guide people's decisions to undertake preventive health-related measures (5).

health psychology The branch of psychology that explores the relationship between physical and psychological factors (5).

heredity Developmental characteristics transmitted biologically from one's parents (3).

heterosexuality Sexual behavior between a man and a woman (12).

hierarchy of fears List, in order of increasing severity, of stimuli associated with such fears (8).

hierarchy of needs Where fundamental, basic needs must be fulfilled before higher-order, more sophisticated needs can be met (4).

homeostasis Process by which an organism tries to maintain an optimal level of internal biological functioning (4).

homophobia A strong, irrational fear of homosexuals (12).

homosexuality Sexual attraction to members of one's own sex (12).

humanistic model A view of maladaptive behavior that concentrates on what is uniquely human, particularly the way people perceive and view themselves (7).

humanistic therapy Therapy in which the underlying assumption is that people have control of their own behavior. It is up to them to solve their own problems (8).

hypochondriasis A fear of disease and preoccupation with health (7).

hypothalamus Part of the brain affecting the experience of hunger or directing eating behavior (4).

id The raw, unorganized, inherited part of personality whose sole purpose is to reduce tension created by primary drives related to hunger, sex, aggression, and irrational impulses (1).

identity The sense of one's unique value and position in the world (3).

identity crisis A state of unsureness, aimlessness, and confusion about one's identity (3).

identity versus role confusion stage According to Erikson, a time in adolescence of testing to determine one's own unique qualities (3).

illustrators Movements used to modify and augment spoken messages (9).

immune system The body's natural defenses that fight disease (5).

implicit personality theories Theories

reflecting our notions of what traits are found together in individuals (2).

incentives   Stimuli which attract or repel us (4).

industry versus inferiority stage   According to Erikson, the period during which children aged 6 to 12 years may develop positive social interactions with others or may feel inadequate and become less sociable (3).

information overload   Occurs in situations in which we receive so much physical and visual stimulation that we are unable to process and comprehend critical environmental data (15).

inhibited ejaculation   The difficulty resulting when a man is able to have an erection but is unable to ejaculate (12).

initiative versus guilt period   According to Erikson, the period during which children aged 3 to 6 years experience conflict between independence of action and the sometimes negative results of that action (3).

innate   Inborn in a species (13).

insight   A sudden awareness of the relationship between various elements of a problem that had previously appeared to be independent of one another (2).

insomnia   Inability to sleep (4).

instinctual drives   The infantlike wishes, desires, demands, and needs that are hidden from our conscious awareness because of the conflicts and pain they would cause us if they were part of everyday life (1).

intensification   Exaggeration of a facial expression (9).

interactionist view (of development)   Suggests that both nature and nurture interact to determine the course of a specific individual's development (3).

interpsychic phase   Focus on the other person's behavior and evaluation of the extent to which this behavior provides a basis for terminating the relationship (10).

intimacy versus isolation stage   According to Erikson, the stage during which people focus on developing close relationships with others (3).

intimate interaction zone   Close to 18 inches—the comfortable spacing of two people who are close personal friends (15).

intrinsic motivation   Motivation that causes people to participate in work for their own enjoyment, rather than the reward it will bring them (14).

job clarity   Degree of explicitness of the rules that determine what is expected of a worker (14).

job enlargment   A technique in which the number and variety of tasks assigned to a job is increased (14).

kinesics   The study of how body language—movements of the hands, feet, and trunk—is related to communication (9).

latent content (of dreams)   According to Freud, the true meaning of dreams, hidden by more obvious subjects (8).

learned drives   Drives in which no obvious biological need is being fulfilled (4).

learned helplessness   When people's attempts to control a situation are unsuccessful, and they give up trying even though they could be successful if they tried (5).

linguistic relativity hypothesis   The view that language shapes, and may actually determine, the way people of a particular culture perceive, think about, and understand the world (9).

lithium   Form of mineral salts and the most frequently prescribed antidepressant (8).

locus of control   The degree to which we believe we are personally responsible for events in our lives (2).

loneliness   Inability to maintain the level of affiliation desired (4).

looking-glass self The view of one's self that is provided by society and by other specific, significant individuals who populate a person's world (1).

loss-of-control explanation (of crowding) An explanation that suggests that the unpleasantness of crowding is due to the feeling that people cannot control their surroundings (15).

manifest content Surface description of a dream (8).

mantra A sound, word, or syllable repeated in meditation (6).

masturbation Self-stimulation producing sexual arousal (12).

medical model An explanation that suggests the root of maladaptive behavior lies in some physical dysfunction (7).

medical student's disease The feeling that symptoms and illnesses about which one studies are characteristic of oneself (7).

meditation Learned technique for refocusing attention that brings about an altered state of consciousness (6).

mere-exposure phenomenon Repeated exposure to any stimulus is sufficient to increase positivity of the evaluation of the stimulus (10).

midlife crisis Said to occur when people in their thirties and forties begin to question their contributions to the world and the very meaning of their existence (3).

midlife transition Said to occur when people in their thirties and forties begin to question their lives and their own particular "dream" (3).

mind Our individual consciousness, personality, and awareness of ourselves (5).

mind-body question Revolves around the relationship between the workings of the mind and the physical activities of the body (5).

models Systems of interrelated ideas and concepts used to explain phenomena (1).

motivation The factors that arouse, sustain, and direct behavior toward attainment of certain goals (4).

mutuality Occurs when two people share knowledge about themselves with each other, feeling similar degrees of responsibility (10).

narcissistic personality disorder A disorder in which there is a sense of self-importance, and preoccupation with fantasies of unlimited success (7).

need for achievement A stable, learned characteristic in which satisfaction is obtained by striving for and obtaining excellence (4).

need for affiliation A concern with establishing and maintaining relationships with others (4).

need-complementarity hypothesis Suggests that people are attracted to those who fill their needs (10).

negative identity A socially unacceptable identity (3).

neutralization An attempt to show no emotion at all (9).

nondirective counseling A procedure in which therapists clarify or reflect back in some way what the client had said (8).

nonstandard English A variant of English spoken fairly consistently in certain urban areas (9).

nonverbal communication Communication that is distinct from words (9).

norms Generalized expectations that are held by society regarding appropriate behavior in a given social situation (13).

norm of equity Norm stating that people should be rewarded in proportion to their costs and that they should suffer in proportion to their transgressions (13).

norm of reciprocity Norm stating that

one reason for helping others is to receive some future benefit oneself (13).

norm of social responsibility Norm reflecting the expectation that people should respond to the needs of others who are dependent upon them (13).

obesity Occurs when a person weighs over 20 percent more than the average weight of people his or her height (4).

observational learning Learning in which one models one's behavior after another (8).

observational learning theory (explanation of aggression) Suggests we learn to be aggressive, employing processes no different from those that explain the way we learn everything else (13).

obsessions Thoughts or ideas that keep recurring (7).

open communication A process in which couples speak openly of their feelings, employ statements that reveal their own perceptions, and produce reasons for their actions (11).

open marriage A marriage in which sexual encounters with people outside the marriage are acceptable (11).

orgasm Rhythmic muscular contractions of the genitals every eight-tenths of a second at the peak of sexual attraction (12).

ovaries The female reproductive organs (12).

ovulation The monthly release of an egg from an ovary (12).

palimony Financial support for a partner after a nonmarriage relationship has ended (11).

passion component (of love) Motivational drives relating to sex, physical closeness, and romance (10).

passionate (or romantic) love A state of intense absorption in someone (10).

perception The sorting out, interpretation, analysis, and integration of stimuli from our sense organs (2).

personal space Zone around a person's body into which other people may not enter (15).

personal stressors Represent major events in one's life that can produce an immediate stress reaction (6).

personality The set of distinctive and stable characteristics that differentiate us from others and which provide consistency in our behavior across different situations.

personality disorder Enduring, inflexible, maladaptive patterns of behavior, thought, and perception (7).

phobia An intense, irrational fear of specific objects or stimuli (7).

physical attractiveness stereotype Suggests that people who are physically attractive have a number of other desirable qualities (10).

physical self Our image of the physical aspects of our bodies (1).

plateau phase A period in which the maximum level of arousal is attained, the penis and clitoris swell with blood, and the body prepares for orgasm (12).

pleasure principle Operates when the goal is the immediate reduction of tension and the maximization of satisfaction (1).

Polyanna effect A tendency to rate others in a generally positive manner (2).

postconventional morality According to Erikson, invokes universal moral principles that are seen as broader than the particular society in which individuals live (3).

posttraumatic stress syndrome Occurs when original events and feelings associated with a traumatic event are reexperienced in vivid flashbacks or dreams (6).

power semantic Mediates the power or status level that a speaker holds (9).

preconventional morality Morality in which people follow unvarying rules

523

based on rewards and punishments (3).

predisposition model (of schizophrenia) Suggests that people inherit a predisposition or inborn sensitivity to schizophrenia, making them vulnerable to stressful factors in the environment (7).

prefrontal lobotomy A surgical technique that destroys certain portions of a patient's frontal lobes, which are associated with emotions (8).

prejudice Evaluations or judgments of members of a particular group based primarily on membership in that group and not on characteristics of those specific individuals (2).

premature ejaculation Occurs when a man is unable to delay ejaculation (12).

preoperational stage According to Piaget, the period from 2 to 7 years of age that is characterized by language development (3).

primary drives Drives relating to the basic biological functioning of the body (4).

primary orgasmic dysfunction Occurs when a woman has never experienced an orgasm (12).

primary territory Territory in which an individual has a complete, long-term control of an area, perceived in that manner by *both* their owners and other people (15).

primacy effect The weighing of initial information about a person more heavily than information received later (2).

progressive relaxation Meditation technique that focuses on the relaxation of specific muscle groups as well as the body as a whole (6).

projection A defense mechanism in which people attribute their own unacceptable ideas or thoughts to other people (6).

promiscuity Indiscriminate, casual sex (12).

prosocial behavior Helping behavior (13).

psychiatric social worker A social worker with specialized training in working with people in home and community settings (8).

psychiatrist A physician with postgraduate training in abnormal behavior (8).

psychoanalysis Psychodynamic therapy that involves frequent sessions and often lasts for many years (8).

psychoanalyst Physician or psychologist who specializes in psychoanalysis (8).

psychoanalytic model (of maladaptive behavior) Suggests that maladaptive behavior stems from childhood conflicts over opposing desires (7).

psychodynamic model Based on the belief that behavior is brought about by unconscious inner forces over which an individual has little control (1).

psychodynamic therapy A treatment approach based on the premise that the source of maladaptive behavior is unresolved past conflicts (8).

psychology The scientific study of behavior and mental processes (1).

psychosocial development The growth and change of psychological orientation toward oneself and others (3).

psychosomatic disorders Physical disorders in which emotions and thoughts play an important role (6, 7).

psychosurgery Brain surgery carried out to alleviate symptoms of mental disorder (8).

psychotherapy Psychological treatment in which patients attempt to remedy psychological difficulties through discussions and interactions (8).

public interaction zone The 12- to 25-foot space kept between strangers in public places and during impersonal events (lectures, ceremonies, etc.) (15).

public territories Areas of temporary personal control, which normally may be occupied by anyone at any time (for example, a bench in a train station) (15).

Puritan work ethic The notion that work is important in and of itself (14).

push models (of motivation) Suggest that our behavior is motivated primarily by our inner needs and desires (4).

rape trauma syndrome Psychological and physical damage that occurs following rape (12).

rapid eye movement (REM) sleep Phase of sleep during which the heart's rate increases and becomes irregular, blood pressure and respiration rate rise, males have erections, and voluntary muscles act as if they were paralized (4).

rational-emotive therapy A treatment designed to restructure a person's belief system into a more realistic, rational, and logical one (8).

rationalization A defense mechanism in which there is distortion of reality stemming from an attempt to justify thoughts, feelings, or events that make us uncomfortable (6).

realistic period (of career choice) Phase in which specific career options are explored, either through actual work experience or through training (14).

reality principle When instinctual energy is restrained in order to maintain the safety of the individual and help integrate the person into society (1).

reciprocity-of-liking phenomenon A tendency to like those whom we think like us (10).

recreational role Husband and wife share activities of a recreational nature (11).

refractory period Entered by a male after the resolution stage, a period during which he cannot be sexually aroused (12).

regression A defense mechanism in which behavior retreats to an earlier stage of development (6).

repression A defense mechanism in which stressful, anxiety-producing thoughts or feelings are pushed out of conscious awareness (6).

resistance Inability or unwillingness to discuss or reveal particular memories, thoughts, or motivations (8).

resistance stage (of the general adaptation syndrome) Stage in which people prepare to fight the stressor and are generally able to cope with stress-producing situations (6).

resolution stage The final stage of sexual arousal during which the body returns to its normal state (12).

reward-cost analysis (of helping) A person psychologically weighs the rewards that will come from helping against the costs incurred from giving the help (13).

role conflict Contradictory demands placed on a worker by employers, likely to produce dissatisfaction (14).

role exit Termination of an ongoing role.

Romeo and Juliet effect Suggests that greater levels of parental interference in dating relationships lead to greater attraction (10).

schizophrenia Class of disorders whose symptoms include severe distortion of reality, disturbances in thinking, perception, and emotion (7).

secondary territories Areas used regularly by a person but under less permanent control and used by more than one person (15).

security needs Needs to be safe in the world (4).

selective attention A process in which we choose which stimulus to perceive and pay attention to (2).

self-actualization A state in which other needs are fulfilled and the individual focuses on personal growth and reaching his or her highest potential (4).

self-efficacy The belief that people are personally responsible (1).

self-esteem Feelings of personal self-worth (2).

self-fulfilling prophecies Expectations about the possibility of future events or behaviors that act to increase the likelihood that the event or behavior will occur (2).

semen The fluid containing sperm, from the penis (12).

sensate focus A method of sexual therapy in which attention is drawn away from intercourse and toward other behaviors that feel pleasurable to a partner (12).

sensorimotor stage According to Piaget, the stage from birth to 2 years during which a child has little competence in representing the environment using images, language, or other symbols (3).

sexism Negative attitudes and behavior based on an individual's sex (2, 9).

sexual role Marriage provides the only morally acceptable avenue for sexual activities (12).

situational causes (of behavior) Causes brought about by something in the environment and not the person himself or herself (2).

situational orgasmic dysfunction Occurs when a female is able to have an orgasm only under certain conditions (12).

social cognition Relates to the processes that underlie our understanding of the social world (2).

social comparison A phenomenon in which people depend on others to evaluate their own behavior, abilities, expertise, and opinions (1).

social development The changes in relationships and interactions with others (3).

social readjustment rating scale (SRRS) A questionnaire for rating the number of life events, both negative and positive, that a person has experienced during the past year (6).

social self Comprises the various roles that we play in life as part of our interactions with others (1).

social support The knowledge that we are part of a mutual network of caring, interested others, enabling us to experience lower levels of stress and to better cope with stress (6).

sociocultural model (of maladaptive behavior) Considers society to be the source of adjustment problems (7).

social isolation When a person feels cut off from the social support of family and friends (4).

socialization The process of learning and accepting society's values, attitudes, beliefs, and customs (3).

solidarity semantic Degree of shared social experience between two people, indicated during a conversation (9).

somatoform disorders Psychological problems that take on a physical form of some sort (7).

speculative communication A process in which problems are acknowledged, but the conflict is not dealt with in detail (11).

spontaneous remission A process in which a person recovers without treatment (8).

status Evaluation by others of the roles we play in society (14).

stereotype An overly simplified idea or expectation assigned to members of specific groups (2).

stimulus-overload explanation (of crowding) An explanation based on the fact that an overdose of environmental stimuli can lead to withdrawal from the situation (15).

stress The process of appraising events as threatening, challenging, or harmful, and responding to such events on a psychological, emotional, cognitive, or behavioral level (6).

stress-inoculation training Method for coping with and modifying people's thoughts about stress and tension in their lives (6).

stressors The circumstances and events that produce stress (6).

subjective-discomfort approach (to maladaptive behavior) Suggests that a behavior is maladaptive if it produces feelings of distress, anxiety, or guilt, or if it causes harm to other individuals (7).

suppression Voluntary attempt to push unpleasant thoughts out of one's consciousness (6).

sympathetic nervous system The part of the nervous system that is responsible for physiological responses to emergency situations (6).

symptom substitution A phenomenon in which once a maladaptive behavior is eliminated, new ones sometimes crop up (8).

syphilis A sexually transmitted disease which may lead to neurological problems and/or death (12).

systematic desensitization A procedure in which a stimulus that evokes pleasant feelings is repeatedly paired with a stimulus that evokes anxiety in the hope that the anxiety will be alleviated (8).

tabula rasa A "blank slate" (1).

Tay-Sachs disease Rare, but fatal, disease affecting one in 30 children in certain cultural groups (5).

tentative period (of career choice) Phase in which realistic considerations begin to be taken into account (14).

territorial markers Objects and behavior used to personalize and defend territories (15).

territoriality The sense of ownership that people develop over a particular space or geographic area (15).

testes Part of male genitals that produce sperm and androgen (12).

token economy A procedure whereby a person is rewarded for performing certain desired behaviors (8).

transcendence When people see themselves in a spiritual light, in harmony with nature, the world, and the universe (4).

transference A process in which patients come to see the analyst as symbolic of significant others (8).

trust versus mistrust stage According to Erikson, the stage that centers around the development of trust (birth to 1½ years) (3).

two-factor theory of love Suggests that people experience love when two things occur together: intense physiological arousal and situational cues that suggest love (10).

unconditional positive regard Expressions of acceptance, regardless of what a client says or does (8).

unconscious The part of personality of which a person is not aware.

uplifts Events that make one feel good, even temporarily; opposite of hassles (6).

vicarious reinforcement Learning by observing others (13).

wear-and-tear theory Theory that the body just wears out (3).

weight set point A particular weight level the body strives to maintain (4).

References

Adams, G. R., & Huston, T. L. (1975). Social perception of middle-aged persons varying in physical attractiveness. *Developmental Psychology, 11*, 657–658.

Adler, J. (1984, April 23). The fight to conquer fear. *Newsweek*, pp. 66–72.

Agras, W. S. (1987). *Eating disorders: Management of obesity, bulimia, and anorexia.* New York: Pergamon.

Agras, W. S., Southam, M. A., & Taylor, C. B. (1983). Long-term persistence of relaxation-induced blood pressure lowering during the working day. *Journal of Consulting and Clinical Psychology, 51*, 792–794.

Aiello, J. R., Vautier, J. S., & Bernstein, M. D. (1983, August). *Crowding stress: Impact of social support, group formation, and control.* Paper presented at the meeting of the American Psychological Association, Anaheim, CA.

Ainsworth, M. D. S., Blehar, M. C., Waters, E., & Wall, S. (1978). *Patterns of attachment.* Hillsdale, NJ: Erlbaum.

Allport, G. W. (1954). *The nature of prejudice.* Cambridge, MA: Addison-Wesley.

Altman, I. (1975). *The environment and social behavior.* Monterey, CA: Brooks/Cole.

Amir, Y. (1976). The role of intergroup contact in change of prejudice and ethnic relations. In P. Katz (Ed.), *Towards the elimination of racism.* New York: Pergamon.

Amir, Y., & Sharan, S. (1984). *School desegregation.* Hillsdale, NJ: Erlbaum.

Anderson, C. A. (1987). Temperature and aggression: Effects on quarterly, yearly, and city rates of violent and nonviolent crime. *Journal of Personality and Social Psychology, 52*, 1161–1173.

Angell, M. (1985). Disease as a reflection of the psyche (editorial). *New England Journal of Medicine, 312*, 1570–1572.

Arena, J. M. (1984, April). A look at the opposite sex. *Newsweek on Campus*, p. 21.

Asnis, G., & Ryan, N. D. (1983). The psychoneuroendocrinology of schizophrenia. In A. Rifkin (Ed.), *Schizophrenia and affective disorders: Biology and drug treatment* (pp. 205–236). Boston: John Wright.

Au, T. K. (1983). Chinese and English counterfactuals: The Sapir-Whorf hypothesis revisited. *Cognition, 15*, 155–187.

Averill, J. R. (1975). A semantic atlas of emotional concepts. *Catalog of selected documents in psychology, 5*, 330.

Ball-Rokeach, S. J., Rokeach, M., & Grube, J. W. (1984). *The great American values test: Influencing behavior and belief through television.* New York: Free Press.

Bandura, A. (1977). *Social learning theory.* Englewood Cliffs, NJ: Prentice-Hall.

Bandura, A. (1982). Self-efficacy mechanism in human agency. *American Psychologist, 37*, 122–147.

Bandura, A. (1986). *Social foundations of thought and action: A social cognitive theory.* Englewood Cliffs, NJ: Prentice-Hall.

Bandura, A., Grusec, J. E., & Menlove, F. L. (1967). Vicarious extinction of avoidance behavior. *Journal of Per-

sonality and Social Psychology, 5, 16–23.

Bandura, A., Ross, D., & Ross, S. (1963). Imitation of film-mediated aggressive models. *Journal of Abnormal and Social Psychology, 66,* 3–11.

Bandura, A., & Schunk, D. H. (1981). Cultivating competence, self-efficacy, and interest through proximal self-motivation. *Journal of Personality and Social Psychology, 41,* 586–598.

Baron, J. B., & Sternberg, R. J. (1987). *Teaching thinking skills: Theory and practice.* New York: Freeman.

Baron, R. A. (1978). Invasions of personal space and helping: Mediating effects of invader's apparent need. *Journal of Experimental Social Psychology, 14,* 304–312.

Baron, R. M., Mandel, D. R., Adams, C. A. & Griffen, L. M. (1976). Effects of social density in university residential environments. *Journal of Personality and Social Psychology, 34,* 434–446.

Barron, F. (1969). *Creative person and creative process.* New York: Holt.

Barron, F., & Harrington, D. M. (1981). Creativity, intelligence, and personality. *Annual Review of Psychology, 32,* 439–476.

Baruch, G. D., & Barnett, R. C. (1986). Consequences of fathers' participation in family work: Parents' role strain and well-being. *Journal of Personality and Social Psychology, 51,* 983–992.

Basow, S. A. (1980). *Sex role stereotypes: Traditions and alternatives.* Monterey, California: Brooks/Cole.

Bauer, B. G., Anderson, W. P., & Hyatt, R. A. (with contributions by Margaret Flynn). (1986). *Bulimia: Book for therapist and client.* Muncie, IN: Accelerated Development.

Baum, A., Fisher, J. D., & Solomon, S. K. (1981). Type of information, familiarity, and the reduction of crowding stress. *Journal of Personality and Social Psychology, 40,* 11–23.

Baum, A., Fleming, R., & Singer, J. E. (1983). Coping with technological disaster. *Journal of Social Issues, 39,* 117–138.

Baum, A., & Gatchel, R. J. (1981). Cognitive determinants of response to uncontrollable events: Development of reactance and learned helplessness. *Journal of Personality and Social Psychology, 40,* 1078–1089.

Baum, A., & Valins, S. (1977). *Architecture and social behavior: Psychological studies of social density.* Hillsdale, NJ: Erlbaum.

Baum, A., & Valins, S. (1979). Architectural mediation of residential density and control: Crowding and the regulation of social contact. In L. Berkowitz (Ed.), *Advances in experimental social psychology* (Vol. 12). New York: Academic.

Beck, A. T. (1985). Cognitive therapy of depression: New perspectives. In P. J. Clayton and J. E. Barret (Eds.), *Treatment of depression: Old controversies and new approaches.* New York: Raven Press.

Becker, M. H., Kaback, M., Rosenstock, I. M., & Ruth, M. (1975). Some influences of public participation in a genetic screening program. *Journal of Community Health, 1,* 3–14.

Becker, M. H., & Maiman, L. A. (1975). Sociobehavioral determinants of compliance with health and medical care recommendations. *Medical Care, 13,* 10–24.

Beckman, L. (1970). Effects of students' performance on teachers' and observers' attributions of causality. *Journal of Educational Psychology, 61,* 76–82.

Beech, R. P., & Schoeppe, A. (1974). Development of value systems in adolescents. *Developmental Psychology, 10,* 644–656.

Belkin, G. S. (1984). *Introduction to counseling.* Dubuque, IA: Wm. C. Brown.

Belsky, J. (1985). Two waves of day care research: Developmental effects and conditions of quality. In R. Ainslie (Ed.), *The child and the day care setting.* New York: Praeger.

Benjamin, L. T., Jr. (1985, February). Defining aggression: An exercise for classroom discussion. *Teaching of Psychology, 12*(1), 40–42.

Benson, H. (1975). *The relaxation response.* New York: William Morrow.

Benson, H., & Friedman, R. (1985). A rebuttal to the conclusions of Davis S. Holme's article, "Meditation and somatic arousal reduction." *American Psychologist,* 725–726.

Bergener, M., Ermini, M., & Stahelin, H. B. (Eds.). (1985, February). *Thresholds in aging.* The 1984 Sandoz Lectures in Gerontology. Basle, Switzerland.

Berger, C. R., Gardner, R. R., Clatterbuck, G. W., & Schulman, L. S. (1976). Perceptions of information sequencing in relationship development. *Human Communication Research, 3,* 34–39.

Berger, J., Cohen, B. P., & Zelditch, M., Jr. (1973). Status characteristics and social interaction. In R. J. Ofshe (Ed.), *Interpersonal behavior in small groups* (pp. 194–216). Englewood Cliffs, NJ: Prentice-Hall.

Bergler, E. (1974). *Principles of self-damage.* New York: Intercontinental Medical Book Corporation.

Berkowitz, L. (1973). Control of aggression. In B. M. Caldwell & H. Ricciuti (Eds.), *Review of child development research* (Vol. 3, pp. 95–140). Chicago: University of Chicago Press.

Berkowitz, L. (1974). Some determinants of impulsive aggression: The role of mediated associations with reinforcements for aggression. *Psychological Review, 81,* 165–176.

Berkowitz, L. (1984). Aversive conditioning as stimuli to aggression. In R. J. Blanchard and C. Blanchard (Eds.), *Advances in the study of aggression* (Vol. 1). New York: Academic Press.

Berkowitz, L., & Geen, R. G. (1966). Film violence and the cue properties of available targets. *Journal of Personality and Social Psychology, 3,* 525–530.

Berkowitz, L., & LePage, A. (1967). Weapons as aggression-eliciting stimuli. *Journal of Personality and Social Psychology, 7,* 202–207.

Berlyne, D. (1967). Arousal and reinforcement. In D. Levine (Ed.), *Nebraska symposium on motivation.* Lincoln: University of Nebraska Press.

Berman, J. S., Miller, R. C., & Massman, P. J. (1985). Cognitive therapy versus systematic desensitization: Is one treatment superior? *Psychological Bulletin, 97,* 451–461.

Bernard, J. (1972). *The future of marriage.* New York: World.

Bernard, M. E., & Joyce, M. R. (1984). *Rational-emotive therapy with children and adolescents.* Somerset, NJ: Wiley.

Berscheid, E. (1985). Interpersonal attraction. In G. Lindzey and E. Aronson (Eds.), *Handbook of Social Psychology* (Vol. 2). New York: Random House.

Berscheid, E., & Campbell, B. (1981). The changing longevity of heterosexual close relationships: A commentary and forecast. In M. Lerner (Ed.), *The justice motive in times of scarcity and change.* New York: Plenum.

Berscheid, E., & Walster, E. (1974). Physical attractiveness. In L. Berkowitz (Ed.), *Advances in Experimental Social Psychology* (Vol. 7, pp. 157–215). New York: Academic.

Berscheid, E., Walster, E., & Campbell, R. (1974). Grow old with me. Cited in E. Berscheid & E. Walster, Physical attractiveness. In L. Berkowitz (Ed.), *Advances in Experimental Social Psychology* (Vol. 7). New York: Harper.

Birnbaum, M. H., & Mellers, B. A. (1979). Stimulus recognition may mediate exposure effects. *Journal of Personality and Social Psychology, 37,* 391–394.

Birren, J. E. (1986). Aging as a scientific and value-laden field of inquiry. *Journal of Religion and Aging, 2,* 29–39.

Blatt, S. J., D'Affilitti, J. P., & Quinlan, D. M. (1976). Experiences of depression in normal young adults. *Journal of Abnormal Psychology, 85,* 383–389.

Blau, Z. S. (1973). *Old age in a changing society.* New York: New Viewpoints.

Bloom, A. H. (1981). *The linguistic shaping of thought: A study in the impact of language on thinking in China and the West.* Hillsdale, NJ: Erlbaum.

Boakes, R. A., Popplewell, D. A., & Burton, M. J. (Eds.). (1987). *Eating habits: Food, physiology, and learned behaviour.* New York: Wiley.

Bohanan, P. (1970). The six stations of divorce. In P. Bohanan (Ed.), *Divorce and After* (pp. 33–62). New York: Doubleday.

Bolles, R. N. (1987). *What color is your parachute?* Berkeley, CA: Ten Speed Press.

Booth-Kewley, S., & Friedman, H. S. (1987). Psychological predictors of heart disease: A quantitative review. *Psychological Bulletin, 101,* 343–362.

Bourne, L. E., Dominowski, R. L., Loftus, E. F., Healy, A. (1986). *Cognitive processes.* Englewood Cliffs, NJ: Prentice-Hall.

Bowlby, J. (1969). *Attachment and loss: Vol. 1. Attachment.* New York: Basic Books.

Boyd, J. H. & Weissman, M. M. (1981). Epidemiology of affective disorders: A re-examination and future directions. *Archives of General Psychiatry, 38,* 1039–1045.

Brain, R. (1977, October). Somebody else should be your own best friend. *Psychology Today,* 83–84, 120–123.

Brenton, M. (1972). *Sex talk.* New York: Stein and Day.

Bronzaft, A. L., & McCarthy, D. P. (1975). The effect of elevated train noise on reading ability. *Environment and Behavior, 7,* 517–527.

Brown L., & McKinnon, A. (1976). A model for adapting instructional approaches. *Education and Training of the Mentally Retarded, 11,* 223–224.

Brown, R. (1976). Reference: In memorial tribute to Eric Lenneberg. *Cognition, 4,* 125–153.

Brown, R., & Gilman, A. (1960). The pronouns of power and solidarity. In T. A. Sebeok (Ed.), *Style in language* (pp. 253–276). Cambridge, MA: M.I.T. Press.

Brown, R., & Lenneberg, E. H. (1954). A study of language and cognition. *Journal of Abnormal and Social Psychology,* 454–462.

Bryan, J. H., & Test, M. A. (1967). Models and helping: Naturalistic studies in aiding behavior. *Journal of Personality and Social Psychology, 6,* 400–407.

Buck, R. (1984). *Nonverbal behavior and the communication of affect.* New York: Guilford.

Burger, J. M., Oakman, J. A., & Ballard, N. G. (1983). Desire of control and the perception of crowding. *Personality and Social Psychology Bulletin, 9,* 475–479.

Burgess, A. W., & Holmstrom, L. L. (1979). *Rape: Crisis and recovery.* Bowie, MD: Robert J. Brady.

Burgess, E. W., & Wallin, P. (1953). *Engagement and marriage.* Philadelphia: Lippincott.

Burgess, R. L., & Huston, T. L. (Eds.). (1979). *Social exchange in developing relationships.* New York: Academic.

Burleson, J. A. (1984, April). *Reciprocity of interpersonal attraction within acquainted versus unacquainted small groups.* Paper presented at the annual meeting of the Eastern Psychological Association, Baltimore.

Burnam, M. A., Pennebaker, J. W., & Glass, D. C. (1975). Time consciousness, achievement striving, and the Type A coronary-prone behavior pattern. *Journal of Abnormal Psychology, 84,* 76–79.

Burros, M. (1988, February 24). Women: Out of the house but not out of the kitchen. *New York Times,* A1; C10.

Buss, D. M., & Barnes, M. (1986). Preferences in human mate selection. *Journal of Personality and Social Psychology, 50,* 559–570.

Byrne, D. (1969). Attitudes and attraction. In L. Berkowitz (Ed.), *Advances in Experimental Social Psychology* (Vol. 4, pp. 35–89). New York: Academic.

Byrne, D., & Kelley, L. (1981). *An introduction to personality* (3rd ed.). Englewood Cliffs, NJ: Prentice-Hall.

Carlson, M., & Miller, N. (1987). Explanation of the relation between negative mood and helping. *Psychological Bulletin, 102,* 91–108.

Carmi, A., & Schneider, S. (Eds.). (1986). *Drugs and alcohol.* Berlin, Federal Republic of Germany: Springer-Verlag Berlin.

Carson, R. C. (1983). The schizophrenias. In H. E. Adams & P. B. Sutker (Eds.), *Handbook of clinical behavior therapy.* New York: Plenum.

Carver, C. S., DeGregorio, E., & Gillis, R. (1980). Field study of an ego-defensive bias in attribution among two categories of observers. *Personality and Social Psychology Bulletin, 6,* 44–50.

Casey, R. J., & Berman, J. S. (1985). The outcome of psychotherapy with children. *Psychological Bulletin, 98,* 388–400.

Check, J. V. P., & Malamuth, N. M. (1986). Pornography and sexual aggression. A social learning theory analysis. In M. L. McLaughlin (Ed.), *Communication yearbook 9.* Beverly Hills, CA: Sage.

Cherry, E. C. (1953). Some experiments on the recognition of speech with one and two ears. *Journal of the Acoustical Society of America, 25,* 975–979.

Ciminero, A. R., Calhoun, K. S., & Adams, H. E. (Eds.). (1986). *Handbook of behavioral assessment.* (2nd ed.). New York: Wiley.

Clark, H. H. (1985). Language use and language users. In G. Lindzey & E. Aronson (Eds.), *Handbook of social psychology,* (Vol. 2, 3rd ed.). New York: Random House.

Clark, H. H., & Clark, E. V. (1977). *Psychology and language.* New York: Harcourt Brace Jovanovich.

Clark, K. B., & Clark, M. P. (1947). Racial identification and preference in Negro children. In T. M. Newcomb & E. L. Hartley (Eds.), *Readings in social psychology.* New York: Holt, Rinehart, and Winston.

Cloninger, C. R. (1987, April). Neurogenetic adaptive mechanisms in alcoholism. *Science, 236,* 410–416.

Cohen, S. (1980). After-effects of stress on human performance and social behavior: A review of research and theory. *Psychological Bulletin, 88,* 82–108.

Colby, A., Kohlberg, L., Gibbs, J., & Lieberman, M. (1983). A longitudinal study of moral judgment. *Monographs of the Society for Research in Child Development, 48* (200), pp. 77–86.

Coleman, J., et al. (1977). Adolescents and their parents: A study of attitudes. *Journal of Genetic Psychology, 130,* 239–245.

Constantine, J., & Constantine, L. (1970, April). Where is marriage going? *The Futurist,* p. 46.

Cook. R. (1973, May 14). The new doctor's dilemma. *Newsweek.*

Cooper, H. M. (1986). On the social psychology of using research reviews: The case of desegregation and black achievement. In R. S. Feldman (Ed.), *The social psychology of education: Current research and theory* (pp. 341–363). Cambridge: Cambridge University Press.

Corter, C., Trehub, S., Boukydis, C., Ford, L., Clehoffer, L., & Minde, K. (1978). Nurses' judgments of the attractiveness of premature infants. *Infant Behavioral Development, 1,* 373–380.

Costa, P. T., Jr., & McCrae, R. R. (1985). Hypochondriasis, neuroticism, and aging. *American Psychologist, 40,* 19–28.

Cox, V. C., Paulus, P. B., & McCain, G. (1984). Prison crowding research. *American Psychologist, 39,* 1148–1160.

Cox, V. C., Paulus, P. B., McCain, G., & Schkade, J. K. (1979). Field research on the effects of crowding in prisons and on offshore drilling platforms. In J. R. Aiello and A. Baum (Eds.), *Residential Crowding and Design.* New York: Plenum.

Cross, H. A., Halcomb, C. G., & Matter, W. W. (1967). Imprinting and exposure learning in rats given early auditory stimulation. *Psychonomic Science, 10,* 223–234.

Cummings, E., & Henry, W. E. (1961). *Growing old.* New York: Basic Books.

Darley, J. M., & Batson, C. D. (1973). "From Jeruselem to Jericho": A study of situational and dispositional variables in helping behavior. *Journal of Personality and Social Psychology, 27,* 100–108.

Davis, M. S. (1968). Physiological, psychological and demographic factors in patient compliance with doctors' orders. *Medical Care, 6,* 115–122.

Davis, M. S. (1973). *Intimate relations.* New York: Macmillan.

Davison, G. C., & Neale, J. M. (1978). *Abnormal psychology* (2nd ed.). New York: Wiley.

Davison, G. C., & Neale, J. M. (1982). *Abnormal psychology* (3rd ed.). New York: Wiley.

Deci, E. L., & Ryan, R. M. (1985). *Intrinsic Motivation and Self-Determination in Human Behavior.* New York: Plenum.

Delbeckg, A., venDeven, A., & Gustafson, D. (1975). *Group techniques for program planning.* Glenview, IL: Scott, Foresman.

Dembroski, T. M., MacDougall, J. M., Herd, J. A., & Shields, J. L. (1983). Perspectives on coronary-prone behavior. In D. S. Krantz, A. Baum, & J. E. Singer (Eds.), *Handbook of psychology and health, 3.* Hillsdale, NJ: Erlbaum.

Dement, W. C. (1979). Two kinds of sleep. In D. Goleman & R. J. Davidson (Eds.), *Consciousness: Brain, states of awareness and mysticism* (pp. 72–75). New York: Harper & Row.

Dickstein, L. S. (1972). Death concern: Measurement and correlates. *Psychological Reports, 30,* 563–571.

Dion, K. K., & Berscheid, E. (1974). Physical attractiveness and social perception of peers of preschool children. Reported in E. Berscheid and E. Walster, Physical attractiveness. In L. Berkowitz (Ed.), *Advances in experimental social psychology* (Vol. 7). New York: Academic.

Donnerstein, E., & Berkowitz, L. (1981). Victim reactions in aggressive erotic films as a factor in violence against women. *Journal of Personality and Social Psychology, 41,* 710–724.

Driscoll, R., Davis, K. E., & Lipitz, M. E. (1972). Parental interference and romantic love: The Romeo and Juliet effect. *Journal of Personality and Social Psychology, 24,* 1–10.

Drug users, rich and poor, tell of the costs and the anguish. (1984, May 20). *The New York Times,* p. 50.

Duberman, L. (1974). *Marriage and its alternatives.* New York: Praeger.

DuBrin, A. J. (1974). The meeting/mating game: How and where to play. *Single, 2,* 48–51, 72–75.

Duck, S. W. (1982). A topography of relationship disengagement and dissolution. In S. W. Duck (Ed.), *Personal relationships: Vol. 4. Dissolving personal relationships.* New York: Academic Press.

Duffy, M., Bailey, S., Beck, B., & Barker, D. G. (1986). Preferences in nursing home design: A comparison of residents, administrators, and designers. *Environment and Behavior, 28,* 246–257.

Duke, M. P., & Nowicki, S. Jr. (1972). A new measure and social learning model for interpersonal distance. *Journal of Experimental Research in Personality, 6,* 119–132.

Duke, M., & Nowicki, S., Jr. (1979). *Abnormal psychology: Perspectives on being different.* Monterey, CA: Brooks/Cole.

Duncker, K. (1945). On problem solving. *Psychological Monographs, 58* (5, whole no. 270).

Dutton, D., & Aron, A. (1974). Some evidence for heightened sexual attraction under conditions of high anxiety. *Journal of Personality and Social Psychology, 30,* 510–517.

Dwortzky, J. P. (1984). *Introduction to child development* (2nd ed.). St. Paul.

Edney, J. J. (1975). Territoriality and control: A field experiment. *Journal of Personality and Social Psychology, 31,* 1108–1115.

Eisenberg, N. (Eds.) (1987). *Contemporary topics in developmental psychology.* New York: Wiley.

Eisenberg, N., & Miller, P. A. (1987). The relation of empathy to prosocial and related behaviors. *Psychological Bulletin, 101*(1), 91–119.

Eisenberg-Berg, N., & Mussen, P. (1978). Empathy and moral development in adolescence. *Developmental Psychology, 14,* 185–186.

Ekman, P. (1972). Universals and cultural differences in facial expressions of emotion. In J. Cole (Ed.), *Darwin and facial expression: A century of research in review* (pp. 169–222). New York: Academic Press.

Ekman, P. (Ed.). (1982). *Emotion in the human face.* Cambridge, England: Cambridge University Press.

Ekman, P., Friesen, W. V., & Ellsworth, P. (1972). *Emotion in the human face.* Elmsford, NY: Pergamon.

Ekman, P., Friesen, W., & Ellsworth, P. (1982). Does the face provide accurate information? In P. Ekman (Ed.), *Emotion in the human face* (2nd ed.) (pp. 56–97). Cambridge, England: Cambridge University Press.

Ekman, P., Levenson, R. W., & Friesen, W. V. (1983, September 16). Autonomic nervous system activity distinguishes among emotions. *Science, 223,* 1208–1210.

Ellis, A. (1962). *Reason and emotion in psychotherapy.* New York: Lyle Stuart.

Ellis, A. (1975). Creative job and happiness: The humanistic way. *The Humanist, 35* (1), 11–13.

Ellis, A., & Harper, R. A. (1961). *Guide to rational living.* North Hollywood, CA: Wilshire Book Company.

Erickson, E. H. (1963). *Childhood and society* (2nd ed.). New York: Norton.

Erikson, E. H. (1987). *A way of looking at things: Selected papers from 1930 to 1980*. New York: Norton.

Erikson, F. (1979). Talking down: Some cultural sources of miscommunication in interracial interviews. In A. Wolfgang (Ed.), *Nonverbal behavior applications and cultural implications* (pp. 99–126). New York: Academic.

Eron, L. D. (1986). Interventions to mitigate the psychological effects of media violence on aggressive behavior. *Journal of Social Issues, 42,* 155–169.

Eron, L. D., Huesmann, L. R., Lefkowitz, M. M., & Walder, L. O. (1972). Does television violence cause aggression? *American Psychologist, 27,* 253–263.

Evans, G. W. (1974). An examination of the information overload mechanism of personal space. *Man-Environment Systems, 4,* 61.

Exline, R. V., & Winters, L. C. (1965). Affective relations and mutual glances in dyads. In S. S. Tomkins & C. W. Izard (Eds.), *Affect, cognition, and personality.* New York: Springer.

Eysenck, H. J. (1952). The effects of psychotherapy: An evaluation. *Journal of Consulting Psychology, 16,* 319–324.

Feldman, R. S. (Ed.). (1982). *Development of nonverbal behavior in children.* New York: Springer-Verlag.

Festinger, L. (1954). A theory of social comparison processes. *Human Relations, 7,* 117–140.

Festinger, L. (1957). *A theory of cognitive dissonance.* Stanford, CA: Stanford University Press.

Festinger, L., Schachter, S., & Back, K. W. (1950). *Social pressure in informal groups.* New York: Harper.

Fincham, F. D., Beach, S. R. & Baucom, D. H. (1987). Attribution processes in distressed and nondistressed couples: 4. Self-partner attribution differences. *Journal of Personality and Social Psychology, 52,* 739–748.

Fischman, Joshua. (1987, February). Type A on trial. *Psychology Today, 21,* 42–50.

Fisher, J. D., Bell, P. A., & Baum, A. S. (1984). *Environmental Psychology* (2nd ed.). New York: Holt.

Fisher, J. D., Nadler, A., & Whitcher-Alagna, S. (1982). Recipient reactions to aid. *Psychological Bulletin, 91,* 27–54.

Fisher, K. (1985, March). ECT: New studies on how, why, who. *APA Monitor,* 18–19.

Fiske, S. T. (1987). People's reactions to nuclear war: Implications for psychologists. *American Psychologist, 42,* 207–217.

Fiske, S. T., & Taylor, S. E. (1983). *Social cognition.* Reading, MA: Addison-Wesley.

Flaxman, J. (1978). Quitting smoking now or later: Gradual, abrupt, immediate, and delayed quitting. *Behavior Therapy, 9,* 260–270.

Fleming, J. B., & Washburne, C. K. (1977). *For better, for worse.* New York: Scribner.

Fleming, R., Baum, A., and Singer, J. (1984). Toward an integrative approach to the study of stress. *Journal of Personality and Social Psychology, 46,* 939–949.

Folkman, S. (1984). Personal control and stress and coping processes: A theoretical analysis. *Journal of Personality and Social Psychology, 46,* 839–852.

Forsyth, D. R. (1983). *An introduction to group dynamics.* Monterey, CA: Brooks/Cole.

Freedman, J. L. (1979). Reconciling apparent differences between responses to humans and other animals to crowding. *Psychological Review, 86,* 80–85.

Freedman, J. L. (1984). Effect of television violence on aggressiveness. *Psychological Bulletin, 96,* 227–246.

Frenkel-Brunswick, E. (1968). Adjustments and reorientation in the course of the life span. In B. L. Neugarten (Ed.), *Middle age and aging.* Chicago: University of Chicago Press.

Freud, S. (1920). *A general introduction to psychoanalysis.* New York: Boni & Liveright.

Freud, S. (1922/1959). *Group psychology and the analysis of the ego.* London: Hogarth.

Friedman, H. (1986). Science press seminar. Alcohol, Drug Abuse and Mental Health Administration.

Friedman, M., & Rosenman, R. H. (1974). *Type A behavior and your heart.* Greenwich, CT: Fawcett.

Friedman, M., Thoresen, C. E., Gill, J. J., Ulmer, D., Leonti, T., Powell, L., Price, V., Elek, S. R., Robin, D. D., Breall, W. S., Piaget, G., Dixon, T., Bourg, E., Levy, R. A., & Tasto, D. L. (1984). Feasibility of altering Type A behavior pattern after myocardial infarction. *Circulation, 66,* 83–92.

Friedrich-Cofer, L., & Huston, A. C. (1986). Television violence and aggression: The debate continues. *Psychological Bulletin, 100,* 364–371.

Frost, P. J., Moore, L. F., Louis, M. R., Lundberg, C. C., & Martin, J. (Eds.). (1985). *Organizational Culture.* Beverly Hills, CA: Sage.

Fryer, D., & Payne, R. (1986). Being unemployed: A review of the literature on the psychological experience of unemployment. In C. L. Cooper and I. T. Robertson (Eds.), *International Review of Industrial and Organizational Psychology.* Chichester, England: Wiley.

Funder, D. C. (1987). Errors and mistakes: Evaluating the accuracy of social judgment. *Psychological Bulletin, 101,* 75–90.

Galanter, E. (1962). Contemporary psychophysics. In R. Brown, E. Galanter, E. Hess, & G. Maroler (Eds.), *New directions in psychology.* New York: Holt.

Garfield, S. L., & Bergin, A. E. (Eds.). (1986). *Handbook of psychotherapy and behavior change* (3rd ed.). New York: Wiley.

Garson, B. (1975). *All the Livelong Day.* New York: Penguin.

Gastorf, J. W. (1980). Time urgency of the Type A behavior pattern. *Journal of Consulting and Clinical Psychology, 48,* 299.

Geen, R. G., & Thomas, S. L. (1986). The immediate effects of media violence on behavior. *Journal of Social Issues, 42,* 7–27.

Gerbner, G., Gross, L., Jackson-Beek, M., Jeffries-Fox, S., & Signorielli, N. (1978). Cultural indicators: Violence profile. *Journal of Communication, 28,* 176–207.

Gergen, K. H. (1965). The effects of interaction goals and personalistic feedback on presentation of self. *Journal of Personality and Social Psychology, 26,* 309–320.

Gerson, K. (1985). *Hard choices: How women decide about work, career, and motherhood.* Berkeley: University of California Press.

Gilligan, C. (1982). *In a different voice.* Cambridge: Harvard University Press.

Ginzberg, E. (1972). Toward a theory of occupational choice: A restatement. *Vocational Guidance Quarterly, 12,* 10–14.

Glenn, N. D., & Weaver, C. N. (1977). The marital happiness of remarried divorced persons. *Journal of Marriage and the Family, 39,* 331–337.

Glick, P., & Spanier, G. B. (1980). Married and unmarried cohabitation in the United States. *Journal of Marriage and Family, 42,* 19–30.

Goethals, G. R. (1986). Social comparison theory: Psychology from the lost and found. *Personality and Social Psychology Bulletin, 12,* 261–278.

Goldstein, A. P., & Kanfer, F. H. (1986). *Helping people change: A textbook of methods* (3rd ed.). New York: Pergamon.

Goldstein, M. J., Baker, B. L., & Jamison, K. R. (1980). *Abnormal psychology: Experiences, origins, and interventions.* Boston: Little, Brown.

Goleman, D. (1985, February 5). Mourning: New studies affirm its benefits. *The New York Times,* pp. C1–C2.

Goode, W. J. (1976). Family disorganization. In R. Merton & R. Nisbett (Eds.), *Contemporary social problems* (4th ed.). New York: Harcourt Brace Jovanovich.

Gordon, S. E., Wyer, R. S., Jr. (1987). Person memory: Category-set-size effects on the recall of a person's behavior. *Journal of Personality and Social Psychology, 53,* 648–662.

Gould, R. L. (1978). *Transformations.* New York: Simon and Schuster.

Gray, L. B., & Applebaum, M. I. (1979). Instrumental effects in the assessment of racial differences in self-esteem. *Journal of Personality and Social Psychology, 37,* 1221–1229.

Green, B. L. (1986). On the confounding of 'hassles' stress and outcome. *American Psychologist, 41,* 714–715.

Greenblatt, M. (1978). The grieving spouse. *American Journal of Psychiatry, 135,* 43–47.

Greene, L., & Riess, M. (1984, April). *The role of gaze in managing impressions of dominance and submission.* Paper presented at the annual meeting of the Eastern Psychological Association, Baltimore.

Gribbons, W. D., & Lohnes, P. R. (1965). Shifts in adolescents' vocational values. *Personal and Guidance Journal, 43,* 248–252.

Groth, A. N. (1979). *Men who rape: The psychology of the offender.* New York: Plenum.

Grusec, J. E., Kuczynski, L., Rushton, J. P., & Simutis, Z. M. (1978). Modeling, direct instruction, and attributions: Effects on altruism. *Developmental Psychology, 14,* 51–57.

Grusec, J. E., & Skubiski, S. L. (1970). Model nurturance, demand characteristics of the modeling experiment, and altruism. *Journal of Personality and Social Psychology, 14,* 352–359.

Gubrium, J. G. (1973). *The myth of the golden years: A socioenvironmental theory of aging.* Springfield, IL: Thomas.

Hall, E. T. (1966). *Beyond Culture.* New York: Anchor/Doubleday.

Hall, J. (1985). *Nonverbal sex differences: Communication accuracy and expressive style.* Baltimore: Johns Hopkins University Press.

Harackiewicz, J. M., & Larson, J. R. (1986). Managing motivation: The impact of supervisor feedback on subordinate task interest. *Journal of Personality and Social Psychology, 51,* 547–556.

Harlow, H. F., & Zimmerman, R. R. (1959). Affectional responses in the infant monkey. *Science, 130,* 421–432.

Harris, L. (1987). *Inside America.* New York: Vintage.

Harris, R. L., Ellicott, A. M., & Holmes, D. S. (1986). The timing of psychosocial transitions and changes in women's lives: An examination of women aged 45 to 60. *Journal of Personality and Social Psychology, 51,* 409–416.

Hart, R. P., Friedrich, G. W., & Brooks, W. D. (1975). *Public communication.* New York: Harper & Row.

Hartmen, W., & Fithian, M. (1984). *Any man can.* New York: St. Martin's.

Hathaway, B. (1984, July). Running to ruin. *Psychology Today, 18,* 14–15.

Hayduk, L. A. (1978). Personal space: An evaluation and orienting review. *Psychological Bulletin, 85*, 117–134.

Hayduk, L. A. (1983). Personal space: Where we now stand. *Psychological Bulletin, 94*, 293–335.

Heather, N., Robertson, I., & Davies, P. (Eds.). (1985). *In misuse of alcohol: Crucial issues in dependence treatment and prevention.* New York: New York University Press.

Heckhausen, H., Schmalt, H., & Schneider, K. (1985). *Achievement motivation in perspective.* (Margaret Woodruff & Robert Wicklund, Trans.). Orlando, FL: Academic.

Heider, F. (1958). *The psychology of interpersonal relations.* New York: Wiley.

Heiman, J., LoPiccolo, L., & LoPiccolo, J. (1976). *Becoming orgasmic: A sexual growth program for women.* Englewood Cliffs, NJ: Prentice-Hall.

Hendrick, C., & Hendrick, S. (1983). *Liking, loving, and relating.* Monterey, CA: Brooks/Cole.

Henley, N. M. (1977). *The body politics.* Englewood Cliffs, NJ: Prentice-Hall.

Hensen, W. B., & Altman, I. (1976). Decorating personal places: A descriptive analysis. *Environment and Behavior, 8*, 491–504.

Herschman, R. S., Leventhal, H., & Glynn, K. (1984). The development of smoking behavior: Conceptualization and supportive cross-sectional survey data. *Journal of Applied Social Psychology, 14*, 184–206.

Hersh, R. H., Paolitto, D. P., & Reimer, J. (1979). *Promoting moral growth.* New York: Longmans.

Hess, E. H. (1975). *The tell-tale eye.* New York: Van Nostrand-Reinhold.

Hill, C. J., & Stull, D. E. (1981). Sex differences in effects of social and value similarity in same-sex friendship. *Journal of Personality and Social Psychology, 41*, 488–502.

Hirschman, R. S., Leventhal, H. & Glynn, K. (1984.) The development of smoking behavior: Conceptualization and supportive cross-sectional survey data. *Journal of Applied Social Psychology, 14*, 184–206.

Holahan, C. J. (1982). *Environmental psychology.* New York: Random House.

Holahan, C. J. (1986). Environmental psychology. In M. R. Rosenweig and L. W. Porter (Eds.), *Annual review of psychology.* Palo Alto, CA: Annual Reviews.

Holahan, C. J., & Moos, R. H. (1987). Personal and contextual determinants of coping strategies. *Journal of Personality and Social Psychology, 52*, 946–955.

Holden, C. (1985). A guarded endorsement for shock therapy. *Science, 1228*, 1510–1511.

Holmes, D. S. (1985). To meditate or rest? The answer is rest. *American Psychologist, 40*, 728–731.

Holmes, T. H., & Rahe, R. H. (1967). The social readjustment rating scale. *Journal of Psychosomatic Research, 11*, 213–218.

Hopson, J. L. (1986, June). The unraveling of insomnia. *Psychology Today, 20*, 43–49.

Horn, M. C., & Bachrach, C. A. (1985). *1982 National Survey of Family Growth.* Washington, DC: National Center for Health Statistics.

Horner, M. S. (1972). Toward an understanding of achievement related conflicts. *Journal of Social Issues, 28*, 157–176.

Howard, J. (1978). *Families.* New York: Simon and Schuster.

Howells, J. G., & Osborn, M. L. (1984). *A reference companion to the history of abnormal psychology.* Westport, CT: Greenwood Press.

Hoyenga, K. B., & Hoyenga, K. T. (1984). *Motivational explanations of behavior: Evolutionary, psychological, and cognitive ideas.* Monterey, CA: Brooks/Cole.

Hunt, M. (1974). *Sexual behaviors in the 1970s.* New York: Dell.

Huntley, C. W., & Davis, F. (1983). Undergraduate study of value scores as predictors of occupation 25 years later. *Journal of Personality and Social Psychology, 45,* 1148–1155.

Hyde, J. (1986). *Understanding human sexuality.* New York: McGraw-Hill.

Hyland, M. E., Curtis, C., & Mason, D. (1985). Fear of success: Motive and cognition. *Journal of Personality and Social Psychology, 49,* 1669–1677.

Iaffaldano, M. T., & Muchinsky, P. M. (1985). Job satisfaction and job performance: A meta-analysis. *Psychological Bulletin, 97,* 151–173.

Isen, A. M., & Levin, P. F. (1972). Effect of feeling good on helping: Cookies and kindness. *Journal of Personality and Social Psychology, 21,* 384–388.

Izard, C. E. (1977). *Human emotions.* New York: Plenum.

Jacobson, E. (1938). *Progressive relaxation.* Chicago: University of Chicago Press.

Jahoda, M. (1982). *Employment and unemployment.* Cambridge, England: Cambridge University Press.

Janda, L. H., & Klenke-Hamel, K. E. (1980). *Human sexuality.* New York: Van Nostrand.

Janis, I., & Mann, L. (1977). *Decision-making.* New York: Free Press.

Janis, I., & Wheeler, D. (1978). Thinking clearly about career choices. *Psychology Today,* pp. 66–76, 121–122.

Jones, E. E., & Goethals, G. R. (1972). *Order effects in impression formation: Attribution context and the nature of the entity.* Morristown, NJ: General Learning Press.

Jourard, S. M. (1970). Experimenter-subject distance and self disclosure. *Journal of Personality and Social Psychology, 15,* 278–282.

Jourard, S. M. (1971). *Self-disclosure.* New York: Wiley.

Jussim, L., Coleman, L. M., & Lerch, L. (1987). The nature of stereotypes: A comparison and integration of three theories. *Journal of Personality and Social Psychology, 52,* 536–546.

Kane, J. M. (1983). Hypothesis regarding the mechanism of action of anti-depressant drugs: Neurotransmitters in affective disorders. In A. Rifkin (Ed.), *Schizophrenia and affective disorders: Biology and drug treatment* (pp. 19–34). Boston: John Wright.

Kanner, A. D., Coyne, J. C., Schaefer, C., & Lazarus, R. (1981). Comparison of two modes of stress measurement: Daily hassles and uplifts versus major life events. *Journal of Behavioral Medicine, 4,* 14.

Kantrowitz, B. (1986, September 1). Three's a crowd. *Newsweek,* pp. 68–76.

Kaplan, H. S. (1974). *The new sex therapy.* New York: Brunner-Mazel.

Kaplan, M. F. (1983, May). *Effect of training on reasoning in moral choice.* Paper presented at the meeting of the Midwestern Psychological Association, Chicago.

Karoly, P., & Kanfer, F. H. (1982). *Self management and behavior change.* New York: Pergamon.

Kaufmann, Yoram. (1979). Analytical psychotherapy. In Raymond J. Corsini and contributors, *Current psychotherapies* (p. 111). Itasca, IL: F. E. Peacock.

Kazdin, A. E., & Wilson, G. T. (1978). *Evaluation of behavior therapy: Is-*

sues, evidence, and research strate-gies. Cambridge, MA: Ballinger.

Keating, D. P., & Clark, L. V. (1980). Development of physical and social reasoning in adolescence. *Developmental Psychology, 16,* 23–30.

Kelley, H. H. (1983). Love and commitment. In H. H. Kelley, E. Berscheid, A. Christensen, J. Harvey, T. L. Huston, G. Levinger, E. McClintock, A. Peplau, & D. R. Peterson, (Eds.). *Close relationships.* San Francisco: Freeman.

Kelley, H. (1950). The warm-cold variable in first impressions of persons. *Journal of Personality and Social Psychology, 18,* 431–439.

Kerr, P. (1986, May 18). Opium dens for the crack era. *The New York Times,* pp. 1, 38.

Killman, P. R., & Mills, K. H. (1983). *All about sex therapy.* New York: Plenum.

Kinsey, A. C., Pomeroy, W. B., & Martin, C. E. (1948). *Sexual behavior in the human male.* Philadelphia, Saunders.

Kleinke, C. L. (1986). Gaze and eye contact: A research review. *Psychological Bulletin, 100,* 78–100.

Knapp, M. L. (1984). *Interpersonal communication and human relationships.* Boston: Allyn & Bacon.

Knott, D. H. (1986). *Alcohol problems: Diagnosis and treatment.* New York: Pergamon.

Knox, D. (1979). *Exploring marriage and the family.* Glenview, IL: Scott, Foresman.

Kohlberg, L. (1984). *The psychology of moral development: Essays on moral development* (Vol. 2). San Francisco: Harper & Row.

Konecni, V. (1975). Annoyance, type and duration of postannoyance activity, and aggression: The "cathartic effect." *Journal of Experimental Psychology, 104,* 76–102.

Krantz, D., Baum, A., & Wideman, M. V. (1980). Assessment of preferences for self-treatment and information in health care. *Journal of Personality and Social Psychology, 39,* 977–990.

Kryter, K. (1985). *The effects of noise on man* (2nd ed.). Orlando, FL: Academic.

Kübler-Ross, E. (1969). *On death and dying.* New York: Macmillan.

Kuhn, M. H., & McPartland, T. S. (1954). An empirical investigation of self attitudes. *American Sociological Review, 19,* 68–76.

Kurtines, W. M., & Gewirtz, J. L. (Eds.). (1987). *Moral development through social interaction.* New York: Wiley.

Labov, W. (1973). The logic of nonstandard English. In N. Keddie (Ed.), *Tinker, tailor . . . The myth of cultural deprivation* (pp. 21–66). Harmondsworth, England: Penguin Education.

LaFrance, M., & Mayo, C. (1976). *Moving bodies: Nonverbal communication in social relationships.* Monterey, CA: Brooks/Cole.

Lamb, M. F. (1982). Paternal influences on early socio-economic development. *Journal of Child Psychology and Psychiatry and Allied Disciplines.*

Landis, D., Day, H. R., McGrew, P. L., Thomas, J. A., & Miller, A. B. (1976). Can a black "culture assimilator" increase racial understanding? *Journal of Social Issues, 32,* 169–184.

Landy, F. J. (1985). *The psychology of work behavior.* Homewood, IL: Dorsey.

Latané, B., & Darley, J. M. (1970). *The unresponsive bystander: Why doesn't he help?* New York: Appleton-Crofts.

Latané, B., & Nida, S. (1981). Ten years of research on group size and helping. *Psychological Bulletin, 89,* 308–324.

Lauer, J., & Lauer, R. (1985, June). Marriages made to last. *Psychology Today, 19,* 22–26.

Lawler, E. E. (1981). *Pay and organizational development.* Reading, MA: Addison-Wesley.

Lazarus, R. S., & Cohen, J. B. (1977). Environmental stress. In I. Altman & J. F. Wohlwill (Eds.), *Human behavior and the environment: Current theory and research* (Vol. 2). New York: Plenum.

Leibowitz, H. W., & Owens, D. A. (1986, January). "We drive by night." *Psychology Today,* 55–58.

Leigh, H., & Reiser, M. F. (1980). *The patient.* New York: Plenum.

LeMagnen, J. (1985). *Hunger.* Cambridge, England: Cambridge University Press.

LeMasters, E. E. (1977). *Parents in modern America: A sociological analysis* (3rd ed.). Homewood, IL: Dorsey.

Lepper, M. R., Greene, D., & Nisbett, R. E. (1973). Undermining children's intrinsic interest with extrinsic reward: A test of the overjustification hypothesis. *Journal of Personality and Social Psychology, 23,* 129–137.

Leventhal, H., & Cleary, P. D. (1980). The smoking problem: A review of the research and theory in behavioral risk modification. *Psychological Bulletin, 88,* 370–405.

Leventhal, H., Nerenz, D., & Leventhal, E. (1985). Feelings of threat and private views of illness: Factors in dehumanizing in the medical care system. In A. Baum and J. E. Singer (Eds.), *Advances in environmental psychology* (Vol. 4). Hillsdale, NJ: Erlbaum.

Levinger, G. A. (1974). A three-level approach to attraction: Toward an understanding of pair relatedness. In T. L. Huston (Ed.), *Foundations of interpersonal attraction.* New York: Academic.

Levinger, G. (1979). A social psychological perspective on marital dissolution. In G. Levinger and D. C. Moles (Eds.), *Divorce and separation.* New York: Basic Books.

Levinson, D. J. (1986). A conception of adult development. *American Psychologist, 41,* 3–13.

Ley, D., & Cybriwsky, R. (1974). Urban graffiti as territorial markers. *Annals of the Association of American Geographers, 64,* 491–505.

Ley, P., & Spelman, M. S. (1967). *Communicating with the patient.* London: Staples Press.

Lieberman, M. A. (1982). The effects of social supports on responses to stress. In L. Goldberger and L. Breznitz (Eds.), *Handbook of stress.* New York: Free Press.

Locke, E. A. (1976). The nature and causes of job satisfaction. In M. D. Dunnette (Ed.), *Handbook of industrial and organizational psychology.* Chicago: Rand McNally.

Locke, E. A., & Henne, D. (1986). Work motivation theories. In C. L. Cooper and I. T. Robertson (Eds.), *International Review of Industrial and Organizational Psychology.* Chichester, England: Wiley.

Locke, E. A., & Schweiger, D. M. (1979). Participation in decision making: One more look. In B. Staw (Eds.), *Research in Organizational Behavior* (Vol. 1). Greenwich, Conn.: JAI Press.

Locksley, A., Ortiz, V., & Hepburn, C. (1980). Social categorization and discriminatory behavior: Extinguishing the minimal intergroup discrimination effect. *Journal of Personality and Social Psychology, 39,* 773–783.

Long, T. E., & Richard, W. C. (1986). *Community post-tornado support groups: Conceptual issues and personal themes.* Paper presented at the meeting of the American Psychological Association, Washington, DC.

Longyear, M. (1983) (Ed.). *The McGraw-Hill style manual*. New York: McGraw-Hill.

Lorenz, K. (1974). *Civilized man's eight deadly sins*. New York: Harcourt Brace Jovanovich.

Luchins, A. S. (1957). Experimental attempts to minimize the impact of first impressions. In C. I. Hovland (Ed.), *The order of presentation in persuasion* (pp. 62–75). New Haven, CT: Yale University Press.

Lynch, J. G., Jr., & Cohen, J. L. (1978). The use of subjective expected utility theory as an aid to understanding variables that influence helping behavior. *Journal of Personality and Social Psychology, 36*, 1138–1151.

MacDonald, M. L., & Tobias, L. L. (1976). Withdrawal causes relapse? Our response. *Psychological Bulletin, 83*, 448–451.

MacDonald, M. R., & Kulper, N. A. (1983). Cognitive-behavioral preparations for surgery: Some theoretical and methodological concerns. *Clinical Psychology Review, 3*, 27–39.

MacDonald, N. (1960). Living with schizophrenia. *The Canadian Medical Association Journal, 82*.

Maddi, S. R., Bartone, P. T., & Puccetti, M. C. (1987). Stressful events are indeed a factor in physical illness: Reply to Schroeder and Costa (1984). *Journal of Personality and Social Psychology, 52*, 833–843.

Mahoney, E. R. (1983). *Human sexuality*. New York: McGraw-Hill.

Maier, N. R. F. (1967). Assets and liabilities in group problem solving: The need for an integrative function. *Psychological Review, 47*, 239–247.

Malamuth, N. M. (1981). Rape proclivity in males. *Journal of Social Issues, 37*(4), 138–157.

Malamuth, N., & Donnerstein, E. (1982). The effects of aggressive-pornographic mass media stimuli. In L. Berkowitz (Ed.), *Advances in experimental social psychology* (Vol. 15). New York: Academic.

Malanka, P. A. (1986, February). Quit smoking for someone you love. *Health, 18*, 27–36.

Malinak, D. P., Hoyt, M. F., & Patterson, V. (1979). Adults' reactions to the death of a parent: A preliminary study. *American Journal of Psychiatry, 136*.

Marini, M. M. (1978). Sex differences in the determination of adolescent aspirations: A review of research. *Sex Roles, 4*, 723–753.

Markson, Elizabeth W. (1985). After deinstitutionalization, what? *Journal of Geriatric Psychiatry, 18*, 37–56.

Martin, A. J. (1975). *One man, hurt*. New York: Macmillan.

Martin C. L. (1987). A ratio measure of sex stereotyping. *Journal of Personality and Social Psychology, 52*, 489–499.

Martin, D., & Martin, M. (1984). Selected attitudes toward marriage and family life among college students. *Family Relations, 33*, 293–300.

Martz, L. (1986, August 11). Trying to say "no." *Newsweek*, pp. 14–19.

Marx, M. B., Garrity, T. F., & Bowers, F. R. (1975). The influence of recent life experience on the health of college freshmen. *Journal of Psychosomatic Research, 19*, 87–98.

Maslach, C. (1982). *Burnout—the cost of caring*. Englewood Cliffs, NJ: Prentice-Hall.

Maslow, A. (1970). *Motivation and personality*. New York: Harper & Row.

Masters, J. C., Buriski, T. G., Hollon, S. D., & Rimm, D. C. (1987). *Behavior therapy* (3rd ed.). San Diego: Harcourt Brace Jovanovich.

Masters, W. H., & Johnson, V. E. (1966). *Human sexual response*. Boston: Little, Brown.

Masters, W. H., Johnson, V. E., & Kolodny, R. C. (1988). *Crisis: Heterosexual Behavior in the Age of AIDS*. New York: Grove Press.

Masters, W. H., Johnson, V. E., & Kolodny, R. C. (1985). *Human sexuality*. Boston: Little, Brown.

Mathes, E. W. (1975). The effects of physical attractiveness and anxiety on heterosexual attraction over a series of five encounters. *Journal of Marriage and the Family*, 769–773.

Matthews, K. A. (1982). Psychological perspectives on the Type A behavior pattern. *Psychological Bulletin, 91,* 293–323.

Mayo, E. (1933). *The Human Problems of an Industrial Civilization*. New York: Macmillan.

McCammon, S., Parker, L., & Horton, R. (1986). Community post-tornado support groups: Intervention and evaluation. Paper presented at the annual meeting of the American Psychological Association.

McClelland, D. C., Atkinson, J. W., Clark, R. A., & Lowell, E. L. (1953). *The achievement motive*. New York: Appleton-Century-Crofts.

McKusick, L., Coates, T., & Horstman, W. (1985). *HTLV-III transmitting behavior and desire for HTLV-III: Antibody testing in San Francisco on men at risk from AIDS 1982–1985*. Report from the AIDS Behavioral Research Project. The Public Health Department of the City and County of San Francisco.

McNeal, E. T., & Cimbolic, P. (1986). Antidepressants and biochemic theories of depression. *Psychological Bulletin, 99,* 361–374.

McNeil, E. (1967). *The quiet furies*. Englewood Cliffs, NJ: Prentice-Hall.

Mead, G. H. (1934). *Mind, self, and society*. Chicago, IL: University of Chicago.

Mehrabian, A. (1968a). Interference of attitude from the posture orientation and distance of a communicator. *Journal of Consulting and Clinical Psychology, 32,* 296–308.

Mehrabian, A. (1968b). Relationship of attitude to seated posture, orientation, and distance. *Journal of Personality and Social Psychology, 10,* 26–30.

Meichenbaum, D. (1977). *Cognitive-behavior modification: An integrative approach*. New York: Plenum.

Mentzer, S. J., & Snyder, M. L. (1982). The doctor and the patient: A psychological perspective. In G. S. Sanders and J. Suls (Eds.), *Social Psychology of health and illness* (pp. 161–181). Hillsdale, NJ: Erlbaum.

Mettee, D. R., & Aronson, E. (1974). Affective reactions to appraisal from others. In T. L. Huston (Ed.), *Foundations of interpersonal attraction* (pp. 235–283). New York: Academic.

Meyer, J. P., & Pepper, S. (1977). Need compatibility and marital adjustment in young married couples. *Journal of Personality and Social Psychology, 35,* 331–342.

Meyer, T. J. (1984, December 5). "Date rape": A serious campus problem that few talk about. *Chronicle of Higher Education, 29,* 1, 12.

Middlebrook, P. (1974). *Social psychology and modern life*. New York: Knopf.

Milgram, J. (1974). *Obedience to authority*. New York: Harper & Row.

Miller, G. R., Bauchner, J. E., Hocking, J. E., Fontes, N. E., Kaminski, E. P., & Brandt, D. R. (1981). "... and nothing but the truth": How well can observers detect deceptive testimony? *Perspectives in law and psychology: Vol. 2. The trial process*. New York: Plenum.

Miller, G. R., & Burgoon, J. K. (1982). Factors affecting assessment of witness credibility. In N. N. Kerr & R. Bray

(Eds.), *The psychology of the court-room* (pp. 176–177). New York: Academic.

Miller, L. L. (Ed.). (1975). *Marijuana: Current research.* New York: Academic.

Miller, N. E. (1985, February). Rx: Biofeedback. *Psychology Today,* pp. 54–59.

Miller, R., & Sperry, R. (1987). The socialization of anger and aggression. *Merrill Palmer Quarterly, 33,* 1–31.

Miller, W. R., & Lief, H. I. (1976). Masturbatory attitudes, knowledge, and experience. Data from the Sex Knowledge and Attitude Test (SKAT). *Archives of Sexual Behavior, 5,* 447–458.

Millon, T. (1981). *Disorders of personality: DSM-III: Axis II.* New York: Wiley.

Mineka, S., & Henderson, R. W. (1985). Controllability and predictability in acquired motivation. *Annual Review of Psychology, 36,* 495–529.

Mitchell, T. R. (1982). *People in organizations: An introduction to organizational behavior* (2nd ed.). New York: McGraw-Hill.

Mobley, W. H., Horner, S. O., & Hollingsworth, A. T. (1978). An evaluation of precursors of hospital employee turnover. *Journal of Applied Psychology, 63,* 408–414.

Moos, R. H., & Schaefer, J. A. (1986). Life transitions and crises: A conceptual overview. In R. H. Moos (Ed.), *Coping with life crises: An integrated approach.* New York: Plenum.

Morganthau, T. (1986, November 24). Future shock. *Newsweek,* pp. 30–39.

Morin, S. F., Charles, K. A., & Malyon, A. K. (1984). The psychological impact of AIDS on gay men. *American Psychologist, 39,* 1288–1293.

Motley, M. T. (1987, February). What I meant to say. *Psychology Today,* pp. 24–28.

Nahemow, L., & Lawton, M. P. (1976). Similarity and propinquity in friendship formation. *Journal of Personality and Social Psychology, 32,* 205–213.

Nass, G. D. (1978). *Marriage and the family.* Reading, MA: Addison-Wesley.

National Academy of Sciences. (1982). *Marijuana and health.* Washington, DC: National Academy Press.

Nelson, B. (1983, April 2). Despair among jobless is on the rise, studies find. *The New York Times,* p. 22.

The new addicts. (1984, May 20). *The New York Times,* p. 50.

Nickerson, R. S. (1986). *Reflections on reasoning.* Hillsdale, NJ: Erlbaum.

Nisbett, R. E. (1968). Taste, deprivation, and weight determinants of eating behavior. *Journal of Personality and Social Psychology, 10,* 107–116.

Nisbett, R. E. (1972). Hunger, obesity, and the ventromedial hypothalamus. *Psychological Review, 79,* 433–453.

Nisbett, R., & Ross, L. (1980). *Human inference: Strategies and shortcomings.* Englewood Cliffs, NJ: Prentice-Hall.

Noll, K. M., Davis, J. M., & DeLeon-Jones, F. (1985). Medication and somatic therapies in the treatment of depression. In E. E. Beckhman & W. R. Leber (Eds.), *Handbook of depression: Treatment, assessment, and research.* Homewood, IL: Dorsey.

NORC (National Opinion Research Center) (1982). *General social surveys, 1972–1982: Cumulative codebook.* Chicago: National Opinion Research Center.

Norvell, N., & Worchel, S. (1981). A reexamination of the relation between equal status contact and intergroup attraction. *Journal of Personality and Social Psychology, 41,* 902–908.

Nunnally, E. W., Miller, S., & Wackman, D. B. (1975). The Minnesota couples communication program. *Small Group Behavior, 6,* 57–71.

O'Neill, N., & O'Neill, G. (1972). *Open marriage: A new lifestyle for couples.* New York: M. Evans & Company.

Orford, J. (1985). *Excessive appetites: A psychological view of addictions.* Chichester, England: Wiley.

Orwin, R. G., & Condray, D. S. (1984). Smith and Glass' psychotherapy conclusions need further probing: On Landsman and Dawes' re-analysis. *American Psychologist, 39,* 71–72.

Osborne, A. F. (1957). *Applied imagination.* New York: Scribner.

Papalia, D. (1972). The status of several conservation abilities across the life span. *Human Development, 15,* 229–243.

Paterson, R. J., & Neufeld, R. W. J. (1987). Clear danger: Situational determinants of the appraisal of threat. *Psychological Bulletin, 101,* 404–416.

Paulus, P. B., & McCain, G. (1983). Crowding in jails. *Basic and Applied Social Psychology, 4,* 89–107.

Peplau, L. A., Miceli, M., & Moras, B. (1982). Loneliness and self-evaluation. In L. A. Peplau & D. Perlman (Eds.), *Loneliness.* New York: Wiley.

Peplau, L. A., Rubin, Z., & Hill, C. T. (1977). Sexual intimacy in dating relationships. *Journal of Social Issues, 33*(2), 76–109.

Perls, F. S. (1967). Group vs. individual therapy. *ETC: A review of general semantics, 34,* 306–312.

Perls, F. S. (1970). *Gestalt therapy now: Therapy, techniques, applications.* Palo Alto, CA: Science and Behavior Books.

Peterson, C., Semmel, A., von Baeyer, C., Abramson, L. Y., Metalsky, G. I., & Seligman, M. E. P. (1982). The attributional style questionnaire. *Cognitive Therapy and Research, 6,* 287–300.

Pettingale, K. W., Morris, T., Greer, S., & Haybittle, J. L. (1985). Mental attitudes to cancer: An additional prognostic factor. *Lancet,* 750.

Pfeiffer, E., Verwoerdt, A., & Wang, H. S. (1968). Sexual behavior in aged men and women. *Archives of General Psychiatry, 19,* 753–758.

Piaget, J. (1970). Piaget's theory. In P. H. Mussen (Ed.), *Carmichael's manual of child psychology* (Vol. 1, 3rd ed.). New York: Wiley.

Polivy, J., & Herman, L. P. (1985). Dieting and binging: A causal analysis. *American Psychologist, 40,* 193–201.

Pomerleau, O. F., & Pomerleau, C. S. (1977). *Breaking the smoking habit: A behavioral program for giving up cigarettes.* Champaign, IL: Research Press.

Pritchard, C. (1985). *Avoiding rape on and off campus.* Wenonah, NJ: State College Publishing Company.

Rachman, S., & Hodgson, R. (1980). *Obsessions and compulsions.* Englewood Cliffs, NJ: Prentice-Hall.

Ragozin, A. S. (1980). Attachment behavior of day care children: Naturalistic and laboratory observations. *Child Development, 51,* 409–415.

Reese, H. W., Treffinger, D. J., Parnes, S. J., & Kaltsounis, G. (1976). Effects of a creative studies program on structure-of-intellect factors. *Journal of Educational Psychology, 68,* 401–410.

Reinke, B. J., Holmes, D. S., & Harris, R. L. (1985). The timing of psychosocial changes in women's lives: The years 25–45. *Journal of Personality and Social Psychology, 48,* 1353–1364.

Reiss, B. F. (1980). Psychological tests in homosexuality. In J. Marmor (Ed.), *Homosexual behavior* (pp. 296–311). New York: Basic Books.

Reiss, M. (1985, April). "Dear God, help me—I can't hang on." *Readers' Digest,* 60–64.

Repetti, R. L. (1987). Individual and common components of the social environment at work and psychological well-being. *Journal of Personality and Social Psychology, 52,* 710–720.

Rinn, W. E. (1984). The neuropsychology of facial expression: A review of neurological and psychological mechanisms for producing facial expressions. *Psychological Bulletin, 95,* 52–77.

Robbins, M., & Jensen, G. D. (1978). Multiple orgasm in males. *Journal of Sex Research, 14,* 21–26.

Roberts, A. H. (1985). Biofeedback: Research, training, and clinical roles. *American Psychologist, 40,* 938–941.

Rodin, J. (1986, September 19). Aging and health: Effects of the sense of control. *Science, 233,* 1271–1276.

Rodin, J., & Langer, E. (1980). Aging labels: The decline of control and the fall of self-esteem. *Journal of Social Issues, 36,* 12–29.

Roethlisberger, F. J., & Dickson, W. V. (1939). *Management and the worker.* Cambridge: Harvard University Press.

Rogers, C. R. (1951). *Client-centered therapy.* Boston: Houghton Mifflin.

Rogers, C. R. (1971). A theory of personality. In S. Maddi (Ed.), *Perspectives on personality.* Boston: Little, Brown.

Rogers, C. R. (1980). *A way of being.* Boston: Houghton Mifflin.

Rosenhan, D. L., Moore, B. S., & Underwood, B. (1976). The social psychology of moral behavior. In T. Lickona (Ed.), *Moral development and behavior: Theory, research, and social issues.* New York: Holt.

Rosenman, R. H., Brand, R. J., Jenkins, C. D., Friedman, M., Straus, R., & Wurn, M. (1975). Coronary heart disease in the Western Collaborative Group Study: Final follow-up experience of 8½ years. *Journal of the American Medical Association, 233,* 872–877.

Rosenstock, I. M. (1966). Why people use health services. *Milbank Memorial Fund Quarterly, 44,* 94–127.

Ross, L., Greene, D., & House, P. (1977). The "false consensus effect": An egocentric bias in social perception and attribution processes. *Journal of Experimental Social Psychology, 13,* 279–301.

Roth, S., & Cohen, L. J. (1986). Approach, avoidance, and coping with stress. *American Psychologist, 41,* 813–819.

Rotter, J. B. (1966). Generalized expectancies for internal versus external control of reinforcement. *Psychological Monographs, 80* (Whole No. 609).

Rowe, J. W., & Kahn, R. L. (1987, July 10). Human aging: Usual and successful. *Science, 237,* 143–149.

Royer, J. M., & Feldman, R. S. (1984). *Educational psychology: Applications and theory.* New York: Knopf.

Rubeck, R. B., Dabbs, J. M., Jr., & Hopper, C. H. (1984). The process of brainstorming: An analysis with individual and group vocal parameters. *Journal of Personality and Social Psychology, 47,* 558–567.

Rubin, Z. (1973). *Liking and loving: An invitation to social psychology.* New York: Holt.

Russell, C. (1985, October). The new homemakers. *American Demographics,* 23–27.

Russell, D. E. H., & Howell, Nancy (1983). The prevalence of rape in the United States revisited. *Signs, 8,* 688–695.

Ruth, J. E., and Birren, J. E. (1985). Creativity in adulthood and old age: Relations to intelligence, sex and mode of testing. *International Journal of Behavioral Development, 8,* 99–109.

Rutter, M. (1982). Social-emotional consequences of day care for preschool children. In E. F. Zigler & E. W. Gordon

(Eds.), *Day care: Scientific and social policy issues.* Boston: Auburn House.

Sackheim, H. A. (1985, June). The case for E.C.T. *Psychology Today, 19,* 36–40.

Sacks, H., Schegloff, E. A., & Jefferson, G. (1974). A simplest systematics for the organization of turn-taking for conversation. *Language, 50,* 696–735.

Salber, E. J., Freeman, H. E., & Abelin, T. (1968). Needed research on smoking: Lessons from the Newton study. In E. F. Borgatta & R. R. Evans (Eds.), *Smoking, health and behavior.* Chicago: Aldine.

Sapir, E. (1949). *Selected writings of Edward Sapir.* D. G. Mandelbaum (Ed.). Berkeley and Los Angeles: University of California Press.

Sarason, I. G. (1976). A modeling and informational approach to delinquency. In E. Rebes-Inesta & A. Bandura (Eds.), *Analysis of delinquency and aggression.* Hillsdale, NJ: Erlbaum.

Savinar, J. (1975). The effect of ceiling height on personal space. *Man-Environment Systems, 5,* 321–324.

Schachter, S. (1982). Recidivism and self-cure of smoking and obesity. *American Psychologist, 37,* 436–444.

Schachter, S. (1971). Some extraordinary facts about obese humans and rats. *American Psychologist, 26,* 129–144.

Schaefer, C., Coyne, J. C., & Lazarus, R. S. (1981). The health-related functions of social support. *Journal of Behavioral Medicine, 4,* 381–406.

Scheibel, A., & Kovelman, B. (1986). Biological substrates of schizophrenia. *Acta Neurologica Scandinavica, 73,* 1–32.

Scherer, K. R., & Ekman, P. (Eds.). (1984). *Approaches to emotion.* Hillsdale, NJ: Erlbaum.

Schneidman, E. (1985). *Definition of suicide.* New York: Wiley.

Schneidman, E. (1971, June). You and death. *Psychology Today,* pp. 43–45, 74–80.

Schoeneman, T. J., & Rubanowitz, D. E. (1985). Attributions in the advice columns: Actors and observers, causes and reasons. *Journal of Personality and Social Psychology, 11,* 315–325.

Schofield, A. T., & Vaughan-Jackson, P. (1913). *What a boy should know.* New York: Cassell.

Schofield, W. (1964). *Psychotherapy: The purchase of friendship.* Englewood Cliffs, NJ: Prentice-Hall.

Schroeder, D. H., & Costa, P. T., Jr. (1984). Influence of life events' stress on physical illness: Substantive effects on methodological flaws? *Journal of Personality and Social Psychology, 46,* 853–863.

Schultz, K. A., Schmitt, F. A., Logue, P. A., & Rubin, D. C. (1986). Unit analysis of prose memory in clinical and elderly populations. *Developmental Neuropsychology, 2,* 77–87.

Schwartz, S. H. (1977). Normative influences on altruism. In L. Berkowitz (Ed.), *Advances in experimental social psychology* (Vol. 10). New York: Academic.

Sears. D. O. (1982). The person-positivity bias. *Journal of Personality and Social Psychology, 44,* 233–250.

Seligman, M. E. P. (1975). *Helplessness: On depression, development, and death.* San Francisco: Freeman.

Selye, H. (1976). *The stress of life.* New York: McGraw-Hill.

Shiffman, S., Read, L., & Jarvik, M. E. (1985). Smoking relapse situations: A preliminary typology. *International Journal of the Addictions, 20,* 311–318.

Simberg, A. L. (1971). *Obstacles to creative thinking.* New York: Holt.

Simpson, G. E., & Yinger, J. M. (1985). *Racial and cultural minorities: An analysis of prejudice and discrimination* (5th ed.). New York: Plenum.

Simpson, J. A., Campbell, B., & Berscheid, E. (1986). The association between romantic love and marriage: Kephart (1967) twice revisited. *Journal of Personality and Social Psychology Bulletin, 12,* 363–372.

Singer, J. L., & Singer, D. G. (1981). *Television, imagination, and aggression: A study of preschoolers.* Hillsdale, NJ: Erlbaum.

Siris, S. G., & Rifkin, A. (1983). Side effects of drugs used in the treatment of affective disorders. In A. Rifkin (Ed.), *Schizophrenia and affective disorders: Biology and drug treatment* (pp. 117–138). Boston: John Wright.

Skinner, B. F. (1975). The steep and thorny road to a science of behavior. *American Psychologist, 30,* 42–49.

Skinner, D. A. (1986). Dual-career family stress and coping. In R. H. Moos (Ed.), *Coping with life crises: An integrated approach.* New York: Plenum.

Skrypnek, B. J., & Snyder, M. (1982). On the self-perpetuating nature of stereotypes about women and men. *Journal of Experimental and Social Psychology, 18,* 277–291.

Smith, M. J. L., Glass, G. V., & Miller, T. J. (1980). *The benefits of psychotherapy.* Baltimore: Johns Hopkins.

Snyder, M., & Swann, W. B., Jr. (1978). Hypothesis testing processes in social interaction. *Journal of Personality and Social Psychology, 36,* 1202–1212.

Sommer, R. (1969). *Personal space: The behavioral basis of design.* Englewood Cliffs, NJ: Prentice-Hall.

Sommer, R. (1974). *Tight spaces: Hard architecture and how to humanize it.* Englewood Cliffs, NJ: Prentice-Hall.

Sommer, R., & Becker, F. D. (1969). Territorial defense and the good neighbor. *Journal of Personality and Social Psychology, 11,* 85–92.

Sorrentino, R. M., & Higgins, E. T. (Eds.). (1986). *Handbook of motivation and cognition: Foundations of social behavior.* New York: Guilford Publications.

Sotile, W. M., & Kilmann, P. R. (1977). Treatments of psychogenic female sexual dysfunctions. *Psychological Bulletin, 84,* 619–633.

Stark, S. D. (1987, August 20). Housekeeping today: Just a lick and a promise. *The New York Times,* p. C1.

Staub, E. (1971). A child in distress: The influence of nurturance and modeling on children's attempts to help. *Developmental Psychology, 5,* 124–133.

Staub, E. (Ed.). (1978). *Positive social behavior and morality: Vol. 2. Social and personal influences.* New York: Academic.

Steel, D. (1983). *Thurston House.* New York: Dell.

Steers, R. M., & Porter, L. W. (1983). *Motivation and work behavior* (3rd ed.). New York: McGraw-Hill.

Steers, R. M., & Rhodes, S. R. (1978). Major influences on employee attendance: A process model. *Journal of Applied Psychology, 63,* 391–407.

Sternberg, R. J. (1986a). Intelligence, wisdom, and creativity: Three is better than one. *Educational Psychologist, 21,* 175–190.

Sternberg, R. J. (1986b). Triangular theory of love. *Psychological Review.*

Stires, L. (1980). Classroom seating location, student grades, and attitudes: Environment or self-selection? *Environment and Behavior, 12,* 241–254.

Streib, G. F. (1977). Older people in a family context. In R. A. Kalish (Ed.), *The later years: Social applications of gerontology.* Monterey, CA: Brooks/Cole.

Stricker, E. M., & Zigmond, M. J. (1976). Recovery of function after damage to catecholamine-containing neurons: A neurochemical model for hypothalmic syndrome. In J. M. Sprague & A. N. Epstein (Eds.), *Progress in psychobiology and physiological psychology* (Vol. 6). New York: Academic.

Strupp, H. (1981). Clinical research, practice, and the crisis of confidence. *Journal of Consulting and Clinical Psychology, 49,* 216–219.

Subway altruism. (1982, December 21). *The New York Times,* p. A1.

Sue, D. (1979). Erotic fantasies of college students during coitus. *Journal of Sex Research, 15,* 299–305.

Sulzer-Azaroff, B., & Mayer, G. R. (1986). *Achieving educational excellence with behavioral strategies.* New York: Holt.

Svarstad, B. (1976). Physician-patient communication and patient conformity with medical advice. In D. Mechanic (Eds.), *The growth of bureaucratic medicine.* New York: Wiley.

Sweet, E. (1985, October). Date rape: The story of an epidemic and those who deny it. *MS/Campus Times,* pp. 56–59.

Swenson, C. H. (1972). The behavior of love. In H. A. Otto (Ed.), *Love today: A new exploration.* New York: Association Press.

Szasz, T. (1982). The psychiatric will: A new mechanism for protecting persons against "psychosis" and psychiatry. *American Psychologist, 37,* 762–770.

Szilagyi, A. D., Jr., & Wallace, M. J., Jr. (1987). *Organizational Behavior and Performance* (4th ed.). Glenview, IL: Scott, Foresman.

Tamir, L. M. (1986). Men at middle age: Developmental transitions. In Moos, R. H. (Eds.), *Coping with life crises: An understanding approach.* New York: Plenum.

Tavris, C. (1983). *Anger: The misunderstood emotion.* New York: Simon and Schuster.

Tavris, C., & Jayaratne, T. E. (1976, June). How happy is your marriage? What 75,000 wives say about their most intimate relationship. *Redbook,* pp. 90–92, 132–134.

Tavris, C., & Sadd, S. (1977). *The Redbook report on female sexuality.* New York: Delacorte.

Taylor, J. (1953). A personality scale of manifest anxiety. *Journal of Abnormal and Social Psychology, 48,* 285–290.

Taylor, R. B., & Stough, R. R. (1978). Territorial cognition: Assessing Altman's typology. *Journal of Personality and Social Psychology, 36,* 418–423.

Taylor, S. (1986). *Health psychology.* New York: Random House.

Taylor, S. E. (1982). Hospital patient behavior: Reactance, helplessness, or control. In H. S. Friedman & M. R. DiMatteo (Eds.), *Interpersonal issues in health care.* New York: Academic.

Tennis, G. H., & Dabbs, J. M. (1975). Sex, setting, and personal space: First grade through college. *Sociometry, 38,* 385–394.

Thomas, C. B., Duszynski, K. R., & Schaffer, J. W. (1979). Family attitudes reported in youth as potential predictors of cancer. *Psychosomatic Medicine, 41,* 287–302.

Thompson, Anthony P. (1983). Extramarital sex: A review of the research literature. *Journal of Sex Research, 19,* 1–22.

Tjosvold, D. (1982). Effects of approach to controversy on superiors' incorporation of subordinates' information in decision making. *Journal of Applied Psychology, 67,* 189–193.

Triandis, H. C., & Vassiliou, V. (1967). Frequency of contacts and stereotyping. *Journal of Personality and Social Psychology, 7,* 316–328.

Truax, C. B., & Mitchell, K. M. (1971). Research on certain therapist interpersonal skills in relation to process and outcome. In A. E. Bergin & S. L. Garfield (Eds.), *Handbook of psychotherapy and behavior change.* New York: Wiley.

U. S. Department of Commerce (1980). *The social and economic status of the black population in the United States: An Historical View, 1790–1978.* Washington, DC: Bureau of the Census.

U.S. Department of Justice. (1986, July). *Attorney General's Commission on Pornography.* (Final Report). Washington, D.C.: U.S. Government Printing Office.

Valenstein, E. S. (1986). *Great and desperate cures: The rise and decline of psychosurgery and other radical treatments for mental illness.* New York: Basic Books.

VanSell, M., Brief, A. D., & Schuler, R. S. (1981). Role conflict and role ambiguity: Integration of the literature and directions for future research. *Human Relations, 34,* 43–71.

Vonnegut, M. (1975). *The Eden express.* New York: Bantam.

Wachowiak, D., & Bragg, H. (1980). Open marriage and marital adjustment. *Journal of Marriage and the Family, 42,* 57–62.

Walker, I., & Mann, L. (1987). Unemployment, relative deprivation, and social protest. *Personality and Social Psychology Bulletin, 13,* 275–283.

Wallace, R. K., & Benson, H. (1972, February). The physiology of meditation. *Scientific American,* 84–90.

Wallerstein, J. S., & Kelly, J. B. (1980). *Surviving the breakup: How children and parents cope with divorce.* New York: Basic Books.

Walster, E., & Walster, G. W. (1978). *Love.* Reading, MA: Addison-Wesley.

Walters, R. H., & Brown, M. (1963). Studies of reinforcement of aggression: III. Transfer of responses to an interpersonal situation. *Child Development, 34,* 536–571.

Ward, W. C., Kogan, N., & Pankove, E. (1972). Incentive effects in children's creativity. *Child Development, 43,* 669–676.

Warr, P. B. (1983). Work, jobs, and unemployment. *Bulletin of the British Psychological Society, 36,* 305–311.

Watkins, L. R., & Mayer, D. J. (1982). Organization of endogenous opiate and non-opiate pain control systems. *Science, 216,* 1185–1192.

Watson, D. (1982). The actor and the observer: How are their perceptions of causality divergent? *Psychological Bulletin, 92,* 682–700.

Watson, D. M., & Graves, T. D. (1966). Quantitative research in proxemic behavior. *American Anthropologist, 68,* 971–985.

Watson, J. B. (1924). *Behaviorism.* New York: Norton.

Watson, J. B., & Rayner, R. (1922). Conditioned emotional reactions. *Journal of Experimental Psychology, 3,* 1–14.

Watt, N. (Ed.). (1985). *Children at risk for schizophrenia.* Cambridge, England: Cambridge University Press.

Webb, B., Worchel, S., Riechers, L., & Wayne, W. (1986). The influence of categorization on perceptions of crowding. *Personality and Social Psychology Bulletin, 12,* 539–546.

Weber, E. (1970). *How to pick up girls.* New York: Symphony Press.

Weber, R., & Crocker, J. (1983). Cognitive processes in the revision of stereotypic beliefs. *Journal of Personality and Social Psychology, 45,* 961–977.

Wedding, D., & Corsini, R. (1979). *Great cases in psychotherapy.* Itasca, IL: F. E. Peacock.

Westoff, C. F. (1974). Coital frequency and contraception. *Family Planning Perspectives, 8,* 54–57.

Westoff, C. F. (1986, October 31). Fertility in the United States. *Science, 234,* 554–558.

Whitbourne, S. K. (1986). *The me I know: A study of adult identity.* New York: Springer-Verlag.

White, Burton. (1988). *Educating the infant and the toddler.* Lexington, MA: Lexington Books.

Whorf, B. L. (1956). *Language, thought, and reality.* New York: Wiley.

Wilson, T. (1552). *Arte and rhetorique.* Gainesville: Scholars Facsimiles and Reprints.

Wilson, T. D., & Linville, P. (1982). Improving academic performance of college freshmen: Attribution therapy revisited. *Journal of Personality and Social Psychology, 42,* 367–376.

Wilson, T. D., & Linville, P. (1985). Improving the performance of college freshmen with attributional techniques. *Journal of Personality and Social Psychology, 49,* 287–293.

Winch, R. F. (1958). *Mate selection: A study of complementary needs.* New York: Harper & Row.

Winokur, G. (1983). Alcoholism and depression. *Substance and Alcohol Actions/misuse, 4,* 11–119.

Wolpe, J. (1969). *The practice of behavior therapy.* New York: Pergamon.

Woodruff, R. A., Clayton, P. J., & Guze, S. B. (1975). Is everyone depressed? *American Journal of Psychiatry, 132,* 627–628.

Worchel, S., & Brown, E. H. (1984). The role of plausibility in influencing environmental attributions. *Journal of Experimental Social Psychology, 20,* 86–96.

Yankelovich, D. (1974). *The new morality.* New York: McGraw-Hill.

Yarnold, P. R., & Grimm, L. G. (1982). Time urgency among coronary-prone individuals. *Journal of Abnormal Psychology, 91,* 175–177.

Yerkes, R. M., & Margulis, S. (1909). The method of Pavlov in animal psychology. *Psychological Bulletin, 6,* 257–273.

Zajonc, R. B. (1968). The attitudinal effects of mere exposure. *Journal of Personality and Social Psychology, 9* (Pt. 2), 1–27.

Zilbergeld, B. (1978). *Male sexuality.* Boston: Little, Brown.

Zivin, G. (Ed.). (1985). *The development of expressive behavior: Biology-environmental interactions.* New York: Academic.

Zubin, J., & Spring, B. (1977). Vulnerability: New view of schizophrenia. *Journal of Abnormal Psychology, 86,* 103–126.

Zuckerman, M. (1978). The search for high sensation. *Psychology Today,* pp. 30–46.

Zuckerman, M., DePaulo, B. M., & Rosenthal, R. (1981). Verbal and nonverbal communication of deception. *Advances in Experimental Social Psychology, 14,* 163–171.

Zuckerman, M., Lipets, M. S., Koivumaki, J. H., & Rosenthal, R. (1975). Encoding and decoding nonverbal cues of emotion. *Journal of Personality and Social Psychology, 32,* 1068–1076.

Zurcher, L. A. (1977). *The Mutable Self: A Self-Concept for Social Change.* Beverly Hills, CA: Sage.

Acknowledgments

Questionnaire, pages 28–30. Donn Byrne/Kathryn Kelley, *An introduction to personality*, 3/e, © 1981, p. 103. Reprinted by permission of Prentice-Hall, Inc., Englewood Cliffs, New Jersey.

Figure 2-2. Reprinted by permission of the publisher.

Questionnaire, pages 107–108. Reprinted with permission of author and publisher. Dickstein, L. S. Death concern: Measurement and correlates. *Psychological Reports,* 1972, *30,* 563–571.

Questionnaire, pages 123–124. Copyright © 1978 by the American Psychological Association. Reprinted by permission of author.

Questionnaire, pages 140–141. Ball-Rokeach, S. J., Rokeach, M., and Grube, J. S., *The Great American Values Test: Influencing behavior and belief through television,* © 1984. Reprinted by permission of the Free Press Publishers, Monroe, Louisiana.

Questionnaire, pages 145–146. Goldstein, J. J., Baker, B. L., and Jamison, K. R., *Abnormal psychology: Experiences, origins, and interventions,* © 1980. Reprinted with permission of Little, Brown Publishers, Boston, MA.

Figure 5-1. Reprinted with permission of author and publisher (Pettingale, K. W., Morris, T., Greer, S., and Haybittle, J. S. (1985). Mental attitudes to cancer: An additional prognostic factor. *Lancet,* 750).

Table 5-1. Reprinted with permission of Taylor, S. E., "Hospital patient behavior: Reactance, helplessness, or control?" *Journal of Social Issues, 35,* 175.

Questionnaire, pages 169–170. Copyright © 1980 by the American Psychological Association. Reprinted by permission of the authors.

Figure 5-2. Copyright © 1975 by the Lippincott Company. Reprinted by permission of the publisher.

Questionnaire, pages 179–180. Copyright © 1986 by the Family Media, Inc. Reprinted by permission of the publisher.

Questionnaire, page 192. Reprinted by permission of the publisher.

Table 6-1. Reprinted by permission of Plenum Publishing Corporation, New York, New York.

Figure 6-1. © 1976. Reprinted by permission of McGraw-Hill, New York, New York.

Questionnaire, pages 203–205. Copyright © 1953 by the American Psychological Association. Reprinted by permission of the publisher.

Questionnaire, pages 212–213. Reprinted by permission of William Morrow and Co, Inc., New York, New York.

Table 6-3 from Meichenbaum, D., *Cognitive behavior modification: An integration,* © 1977. Reprinted by permission of Plenum Publishing Corporation, New York, New York.

Passage from a poem, pages 226–227. Kerouac, J. *On the road,* © 1957. Reprinted by permission of Penguin Books, Inc., New York, New York.

Quote, page 237. © 1980. Reprinted by permission of Little, Brown and Company, Boston, MA.

Quote, page 243. Reprinted by permission of Bergler, E., *Principles of self-damage,* Thieme Medical Publishers, New York, 1974.

Quote, pages 244–245. Originally published in *Canadian Medical Association Journal, 82,* January 23, 1960.

Quote, page 247. © 1967. Reprinted by permission of Prentice-Hall, Inc., Englewood Cliffs, New Jersey.

Questionnaire, page 261. Reprinted by permission of F. E. Peacock Publishers, Inc., Itasca, IL.

Quote, pages 270–271. Reprinted by permission of the authors.

Diaglogue, page 297. Labov, W., *Tinker, Tailor . . . The myth of cultural deprivation.* Copyright © 1973 by Penguin Education Books, Ltd. Adapted by permission.

Table 10-1. From *Liking and loving: An invitation to social psychology* by Zick Rubin. Copyright © 1973 by Holt, Rinehart and Winston, Inc. Reprinted by permission of CBS Publishing.

Table 10-2. Copyright © 1986 by the American Psychological Association. Reprinted by permission of the authors.

Table 10-3. Adapted from "Breakups before marriage: The end of 103 affairs," by Charles T. Hill, Zick Rubin, and Letitia Anne Peplau, in *Divorce and Separation: Context, Causes, and Consequences.* Edited by George Levinger and Oliver C. Moles. Copyright © 1979 by the Society for the Psychological Study of Social Issues. Reprinted by permission of Basic Books, Inc., Publishers.

Figure 10-2. Copyright © 1982 by Academic Press, Inc. Reprinted with permission.

Figure 11-1. From Janda, L. H., & Klenke-Hamel, K. E., *Human Sexuality,* © 1980 by Van Nostrand Reinhold Co., Inc., New York, New York. Reprinted by permission of the publisher.

Table 11-1. Copyright © 1986 by the American Psychological Association. Reprinted by permission of the authors.

Questionnaire, page 364. Reprinted with permission from *Psychology Today* magazine. Copyright © 1985, American Psychological Association.

Table 11-2. From Goode, William J., Family disorganization, in R. Merton and R. Nisbet (Eds.), *Contemporary Social Problems,* © 1976 Harcourt Brace Jovanovich, Inc. Reprinted by permission of the publishers.

Questionnaire, page 369. From Martin, M., & Martin, D., Counseling the child of divorce: Emphasizing the positive aspects, in *Individual Psychology:* *Journal of Alderian Theory, Research, and Practice, 31,* 1083. Reprinted by permission of the University of Texas, Austin, Texas.

Questionnaire, page 377. Copyrighted by the National Council on Family Relations, 1910 West County Road B., Suite 147, St. Paul, MN 55113. Reprinted by permission.

Letter to Abby, page 380. Reprinted by permission of the *Daily Hampshire Gazette.*

Figure 12-5. Reprinted by permission of the Kinsey Institute for Research in Sex, Gender, and Reproduction, Inc.

Figure 12-2. Copyright © 1979 by the Society for Scientific Study of Sex. Reprinted by permission of the publisher.

Figure 12-4. Copyright © 1974 by the Alan Guttmacher Institute. Reprinted by permission of the publisher.

Figure 12-6. Reprinted by permission of author.

Quote, page 409. Reprinted with permission from *Newsweek* magazine, copyright © 1986.

Questionnaire, page 429. Copyright © 1977 by Academic Press, Inc. Reprinted with permission of publisher.

Questionnaire, page 436. From Benjamin, L. T., Jr. Defining aggression: An exercise for classroom discussion. *Teaching of Psychology, 12*(1). Copyright © 1985 by Lawrence Erlbaum, Associates, Inc. Reprinted with permission of the publisher.

Table 14-1. Reprinted with permission from National Opinion Research Center.

Quote, page 472. From Garson, B. *All the livelong day,* 1975. Reprinted by permission of Penguin Books, Inc., New York, New York.

Questionnaire, page 473. From Locke, E. A., The nature and causes of job satisfaction in *Handbook of Industrial and Organizational Psychology,* 1976. Reprinted by permission of John Wiley & Sons, Inc., New York, New York.

Table 14-2. Copyright © 1985 by The Dorsey Press, Chicago, Illinois. Reprinted by permission of the publisher.

Figure 15-2. From *Personal Space* by Robert Sommer, © 1969. Reprinted by permission of the publisher, Prentice-Hall, Inc., Englewood Cliffs, New Jersey.

Figure 15-4. Copyright © 1978 by the American Psychological Association. Reprinted with permission of the author.

Figure 15-5. Copyright © 1972 by Academic Press. Reprinted with permission of the publisher.

Figure 15-6. Reprinted with permission of author.

Figure 15-7. From Baum, A., & Valins, S., *Architecture and social behavior: Psychological studies of social density,* © 1977 by Lawrence Erlbaum, Associates, Inc., Hillsdale, New Jersey. Reprinted with permission of the publisher.

PART-OPENING AND CHAPTER-OPENING PHOTOGRAPHS

Part I: Hazel Hankin
Chapter 1: Peter Menzel/Stock, Boston

Part II: Joel Gordon
Chapter 2: Susan Lapides/Design Conceptions
Chapter 3: Peter Menzel/Stock, Boston
Chapter 4: Peter Menzel/Stock, Boston

Part III: Peter Menzel/Stock, Boston
Chapter 5: Hazel Hankin
Chapter 6: Joel Gordon
Chapter 7: David Witbeck/The Picture Cube
Chapter 8: Enrico Ferorelli/Dot

Part VI: Joel Gordon
Chapter 9: Howard Dratch/The Image Works
Chapter 10: Tom Grill/Comstock
Chapter 11: Hazel Hankin
Chapter 12: Joel Gordon

Part V: Joel Gordon
Chapter 13: (a) Reuters/Bettmann Newsphotos
(b) Alan Carey/The Image Works
Chapter 14: Ulrike Welsch/Photo Researchers
Chapter 15: George Gardner/The Image Works

Name Index

NAME INDEX

Subject Index

SUBJECT INDEX

SUBJECT INDEX

SUBJECT INDEX